T0181522

Lecture Notes in Computer Science 13305

More information about this series at https://link.springer.com/bookseries/558

Lecture Notes in Computer Science   13305

More information about this series at https://link.springer.com/bookseries/558

Sakae Yamamoto · Hirohiko Mori (Eds.)

Human Interface and the Management of Information

Visual and Information Design

Thematic Area, HIMI 2022
Held as Part of the 24th HCI International Conference, HCII 2022
Virtual Event, June 26 – July 1, 2022
Proceedings, Part I

Springer

Editors
Sakae Yamamoto
Tokyo University of Science
Tokyo, Saitama, Japan

Hirohiko Mori
Tokyo City University
Tokyo, Japan

ISSN 0302-9743 ISSN 1611-3349 (electronic)
Lecture Notes in Computer Science
ISBN 978-3-031-06423-4 ISBN 978-3-031-06424-1 (eBook)
https://doi.org/10.1007/978-3-031-06424-1

This Springer imprint is published by the registered company Springer Nature Switzerland AG
The registered company address is: Gewerbestrasse 11, 6330 Cham, Switzerland

Foreword

Human-computer interaction (HCI) is acquiring an ever-increasing scientific and industrial importance, as well as having more impact on people's everyday life, as an ever-growing number of human activities are progressively moving from the physical to the digital world. This process, which has been ongoing for some time now, has been dramatically accelerated by the COVID-19 pandemic. The HCI International (HCII) conference series, held yearly, aims to respond to the compelling need to advance the exchange of knowledge and research and development efforts on the human aspects of design and use of computing systems.

The 24th International Conference on Human-Computer Interaction, HCI International 2022 (HCII 2022), was planned to be held at the Gothia Towers Hotel and Swedish Exhibition & Congress Centre, Göteborg, Sweden, during June 26 to July 1, 2022. Due to the COVID-19 pandemic and with everyone's health and safety in mind, HCII 2022 was organized and run as a virtual conference. It incorporated the 21 thematic areas and affiliated conferences listed on the following page.

A total of 5583 individuals from academia, research institutes, industry, and governmental agencies from 88 countries submitted contributions, and 1276 papers and 275 posters were included in the proceedings to appear just before the start of the conference. The contributions thoroughly cover the entire field of human-computer interaction, addressing major advances in knowledge and effective use of computers in a variety of application areas. These papers provide academics, researchers, engineers, scientists, practitioners, and students with state-of-the-art information on the most recent advances in HCI. The volumes constituting the set of proceedings to appear before the start of the conference are listed in the following pages.

The HCI International (HCII) conference also offers the option of 'Late Breaking Work' which applies both for papers and posters, and the corresponding volume(s) of the proceedings will appear after the conference. Full papers will be included in the 'HCII 2022 - Late Breaking Papers' volumes of the proceedings to be published in the Springer LNCS series, while 'Poster Extended Abstracts' will be included as short research papers in the 'HCII 2022 - Late Breaking Posters' volumes to be published in the Springer CCIS series.

I would like to thank the Program Board Chairs and the members of the Program Boards of all thematic areas and affiliated conferences for their contribution and support towards the highest scientific quality and overall success of the HCI International 2022 conference; they have helped in so many ways, including session organization, paper reviewing (single-blind review process, with a minimum of two reviews per submission) and, more generally, acting as goodwill ambassadors for the HCII conference.

This conference would not have been possible without the continuous and unwavering support and advice of Gavriel Salvendy, founder, General Chair Emeritus, and Scientific Advisor. For his outstanding efforts, I would like to express my appreciation to Abbas Moallem, Communications Chair and Editor of HCI International News.

June 2022   Constantine Stephanidis

HCI International 2022 Thematic Areas and Affiliated Conferences

Thematic Areas

- HCI: Human-Computer Interaction
- HIMI: Human Interface and the Management of Information

Affiliated Conferences

- EPCE: 19th International Conference on Engineering Psychology and Cognitive Ergonomics
- AC: 16th International Conference on Augmented Cognition
- UAHCI: 16th International Conference on Universal Access in Human-Computer Interaction
- CCD: 14th International Conference on Cross-Cultural Design
- SCSM: 14th International Conference on Social Computing and Social Media
- VAMR: 14th International Conference on Virtual, Augmented and Mixed Reality
- DHM: 13th International Conference on Digital Human Modeling and Applications in Health, Safety, Ergonomics and Risk Management
- DUXU: 11th International Conference on Design, User Experience and Usability
- C&C: 10th International Conference on Culture and Computing
- DAPI: 10th International Conference on Distributed, Ambient and Pervasive Interactions
- HCIBGO: 9th International Conference on HCI in Business, Government and Organizations
- LCT: 9th International Conference on Learning and Collaboration Technologies
- ITAP: 8th International Conference on Human Aspects of IT for the Aged Population
- AIS: 4th International Conference on Adaptive Instructional Systems
- HCI-CPT: 4th International Conference on HCI for Cybersecurity, Privacy and Trust
- HCI-Games: 4th International Conference on HCI in Games
- MobiTAS: 4th International Conference on HCI in Mobility, Transport and Automotive Systems
- AI-HCI: 3rd International Conference on Artificial Intelligence in HCI
- MOBILE: 3rd International Conference on Design, Operation and Evaluation of Mobile Communications

List of Conference Proceedings Volumes Appearing Before the Conference

1. LNCS 13302, Human-Computer Interaction: Theoretical Approaches and Design Methods (Part I), edited by Masaaki Kurosu
2. LNCS 13303, Human-Computer Interaction: Technological Innovation (Part II), edited by Masaaki Kurosu
3. LNCS 13304, Human-Computer Interaction: User Experience and Behavior (Part III), edited by Masaaki Kurosu
4. LNCS 13305, Human Interface and the Management of Information: Visual and Information Design (Part I), edited by Sakae Yamamoto and Hirohiko Mori
5. LNCS 13306, Human Interface and the Management of Information: Applications in Complex Technological Environments (Part II), edited by Sakae Yamamoto and Hirohiko Mori
6. LNAI 13307, Engineering Psychology and Cognitive Ergonomics, edited by Don Harris and Wen-Chin Li
7. LNCS 13308, Universal Access in Human-Computer Interaction: Novel Design Approaches and Technologies (Part I), edited by Margherita Antona and Constantine Stephanidis
8. LNCS 13309, Universal Access in Human-Computer Interaction: User and Context Diversity (Part II), edited by Margherita Antona and Constantine Stephanidis
9. LNAI 13310, Augmented Cognition, edited by Dylan D. Schmorrow and Cali M. Fidopiastis
10. LNCS 13311, Cross-Cultural Design: Interaction Design Across Cultures (Part I), edited by Pei-Luen Patrick Rau
11. LNCS 13312, Cross-Cultural Design: Applications in Learning, Arts, Cultural Heritage, Creative Industries, and Virtual Reality (Part II), edited by Pei-Luen Patrick Rau
12. LNCS 13313, Cross-Cultural Design: Applications in Business, Communication, Health, Well-being, and Inclusiveness (Part III), edited by Pei-Luen Patrick Rau
13. LNCS 13314, Cross-Cultural Design: Product and Service Design, Mobility and Automotive Design, Cities, Urban Areas, and Intelligent Environments Design (Part IV), edited by Pei-Luen Patrick Rau
14. LNCS 13315, Social Computing and Social Media: Design, User Experience and Impact (Part I), edited by Gabriele Meiselwitz
15. LNCS 13316, Social Computing and Social Media: Applications in Education and Commerce (Part II), edited by Gabriele Meiselwitz
16. LNCS 13317, Virtual, Augmented and Mixed Reality: Design and Development (Part I), edited by Jessie Y. C. Chen and Gino Fragomeni
17. LNCS 13318, Virtual, Augmented and Mixed Reality: Applications in Education, Aviation and Industry (Part II), edited by Jessie Y. C. Chen and Gino Fragomeni

39. CCIS 1582, HCI International 2022 Posters - Part III, edited by Constantine Stephanidis, Margherita Antona and Stavroula Ntoa
40. CCIS 1583, HCI International 2022 Posters - Part IV, edited by Constantine Stephanidis, Margherita Antona and Stavroula Ntoa

http://2022.hci.international/proceedings

Preface

Human Interface and the Management of Information (HIMI) is a Thematic Area of the International Conference on Human-Computer Interaction (HCII), addressing topics related to information and data design, retrieval, presentation and visualization, management, and evaluation in human computer interaction in a variety of application domains, such as, for example, learning, work, decision, collaboration, medical support, and service engineering. This area of research is acquiring rapidly increasing importance towards developing new and more effective types of human interfaces addressing the new emerging challenges, and evaluating their effectiveness. The ultimate goal is for information to be provided in such a way as to satisfy human needs and enhance quality of life.

The related topics include, but are not limited to the following:

- Service Engineering: Business Integration, Community Computing, E-commerce, E-learning and e-education, Harmonized Work, IoT and Human Behavior, Knowledge Management, Organizational Design and Management, Service Applications, Service Design, Sustainable Design, and User Experience Design.
- New HI (Human Interface) and Human of QOL (Quality of Life): Electric Instrumentation, Evaluating Information, Health Promotion, E-health and its Application, Human Centered Organization, Legal Issues in IT, Mobile Networking, and Disasters and HCI.
- Information in VR, AR, and MR: Application of VR, AR, and MR in Human Activity, Art with New Technology, Digital Museum, Gesture/movement Studies, New Haptic and Tactile Interaction, Information of Presentation, Multimodal Interaction, and Sense of Embodiment (SoE) in VR and HCI.
- AI, Human Performance, and Collaboration: Automatic Driving Vehicles, Collaborative Work, Data Visualization and Big Data, Decision Support Systems, Human AI Collaboration, Human Robot Interaction, Humanization of Work, Intellectual Property, Intelligent System, Medical Information System and Its Application, and Participatory Design.

Two volumes of the HCII 2022 proceedings are dedicated to this year's edition of the HIMI Thematic Area, entitled Human Interface and the Management of Information: Visual and Information Design (Part I) and Human Interface and the Management of Information: Applications in Complex Technological Environments (Part II). The first focuses on topics related to human-centred design approaches, information design and quality, visual design, visualization and big data, and information, cognition and learning, while the second focuses on topics related to the appearance and embodiment of robots and avatars, information in virtual and augmented reality, and information in complex technological environments.

Papers of these volumes are included for publication after a minimum of two single-blind reviews from the members of the HIMI Program Board or, in some cases, from members of the Program Boards of other affiliated conferences. We would like to thank all of them for their invaluable contribution, support, and efforts.

June 2022   Sakae Yamamoto
                                                                  Hirohiko Mori

Human Interface and the Management of Information Thematic Area (HIMI 2022)

Program Board Chairs: **Sakae Yamamoto,** Tokyo University of Science, Tokyo, Japan, and **Hirohiko Mori,** Tokyo City University, Tokyo, Japan

- Yumi Asahi, Tokyo University of Science, Japan
- Michitaka Hirose, University of Tokyo, Japan
- Yasushi Ikei, University of Tokyo, Japan
- Keiko Kasamatsu, Tokyo Metropolitan University, Japan
- Daiji Kobayashi, Chitose Institute of Science and Technology, Japan
- Kentaro Kotani, Kansai University, Japan
- Hiroyuki Miki, Oki Consulting Solutions, Japan
- Miwa Nakanishi, Keio University, Japan
- Ryosuke Saga, Osaka Prefecture University, Japan
- Katsunori Shimohara, Doshisha University, Japan
- Yoshinobu Tamura, Yamaguchi University, Japan
- Takahito Tomoto, Tokyo Polytechnic University, Japan
- Kim-Phuong L. Vu, California State University, USA
- Tomio Watanabe, Okayama Prefectural University, Japan
- Takehiko Yamaguchi, Suwa University of Science, Japan

The full list with the Program Board Chairs and the members of the Program Boards of all thematic areas and affiliated conferences is available online at

http://www.hci.international/board-members-2022.php

HCI International 2023

The 25th International Conference on Human-Computer Interaction, HCI International 2023, will be held jointly with the affiliated conferences at the AC Bella Sky Hotel and Bella Center, Copenhagen, Denmark, 23–28 July 2023. It will cover a broad spectrum of themes related to human-computer interaction, including theoretical issues, methods, tools, processes, and case studies in HCI design, as well as novel interaction techniques, interfaces, and applications. The proceedings will be published by Springer. More information will be available on the conference website: http://2023.hci.international/.

General Chair
Constantine Stephanidis
University of Crete and ICS-FORTH
Heraklion, Crete, Greece
Email: general_chair@hcii2023.org

http://2023.hci.international/

Contents – Part I

Visual Design

Visualization and Big Data

Information, Cognition and Learning

Contents – Part II

Information in Virtual and Augmented Reality

Information in Complex Technological Environments

Human-Centred Design Approaches

Proposal of the Warm Product for HSP/HSC

Takeo Ainoya[1]([✉]), Miharu Asaka[1], Fuko Oura[2], and Keiko Kasamatsu[2]

[1] Tokyo University of Technology, 5-23-22, Nishi-Kamata, Ota, Tokyo, Japan
ainoyatk@stf.teu.ac.jp
[2] Tokyo Metropolitan University, 6-6, Asahigaoka, Hino, Tokyo, Japan

Abstract. In this research, we consider HSP/HSC as users, not as a medical treatment for HSP/HSC, and introduce the process of considering what value can be provided to them and proposing products. In this study, design students used design thinking to create an experiential prototyping of a product proposal for HSP/ HSC. The process could be divided into five parts. By guiding the student's interest and illustrating and carding the research, we were able to identify points for co-creation. In addition, the question of what is valuable for HSP/HSC was prototyped, focusing on physical perception and psychological states. This prototype uses the sense of warmth and a teddy bear-like shape, a metaphor for acceptance, to support a state of relaxation. The next step is to test the effectiveness of this prototype. Furthermore, in order to achieve co-creation, it is necessary to examine the development process using prototypes in order to involve all participants and stakeholders and have specific discussions. It is also necessary to develop skills and approaches for development process.

Keywords: Product design · Prototyping · Co-creation · HSP/HSCS

1 Introduction

This study is a product proposal for HSP/HSC (Highly Sensitive Person/ Highly Sensitive Children) using the HCD(Human Centered Design) approach. In the development of the KADEN project [1] and the robot door [2], we have been using design thinking to think about the value for the user and what kind of experience can be provided, and to derive design requirements and conduct prototyping [3, 4].

HSP/ HSC has been studied by Elaine N. Aaron and others, and it is estimated that 20% of children are predisposed to it [5]. HSP/HSC refers to people with a high level of sensory processing sensitivity (SPS), an innate trait that makes them more sensitive to a variety of external stimuli than other people. According to Aron & Aron [6], SPS is defined as follows: SPS is an innate trait, a fundamental personal characteristic of the brain's processing of sensory information rather than of the sensory organs themselves. People with high SPS, which is estimated to be about 15%, are sensitive to subtle stimuli, prone to overstimulation, and tend to check novel stimuli against their previous experience before deciding what to do next. HSP/HSC are said to have four characteristics [7]. They are sensitive to small changes in their environment (sensory sensitivity), easily fatigued (overarousal), have high emotional intensity (emotional intensity), and think

S. Yamamoto and H. Mori (Eds.): HCII 2022, LNCS 13305, pp. 3–11, 2022.
https://doi.org/10.1007/978-3-031-06424-1_1

deeply (depth of processing). In addition, while highly sensitive persons are highly empathic [8–11], they are also more likely to be influenced by others. Research on HSP/HSC has only just begun in Japan.

In this research, we consider HSP/HSC as users, not as a medical treatment for HSP/HSC, and introduce the process of considering what value can be provided to them and proposing products. This research aims to share the process for product design in design education by looking over this process.

2 Methods

In this study, design students used design thinking to create an experiential prototyping of a product proposal for HSP/ HSC. The process could be divided into five parts.

2.1 Motivation

Through discussion of the interests of design students, we derive issues that can be considered as a personal matter. Traditionally, design has often been about solving problems. However, it is important for future product development that students discover issues as their own, as they did in this case. Because we consider that by getting to know the people involved, getting to know the UX and getting to know the awareness, we can provide real value for the user.

2.2 Investigation

In response to the multiple issues identified by the students, the research was conducted while the students themselves considered the value they could offer as designers when they perceived the subject as a user.

2.3 Empathy

We discussed ways of sharing our understanding of the research, not only in writing, but also in order to deepen our understanding.

2.4 Cardification as a Sharing Tool

In order to find a way to share the information, we illustrated the survey contents and made a card based on it. Based on the content of the cards, we discussed what value they could provide to their users.

2.5 Prototyping

A prototype was created to realize the values discussed in 2.4.

3 Results

The results for each process are described below.

3.1 Motivation

The topics of interest to the students were those related to HSP/HSC. The design students' interest in HSP/HSC was sparked by their own experiences and a desire to make HSP/HSC more accessible and understood in society.

3.2 Investigation

The design student was interested in HSP/HSC, but did not understand what HSP/HSC needed or how to support it. The students read a book called The Highly Sensitive Child [] which is about HSP/ HSC and tried to understand its characteristics.

3.3 Empathy

We decided to illustrate examples of the content of the research as well as the written understanding of the content. The teachers had little knowledge of HSP/ HSC, but this illustration has made it easier for them to understand (Fig. 1 and 2).

Fig. 1. The sample 1 of illustration

Fig. 2. The sample 2 of illustration

3.4 Cardification as a Sharing Tool

Based on the results of 3.3, we decided that illustration would be an effective tool for co-creation and decided to make cards of illustrations. From the illustrations, we examined the design requirements to realize the value for HSP/HSC as a user. In the end, these illustrations were made into 3D models, which were used in the exhibition, aiming to attract and empathize with as many people as possible.

Of the 70 or so contents surveyed, five were illustrated. Some of the illustrations are shown in Fig. 3 and 4. 3D model is shown in Fig. 5.

Fig. 3. The sample 1 of card

Fig. 4. The sample 2 of card

Fig. 5. The 3D model

3.5   Prototyping

A prototype was created to realize the values discussed in 3.4.

As a specific prototyping theme, we focused on physical perception and psychological states. It was inspired by the contents of a book on tactile sensation (触楽入門 (in Japanese)). It is as follows; Linus, the character in the cartoon "Snoopy", always has a blue blanket. Linus performs at his best when he has a blanket. That's how Charlie Brown explains the effect of the blanket: "It calms the mind and gets the brain working." It is well known that children, like Linus, tend to become attached to the things that used to surround them. This is known as the 'security blanket' phenomenon. Children can be calmed by being exposed to their favourite things even when their mother is not around. Touch changes our bodies, both physiologically and psychologically. For this reason, we focused on physical perception and psychological states. So we decided to prototype "something" that would stimulate perception.

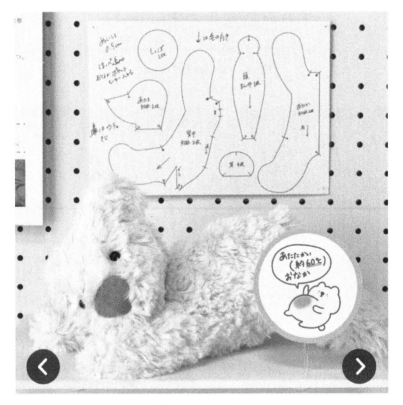

Fig. 6. Prototype

As a stimulating perception, it was defined as a sensation of warmth. Warmth is generally used for relaxation and pain relief. For the shape, we decided to use a teddy bear-like shape, referring to "the teddy bear is a metaphor for acceptance" (from 触楽 入門). The surface material chosen is the softest and fuzziest of all plush toys. (Fig. 5)

As a mechanism, we decided to create a pocket that can contain the heat source and put a disposable body warmer in it. (Fig. 6) This allowed the temperature of about 60 °C to be maintained for about 8 h. In the process of deciding on this disposable body warmer, we also considered several USB body warmers. However, when commercial products are used, they were not used in this study because the shape of the ready-made products can affect the grip and holding comfort (Fig. 7).

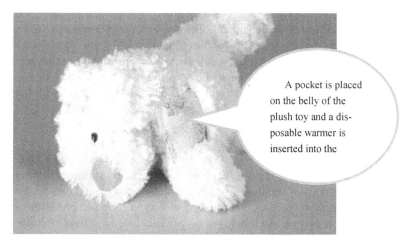

A pocket is placed on the belly of the plush toy and a disposable warmer is inserted into the

Fig. 7. Disposable warmer position

4 Discussion

By following the five processes described above, we could have made the intended proposal by prototyping the production envisaged by the student.

However, we consider the following points to be issues for the future.

1. to verify the effectiveness of the product for HSP/ HSC
2. develop a prototyping method and evaluation items for design research (for design education)
3. develop a process for co-creation

4.1 Verify the Effectiveness of the Product for HSP/ HSC

In this paper we have only made suggestions, but we consider that in the future it will be necessary not only to make suggestions but also to verify their effectiveness. The design process in Japanese art universities often does not provide enough technical problems and validation methods for the production of mechanisms and workable prototypes. In this respect, we need to further develop the co-creation environment. There is also a need to design across a number of methodologies, including medical, nursing and support tool methodologies to address issues that are not fully understood, such as HSP/ HSC.

With such a guideline approach to method selection, it is possible to flow through the approaches and the considerations in the process. Such a flow makes the purpose of the thinking and the setting of the tasks clear, facilitates the participation of a large number of novice designers, and is considered to be a co-creation process.

4.2 Develop a Prototyping Method and Evaluation Items for Design Research (for Design Education)

At present, design education in Japan still often focuses on the evaluation of exterior design. In this review, the review was not of the product for HSP/ HSC, but of the styling of the product design, and not of the approach as a whole. However, it is also important to take an approach to product design that allows us to understand the function and use of the product at a glance, to empathize with the use of the product, and to understand the meaning of the shape and the symbolic meaning of the design.

4.3 Develop a Process for Co-Creation

The potential of prototyping as an effective process for co-creation will also be discussed.

There are six prototypes and three objectives of prototyping by takram design engineering. [12] The six prototypes are: sketch, dirty prototype, technical prototype, styling prototype, working prototype and movie prototype. The three objectives of prototyping are creation, improvement and communication. The takram design engineering defines the process from phase 1 to 9 and practices product development.

In addition to the development process in the actual field, we consider that phase 0, as examined in this study, is necessary to create new value in the future. The use of prototyping as design research for Phase 0 and the mindset for this is considered to be important. In the future, it will be essential for product designers to consider not only the product itself, but also the relationship with users and other stakeholders. In addition, knowledge of the technology is required, and we recognize that the ability to create value through user-driven ideation, rather than technology-driven ideation, is desirable. It is important to use prototyping as a way to find out what value can be provided to the user. In order to achieve better co-creation, we consider that there is a need for prototypes to bring together all involved parties for concrete discussions, and to develop the skills and approaches to achieve this.

References

1. Ainoya, T.: KADEN project-towards the construction of model for sharing cognition in manufacturing, Human Interface and the Management of Information, Part I, ©Springer International Publishing, pp. 291–297 (2014). https://doi.org/10.1007/978-3-319-07731-4_30.
2. Ainoya, T., Kasamatsu, K.: PXD Process for innovative product development. In: ISIS2019&ICBAKE2019 The 20th International Symposium on Advanced Intelligent Systems and 2019 International Conference on Biometrics and Kansei Engineering, pp. 539–545 (2019)

3. Chen, L., Kasamatsu, K., Ainoya, T.: Study on process for product design applying user experience, human interface and the management of information. Information in Applications and Services, P. 67. Springer International Publishing (2018). https://doi.org/10.1007/978-3-319-92046-7_6

4. Oura, F., Ainoya, T., Kasamatsu, K.: A Study on design process model based on user experience, Development for the Concept of Service for Vision-impaired People-, Human Interface and the Management of Information. Information in Intelligent Systems, HIMI 2019. (LNCS, vol. 11570), Springer, pp. 523–533 (2019). https://doi.org/10.1007/978-3-030-22649-7_42

5. Aron, E.N.: The Highly Sensitive Child: Helping Our Children Thrive When the World Overwhelms. Harmony, Them (2002)

6. Aron, E.N., Aron, A.: Sensory-processing sensitivity and its relation to introversion and emotionality. J. Pers. Soc. Psychol. **73**, 345–368 (1997)

7. Aron, E.N., Aron, A., Jagiellowicz, J.: Sensory processing sensitivity: a review in the light of the evolution of biological responsivity. Pers. Soc. Psychol. Rev. **16**(3), 262–282 (2012)

8. Acevedo, B.P., Aron, E.N., Aron, A., Sangster, M.D., Collins, N., Brown, L.L.: The highly sensitive brain: an fMRI study of sensory processing sensitivity and response to others' emotions. Brain and Behavior **4**(4), 580–594 (2014)

9. Acevedo, B., Aron, E., Pospos, S., Jessen, D.: The functional highly sensitive brain: a review of the brain circuits underlying sensory processing sensitivity and seemingly related disorders. Philosophical Trans. Royal Soc. B Biol. Sci. **373**(1744), 20170161 (2018)

10. Carney, D.R., Harrigan, J.A.: It takes one to know one: Interpersonal sensitivity is related to accurate assessments of others' interpersonal sensitivity. Emotion **3**(2), 194–200 (2003). https://doi.org/10.1037/1528-3542.3.2.194

11. Iimura, S.: Development of the Junior High School Students Version of the Sensory Sensitivity Index (SSSI).The Japanese Journal of Personality, **25**(2), 154–157 (2016). 10. Masashi, N., Yasuaki, K., Soichiroa,M., Kota, M.: Shokuraku Nyumon (Introduction to Shokuraku – Rediscovering the world through touch), Asahi Press (2016)

12. Tagawa, K.: Takram design engineering and its design process. KEIO SFC Journal **10**(1), 17–25 (2010)

The Effect of the Gap Between Expectation and Satisfaction on Corporate Brand Value

Rikuto Koshi[✉] and Yumi Asahi

Graduate School of Business Administration, Tokyo University of Science, Tokyo, Japan
8621503@ed.tus.ac.jp, asahi@rs.tus.ac.jp

Abstract. In recent years, with the advancement of technology and globalization, commoditization has been progressing in various markets in Japan. Therefore, in recent years, brand building has been attracting a lot of attention as a means of "de-commoditization" to break away from the current market. However, due to the lack of knowledge about branding among Japanese managers, few companies are working on it.

In this study, we focused on the beauty esthetic industry in Japan and analyzed the effects of prior expectations and satisfaction on the brand value of companies.

The results showed that there was no significant difference in the positive impact on brand value between high and low prior expectations. On the other hand, the negative impact of low prior expectations on brand value was more than twice as large as the negative impact of high prior expectations.

Considering the negative impact on the brand, this study suggests the necessity of increasing the level of prior expectations, contrary to the argument that prior expectations should be controlled not to be too high to prevent the negative divergence between expectations and satisfaction. As for the negative divergence, it is necessary to control it using causal attribution and Cognitive Dissonance theory.

Since the results of this research are very abstract, it is unlikely that individual managers will implement strategies based on these results. We will analyze what specific items are more effective in managing expectations and study them to the point where they can be incorporated into concrete strategies.

Keywords: Brand equity · Ordered probit model · Expectation management

1 Introduction

In recent years, with the advancement of technology and globalization, commoditization has been progressing in various markets in Japan. Commoditization is defined as "a situation in which the level of technology among companies gradually becomes homogeneous, making it difficult to differentiate the essential aspects of products and services, and in which customers can find little or no difference between brands. A company cannot survive unless it continues to create value for its customers and generate profits. For this reason, "decommodification" to break out of the current market has become a marketing issue of the day. In recent years, brand building (branding) has attracted a lot of attention as a means of decommodification. The objective is not to improve the performance or quality of the product or service itself, but to gain an advantage in a homogenous market by improving the brand value.

However, branding costs a great deal of money and is often neglected by business managers due to the lack of visible results and lack of knowledge about branding. Therefore, there are few companies (especially small and medium-sized companies) that actually conduct in branding. In this study, we focused on the gap between the level of expectation and the level of satisfaction with a company and examined how it affects the brand evaluation (customer loyalty).

2 Purposes of This Study

In this study, we focused on the beauty esthetic industry, which is one of the industries in Japan where market commoditization is a serious problem and corporate branding is said to be important as a solution to this problem. The current market size of the beauty esthetic industry in Japan has been almost flat for the past several years, although there has been a slight decrease due to the impact of the COVID-19 (see Fig. 1). In contrast, however, competition in the beauty treatment industry has intensified due to the entry of medical institutions that can be expected to provide highly effective treatments and the increase in the number of beauty salons that can provide not only beauty treatments but also haircuts at the same time. In addition to the intensifying market competition, 61.7% of the beauty salon industry in Japan is privately owned, and the lack of knowledge on how to run a business is also an issue. Due to this, the number of companies going bankrupt is increasing every year (see Fig. 1). In fact, in recent years, we have frequently seen advertisements related to the beauty esthetic industry in Japan that use social networking

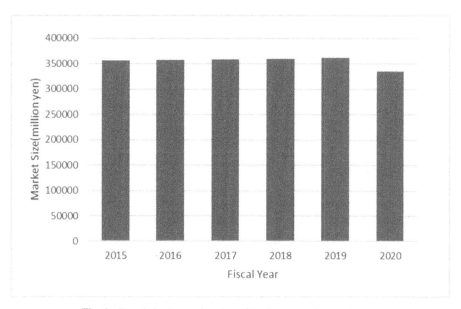

Fig. 1. Trends in the market size of the beauty esthetic industry.

services (Instagram, YouTube, etc.) to excessively advertise their effectiveness and low prices, or to denigrate those who do not attend esthetic clinics. Although these advertising methods may have a temporary effect on attracting customers, it is difficult to run a sustainable company.

Under these circumstances, in order for a company to survive, it is necessary for the manager to acquire appropriate management knowledge and to manage the company to improve the value of the corporate brand. In this study, we focused on the discrepancy between the level of expectation before using a beauty salon and the level of satisfaction after using a beauty salon and analyzed how it affects the value of the corporate brand. Based on the results of this analysis, we suggest a method for managing expectations in order to maintain or increase brand value, and thereby improve the lack of knowledge about management in the beauty esthetic industry in Japan. As a result, we aim to create as many brand companies as possible in Japan (Fig. 2).

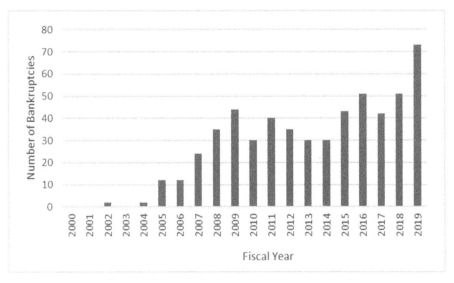

Fig. 2. Annual Bankruptcies in the Japanese Beauty Esthetic Industry.

3   Data Summary

Of the 6191 questionnaires that were administered to esthetic users in 2017, 3760 were used for the analysis of this study after removing missing values. The details of the data are shown in the table below (see Table 1).

3.1   Objective Variable

The objective variable is the brand value of the company. However, since brand value is intangible and invisible, it is difficult to measure. In this study, we refer to Dr. Kevin

Table 1. Details of data used.

Industry	Survey year	Number of samples	Sex	Age	Conditions for Survey Subjects
Beauty Esthetics	2,017	6,191	female	Over 20 years old	Have used the services of a domestic beauty salon within the past two years

Keller's Customer-based Brand Equity Pyramid and use Resonance (brand loyalty), which is the top of the pyramid and the ultimate goal of branding, as the objective variable. Brand loyalty is measured by the NPS (Net Promoter Score), which is an index that measures the degree of attachment to and trust in a brand based on the degree of recommendation to others. The calculation method is shown below (see Fig. 3).

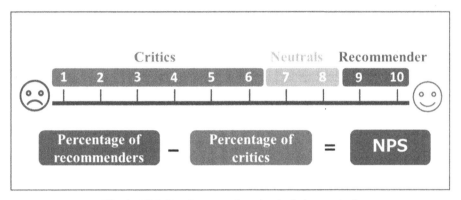

Fig. 3. NPS (Net Promoter Score) calculation method.

3.2 Explanatory Variables

The data used to create the explanatory variables consisted of answers to 12 questions on a 10-point rating scale to indicate the level of expectation before and satisfaction after using a beauty salon. The questions are shown in the table below (see Table 2). Those who answered 10 to 8 for pre-use expectation were " High Expectations", those who answered 3 to 1 for pre-use expectation were "Low Expectations", those who answered 10 to 8 for post-use satisfaction were "Satisfied", and those who answered 3 to 1 for post-use satisfaction were "Dissatisfied". Since the data does not directly examine the discrepancy between expectation and satisfaction, the discrepancy variable between expectation and satisfaction was defined as follows.

$$HH \; x = \begin{cases} 1 & \text{"High Expectations"} and \text{"Satisfied"} \\ 0 & \text{Other} \end{cases}$$

$$HL \; x = \begin{cases} 1 & \text{"High Expectations"} and \text{"Satisfied"} \\ 0 & \text{Other} \end{cases}$$

$$LH \; x = \begin{cases} 1 & \text{"High Expectations"} and \text{"Satisfied"} \\ 0 & \text{Other} \end{cases}$$

$$LL \; x = \begin{cases} 1 & \text{"High Expectations"} and \text{"Satisfied"} \\ 0 & \text{Other} \end{cases}$$

Table 2. Questions.

Q1)	Expectations and satisfaction with website usability, including ease of viewing and use of the website (various devices) Level of expectation and satisfaction
Q2)	Expectation and satisfaction with "ease of making an appointment", such as providing information on the availability of appointments
Q3)	Level of expectation and satisfaction with the treatment staff's manner, appearance, friendliness, and other aspects of the treatment staff.
Q4)	Level of expectation and satisfaction with "skills of the practitioner," such as the practitioner's ease of explanation, the practitioner's wealth of knowledge, and the practitioner's ability to listen
Q5)	Perceived effectiveness Expectation and satisfaction with "treatment effectiveness" including the balance between cost and effectiveness
Q6)	Level of expectation and satisfaction with "treatment menu" such as variety of treatment menu and ease of understanding of treatment menu
Q7)	Facility atmosphere Expectation and satisfaction with "facility atmosphere" such as cleanliness of the facility
Q8)	Quality of facilities (equipment, etc.) Level of expectation and satisfaction regarding the "quality of beauty supplies and equipment," including the quality of products (cosmetics, etc.) handled during treatment."
Q9)	Level of expectation and satisfaction with "ease of use" (e.g., length of business hours, location and accessibility)
Q10)	Expectations and satisfaction with "cost performance" such as clarity of fee structure and balance between treatment cost and service quality
Q11)	Level of expectation and satisfaction with "support services" such as e-mail and telephone inquiries and after-sales follow-up
Q12)	Level of expectation and satisfaction with "reliability of the company" such as trust in the company

Each "x" stands for a question number. Therefore, the total number of explanatory variables used in the analysis is 48.

4   Results

Table 3. Analysis results (high expectations and satisfaction, or dissatisfaction).

Explanatory variables	coefficient	Standard deviation	t-value	p-value	
HH1	0.104	0.059	1.765	0.078	
HL1	0.087	0.055	1.569	0.117	
HH2	0.057	0.060	0.946	0.344	
HL2	0.064	0.056	1.146	0.252	
HH3	0.218	0.080	2.738	0.006	**
HL3	-0.042	0.070	-0.606	0.545	
HH4	0.268	0.085	3.155	0.002	**
HL3	-0.030	0.074	-0.407	0.684	
HH5	0.383	0.079	4.823	0.000	***
HL5	-0.241	0.069	-3.486	0.000	***
HH6	0.270	0.079	3.440	0.001	***
HL6	-0.093	0.069	-1.337	0.181	
HH7	-0.021	0.081	-0.254	0.799	
HL7	-0.005	0.072	-0.071	0.943	
HH8	0.144	0.084	1.714	0.086	
HL8	-0.087	0.073	-1.186	0.235	
HH9	0.132	0.068	1.956	0.051	
HL9	-0.091	0.063	-1.434	0.152	
HH10	0.482	0.071	6.769	0.000	*
HL10	-0.186	0.064	-2.914	0.004	**
HH11	0.327	0.070	4.652	0.000	***
HL11	-0.179	0.063	-2.816	0.005	**
HH12	0.485	0.061	7.977	0.000	***
HL12	-0.097	0.060	-1.606	0.108	

'***' $p < 0.001$, '***' $p < 0.01$, '*' $p < 0.05$

The results of the analysis using the deviating variables of high prior expectation and satisfaction, or high prior expectation and dissatisfaction are shown below (see Table 3). 10 of the 24 explanatory variables were significant in the t-test at a significance level of 5% or less.

Table 4. Analysis Results (low expectations and satisfaction, or dissatisfaction).

Explanatory variables	coefficient	Standard deviation	t-value	p-value	
LH1	0.108	0.050	0.363	0.717	
LL1	-0.145	0.083	-1.747	0.081	
LH2	-0.063	0.050	-1.245	0.213	
LL2	0.085	0.084	1.017	0.309	
LH3	0.057	0.062	0.909	0.363	
LL3	-0.501	0.144	-3.469	0.001	***
LH4	0.314	0.067	4.712	0.000	***
LL4	-0.335	0.148	-2.257	0.024	*
LH5	0.386	0.060	6.448	0.000	***
LL5	-0.861	0.118	-7.315	0.000	***
LH6	0.179	0.062	2.896	0.004	**
LL6	-0.131	0.143	-0.913	0.361	
LH7	0.081	0.058	1.401	0.161	
LL7	-0.174	0.141	-1.239	0.216	
LH8	0.090	0.061	1.467	0.142	
LL8	-0.124	0.148	-0.836	0.403	
LH9	0.015	0.047	0.319	0.750	
LL9	-0.012	0.102	-0.115	0.909	
LH10	0.411	0.056	7.299	0.000	***
LL10	-0.498	0.107	-4.644	0.000	***
LH11	0.193	0.054	3.569	0.000	***
LL11	-0.188	0.100	-1.885	0.059	
LH12	0.462	0.047	9.903	0.000	***
LL12	-0.668	0.103	-6.469	0.000	***

'***' $p < 0.001$, '***' $p < 0.01$, '*' $p < 0.05$

The results of the analysis using the deviating variables of low prior expectation and satisfaction, or low prior expectation and dissatisfaction are shown below (see Table 4).

In the t-test with a significance level of 5% or less, 11 of the 24 explanatory variables were significant.

5   Discussion

In this section, I will discuss the results based on the coefficients of the results in Table 3 and Table 4. Before conducting the analysis of this study, I had made a hypothesis regarding the results of this study. The hypothesis is based on the Expectation Disconfirmation Theory proposed by Oliver (1980). This Expectation Disconfirmation Theory states that customer satisfaction is formed from two factors: the level of expectation formed from the customer's past knowledge and experience in the pre-purchase stage, and the level of perception of product performance felt in the actual consumption experience in the post-purchase stage. In other words, based on pre-purchase expectations, customers are satisfied and happy if their expectations are exceeded after purchase, disinterested if their expectations are met, and dissatisfied, angry, and disappointed if their expectations are not met.

Since customer satisfaction and brand value have been said to be related, based on Oliver's theory, a negative deviation variable (HLx) that indicates dissatisfaction with high expectations has a greater negative impact on a company's brand value than other variables, while a positive deviation variable (LHx) that indicates satisfaction with low expectations has a greater negative impact than other variables. The positive deviation variable (LHx) was expected to have a greater positive impact than the other variables. The variables that did not diverge between prior expectations and post-use satisfaction (HHx and LLx) were expected to have a positive or negative impact on corporate brand value, respectively, but less than the positive divergence variable (LHx) and the negative divergence variable (HLx).

However, the results were not as expected. Of the variables that showed significant differences in the analysis, the mean values for each of the deviating variables were HH = 0.347, LH = 0.324, HL = −0.202, and LL = −0.572. In the following, we will discuss why the results were not as expected and propose an expectation management method to increase brand value.

5.1   Positive Impact on Corporate Brand

Of the variables that were found to be significant in the analysis, 13 variables, HH (3,4,5,6,10,11,12) and LH (4,5,6,10,11,12), had a positive impact on the brand value of the company. The mean coefficients of HH and LH for these 13 variables were HH = 0.347 and LH = 0.324, indicating that there was no significant difference between them. Compared to HH, LH is considered to have lower brand evaluation before use due to lower prior expectation. However, the positive discrepancy caused by the use of a beauty salon increased the brand value. On the other hand, the reason why the value of HH was the same as that of LH despite the high level of prior expectations is because HH could not exceed the level of prior expectations and made customers feel that their expectations were met. This is the same result as in the Expectation Disconfirmation Theory, where a large positive discrepancy occurred for LH because the initial expectation level was low, while HH failed to produce a positive discrepancy because the initial expectation level was high. This suggests that the initial expectation level of HH was higher than that of LH but similar to that of LH.

5.2 Negative Impact on Corporate Brand

Of the variables that showed significance as a result of the analysis, the eight variables that had a negative impact on corporate brand value were HL (5,10,11) and LL (3,4,5,10,12). The mean coefficients of HL and LL for these eight variables were HL = 0.202 and LL = 0.572, indicating that LL has a greater negative impact on corporate brand value than HL. Based on the Expectation Disconfirmation Theory, HL is considered to have a large negative impact in that it causes people to have high expectations and then disappoints them, while LL has a larger negative impact.

However, the results showed that LL had a greater negative impact than LL. This result needs to be considered in the context of the theory of causal attribution. Causal attribution is the perception that people have of the factors behind their own behavior, the behavior of others, or the events they observe. Causal attribution is also said to affect emotions, especially when negative and unexpected outcomes or events occur. Causal attribution is based on three properties: Locus, Stability, and Controllability (Locus, what is the center of the cause; Stability, does the cause occur frequently; Controllability, is the center of the cause controllable) In this case, HL was more negative. The reason why the negative effect of HL was smaller than that of HL was that the prior expectation was higher, and the actual satisfaction was lower, which led to causal attribution, and the cognitive dissonance theory, which justifies oneself when one's thoughts are contradicted, arose in the thought.

5.3 Expectation Management to Increase Brand Value

In recent years, we have seen the argument that we should control prior expectations so that they are not too high. However, in reality, in a market where there are many competitors, in order for a company's product to catch the attention of customers and be purchased, it is necessary to create a sense of expectation in customers. The results of this study show that there is no significant difference in the results of increasing brand value depending on prior expectations. However, for the results of lowering brand value, lower prior expectations had a negative impact more than twice as much. This result suggests the need to raise expectations along with satisfaction, rather than managing expectations out of fear of negative deviations. With regard to negative deviations, it is necessary to use causal attribution and cognitive dissonance theory, and at the same time manage customers to interpret that the cause of the negative deviation is something that happened by accident this time and can be controlled by the company.

6 Conclusion

The results of this study show that raising the level of expectation reduces the risk of lowering the brand value, rather than lowering the level of expectation. However, this result is abstract. In the future, we will analyze what specific items are more effective in managing expectation levels.

References

1. Yukihiro, A.: Recent developments in consumer behavior research- considering new research directions and possibilities. Japan Business Association "Circulation Research" **16**(2), (2014)
2. Mototaka, S.: Influence of brands on purchase decisions. Japan Business Associa tion "Circulation Research" **4**(2), (2001)
3. Yuka, K., Masuko, S., Tosimasa, Y.: Cognitive dissonance, and online reviews in consumer purchasing. J. Japan Soc. Sens. Eng. **17**(4), (2018)
4. Hikaru, H.: Tourist expectations and satisfaction. Consum. Behav. Res.**16**, 275–288 (2010)
5. Naoto, O.: The Marketing Logic of Commoditized Markets. Yuhikaku Publishing Co., Ltd. (2007)
6. Nobuhiko, N.: An Empirical study on improving customer satisfaction by reducing prior expectations. Japan Adv. Inst. Sci. Technol. (2013)
7. Gosen, I.: Challenges in improving service quality in the beauty service industry "from a service profit chain perspective". Social Syst. Res. **23**, (2011)
8. Souyu, O.: Expectation management pre "control of customer satisfaction by marketing communication". J. Manage. Stud. **36**, 233–242 (2012)
9. Chihiro, M.: The importance of expectations in marketing. Kwansei Gakuin University management strategy research group business administration research, **3**, 21-34 (2009)
10. Song Ming, S., Miseon, L.: A Study on Execution Task of Branding Strategy of
11. SMEs and its solution "focusing on the case study of general foundation corpo ration association for the certification of brand managers Japan". Econ. Bus. Rev. **26**(2), 29-41 (2019)
12. Shigeru, F., Takaaki, S., Takuya, H., Kazuo S.: Visualization for controlling the expectation of customer satisfaction "framework of service design". Japan Soc. Design Stud. Design Stud. (2014)
13. Aaker, D.A.: Aaker on Branding"20 Principles that Drive Success". Morgan James Publisher, New York (2014)
14. Yano Research Institute Ltd: https://www.yano.co.jp/press-release/show/press_id/2901. Accessed 21 Feb 2022
15. Tokyo shoko research Ltd: https://www.tsr-net.co.jp/news/analysis/20200114_02.html. Accessed 21 Feb 2022
16. PR TIMES Inc.: https://prtimes.jp/main/html/rd/p/000000006.000019959.html. Accessed 24 Feb 2022
17. Oliver, R.L.: A cognitive model of the antecedents and consequences of satisfaction decisions. J. Mark. Res. **17**(4), 460–469 (1980)

Wisdom Science of Image Conceptualization

Tetsuya Maeshiro[1(✉)], Yuri Ozawa[2], and Midori Maeshiro[3]

[1] Faculty of Library, Information and Media Studies,
University of Tsukuba, Tsukuba 305-8550, Japan
`maeshiro@slis.tsukuba.ac.jp`
[2] Ozawa Clinic, Tokyo, Japan
[3] School of Music, Federal University of Rio de Janeiro, Rio de Janeiro, Brazil

Abstract. This paper proposes a model of human creative activities using the framework of wisdom science. The two main components of the model are the concept processing and image processing modules, which function in parallel with information exchange links between them. The model is also discussed related to the model of tacit and explicit knowledge. The concept of system science serves as the basic framework for the modeling and analysis.

Keywords: Concept · Image · Tacit knowledge · Explicit knowledge · Relationality · Quantitative · Facets

1 Introduction

This paper describes a model and theoretical basis to study creative activities by human beings using the framework of wisdom science [1].

We assume that human creative activities are the results of a parallel interaction between language based processing and image based processing (Fig. 1). The former is associated with logic, and the latter with emotion. We denote the former as *concept processing* and the latter as *image processing*. The term "image" does not imply that the image processing is abstract or vague. On the contrary, most images are clear, although their description, usually using natural language, is difficult, but their mental manipulation is possible. Such operation would not be possible if images were vague.

Creative activity is a result of knowledge manipulation. As such, explicit knowledge corresponds to concept processing, and tacit knowledge to image processing. Another interpretation is that concept processing manipulates explicit knowledge, and image processing manipulates tacit knowledge.

Wisdom science, upon which the present study is based, treats both explicit and tacit knowledge as two different facets of collection of knowledge elements, denoted as *knowledge ocean* (Fig. 2). Explicit knowledge and tacit knowledge have contrasting properties, where the former can be explicitly described, is

S. Yamamoto and H. Mori (Eds.): HCII 2022, LNCS 13305, pp. 22–34, 2022.
https://doi.org/10.1007/978-3-031-06424-1_3

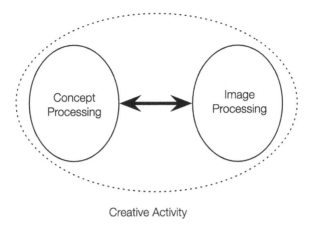

Creative Activity

Fig. 1. Parallel processes of concept processing and image processing

objective, can be communicated through text, shared by a group of people, and represents a consensus of a group of people. On the other hand, tacit knowledge cannot be described by text, is individual, subjective and internal, thus not shared by people, and is strongly associated with the body of each person and personal feelings.

The basic framework of wisdom science is that the elements of knowledge of a person is activated and manipulated consciously for explicit knowledge or unconsciously for tacit knowledge. Our model of tacit and explicit knowledge is fundamentally different from the conventional frameworks where tacit and explicit knowledge constitute knowledge of a person and the two types of knowledge are distinct elements of knowledge of a person (Fig. 3). Therefore, a given knowledge element may be activated as explicit knowledge in one instance and activated as tacit knowledge in another instance. Questioning and answering process is an example of knowledge elements being used in tacit or explicit knowledge depending on situation, represented as small circles in the bottom linked to explicit knowledge and tacit knowledge in Fig. 2. When a person is asked a question, for instance in a interview, the asked person sometimes say opinions, thoughts or ideas that the person has never said before or the person himself was not aware of. And the person himself feels surprised the recognize how the person was thinking about the asked issue. Formulating a sentence to talk involves gathering knowledge elements or concepts related to the content of the speech. In this (i) collecting process and (ii) the meaning generated by the formulated sentence activates the knowledge elements that belong to tacit knowledge. In conventional interpretation, this process is a tacit concept being transformed to an explicit concept. However, wisdom science models this process as a concept element that was already evoked as tacit knowledge became also evoked as explicit knowledge. As stated before, tacit knowledge and explicit knowledge are the representations of knowledge elements linked to the consciousness of the person possessing that knowledge.

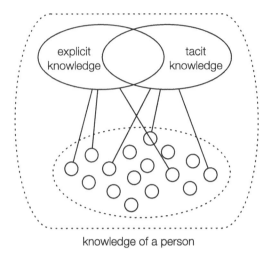

Fig. 2. Wisdom science interpretation of knowledge of a person. Explicit knowledge and tacit knowledge as activated from the ocean of knowledge elements. Bottom dotted circle represents the core of knowledge of a person, and small circles in the bottom dotted circle denote "knowledge elements".

Tacit knowledge is contrasted to explicit knowledge primarily on the describability by a text. Explicit knowledge and tacit knowledge are closely related with memory skill and imagination skill, respectively. While the memorization skill is related to rationality, imagination skill is related to emotions and feelings. However, memorization of images is also linked to emotions and feelings (Fig. 4).

Few attempts to model the simultaneous use of explicit and tacit knowledge have been reported. For instance, from the facet related to the individuality of knowledge, Nonaka treated the tacit knowledge based on the innovation process, which is a creative activity, of a group of individuals, and proposed the SECI model [2]. The SECI model connects the explicit and tacit knowledge by proposing the mechanisms involved in the endless cycle of explicit knowledge ⇒ tacit knowledge ⇒ explicit knowledge ⇒ tacit knowledge ⋯⋯. It offers a general framework, but lacks the detailed mechanism of individual processes described in the model, particularly the mechanism of transitions among tacit and explicit knowledge. In other words, it fits the observed process because the description is abstract and models abstract phenomena, but no concrete mechanism has been proposed, for instance a structure that might enable computer based implementations, for instance.

Tacit knowledge is so denoted because the person cannot describe his own tacit knowledge, particularly by natural language, and is even more difficult, if not impossible, to be described by the others. However, it is often possible to describe vaguely using images or feelings. The author agrees with Polanyi's statement that the inability of description does not negate its existence.

A focus of this paper is the integrated treatment of human creative activity. Activities using the knowledge, which is not limited to "intellectual" activities, is primarily an individual act. Any activity using the knowledge involves not only the explicit knowledge, but also the tacit knowledge. Conventional studies tend to treat explicit knowledge as an external layer of the tacit knowledge or explicit and tacit knowledge as two independent modules, but this paper treats the both explicit and tacit knowledge as two facets of the knowledge of a person.

2   Model of Human Creative Activity

2.1   Concept Processing

Figure 5 illustrates the concept processing model. There is a set of entities, denoted 'concept ocean'. A concept *emerges* from the ocean by invoking multiple entities in the ocean and connecting them based on some relationships.

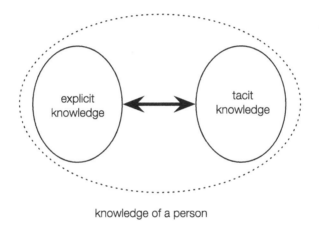

Fig. 3. Conventional interpretation of knowledge of a person

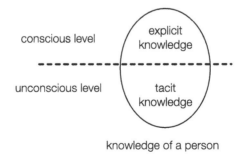

Fig. 4. Another representation of knowledge of a person, where explicit and tacit knowledge are associated with conscious level

The system description consists basically of elements and relationships among elements. Conventional representation models used for system description are mathematically equivalent to graphs [3]. However, conventional models present following defects: (1) unable to represent N-ary relationships or relationships among more than two nodes; (2) unable to represent relationships among relationships; (3) unable to specify relationships or assign attributes; (4) unable to represent multiple facets of quantitative relationships. The hypernetwork model solves these issues.

Details of individual relationships are described using the hypernetwork model [4,5]. Similar descriptions are impossible with other conventional models.

The system description of a phenomenon based on a given viewpoint is actualized by a set of elements and links (relationships) among them.

The elements and related concepts constitute a set

$$V = \{v_1, v_2, \ldots, v_N\} \tag{1}$$

where v_i, $i = 1 \ldots N$, is an element, and N is the number of elements. Conceptually, all the elements used to describe some aspect of the phenomena constitute a set of nodes V, which is a collection of elements. We denote this collection a *pool* of elements. Elements in the *pool* can be generated, modified and deleted.

Then a set of elements S_V, $S_V \subseteq V$, constitute a concept viewpoint P_C.

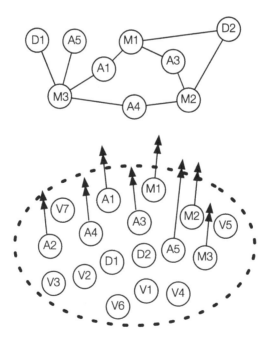

Fig. 5. Concept ocean and emerged concept of concept processing

A concept viewpoint P_C is defined as

$$P_C = C \times R \times A, \text{ where } E \subseteq V,\ R \subseteq V,\ E \cap R = \emptyset \qquad (2)$$

where

$$C \subseteq V,\ R \subseteq V,\ A \subseteq V \qquad (3)$$

and

$$C \cap R = \emptyset,\ C \cap A = \emptyset,\ R \cap A = \emptyset \qquad (4)$$

where C denotes the set of nodes (elements) functioning as Concept nodes, R the set of nodes functioning as Relation nodes, and A the set of nodes functioning as Attribute nodes. C, R and A are subsets of all elements V, and the role (Concept, Relation and Attribute) of a node is only one under a given viewpoint, and no simultaneous assignment of multiple roles is allowed under the same viewpoint P_C.

Since the role of a node and connections among nodes are viewpoint dependent, the set of elements in the *ocean* V is simply a set of isolated elements

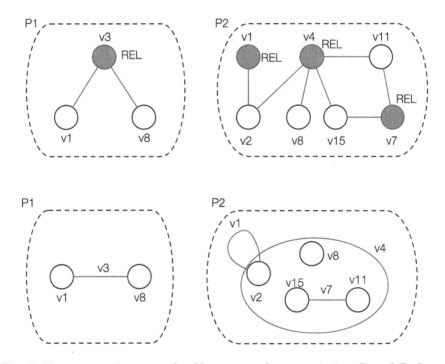

Fig. 6. The *ocean* and an example of hypernetwork representation. P_1 and P_2 denote the viewpoints. Also shown are conventional hypergraph representations. White nodes denote nodes functioning as elements, and filled nodes (labeled "REL") represent nodes defining the relationships among connected nodes. For instance, the Relation node "v_3" is a relationship between nodes "v_1" and "v_8" in facet P_1. While the element v_1 functions as a concept or attribute in facet P_1, it is a relationship in facet P_2.

without any connection among them. Nodes are connected once the viewpoint is selected and connections appear between the nodes used to represent the viewpoint. In other words, the viewpoint determines the role of elements (nodes) and connections among them. Distinct viewpoints usually consist of different sets of nodes, but when they are identical, connections among nodes are different.

The details of concepts and relationships can be specified by connecting other elements as attribute nodes. An attribute may specify multiple nodes, and Concept and Relation nodes function as Attribute nodes of other nodes. Figure 6 is a graph representation of a description based on the hypernetwork model.

2.2   Image Processing

Figure 7 illustrates the proposed basic model of image processing. Analogous to the concept processing model, there is a set of image entities or elements, denoted "image ocean". An image *emerges* from the image ocean by invoking multiple images in the ocean and fused. Although denoted "image", it denotes non-linguistic entities and is not limited to two dimensional images, and includes sensory information such as odor, taste, sound, and feelings.

The activation process of image processing is also different from concept processing. In the case of concept processing, relationships among entities are also activated, but no such role exists in image processing. Differing from the concept processing, no role (Concept, Relation, Attribute) is associated with activated elements v_i. As stated before, the entities are fused and generates a new image. The generated image may be added to the image ocean depending on its importance or value, but calculation of these values will not be discussed in this paper. Such *feedback process* is not required in concept processing, as activated entities include relationships among concepts, and no strictly speaking "new" concepts are generated, as relationships are representations of entities with Relation as their roles.

A crucial difference from concept processing is that the emerged entity, which is a combination of activated entities, is not decomposable. Contrary to the concept processing, where the components of the generated entity have one-to-one correspondences with entities in the concept ocean and individual components can be identified and extracted, individual components are roughly identified but blurred boundaries among components (Fig. 7 (B)), In some cases, identification of individual components might be impossible. Furthermore, the role of each entity (Concept, Attribute or Relation) is also difficult to be defined, possibly impossible, differing from defined roles of concept, relation and attribute of the concept processing.

A viewpoint P_I is defined as

$$P_I = v_1 \circledast v_2 \circledast \cdots \circledast v_n \tag{5}$$

$$S_V = \{v_1, v_2, \ldots, v_N\}, \quad S_V \subseteq V \tag{6}$$

where "$\circledast$" denotes the fusion operator, which denotes the image fusion.

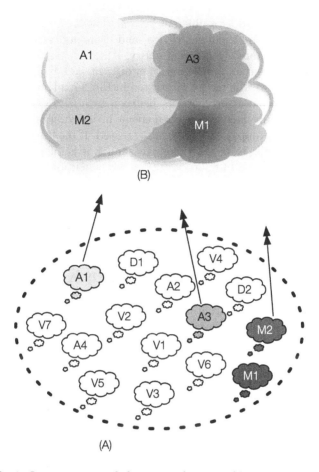

Fig. 7. Image ocean and the emerged image of Image processing

The fusion operator $\circledast$ is non-commutative and non-associative. Therefore,

$$v_1 \circledast v_2 \neq v_2 \circledast v_1 \tag{7}$$

$$(v_1 \circledast v_2) \circledast v_3 \neq v_1 \circledast (v_2 \circledast v_3) \tag{8}$$

3   Model of Knowledge of a Person

The author's viewpoint about the relationship between explicit and tacit knowledge is different from conventional standpoints. Conventionally the explicit and tacit knowledge are characterized as distinct entities. Treating as two different facets of an entity implies that each of explicit knowledge and tacit knowledge can be treated as two independent systems. One viewpoint is to model the knowledge of a person as a system of systems. However, wisdom science treats the knowledge of a person as a different system that is the result of the fusion of explicit knowledge and tacit knowledge, and elements employed by tacit or explicit knowledge is stored in different entity.

Compared to conventional interpretation of tacit and explicit knowledge as distinct entities (Fig. 3), the model illustrated in Fig. 2 explains better the transitions of knowledge pieces or elements between tacit and explicit knowledge. Wisdom science mainly focuses on phenomena in individuals, although social knowledge involving groups of people is also treated. If tacit and explicit knowledge are distinct entities as conventionally assumed, it is difficult to explain the transformation mechanism of tacit knowledge to explicit and vice-versa without the existence of *something* that transitions between tacit and explicit knowledge.

Wisdom science also studies how knowledge elements are activated as tacit or explicit knowledge, including temporal development of knowledge elements including their state and handling when deployed as tacit or explicit knowledge. The author proposes that both tacit and explicit knowledge are two facets of knowledge of a person, or *emerged* state of some of knowledge elements that belong to the core of knowledge of a person (Fig. 2). A defect of conventional interpretation (Fig. 3) is that knowledge elements, usually concepts at finest grain level, may not *emerge* from unconscious to conscious level, because some knowledge elements are employed simultaneously by both tacit and explicit knowledge.

4   Image Conceptualization Hypothesis

Human creative activities involve employment of personal knowledge. The proposed model of creative activity focus on the different aspect of knowledge, as the concept processing corresponds to explicit knowledge, and the image processing to tacit knowledge. From the viewpoint of describability, tacit and explicit knowledge share the same ocean that is the set of knowledge elements (Fig. 2). Compared to the model illustrated in Fig. 8, it focuses on static aspect of creative activity. On the other hand, the creative activity model focuses on more dynamic aspect, and includes additional property of *describability*, which is what differentiates tacit and explicit knowledge.

Concept ocean and image ocean are represented as distinctive entities (Fig. 8), contrary to the ocean of concept elements shared by tacit and explicit knowledge (Fig. 2). We introduced the concept of image in knowledge representation and manipulation as an element with fundamentally different properties from the concept element. The possible operations are also fundamentally distinct, as images can be fused, partially removed or gradually changed, which is impossible with concepts. Therefore, our creative activity model composed of concept and image processing offers a new facet of knowledge manipulation, describing different viewpoint from the conventional treatment of tacit and explicit knowledge.

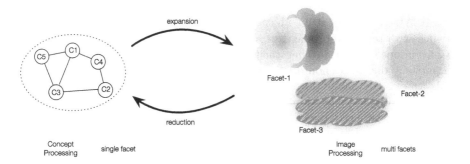

Fig. 8. Functional interactions between parallel processes of concept processing and image processing

The image ocean can be interpreted as the set of knowledge elements belonging to the ocean (Fig. 2) interpreted as image elements. Similarly, the concept ocean consists of knowledge elements focusing on their describable aspects. Such classification based on concept and image aspect is completely different from the conventional classification of tacit or explicit, which is based on the describability by the person himself. The proposed model focuses on individual activity, and is related to Polanyi's treatments [6]. Our model offers more concrete aspects than conventional studies, by introducing two processes that manipulates two distinct objects, the concept ocean and the image ocean.

The model of concept and image processing offers a different perspective from the conventional explicit and tacit knowledge model. Both offer possible interpretations of human knowledge. In our framework, the oceans, which contain the respective functional and descriptive elements, are the shared components among models. We propose that the elements in the oceans correspond to single or groups of neurons. The existence of shared component ensures the compatibility between the two models, and the two models represent different facets of the knowledge. Compared to the model of explicit and tacit knowledge, the model of concept and image processing is function oriented, focusing on the invocation of concepts and images, and the expansion and reduction entities involved in creative activities.

The authors assume that creative activity is based on neural activities. Polanyi also used the concept of emergence in the process of scientific discovery, the relationship between the elements (subsidiary particulars) and the image generated from the result of focusing the whole. The integrated image of the whole disappears if any of elements is focused. This corresponds to the "reduction" in Fig. 8, where a concept is focused from the set of activated images.

A model framework with enough description capability is necessary to describe integrated personal knowledge of tacit and explicit knowledge. Namely, the model should be able to integrate multiple facets, no prerequisite of precise structure, and no fixed boundaries. The three features are interrelated. The hypernetwork model [5] is the model framework used to describe. No other conventional model framework presents the three properties related to multiple facets. No restrictions exist on what an element represents. It can be a concept described with terms, and image, or an abstract or a fuzzy entity.

Conventional definition that tacit knowledge is processed on unconscious level partially due to its non-describability does not apply to image processing. In this aspect, the image processing is different from tacit knowledge because image processing is executed on conscious level. Undoubtedly image processing is not executed only at conscious level, and images operated in image processing associated with tacit knowledge are manipulated at unconscious level. The basic features to define tacit knowledge are the unconscious and automatic process and inability of description. Therefore, the execution at unconscious level is an essential feature of tacit knowledge, which is not for image processing, then tacit knowledge and image processing are incompatible and are models based on different viewpoints. Consequently, image processing is distinct from tacit knowledge, and they denote different aspects of human intellectual activities. One of main similarities between image processing and tacit knowledge is the difficulty to describe manipulated elements (knowledge or image) using language. Therefore, Figs. 1, 3 and 2 are distinct models of personal knowledge, but compatible as these models share the basic elements belonging to oceans of respective models.

Figure 9 illustrates the compatibility between the conventional concept of explicit and tacit knowledge and the proposed model of concept and image processing, based on the describability by the person himself who operates the involved knowledge elements. Explicit and tacit knowledge are distinct, and the same applies to concept and image processing, drawn as non-overlapping shapes in Fig. 9. The differences of size of the shapes of explicit knowledge and concept processing are irrelevant, drawn for easier visual cognition. Where explicit knowledge and concept processing occupy the similar region in the graph, tacit knowledge and image processing do not. As discussed above, images can be manipulated unconsciously or consciously, which differentiates the image processing from tacit knowledge, which is operated unconsciously by definition. Furthermore, the area enclosed by concept and image processings is larger than the area filled by explicit and tacit knowledge, indicating that the proposed model explains more diverse knowledge manipulation phenomena. The wider coverage of image processing suggests that the proposed model of concept and image processing is able to explain wider range of knowledge manipulation than conventional models.

This paper does not discuss the representation mechanism of concepts and images by neurons. However, some experimental results have been reported [7], and although detailed mechanism is still unknown, no problems exist with neuron representation hypothesis.

The generation of image and concept elements in image ocean and concept ocean will be discussed elsewhere.

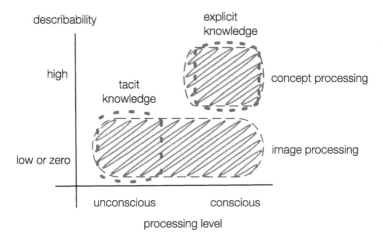

Fig. 9. Comparison of concept processing and image processing with explicit and tacit knowledge based on describability and consciousness level of the processes

5   Conclusions

This paper proposes a model of human creative activities using the framework of wisdom science. The two main components of the model are the concept processing and image processing modules, which function side by side. The hypernetwork model is used, which is capable of representing structures that cannot be described by conventional system models. The concept of system science serves as the basic framework for the modeling and analysis. Wisdom science aims to describe knowledge based on neuron level phenomena, differing from conventional knowledge studies that rely on vague and abstract level. Use of neuron activities permits quantitative investigation of creative activities, which has not been done before.

The concept processing and image processing are not independent mechanisms from conventional treatments of tacit and explicit knowledge, but should be interpreted as a new viewpoint or facet to understand human creative activities.

References

1. Maeshiro, T.: Proposal of wisdom science. In: Yamamoto, S., Mori, H. (eds.) HCII 2021. LNCS, vol. 12766, pp. 406–418. Springer, Cham (2021). https://doi.org/10. 1007/978-3-030-78361-7_31
2. Nonaka, I.: A dynamic theory of organizational knowledge creation. Organ. Sci. **5**, 14–37 (1994)
3. Berge, C.: The Theory of Graphs. Dover (2001)
4. Maeshiro, T., Ozawa, Y., Maeshiro, M.: A system description model with fuzzy boundaries. In: Yamamoto, S. (ed.) HIMI 2017. LNCS, vol. 10274, pp. 390–402. Springer, Cham (2017). https://doi.org/10.1007/978-3-319-58524-6_31

5. Maeshiro, T.: Framework based on relationship to describe non-hierarchical, bound-aryless and multi-perspective phenomena. SICE J. Control Measur. Syst. Integr. **11**, 381–389 (2019)
6. Polanyi, M.: Genius in science. Encounter **38**, 43–50 (1972)
7. Quiroga, R.Q., Reddy, L., Kreiman, G., Koch, C., Fried, I.: Invariant visual repre-sentation by single neurons in the human brain. Nature **435**, 1102–1107 (2005)

Service Design Approach for Regional Issues
-Case Study of the Audio Company-

Tappei Mori[1]([⊠]), Suzuka Mori[1], Miho Suto[1], Keiko Kasamatsu[1], and Takeo Ainoya[2,3]

[1] Tokyo Metropolitan University, Asahigaoka, Hino, Tokyo, Japan
t.mori48ppp@icloud.com
[2] Tokyo University of Technology, Nishi-Kamata, Ota, Tokyo, Japan
[3] VDS Co., Ltd., Higashiyama, Meguro, Tokyo, Japan

Abstract. The purpose of this study is to rebrand the Forest Notes product and service through a case study with an audio company. First, we conducted a research on the image of the audio company. Among college students around the age of 20 who were researched, the awareness of the audio company was low. This is thought to be because there are few touch points in media familiar to university students. On the other hand, research has shown that there is trust in technology. Next, we researched which companies made good impressions on us. The five companies that came up as the most impressive were Starbucks, Oriental Land, Nintendo, Apple, and Patagonia. The analysis revealed that all of the companies have developed a clear vision. It is thought that a clear vision and the creation of touch points based on a thorough vision have led to the formation of an image. The next step was to evaluate Forest Notes. From the evaluation, it became clear that although Forest Notes has a high level of performance, it is difficult to create value for users because it does not convey its purpose and intent. We need to clarify our targets and clarify the meaning of Forest Notes. In the future, we will decide on the target, think about UX, and propose a new Forest Notes.

Keywords: Service design · Rebranding · Vision

1 Introduction

1.1 Background

In conducting joint research with the audio company, we thought that we could make new proposals to the audio company not only by evaluating audio products, but also by taking a unique university approach using our research on UX and design management.

1.2 Purpose

The main purpose of this project is to rebrand the "Forest Notes" service and product offered by the audio company. In addition, the sub-purpose is to analyze and research the company, and to rebrand the audio company through the rebranding of "Forest Notes".

S. Yamamoto and H. Mori (Eds.): HCII 2022, LNCS 13305, pp. 35–45, 2022.
https://doi.org/10.1007/978-3-031-06424-1_4

1.3   What is Forest Notes?

Forest Notes is an internet service [1] that allows users to listen to the sounds of eight forests in Japan in real time, and a speaker [2] that works with the application. The speakers come in two different sizes, the larger one being in the shape of a cube with a volume of thirty liters. Thirty liters is the amount of oxygen that a tree produces in a day. The wood used is domestic chestnut wood, which is characterized by its strength, and is selected, processed, and assembled by hand by skilled craftsmen. The surface of the wood is coated with oil, mainly linseed oil, which makes it moist and comfortable to the touch. While there are various particulars, the price of the larger Forest Notes is around 320,000 yen because it is difficult to secure a large area of wood and difficult to process (Fig. 1).

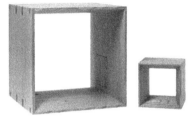

Fig. 1. Forest notes and forest notes mini [2]

2   Research

2.1   Image of the Audio Company

First of all, we researched the image of the audio company. Of the 44 s-year university students who attended the class, only 3 knew about the audio company. The opinions from the research on the audio company included "little advertising" and "little exposure on Twitter and YouTube, so there are few opportunities to be recognized by young people. It is thought that the result of 3 out of 44 students was due to the lack of touch points in the media familiar to the students. Many of the images of audio companies obtained from the students" research were "good cost performance," "trust in products," and "little change". Furthermore, the research revealed that there was a high level of awareness about the subsidiary entertainment company, but not about the fact that the company was a subsidiary of the audio company. Since many of the artists belonging to the entertainment company are touch points, the subsidiary company is considered to be more widely known.

2.2   Companies of Good Impressions

Next, we researched the companies that the students had a good impression of. The companies that came up with a good impression were Starbucks, Oriental Land (the company that runs Tokyo Disneyland and Tokyo DisneySea), Nintendo, Apple, and Patagonia. Two out of the six groups of students listed all of these companies as companies they had a good impression of.

These five companies were categorized into four companies: Starbucks, Oriental Land, Nintendo, Apple, and and one company: Patagonia. The first four companies are considered to have a high level of recognition because many users have used them, while Patagonia is considered to have a lower level of both experience and recognition than the other four companies, hence this classification. Based on the above categorization, we tried to figure out why this company came up as a company with a good impression. In the case of Starbucks, Oriental Land, Nintendo, and Apple, and the entire experience with the products and services provided by the company is connected to the image of the company, and the experience itself has value, so it is thought that people have a good impression of the company. When we researched what kinds of experiences are leading to value, it became clear that each company has a variety of approaches.

Starbucks has a variety of initiatives, including a strategy of opening stores in high-traffic urban areas [3], regional land stores to enhance coexistence with local communities [4], customized drinks to create a special feeling, messages on drinks drawn by store staff, design of spaces with a relaxed atmosphere, and mobile ordering to reduce the stress of waiting in line [5]. It became clear that all of these initiatives are connected to the company's role as a third place (not just a place to drink coffee, but a place where people can enjoy the atmosphere and build relationships [4]), which has been its mission since its establishment (Fig. 2).

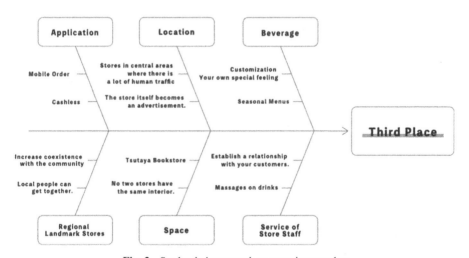

Fig. 2. Starbucks' approach to experience value

Oriental Land's cast members, attractions, shows, restaurants, etc. are all connected to Disney's philosophy of providing happiness [6], which makes the experience worthwhile (Fig. 3).

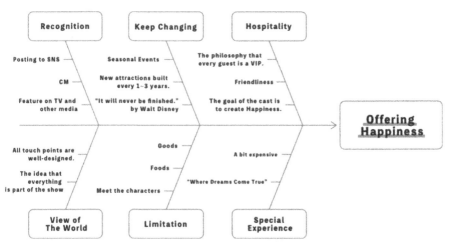

Fig. 3. Oriental land's approach to experience value

For Nintendo, the high recognition of Mario, the wide range of game software available, from single player to family friendly, and the UI [7] that is easy for children to understand all contribute to a worthwhile experience (Fig. 4).

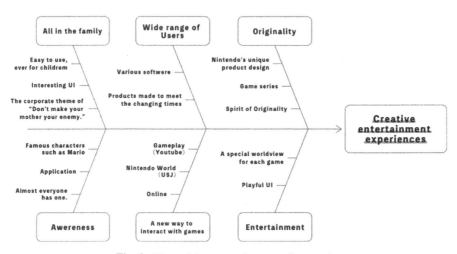

Fig. 4. Nintendo's approach to experience value

For Apple, simple and stylish products, unified branding, and the philosophy of Steve Jobs have made the company what it is today (Fig. 5).

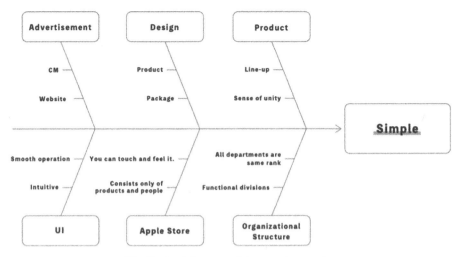

Fig. 5. Apple's approach to experience value

The other company, Patagonia, has been strongly promoting its environmental initiatives on its SNS [8], website [9], and advertisements [10]. Environmental efforts are an easy-to-understand social contribution activity, and the fact that the entire company is working on environmental issues and communicating them in a positive manner is thought to be leading to a good impression (Fig. 6).

Fig. 6. Patagonia's SNS [8], website [9] and advertisement [10]

2.3 Discussion

What became clear from the research was that the four companies that came up as having a good impression of us all had a clear vision in common. If we were to categorize visions, Starbucks and Oriental Land have a vision to provide a good experience for users; Apple and Nintendo have a vision to provide an experience that is different from other companies. In addition, all companies are thoroughly creating touch points based on their vision. Since the vision is clear, it may be easy to form an image of the company. In light of the above, when we consider the audio company, we find that it was formed by the merger of three electronics manufacturers and has no clear vision. The nature of the business varies, and it is considered difficult to form an image of what the company does.

3 Evaluate Forest Notes

3.1 Purpose of the Evaluation

The class was divided into six groups to evaluate Forest Notes. The purpose of this evaluation was to understand the value of Forest Notes from the user's perspective by assuming actual usage scenarios.

3.2 Evaluation Method

The evaluation of Forest Notes was done using the QDA (Quantitative Descriptive Analysis) method.

Procedure of QDA Method. The QDA method is based on the following steps.

1. Decide which products to evaluate. (In addition to the Forest Notes, the class had three or four other products from the same audio company.)
2. Determine the scene in which the product will be used.
3. Produce a number of evaluation terms.
4. Reduce the number of evaluation terms to 10.
5. Prepare one word for the overall assessment.
6. Create a seven-step evaluation sheet.
7. Ask them to evaluate it.

Product Usage Scenarios. The usage scenes of the products set by each group are as follows.

Group1: Selecting a gift for a friend at an electronics store, relying on the advice of the staff.

Group2: A gift for a family member who lives with you. Similar products are not available at home, and I use them myself.

Group3: See tie-up ads with celebrities or characters.

Group4: Use it in the living room of your house.

Group5: Listen to it when you want to relax, such as while studying.

Group6: Use in the office bathroom.

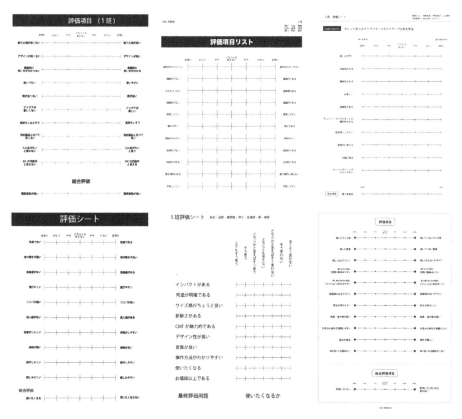

Fig. 7. Evaluation sheets for groups 1, 2, 3, 4, 5, and 6

Evaluation sheets. The evaluation sheet for each group is as follows (Fig. 7).

3.3   Evaluation Results

The results of the Forest Notes evaluation for each group were as follows.

Group1: The intuitive use of the product was rated low, but the idea of the product was rated high. The data for the item of whether or not you want to give it to a friend related to the scene you set was uneven (Fig. 8).

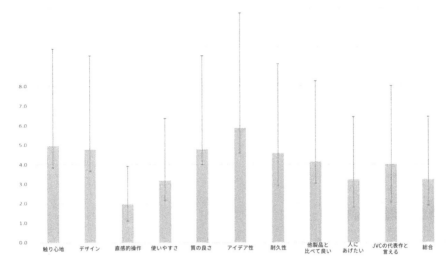

Fig. 8. Evaluation results of Group1

Group2: Many people consider the product to be revolutionary. The mean for ease of learning was high, but the standard deviation values were high and varied from person to person. It is thought that the user needs to be narrowed down quite specifically (Fig. 9).

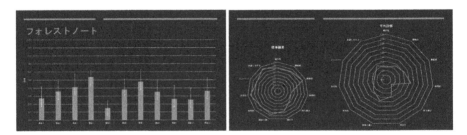

Fig. 9. Evaluation results of Group2

Group3: There was a lot of appreciation for the novelty. On the other hand, there were many evaluations that said it was difficult to use on a daily basis and not intuitive to use. This may be due to the characteristic of Forest Notes to provide unprecedented experience value. It is necessary to appeal to the newness and rarity of the product and carefully follow up on its usage (Fig. 10).

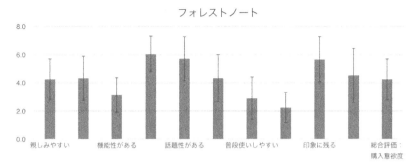

Fig. 10. Evaluation results of Group3

Group4: Not a single category scored above the middle of the average score (5 points), and the overall rating, whether or not I would like to purchase the product, was 3.5 points, indicating that the product does not seem to be popular overall. The low ratings for ease of transport, cost performance, storage, and operability suggest the need for innovations in CMF and overall shape. Having to pay attention to moisture and insect infestation may lead to stress when using them. The high ratings for sound and immersion indicate that users feel as if they are in a forest (Fig. 11).

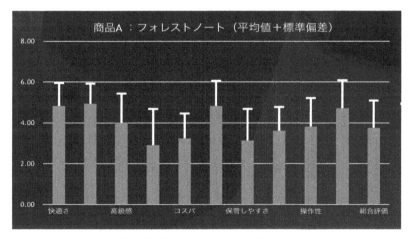

Fig. 11. Evaluation results of Group4

Group5: The impact and freshness items were rated highly. Many respondents rated the operation method as difficult to understand. They expected CMF to be highly rated, but it is not outstandingly high compared to other products. The standard deviation for the category "clear use" was 1.9, which was more varied than the other categories. Since the people who were asked to evaluate the product were students of the same class, many of them knew about its use, and it is unclear whether they were able to evaluate it assuming that they did not know about it (Fig. 12).

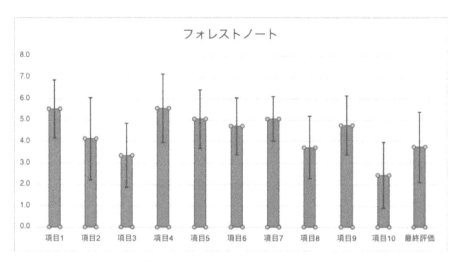

Fig. 12. Evaluation results of Group5

Group6: As a result of its suitable size and its ability to fit into the space, it has an interior design that fits in well even when installed in public spaces. They hypothesized that sound quality would not be an appealing point, but many people rated the sound quality as good, and the functionality of the product was readily apparent. It was difficult to understand the operability of the system from its appearance, and many evaluated it as difficult to operate. The category of "would recommend to acquaintances" was low, suggesting that the touch points are narrow (Fig. 13).

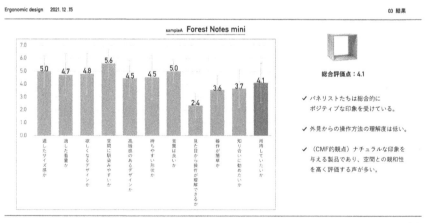

Fig. 13. Evaluation results of Group6

3.4 Discussion

The performance of the system is highly technical, based on evaluations such as good sound, immersion, and sound quality. Including the results of the audio company's image survey, it is clear that the company has high technology and a high level of trust in its technology. Many people are aware that Forest Notes is something new, as it has been highly evaluated as innovative, impactful, and novel. However, the low evaluation of operability suggests that people do not understand how to use it and what it is used for. The product is of high quality and novelty, but it is difficult to imagine its value to the user because the purpose and intent are not clear. It would be difficult for a 320,000 yen speaker that specializes in listening to the sound of a forest, whose intentions are unclear, to be attractive to users.

4 Conclusions

4.1 What You Need for Forest Notes

The corporate research revealed that companies that make a good impression have a clear vision, and that their services and products are thoroughly based on the vision. It is thought that a clear impression is formed by the vision. Forest Notes is a product, but it also needs a clear vision. A vision in a product is a concept. The concept of Forest Notes in its current state is vague and not communicated to users. It is a product and service that specializes in listening to the sounds of the forest. Although it is aimed at a niche market, the concept is considered to be vague because the target users have not been determined. It is necessary to define the target users, determine the concept, and clarify the intent of Forest Notes.

4.2 Future Work

At this stage, this research is not finished. After deciding on the target, think about the UX for the target. Propose new products and services based on UX. We would like to come up with a UX where the recognition of the product/service leads to the recognition of the audio company.

References

1. Forest Notes Homepage. https://www.forestnotes.jp/
2. ITmedia News. https://www.itmedia.co.jp/lifestyle/articles/1302/28/news090.html
3. BRANDINGLAB. https://www.is-assoc.co.jp/brandinglab/starbucks-4p4c
4. TV Tokyo plus. https://www.tv-tokyo.co.jp/plus/business/entry/2021/024050.html
5. ModuleApps 2.0. https://moduleapps.com/mobile-marketing/17180rpt/
6. OLC Group Homepage. http://www.olc.co.jp/ja/sustainability/social/safety/scse.html
7. Career Hack. https://careerhack.en-japan.com/report/detail/965
8. Patagonia Japan Instagram. https://www.instagram.com/patagoniajp/?hl=ja
9. Patagonia Japan Homepage. https://www.patagonia.jp/home/
10. Patagonia Japan Homepage. https://www.patagonia.jp/stories/dont-buy-this-jacket-black-fri day-and-the-new-york-times/story-18615.html

The Study on Process for Co-creation of Value Focused on Ideation Pattern

Fuko Oura[1,2(✉)], Takeo Ainoya[3,4], Eibo Ahmad[5], and Keiko Kasamatsu[1]

[1] Tokyo Metropolitan University, 6-6 Asahigaoka, Hino, Tokyo, Japan
fu.a7te@gmail.com
[2] National Institute of Advanced Industrial Science and Technology, Chiba, Japan
[3] Tokyo University of Technology, Tokyo, Japan
[4] VDS Co., Ltd., Otsu, Japan
[5] Eibo Enterprise, LLC, Tokyo, Japan

Abstract. In order to deal with complex social issues and/or to create innovative designs that create new values, the co-creation approach, in which not only designers but also various disciplines and stakeholders are involved in the design process and create together, is gaining attention. The research field of co-creation dialogue scenes and creative processes has not yet matured, and there is still room for further research on the design of co-creation dialogue scenes. There is still little knowledge analyzed from actual co-creation scenes about what kind of dialogue styles occur and how design requirements are defined. In this study, we will conduct a workshop that includes elements of co-creation, and analyze the processes of three different teams in order to see the patterns of ideas in the team processes. From the analysis of a case study of a UX-based workshop that included prototyping, the characteristics of the team's conception patterns are reported as results.

Keywords: Co-creation · Team creativity · UX based workshop · Prototyping

1 Introduction

1.1 Team Dialogue Research for Co-creation

In order to deal with complex social issues and/or to create innovative designs that create new values, the co-creation approach, in which not only designers but also various disciplines and stakeholders are involved in the design process and create together, is gaining attention. In the academic field as well, there have been many research reports on co-creation methods and frameworks obtained from actual practice, but the research field of co-creation dialogue scenes and creative processes has not yet matured, and there is still room for further research on the design of dialogue spaces for co-creation. However, the research field of co-creation dialogue scenes and creative process is not yet mature.

Although there are many studies on the creative process, it is expected that various forms such as the use of tools and styles of discussion will be created when promoting

S. Yamamoto and H. Mori (Eds.): HCII 2022, LNCS 13305, pp. 46–57, 2022.
https://doi.org/10.1007/978-3-031-06424-1_5

design in teams like co-creation. However, there are still few findings that have been analyzed from actual co-creation situations regarding what kind of interaction styles occur and how design requirements are defined.

In this study, we conducted a workshop that included elements of co-creation and analyzed the processes of three different teams in order to see the patterns of ideation in the team processes. In this study, prototyping was used as a means of value expression in a UX-based workshop conducted as part of a cross-disciplinary design education program at a university. In this paper, we will discuss the differences and characteristics of the idea patterns in different teams by extracting the ideation patterns from the team process to see how design ideas created in the process of value expression through prototyping.

1.2 UX Based Workshop

Human Centered Design (HCD) in ISO 9241–210 emphasizes the importance of considering functions from the user's (human) point of view. UI (User Interface) is a tool for performing tasks, and the object of operation is the object of desire. In HCD, value is handled by considering not only UI but also how to use tools as HI (Human Interface)

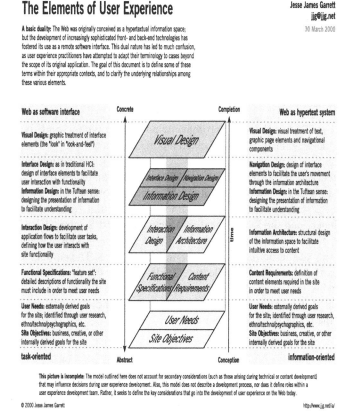

Fig. 1. The Elements of User Experience [2]

to achieve goals. In particular, since around 2000, "what users experience" has been treated as value, and has been incorporated into ISO 9241–210.

In Garrett's Key Considerations for Developing UX on the Web as Elements of User Experience, the model shown in the figure below (see Fig. 1) is proposed, and user demand is mentioned in the concept definition [1, 2]. In other words, UX is considered important in the early stages of design.

In their work on the research core SerBOTinQ [3], the authors used design thinking to analyze the user experience in service development, which led to the conception of ideas, and from there to the concretization of design requirements. In the process of service development, design thinking is used to analyze the user experience, which leads to idea generation, and from there to specifying design requirements [4, 5].

1.3 Prototyping

According to Exner et al. prototypes can visualize mental ideas, support understanding of complexity, enable communication by removing cultural and linguistic barriers, or test functions and requirements [6]. For situations where it is difficult to visualize the finished product in the early stages of design, bringing in prototyping can make the experience possible [7]. Also, prototyping can take many types, and it be necessary for those planning design activities to choose the form that best suits the situation, depending on the stage of design and the purpose.

2   Method

2.1   Research Method

We conducted a UX-based workshop that included prototyping, and focused on the differences in the way ideas were conceived among the teams.

The workshop was recorded via ZOOM. Since some of the participants were from overseas, the workshop was held in a hybrid format using an online teleconference tool (ZOOM) and an online whiteboard tool (Miro) to enable online participation. The participants were 22 students from the Department of Industrial Arts, the Department of Computer Science, and the Department of Mechanical and Systems Engineering. The students were divided into three groups to ensure that the groups were not unevenly distributed among the participating students' academic areas. The number and composition of each team is shown in the table. (see Table 1) After the workshop, two members of each team were interviewed to reflect on the team activities in the workshop. From the data collected, we extracted patterns of ideas from the dialogue among the team members and the forms of expression used.

Table 1. Composition and remote participation status of each team

	Number of people	Participant's academic area	Remote participation situation
Team1	9 people	· Computer Science · Mechanical Systems Engineering · Industrial Arts	Students from Malaysia and China were included as remote participants
Team2	7 people	· Mechanical Systems Engineering · Industrial Arts	Students from China were included as remote participants
Team3	6 people	· Mechanical Systems Engineering · Industrial Arts	No remote participants

2.2 Workshop Overview

The purpose of this workshop was to reframe everyday behavior and thinking using design thinking on the theme of Japanese courtesy, and to propose idea scenarios that would lead to new services. The workshop also focused on acquiring the basics of design thinking and broadening the research perspectives of the participating students regardless of their fields of expertise.

In this workshop, as a development process that emphasizes user experience, we shared the value of experience based on experience, with the aim of expressing it in an application as one means of providing a service that defines UX value.

The process of the workshop was as follows. The goal of the workshop was to "transform bad shopping experiences into fun applications" by following this process.

During the ice break, we introduced ourselves to the team and discussed our impressions of sight and taste and our own past experiences using Japanese sweets. The purpose of this discussion was to compare the sense of taste one gets when looking at a package of sweets and the taste one gets when actually eating them. The goal was to have the students compare their own country's sweets with sweets that are commonly eaten in Japanese daily life and to learn about each other's background by discussing their childhood experiences. The sweets were placed on individual plates and eaten with chopsticks to prevent infection.

As a result, there was a lot of discussion about the different taste from what they expected from the package, the sweets of their own countries, and the stories behind the sweets.

This was followed by an introduction to the basics of UX and research examples. Dr. Eibo, a special lecturer, introduced research on packaging that takes into account regional characteristics, and lectured on the development of such packaging into products that are actually sold in the market.

In the workshop on Japanese courtesy, special lecturer Prof. Ainoya and Prof. Eibo gave a lecture on Japanese courtesy, and we started to work based on the workflow.

Using the theme of Japanese courtesy, we discussed our own experiences with shopping using design thinking, and discussed how we could turn an unpleasant experience into an enjoyable one, discovering new values as new points of awareness. The final objective was to create a scenario for an enjoyable experience based on this, propose a service for a new shopping experience, and express it in an application. We used Miro as a common tool to exchange opinions and ideas, and Figma as the final product. Each team used Miro and came up with ideas using sketches as shown below (see Fig. 2).

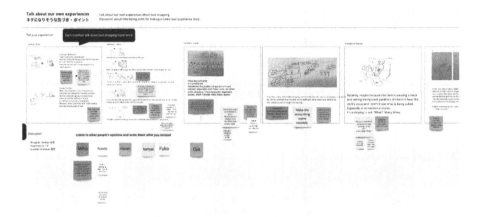

Fig. 2. View of ideation by miro

3   Analysis

3.1   Observation and Process Analysis

Team 1 was the fastest team to complete the development of the app, although it took some time to get online due to network problems at the beginning of the team's activities. The developed app is targeted at people who work late, telling them not to miss dinner and allowing them to order food. The app can also be used for health management and maintenance.

Team 2 spent a lot of time discussing the value of the experience and shared their values with each other in great depth. The application developed was a home delivery application, but one that could provide a higher level of trust by allowing users to see the process of making the food they ordered. The app focuses on trust, which is an important point when dealing with systems such as applications, and was commented on as a service that could be added to current delivery apps immediately.

Team 3 focused on the fact that electronic payments for online shopping, etc., weaken the sense of payment, and developed an app to prevent overspending by making the user feel that they are paying for something, even with electronic payments. There was a lively discussion on how to express the feeling of spending money, and the idea was to provide the perception of "paying" through the swiping motion and animation on the smartphone. They came up with the idea of providing experience containing the perception of "paying" with such interaction, and implemented it.

4   Result

4.1   Ideation Patterns in Three Different Teams

The characteristics of the team process observed for each team's ideation scene are shown below.

First, individual experiences were shared in each of the three teams, and those that were shared among the members were selected as the target user experiences.

Team 1. The following is a description of the ideas generated by each team. First, Team 1 had a discussion about the conceptualization of a service to address the issue. One of the participants, who was the most active in the team and had a lot to say about the team's progress, proposed a scenario about missed dinners and lost lunches at the supermarket as a service concept because it was an interesting and sympathetic experience among the shared experiences. The other members agreed with the proposal and the decision was made. The group was then divided into three work groups: logo and illustration creation, user experience scenario creation, and Figma UI creation. The group that had completed their work joined the group that was creating the Figma, with one person playing a facilitating role in the Figma, while the rest of the group watched the work, answering questions from the workers and making comments on points of concern. It was observed Team 1 was leader-driven throughout the entire process, with dialogue-based ideas in the service scenario building phase, and Figma-based interfaces and dialogue-based ideas in the Figma prototyping phase.

Team 2. Team 2 decided to use a food and beverage delivery service as the target scenario, as there was a high degree of sympathy among the team members for the issue of the gap between the image of online purchases and the actual product. After that, a simple UX map was created in order to find out the specific issues from the user's usage process. At this stage as well, after deciding on the theme of creating a UX map, each team member first wrote down their UX in Miro, and after everyone had finished, the maps were shared and discussed. The flow of the team's dialogues up to this point was as follows: the team decided on a mini-topic for the discussion, wrote down their individual experiences and thoughts on the miro, and then shared and discussed them through dialogues using the miro. At the beginning of prototyping with Figma, there was an interactive discussion on what functions the application should have and what the process of the application should be. One of the participants made a sketch on paper of the general flow of the application and the screens to be created in the prototype based on the dialogue. The sketches were shared on Figma, and a person was assigned to each screen, and the work was divided among the participants. As you can see, Team 2 did not seem to have a strong leader, and they seemed to confirm each other's discussions and design procedures as they went along. At the stage of building the scenario of the service, individual ideas were first written down in text, illustrations, or diagrams, and discussions were held based on these.

Team 3. Team 3 discussed the experience of wasting money when shopping online. The question "Why do we waste money when we shop online?" was created, and the team members wrote down the advantage and disadvantage factors of electronic payment on the miro. After that, the participants wrote down their ideas and points of view on sticky notes on the miro again. The ideas were expressed in the form of text for the elements and functions to be focused on, or illustrated with images of how they would be expressed in the application. The ideas were introduced and discussed, and the image of the main function of the application was decided by integrating several ideas that the members thought looked good. After that, the design motif for the main function of the payment screen was discussed in an interactive manner. Once the motif was decided, one of the participants made a sketch of the screen image using an iPad. Once the sketch was shared with the members, it was observed that there was a lively discussion about the specific elements of expression, such as the change of the character's expression and color according to the remaining balance. Once the screen image of the main function was solidified, the member in charge of Figma started to create the application, while the other members discussed other necessary pages and elements of the application by drawing illustrations and pasting reference materials on Miro. At this stage, they also discussed the UX of the app in preparation for the presentation. The team members, including Figma's creator, discussed the UX of the application in an interactive manner, and it was apparent that they were struggling to come up with a feasible model for the application's operation and usage scenarios. In Team 3, there was a co-leadership style in which a few specific people made comments on the progress. At the stage of building the service scenario, each team member first wrote down their thoughts in text and illustrations according to the framework created by the team, and then shared and discussed their ideas. In the prototyping stage, a partial division of labor was observed, such as all team members working together to solidify the image of the main functions to be conveyed in the prototype using sketches, and then discussing the other functions and screen details while creating the application using figma. We observed a partial division of labor. Rather than each team member deciding on the elements, all the team members discussed them together in a dialogue style while looking at the miro.

4.2 Workshop Outputs

The following figure shows the prototypes of each team's app that were created using Figma during the workshop.

Team 1 put a lot of effort into creating the logo, and the visual design of the app was especially designed with visibility in mind. Team 1 completed their prototype within the time frame, which showed the flow of the app and resulted in a unified visual design. (see Fig. 3).

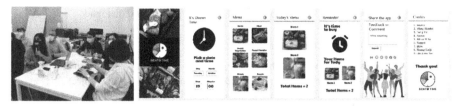

Fig. 3. Prototype created (Team1)

Team 2's prototype was focused on how to present information on the app, such as how to show the location of the store on a map, how to show product information and reviews, and how to show product videos (see Fig. 4).

Due to the time constraint of the workshop, Team 3 prototyped only the main function of the app, which was the UI expression that the remaining amount of money decreases when you make a payment. They used animation effects to convey the experience of swiping money out of the piggy bank and changing the expression of the piggy bank in a realistic way (see Fig. 5).

Fig. 4. Prototype created (Team2)

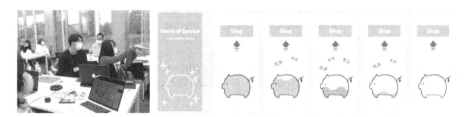

Fig. 5. Prototype created (Team3)

4.3 Result of Interview

The results of the interviews are summarized in the following table (see Table 2) (see Table 3). The following table summarizes the participants' own reflections on the workshop, including their reflections on the team process and dialogue, and their thoughts on the value of prototyping in their own team.

Table 2. Interview remarks about the team process and dialogue

	About the team process and dialogue
Team 1	· "What went well was, maybe, the clear division of labor depending on the characteristics of the team members and the smooth running of the project" · "I felt that there was too much sence of the division of roles and not enough sence of the team. For example, at the final presentation, the leader said that each person in charge would present his or her part of the project. However, ended up, the leader presented the entire content" · "Everyone was too kind. Feeling that anything is fine. Maybe a passive feeling" · "One part of us thought that the UX map was necessary to explain, but the leader's opinion was probably that our app should be used at what time and for what people, and that we should focus on these things. In the last presentation, the leader focused on Figma's part"
Team 2	· "What went well… I' think the best part of the discussion is when someone mentions a theme and everyone explains their ideas around this theme. At this time, everyone is focused and actively thinking about their own design. I think this was the best part" · "This happened sometimes. This is when no one speaks, when there is a long period of silence, no one says anything. The feeling that no one is doing their own thing is simply working on their own, not as a team" · "We first decide what this app can do, then we design the screen, this is a team effort, so eventually we discuss the features, and at this time one member draws a sketch, and everyone says, "I have this design pattern " or "there's a map," and then we decide on the position, and then we divide up who makes this first page, who makes this fourth page for example, and I make the pages that I work on. That's how it works. (…) After this, one member took a picture of the sketch, uploaded it to Figma, and everyone designed "based on this picture. But the final product is not what we imagined…"
Team 3	· "During the idea generation stage, everyone was able to express their own opinions, so I think we were able to work well together" · "When we decided to start working on the actual service at Figma, I think for the first half of the project, I was working on the system side and the other people were discussing the other parts of App. There was a part where one of the international students seemed to be at a loss as to what to do. I thought it would have been better if we could have divided the work better" · "There were international students, and it was difficult to communicate in English with members with different languages and discipline, so it took time to understand what each other wanted to say. (…) It would have been good to discuss how to communicate with them at the beginning"

Table 3. Interview remarks about the value discussed on team

	About value
Team 1	"I heard sensitivities from members of different languages. I think this is the most important takeaway from these teamwork for me. I may not agree with their views, but I need a different perspective from the outside world. I may not agree with this information or this concept, but I need these voices"
Team 2	"The focus is on the trust between the shopper, and the shopkeeper.People who sell things show the best state of what they sell, but the actual thing they sell is not. There is always this situation. This is not just food, but shoes and clothes, for example, also have this situation. I feel that this is the cause of trust. I feel that this is not only in China, but in other countries as well"
Team 3	"The idea we came up with was the exact opposite of what the current services are aiming for, it was like we were just saying what the users wanted. I think the companies that make the current services are thinking about the value of making people spend money, and that if they can make payments easily, people will buy a lot and it's a win-win situation. I'm sure the company understands that there are some selfish things that users do, but those things are probably detrimental to the company, so to be honest, I think they are easily ignored by the company. I think we were able to have a great discussion about the value of the selfishness of users and the value of the parts that should not be discarded just because they are detrimental to the company"

5 Discussion

5.1 Differences in Ideation Patterns in Different Teams

Individual work and division of labor in team processes

In all groups, we observed that in addition to discussion, there was division of labor and individual work. However, the timing of these activities, how they were conducted, and the style in which they were conducted differed among the teams.

Individual Work. First of all, individual work was observed when the team members externalized their individual experiences and thoughts about the work tasks and discussion topics decided within the team at a certain point of the team process into information using text and illustrations. Especially in the early stages of the workshop, when individual experiences were shared, all teams had time for this kind of individual work, followed by sharing and discussion. In the later stages of the process, Team 1 did not engage in complete individual work, while Team 3 sometimes had time for individual work, but gradually shifted to a more casual style of work and dialogue. Team 2 decided on work tasks and themes for discussion, and continued the discussion style of individual work, sharing, and discussion until the latter half of the workshop. One of the characteristics of individual work is that it allows members to work in parallel, so that information from individual perspectives can be expressed by each member. In dialogue, if too many people talk at the same time, dialogue will not be possible, so some participants may not be able to express their opinions as a result of asking for opportunities to speak. In the case of individual work, this can be a problem. In this respect, individual work is characterized by the fact that it is easier for each individual to provide information in a fair manner. In addition, the interviewees mentioned that this kind of individual work time is good because it allows them to concentrate and think. When reflecting on one's own experiences and thinking about ideas, they can be elicited and generated through interaction with others, but apart from that, incorporating time for individual thinking may also lead to stimulation of creativity.

Division of Labor. Division of labor was also seen in the prototyping stage for both teams. In Team 1, there were three divisions of labor: logo, Figma, and UX scenario, and each team interacted with each other. Team 2 was divided into individual teams, and each team was responsible for creating their own UI screens. Team 3 had a designated person in charge of Figma creation, but often participated in the dialogue by listening to the members discussing at the same desk.

There seemed to be differences between the teams, especially in terms of the degree of dialogue that took place between the teams or individuals divided during the division of labor. Even though the concepts, requirements, and functions were shared in the discussions, the concrete images in the minds of the individuals differed, so I think one of the key points in the division of labor is to match the images when creating the prototypes. One of the comments from the interviewees was that they had made rough sketches of the screen design and functions based on the discussion before the division of labor, but the final product was not what they had imagined. The division of labor can be efficient especially when prototyping is required in a short period of time, but this workshop also suggests that communication is necessary to confirm and adjust the image during the division of labor.

Tools and Expressions Used in the Dialogue. The tools and expressions used during the workshop were also different among the three teams. While teams 2 and 3 shared and organized information and shared ideas while writing them down in Miro, team 1 used almost no tools in the early stages of the workshop. As for the communication using miro, as mentioned in the result of Team 2, it was difficult to convey the experience by text only. As for the communication using MIRO, as mentioned in the result of Team 2, it was difficult to convey the experience when only text was used, and we observed an attempt to facilitate communication by changing the expression method to include illustrations. In addition, not only in the experience sharing phase, but also in the idea sharing phase of Team 3, the use of illustrations was seen to promote the sharing of images and sympathy for the ideas within the team. It is suggested that communication using illustrations as well as text may make the image sharing in the team more concrete and acceptable in both the experience sharing and idea sharing phases.

Participant Who Have Leadership. Looking at the participants in each team, it is suggested that the behavior of the participants with leadership skills has a significant impact on the team process and dialogue style. This was most evident in Team 1. In Team 1, there was one participant who spoke a lot within the team, leading the dialogue and making comments on how to proceed with the design. Except for the time when they were divided into groups for division of labor, this participant was the main focus of the dialogues and design activities throughout. Team 1, which was led by a participant with strong leadership skills, progressed quickly in determining the target scenario and setting the concept of the application, and started prototyping earlier than any other team. On the other hand, insights from the interviews and the discussions during the workshop suggest that members other than the participants with leadership roles seemed to be relatively aligned in their opinions. While it is possible for a design to progress steadily with one person at the center, it is also possible for a team to become one in which the other participants tend to agree with the opinions of the others as followers. In such a case, the opportunity for creation through interaction among participants with diverse viewpoints may be compromised, and therefore, knowledge on the method of dialogue is needed from the perspective of the role of participants in terms of the behavior of the leader and the resulting relationship with other members in the co-creation space. It is also thought that knowledge of dialogue methods is necessary from the perspective of the role of the participants in terms of the behavior of the leader in the co-creation field and the resulting relationships with other members. In addition, if the roles of the participants in the dialogue and the relationships between them are well established, the participants will be able to feel their own contribution to the dialogue, and this may lead to a reduction in the sense of anxiety they have about the dialogue.

References

1. Garrett, J.J.: The Elements of User Experience: User-Centered Design for the Web. Goodwill of Silicon Valley, California (2016)
2. http://www.jjg.net/elements/. Accessed 28 Jan 2022
3. SerBOTinQ Homepage. https://www.comp.sd.tmu.ac.jp/serbotinq/index.html. Accessed 2 Feb 2022
4. Kasamatsu, K., Ainoya, T., Motegi, R., Kubota, N., Takesue, N., Ikei, Y.: Our approach for revitalization on Hachijojima using PXD. In: The 20th International Symposium on Advanced Intelligent Systems and 2019 International Conference on Biometrics and Kansei Engineering, pp. 528–532 (2019)
5. Kasamatsu, K., Ainoya, T., Motegi, R., Kubota, N., Takesue, N., Ikei, Y.: Idea prototyping for co-creation using PXD method -Case study of Izu Oshima project. In: The 20th International Symposium on Advanced Intelligent Systems and 2019 International Conference on Biometrics and Kansei Engineering, pp. 533–538 (2019)
6. Exner, K., Lindow, K., Stark, R., Stark, R., Ängeslevä, J., Bähr, B., Nagy, E.: A transdisciplinary perspective on prototyping. In: 2015 IEEE International Conference on Engineering, Technology and Innovation/ International Technology Management Conference (ICE/ITMC), pp. 1–8 (2016)
7. Tagawa, K.: Takram design engineering and its design process. Keio SFC Journal 10(1), 17–25 (2010)

Multiple Perspectives Co-creation Process and Human-Centered Scenario-Oriented Activity Design

Der-Jang Yu[✉], Wen-Chi Lin, and I-Lin Chen

Providence University, 200, Sec. 7, Taiwan Boulevard, Shalu Dist.,
Taichung City 43301, Taiwan R.O.C.
djyu@scenariolab.com.tw

Abstract. Design is changing. The object of design has changed from users and products to customers and services, from the interface of products to the touch points of the journey, and from the interaction of digital products to activities in the digital world. In the past, the division of labor in which the designer made the design first, and then provided the design to the user after completion, will become a continuous co-creation activity between the customer and the designer in the future.

Scenario was originally a design tool, but now it has become a design object. This article explores how to carry out human-centered, Scenario-Oriented Activity Design through a multi-perspective co-creation process under such changes.

This paper proposes a framework for connecting activities and scenarios with narratives. The visual narrative combined with the guidance method of switching from multiple perspectives allows the co-creation team to generate multiple empathy, and conduct usage activities, design activities, and facilitating activities at the same time. This paper also proposes a co-creative narrative guiding structure O-S-M-C that echoes the dynamic sequence of activity theory to assist the design of innovative activities. This paper also illustrates with practical examples.

Keywords: Scenario-based design · Human-centered design · Design thinking · Co-creation · Design method · Activity theory

1 Scenario, Activity, and Narrative Empathy

Storytelling is an essential partner in the design journey. While we do design, we tell the story of design objects. Scenario-based design is a representative method, which combines people, environment, objects, activities, intentions and experiences, from problem domain to solution domain, to help us complete the work of designing good products. However, the object of design is changing from products and functions to journeys and activities, such as service design, experience design. And the use of the scenario-based description of the product function has also become an activity scenario description of the journey touch points. Scenario-based product design, also becomes Scenario-oriented activity design.

© The Author(s), under exclusive license to Springer Nature Switzerland AG 2022
S. Yamamoto and H. Mori (Eds.): HCII 2022, LNCS 13305, pp. 58–72, 2022.
https://doi.org/10.1007/978-3-031-06424-1_6

Scenario-oriented activity design has three operational objects: activity, activity scenario, and activity narrative. In this article, we use the simplified activity schema image to represent the activity, the activity schema with the document frame to represent the activity scenario, and the dialog box to represent the activity narrative (see Fig. 1).

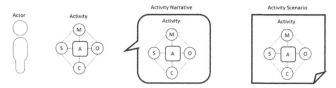

Fig. 1. Activity, activity scenario, and activity narrative.

In the field of collaborative design, an activity theory schema is a framework for describing activities. The activity schema contains four elements: subject, object, mediator and community. If the subject wants to operate the object, he will use the mediator tool or the environmental community to perform activities, and at the same time feel the tensions between the elements.

The activity scenario contains a complete description of people, environments, things, and activities. A complete set of structural scenario description methods has been provided [3], including value scenarios, activity scenarios, and action scenarios. Participants can perform activities according to its scenario data sheet.

Activity narrative is the statement of the activity by the participants of the activity, including the systematic recitation of an event or series of events, or the narration of the actions of part of the event. Sometimes, activity narrative are the emotional points that the narrator wants to convey.

Activity participants can refer to the activity scenario for activities, and express the process and experience with activity narrative. Activity participants can also generate scenarios through activity narrative. Through narrative, the scenarios of the activity can be passed on to another person to perform a similar activity (see Fig. 2).

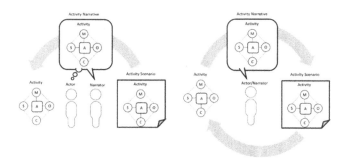

Fig. 2. Narrative is the transition key between activity and scenario.

Activities are intangible sequences, activity scenarios are specific documents, and activity narratives are the key way for people to convert scenarios into activities, or convert activities into scenarios, as well as a key tool for human-centered design.

■ "Being" narrative, "Becoming" narrative, empathy and co-creation.

Establishing two opposing states of "Being" and "Becoming" at the same time can drive innovation. People share the story of "Being" together through narrative, share everyone's expectations and their own experiences, and connect possible implementation methods and ideas to co-create a "Becoming" scenario that doesn't yet exist (Fig. 3).

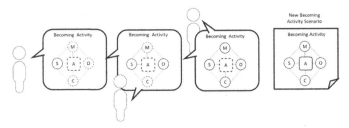

Fig. 3. Share being narratives create becoming scenarios.

Wistron's fitness magic mirror case illustrates such a process. In 2014, we assisted a Taiwanese manufacturer to discuss the future type of large-scale displays. We led a group of four to share the narrative and created a LEGO storyboard script describing a woman's fitness activities using a large smart display with her trainer and her own reflection in the mirror. And the same scene appeared in the commercial product service in 2020 (Qiaoshan Magic Mirror). The product advertisement video also featured a situational picture that was almost identical to the original concept (see Fig. 4), and the display used by the commercial product company happened to be provided by the manufacturer. This case illustrates how a small team co-created a "Becoming" script through scenario-oriented activity design to truly become a "Being" story that everyone can accept.

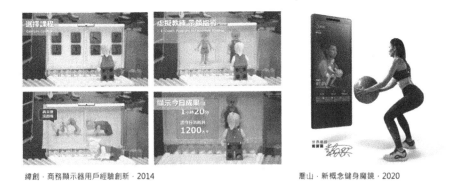

Fig. 4. Two sets of fitness magic mirror scenarios.

2 Scenario Combined with Narrative to Facilitate Co-creation Activities

There are three types of activities in the innovation process, Scenario-Oriented Activity Design produces user scenarios for user groups, supporting user activities and narratives. Similarly, in innovative activities, Scenario-Oriented Activity Design produces design scenarios for designer groups to assist in designing activities. It can also generate facilitating scenarios of facilitators to help guide co-creation activities. (dotted arrow in the Fig. 5 below).

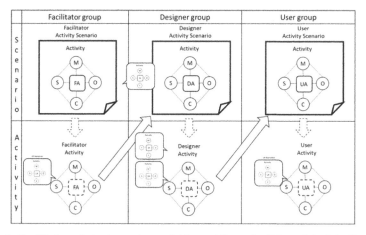

Fig. 5. Facilitating, designing, using activities and Scenario-Oriented Activity Design.

In addition to being used in the same ethnic group, Scenario-Oriented Activity Design must also cross different ethnic groups, connecting the activities of facilitators, designers, and users. The facilitator uses the facilitator scenario to carry out the facilitating activity, assists in generating the designer scenario, and guides the designer to carry out the design activity. The designer uses the designer scenario to generate the user scenario and guide the user to perform the user activity (as shown by the solid arrow in the Fig. 5 above).

Since design submissions have changed from products to current activities and interactions, Scenario-oriented Activity Design also faces a co-creation situation where facilitating, design, and using occur at the same time. Through the activity narrative to drive empathy and mirroring, the participants of innovative activities can quickly integrate into different roles such as facilitator, designer, user, and carry out corresponding activities according to different scenarios. In the image below, the designer activity scenario on the screen, with the addition of a visual facilitator activity narrative, integrates the facilitator activity with the designer activity scenario. Designers can collaborate and co-create more smoothly through dual empathy.

In the image below (see Fig. 6), on the screen, the design activity scenario plus the visual facilitator activity narrative presents two sets of activity scenarios. Designers can collaborate and co-create more smoothly through dual empathy.

Fig. 6. Visual narrative drives the dual empathy of facilitating and design.

■ Narrative perspective presentation, interaction and use of props.

Visual narration provides the positioning of the narrator, defines the empathy perspective of the reader, and drives empathy, dialogue and interaction between them. The presentation of multi-perspective narrative requires the support of narrative tools with activity descriptive power, including personnel setting, object operation and scene evolution, and the transfer of experience.

LEGO bricks, manga figures, large digital displays and smart glasses are all good materials and props. Through these narrative visualization support tools, members of the co-creation ecosystem can perform creative tasks while empathizing with the narrative. The following images are use cases for LEGO mini-figures, manga figures, and smart displays (see Fig. 7).

Fig. 7. LEGO bricks, manga figures, large displays and smart glasses as design props.

■ Activity schema and narrative perspective presentation.

Activity schema takes the subject as the starting point, and describes the interaction dynamics between the subject and the objects, mediators and communities in the activity system. Taking the subject as the center, combined with the position of the narrator's different perspectives, can produce different empathy as shown below (see Fig. 8).

Fig. 8. Presentation of multiple perspectives.

The first-person perspective starts from "I…", which is to watch the activities from the perspective of the subject, and the narrator himself will also strongly feel various tensions and response motives, as shown on the Fig. 8. left image.

The second-person perspective starts with "You…", you can watch the subject's activities from the opposite angle of the subject, and you will clearly feel the next interaction between the subject and yourself when narrating, as shown on the middle image.

From a third-person perspective, the subject's activities can be viewed from a bystander's perspective. The narration starts with "He…", and the narrator will feel the surroundings of the bystander, and the connection between the community and the environment. Through narratives from different perspectives, designers can better understand user feelings, object intentions, and operation appearances, as shown on the Fig. 8. Right image.

Furthermore, activity theory divides activities into activity-levels with motivation and ambiguous actions, and action-levels with goals and clear processes. Bringing innovation participants back and forth between the fuzzy motivation level and the clear execution level creates opportunities for dialogue, interaction and innovation.

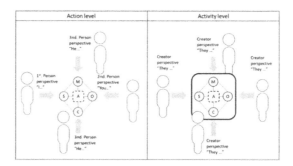

Fig. 9. Multiple perspective switching between active level and action level.

We propose a creator's perspective to assist activity-level narratives with only motives but unclear actions. The design activities from the creator's perspective are carried out on a mini-stage mainly constructed by LEGO minifigures. The designers are like the Greek gods in Greek mythology, not only creating users, but also constructing various possible scenarios that users may experience.

With vague activity-level and clear action-level narrative presentation props, designers can freely enter and exit the two levels, and use the activity-level negative space perspective and action-level positive space perspective to make innovative connections, combining the subjective narrative of "Becoming" with the objective scenario of "Being" into a future narrative of "Become being".

The picture below shows the Taoyuan Airport team discussing the "Becoming" scenarios of Airport 4.0 digital transformation from the creator perspective. The team created the activity scenarios from the creator's perspective, and then enlarged the action scene into a life-size image. Designers can switch themselves from the creator's perspective of "Becoming" scenarios to the first-person or the third-person perspective to discuss the "Being" details of the actions, and finally get the concrete "Become being" scenarios. (See Fig. 10).

Fig. 10. Switch perspective activity in Taoyuan Airport collaborative design.

■ WOZ narrative of positive and negative spaces.

WOZ Wizard of Oz is a narrative approach to HCD (Human-Centered Design) collaborative design. WOZ has an activity state of facilitation, design and using at the same time The WOZ facilitating scenarios is to let the designer act as a product, facilitate user interaction, observe the usage status, and design at the same time. Taking ATM (automatic teller machine) as an example (as shown in the Fig. 11 below), according to the facilitating scenarios, the designer hides behind the ATM and proposes a low-fidelity prototype to facilitate the user to withdraw money in front of the ATM with a low-fidelity interface machine use.

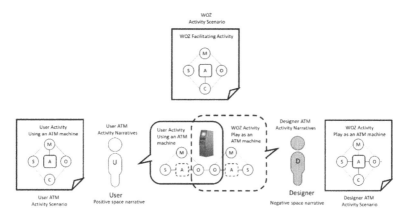

Fig. 11. ATM WOZ narrative interactions.

What the designer provides on the product side is a selective negative space narrative. The user side is a decision-making positive space narrative. Through such design co-creation activities, designers experience the activities, interactions, and even tension between user and product, and establish appropriate physical appearances of product and interfaces.

The WOZ method provides a unique product perspective, coupled with structured positive and negative space narrative interactions, facilitates the design activity groups, and uses activity groups to co-create new product activities together, resulting in human-centered outcomes.

3   The "O-S-M-C" Narrative Process

The feature of WOZ is that the designer plays the product and interacts with the user from the product perspective. However, if the design object becomes an abstract activity, how can we use the activity perspective to carry out the WOZ co-creation activities? We propose to use the four basic elements of activity schema as the entity of WOZ perspective. This entity is like an assemblable transformer robot of Japanese manga, which is activated individually from subject perspective, object perspective, mediator perspective, and community perspective, and can become a whole activity perspective finally. This four-in-one composite entity is more responsive to the challenges of designing journey-style activities.

Let's break down the process of changing the perspective of WOZ facilitation. WOZ first stands on the perspective of the object product, narrates from the perspective of "you", understands the interaction between me (the product) and you (the user), and then stands on the subject user's perspective. From the perspective of "I", establish a common sense with the user, and finally observe the activities of the subject user from the perspective of mediator or community, and narrate from the perspective of "he", producing methods that can assist the subject. The WOZ process completely echoes the execution order of O-S-M-C (Object-Subject-Mediator-Community).

Because the "O-S-M-C" activity schema elements have the characteristics of dynamic response and mutual enabling, combined with the narrative guidance sequence of "O-S-M-C", and the perspective variation of "you-me-he-them", "O-S-M-C" narrative facilitating mechanism will become an effective structure to drive co-creation activities:

1. Narrate from the perspective of "Object", establish a common sense of "you", and understand your "Becoming" goals and interactions.
2. Tell the story from the perspective of "Subject", establish a empathy of "I", and understand my "Becoming" feeling.
3. Finally, watch the subject's activities from the perspective of "Mediator" or "Community", start with "him", empathize and understand, and produce the "Becoming" assistance he needs.
4. Finally, watch the subject's activities from the perspective of the creator, starting from "them", empathizing with and understanding their "Becoming" scenarios, and producing methods to assist the subject. (See Fig. 12).

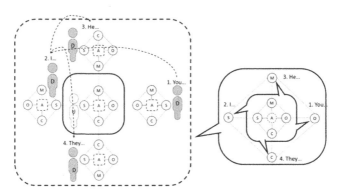

Fig. 12. The "O-S-M-C" narrative process.

4   Two Case Studies

Finally, we analyze the service design course of Tsinghua University and the bilingual training system of Providence University from the perspective of "O-S-M-C" four-in-one mechanism, and the facilitating design of the two human -centered co-creation activity cases.

Case 1: Service Design Self-taught and Cocreation Process
Tsinghua University's service design course faces the challenge of doing co-creating and learning design methods at the same time. We decided to use a co-creation system that could simultaneously support facilitation activities, design activities, and use activities to assist in the course. This course is completely self-study by the students, five weeks and 15 h without teachers' teaching, and the collaborative innovation output has been

rated positively by each other. We analyze the interaction between students and learning activities from the perspective of "O-S-M-C" as a service design course activity entity:

1. The design activities will be carried out by the "Object" perspective to guide "you"::

The service design facilitating activity entity stands in the position of Object, faces the designer with the prompt of "You becoming", and allows the designer to expand into a series of states to be completed. As shown in the Fig. 13, the facilitator in this service design program is a cartoon character, providing appropriate design tools, such as customer journey map, and assisting design students to complete collaborative work by themselves through the dual empathy of guiding activities and design activities.

Fig. 13. The "Object" perspective guides the design activities via customer journey map.

2. The design activities are conducted by the "Subject" perspective, "I"::

The service design facilitating activity entity stands in the position of the Subject, and makes the designer becoming aware of the dilemma or need of each target to be accomplished by the prompting method of "I becoming". The service design program is transformed into a guiding comic character, providing empathy tools for service exploration, cool hunting, persona, etc. Assist student groups with empathic research work. (See Fig. 14).

Fig. 14. The " Subject " perspective guides the design activities via persona.

3. The design activities will be facilitated by the "Mediator" perspective to guide the creator to find the user's need":

The service design facilitating activity entity stands in the perspective of "he", with the prompt of "helping him in the way…", so that the designer "Becoming" can find the solution of mediating ideas or concepts.

This stage will use innovative tools such as Brain writing 653, Innovation Matrix, Storyboards, Paper Prototypes, etc. The guided narrative here will include the first and second person perspectives of the comic book characters, as well as the creator's perspective established in the context of the LEGO story, guiding the designer in and out of the usage and design activities.

The left side of the image below (See Fig. 15)shows the space the design team travel between the first and second-person perspectives and the creator's perspective.

Fig. 15. The "Mediator" perspective guides the design activities via story boards.

4. The design activities will be incorporated by the "Community" perspective to assist the creator in finding "their" needs:

The guidance service design activity entity is prompted from the perspective of "they", so that the designer "Becoming" can complete the design output that is commonly recognized in the way of separate and co-constructed stories for the ultimate goal of the whole. The methods used include mini-figure micro-movies, service blueprints, and more.

The left side of the Fig. 16 below shows the narrative space of the LEGO Storyboard, which provides the design team with the co-creation of the stories of mortal characters from the perspective of Greek gods.

Case 2: Co-creation Activity of Bilingual Development System
Taiwan has been promoting bilingualism in recent years, and in a short period of time,

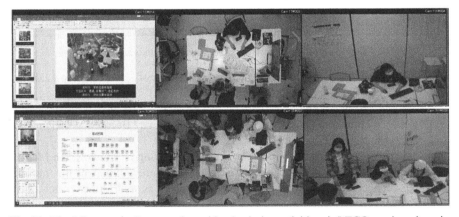

Fig. 16. The " Community " perspective guides the design activities via LEGO movie and service blueprint.

the narrative ability will become both Chinese and English. From the perspective of co-creation activities, it is to transform a field that used to be activities in the mother tongue into a field that "will become a field for activities in bilinguals": The content of the activity must becoming bilingual, the people involved in the activity must becoming bilingual, the tools of the activity must becoming bilingual, and the community related to the activity must becoming bilingual, as shown in the Fig. 17 below.

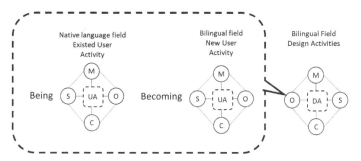

Fig. 17. Bilingual field design activity

At Providence University, we have developed a bilingual development system that includes collection, production, practice and sharing through cross-team co-creation. The entire bilingual co-creation service can be explained by the "O-S-M-C-you-me-he" activity-facilitated perspective narrative.

1. The "Object" perspective, standing in the position of the Object, lists key activities based on what you will do in the field that requires bilingualism, and drives the subject's perspective to externalize these activities.

Actual design and operation: Combined with smart glasses, conduct field tours in the first-person way, and record with the mobile phone in the third-person way, and collect the field activities that the field stakeholders will carry out. (See Fig. 18).

Fig. 18. The collection activity of first person view.

2. From the perspective of "Subject", stand in the position of Subject, experience how users can use bilingualism, and understand the difficulties that users will face, such as not knowing how to translate into English, unable to express in English, and not knowing what the other party needs.

Actual design and operation: We use the collected audio and video records to create bilingual key images and interactive narratives, and invite bilingual users to experience and narrate from a first-person perspective and a third-person perspective to understand their usage behaviors and obstacles. (See Fig. 19).

Fig. 19. The interaction of bilingual learners.

3. The "Mediator" perspective, standing in the Mediator's position, assists the system to establish the possibility of bilingual interaction and the "Becoming" method. How does the object in the bilingual activity system establish bilingual content, how does the subject establish bilingual ability, and how does the mediator assist bilingualism? In response to such needs, various prototypes of mediating methods or tools are proposed.

Actual design and operation: We build smart AR glasses and a large display screen to carry bilingual learning content. We also provide learners with different usage scenarios and bilingual dialogue interactions from different perspectives. These scenarios can be recorded and played repeatedly for learners to practice. (See Fig. 20).

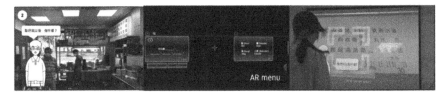

Fig. 20. The interaction of bilingual learning through mart display.

4. The "Community" perspective, from the creator's perspective, establishes activity scenarios for different subjects and objects, and convert it into an action script, enrich the program, and continue to expand bilingual activities.

Actual design and operation: Build a minifigure storyboard, provide basic activity concepts, and guide the team to complete innovation based on the creator's perspective. We guide the field users (including hosts and customers) to externalize the key activities of the field; we look for foreign language students to collaborate on the production of bilingual textbooks; we help field stakeholders through mediator innovation to establish key field activity scenarios. (See Fig. 21).

Fig. 21. The creator perspective scenarios for communities.

This case shows how to design activities, from the guiding perspective of "Object-Subject- Mediator- Community", to establish different activities to form a bilingual environment to guide the field and related people, from the old scenarios of Being's native language, Becoming to bilingual new scenarios. Through the mediation tools of new display technology and smart glasses, the new possibility of multi-perspective narrative and multi-activity crossing has been brought forward.

5 Conclusion and Finding

The system dynamics of Activity Theory is to initiate activities under the mutual contradictions of system elements and to interact until the contradiction disappears.

Through the O-S-M-C facilitating structure, a human-centered scenario-oriented co-creation system will encounters obstacles to its goals, and will choose to mediate innovative solutions or call the community for assistance according to the rules of the participants. Then from an existed being scenario to a becoming scenario that meets the needs of the participants.

The bilingual training case in Providence University, such as the on-site collection of target activities, to user obstacles, and the visual narrative guidance method of bilingual ability improvement, echoes the innovative activity dynamics of the bilingual activity system. The Tsinghua University service design self-learning case is to provide a self-learning and co-creation environment to support innovation teams to shuttle between design, use, and guiding activities, carry out self-learning and cooperation, and complete innovation activities.

This paper proposes a framework for connecting activities and scenarios with narratives allows the co-creation team to generate multiple empathy, and conduct usage activities, design activities, and facilitating activities at the same time. This paper also proposes a co-creative narrative facilitating structure O-S-M-C that echoes the dynamic sequence of activity theory to assist the design of innovative activities.

Such co-creation activities are connected by the narrative of the participants, guided by the changes of perspective, and carried out with the assistance of visual scenario tools. Thanks to better displays and smart glasses, it will be easier to switch perspectives and visualize narratives, making the aforementioned human-centered co-creation more possible.

References

1. Yu, D.-J., Lin, W.-C.: Facilitating idea generation using personas. In: Human Centered Design (2009)

2. Nardi, B.A. (ed.): Context and Consciousness: Activity Theory and Human-Computer Interaction. MIT Press, Cambridge (1996)
3. Kurosu, M. (ed.): HCD 2009. LNCS, vol. 5619. Springer, Heidelberg (2009). https://doi.org/10.1007/978-3-642-02806-9
4. Yu, D.-J., Chuang, M.-C., Tseng, S.: Case study for experience vision designing Notebook PC. In: Human-Computer Interaction. Human-Centred Design (2013)
5. Schank, R.: Tell Me a Story: Narrative and Intelligence. Northwestern University Press, Evanston (1995, 2001)
6. Carroll, J.M.: Scenarios and design cognition. In: Proceedings of the IEEE Joint International Conference on Requirement Engineering (2002)
7. Yu, D.J., Lin, W.C., Wang, J.C.: Scenario-Oriented Design, Garden City, Taipei (2000)
8. Yu, D.-J., Yeh, H.-J.: Scenario-based product design, a real case. In: Human-Computer Interaction. Interaction Design and Usability (2007)
9. Okamoto, M., Komatsu, H.: Participatory design using scenarios in different cultures. In: Human-Computer Interaction (2007)
10. Yu, D.-J., Lin, W.-C., Wun, M.-Y., Yeu, T., Lee, T., Yu, T.-T.: A scenario-based, self-taught and collaborative system for human-centered and innovative solutions. In: HCI International (2021)

Information Design and Quality

Effect of Self-efficacy on Open Card Sorts for Websites

Christos Katsanos[1]([✉]) [iD], Georgia Zafeiriou[1], and Alexandros Liapis[2,3]

[1] Department of Informatics, Aristotle University of Thessaloniki, Thessaloniki, Greece
{ckatsanos,georgiaza}@csd.auth.gr
[2] Department of Electrical and Computer Engineering, University of Peloponnese, Patras, Greece
a.liapis@esdalab.ece.uop.gr
[3] School of Science and Technology, Hellenic Open University, Patras, Greece

Abstract. Card sorting is a popular way for creating website information architectures based on users' mental models. This paper explores the effect of participants' self-efficacy on card sorting results. A two-phase study was carried out. The first phase involved 40 participants rating their self-efficacy on a standardized scale, followed by an open card sort experiment. The median self-efficacy score was used to split the open card sort data into two groups: one for low and one for high participants' self-efficacy. These two datasets were analyzed following state-of-the-art techniques for open card sort data analysis, which resulted in two information architectures for the eshop. In the second phase, two functional prototypes were first created for the eshop, one for each information architecture of the first phase. Subsequently, 30 participants interacted with both prototypes in a user testing study. This paper found that users interacting with the information architecture produced by open card sort participants with low self-efficacy made statistically significantly more correct first clicks, significantly less time to find content items, rated the tasks as significantly easier, and provided higher perceived usability ratings compared to when they interacted with the information architecture produced by users with high self-efficacy.

Keywords: Card sorting · Information architecture · Self-efficacy

1 Introduction

Website Information Architecture (IA) refers to the practice of organizing and labelling website content to support findability and usability [1, 2]. The most popular HCI practice to support the design of user-centered website IAs is open card sorting [2-4].

In an open card sort, participants place cards (i.e., content items), written on paper or on any card sorting software tool, into categories that make sense to them and label each category. Analysis of these data can reveal how people understand and categorize website content items, and thus support the creation of a user-centered website IA [5]. Open card sorting has been also used in many other contexts, such as to group design guidelines [6–8], to assess technologies for automatic content categorization on websites [9, 10]

S. Yamamoto and H. Mori (Eds.): HCII 2022, LNCS 13305, pp. 75–87, 2022.
https://doi.org/10.1007/978-3-031-06424-1_7

and applications in multipurpose public displays [11], and to understand users' mental models for mobile games categorization [12], haptic devices [13], web programming [14], cybersecurity warnings [15], and self-tracking for mental wellness [16].

Given the importance of the open card sorting method, there is a lot of research on how to conduct it and analyze the produced data. Examples of research questions that have been explored relate to the minimum sample size required [17, 18], the number of cards to be sorted [19], reliability of the method [20, 21], the use of software tools to mediate card sorting [22–26], and data analysis [4, 5, 27–30]. However, little study has been done on participants' characteristics that might influence the method's results. One such study was done in our previous research [31] that found that participants' spatial visualization ability affects open card sort results.

This paper investigates the effect of participants' self-efficacy on the results of an open card sort for website IA design. Self-efficacy is defined as the belief in one's ability to effectively complete a task or exhibit a particular behavior [32]. Self-efficacy has been shown to correlate with one's computer performance, education, and technology acceptance [33]. People with high self-efficacy are less anxious about possible future changes, set demanding goals, make more effort, persist when faced with difficulties, and achieve higher performance [32]. As a result, we hypothesized that a participant with high self-efficacy might be also better at creating good information structures when engaged in an open card sort. The following are the specific research questions addressed in this paper:

- RQ1: Is there any effect of open card sorting participants' self-efficacy on interaction effectiveness of the produced IA?
- RQ2: Is there any effect of open card sorting participants' self-efficacy on interaction efficiency of the produced IA?
- RQ3: Is there any effect of open card sorting participants' self-efficacy on perceived task difficulty while interacting with the produced IA?
- RQ4: Is there any effect of open card sorting participants' self-efficacy on perceived usability of the produced IA?

2   Card Sorting Study

2.1   Methodology

Forty participants were involved in the card sorting study, 27 females, with mean age 27.5 years (SD = 12.7). The participants were first asked to fill a questionnaire and then perform an open card sort for an existing eshop. All of the participants were native Greek speakers, and the cards and questions were presented in Greek.

The questionnaire asked participants to provide demographic information (gender, age) and complete the standardized General Self-Efficacy Scale (GSE) [34]. The GSE was developed by Schwarzer and Jerusalem [34] and is used to assess the general sense of self-efficacy of individuals. The scale has 10 items rated between 1 (not at all true) and 4 (exactly true) and produces an overall score between 10 and 40, where the higher the score the better the perceived self-efficacy of the respondent. The GSE scale has been found both valid and reliable [35]. It has been translated into 32 languages; we used the Greek version available at http://userpage.fu-berlin.de/~health/greek.htm. For our dataset, the Greek GSE was found to have high internal reliability; Cronbach's $\alpha = 0.774$. Google forms mediated the questionnaire completion.

Next, participants completed an open card sort with 45 cards. The cards were chosen from an existing eshop following Spencer's recommendations [2] so that they were similar enough to enable participants to propose potential groups but not so similar that they would lead participants to a certain grouping. Examples of the selected cards are the following: "Table clock", "Mirror", "Poster", "Wall lamp", Sofa-bed", "Desk", "Swivel chair", "Bookcase", "Gas hob", "Tea towel", and "Cutlery tray". The labeling and explanations on the cards were straightforward to grasp and indicative of the website domain, according to the pilot testers. The card sort was mediated by USort [36]. The collected data were analyzed using Microsoft Excel 2016 and EZCalc [36].

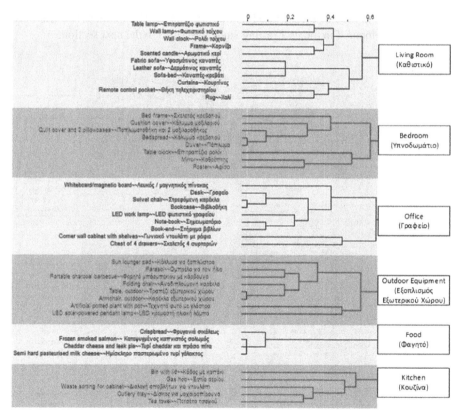

Fig. 1. Proposed information architecture for the eshop based on the open card sort involving participants with low self-efficacy (Low-GSE). Items were made available in participants' native language (Greek) but are also translated into English for presentation purposes.

2.2   Results

The median GSE score (Mdn = 27.0) was used to split the open card sort data into two groups: the Low-GSE group (N = 20) with scores below or equal to the median and the High-GSE group (N = 20) with scores above the median. The minimum sample size for a reliable open card sort is 15 [17, 18], thus our groups had adequate sample size.

The open card sort datasets for the two groups (Low-GSE, High-GSE) were analyzed following state-of-the-art techniques [2, 28]. Qualitative analysis was conducted using Spencer's Excel spreadsheet template. This spreadsheet offers the ability to explore the data, standardize category labels and produce summative matrixes. Quantitative analysis of the open card sort data was conducted using EZCalc [36]. We used the average-linkage hierarchical clustering algorithm on the open card sort datasets.

The data analysis yielded two suggested IAs for the eshop, one based on data from participants with low self-efficacy (see Fig. 1), and the other one based on data from participants with high self-efficacy (see Fig. 2). Usability metrics for these two IAs were collected and compared in the user testing study described in the next section.

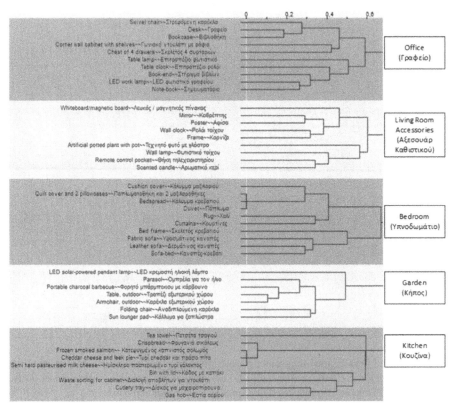

Fig. 2. Proposed information architecture for the eshop based on the open card sort involving participants with high self-efficacy (High-GSE). Items were made available in participants' native language (Greek) but are also translated into English for presentation purposes.

3   User Testing Study

3.1   Methodology

First, two functional prototypes were created for the eshop using Adobe XD. The prototypes had the same overall appearance and featured a top navigation menu. They differed only in their IA: one used the IA created by data from participants with low self-efficacy and the other eshop the IA produced by data from participants with high self-efficacy.

Next, these prototypes were user tested by 30 participants, 19 females, with mean age 26.0 years (SD = 11.2). All of the participants were native Greek speakers, and the prototypes and questionnaires presented were in Greek. A within-subjects design was employed and thus all participants used both prototypes. Videoconferencing and remote control of the facilitator's laptop were used to conduct the research remotely. The participants performed five tasks which were selected so that the item to be found was placed under a different category in the two eshop versions. To reduce order effects, the eshop versions and tasks were randomized per user.

The following dependent variables were measured: first click success, time on task, Singe Ease Question (SEQ) [37] and System Usability Scale (SUS) [38]. First click success and time on task were recorded by the facilitator while observing the participants. Each user interaction session was also recorded as a screencast, which was then reviewed to double-check the data supplied by the facilitator.

SEQ is a question answered on a seven-point grading scale with anchors "Very Difficult 1" and "Very Easy 7". Research [37] has shown that it measures perceived task complexity as well as or better than equivalent other tools. In our study, SEQ was completed immediately after each task.

SUS has 10 items rated between 1 and 5 and produces an overall SUS score between 0 and 100, where the higher the score the better the perceived usability of the system. Research [39–41] has shown that it is a valid and reliable instrument for measuring perceived usability. In our study, we used the standardized Greek version of SUS [42, 43], which was completed per eshop version after the participants had performed all the assigned tasks. For our dataset, the Greek SUS was found to have high internal reliability; Cronbach's $\alpha = 0.881$.

Google forms mediated the questionnaire completion. The collected data were organized using Microsoft Excel 2016 and were analyzed using IBM SPSS Statistics 26.

3.2   Results

Descriptive statistics for the dependent variables used in this study are shown in Table 1. In the following statistical analyses, the effect size r was calculated using the formulas mentioned in [44].

RQ1: Effect of Open Card Sort Participants' Self-efficacy on First Click Success.
Figure 3 displays the participants' mean first click success per IA version. Shapiro-Wilk analysis showed that the assumption of normality was violated for the differences in the first click success of the two conditions; $W(30) = 0.898$, $p = 0.008$. Thus, a

Table 1. Descriptive statistics of the dependent variables measured in the user testing study.

IA version	Variable	Mean	Median	SD	95% C.I
Low-GSE	First click success (%)	53.3	60.0	19.9	(45.9, 60.8)
High-GSE	First click success (%)	18.0	20.0	19.9	(10.6, 25.4)
Low-GSE	Time on task (sec)	9.9	9.2	3.8	(8.5, 11.3)
High-GSE	Time on task (sec)	12.2	11.8	4.0	(10.7, 13.7)
Low-GSE	SEQ score (1–7)	5.8	6.0	0.8	(5.5, 6.1)
High-GSE	SEQ score (1–7)	5.2	5.2	0.8	(4.9, 5.5)
Low-GSE	SUS score (0–100)	81.3	85.0	16.3	(75.2, 87.3)
High-GSE	SUS score (0–100)	67.5	67.5	20.2	(59.9, 75.1)

non-parametric test was used to compare participants' first click success between the Low-GSE eshop and the High-GSE eshop. A two-tailed Wilcoxon signed-rank test found that users were significantly more successful with their first click in the Low-GSE eshop (Mdn = 60%) compared to the High-GSE eshop (Mdn = 20%); z = 4.238, p < 0.001, r = 0.547.

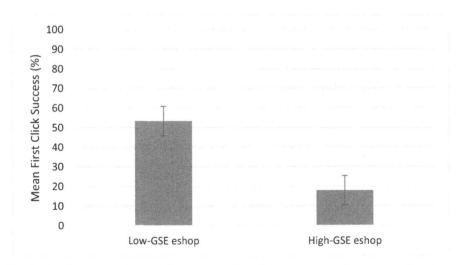

Fig. 3. Bar chart presenting participants' mean first click success per eshop version. Error bars represent the 95% confidence interval.

RQ2: Effect of Open Card Sort Participants' Self-efficacy on Time on Task. Figure 4 shows the participants' mean time on task per eshop version. A Shapiro-Wilk test found that the distribution of the differences in the time on task for the Low-GSE eshop and the High-GSE eshop did not deviate significantly from a normal distribution; W(30) = 0.968, p = 0.487. Thus, a parametric test was used to compare participants' time on task between the two conditions. A two-tailed dependent t-test found that participants were significantly faster when navigating in the Low-GSE eshop (M = 9.9, SD = 3.8) than when they did so in the High-GSE eshop (M = 12.2, SD = 4.0); t(29) = 3.395, p = 0.002, r = 0.533.

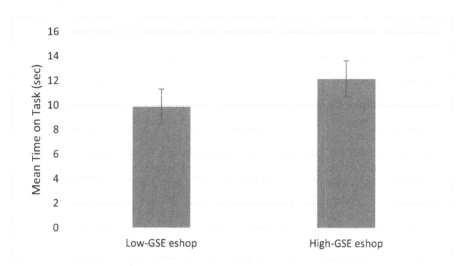

Fig. 4. Bar chart presenting participants' mean time on task per eshop version. Error bars represent the 95% confidence interval.

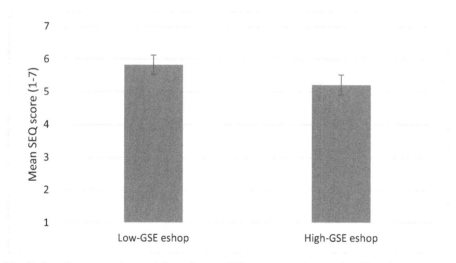

Fig. 5. Bar chart presenting participants' mean SEQ score per eshop version. Error bars represent the 95% confidence interval.

RQ3: Effect of Open Card Sort Participants' Self-efficacy on SEQ Score. Figure 5 shows the participants' mean SEQ score per eshop version. Shapiro-Wilk analysis showed that the assumption of normality was not violated for the differences in the SEQ score of the two conditions; $W(30) = 0.966$, $p = 0.441$. Thus, a parametric test was used to compare participants' perceived task difficulty score between the Low-GSE eshop and the High-GSE eshop. A two-tailed dependent t-test showed that participants using the Low-GSE eshop ($M = 5.8$, $SD = 0.8$) found the tasks significantly easier than when using the High-GSE eshop ($M = 5.2$, $SD = 0.8$); $t(29) = 3.491$, $p = 0.002$, $r = 0.544$. The mean SEQ score is around 5.5 across a dataset of over 400 tasks and 10000 users [45]. This means that our study participants found the tasks to be rather hard while interacting with the High-GSE eshop and rather easy when performing them in the Low-GSE eshop.

RQ4: Effect of Open Card Sort Participants' Self-efficacy on SUS Score. Figure 6 illustrates the participants' SUS score per eshop version. A Shapiro-Wilk test found that the distribution of the differences in the SUS score for the Low-GSE eshop and the High-GSE eshop did not deviate significantly from a normal distribution; $W(30) = 0.934$, $p = 0.061$. Thus, a parametric two-tailed dependent t-test was used. It found that participants provided significantly higher SUS scores for the Low-GSE eshop ($M = 81.3$, $SD = 16.3$) compared to the High-GSE eshop ($M = 67.5$, $SD = 20.2$); $t(29) = 3.095$, $p = 0.004$, $r = 0.498$. According to [40], the users found the Low-GSE shop as "Good to Excellent" (SUS score from 71.4 to 85.5) and the High-GSE shop as "OK to Good" (SUS score from 50.9 to 71.4) in terms of perceived usability.

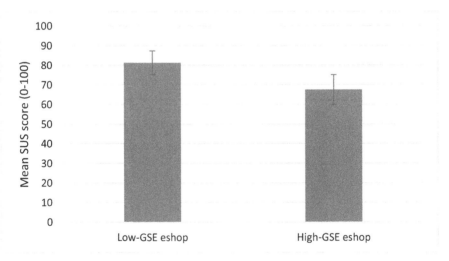

Fig. 6. Bar chart presenting participants' mean SUS score per eshop version. Error bars represent the 95% confidence interval.

4   Discussion and Conclusions

Information architecture plays an important role in the findability and usability of a website. Open card sorting is typically used to facilitate the design or evaluation of website IAs. This paper explores the influence of participants' self-efficacy on the IA produced based on state-of-the-art analysis of open card sort data.

To this end, a two-phase study was conducted. In the first phase, 40 participants rated their self-efficacy on a standardized scale and completed an open card sort for an eshop. A median-split based on their mean self-efficacy score was performed to produce two open card sort datasets: one for participants with low self-efficacy (N = 20) and one for participants with high self-efficacy (N = 20). These datasets were analyzed to produce two IAs for the eshop. In the second phase, two interactive prototypes were developed that implemented the IAs produced in the first phase. Usability metrics were collected and compared for these two interactive prototypes in a within-subjects user testing study involving 30 participants.

This paper found that users interacting with the IA produced by users with low self-efficacy made statistically significantly more correct first clicks, significantly less time to find content items, rated the tasks as significantly easier, and provided higher perceived usability ratings compared to when they interacted with the IA produced by users with high self-efficacy. In addition, all observed effect sizes were large; r from 0.498 to 0.547 [46].

These findings were unexpected and might seem counterintuitive. However, Pajares [47] argues that high self-efficacy does not always guarantee positive expectations for the quality of the results. High self-efficacy can make people overly self-confident and ignore weaknesses that they have not realized that they have [48] and thus their performance in the given tasks may not be the best. In our case, such weaknesses might have affected the card sorting task result that was produced by the high self-efficacy group of participants.

One other possible explanation could be that a third variable might be responsible for the observed finding. In our previous research [31], we have found that participants' sense of direction affects open card sort results. The standardized Santa Barbara Sense of Direction scale (SBSOD) [49] was used for measuring participants' sense of direction in [31]. The same participants were involved in [31] and the open card sort reported in this paper, thus we first aggregated in a single dataset the participants' self-reported ratings for their sense of direction and self-efficacy. Next, we performed a correlation analysis between participants' SBSOD and GSE scores. A low and non-significant correlation was found between participants' sense of direction and self-efficacy; r = 0.233, p = 0.148. In addition, we found that 9 users (22.5%) were placed in both the Low-GSE and High-SBSOD groups, and 8 users (20.0%) were placed in both the High-GSE and Low-SBSOD groups. All the rest participants were placed in the low or high group for both user characteristics. These results tend to suggest that participants' sense of direction is not responsible for the somehow surprising finding in this paper. However, some other third variable that was not measured in our research could be responsible, and future research should investigate it.

In conclusion, the effectiveness of the card sorting approach for producing usable IAs for websites tends to be influenced by participants' self-efficacy. Additional research with websites from other domains is needed, however, to confirm that the findings are generalizable. Future steps for this research also include looking at the influence of other user characteristics on open card sort results for websites. We plan to first focus on personality traits that have been found to affect other HCI methods [50]. We also plan to investigate how the continuous monitoring of a participant's physiological state while performing an open card sort might provide useful qualitative insights for facilitating IA design. For instance, the automatic detection of stress episodes [51–54] might be associated with cards that are hard to group in only one category or difficult to understand, and thus require additional attention while analyzing the results.

References

1. Rosenfeld, L., Morville, P., Arango, J.: Information architecture: For the Web and beyond. O'Reilly Media, Sebastopol (2015)
2. Spencer, D.: Card sorting: designing usable categories. Rosenfeld Media, Brooklyn (2009)
3. Albert, W., Tullis, T.S.: Measuring the User Experience: Collecting, Analyzing, and Presenting Usability Metrics. Morgan Kaufmann (2013)
4. Paul, C.: Analyzing card-sorting data using graph visualization. J. Usability Stud. **9**, 87–104 (2014)
5. Wood, J., Wood, L.: Card sorting: Current practices and beyond. J. Usability Stud. **4**, 1–6 (2008)
6. Adamides, G., Christou, G., Katsanos, C., Xenos, M., Hadzilacos, T.: Usability guidelines for the design of robot teleoperation: A taxonomy. IEEE Trans. Hum. Mach. Syst. **45**, 256–262 (2015). https://doi.org/10.1109/THMS.2014.2371048
7. Kappel, K., Tomitsch, M., Költringer, T., Grechenig, T.: Developing user interface guidelines for DVD menus. In: Extended Abstracts of the 2006 CHI Conference on Human Factors in Computing Systems, pp. 177–182. ACM, New York (2006). https://doi.org/10.1145/112 5451.1125490
8. Zaphiris, P., Ghiawadwala, M., Mughal, S.: Age-centered research-based web design guidelines. In: Extended Abstracts of the 2005 CHI Conference on Human Factors in Computing Systems, pp. 1897–1900. ACM, New York (2005). https://doi.org/10.1145/1056808.1057050
9. Katsanos, C., Tselios, N., Avouris, N.: AutoCardSorter: Designing the information architecture of a web site using latent semantic analysis. In: Proceedings of the 2008 CHI Conference on Human Factors in Computing Systems, pp. 875–878. ACM, Florence (2008). https://doi.org/10.1145/1357054.1357192
10. Katsanos, C., Tselios, N., Avouris, N.: Automated semantic elaboration of web site information architecture. Interact. Comput. **20**, 535–544 (2008). https://doi.org/10.1016/j.intcom.2008.08.002
11. Katsanos, C., Tselios, N., Goncalves, J., Juntunen, T., Kostakos, V.: Multipurpose public displays: Can automated grouping of applications and services enhance user experience? Int. J. Hum. Comput. Interact. **30**, 237–249 (2014). https://doi.org/10.1080/10447318.2013.849547
12. Cassidy, B., Antani, D.S., Read, J.C.C.: Using an open card sort with children to categorize games in a mobile phone application store. In: Proceedings of the 2013 CHI Conference on Human Factors in Computing Systems, pp. 2287–2290. ACM, New York (2013). https://doi.org/10.1145/2470654.2481315
13. Seifi, H., Oppermann, M., Bullard, J., MacLean, K.E., Kuchenbecker, K.J.: Capturing experts' mental models to organize a collection of haptic devices: affordances outweigh attributes. In: Proceedings of the 2020 CHI Conference on Human Factors in Computing Systems, p. 13. ACM, New York (2020). https://doi.org/10.1145/3313831.3376395
14. Dorn, B., Guzdial, M.: Learning on the job: Characterizing the programming knowledge and learning strategies of web designers. In: Proceedings of the 2010 CHI Conference on Human Factors in Computing Systems, Atlanta, pp. 703–712 (2010). https://doi.org/10.1145/175 3326.1753430

15. Jeong, R., Chiasson, S.: "Lime", "open lock", and "blocked": children's perception of colors, symbols, and words in cybersecurity warnings. In: Proceedings of the 2020 CHI Conference on Human Factors in Computing Systems, p. 14. ACM, New York (2020). https://doi.org/10.1145/3313831.3376611

16. Kelley, C., Lee, B., Wilcox, L.: Self-tracking for mental wellness: Understanding expert perspectives and student experiences. In: Proceedings of the 2017 CHI Conference on Human Factors in Computing Systems, pp. 629–641. ACM, New York (2017). https://doi.org/10.1145/3025453.3025750

17. Nielsen, J.: Card Sorting: How many users to test. http://www.useit.com/alertbox/20040719.html

18. Tullis, T., Wood, L.: How many users are enough for a card-sorting study? In: Proceedings of the 2004 Conference on Usability Professionals Association (UPA), Minneapolis (2004)

19. Tullis, T., Wood, L.: How can you do a card-sorting study with LOTS of cards? In: Proceedings of the 2004 Conference on Usability Professionals Association (UPA), Minneapolis (2004)

20. Pampoukidou, S., Katsanos, C.: Test-retest reliability of the open card sorting method. In: Extended Abstracts of the 2021 CHI Conference on Human Factors in Computing Systems, pp. Article330:1–Article330:7. Association for Computing Machinery, New York (2021). https://doi.org/10.1145/3411763.3451750

21. Katsanos, C., Tselios, N., Avouris, N., Demetriadis, S., Stamelos, I., Angelis, L.: Cross-study reliability of the open card sorting method. In: Extended Abstracts of the 2019 CHI Conference on Human Factors in Computing Systems, pp. LBW2718:1–LBW2718:6. ACM, New York (2019). https://doi.org/10.1145/3290607.3312999

22. Harper, M.E., Jentsch, F., Van Duyne, L.R., Smith-Jentsch, K., Sanchez, A.D.: Computerized card sort training tool: Is it comparable to manual card sorting? In: Proceedings of the Human Factors and Ergonomics Society Annual Meeting, pp. 2049–2053. SAGE Publications Inc. (2002). https://doi.org/10.1177/154193120204602512

23. Petrie, H., Power, C., Cairns, P., Seneler, C.: Using card sorts for understanding website information architectures: Technological, methodological and cultural issues. In: Campos, P., Graham, N., Jorge, J., Nunes, N., Palanque, P., Winckler, M. (eds.) INTERACT 2011. LNCS, vol. 6949, pp. 309–322. Springer, Heidelberg (2011). https://doi.org/10.1007/978-3-642-23768-3_26

24. Bussolon, S., Russi, B., Missier, F.D.: Online card sorting: As good as the paper version. In: Proceedings of the 13th European Conference on Cognitive Ergonomics: Trust and Control in Complex Socio-Technical Systems, pp. 113–114. Association for Computing Machinery, New York (2006). https://doi.org/10.1145/1274892.1274912

25. Chaparro, B.S., Hinkle, V.D., Riley, S.K.: The usability of computerized card sorting: A comparison of three applications by researchers and end users. J. Usability Stud. **4**, 31–48 (2008)

26. Melissourgos, G., Katsanos, C.: CardSorter: Towards an open source tool for online card sorts. In: Proceedings of the 24th Pan-Hellenic Conference on Informatics, pp. 77–81. ACM, New York (2020). https://doi.org/10.1145/3437120.3437279

27. Nawaz, A.: A Comparison of card-sorting analysis methods. In: Proceedings of the 10th Asia Pacific Conference on Computer-Human Interaction, APCHI 2012, pp. 583–592. ACM Press (2012)

28. Righi, C., et al.: Card sort analysis best practices. J. Usability Stud. **8**, 69–89 (2013)

29. Paea, S., Baird, R.: Information Architecture (IA): Using multidimensional scaling (MDS) and K-Means clustering algorithm for analysis of card sorting data. J. Usability Stud. **13**, 138–157 (2018)

30. Capra, M.G.: Factor analysis of card sort data: An alternative to hierarchical cluster analysis. In: Proceedings of the Human Factors and Ergonomics Society 49th Annual Meeting, pp. 691–695. HFES, Santa Monica (2005)

31. Zafeiriou, G., Katsanos, C., Liapis, A.: Effect of sense of direction on open card sorts for websites. In: Proceedings of the CHI Greece 2021: 1st International Conference of the ACM Greek SIGCHI Chapter, pp. 1–8. Association for Computing Machinery, New York (2021). https://doi.org/10.1145/3489410.3489416

32. Jawahar, I.M., Elango, B.: The effect of attitudes, goal setting and self-efficacy on end user performance. J. End User Comput. **13**, 40–45 (2001). https://doi.org/10.4018/joeuc.200104 0104

33. Igbaria, M., Iivari, J.: The effects of self-efficacy on computer usage. Omega **23**, 587–605 (1995). https://doi.org/10.1016/0305-0483(95)00035-6

34. Schwarzer, R., Jerusalem, M.: Generalized self-efficacy scale. In: Proceedings of the Measures in Health Psychology: A User's Portfolio Causal and Control Beliefs, pp. 35–37. NFER-NELSON, Windsor (1995)

35. Scholz, U., Gutiérrez Doña, B., Sud, S., Schwarzer, R.: Is General self-efficacy a universal construct? Eur. J. Psychol. Assess. **18**, 242–251 (2002). https://doi.org/10.1027//1015-5759. 18.3.242

36. Dong, J., Martin, S., Waldo, P.: A user input and analysis tool for information architecture. In: Extended Abstracts of the 2001 CHI Conference on Human Factors in Computing Systems, pp. 23–24. ACM, Seattle (2001). https://doi.org/10.1145/634067.634085

37. Sauro, J., Dumas, J.S.: Comparison of three one-question, post-task usability questionnaires. In: Proceedings of the 2009 CHI Conference on Human Factors in Computing Systems, pp. 1599–1608. ACM, New York (2009). https://doi.org/10.1145/1518701.1518946

38. Brooke, J.: SUS: A "quick and dirty" usability scale. In: Jordan, P.W., Thomas, B., Weerd-meester, B.A., McClelland, A.L. (eds.) Usability Evaluation in Industry. Taylor and Francis, London (1996)

39. Bangor, A., Kortum, P., Miller, J.: An empirical evaluation of the system usability scale. Int. J. Hum. Comput. Interact. **24**, 574–594 (2008). https://doi.org/10.1080/10447310802205776

40. Bangor, A., Kortum, P., Miller, J.: Determining what individual SUS Scores mean: Adding an adjective rating scale. J. Usability Stud. **4**, 114–123 (2009)

41. Tullis, T., Stetson, J.: A comparison of questionnaires for assessing website usability. In: Proceedings of the 2004 Conference Usability Professionals Association (UPA), pp. 7–11 (2004)

42. Katsanos, C., Tselios, N., Xenos, M.: Perceived usability evaluation of learning management systems: A first step towards standardization of the system usability scale in greek. In: Proceedings of the 2012 16th Panhellenic Conference on Informatics, pp. 302–307 (2012). https://doi.org/10.1109/PCi.2012.38

43. Orfanou, K., Tselios, N., Katsanos, C.: Perceived usability evaluation of learning management systems: Empirical evaluation of the system usability scale. Int. Rev. Res. Open Distrib. Learn. **16**, 227–246 (2015). https://doi.org/10.19173/irrodl.v16i2.1955

44. Field, A.P.: Discovering statistics using SPSS. SAGE, Los Angeles (2009)

45. Sauro, J.: 10 Things to Know About the Single Ease Question (SEQ), http://www.measuringu.com/blog/seq10.php.

46. Cohen, J.: A power primer. Psychol. Bull. **112**, 155–159 (1992)

47. Pajares, F.: Current directions in self-efficacy research. Adv. Motiv. Achiev. **10**, 1–49 (1997)

48. Ormrod, J.E.: Human Learning. Pearson, Upper Saddle River (2007)

49. Hegarty, M., Richardson, A.E., Montello, D.R., Lovelace, K., Subbiah, I.: Development of a self-report measure of environmental spatial ability. Intell. **30**, 425–447 (2002). https://doi.org/10.1016/S0160-2896(02)00116-2

50. Liapis, A., Katsanos, C., Xenos, M., Orphanoudakis, T.: Effect of personality traits on UX evaluation metrics: A study on usability issues, valence-arousal and skin conductance. In: Extended Abstracts of the 2019 CHI Conference on Human Factors in Computing Systems, pp. LBW2721:1-LBW2721:6. ACM, New York (2019). https://doi.org/10.1145/3290607.331 2995
51. Liapis, A., Katsanos, C., Karousos, N., Xenos, M., Orphanoudakis, T.: User experience evaluation: A validation study of a tool-based approach for automatic stress detection using physiological signals. Int. J. Hum. Comput. Interact. **37**, 470–483 (2021). https://doi.org/10. 1080/10447318.2020.1825205
52. Liapis, A., Katsanos, C., Karousos, N., Sotiropoulos, D., Xenos, M., Orphanoudakis, T.: Stress heatmaps: A fuzzy-based approach that uses physiological signals. In: Marcus, A., Rosenzweig, E. (eds.) HCII 2020. LNCS, vol. 12202, pp. 268–277. Springer, Cham (2020). https://doi.org/10.1007/978-3-030-49757-6_19
53. Liapis, A., Katsanos, C., Sotiropoulos, D., Xenos, M., Karousos, N.: Recognizing emotions in human computer interaction: Studying stress using skin conductance. In: Abascal, J., Barbosa, S., Fetter, M., Gross, T., Palanque, P., Winckler, M. (eds.) INTERACT 2015. LNCS, vol. 9296, pp. 255–262. Springer, Cham (2015). https://doi.org/10.1007/978-3-319-22701-6_18
54. Liapis, A., Karousos, N., Katsanos, C., Xenos, M.: Evaluating user's emotional experience in HCI: The PhysiOBS approach. In: Kurosu, M. (ed.) HCII 2014. LNCS, vol. 8511, pp. 758–767. Springer, Cham (2014). https://doi.org/10.1007/978-3-319-07230-2_72

Consideration on Must-Be Quality About ICT Tools

Suzuka Mori[1]([✉]), Keiko Kasamatsu[1], and Takeo Ainoya[2]

[1] Graduate School of System Design, Tokyo Metropolitan University, Hachioji, Japan
`suzuka7498@gmail.com, kasamatu@tmu.ac.jp`
[2] Tokyo University of Technology, VDS Co., Ltd., Hachioji, Japan

Abstract. With the spread of "ICT tools" such as smartphones, which allow us to connect to the Internet anytime, anywhere and obtain information, the number of things we can do easily has increased and our lives have become more convenient. On the other hand, I felt that there are many things that we no longer value because the number of things that frustrate us when we can't do something, but only make us feel "normal" when we can, has increased.

Therefore, this research aims to build a model that includes experiences and emotions related to ICT tools, referring to" the Kano model", which is a concept that models the quality required by customers. Based on this model, the goal of this research is to provide a means to offer new attractions, and to find a way to create value in experiences that have become commonplace over time.

As an indicator for building a model, we will conduct a factor analysis of "what is taken for granted" and "what is attractive" in ICT tools and applications used in conjunction with them. In this paper, I introduce the survey I conducted as a preliminary step to gather information.

Keywords: ICT tools · Must-be quality · Communication

1 Introduction

1.1 Background

With the spread of "ICT tools" such as smartphones, which allow us to connect to the Internet anytime, anywhere and obtain information, the number of things we can do easily has increased and our lives have become more convenient. On the other hand, we felt that there are many things that we no longer value because the number of things that frustrate us when we can't do something, but only make us feel "normal" when we can, has increased.

S. Yamamoto and H. Mori (Eds.): HCII 2022, LNCS 13305, pp. 88–98, 2022.
https://doi.org/10.1007/978-3-031-06424-1_8

The "must-be quality" defined in the Kano model is an element of the model of quality that customers demand and is something that is only ordinary when it is satisfied, but is unsatisfactory when it is not. Similarly, "attractiveness quality," which is listed as one of the elements of the model, is the counterpart of must-be quality, and is considered a quality element that is satisfying if it is satisfied, but does not cause dissatisfaction even if it is not.

In addition, "ICT tools" in this study are defined as those that "allow communication with others" and "provide necessary information at any time," such as smartphones Fig. 1.

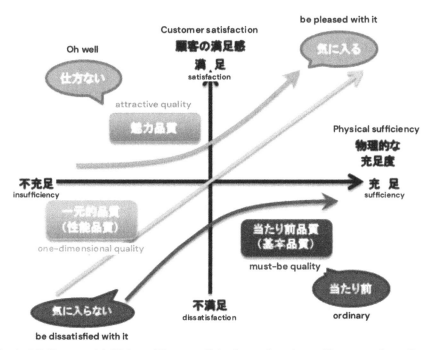

Fig. 1. [1] Kano model (Union of Japanese Scientists and engineers Homepage, https://www.juse.or.jp/departmental/point02/08.html, last accessed 2022/2/10)

1.2 Purpose

In this research, we aim to build a model that includes experiences and emotions related to ICT tools, referring to the Kano model, which is a concept that models the quality required by customers. Based on this model, the goal of this research is to provide a means to offer new attractions, and to find a way to create value in experiences that have become commonplace over time [1].

As an indicator for model building, elemental analysis of "what is taken for granted" and "what is attractive" in ICT tools and applications used in conjunction with them will be conducted. In this paper, we introduce the survey I conducted as a preliminary step to gather information Fig. 2.

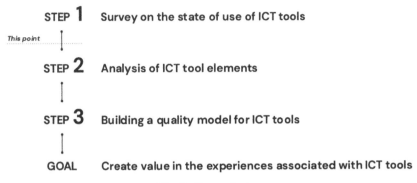

Fig. 2. Research plan

2   Prior Experiment

2.1   Outline

In this study, we conducted a "meeting without a smartphone" as a preliminary experiment. The condition was no contact from the time you leave your house until you meet your partner at the meeting place.

There were three participants in the experiment, two working adults and one graduate student, all of whom were female, and their average age was 22.7 years old.

They met up with one of us, the experimenter, one-on-one. The three locations were Nishiogikubo Station, Tachikawa Station, and Noborito Station.

2.2   Result

The main overall result was that all participants were able to meet up with each other without any major problems. One conditional factor was that the stations were all small.

Meeting at Nishiogikubo Station

Participant	: Ms. A (24 years old student)
Ticket gates	: one
Intimacy with partner	: excellent
Familiarity with the place	: just visited together recently

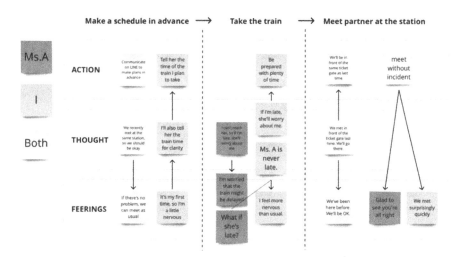

Fig. 3. Results of prior experiments 1

Details of experimental situation and a summary of the behavior, thoughts, and feelings of each of the experimental participants and myself from the time we made plans to the time we met are shown in Fig. 3-Fig. 5.

Figure 3 shows a case where Ms. A and one of us (Fig. 3-Fig. 5: I) met at Nishiogikubo station. The location was a station with a single ticket gate, and they had only recently met up together at that station.

As a result, there was consideration for each other to be punctual so as not to worry the other. On the emotional side, she was anxious about the possibility of trouble and being late due to lack of contact, and nervous about trying not to be late. Since they had the experience of meeting at the same place last time and the station was not large, they were able to meet right away without having to decide on a detailed meeting place in advance. It is thought that both felt that they would be able to meet at that location.

Meeting at Tachikawa Station

Participant	: Ms. B (23 years old, working adult)
Ticket gates	: two
Intimacy with partner	: excellent
Familiarity with the place	: had a few meet-ups together

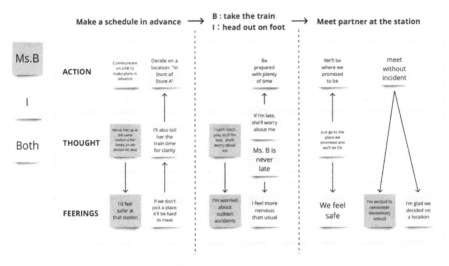

Fig. 4. Results of prior experiments 2

Figure 4 shows a case where Ms. B and one of us met up at Tachikawa station. The location was a station with two ticket gates, and Ms. B's familiarity with the place was such that she would meet up with her frequently.

Normally, Ms. B and she would meet after arriving at the meeting place by exchanging "Where are you? " However, under this experiment, there was a change in determining the detailed location in advance. On the emotional side, we received comments that they felt relieved to be in a place they were familiar with, and that not using their phones made her feel excited, reminding her of meeting up with friends in elementary school.

Meeting at Nonborito Station

Participant	: Ms. C (22 years old, working adult)
Ticket gates	: two
Intimacy with partner	: excellent
Familiarity with the place	: first time for both of us

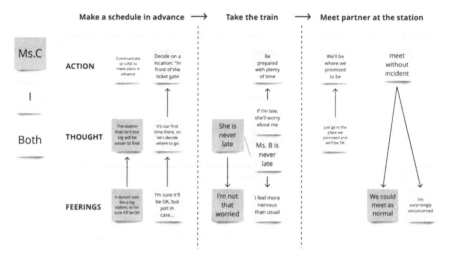

Fig. 5. Results of prior experiments 3

Figure 5 shows a case where Ms. C and one of us met up at Noborito station. The location was a station with two ticket gates, it was the first time for both to visit this place. Since it was the first time for both to be there, they specified the location of the ticket gate in advance and were able to meet smoothly. On the emotional side, she said that she did not feel particularly anxious because she felt more secure when she knew that the other person would not be late.

2.3   Consideration

The results of the preliminary experiment did not show any difference in the result itself that the meeting was possible even without smartphone. However, it turns out that people do things to make up for the lack of a smartphone. These are thought to be linked to the values and behavioral devices for meeting up before the spread of ICT tools.

On the emotional side, we found that while they felt anxious, it did not affect them as much depending on our trust and intimacy with the other person, and that they were excited by the nostalgia.

As a consideration, changes in the way information is exchanged are likely to affect people's behavior and emotions. It could also be said that ICT tools have taken root as a sense of security that allows people to contact each other anytime, anywhere.

3 Survey1

3.1 Outline

Based on the results of the preliminary experiment, a comparison was made between the conventions that faded with the spread of ICT tools and the substitution behavior in the present day to understand how the spread of ICT tools has changed the way information is exchanged and communicated.

To extract practices for comparison, we interviewed 55-year-old working woman, about the practices that have disappeared or have fewer opportunities now that ICT tools have become widespread, and selected events related to the exchange of information. As a result, three types of information were extracted: writing letters, using public telephones, and obtaining information through oral communication.

We set up possible purposes for these actions and wrote down the process of carrying out these purposes before and after the spread of. ICT tools, and compared them.

3.2 Result

Figure 6 shows the process and characteristics of achieving each objective before and after the diffusion of ICT tools and summarizes the common elements.

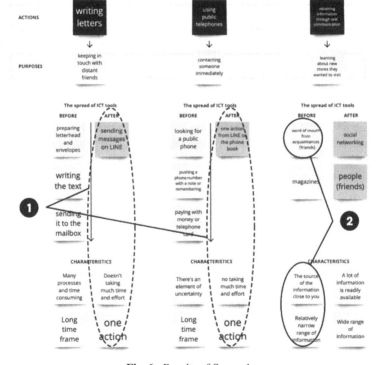

Fig. 6. Results of Survey1

First, before the spread of ICT tools, the purpose of the act of "letter writing" was to keep in touch with distant friends. The process of "keeping in touch with distant friends" before the spread of ICT tools is thought to include at least three actions: preparing letterhead and envelopes, writing the text, and sending it to the mailbox. On the other hand, now that ICT tools have become widespread, it is possible to send messages such as "How are you?" on LINE. Comparing these, we can see that the length of the timeline to achieve the goal is very different.

Second, the purpose of the act of "using a public phone" before the spread of ICT tools was to contact someone immediately. The process before the diffusion of ICT tools in "contacting someone immediately" includes at least three behaviors: "looking for a public phone," "pushing a phone number with a note or remembering it" and "paying with money or telephone card. On the other hand, nowadays, people can be contacted immediately with one action from LINE or the phone book. This also shows that the time axis is very different, and the time and effort has been reduced.

Third, before the spread of ICT tools, when people obtained information about unfamiliar stores, they may have had the goal of learning about new stores they wanted to visit. Before the spread of ICT tools, the most common sources of information were "word of mouth from acquaintances" and "magazines". The source of the information was often close to home, as it was basically passed on through word of mouth to acquaintances. On the other hand, "social networking" and "people (friends)" are the main ones nowadays. A vast amount of information can be easily obtained from social networking sites. In addition, even if you hear about it from others, you probably get additional information by searching on your own later. In comparison, the breadth and quantity of information is very different.

3.3 Consideration

From the results of the survey, the following two considerations were made.

The first is that it has become so easy to exchange information that the method has become univocal, regardless of the person or situation. (Fig. 6. - ①) As a result, we may be experiencing a lack of emotional change.

Second, before the spread of ICT tools, it is thought that people basically exchanged information with people they or their relatives knew. (Fig. 6. - ②) As a result, it was probably easier to grasp the source of the information and judge its reliability than it is today.

4 Survey2

4.1 Outline

Next, we conducted an interview survey to find out how people exchange information and communicate with others.

The four interview items were: what you currently use to communicate (1), what you currently use when you have information you want to know (2), what you can get unexpected information from (3), and the moment when you feel you might have been better off without a smartphone (4).

There were four participants in this study, of which two were working adults and two were graduate students, three were women and one was a man, and their average age was 23.5 years.

By learning how people exchange information and communicate with others, we aim to discover the elements that are taken for granted in the way people interact with ICT tools and the applications they use, and what has become commonplace.

4.2 Result

The main responses to each of the interview items are summarized in Figures Fig. 7- Fig. 10.

1. What you use to communicate

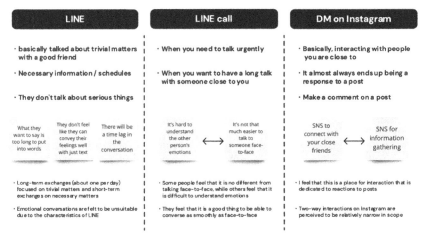

Fig. 7. Results of interview (1)

The results of the interview (1) showed that the participants mainly used three main methods to contact each other: LINE, LINE calls, and direct messages on Instagram. It was felt that having serious and emotional conversations on LINE was not suitable since it is only text information, the amount of text when converted, and the time lag. Therefore, they basically talked about trivial matters, information, and schedules. They felt that the good thing about LINE calls was that conversations proceeded as smoothly as when they were face-to-face. However, some felt that it was difficult to understand their emotions because they could not see their facial expressions Fig. 8.

2. What you use when you have information you want to know

Google	People	Intagram
At first, look it up on Google	When there are people around them who are good at what they want to know	When researching hobbies and interests, such as clothes and restaurants

Get to know the broad and shallow Weak on questions without certainty ex."Fashionable" can't be trusted so easily Information is unidirectional

· Google is all-powerful, but perceived as weak on unanswered questions

· The vast amount of information is appealing, but we need to figure out the right one ourselves

Information with different answers depending on the person School and personal things that Google can't tell their It's easy to believe information when it comes from someone you trust bidirectional communication

· They often ask about the person's experiences that are useful and personal

· Information from people you know is easier to trust, and you can dig deeper

t's easy to find what you like Mainstream use as information gathering from stores and influencers

· It's easy to find information that matches your interests from people you can relate to

· It's easy to see what kind of people are sending

Twitter	Other Apps	Book
Learn about the "current" information from the world's trend searches	Tabelog / Wether / train transfer... Apps that focus on the information you want to know	Participants use it to gather information related to their studies

Fig. 8. Results of interview (2)

The results of interview (2) showed that the participants mainly rely on three sources when they want to know something: Google, people, and Instagram. Many of the participants said that they would do search once anyway, as Google is a quick and easy way to get answers. However, it was felt that they were not well suited for sensitive and unanswerable questions such as "fashionable". Many of the participants asked people if they could use their experience or if they wanted to ask something informal, and they felt that the reliability of the information and the ability to dig deeper was a good thing. Many of the participants use Instagram to look up things like hobbies and preferences, and this is thought to be related to the fact that it is easy to understand who the person transmitting the message is, making it easier to gain trust and empathy Fig. 9.

3. What you can get unexpected information from

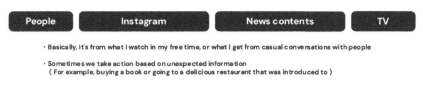

Fig. 9. Results of interview (3)

The results of interview (3) included uneventful conversations with people, Instagram, and news content. While most of the responses were passive, such as watching the videos in their free time, some respondents acted based on the information they received.

The results of interview (4) included the feeling of wasting time by watching smart phone too much, and the fear of being easily connected with many people.

It turns out that there are some problems that arise when we take for granted that we can access the Internet anytime, anywhere.

4. The moment you think you might be better off without your phone

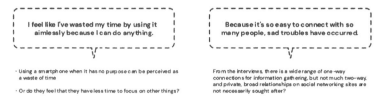

Fig. 10. Results of interview (4)

4.3 Consideration

The results of these interviews showed that while each participant had different impressions and uses of ICT tools in communication and information gathering, there were some things in common.

We thought that the fact that the usage of ICT tools and applications is common among people who can use them freely may be since there are factors that form the "usual" (factors that make people use them and the way they use them) in some elements of ICT tools and applications. I would like to explore the elements of this, considering the lifestyle of people today, which is thought to have been changed by ICT tools.

5 Conclusion

From the previous surveys, it can be assumed that the method of communication, the use of information tools and applications, and the emotions associated with them will vary depending on the purpose and situation.

It was also found that there were some things that were established as "usual" among the interview participants, such as "they don't talk much about emotional things on LINE" and "They look it up once on Google anyway".

Based on this, an elemental analysis of "what is taken for granted" and "what is attractive" in ICT tools and applications used in conjunction with them will be conducted as an indicator for building the model. By doing so, we would like to discover the relationship between experiences and emotions through ICT tools for each purpose and situation and use this to build a model.

References

1. Union of Japanese Scientists and engineers Homepage. https://www.juse.or.jp/departmental/point02/08.html (last accessed 2022/2/10)
2. Takagi, S., Uesu, H.: An analysis of students' needs at mathematics lectures. In: Proceedings of the 28th Annual Conference of Biomedical Fuzzy System Association (BMFSA2015), Kumamoto (2015)
3. Hsu, Y.-L., Hsu, C.-C., Bing, P.-C.: Sharpening passenger service strategy planning by applyingkano'squality element classification: A case study in the airline industry. In: Proceedings of the Eastern Asia Society for Transportation Studies, vol. 6 (2007)

Examination of Conditions that the Point System Contributes to the Activation of Local Communication

Yurika Shiozu[1]([✉]), Soichi Arai[2], Hiromu Aso[3], Yuto Ohara[3], and Katsunori Shimohara[3]

[1] Kyoto Sangyo University, Kyoto 603-8555, Kyoto, Japan
yshiozu@cc.kyoto-su.ac.jp
[2] Akita University, Akita 010-8502, Akita, Japan
[3] Graduate School of Science and Engineering, Doshisha University, Kyotanabe 610-0394, Japan

Abstract. In recent years, social media has been used by many businesses, governments and individuals. Social media is helping to build new relationships as well as strengthen existing ones. Many individuals are said to exist merely as searchers of information. However, including anonymous engagement behaviors such as "likes", they are also considered to be expressing their intentions. We call them Lurker, but can we use Lurker's principles of action to revitalize the local community?

This paper presents the results of an experiment featuring a smart phone social media application (app) intended to incentivize communication during certain health behavior, namely walking, among participating users in Japan, through a non-monetary point system. Our research question is to clarify the point system that have no economic value activate reciprocal motivation and communication by making connections between individuals visible in a non-anonymous manner. Upon analysis of the data obtained, two main findings were revealed. First, over time, the non-anonymous point system where points have no economic value did not effectively activate communication among participants given the experimental conditions. However, when the rules and goals for using points are clearly defined, when point use targets not only individuals but also places or events (as will be explained), and when approval is anonymously and easy to express and feedback easy to obtain, app use becomes sustainable.

Keywords: Point system · Anonymity · Lurker

1 Introduction

This paper presents the results of an experiment featuring a smart phone social media application (app) intended to incentivize communication during certain health behavior, namely walking, among participating users in Japan, through a non-monetary point system.

S. Yamamoto and H. Mori (Eds.): HCII 2022, LNCS 13305, pp. 99–117, 2022.
https://doi.org/10.1007/978-3-031-06424-1_9

Social media use is not generally limited by user attributes other than age. This wide appeal supports not only connection-building among experienced users but also relationship-building for new users. Commercial companies take advantage of social media for marketing, and politicians and governments use it for information dissemination. For instance, the importance of human connections within communities has been well recognized in the context of disaster response. However, the opportunity cost of participation in traditional community association activities is high, and the maintenance of community ties through such participation is no longer easy. Against this backdrop, there moves have been in recent years to incorporate social media into, for example, community association and PTA activities to reduce the burden of participation and revitalize communication among members. That said, it is not enough to use social media to simply send out messages; operational innovations are also necessary.

In general, when encouraging others to change their behaviors, appropriate incentives must be designed, as has been shown in accumulated research on health behaviors and waste problems. For example, Okamoto et al. (2017) found that to effectively encourage continuous practice of certain health behaviors, incentives should function similarly to cash, such as being exchangeable for prizes, and should consider the original health status of participants. In response to these research results, some non-profit organizations and governments have introduced point systems to encourage the public to practice certain health behaviors. For example, in the health point program implemented by local governments throughout Japan, community residents receive points that they can be exchange for prizes or discount coupons when they take actions that contribute to their health.

Commercial companies, on the other hand, deploy point systems, often in the form of loyalty programs, aimed at retaining customers through price discrimination strategies such as the issuance of coupons. When profit companies provide accounting allowance when issuing points, allowing them to be exchanged for goods and services at their own stores or affiliated stores.

In contrast, premiums and discount coupons issued by non-profit organizations and governments are funded through subsidies and corporate social contributions. Limited financial resources often make such systems difficult to sustain in non-profit and government sectors. We should also consider that when points are issued since transactions with specific companies, as is the case with corporate point systems, there are problems with of lack of convenience and limited number of users.

On the other hand, systems with tools that allow consumers to express approval, such as the "like" function in social media platforms, have been in continual use despite the lack of direct economic value involved. There are though problems associated with approval being expressed in this way. For example, some people stop participating in social media due to anonymity and trust issues. For example, they stop endorsing social media posts because others can see their endorsements or because they fear the information sender is using social media for stealth marketing. The former problem is an issue with any system wherein user approval statements are not anonymized, and the latter is often a marketing-related problem.

Is it possible to alleviate the funding problems nonprofits and governments face when designing incentives by using social media to lower the opportunity cost of communication among community residents? More specifically, can points that have no economic value activate reciprocal motivation and communication by making connections between individuals visible in a non-anonymous manner? That is the guiding question of this research. Toward gaining clear insight on the matter, we developed the original mobile social media app intended to activate communication within local communities and implemented a unique point system; points have no economic value in and of themselves but rather function as indicators of intention. We implemented the system and conducted the social experiment in two phases. Upon analysis of the data obtained, two main findings were revealed. First, over time, the non-anonymous point system where points have no economic value did not effectively activate communication among participants given the experimental conditions. However, when the rules and goals for using points are clearly defined, when point use targets not only individuals but also places or events (as will be explained), and when approval is anonymously and easy to express and feedback easy to obtain, app use becomes sustainable.

In the following, Sect. 2 overviews previous studies, Sect. 3 describes the social experiment, Sect. 4 presents the data analysis results, Sect. 5 discusses those results, and Sect. 6 presents conclusions and plans for future research.

2 Literature Review

2.1 Altruism and Reciprocity

Contract theory by [3] and [8] has shown that appropriately designed incentives can be used to improve community members' social welfare. While contract theory focuses primarily on monetary rewards as incentives, behavioral economics studies not only monetary rewards but also non-monetary rewards such as altruism and the desire for approval, with application to various fields. Accordingly, enjoyment is considered a non-monetary reward, and gamification, which incorporates game elements into non-game activities, is a method for producing such enjoyment. According to [5] shows metanalysis, gamification strategies have been effectively applied in encouraging cleanliness on public transportation and garbage recycling and in promoting civic participation in urban areas. That is, it has been shown that introducing game elements or "fun" when raising people's awareness of local issues may positively impact their behavior toward solving the issue. In addition, the use of points and donations is proposed as an effective means of encouraging continued participation in each game, based on human desires for both reward and altruism.

The point systems found in corporate loyalty programs are means for commercial companies to differentiate themselves from competitors, retain customers, and engage in price discrimination strategies. Microeconomics explains that when a company cannot fully grasp consumer demand for its products, it can secure sales volume and earn more profit by classifying consumers according to their price sensitivity and offering appropriate discounts accordingly. For example, companies can implement indirect price discrimination strategies through a point system for the issuance of coupons based on past purchase behavior. That is, satisfying the desire for reward through points as a means of encouraging consumers' continuous game participation is nothing more than maintaining behavioral changes through monetary rewards.

[1] suggests that when donors' giving involves perceived utility or "impure altruism," the act of giving is not affected by increases in government subsidies, number of donors, or increases in the amount of other donors' contributions. However, in the case of pure altruism, i.e., motivated solely by the desire to be of service to others, the act of donation is affected by the government's subsidy policy and the behavior of other donors. Due to its relative stability, impure altruism is considered a useful tool to encourage continued participation in a game.

Relatedly, reciprocity posits that human beings react favorably to favorable actions by others and with disfavor against malicious actions. For example, [9] shows that when participants receive point donations, the probability that they will in turn donate points becomes 17 times, even when the points have no economic value. That reciprocity occurs even with non-monetary rewards indicates that it may be useful in promoting continual game participation.

2.2 Donor SOC

What characteristics are attributable to individuals who work toward solving social problems? Antonovsky's Sense of Coherence (SOC) is a useful construct here. SOC, roughly, measures our perceived ability to live healthily and has three components: comprehensibility, processability, and meaningfulness. Comprehensibility is our sense of our ability to understand life problems, processability is our sense of access to problem-solving resources, and meaningfulness is our sense that solving these problems is worthwhile. Although SOC is thought to remain in development through age 30 or so and then remain constant, [4] finds that SOC increases when we feel useful to others, irrespective of age. Notably, through a large-scale survey conducted across Japan, [11] found that people who participate in municipal councils and neighborhood associations, volunteer activities, and hobby circles have high SOC, while those who only participate in internet communities have low SOC.

It is well known that there are two types of social media users or internet community members: those who actively transmit information and "lurkers" who do not. According to [7], nearly 80% of Japan's social media users are lurkers, a higher ratio than in Europe or the United States. Withing traditional social media marketing, the lurker has been viewed negatively as a "free rider" or consumer of information. However, [2] points out that the lurker plays an important role in social media marketing, and it is important to clarify the mechanisms driving such a role. [6] acknowledges that although lurkers avoid transmitting information, they still present engagement behaviors such as liking and sharing, posts and points out that the functional characteristics of social media make engagement behaviors visible and thus influence consumer behavior.

In the context of SOC, problem-solving resources are thought to be accessible through social media interactions that increase recipient's sense of processability and donor's sense of meaningfulness. Depending on the content of the social issue, when an entity sends out or "donates" information, they may welcome even seemingly passive recipients, i.e., lurkers or free riders, because a connection can nonetheless be secured with such recipients. When lurkers practice diffusion and engagement behaviors such as expressing their support for social action efforts through liking and sharing, sense of meaningfulness may increase for both lurkers and information senders. As such, the relationship between SOC and social media use remains a relevant issue.

3 Methods

3.1 The Social Experiment

To conduct this experiment, we developed an original Community System Design (CSD) mobile social media app and used it along with an Omron activity meter (step-measurer). Toward enhancing the continuity of the application, points, an element of gamification, were introduced into the app. The points have no economic value; they are meaningful as indicators of intention only. The experiment was conducted in two phases.

3.2 Participants and Study Phases

The social experiment was conducted in two two-month phases: from October 12, 2020 to December 12, 2020 (Phase I) and from October 17, 2021 to December 17, 2021 (Phase II). Phase I participants comprised 10 men and 8 women who are members of a community development NPO in the Makishima area, Uji City, Kyoto Prefecture. Participants were aged 40 to 80 years old, with most being in their 70s. Phase II included participants from the first group as well as two female members of a child-rearing NPO who are in their 30s and 40s and four female members of a musicians' circle in Noshiro City, Akita Prefecture who are in their 60s to 80s.

In Phase I, researchers provided participants with a smartphone with the CSD application installed and an Omron activity meter for use during the experiment. In Phase I, participants had the option of using the provided smartphone or installing the CSD app on their personal smartphone. Omron activity meters were distributed to all Phase II participants. Training sessions were held in various locations before each phase to explain how to operate the app[1].

3.3 App Features

The CSD app has five main functions: 1) it transfers step data from the Omron activity meter and awards unique points based on the number of steps taken; 2) it allows participants to gift one other with unique points; 3) it allows participants to post photos on a

---

[1] Prior to conducting all social experiments and questionnaires, the project underwent an ethical review by Kyoto Sangyo University and Doshisha University and obtained their approval before conducting the surveys.

map, share them with other participants, and express approval of posted photos; and 4) it awards participants unique points for expressing their approval of the app via Bluetooth when another device with the CSD app installed is detected nearby. Finally, function 5) divides participants into two teams to play a monthly battle game. In this paper, we discuss the second, third, and fourth functions.

First, let us look at the second function in detail. As illustrated in Fig. 1, participants can non-anonymously gift their points to other participants by name. The four steps to donate points are as follows: 1) tap the "donate points" icon, 2) select the recipient, 3) enter the number of points to donate, and 4) send (with the option of including a comment). The point-gifting activity is visible to all participants. It includes the names of the donors and the recipients, the number of points gifted, and the date of the gift. When the red button (Fig. 1, far left) is tapped, the rightmost image in Fig. 1 appears, and the information within the yellow circle can be viewed.

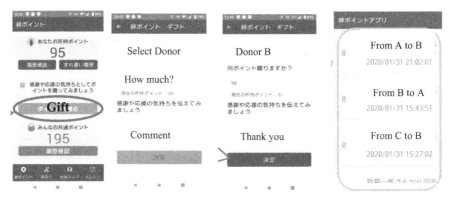

Fig. 1. Point-gifting function screen

Next, we look at the third function, posting photos on the map. Participants can earn unique points by posting photos. The posted photos are viewable by all participants, and all photos can be liked. To express approval of a posted photo, users 1) tap the red circle (Fig. 2, left) to open the map, 2) tap the purple pin (Fig. 2, center, and 3) when the photo appears, tap like (Fig. 2, right). Participants also receive unique points for liking other's photos. A notable feature here is that the date of posting and the identities of both posters and likers are hidden. Only the number of likes is visible.

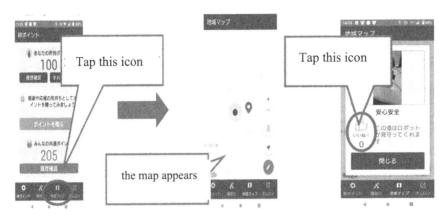

Fig. 2. Screenshot of CSD application. Process of expressing approval of a submitted photo

The system is designed such that the gifting of points is done in a non-anonymous manner, and the expression of approval for the posted photos is done anonymously. Although sthe point targets points are named individuals, like targets are anonymously submitted photos of places and events.

4 Data Analysis and Results

4.1 Data

In the following, we overview the data collected from Phases I and II of the social experiment using the CSD app.

Data Obtained from Use of the CSD App. In this paper, we examine the app's effectiveness in activating communication among participants by comparing 1) the non-anonymous, publicly announced gifting of unique points that have no economic value compared to 2) anonymous expressions of approval of posted photos and 3) proximity connectivity (app-facilitated face-to face meet ups) among participants. We compare the distribution of the time series of 1) the number of gifts of unique points made, 2) the number of expressions of approval of posted photos, and 3) the number of proximity connections made in Phases I and II.

First, a total of 93 unique point gifts were observed in Phase I and 69 in Phase II (see Fig. 3 and Fig. 4 for distribution details). It took 43 days to reach 80% cumulative density in in Phase I and 19 days in Phase II.

The maximum number of point gifts per day was nine in Phase I, reaching 15 in Phase II. There were 29 days with no gifts made in Phase I and 41 such days in Phase II. Table 1 presents the basic statistics on the number of gifts in Phases I and II for comparison. The large difference in kurtosis confirms that although there were fewer gifts given per day in Phase I, gifts were given on more days. Moreover, point gifts were more frequently accompanied by comments in Phase I than in Phase II.

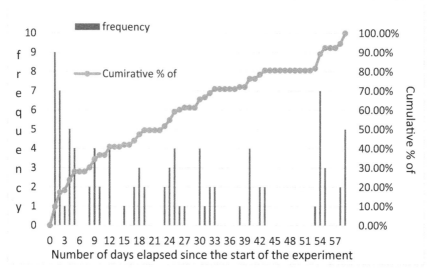

Fig. 3. Histogram: number of point gifts in Phase I, points were gifted a total of 93 times (88 times with comments).

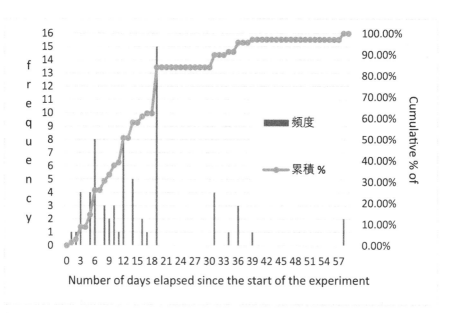

Fig. 4. Histogram: Number of point gifts in Phase II, points were gifted a total of 69 times (33 times with comments).

Table 1. Descriptive statistics of gifted point at phase I and II

	Average	Median	Mode	S.D.	Distribution	Kurtosis	Skewness
Phase I	1.55	1	0	2.07	4.32	2.40	1.58
Phase II	1.15	0	0	2.57	6.64	14.61	3.47

Next, we analyze the distribution of liked photos.

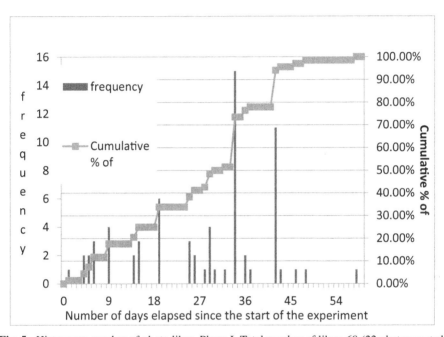

Fig. 5. Histogram: number of photo likes, Phase I, Total number of likes: 68 (22 photos posted, 3.09 likes per photo)

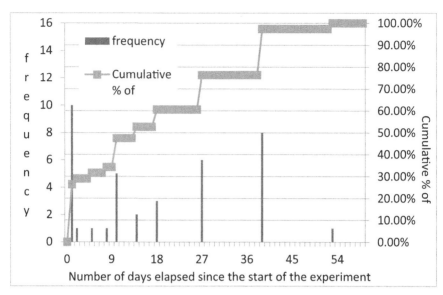

Fig. 6. Histogram: number of photo likes, Phase II, Total number of likes: 38 (11 photos posted, 3.45 likes per photo)

First, a total of 68 photo likes were observed in Phase I and 38 in Phase II. (see Fig. 5 and Fig. 6 above for the distribution. It took 34 days to reach 80% cumulative density in Phase I and 39 in Phase II. The maximum number of likes per day was 15 in Phase I and 10 in Phase II. There were 38 days with no likes in Phase I and 50 such days in Phase II. See Table 2 to compare basic statistics on number of likes in Phases I and II. The large differences in mean and variance confirm that there were more likes per day and more days with likes in Phase I than Phase II.

Table 2. Descriptive statistics: number of likes, Phases I and II

	Average	Median	Mode	S.D.	Distribution	Kurtosis	Skewness
Phase I	1.13	0	0	2.58	6.66	16.83	3.83
Phase II	0.63	0	0	1.92	3.70	13.18	3.61

Although 22 photos were posted in Phase I and only 11 in Phase II, the difference in the number of likes per photo between the two phases was not significant at 3.09 and 3.45, respectively.

Finally, we check for changes in the time distribution for Bluetooth proximity connections.

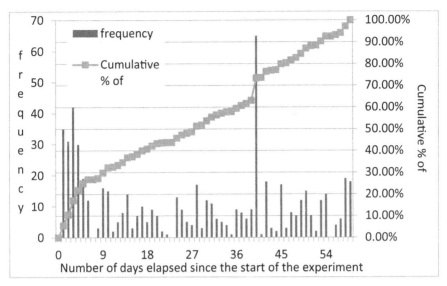

Fig. 7. Histogram: Number of proximity connections, Phase I, Participants were within Bluetooth proximity of one another a total of 631 times.

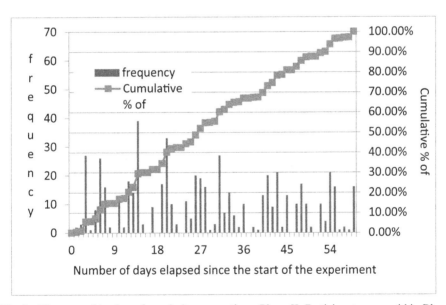

Fig. 8. Histogram: Number of proximity connections, Phase II, Participants were within Bluetooth proximity of one another a total of 578 times.

The COVID-19 disaster made face-to-face communication difficult during both phases. However, Fig. 7 shows that there were only four days during phase ? when proximity did not appear, and Fig. 8 shows that there were only eight days during the phase

? when proximity could not be observed. It means that participants secured numerous opportunities to meet face-to-face.

4.2 Social Network Analysis

Prior research has confirmed that reciprocity comes into play even when points have no economic value. Figure 9 illustrates a reciprocal network where all participants attempt to reciprocate with all other participants.

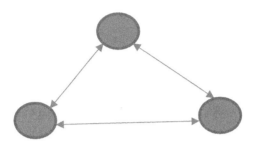

Fig. 9. Reciprocal network

Consider our research question, (i.e., Can points, which have no economic value, activate reciprocal motivation and communication by making connections between individuals visible in a non-anonymous manner?), if we can confirm a strongly connected directed graph with respect to participants' behavior in gifting economically valueless points, we can argue that the system enhances communication between individuals even though it is non-anonymous. Strong connectedness is determined by analyzing diameter, network density, modularity, modularity class, and average clustering coefficient, which are among the indicators to be derived during social network analysis. Diameter indicates the frequency of point-giving among social network participants, and network density indicates the frequency of point-giving. By determining modularity class, we identify the existence of clusters, which are subsets of the whole body of participants. The modularity determines whether the exchange of points within each cluster is active, and the clustering coefficient indicates the degree to which each participant is connected to others. If the degree of connectedness is higher in Phase I than in Phase II, the program is considered to have continuity.

The Overall Network Structure for Point-Gifting. First, 16 participants gifted unique points in Phase I and 17 in Phase II. Gephi0.9.2 was used for the analysis. Whole-network indicators by social network analysis are reported in Table 3.

Table 3. Network-wide indicators

	Phase I	Phase II
Number of times points can be gifted (A gift between the same participant is counted as one gift.)	51	21
Network diameter	4	5
Graph density	0.212	0.077
Modularity	0.34	0.27
Modularity class	2	4
Average clustering coefficient	0.532	0.122

We can see that the number of point gifts decreased by half in Phase II. Accordingly, the graph density also decreased in Phase II. Although the modularity class doubled over Phase I, the decrease in modularity indicates that the number of point gifts within each cluster also decreased. The clustering coefficient is 1 for network members who engaged in point-gifting with anyone except themselves. The clustering coefficient is 0 for network members who had points to available to gift to others but did not gift them. The average clustering coefficient in Phase I is 0.532, suggesting that point-gifting among the participants in the social experiment did take place to a certain extent. Figure 10 visualizes each participant's clustering coefficient ranking in Phase I. The darker the circle color, the higher the clustering coefficient; the darker the line color, the higher the frequency; the thicker the line, the greater the number of points gifted. As illustrated, all participants are connected by a path. That is, there is no isolated vertex. In addition, as there are several dark circles, two-way communication can be confirmed. As such, the Phase I network is characterized by a large proportion of strong connections.

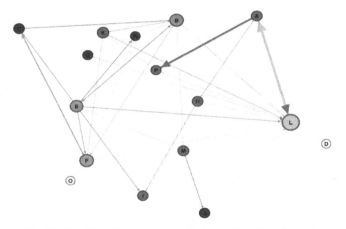

Fig. 10. Ranking of clustering coefficients, Phase I participants.

On the other hand, the average clustering coefficient in Phase II is 0.122, which is close to zero, indicating that point-gifting between participants is less likely to take place under the conditions. Figure 11 visualizes the clustering coefficient for each participant in Phase II. Figure 11 indicates independent point-gifting by participants B, Q, C, and S. This means that they are separatable by two modularity classes. Furthermore, as there is only one dark circle, it can be confirmed that the points are one-way and not exchanged mutually, indicating a lower proportion of strong connections.

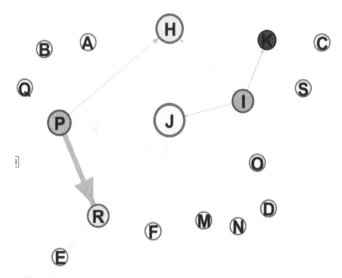

Fig. 11. Ranking of clustering coefficients, Phase II participants

The clustering coefficients and the indegree and outdegree for each participant in Phases I and II are reported in the Table 4. In general, the order of each participant is smaller in Phase I than in Phase II for both indegree and outdegree. In Phase I, there were no participants with point sources, and 3 participants, 18.7% of the total, with point sinks. In Phase II, there were 2 participants with point sources and one participant with a point sink, which is 58. In Phase II, there were 2 participants with source points and one with a point sink, which is 18.7% of the total. Thus, it can be seen that both giving and receiving points decreased in Phase II; especially, the number of people who gave points to others decreased significantly. This is why the clustering coefficient is higher for participants in Phase I. To confirm whether participants ceased giving points to others in return for receiving points, we use hub and authority score indices. A high authority score indicates participant received many points from other participants, and a high hub score indicates that the participant gifted many points to other participants.

Table 4. Clustering coefficients and indegree and outdegree, Phase I and II

Phase I				Phase II			
Id	In degree	Out degree	Clustering Coefficient	Id	In degree	Out degree	Clustering Coefficient
C	3	2	1	K	2	0	1
G	2	1	1	P	3	2	0.333
N	2	0	1	I	1	3	0.333
J	2	2	1	R	2	5	0.167
A	2	3	0.667	H	2	7	0.15
H	2	3	0.667	J	2	0	0.083
P	3	0	0.667	A	1	1	0
K	3	4	0.667	B	0	1	0
M	4	1	0.667	C	1	0	0
I	3	1	0.667	D	1	0	0
B	5	7	0.476	E	1	0	0
E	3	7	0.429	F	1	0	0
F	5	7	0.381	M	1	0	0
L	10	12	0.212	N	1	0	0
D	1	1	0	O	1	0	0
O	1	0	0	Q	1	0	0
				S	0	1	0

The Phase I authority and hub rankings are illustrated in Fig. 12 below. The darker the color, the higher the ranking. In Fig. 12 we can see that participants with high authority rankings also had high bub rankings. That is, those who gave the most points also received the most points, indicating strong reciprocity.

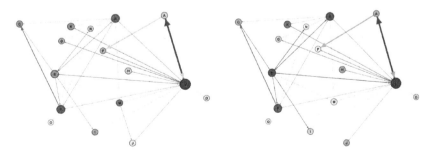

Fig. 12. Authority ranking left (left) and hub ranking (right), Phase I

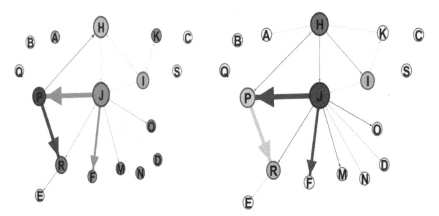

Fig. 13. Authority ranking (left) and hub ranking (right), Phase II

Figure 13 illustrates that in Phase II, participants with high authority rankings were not the same participants who had high hub rankings. That is, there were more participants who only gave or only received give points, indicating weaker reciprocity compared to Phase I.

5 Discussion

Social network analysis reveals that in Phase II the number of giving point was reduced by half, with the substantial increase in the number of point sinks indicating that one-way giving was more prevalent than two-way exchange. In Phase I, participants were 17 times more likely to send reciprocal points than they were to initiate point-giving; in Phase II, the likelihood that participants would reciprocate a gift decreased. Phase I results demonstrate that even when points have no economic value, reciprocity is a powerful motive; when a participant received a point from another, they reciprocated in kind. In Phase II, this reciprocity effect was weakened.

In Phase II, installation of the app on participants' smartphones was time consuming, and replacement of the researcher's cloud computing system coincided with the start of the experiment. This decreased app use as well as the number of gift point exchanges, photo submissions, and proximity detection events. This is thought to have impacted the results. However, while the changes in the cumulative density of proximity detection and expressions of approval of posted photos did not change significantly between Phases I and II, changes in the cumulative density for point-giving are observed. If this is purely the effect of the decline in app use, similar time-series changes would be observable for all functions; that said, use of the point-giving function may have been biased toward the early stage of the experiment due to other factors.

In the first period, 94.6% of point gifts were accompanied by comments; the percentage reduced to almost half, 47.8%, in Phase II. This may suggest that the point-gifting function was used as a direct message tool in Phase I but was no longer used as such in Phase II. It may be that, as described in Sect. 3, point-gifting required multiple operations and was thus cumbersome. In contrast to the point-giving function, the photo approval function was relatively easy to use because when a user viewed a photo, a like button was displayed simultaneously, and the user could express approval simply by tapping the symbol. The number of likes per posted photo was 3.09 in Phase I and 3.45 in Phase II. This indicates no significant changes in users' behavior when expressing approval for posted photos. These findings suggest that if the operation is easy, users will probably react to transmissions from others in a sustained manner.

As noted, when points are gifted in the CSD app, the giver, the receiver, and the number of points can be viewed by all participants, so it has the same effect as an open ballet voting system, so to speak. On the other hand, the app's function for expressing approval for posted photos ensures anonymity. The major difference between the point-giving function and the approval function is that one is anonymous, and the other is not, and so it appears that participants avoided non-anonymous actions. In general, even in the context of individual donations to charitable organizations, donors may either wish to remain anonymous or be adamant that the donations be widely publicized. In this case, lack of anonymity increased the cost of communication among participants.

Another reason that point-gifting function was not more widely utilized may be that face-to-face communication was easier than operating the app. Crossover detection was recorded in both phases, so it is highly likely that participants communicated face-to-face. In Phase I, participants used the point-giving function out of curiosity, but in Phase II, it was easier for participants to communicate face-to-face without needing to operate the app and gift each other points.

Ultimately, the apps' point-giving function was difficult for participants to operate. They also felt psychologically burdened by the name and announcement method. Importantly, because the value of the points was not specified but left to the participants, they did not recognize non-economic or economic value in such points. The important implication here is that when goals and rules for points are not clarified, point-giving functions might not be used.

6 Conclusion and Remarks

In this paper, social network analysis is applied to examine whether the visualization of non-anonymous connections through a point-giving system among users of a CSD application originally developed for the purpose of regional revitalization can activate reciprocal motivation and communication among participants engaged in a common health behavior (in this case step-counting), even when the points involved have no economic value.

The analysis revealed that points without economic value did not effectively activate communication among participants. In this study, we introduced points as a gamification element but left determination of the points' value to the participants. That is, we did not establish the goals to be reached through accumulation of points nor other rules for point use. Accordingly, demonstration of neither economic nor non-economic value was possible. Without such clarification, the cost of communicating using the points was greater than the utility of simply holding the points.

In conclusion, we reiterate that when designing point systems to activate communication in virtual space, goals to be reached through accumulation of points and relevant rules must be included. Moreover, the utility of holding the points must not exceed the cost of giving the points. That is, it is necessary to assign an economic value to the points and specify the exchange rate. Alternatively, non-economic value can be assigned so that participants can obtain utility. Further, any point-giving system must be anonymous and simple, and feedback must be obtainable.

Previous studies show that assigning economic value poses a challenge to sustainability due to restrictions on financial resources. As such, from a sustainability perspective, definition of a non-economic value that allows participants to gain utility from gifts of points is more desirable. When considering non-economic value, it is important to note that there are different types of participants and to design accordingly.

As outlined in Sect. 2, while some people are motivated by pure altruism, others are motivated by impure altruism, warm glow, strategic reciprocity, and others. Additionally, [10] shows that different game mechanisms are effective with different types of human desires. For example, virtual plant growth and ranking displays can be combined in point-gifting systems to fulfill such desires.

Even if the system is limited to point donations, anonymization, simplification, and feedback provision are important issues to consider. In particular, it should be care taken to encourage a sense of meaningfulness for participants, including lurkers who may only participate through likes. For example in the case of road improvement proposals, if the proposer is an information provider who gains supporters, including lurkers, through social media posting, and if improvements are actually made, sense of meaningfulness will increase for both the information provider and the lurker who took the engagement action. When designing apps for adjusting behaviors, governments and nonprofits should gain understanding of the intentions of not only the specific residents targeted but also of other residents in the area. At the same time, systems must be designed so that the point-giving function cannot be used to satisfy desires for approval or used maliciously due to anonymization.

In future studies, we hope to present a point system wherein the non-economic value of points is defined so that participants can actually use the points. We hope to develop another app that combines multiple game mechanisms in consideration of various motivations, and which also includes mechanisms for selecting gifting targets and preventing abuses due to anonymization.

Acknowledgement. The authors acknowledge and thank the members of the Makishima Kizuna Association non-profit organization, Kokarina-no-kai and Kosodate circle in Noshiro for their cooperation in preparation of this paper. This study was funded by JSPS Kakenhi (Grants-in-Aid for Scientific Research by Japan Society for the Promotion of Science) No. JP21K12554.

References

1. Andreoni, J.: Impure altruism and donations to public goods: A theory of warm-glow giving. Econ. J. **100**(401), 464–477 (1990)
2. Edelmann, N.: Reviewing the definitions of "lurkers" and some implications for online research. Cyberpsychol. Behav. Soc. Netw. **16**(9), 645–649 (2013)
3. Laffont, J.-J., Tirole, J.: A Theory of Incentives in Procurement and Regulation. The MIT Press, Cambridge (1993)

4. Langeland, E., Wahl, A.K.: The impact of social support on mental health service users' sense of coherence: A longitudinal panel survey. Int. J. Nurs. Stud. **46**, 830–837 (2009)

5. Latifi, G.R., Monfared, M.P., Khojasteh, H.A.: Gamification and citizen motivation and vitality in smart cities: A qualitative meta-analysis study. Geo J. **87**, 1–14 (2020). https://doi.org/10.1007/s10708-020-10295-0

6. Matui, A.: The importance of lurker on social media. In: Proceedings of the 2019 Japan Marketing Academy Proceedings (In Japanese, SNS- ni-okeru-hihatsugensha-no-jyuyosei). Japan marketing Academy, Tokyo, pp. 362–368 (2019)

7. Ministry of Internal Affairs and Communications Homepage, https://www.soumu.go.jp/johotsusintokei/whitepaper/ja/h30/pdf/n4200000.pdf. (last accessed 2022/02/04)

8. Salanie, B.: The Economics of Contracts, 2nd edn. The MIT Press, Cambridge (2005)

9. Shiozu, Y. et. al.: Can a community point system promote interaction between residents?. In: Yamamoto, S., Mori, H. (eds.) Proceedings of the Conference 2021, LNCS. Springer, Heidelberg, vol. 12766, pp. 312–325 (2021)

10. Stieglitz, S., Lattemann, C., Robra-Bissantz, S., Zarnekow, R., Brockmann, T.: Gamification Using Game Elements in Serious Contexts. Springer, Heidelberg (2017)

11. Yokoyama, Y.: What is the relationship with society seen by people with high SOC?. In: Yamazaki, K., Togari, T., (eds.) Proceedings of the Sense of Coherence, Life, and Society: National Representative Sample Survey and Analysis (in Japanese, SOC-ga- takai-hito-ni-mirareru-shakai-tono-kakawari-toha). Yushin-do, Tokyo (2017)

Inspiring Heterogeneous Perspectives in News Media Comment Sections

Jan Steimann[(⊠)] [iD], Marc Feger, and Martin Mauve

Heinrich Heine University, Universitätsstraße 1, 40225 Düsseldorf, Germany
`jan.steimann@hhu.de`

Abstract. Discussions in the comment sections of news articles are often characterized by highly one-sided arguments. One reason for this is that users primarily consume information that fit into their worldview and consequently argue from their echo chamber when responding to a comment. In this paper we introduce a new approach to comment recommendation. To this end, we present a model that makes recommendations based on a specific comment the user is interested in. These recommendations provide the user with alternative related comments and thereby broaden the perspective of the user before reacting to the specific comment that was originally selected. This is in contrast to previous work that tries to recommend comments based on the interests and previous behavior of the user and therefore fueling the filter bubble by providing information that fit into the worldview of the user.

Keywords: Artificial intelligence and IoT · Evaluation methods and techniques · Information bubble and echo chamber

1 Introduction

In the comment section of news media, people exchange arguments and opinions on the content of the article they have read. These comment sections are often characterized by highly one-sided arguments due to the reason that news agencies often attract reader with a political orientation that coincide to their own [4]. Therefore, we have a rather homogeneous argumentation in the comment section and people tend to behave differently as in a heterogeneous environment [1,2,8]. We believe that comment sections would be much more interesting and beneficial to the user and the society if they would include more diversity.

Our approach to solve this problem is to provide a heterogeneous but well balanced selection of comments from different discussions of other articles and news agencies based on a specific comment the user has selected. This way, we do not focus on the user but rather on the comment for our recommendation. To provide this new perspectives for the discussion, we are developing an ecosystem of components to extract relevant comments from a database for the comment the user is interested in real-time. For this, we create a database that is updated on a regular basis with articles and comments from various news agencies of

S. Yamamoto and H. Mori (Eds.): HCII 2022, LNCS 13305, pp. 118–131, 2022.
https://doi.org/10.1007/978-3-031-06424-1_10

the political spectrum so that the system can provide the user with the latest comments.

In this paper, we propose a solution for one problem of this ecosystem. How to extract and present a relevant selection of comments given a individual comment selected by the user from a large dataset of comments in a reasonable time. Therefore, we present our model that makes recommendations based on the selected comment, i.e. a comment-centric-comment recommendation.

In the following chapter, we take look at related work in the field of comment recommendation. The third chapter will explain our model. After this, we discuss the evaluation of the model and its limitations.

2   Related Work

Previous work in the field of comment recommendation, such as [7,12,13], present a selection of the most interesting comments for the user based on the previous behavior and interests of the user. This way, it is easier for the user to navigate the flood of comments that are posted every day and to find discussions where they can share their expertise.

[7] suggested to promote the general quality of online debates in the comment sections by filtering low quality comments and identifying and highlighting high quality contributions for the user. They try to achieve this by developing a comment moderation system with a flexible interface that interactively identifies high quality comments for the moderator. For this, the comments are scored by several quality criteria like *Article Relevance, Conversational Relevance, Readability etc.*. Afterwards, the comments are ranked by these scores and presented to the moderator with additional meta information, who decides if the comment is accepted, rejected or highlighted as a high quality contribution. Different from our work, the authors focus on a tool to assist the moderator of the comment section of a news agency to find high quality comments in a discussion. Our model tries to suggest highly relevant comments based on the comment the user is interested in. To do this, we search various discussions that might have happened a while ago but still contain relevant perspectives and ideas that differ from the perspective of the comment the user is interested. By this, we provide the user the possibility to build upon those ideas formulated by other users that have a different view on the topic and by this write a much more sophisticated response.

[13] presented an approach for a personalized news comment recommendation system to navigate the flood of comments. They designed a three part system to find the most relevant comments for the user. In the first phase, they filter out comments which contain much repeated or unrelated information by searching for comments that contain joking words, advertisements, and repeating words. Following, the system classifies the comments in *insightful view* or *informal comment* by various dimensions like similarity between the comment and the article, the length of the comment, or the attitude. In the final step, the system provides personalized recommendations based on the record of the user which comment

he or she wrote or liked. In our work, however, we focus on providing comments to the user based on the comment they are interested in. We believe if the user is presented comments only based on their record, it will most likely enforce the filter bubble and echo chamber which in return leads to a one-sided argumentation. The user can formulate a much more thoughtful response if they consider different opinions for the topic of the discussion.

[12] discussed different design goals a personalized comment section system should fulfill. The author considers three main points such a system needs to address to avoid user concerns like filter bubbles or missing the bigger picture. First, any comment proposed to a user needs to be relevant for the user. Second, to avoid being trapped in the filter bubble, the proposed comments need to consider different point of views. At last, the system should also help the user to find comments where they can share their expertise and also point to comments that could deepen their knowledge about the topic of the article. With our work, we try to complement prior work in the field of comment recommendation which proposes comments to the user based on their interest, like [13]. Such work fulfills the first design goal to find relevant comments for the user and to find comments where they can share their expertise. Our model addresses the rest of the design goals by offering different point of views to combat the filter bubble and allow the user to gain new insights through other user comments.

3   Model to Find Relevant Comments

In the following section, we introduce our model to find relevant comments based on the comment C of the current discussion the user would like to argue about. In our future work, this model will be part of a greater ecosystem that should support the user while debating in the comment sections. In this ecosystem the model will extract relevant comments for C from a database that will be updated on a regular basis with comments from discussions from various news agencies.

In order to suggest comments to the user based on the comment they are interested in, and to do this sufficiently quickly, so that they can use the suggestions to formulate their response, it is critical that the model can make the suggestions in an a short time.

For this reason, our model[1] consists of a two-step approach. In the first, step the model makes a preselection to reduce the amount of possible comments to a manageable amount and therefore generates a candidate set of possible comments from which we extract the best suggestions for the user in the second step, like [3] for argument search.

To generate the candidate set, we first consider the article A for the discussion the user is currently participating in. We use the article to find other discussions that deal with the same topic. For example, arguments and opinions about climate change under a article about renewable energies could be useful for an article about the harmful effects of a coal-fired powered plants. Likewise,

---

[1] https://github.com/hhucn/Inspiring-Heterogeneous-Perspectives-in-News-Media-Comment-Sections.

articles that seek to explain a need for coal power plants may be relevant, as they are likely to have different opinions and perspectives that will add value to a discussion about renewable energies. Of course, not every comment from these discussions will be useful for our current discussion but it will help to reduce the amount of possible candidates to a more manageable amount. To create the candidate set, we use the keywords of the article **A** under which the comment **C** appeared for which we want to generate suggestions. The keywords summarize the content of the article and therefore, we can use them to finde articles with a similar content. First, we embed the keywords of all articles in a vectorspace. For this, we calculate the average vector for every keyword and use a k-nearest neighbor search to finde the most similar articles to our article **A** (Fig. 1 left). Afterwards, we store all comments that have appeared under these k articles in the candidateset for the second step where we extract the n most suitable suggestions.

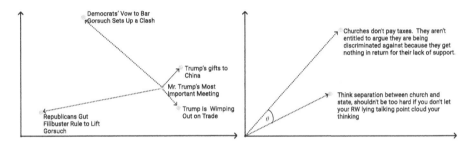

Fig. 1. Left figure: Find the most similar article with k-nearest neighbor. Right figure: Calculate the semantic similarity θ between the comment vectors. Comment and article source: footnote 4

In this last step, we then sort the comment candidate set based on the semantic similarity to our comment **C**. This is calculated using the cosine similarity of the vector space embeddings (Fig. 1 right). Here, we also calculate the average vector for the comments like we did for the keywords of the articles. Because the embedding process is very time consuming, we precompute the vector embeddings for all comments in our dataset. Finally, the n best comments with the highest semantic similarity are presented to the user in a ranked list.

4   Evaluation of the Model

In the following, we describe the evaluation of our approach for the comment-centric-comment recommendation. First, we explain the embedding models and the dataset we used for the experiment. Then, we describe the annotation tool we developed to assess the quality of the suggestions of the model. Finally, we present the results of our evaluation.

4.1   Embedding Model

During the development of our model, we noticed, like [11], that the choice of the embedding model used is important. Therefore, we have decided to test different pre-trained embedding models and compared the results to decide which embedding model is the best for our approach.

For this, we used the PyPi framework sentence-transformers[2][9] of the UKPLab. This package provides simple methods to generate vector representations of sentences and paragraphs, providing a large number of general purpose models trained on more than 1 billion training pairs.

From this set of models we selected five models and compared them with each other in the course of the evaluation:

- Paraphrase-MiniLM-L12-v2 (PML12)
- Bert-Large-Uncased (BLU)
- Paraphrase-Mpnet-Base-v2 (PMB)
- Stsb-Mpnet-Base-v2 (SMB)
- Stsb-Roberta-Base-v2 (SRB)

4.2   Dataset

To the best of our knowledge, there is no annotated dataset with comment suggestions for a give comment. For this reason, we searched for a promising dataset to extract comments from and asses these recommendation in an evaluation.

In this process, we came across a Kaggle dataset of comments from the New York Times[3]. The dataset consists of over 2 million comments from 9000 articles published in the New York Times from Jan-May 2017 and Jan-April 2018.

For the evaluation of the embedding models, fifteen comments from different topics like politics, trade etc. have been chosen. Six comments were extracted for each comment as proposals and were then evaluated by the annotators. We made sure to select both longer and shorter comments. This way, it was investigated whether the model could find good suggestions for both long and short comments. This was important because during the embedding process, as explained in Sect. 3, we generate an average vector representation for the comment that we want to find suggestions for. Therefore, the question is if short comments have enough information to find a suitable suggestions or if long comments have too much information so that the information overlap and the vector has no clear direction.

4.3   Annotation Tool

As mentioned in the previous section, there is no annotated dataset that allows us to evaluate our model and the different embedding models. Therefore, we

---

[2] https://pypi.org/project/sentence-transformers/.

[3] https://www.kaggle.com/aashita/nyt-comments accessed 09/21/2021.

evaluated the suggestions made by the respective embedding models with the help of four annotators from the field of computer science. In order to keep the annotation as simple as possible, we developed an annotation tool with an easy-to-use interface to help the annotators with assessing the quality of the suggestions (Fig. 2).

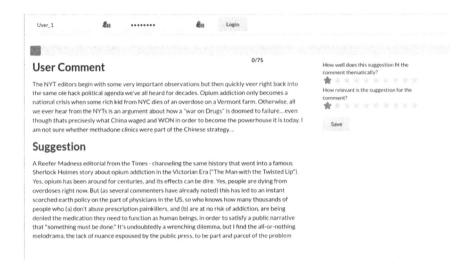

Fig. 2. Screenshot of the annotation tool. The annotators asses the thematic affiliation and the relevance of the suggestion for the given user comment. The annotators rates the suggestions on a 1 to 10 scale.

The annotators were presented with each of the six proposals per comment in a separate step, so that the proposals are first evaluated independently. For each proposal, the annotators are asked to rate on a scale of 1 to 10 whether the proposal fits thematically and whether it is a relevant proposal. "Relevant" means that the suggestion offers new insights, perspectives, or information for the topic. Following, the annotators are presented with the six suggestions as a ranked list, with the most relevant comment at the top. They are then asked to rate the order of comments. Does the ranking fit the relevance of the comments? This results in a total of 525 pairs of annotations for all five models, which every annotator has to evaluate.

To prevent a bias in the evaluation, the comments and models are presented to the annotator in a random order as packages. This means that the six suggestions followed by the ranked list of suggestions for a comment were presented to the annotator as a contiguous package and then a new comment with six suggestions and a ranked list is selected randomly.

4.4   Evaluation

Model Performance. One of the most important qualities of a model for real-time comment suggestion, besides the quality of the suggestion, is of course the performance of the model. A model that cannot generate the suggestions in feasible time would defeat its purpose to help the user in an online discussion because online discussion move at a fast pace.

For this reason, in addition to annotating the proposals, we also have measured the average time our model needs to find a suggestion for a given comment per model. The experiment was conducted on a Lenovo ThinkPad-T15p-Gen-1 with an Intel Core i5 with 8x2.60GHz and 64 GB RAM:

Table 1. Time measurement for extracting one proposal per model

Modelname	Time (s)
stsb-mpnet-base-v2	1.2
bert-large-uncased	1.9
paraphrase-mpnet-base-v2	1.3
stsb-roberta-base-v2	1.3
paraphrase-MiniLM-L12-v2	1.0

Suggestion Quality. In the following paragraph, we evaluate the quality of the suggestions for the different embedding models. As explained in Sect. 4.3, we have three different parameter to assess our model. First, we evaluate the six suggestions $S_1, ..., S_6$ for every comment C the user is interested in seperatly. Here, we rate two quality dimensions. On the one hand, we rate how good the suggestion fits thematically to the comment C and on the other hand, we evaluate how relevant the proposal S_i is. We rate these two dimensions because a suggestion, which is not at all or hardly connected to the comment the user is interested in, cannot be relevant for the user. However, only because a suggestion fits thematically to C, it does not mean it is also relevant for the user. For example, if the comment the user is interested in reads like this:

> I relate to this completely. I remedied the situation by getting off Facebook completely and I do not miss it one bit. I used to log on to my computer and without thinking type Facebook.com but no more. I am so relieved it's incredible how much people are sucked into that. No more distant people I wish were gone than lingering. I have whatsapp notifications muted it's on my time I check my msgs. I highly recommend you utilize the tech in your phone and get yourself some much needed privacy. Cheers[4]

A suggestion like the following would fit thematically, but is hardly relevant for the user because the suggestion does not contribute any relevant information to the discussion or shows new insights:

---

[4] https://www.kaggle.com/aashita/nyt-comments accessed 09/21/2021

Wow! Instagram has really boosted my self-esteem and provided long-term happiness! Said no kid, ever.[5]

As a final parameter, we looked at the ranking of the suggestions by the semantic similarity. With this parameter, we investigate if the semantic similarity is sufficient to be the foundation for the extraction of relevant suggestions or whether further parameters need to be used in future experiments.

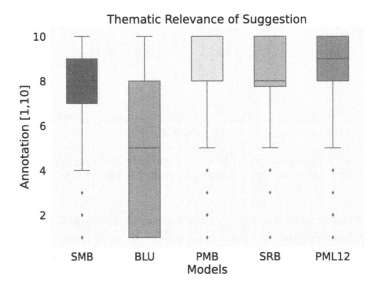

Fig. 3. Boxplot with the scores to asses how good the different embedding models extract suggestions that fit thematically to the comment the user is interested in; higher scores are better

In Fig. 3, we see the results of the evaluation for the quality dimension of how good the respective suggestions $S_1, ..., S_6$ fit thematically to the comment C the user is interested in as boxplots. We notice that all models except for Bert-Large-Uncased (BLU) produce very good results. The median for stsb-mpnet-base-v2 (SMB), paraphrase-mpnet-base-v2 (PMB), and stsb-roberta-base-v2 (SRB) lies at 8 and 75% of the scores are above 7 respectively 8. Only Paraphrase-MiniLM-L12-v2 (PML12) produces higher results with a median of 9 and 75% of the scores are above 8. Therefore, we can state that these four embedding modes produce good and reliable results. In contrast to this, the median of Bert-Large-Uncased (BLU) lies at 5 and the scores scatter very much from 1 to 8. Therefore, the suggestions extracted with Bert have a high variance and do not produce a reliable quality. We observe that with the other four embedding models, we can extract suggestions from the dataset that fit thematically much better and are more consistent in the quality than these extracted with Bert.

---

[5] See footnote 4

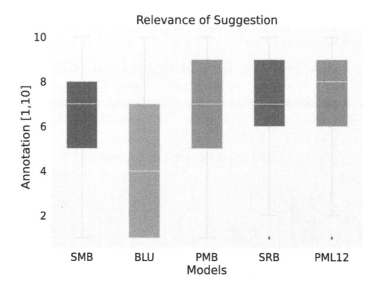

Fig. 4. Boxplot with the scores to asses how good the different embedding models extract relevant suggestions for the comment the user is interested in

Figure 4 shows a similar picture as Fig. 3. Again Stsb-Mpnet-Base-v2 (SMB), Paraphrase-MiniLM-L12-v2 (PML12), and Stsb-Roberta-Base-v2 (SRB) have the same median. Here with a value 7 with 75% of the scores above 5 respectively 6. Paraphrase-MiniLM-L12-v2 (PML12) has the highest median of all models with a value of 8 with first quartile at the score of 6. The worst results are, again, these of Bert-Large-Uncased (BLU). The median for it is 4 and the first quartile lies at 1 and the third quartile at 7. Therefore, the results scatter again very strongly and are much worse and much less reliable as the results of the other models. However, we must note that for the relevance the other models scatter more as for the thematic affiliation. This is not surprising since it is much easier to determine the thematic affiliation by the semantic similarity as the relevance of a suggestion. However, the relevance represents the more important quality dimension for our model, since the thematic affiliation is only a prerequisite for the relevance, but does not add any value on its own as we can see in the quote at the beginning of the Sect. 4.4.

Figure 5 shows the last parameter we have examined in our evaluation, the ranking of the suggestions. We notice the same trend as in the figures above that Bert-Large-Uncased (BLU) produces the weakest results. However, the results of the different embedding models are much closer to each other than above. Here, Paraphrase-MiniLM-L12-v2 (PML12), Stsb-Roberta-Base-v2 (SRB), and Paraphrase-Mpnet-Base-v2 (PMB) have a median of 7 with the first quartile at 5 respectively 6. Stsb-Mpnet-Base-v2 (SMB) has a median of 6 with 75% of the scores above a value of 5. The worst results are, again, produced by Bert. Here, we have a median of 5 with the first quartile at 3. Again, we can state that the

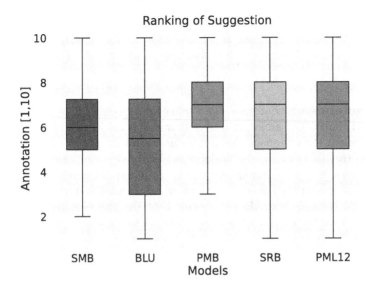

Fig. 5. Boxplot with the scores to asses how good the different embedding models rank the suggestions for the comment the user is interested in

other embedding models produce better results with more consistency. However, the distance to Bert here is much closer than before. Overall, we can see here that the ranking results are good but improvable. This indicates that the semantic similarity is a good starting point for our approach and this model provides a solid baseline for future experiments. Nevertheless, we need to consider other parameters for future models to improve these results.

Model Performance for Long and Short Comments. As explained in Sect. 4.2, we selected both short and long comments to investigate how the model performs for comments of various length because short comments might not contain enough information to find suitable suggestions for and long comments could contain to much information so they might overlap in the process of calculating the average vector for the comment.

Table 2 shows the average scores for the three quality dimension where we considered a comment as short if it contains less that 50 words:

Table 2. Average scores for the different quality dimensions for short and long comments

Model name	Thematic (short/long)	Relevance (short/long)	Ranking (short/long)
stsb-mpnet-base-v2	(6/6)	(8/7)	(6/6)
Bert-large-uncased	(6/7)	(8/8)	(5/6)
paraphrase-mpnet-base-v2	(3/4)	(4/5)	(4/5)
stsb-roberta-base-v2	(6/7)	(8/8)	(6/6)
paraphrase-MiniLM-L12-v2	(7/6)	(8/8)	(6/6)

Scores for short and long comments only differ by a score of 1 point on a scale from 1 to 10, if they differ at all. Therefor, we can affirm that the model produces consistent results for all embedding model despite the length of the comment.

Inter-Annotator-Agreement. The evaluation of the suggestions for a comment is a very subjective annotation task. Some users might consider a suggestion very relevant for the comment the user is interested in, while others do not. In many cases this depends on the background knowledge and experiences of the user. Therefore, it is very important to have a quantitative value to determine the agreement among the annotators. Otherwise it is hard to interpret the results from Sect. 4.4 because it would be possible that the scattering of the boxplots results come from the fact that the annotators are divided in their opinion about the model and some asses the quality of the model very poorly while others very good. However, if the annotators are very consistent in their judgment of the model then we can explain the scattering as an inconsistency in the quality of the suggestions the model produces.

For this reason, we have calculated the Inter-Annotator-Agreement (IAA) of the annotators. Due to the high subjectivity of the annotation task, we have decided to calculate the IAA for the quality dimension if the annotators considered the proposal for a comment as good and calculated the percentage of annotations with a score ≥ 6:

Table 3. Proportion of annotation values greater than or equal to 6

Modelname	Thematic	Relevance	Ranking
stsb-mpnet-base-v2	0.91	0.71	0.72
Bert-large-uncased	0.49	0.41	0.50
paraphrase-mpnet-base-v2	0.95	0.75	**0.77**
stsb-roberta-base-v2	**0.96**	**0.78**	0.68
paraphrase-MiniLM-L12-v2	0.93	0.77	0.70

Besides allowing us to calculate an Inter-Annotator-Agreement, it also gives us an quantifiable value for the quality of the suggestions produced by the embedding models. Looking at Table 3, we see that the model Stsb-Roberta-Base-v2 extracts the suggestions that fit thematically the best and are most relevant, while Paraphrase-Mpnet-Base-v2 provides the best ranking. However, one also finds that the difference with Stsb-Mpnet-Base-v2, Paraphrase-Mpnet-Base-v2, and Paraphrase-MiniLM-L12-v2 is insignificant. Not so with Bert-Large-Uncased. Here, the results are much worse than for the other embedding models. This reflects more or the less the results from Sect. 4.4 where Bert provided the worst results and the other embedding models are very close to each other.

To then calculate the Inter-Annotator-Agreement, we have used Krippendorf Alpha $(\alpha)^6$[5]. We achieved an α of **0.46** for the relevance, **0.70** for the thematical relevance, and **0.69** for the ranking. Thus, there is a high agreement between the annotators despite the high subjectivity of the annotation task.

Self-Agreement of Annotators. It happens from time to time that some models propose the same suggestion for a comment. Furthermore, this is a very laborious annotation task that the annotators have performed over a few weeks. To ensure the consistency of the annotation, we also examined how much the annotators agreed with themselves over the course of the annotation. For this purpose, the mean of the deviation of all annotators with themself was calculated. It only makes sense to look at the thematic agreement and the relevance, since no two models produced exactly the same sequence for the ranked list of suggestions. For the thematic agreement, we have an average deviation of **0.53** and for the relevance of **0.7**[7]. This indicates a high self-agreement among the annotators because on average the difference in the scores for the same proposal made by a different embedding model is below **1**.

4.5   Discussion

After reviewing the results of our evaluation, we can state that our model produces good and consistent results for proposing suggestions for the comment the user is interested in. Furthermore, we have a high agreement among our annotators with and among themselves which means that despite having a very subjective annotation task the annotators agree in their assessment of the model.

However, we can not definitively determine why Bert produces the worst results in all quality dimension we have considered, we assume that in the process of generating the average vector representation of the comment we loose information of the content of the comment because Bert produces very context-sensitive vector representation.

The results of the model depend on which embedding model one chooses. Many publications in the field of argument search and the like use Bert as the embedding model of choice [3,6,10], since it can produce excellent embeddings through the use of context. However, for our problem BERT was not the model of choice.

5   Conclusion and Future Work

In our work, we introduced a new approach to the field of comment recommendation and presented our model that will serve as a baseline for future experiments. In contrast to previous work, we shift the focus away from the user to the comment the user is interested in. By this, we try to offer new perspectives and

---

[6] Range: -1 (perfect disagreement) to 1 (perfect agreement).

[7] Range: 0 (perfect agreement) to 10 (perfect disagreement).

insights to the user. To do this, we made use of a similar approach like [3] to create a candidate set of comments and select the six most interesting suggestions from it by their semantic similarity to the comment. For this, we use very basic machine learning methods like k-nearest-neighbor and vector embeddings. Due to the lack of an annotated dataset to evaluate our results, we asked four annotators to assess the quality of the suggestions for the three parameter. How does the suggestion fits the comment thematically? How relevant is the suggestion to the comment? How good is the ranking of the six suggestions for the comment? Taking into account the simplicity of the model and that we have a very subjective annotation task, we can conclude that our model serves as a very good baseline for future experiments and is a good approach for comment-centric-comment recommendation. We also note that semantic similarity is a good start for our model, but is not sufficient as the only parameter for the model and we need to consider other in future experiments.

In future work we will continue our work in two directions. First, we want to transition our model into an ecosystem of tools that will allow us to test our approach and model in real world discussions under news articles. For this, we develop a browser plugin that allows the user to get suggestions for every possible comment under any news article and a web scrapper to keep our knowledge base up-to-date by retrieving comments from discussion of different news agencies. Second, we want to try different approaches to improve upon our baseline model and to ensure a well balanced selection of comments. If we want to make a significant contribution to online debates and to combat the echo-chamber, we have to put emphasize on a selection of suggestions that represents different views and political orientations on a topic.

Acknowledgment. We would like to thank Markus Brenneis and Björn Ebbinghaus for their help with the annotations.

References

1. An, J., Kwak, H., Posegga, O., Jungherr, A.: Political discussions in homogeneous and cross-cutting communication spaces. In: Proceedings of the International AAAI Conference on Web and Social Media, vol. 13, pp. 68–79 (2019)
2. Del Vicario, M., Zollo, F., Caldarelli, G., Scala, A., Quattrociocchi, W.: Mapping social dynamics on Facebook: The Brexit debate. Social Netw. **50**, 6–16 (2017)
3. Dumani, L., Neumann, P.J., Schenkel, R.: A framework for argument retrieval: Ranking argument clusters by frequency and specificity. Adv. Inf. Retrieval **12035**, 431 (2020)
4. Flaxman, S., Goel, S., Rao, J.M.: Filter bubbles, echo chambers, and online news consumption. Public Opinion Q. **80**(S1), 298–320 (2016)
5. Krippendorff, K.: Computing krippendorff's alpha-reliability (2011)
6. Ollinger, S., Dumani, L., Sahitaj, P., Bergmann, R., Schenkel, R.: Same side stance classification task: Facilitating argument stance classification by fine-tuning a Bert model. arXiv preprint arXiv:2004.11163 (2020)
7. Park, D., Sachar, S., Diakopoulos, N., Elmqvist, N.: Supporting comment moderators in identifying high quality online news comments. In: Proceedings of the 2016 CHI Conference on Human Factors in Computing Systems, pp. 1114–1125 (2016)

8. Quattrociocchi, W., Scala, A., Sunstein, C.R.: Echo chambers on Facebook. Available at SSRN 2795110 (2016)
9. Reimers, N., Gurevych, I.: Sentence-Bert: Sentence embeddings using Siamese Bert-networks. arXiv preprint arXiv:1908.10084 (2019)
10. Reimers, N., Schiller, B., Beck, T., Daxenberger, J., Stab, C., Gurevych, I.: Classification and clustering of arguments with contextualized word embeddings. arXiv preprint arXiv:1906.09821 (2019)
11. Schaefer, R., Stede, M.: Improving implicit stance classification in tweets using word and sentence embeddings. In: Benzmüller, C., Stuckenschmidt, H. (eds.) KI 2019. LNCS (LNAI), vol. 11793, pp. 299–307. Springer, Cham (2019). https://doi.org/10.1007/978-3-030-30179-8_26
12. Wang, Y.: Comment section personalization: Algorithmic, interface, and interaction design. In: Proceedings of the EACL Hackashop on News Media Content Analysis and Automated Report Generation, pp. 84–88 (2021)
13. Zhou, M., Shi, R., Xu, Z., He, Y., Zhou, Y., Lan, L.: Design of personalized news comments recommendation system. In: Zhang, C., et al. (eds.) ICDS 2015. LNCS, vol. 9208, pp. 1–5. Springer, Cham (2015). https://doi.org/10.1007/978-3-319-24474-7_1

Which Method of Fact-Checking is Beneficial in Fighting Misinformation?

Cindy Su$^{(\boxtimes)}$, Timothy Diep, and Kim-Phuong L. Vu

California State University, Long Beach, Long Beach, CA, USA
CindySu151@gmail.com, kim.vu@csulb.edu

Abstract. When users unknowingly interact with false information online, they may be susceptible to the influence of misinformation. Using a fact-checker to analyze whether the information presented is accurate or misleading can help users identify false information. The present study examined two different methods: use of a correction or warning, presented by a fact-checker, to identify which is more effective in reducing misinformation. One hundred and twenty-four participants were recruited from MTurk and Introductory Psychology courses to participate in the study. Participants were asked to read short stories, followed by statements that are related to the short stories (e.g., media posts about the short stories) that were or were not verified by a fact-checker. Then, participants were asked to answer questions related to the original short story to measure their memory of the information as well as the number of references to the misinformation. At the end of the study, participants were asked to rate their level of trust in online information sources and the fact-checker used in the present study, which always provided accurate information. Results showed that participants used a fact-checker about 70% of the time when one was made available to them. Having a choice to use a fact-checker increased participants' accuracy scores on a memory check test, and the presence of a fact-checker reduced the number of references to misinformation.

Keywords: Fact-checker · Misinformation · Correction · Warning

1 Introduction

With news and information being accessible with few restrictions on the internet, identifying accurate information may be difficult. There are fake news articles circulating that were created to mimic legitimate news sources intended to misinform readers [10]. Oversimplified information may cause a misunderstanding of the actual event [7]. When users online unknowingly encounter misinformation, this can negatively affect their memory. Alcott and colleagues found there was an increase in interactions with fake news sites over the years through social media platforms such as Facebook and Twitter [1]. Because of an increase in social media users, there is also an increase in the volume of information shared online which increased the spread of misinformation [3].

© The Author(s), under exclusive license to Springer Nature Switzerland AG 2022
S. Yamamoto and H. Mori (Eds.): HCII 2022, LNCS 13305, pp. 132–145, 2022.
https://doi.org/10.1007/978-3-031-06424-1_11

Misinformation can be defined as information originally believed as correct, but later proven false; however, the original misinformation has an influence on the person's memory [6]. There are theories about why people are influenced by misinformation. The familiarity backfire effect is one theory where a person is repeatedly exposed to misinformation, and it reinforces false information over facts [7]. Another theory on why people may be susceptible to false information is the world view effect which means when fake news aligns with a person's values and beliefs, this will lead to the person being more likely to believe the inaccurate information [7].

Researchers study misinformation by (a) having participants observe an event, (b) providing participants with post-event information where misinformation may be included, and (c) testing the participant's memory of the main event. This allows researchers to examine if misinformation influences the participants' memory of the original information [2].

After being exposed to misinformation, people may show a continued influence effect which occurs when people rely on misinformation even though there was a retraction to the false statement [7]. Ecker and colleagues conducted a study to evaluate the effectiveness of different methods proposed to reduce the continued influence effect [6]. Participants in the study were asked to read a fictional story of a minibus accident. The misinformation presented in the story was that the victims of the accident were elderly people. Ecker et al. examined four different methods designed to correct the misinformation: retraction only, general warning, specific warning, and an alternative ending. The four methods used different strategies to help reduce the influence of misinformation, and each was compared to a baseline condition of no retraction, which meant participants were not made aware of the misinformation present in the original story [6].

In the reaction only condition, the participants would learn that the minibus passengers were not elderly people. Participants in the general warning condition read a warning which stated the facts presented in the story may not be accurate. In the specific warning condition, participants were made aware of the continued influence effect and were presented with examples of how the continued influence effect can affect a person's memory of the misinformation. Lastly, in the alternative ending condition, participants were told that the minibus had hockey players and not elderly people. Ecker and colleagues measured the number of misinformation references the participants made in each condition [6]. They found that specific warnings were the most effective in reducing the influences of misinformation. Participants in the no retraction condition had the highest number of references to the misinformation ($M = 5.06$). The lowest number of references to misinformation was found for the specific warning ($M = 2.12$), followed by the alternative ending ($M = 2.22$), general warning ($M = 3.36$), and retraction only ($M = 4.04$) conditions. Thus, Ecker et al. showed that different methods can be used to reduce the continued influence of misinformation. Moreover, providing users with specific information (i.e., specific warning or alternative ending conditions) was more effective than general information (i.e., general warning or retraction only conditions) [6].

1.1 Fact-Checker

Automated fact-checking is a potential technology that can be used to assist users in detecting misinformation. Automated fact-checking can be broken down into four parts [8]. First, the automation will identify if the claim is worth verifying. This process is done by ranking all claims to see which ones are important to verify. Next, the fact-checker will check if a claim has been previously fact-checked, and if not, the fact-checker will then collect evidence to identify if that claim is true or false.

The automated verification process has two different methods which are called explainable and non-explainable. In the explainable method, the fact-checker gathers evidence to support whether a claim is accurate or misleading. While in the non-explainable method, the automated fact-checker will predict the accuracy of the claim based on the information it has gathered [8]. The automated fact-checker's knowledge is dependent on the information it obtains from a database created by human experts.

Fact-checking technology should maintain its transparency to facilitate trust between it and the user by explaining the steps of the fact-checking process and how sources are obtained [3]. Although current automated fact-checking technology is not completely reliable, it can be utilized as a method to help warn users about whether the information presented is accurate or not. Warning users of false information can help reduce the spread of misinformation online [9]. The present study utilized a fact-checker, displayed as an icon with text, to convey to users whether the information users are encountering is accurate or misleading. Because not all users will employ a fact-checker, when one is available, we also examined conditions where users would have a choice to use a fact-checker when reading statements that were posted about an online story they previously read.

1.2 Methods to Help Reduce Misinformation

As noted, different methods can be employed to help reduce misinformation. The present study focused on two specific methods: corrections and warnings.

Corrections. As its name implies, corrections typically occur after the misinformation is presented. The person is made aware of the inaccurate information and provided with the accurate information (i.e., the correction). Vraga and colleagues conducted a study to examine whether misinformation can be reduced through different types of corrections [12]. Two corrections conditions, logic-focused debunking, and fact-focused debunking were compared to two warning conditions, logic-focused prebunking, and fact-focused prebunking. A no corrections condition (i.e., misinformation only condition) was included as a baseline. In the prebunking conditions, the correction of misinformation was displayed as a warning before the misinformation post, and in the debunking conditions, the correction was displayed after the misinformation post. The fact-focused conditions provided participants with accurate information while the logic-focused conditions countered the misinformation by describing how the information presented may have been oversimplified. Participants were asked to look at an Instagram feed and complete a questionnaire related to climate change misperception, where they rated their level of agreement to different statements that were made as social media posts. Vraga and colleagues found the logic-focused method, regardless of prebunking or debunking, was significantly more effective at reducing the credibility of misinformation provided in the social media posts compared to fact-focused debunking [12].

Crozier and Strange conducted three studies to examine how specific correction methods can help reduce the spread of misinformation [4]. The first study compared the performance of participants who were given a correction (correction group) to those who were not (no correction group) to measure the effectiveness of providing corrections. Participants were asked to (1) watch a short film, (2) complete a filler task which was card sorting, and (3) read a post-event narrative. The post-event narrative contained information related to the short film and it had a total of 40 statements, where there were 8 inaccurate items. From the 8 inaccurate items, half received no correction (control items) and the other half received corrections (misleading items). This was done to identify if the correction was effective at reducing the misinformation effect for the participants in the correction group. Participants in the correction group were better at identifying the misleading items, showing a 65.7% accuracy score compared to the no correction group which obtained a 48.6% accuracy score.

In the second study, Crozier and Strange explored how the correction was implemented: misleading narrative, accurate narrative, corrections narrative, and corrections only [4]. The four different methods determined what post-event narrative the participants were assigned to read. In the misleading narrative, participants were given only misleading information in the post-event narrative. Participants in the accurate narrative, read a post-event narrative which contained no misleading information or correction statements. In the correction narrative, participants received a correction to misinformation immediately after misinformation was presented during the post-event narrative task. Lastly, participants in the correction-only statement read eight critical statements followed by corrections. The critical statements were four misleading items and four control items (i.e., items that received no correction). Participants were asked to watch a short film, complete a filler task, and read the post-event narrative which contained misinformation for all conditions. Results showed that participants were more accurate in identifying the control items in the accurate narrative (72.4%); correction narrative (72.3%), and corrections only (71.1%) conditions, compared to when no corrections were provided in the misleading narrative condition (70.3%). Corrections had a larger effect in helping participants identify the misleading items, with the highest accuracy score obtained for the accurate narrative condition (68%) followed the corrections narrative (64.1%) condition and the corrections only (55.6%) condition. Participants in the misleading narrative had the lowest accuracy score (50.6%) in identifying the misleading items.

In the third study, the order of the post-event narratives was manipulated in three ways: no corrections, accurate corrections, and inaccurate corrections. In the no correction condition, misleading information found in the post-event narrative was not corrected. In the accurate corrections condition, misleading information found in the post-event narrative was immediately corrected. Lastly, in the inaccurate corrections condition, some of the corrections were inaccurate and did not correct the misleading information. It was hypothesized that participants in the inaccurate condition would have the best performance since they would be more aware of the inaccurate information and be more careful when reviewing the information. As Crozier and Strange (2018) expected, participants in the inaccurate corrections condition performed the best: they had a 74.4% accuracy score in identifying the control items and an 81.6% score accuracy in identifying the misleading items. Participants in the accurate corrections performed less well, having a 74% accuracy score in identifying the control items and a 59.5% accuracy score in identifying the misleading items. Participants in the no corrections condition performed the worst, with a 70.6% accuracy score in identifying the control items and a 41.9% accuracy score in identifying the misleading items.

Warnings. The warning method is when a person is alerted that the information being presented may not be accurate. Pennycook and colleagues examined how users rated the accuracy of information when it was accompanied by a warning compared to when it was not [11]. Participants rated the accuracy of a fact-checker's analysis of news headlines using a 4-point scale ranging from not at all accurate to very accurate. They found that participants in the warning group rated false headlines as being less accurate compared to the control group that did not receive the warnings [11].

Bailey and colleagues examined three different techniques to help reduce misinformation: change-detection, general warning, and a combination of both change-detection and warning [2]. Participants were asked to watch a 7-min video, read a post-event narrative, and complete a recognition questionnaire. In the change-detection conditions, participants were asked if the information presented in the post-event narrative corresponded to the main event. For the warning conditions, half of the participants received a general warning before viewing the post-event information and half the participants did not receive the warning. Bailey et al. found that the combination of both change-detection and general warning to be the most effective in reducing misinformation since the lowest percentage (32%) of participants experiencing misinformation was from that condition. The change detection method was the second most effective method with 39% of participants in that condition being affected by the misleading information in the post-event narrative. The percentage of participants showing an effect of misinformation was 43% in the warning condition and 45% in the no warning condition. Based on these findings, Bailey et al. noted that the change-detection method could function as a repeated warning since participants were reminded that there were differences between the event and post-event information in every question [2].

To summarize, both corrections and warnings can be effective methods in reducing misinformation. Moreover, warnings issued by fact-checkers can also be effective, but corrections issued by fact-checkers have not been examined. Thus, the purpose of the present study is to directly compare the effectiveness of warnings and corrections in terms of reducing the effects of misinformation when they are presented by an automated fact-checking display.

1.3 Pilot Study for the Fact-Checker Display

A pilot study was conducted to examine which of five different types of displays (see Fig. 1) was rated as being the most effective for conveying fact-checking information. Participants (N = 19) were asked to read 10 short stories, 5 with accurate titles and 5 with inaccurate titles, and rated the effectiveness of different types of fact-checker displays. The fact-checker was always accurate (i.e., 100% reliable). Participants rated each display in terms of the fact-checkers level of helpfulness (scale of 1–5; 1 = not helpful at all, 5 = very helpful) and effectiveness (1 = not effective at all, 5 = very effective). Additionally, participants were asked to select their preferred display.

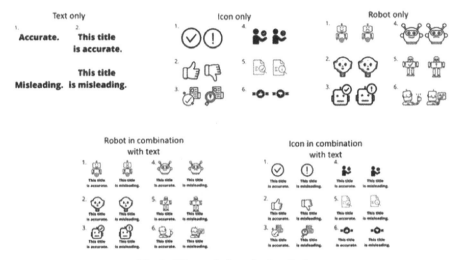

Fig. 1. Pilot study fact-checker displays.

The results of the pilot study showed that the text-only display was rated to be the most helpful. Additionally, participants rated the icon in combination with text display method to be the most effective display for conveying fact-checked information. Overall, 68% of the participants selected the icon in combination with text as their preferred method for the display of a fact-checker. Thus, this display was used for the fact-checker in the present study.

1.4 Present Study

Information found online may not always be accurate since there are no regulations about who can post information and whether the information that is posted contains accurate information or not. Using a fact-checker can assist users by reducing the influence of misleading information when encountering it online. Since it is important for users to trust an automated fact-checker, the one used in this study was 100% in accurate. That is, the fact-checker correctly identified accurate and misleading statements presented to the users all of the time. The purpose of this study was to examine which method, corrections or warnings, is the most effective in reducing the influence of misinformation when presented through a fact-checker display. Moreover, the study examined whether participants would use a fact-checker, if one was made available to them in specific "Choice" conditions. It was hypothesized that:

1. The fact-checker will be effective in reducing the effects of misinformation. Participants in the correction or warning conditions will have a higher accuracy on the memory test and be less influenced by misinformation compared to participants in the no fact-checker condition.
2. Participants in the choice condition will perform better than participants in the no-choice condition. Having a choice will empower users to determine whether to use the fact-checker, and when doing so pay more attention to the fact-checker's analysis.
3. Participants in the choice and warning condition will have the best performance compared to all the other conditions.

2 Methods

2.1 Participants

One-hundred twenty-four participants were recruited from Amazon Mechanical Turk (MTurk) and California State University Long Beach's Introductory Psychology Subject Pool (SONA). One participant in the choice × warning condition was excluded from the data analysis because their time spent on the survey was under five minutes. Table 1 provides the demographic information of participants by condition. Participants' ages ranged from 18 to 64 years old ($M_{age} = 29.53$, $SD = 11.63$), with four participants declining to respond. Sixty-six participants identified as female (53.66%), fifty-one participants (41.46%) identified as male, and six participants declined to respond (4.88%). Participants self-identified as White (48.78%), Hispanic (20.33%), as Asian (12.19%), Black (6.5%), Native American (2.5%), Pacific Islander (.8%) or declined to respond to the ethnicity question (8.9%).

2.2 Design

This study employed 2 (Option of choice to use fact-checker: Choice vs No choice) × 3 (Method of fact-checking: Correction vs Warning vs None) design, where both independent variables were between-subjects factors. The dependent variables were the accuracy score of memory check questions, the number of references to misinformation when selecting incorrect answers to the memory check questions, and ratings of trust to items on a questionnaire.

Table 1. Breakdown of age, gender, and ethnicity by conditions.

Condition	Age	Gender	Ethnicity
Choice × Correction (N = 21)	$M_{Age} = 25.22$	$N_{Female} = 12$ $N_{Male} = 6$ $N_{Omit} = 3$	$N_{White} = 10$ $N_{Black} = 2$ $N_{Hispanic} = 4$ $N_{Asian} = 1$ $N_{PacificIs.} = 1$ $N_{Omit} = 3$
No choice × Correction (N = 20)	$M_{Age} = 27.26$	$N_{Female} = 10$ $N_{Male} = 8$ $N_{Omit} = 2$	$N_{White} = 8$ $N_{Hispanic} = 5$ $N_{Asian} = 2$ $N_{Black} = 2$ $N_{Native} = 1$ $N_{Omit} = 2$
Choice × Warning (N = 21)	$M_{Age} = 31.29$	$N_{Female} = 13$ $N_{Male} = 7$ $N_{Omit} = 1$	$N_{White} = 10$ $N_{Hispanic} = 4$ $N_{Asian} = 3$ $N_{Black} = 2$ $N_{Omit} = 2$
No choice × Warning (N = 21)	$M_{Age} = 27.76$	$N_{Female} = 12$ $N_{Male} = 9$	$N_{White} = 9$ $N_{Hispanic} = 8$ $N_{Asian} = 2$ $N_{Black} = 1$ $N_{Omit} = 1$
Choice × None (N = 20)	$M_{Age} = 34.55$	$N_{Female} = 5$ $N_{Male} = 15$	$N_{White} = 15$ $N_{Asian} = 2$ $N_{Hispanic} = 1$ $N_{Native} = 1$ $N_{Omit} = 1$
No choice × None (N = 20)	$M_{Age} = 30.55$	$N_{Female} = 14$ $N_{Male} = 6$	$N_{White} = 8$ $N_{Asian} = 5$ $N_{Hispanic} = 3$ $N_{Black} = 1$ $N_{Native} = 1$ $N_{Omit} = 2$

2.3 Apparatus and Stimuli

The survey is conducted through Qualtrics, a platform for online surveys, and participants completed the survey with their own devices. The survey was used to collect information online, it contained four fictional short stories followed by statements related to the short stories, that could be accurate or misleading [5]. The fact-checker display used in the present study was an icon in combination with text display (see Fig. 2) since it was found to be the most effective way to convey this information based on the pilot study described earlier. The fact-checker was available in the Warnings and Corrections conditions, and participants had the choice of using the fact-checker in the Choice conditions. For the Choice × None condition, no fact-checker was available, and users were asked if they would use a fact-checker if one was available.

Fig. 2. Icon in combination with text fact-checker display. Each statement in the correction and warning conditions were judged by the automated fact-checker as accurate or misleading. The fact-checker was 100% reliable.

2.4   Procedure

Participants received the Qualtrics survey link after signing up for the study through SONA for introductory psychology students and MTurk for general participants. After the participants activated the survey link, they were asked to read the consent form. Once the participant agreed to participate in the study, the participant was redirected to the first short story. Next, the participant was shown four statements related to the short story that participants were told to be found on social media. Then, participants were asked to complete memory check questions about the original story. The order in which participants were presented with the four short stories was random. After participants completed the four sets of short stories, they were asked to complete a questionnaire on their trust in online information and the automated fact-checker used in the present study and to provide demographic information. Table 2 depicts the flow of tasks in the present study by condition. At the end of the survey, participants were thanked for their participation and received their compensation for completing the survey (1 h of experiment credit for introductory psychology students and $3 for MTurk participants).

Table 2. There were six conditions in this study, reflecting the 2 (Option of choice to use fact-checker: Choice vs No choice) × 3 (Method of fact-checking: Correction vs Warning vs None) design. The table depicts the flow of tasks for each condition.

Condition	Flow of Tasks: Repeated for each of the four sets of short stories. The statements about the short stories can be accurate or misleading				Trust Survey & Demographics
Choice × Correction	Short story	Statements	Option to use fact-checker presented after each statement	Memory check questions	Questionnaires
No choice × Correction	Short story	Statements	Fact-checker displayed after each statement	Memory check questions	Questionnaires
Choice × Warning	Short story	Option to use fact-checker presented before each statement	Statements	Memory check questions	Questionnaires

(*continued*)

Table 2. (*continued*)

No choice x Warning	Short story	Fact-checker displayed before each statement	Statements	Memory check questions	Questionnaires
Choice × None	Short story	Statements	Question about whether the participants would use a fact-checker if one was available	Memory check questions	Questionnaires
No choice × None	Short story	Statements only		Memory check questions	Questionnaires

2.5 Analysis

2 (Option of choice: Choice vs. No choice) × 3 (Type of fact-checker: Correction vs Warning vs. None) ANOVAs were conducted on the accuracy scores for the memory check questions, the number of references to misleading information when answering the memory check questions incorrectly, and trust ratings provided to statements on the questionnaires.

3 Results

3.1 Choice to Use Fact-Checker

For the choice conditions, participant's use of the fact-checker was calculated based on the number of times the participants chose to view the fact-checker's analysis of the statements. The usage rate was 72.32% overall (69.64% in the warning and 75% in the corrections conditions).

3.2 Memory of Information and Misinformation

Table 3 contains the mean accuracy scores to the memory check questions and the mean number of references to misinformation for each of the six conditions.

For accuracy of responses to the memory check questions, there was a main effect of choice, $F(1,123) = 4.84$, $p = .03$, with the accuracy for Choice conditions ($M = 68.05\%$) being higher than that for No Choice conditions ($M = 57.41\%$). There was no main effect in the method of fact-checking, $F(2,123) = 1.687, p = .19$. In addition, there was no interaction between the choice and method of fact-checking $F(2,123) = 2.139$, $p = .122$.

For the number of references to the misinformation items (i.e., selecting the wrong answer that is consistent with the misinformation), there was a main effect in method of fact-checking, $F(2,123) = 11.509, p < .001$. Bonferroni pairwise comparisons showed participants in the correction condition ($M = 1.15$, $SD = .289$, $p < .001$) and warning condition ($M = 1.28$, $SD = .288$, $p < .001$) both performed significantly better than participants in the none condition ($M = 2.35$, SD $= 1.64$). That is, participants who were given the fact-checker made fewer references to misinformation when answering the memory checks. There was no main effect of choice, $F(1,123) = 1.01$, $p = .312$, and no interaction between option of choice and method of fact-checking, $F(2,123) = 1.32$, $p = .271$.

Table 3. Mean accuracy and references to misinformation in each condition

Condition	Mean accuracy	Mean number of references to misinformation
Choice × Correction	$M = 70.24\%$ $SD = .26$	$M = 1.19$ $SD = 1.25$
No choice × Correction	$M = 59.06\%$ $SD = .29$	$M = 1.30$ $SD = 1.30$
Choice × Warning	$M = 78.27\%$ $SD = .24$	$M = .71$ $SD = .96$
No choice × Warning	$M = 55.65\%$ $SD = .30$	$M = 1.48$ $SD = .87$
Choice × None	$M = 55.63\%$ $SD = .25$	$M = 2.40$ $SD = 1.88$
No choice × None	$M = 57.50\%$ $SD = .27$	$M = 2.25$ $SD = 1.41$

3.3 Trust Ratings

Separate ANOVAs were conducted on the trust ratings of information for different online sources (see Table 4 for means). There were no main effects of choice or method of fact-checking, and no interaction between the two independent variables for any of the ratings, $Fs (2,100) < 2.91$, $ps > .06$.

A subsequent analysis was performed with type of information outlet as a factor to determine whether participants trusted information from some outlets more than other outlets. The effect of outlet was significant, $F(5,699) = 10.941$, $p < .001$, indicating that participants' trust ratings differed for information found on the social media, local news website, government website, entertainment websites and personal blogs. A Bonferroni pairwise comparison showed that there was a difference in ratings between social media trust and personal blog trust ($p = .014$), where social media was found to be more trustworthy compared to personal blogs. Participants found the local news websites and government websites to be more trustworthy compared to entertainment websites ($p < .001$) and personal blogs ($p < .001$). Although the fact-checker was 100% accurate in the present study, users' trust ratings averaged $M = 3.69$, which is below the "Agree" rating but above the "Neither agree or disagree" rating based on the 5-point Likert scale. This finding indicates there was not a great amount of trust in the fact-checker. Bonferroni pairwise comparisons showed that participants rated the fact-checker to be more trustworthy compared to an entertainment website ($p = .025$) or personal blog ($p = .001$).

Table 4. Mean ratings of trust in online medias and fact-checker by condition.

Conditions	Social media trust	Local news website trust	Government website trust	Entertainment website trust	Personal blog trust	Fact-checker trust
Choice × Correction	$M = 3.55$ $SD = 1.04$	$M = 3.44$ $SD = .98$	$M = 3.78$ $SD = 1.00$	$M = 3.00$ $SD = 1.14$	$M = 2.89$ $SD = 1.18$	$M = 3.61$ $SD = .61$
No choice × Correction	$M = 3.33$ $SD = 1.11$	$M = 3.73$ $SD = .80$	$M = 3.67$ $SD = 1.23$	$M = 2.73$ $SD = 1.17$	$M = 2.93$ $SD = 1.22$	$M = 3.80$ $SD = .68$
Choice × Warning	$M = 3.47$ $SD = 1.12$	$M = 4.00$ $SD = .68$	$M = 4.32$ $SD = .82$	$M = 2.84$ $SD = 1.12$	$M = 2.74$ $SD = 1.47$	$M = 3.21$ $SD = .92$
No choice × Warning	$M = 3.65$ $SD = 1.06$	$M = 4.09$ $SD = .83$	$M = 4.12$ $SD = .99$	$M = 3.17$ $SD = 1.24$	$M = 3.06$ $SD = 1.30$	$M = 3.47$ $SD = 1.18$
Choice × None	$M = 3.54$ $SD = 1.18$	$M = 3.77$ $SD = 1.09$	$M = 3.71$ $SD = .92$	$M = 3.53$ $SD = 1.18$	$M = 3.35$ $SD = 1.32$	$M = 3.76$ $SD = .90$
No choice × None	$M = 3.07$ $SD = 1.21$	$M = 3.89$ $SD = .93$	$M = 3.86$ $SD = 1.18$	$M = 3.00$ $SD = 1.18$	$M = 2.79$ $SD = 1.05$	$M = 4.00$ $SD = 1.24$

4 Discussion

The present study examined the effectiveness of using fact-checker displays and how it can be used to reduce the spread of misinformation. It was hypothesized that the fact-checker would be effective in reducing the effects of misinformation. Specifically, participants in the correction or warning conditions should have shown a higher accuracy on the memory test and be less influenced by misinformation compared to participants in the no fact-checker condition. This hypothesis was partially supported. Although there was no overall effect of the fact-checking method on accuracy scores, the number of references to misinformation was less when a fact-checker was made available than when it was not.

It was also hypothesized that participants in the choice condition would perform better than participants in the no-choice condition. In the choice conditions, the participants used the fact-checker about 70% of the time. Participants in the choice conditions showed better performance on the memory check questions compared to the participants in the no-choice conditions. This finding suggests that the participants in the choice condition were making a more effortful decision when reading the fact-checkers analysis and statements. Thus, there is evidence supporting the use of a fact-checker to reduce the influence of misinformation on the users.

The final hypothesis was also supported. The choice and warning condition had the highest accuracy with the memory check questions ($M = 78.27\%$) followed by the choice and correction condition ($M = 70.24\%$); all other conditions had an accuracy average below 60%. Moreover, participants in the choice and warning condition ($M = 0.67$) made fewer references to misinformation compared to other conditions ($Ms = 1.19–2.40$).

One limitation of the present study was that participants were recruited to complete this study online and at their own pace. Since the study was unmoderated, there was less control over distractions that could have influenced the participation during the study. There were some participants who completed the study in under 10 min (21.14%) which could imply that they were not reading through all the information thoroughly before completing the memory check questions which could impact their accuracy. The second limitation was the use of a convenience sample. Although MTurk and introductory psychology students are common pools for research studies, there are characteristics of these samples that may not generalize to the broader population. A third limitation was the artificial context of the present study. The study was implemented as an online study and does not have the ecological aspects that users would experience when reading information online.

5   Conclusion

The goal of the present study was to identify if fact-checking was effective to combat the influence of misinformation, and to see if users are willing to use a fact-checker to verify statements if it was available. Although the fact-checker did not help with the participant's accuracy in the memory check questions, it was effective in reducing the number of references made to the misinformation items. Moreover, participants used a fact-checker about 70% of the time. Having a fact-checker available would be beneficial to help users identify false information that users may encounter while reading online media. A future study can explore whether a fact-checker would be effective when the stories appear in conventional media outlets (i.e., a more realistic environment).

References

1. Allcott, H., Gentzkow, M., Yu, C.: Trends in the diffusion of misinformation on social media. Res. Polit. **6**(2), 1–8 (2019). https://doi.org/10.1177/2053168019848554
2. Bailey, N.A., Olaguez, A.P., Klemfuss, J.Z., Loftus, E.F.: Tactics for increasing resistance to misinformation. Appl. Cogn. Psychol. **35**, 863–872 (2021). https://doi.org/10.1002/acp.3812
3. Brandtzaeg, P.B., Følstad, A.: Trust and distrust in online fact-checking services. Commun. ACM **60**(9), 65–71 (2017). https://doi.org/10.1145/3122803
4. Crozier, W.E., Strange, D.: Correcting the misinformation effect. Appl. Cogn. Psychol. **33**, 585–595 (2018). https://doi.org/10.1002/acp.3499
5. Diep, T.T.: The Role of Sharing in Remembering Social Media News (Order No. 22583183). Available from Dissertations & Theses @ California State University, Long Beach; Publicly Available Content Database (2311654536) (2019). http://csulb.idm.oclc.org/login?url= https://www.proquest.com/dissertations-theses/role-sharing-remembering-social-media-news/docview/2311654536/se-2
6. Ecker, U.K., Lewandowsky, S., Tang, D.T.: Explicit warnings reduce but do not eliminate the continued influence of misinformation. Mem. Cognit. **38**(8), 1087–1100 (2010). https://doi.org/10.3758/mc.38.8.1087
7. Lewandowsky, S., Ecker, U.K., Seifert, C.M., Schwarz, N., Cook, J.: Misinformation and its correction: continued influence and successful debiasing. Psychol. Sci. Public Interest **13**(3), 106–131 (2012). https://doi.org/10.1177/1529100612451018
8. Nakov, P., et al.: Automated fact-checking for assisting human fact-checkers. In: Proceedings of the Thirtieth International Joint Conference on Artificial Intelligence (2021). https://doi.org/10.24963/ijcai.2021/619
9. Nekmat, E.: Nudge effect of fact-check alerts: source influence and media skepticism on sharing of news misinformation in social media. Soc. Media + Soc. **6**(1), 1–14 (2020). https://doi.org/10.1177/2056305119897322

10. Pennycook, G., Rand, D.G.: The psychology of fake news. Trends Cogn. Sci. **25**(5), 388–402 (2021). https://doi.org/10.1016/j.tics.2021.02.007

11. Pennycook, G., Bear, A., Collins, E.T., Rand, D.G.: The implied truth effect: attaching warnings to a subset of fake news headlines increases perceived accuracy of headlines without warnings. Manage. Sci. **66**(11), 4944–4957 (2020). https://doi.org/10.1287/mnsc.2019.3478

12. Vraga, E.K., Kim, S.C., Cook, J., Bode, L.: Testing the effectiveness of correction placement and type on Instagram. Int. J. Press/Polit. **25**(4), 632–652 (2020). https://doi.org/10.1177/194 0161220919082

Design of Human-Agent-Group Interaction for Correct Opinion Sharing on Social Media

Fumito Uwano[1](✉) ⓘ, Daiki Yamane[2], and Keiki Takadama[3]

[1] Okayama University, 3-1-1, Tsushima-naka, Kita-ku, Okayama, Japan
uwano@okayama-u.ac.jp
[2] Tokyo Institute of Technology, 2-12-1, Ookayama, Meguro-ku, Tokyo, Japan
dyamane@cas.lab.uec.ac.jp
[3] The University of Electro-Communications, 1-5-1, Chofugaoka,
Chofu-shi, Tokyo, Japan
keiki@inf.uec.ac.jp

Abstract. Social media is popular for us to share some news; however, it is easy for us to receive much fake news and believe them because of its simplicity. A new model is proposed for simulating a cyber-physical system preventing fake news with humans and agents by expanding the opinion sharing model (OSM), and this paper proposes a decision-supporting system based on the model for users to avoid fake news. The experiments investigate the performance of the proposed system in social network simulation based on Twitter. The experimental results show that: (1) the proposed system performed the same simulation in the OSM's situation. (2) The user should inform the received information to the agents straightforward for sharing correct information. (3) The proposed system enabled the agents to suggest the opponent opinion of fake news to the users when they had shared the fake news in the simulation based on Twitter posts.

Keywords: Multiagent network · Social media · Social network · Twitter · Posting frequency.

1 Introduction

Social media is now becoming popular media to share some news in our human society. People often communicate with others to form their own opinions using social media: they discover other users' opinions to form their own opinions. To simulate such decision-making processes, Glinton et al. proposed a multi-agent opinion-sharing model [2] that regards the agents as people who are communicating with others to form their own opinions. In this model, there are a small number of so-called sensor agents and many normal agents. The sensor agents can receive correct information from the environment, while the normal agents can only receive opinions from their neighboring agents. The agents share their opinions as follows.

ⓒ The Author(s), under exclusive license to Springer Nature Switzerland AG 2022
S. Yamamoto and H. Mori (Eds.): HCII 2022, LNCS 13305, pp. 146–165, 2022.
https://doi.org/10.1007/978-3-031-06424-1_12

(1) The sensor agents receive correct information and form their opinions based on it.
(2) The sensor agents convey their opinions to neighboring normal agents.
(3) Normal agents that have received opinions form their own opinions and convey them to neighboring agents.
(4) Neighboring agents that have received opinions also form their own opinions and convey them to others.

It should be noted here that the opinions received need not be correct, leading to communities of agents that wrongly share incorrect opinions. To encourage the agents to form correct opinions despite conveying both correct and incorrect ones, Pryymak proposed the Autonomous Adaptive Tuning (AAT) algorithm [6]. This can improve the proportion of correct opinions shared in networks of various sizes where the agents might convey incorrect opinions. The previous works expanded the OSM as a social network to a real-world situation and proposed the correct opinion-sharing method on that expansion model. Uwano et al. expanded the OSM to a dynamic environment in which network topology is changeable and proposed the conformity-autonomous adaptive tuning algorithm to prevent an incorrect opinion on the expanded OSM [8]. In addition, they expanded to multi-dimensional opinions [9]. However, there is a definite difference between the expanded OSM and real-world social network. Thus, we deal with the OSM as a network system connecting between users to show a new human-agent interaction, or human-agent-group interaction (HAGI), in terms of group interaction with humans and agents, and propose a new decision support system for users connected on a whole network. To tackle this purpose, this paper focuses on proposition of fake news prevention method on the OSM in which users are posting as a goal, and investigated two functions: one is opinion sharing performance on the modified OSM, and the other is similarity between the OSM and real-world circumstance. Concretely, this paper expands the OSM from one layer for agents to the multilayer opinion sharing model (MOSM) that connects two OSMs for human and agent layers. Furthermore, this paper proposes a decision-supporting system based on multilayer opinion sharing model (DSMO). The experiments investigate the performance of the proposed system in social network simulation based on Twitter. Generally, the previous research proposed multilayer model analyzed structure of human society, company, and another network [4,5]. For instance, Kazienko et al. proposed a new measure to analyze circumstance of mutual connections with neighbors in social network [4]. Li et al. proposed detection model for local communities in multi-layer networks by combining two kinds of relation: direct influence relation and indirect influence relation of the network [5]. In short, the previous model simulated only people to simulate something circumstances in human society. However, the proposed model is assumed to simulate both of humans and agents to help humans to overcome something obstacles in human society as novelty.

This paper is organized as follows. OSM and AAT are introduced in Sects. 2 and 3, respectively. The DSMO is proposed in Sect. 4. The experimental details and discussions are described in Sect. 5, and the Twitter simulation details and discussions are in Sect. 6. Finally, Sect. 7 presents our conclusions.

2   Opinion-Sharing Model

The idea of opinion-sharing was formulated to capture the dynamics of the decision-making processes of a network of cooperating agents. In this model, the agents can share their opinions by communicating with their neighbors, while some agents have noisy sensors and can only receive information related to the environment. All agents aim to form correct opinions based on information from their sensors and their neighbors' opinions, and eventually form a consensus.

The agents aim to propagate correct opinions, subject to the following limitations [2].

- Only a few agents with sensors (*i.e.*, the sensor agents) can observe the environment.
- The sensor agents may form incorrect opinions since the sensors can receive incorrect information.
- The agents can only communicate with their neighbors in the network.

2.1   Overview of the Opinion-Sharing Model

In this model, the network $G(A, E)$ consists of a large set of agents $A = \{i_l : l \in 1...N\}, N >> 100$ connected by edges in the edge set E, where l is the number of neighboring agents connected to agent l and N is the total number of agents. Each agent $i \in A$ can only communicate with its neighbors $D_i = \{j : \exists(i, j) \in E\}$, and the average number of neighbors is defined as the degree $d = \sum_{i \in A} |D_i|/N$. The network is sparse because this degree is small for all agents, *i.e.*, $d \ll N$. The environment state b involves only binary values, for example $b \in B$ where $B = \{white, black\}$. Here, *white* and black are regarded as correct and incorrect information/opinions, respectively, and all agents have correct opinions if they all form the opinion *white*. The set B is used because it has been argued that binary choices can be applied to a wide range of real-world situations [2]. The agent community aims to find the true state b observed by some of the sensor agents. In particular, each agent aims to form an opinion o_i that represents the real state of the environment, *i.e.*, $o_i = b$. Note that $o_i = white$ indicates that agent i has formed a correct opinion. Each agent forms its opinion by relying on its neighbors' opinions, while the sensor agents also rely on their noisy sensors. The agents form opinions by having private beliefs $P_i(b = white)$, corresponding to the probability that $b = white$ (denoted as P_i from now on). Likewise, $1 - P_i$ corresponds to the probability that $b = black$. The agents' beliefs are updated by starting from some initial prior P_i'' and then defining later belief states P_i^k, where k is the current belief update step. A small number of sensor agents $S \subset A, |S| \ll N$ have noisy sensors and can observe the environment state b. Each sensor agent $i \in S$ periodically receives an observation $s_i \in B$ that is of low accuracy $r(0.5 < r \leq 1)$. These agents incorporate their sensor observations using a formal update process based on Bayes' theorem [2]:

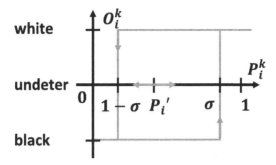

Fig. 1. Update rule of opinion.

$$P_i^k = \frac{C_{upd}P_i^{k-1}}{(1 - C_{upd})(1 - P_i^{k-1}) + C_{upd}P_i^{k-1}} \tag{1}$$

$$where \begin{cases} C_{upd} = r & if \ s_j = white \\ C_{upd} = 1 - r \ if \ s_j = black \end{cases} \tag{2}$$

In these equations, C_{upd} indicates the degree to which the agent believes the neighbors' opinions or the information from the environment. Note that C_{upd} is also utilized for normal agents in Eq. (4): They may be more or less confident of their opinions when updating their beliefs about the true state b of the environment. The agents update their opinions using the following opinion update rule, by comparing their private beliefs P_i^k to a threshold σ.

$$O_i^k = \begin{cases} undeter., initial, if & k = 0 \\ white, & if & P_i^k \geq \sigma \\ black, & if & P_i^k \leq 1 - \sigma \\ o_i^{k-1} & otherwise \end{cases} \tag{3}$$

The thresholds $1 - \sigma$ and σ are the confidence bounds, and the range is $0.5 < \sigma < 1$. Figure 1, taken from Pryymak et al. [6], shows that the opinion update function has a sharp hysteresis loop. An agent will only change its opinion from *white* to *black* if P_i^k decreases below not σ but $1 - \sigma$ and vice versa; we call this a hysteresis loop. If a new observation supports the opposite state, an agent may or may not change its opinion, because the received opinion may be incorrect. The agents send new opinions to their neighbors only when their opinion changes and their neighbors then update their own beliefs and opinions. The agents incorporate their neighbors' opinions using a formal update rule similar to the one for the sensor agents. When an agent receives new opinions from its neighbors $o_j : j \in D_j$, it uses the same belief update rule for each opinion o_j:

$$where \begin{cases} C_{upd} = t_i & if \ o_j = white \\ C_{upd} = 1 - t_i \ if \ o_j = black \end{cases} \tag{4}$$

where $t_i \in [0,1]$ is the importance level and indicates how much weight agent i gives to its neighbors' opinions agents informing its own opinion. Note that t_i does not change the neighbor links because it only affects the number of neighboring agents required to form an opinion. This is a measure of the influence of its neighbors' opinions, and is a conditional probability. The importance level is similar to the accuracy in Eq. (1), but unlike the sensor accuracy, each agent must find its importance level t_i because it is initially unknown. The algorithm for determining t_i is described in Sect. 3. The agents only consider importance levels t_i in the range $t_i \in [0.5, 1]$, with $t_i = 0.5$ indicating that the agents should ignore all opinions received opinions and $t_i = 1$ indicating that it should change its own belief to $P_i^k = \{1,0\}$ and ignore its previous belief P_i^{k-1}.

This model may converge to a false state. Accordingly, the agents are identified with these neighbors in themselves. Regarding this model, we consider that the agents are not equated with these neighbors since it may be quite natural.

2.2   Model Performance Metrics

The model is simulated for $M = \{m_l : l \in 1...|M|\}$ rounds. At the start of each round, the new true state $b^m \in B$ of the environment is randomly selected and the agents reset their opinions and beliefs. At the end of the round, the agents' conclusions are observed and the current true state expires. During the round, the agents are given a limited number of steps for their opinions to converge (*e.g.*, 2000 steps per round). At each step, the agents observe the current state and receive opinions, using them calculate their awareness rates (see below), set their importance levels, and store their accuracies.

As a measure of the average accuracy of the agents' opinions at the end of each round, Glinton et al. proposed using the proportion of agents that formed a correct opinion [3]:

$$R = \frac{1}{N|M|} \sum_{i \in A} |\{m \in M : o_i^m = b^m\}| \cdot 100\% \tag{5}$$

In addition, a performance index was proposed by Pryymak et al. [6] for individual agents. Since an agent cannot determine when it has formed a correct opinion, it measures how often it forms a correct opinion, called the awareness rate:

$$h_i = \frac{|\{m \in M : o_i^m \neq undeter.\}|}{|M|} \tag{6}$$

The value given by Eq. (6) is divided by the number of rounds to calculate the average number of correct opinions formed throughout all rounds. Each agent calculates its awareness rate at the end of every round and sets its importance level so that its awareness rate is as close to the target as possible. Since this is repeated for each round, the awareness rate will steadily increase over time, which is why it is divided by the number of rounds.

This myopic metric can be calculated locally by each agent and is important for the AAT algorithm described in Sect. 3.

3   Autonomous Adaptive Tuning

The AAT algorithm is designed to improve the accuracy R for a variety of complex networks by allowing the agents to share their opinions. In this algorithm, the agents automatically update their beliefs by relying only on local information. In particular, it is based on observing that the accuracy R increases when the opinion-sharing dynamics change phase from a stable state (where opinions are shared only within small communities $\forall i \in A : h_i \ll 1$) to an unstable one (where the opinions are propagated widely, $h_i = 1$). Note that each agent forms its opinion based on only a few other opinions, and may form incorrect opinions due to the unstable sensors when $h_i = 1$. As a result, the agents need to share their opinions with smaller groups before the large cascade occurs so that they do not react to large numbers of incorrect opinions. To optimize the parameters to deal with this issue, the algorithm regulates the agents' importance levels in three stages.

- Each agent creates a list of candidate importance levels to reduce the search space for the following stages. This step happens only once, at the start of the experiment.
- After each round, each agent estimates awareness rates (as described in Sect. 2.2) for each candidate level.
- Each agent sets its importance level by considering how close each of these awareness rates is to the target. It must tune the importance levels gradually when considering the influence of its neighbors.

Note that the importance levels are discrete values, and each agent selects the importance level candidate whose associate awareness rate is closest to the target awareness rate. In the following Sects., we describe these three AAT algorithm stages in detail.

3.1   Importance Level Candidates

In this Sect., we describe how the agents estimate the importance level candidates T_i. Using a set of importance level candidates allows the agents to reduce the problem of selecting an importance level from a continuous range to choosing from a set of consecutive values in the range $[0.5, 1]$. Since there is only a small number of sensor agents, we focus on agents that update their beliefs using only the opinions of neighbors without sensors. Pryymak et al. described the sampling dynamics of the agents' beliefs, where an agent i can change its opinion from *black* to *white* after receiving more *white* opinions [6]. Starting from a prior belief of $P'_i(black)$, an agent may update its opinion to *white*, due to an increase in belief after receiving a series of *white* opinions. The most important aspect of these dynamics is the update step when an agent has just changed its opinion because this is the only time when it sends a new opinion to its neighbors. Consequently, we focus on how many times an agent must update its belief before it changes its opinion. According to the opinion update rule given in Sect. 2.1, we consider the case where the agent's belief matches one of the confidence bounds $P_i^k \in \{\sigma, 1 - \sigma\}$. Given that the maximum number of opinions that the agent can receive is limited by its number of neighbors $|D_i|$, we can pare down the potential candidate importance levels. The agent should find the importance levels where its belief coincides with one of the confidence bounds $P_{i_l} \in \{\sigma, 1 - \sigma\}$ *in* $l \in 1...|D_i|$ updates (see Eq. (3)). After solving this problem, it can obtain the set of importance level candidates that lead to forming an opinion after receiving $1...|D_i|$ opinions, as follows.

$$T_i = \{t_{i_l} : P_{i_l}(t_{i_l}) = \sigma, l \in 1...|D_i|\} \cup$$
$$\{t_{i_l} : P_{i_l}(t_{i_l}) = 1 - \sigma, l \in 1...|D_i|\} \tag{7}$$

The set of importance level candidates is thus limited to twice the number of neighbors, $|T_i| = 2|D_i|$. This is the necessary and sufficient set of importance levels for which the agent forms an opinion after different number update steps, and it need only be initialized once. The agent then only has to estimate the optimal importance level from its set of importance level candidates.

3.2   Estimating Agent Awareness Rates

In this Sect., we describe the criteria used to select an importance level candidate. As mentioned above, the AAT algorithm is based on the observation that the community accuracy R improves when the opinion-sharing dynamics transition between stable and unstable phases. To estimate optimal parameters, each agent has to determine the lowest importance level that allows it to form an opinion. In this opinion-sharing model, the following two conditions help to maximize the accuracy R [7].

- Each agent has to form an opinion, so it should aim for a high awareness rate h_i because agents without correct opinions the community accuracy.
- Each agent has to form its opinion as late as possible with only local information after it has gathered as many opinions from its neighbors as possible.

To satisfy these requirements, the agent must select the importance level $t_{i_l} \in T_i$ from the candidates that allow it to form an opinion ($h_i = 1$). However, since the sensors' values are influenced by random noise, the opinion-sharing dynamics, such as phase transitions, are stochastic. The agents cannot form opinions until opinions are shared on a large scale, due to their awareness rates. The agents should thus select the lowest importance level t_{i_l} from the candidate T_i such that the awareness rate approaches the target h_{trg}, which is slightly lower than maximum, $h_i = 1$. Each agent solves the following optimization problem:

$$t_i = \arg \min_{t_{i_l} \in T_i} |h_i(t_{i_l}) - h_{trg}| \tag{8}$$

In this problem, $h_i(t_{i_l})$ is the awareness rate corresponding to the importance level t_{i_l} that the agent selects. The optimal parameter value for achieving versatile network dynamics is $h_{trg} = 0.9$ [6].

3.3 Importance Level Selection Strategy

Each agent affects the dynamics and awareness rates of all the other agents, due to the dependence of the agents' opinions on those of their neighbors. If an agent selects its optimal importance level greedily, based on the definition of its optimization problem (see Eq. (8)), it may significantly affect the local community dynamics. Instead, the agent should select a strategy that does not dramatically change the dynamics, so that it can estimate community awareness rates accurately and solve the problem more quickly. To select such a strategy, the agent should focus on the following inference. The agents' awareness rates increase monotonically with the importance level. Because the minimum importance level t_i^{min} will require many more updates than the maximum importance level t_i^{max}, if the importance levels are sorted in ascending order, the agent should employ a hill-climbing strategy. In other words, if the awareness rate of the current importance level $t_i = t_{i_l}$ is lower than the target $\hat{h}_{i_l} < h_{trg}$, the agent should increase its importance level by one step (*i.e.*, $l = l + 1$). If reducing the importance level by one step will result in an awareness rate that is below the target $\hat{h}_{i_{l-1}} > h_{trg}$, the agent should use this importance level in the next round (*i.e.*, $l = l - 1$). Using this hill-climbing strategy rather than the greedy strategy allows the agents to achieve higher accuracy [6].

4 Decision-Supporting System Based on Multilayer Opinion Sharing Model

The DSMO simulates opinion sharing including users using the MOSM. In particular, the DSMO has advantage to abolish the premise of the AAT, rate of sensor agents in a network and the sensing rate are given. In short, the DSMO can exchange the agent sensing in the AAT to the user posting (i.e., sensing configuration can be flexible) as a novelty. The next Subsect. explains the details of MOSM.

4.1 User-agent Interaction Assumption

This paper assumes a user is a human, that is, it does not behave in rational, and then a rational agent supports the user to make a decision by showing its opinion as a concierge. Note that the agent does not determine the user's decision but shows one opinion. That is because humans usually have mixed feeing for any news, and each of them might have opponent or different feeling to the same topic each other. Figure 2 shows agents interaction for two users in the proposed method. The users send information to the other user and the counterpart agent, and the agent represents the user to make an opinion through interaction among agents. Afterward, the agent shares the opinion with the user. Note that the user does not know the information confidence or correct in the premise, and the agent cannot be given them.

In addition, this paper focused on a prevention method for evident fake news, and assumed users have the almost same conception each other (i.e., there are

Fig. 2. Decision support by two agents.

correct and incorrect opinions definitely in this paper.) It is out of scope that each of users has different answer like a philosophic topic. However, the proposed system might be utilized to analyze a majority opinion in some society in future work.

4.2   Multilayer Opinion Sharing Model

Figure 3 shows an overview of the MOSM. There are two layers: user-side and agent-side layers. The network topology of both layers assumes to be the same as each other. In this model, users send their own opinion to the counterpart agents and the agents spread it to the neighbor agents by following some rules (explained in Subsect. 4.3). Thus, the agents receive the opinions and decide their own opinion using the AAT algorithm.

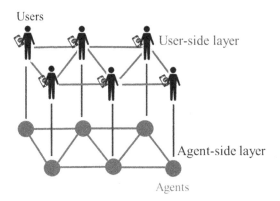

Fig. 3. Multilayer opinion sharing model.

User-Side Architecture. The users send their opinion with the probabilities p_{post} and p_{true} for posting some opinion and true opinion, respectively. Algorithm 1 denotes pseudocode for the user's posting. a user posts some opinion to the counterpart agent by the probability p_{post} every step (line 1), and the posted opinion is also true by the probability p_{true} (lines 2 and 3); otherwise false (lines

Algorithm 1. User's posting function.

1: **if** $rand(0,1) < p_{post}$ **then**
2:    **if** $rand(0,1) < p_{true}$ **then**
3:       The user posts a true opinion
4:    **else**
5:       The user posts a false opinion
6:    **end if**
7: **end if**

---

4 to 6.) The users can have the different p_{post} and p_{true} each other to apply them for a real-world problem.

Agent-Side Architecture. There are two kinds of agents: an agent and a source agent. The source agent spreads the user's opinion to other neighbor agents and the agent decides and shares the opinion by the AAT algorithm. Figure 4 shows the source agents being throughout the agent-side layer. There are some source agents between normal agents like this figure, which seems to be sensor agents and agents in the OSM.

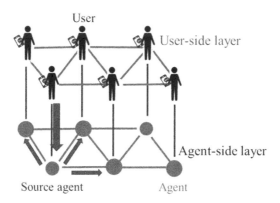

Fig. 4. Source agents and other agents.

4.3   Decision-Supporting System

The source agents have four methods as shown in Fig. 5 to share a correct opinion on the MOSM. Method 1 enables source agents to update their beliefs based on users' posting by the AAT algorithm and send the corresponding opinion to directly connected agents if they decided their opinions. Method 2 is similar to the method 1, however, it modifies the importance level t of the AAT algorithm, or degree C_{upd} of the OSM, to be set for which the source agents can decide an opinion by the number of times of averaged posting-counts. In Method 3, source agents send the received opinion to directly connected agents. In Method

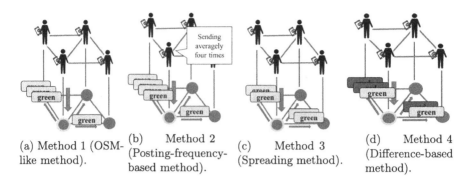

(a) Method 1 (OSM-like method).

(b)   Method 2 (Posting-frequency-based method).

(c)   Method 3 (Spreading method).

(d)   Method 4 (Difference-based method).

Fig. 5. Four methods in DSMO.

4, source agents send the opinion to the directly connected agents if they receive a different opinion from the present received opinion.

4.4   Algorithm

Algorithm 2 is pseudocode of the DSMO. The DSMO executes the process for N rounds (the first line). In this process, all agents initialize their beliefs P and opinions o (lines 2 and 3). In each round, K steps are executed (line 4). In each step, all users send their opinions to the counterpart agents by following the posting function (lines 5 to 8). After that, the agent i send the opinion to other agents by following the four methods if it is a source agent (lines 10 to 12). The agent i receives neighbors' opinions if they send their opinions (line 13). Furthermore, the agent i which receives the opinion updates its belief and decides its opinion by the AAT algorithm, and the agent i which decides the opinion sends it to other agents (lines 14 to 20). Finally, all agents update the importance levels.

5   Experiment

5.1   Experimental Setup

This paper investigated the performance of the DSMO by comparing it with the AAT algorithm and the four methods. There are two cases of investigation: investigating similarity between the DSMO and AAT on OSM, and comparing between four methods. In the first case, we validate the same performance between the DSMO and AAT if the posting probability for users p_{post} is adjusted to be the same as the sensor agents' posting probability. In the second case, we examine the performance of four methods of the DSMO in the same situation as the first case.

Table 1 shows the experimental parameters. We employed Barabasi-Albert (BA) model [1] (line 1). The number of users U and agents N are both 300,

Algorithm 2. DSMO algorithm.

1: **for** $m = 0$ to $M - 1$ **do**
2:    Initialize Beliefs
3:    Initialize Opinions
4:    **for** $k = 0$ to $K - 1$ **do**
5:      **for** $u = 0$ to $U - 1$ **do**
6:        $opinion = PostingFunction()$
7:        User u's counterpart agent receives $opinion$
8:      **end for**
9:      **for** $i = 0$ to $N - 1$ **do**
10:        **if** The agent i is the source agent **then**
11:          $SharingOpinion()$
12:        **end if**
13:        The agent i receives neighbors' opinion
14:        **if** The agent i receives any opinions **then**
15:          The agent i updates its belief
16:          The agent i decides its opinion
17:          **if** The agent i changes its opinion **then**
18:            The agent i sends its opinion
19:          **end if**
20:        **end if**
21:      **end for**
22:    **end for**
23:    The agents update their importance levels
24: **end for**

---

respectively (lines 2 and 3). The posting probability of a true opinion for users and sensor agents is both 0.55, respectively (lines 4 and 5). The agents' beliefs are initialized by a random number following $N(0.5, 0.1)$ (line 6). Total rounds M and steps K are 300 and 2000, respectively (lines 7 and 8). The target awareness rate h_{tar} is 0.95. In addition, correct opinion b is a white color in this experiment.

5.2 Evaluation Criteria

This paper evaluates the performance by correct opinion occupancy rate CR, incorrect opinion occupancy rate FR, and undetermined opinion occupancy rate UR, as following equations, respectively:

$$CR = \frac{1}{N|M|} \sum_{i \in A} |\{m \in M : o^m = b\}|, \tag{9}$$

$$FR = \frac{1}{N|M|} \sum_{i \in A} |\{m \in M : o^m \neq b\}|, \tag{10}$$

$$UR = \frac{1}{N|M|} \sum_{i \in A} |\{m \in M : o_i^m = b\}|. \tag{11}$$

The CR, FR, and UR denote the ratio of the agents which decide a correct opinion, an incorrect opinion, and do not decide, respectively. The CR, FR,

Table 1. Parameters used.

Network topology	BA model
Users' network size U	300
Agents' network size N	300
Posting probability for correct opinion p_{true}	0.55
Sensor agents' posting probability for correct opinion	0.55
Initialized belief	Random number by $N(0.5, 0.1)$
Total rounds M	300
Total steps K	2000
Target awareness rate h_{tar}	0.95

and UR influence each other because all of agents in the MOSM have only three states: decision of a correct opinion and an incorrect opinion, and neither opinions. For example, the high CR decreases the FR and UR, and if two of these criteria are calculated, the other criterion is clearly calculated. Because it is important for an agent to form its opinion at first and to be correct at second, the less UR is the most important, and then the more CR is the next most important.

5.3   Experimental Result

Figure 6 shows the results of the case 1. The vertical and horizontal axes indicate opinion occupancy rate and averaged posting count X in one round, respectively. The left-hand and right-hand sides indicate the results if $p_{post} = X/K$, and p_{post} is a random number by $N(X/K, 1/K)$, respectively. These results examine the results by the different distribution of random numbers. The posting count X is set by 3.5, 6.5, 10.5, and 13.5, respectively. The blue, orange, gray, yellow, light blue, and green lines indicate CR, FR, and UR of AAT and DSMO, respectively. The result shows the method 1 of the DSMO only because the method 1 is similar to the AAT algorithm to any other methods. Figure 6, the DSMO performs almost similar to the AAT every what is set as p_{post}: the CR and UR increase but FR decreases along to X. Thus, sensor and source agents share a correct opinion and prevent an incorrect opinion. The difference between the DSMO and AAT is averagely 1.36×10^{-2} in Fig. 6(a) and 1.95×10^{-2}, which is many close.

Figure 7 shows the results of the case 2. The vertical axis is CR, FR, and UR in Fig. 7(a), 7(b), and 7(c), respectively. The horizontal axis indicates averaged posting count X in one round. The posting probability p_{post} is a random number by $N(X/K, 1/K)$ where the posting count X is set by 3.5, 6.5, 10.5, and 13.5, respectively. The blue, orange, gray, yellow, light blue lines indicate the performance of the AAT, the methods 1, 2, 3, and 4 in the DSMO, respectively. As for the result of CR, the method 3 is better than any other methods without the case if $X = 10.5$, and the FR of the method 3 is the smallest. Therefore, the method 3 is the best. On the other hand, agents did not decide their opinions in

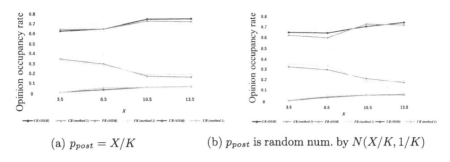

(a) $p_{post} = X/K$ (b) p_{post} is random num. by $N(X/K, 1/K)$

Fig. 6. Result in the case 1.

the method 3: the method 3's UR is highest. Although the UR is entirely small, the method 3 enabled agents to be careful to decide their opinion. The method 1's performance is similar to the AAT also in this result. The method 2 made agents decide false opinions, that is, this method is the worst. The method 4 performs worse if $X = 13.5$ and this method is different from other methods.

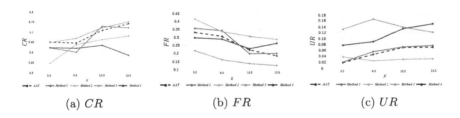

(a) CR (b) FR (c) UR

Fig. 7. Opinion Occupancy Rate.

5.4 Experimental Discussion

Advantage of the Method 3. The results show that the method 3 is the best. The method 3 enable source agents to send the users' opinion to directly connected agents straightforward. Figure 8 shows averaged UR of all methods if p_{post} follows the distribution $N(6.5/K, 1/K)$. The method 3's UR is the largest, which is the method 2's result multiplied by 1.77. In the method 3, agents which connect to source agents directly update their beliefs carefully because the source agents send the counterpart users' opinion straightforward even if the opinion is incorrect. Thus, the neighbor agents cooperatively prevented from incorrect opinions if the users' posting is not stable, and share correct opinions with agents in the whole network, whereas easy to be undetermined.

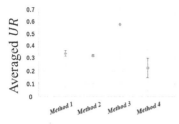

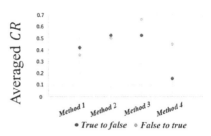

Fig. 8. Averaged UR.   **Fig. 9.** Averaged CR.

The AAT algorithm makes agents converge their opinions, and the opinions cannot change in the late round. However, users change their opinions easily in any round. This paper experimented additionally in the situation that users mainly post a different opinion in the last half rounds. Figure 9 shows the result if p_{post} follows the distribution $N(6.5/K, 1/K)$. The vertical axis indicates averaged CR, and the horizontal axis indicates each method. The blue and orange dots denote the results when the majority opinion in the last half rounds is false and true, respectively. This figure indicates that the method 3 resisted the majority opinion getting worse, and increased CR if the opinion became true. Therefore, the method 3 might be able to the best performance in social media.

Limitation of DSMO. This Sect. analyzes the relationship between p_{post} and the DSMO's performance. Figure 10 shows Fig. 7(a) if X is as long as 20. The method 3 increases its CR, however, that converges at $X = 20$. Other methods are in the same manner however, the method 4 decreases its CR. Although the confidence of opinion sharing becomes better if the posting count is larger, that more than 20 did not affect more.

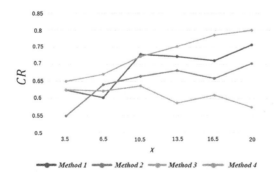

Fig. 10. Analysis of posting.

6   Twitter Data Simulation

6.1   Simulation Setup

In this Sect., we simulate the DSMO based on Twitter posting data and analyze the results. We employ the DSMO with the method 3 because it performs the best in the previous Sect. The data that is posted between February 1st to 8th in 2021 is posted about the effect of wearing two masks overlapped, and the total number of users is 18000 from 15000. The data is analyzed by linguistic sentiment analysis to close Twitter's posting situation to the OSM, and classified to "Positive", "Negative", and "Neutral" as white opinion, black opinion, and undetermined opinion, respectively. Although text sentiment is generally unrelated to confidence of opinion, the positive or negative posting can become approximately confidence in a limited theme in social media. For example, user's sentiment can relate to affirmation or denial about government's arrangement to COVID-19. In addition, the period is converted to 2000 steps. For instance, the posting at 9:08:09 on February 5th is to post "Positive" at step 1095. In this simulation, 60 users are selected from 15000 users to be as the users in the DSMO, and X is set as 3.5 because the 60 users' posting count is 3.5 on averagely. Thus, the 60 users post their opinion along with their posting data on Twitter.

6.2   Simulation Result

Figure 11 shows the result of the Twitter simulation. The left-hand and right-hand sides indicate the users' posting counts and the agents decided opinions, respectively. The vertical axis is posting count and opinion occupancy rate in Figs. 11(a) and 11(b), respectively. The horizontal axis is a time step in both figures. The result shows that a negative opinion is a majority in user-side before step 600, however, a positive opinion finally becomes majority to be posted two times more than negative. On the other hand, agents shared a negative opinion at first to the end, and the rate is 93%.

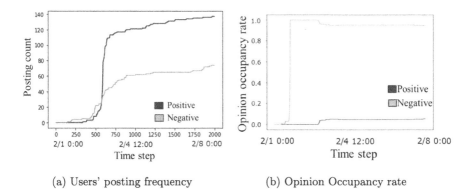

(a) Users' posting frequency   (b) Opinion Occupancy rate

Fig. 11. Results of Twitter simulation.

6.3   Simulation Discussion

In the user-side situation, there is a post that the National institute of allergy and infectious diseases (NIAID) shows an opinion it is effective to wear two masks overlapped around at step 600, and that post influenced users being positive. However, that opinion is not true by the supercomputer Fugaku simulating on the first season in March. Therefore, the users are influenced by one opinion from NIAID to share an incorrect opinion. On the other hand, all agents shared a negative opinion at first and resisted to influence of users to keep their opinions. That is because the agents decide their opinions based on the neighbors' opinions while the users decide their opinions based on one opinion. In short, the agent believes majority opinion by the counterpart user and neighbor agents even if the counterpart user has opposite opinion. The agents share a negative opinion, or a correct opinion, even if the NIAID did not show the positive opinion. However, that is because users and agents shared a negative opinion, or a correct opinion, before the NIAID's show. If almost all of agents and users share a positive opinion, or an incorrect opinion, they require the more negative opinion than the NIAID's information to change their opinion. Note that, the DSMO does not assume the above circumstance, that is, each of agents follows the common-sense majority agents have in agent-network. Therefore, the DSMO can suggest users correct information by modeling the HAGI like Fig. 12.

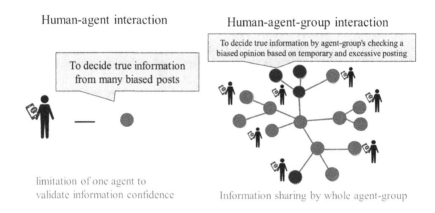

Fig. 12. Difference between HAI and HAGI.

Finally, we compare the Twitter simulation results with the experimental results in Sect. 5. Figure 13 shows users' posting distributions: the left-hand and right-hand sides are in the experiment and Twitter simulation, respectively. The vertical and horizontal axes indicate the number of users and posting frequency, respectively. Thus, each user did not post many times, on averagely two times in the Twitter simulation.

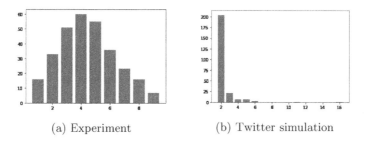

(a) Experiment   (b) Twitter simulation

Fig. 13. Users' posting distributions.

Figure 14 shows transitions of opinion sharing: the top-side and bottom-side are transitions in the experiment and Twitter simulation, respectively. The circles denote agents and they are linked with each other. Blue, red, and green colors are represented as white opinion, black opinion, and undetermined opinion, or positive, negative, and neutral, respectively. The transitions show that the method 3 made agents share their opinion carefully with other agents to share a correct opinion after 1000 steps in the experiment. In the Twitter simulation, agents shared a negative opinion at step 540, or before the influential posting to prevent that influence.

The DSMO assumes the users and agents do not know the confidence of opinion. However, the DSMO has to decide the class, e.g., positive, negative, and neutral in the Twitter simulation. To keep from spreading fake news, the

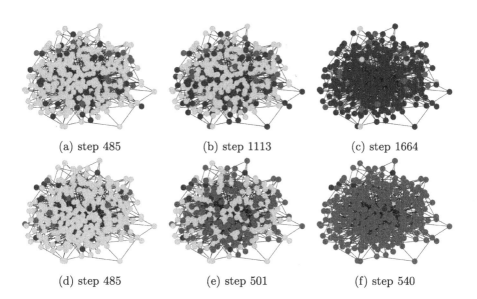

(a) step 485   (b) step 1113   (c) step 1664

(d) step 485   (e) step 501   (f) step 540

Fig. 14. Transitions of opinion sharing (top-side: experiment, bottom-side: Twitter simulation).

DSMO does not have to classify all news, but it has to make users decide all news to fake or not. Thus, to apply it for real-world problem, we must decide whether a user can decide the news to fake or not from the own posting. In the Twitter simulation, the DSMO employed sentiment for the key of decision. That results the better performance of DSMO. However, we have to derive in how to decide the key.

7   Conclusion

This paper proposed the DSMO as a new model for simulating cyber-physical systems preventing fake news with humans and agents by expanding the OSM, and a decision-supporting system based on the model for users to avoid fake news. Concretely, there are four methods as decision-support to prevent fake news: the method 1 enables source agents to update their beliefs based on users' posting by the AAT algorithm and send the corresponding opinion to directly connected agents if they decided their opinions. The method 2 is similar to the method 1, however, it modifies the importance level t of the AAT algorithm, or degree C_{upd} of the OSM, to be set for which the source agents can decide an opinion by the number of times of averaged posting-counts. In the method 3, source agents send the received opinion to directly connected agents. In the method 4, source agents send the opinion to the directly connected agents if they receive the different opinion from the present received opinion.

The experiments investigate the performance of the DSMO in social network simulation based on Twitter. The experimental results show that: (1) the DSMO performed almost the same as the AAT algorithm. (2) The method 3 is the best performance for sharing correct information. (3) The method 3 made source agents share users' opinions straightforward to make the neighbor agents share the opinions carefully. Thus, the method 3 enables agents to share a correct opinion. (4) The DSMO enabled agents to resist the influence of one post on Twitter even if users are influenced that to share an incorrect opinion. Therefore, the DSMO might be able to suggest the opponent opinion of fake news to the users when they have shared the fake news in social media by the simulation based on Twitter posts.

This paper showed the DSMO's performance, however, the DSMO has some limitations yet. The situation is not generalized, e.g., two opinions and the BA model. In addition, this paper did not derive in how to decide key to classify posting information in a real-world problem. Thus, this paper solves these issues to apply the DSMO to real-world social network problems in the future.

Acknowledgement. This research was supported by JSPS Grant on JP21K17807.

References

1. Barabasi, A., Albert, R.: Emergence of scaling in random networks. Science **286**, 509–512 (1999)

2. Glinton, R.T., Scerri, P., Sycara, K.: Towards the understanding of information dynamics in large scale networked systems. In: 2009 12th International Conference on Information Fusion, pp. 794–801, July 2009
3. Glinton, R., Scerri, P., Sycara, K.: An investigation of the vulnerabilities of scale invariant dynamics in large teams. In: The 10th International Conference on Autonomous Agents and Multiagent Systems, AAMAS 2011, vol. 2, pp. 677–684. International Foundation for Autonomous Agents and Multiagent Systems, Richland (2011)
4. Kazienko, P., Brodka, P., Musial, K.: Individual neighbourhood exploration in complex multi-layered social network. In: 2010 IEEE/WIC/ACM International Conference on Web Intelligence and Intelligent Agent Technology, vol. 3, pp. 5–8 (2010)
5. Li, X., Xu, G., Lian, W., Xian, H., Jiao, L., Huang, Y.: Multi-layer network local community detection based on influence relation. IEEE Access **7**, 89051–89062 (2019)
6. Pryymak, O., Rogers, A., Jennings, N.R.: Efficient opinion sharing in large decentralised teams. In: Proceedings of the 11th International Conference on Autonomous Agents and Multiagent Systems, AAMAS 2012, vol. 1, pp. 543–550. International Foundation for Autonomous Agents and Multiagent Systems, Richland (2012)
7. Saito, R., Tatebe, N., Takano, R., Takadama, K.: Network construction for correct opinion sharing by selecting a curator agent. In: 2015 54th Annual Conference of the Society of Instrument and Control Engineers of Japan, SICE, pp. 363–368, July 2015
8. Uwano, F., Saito, R., Takadama, K.: Weighted opinion sharing model for cutting link and changing information among agents as dynamic environment. SICE J. Control Meas. Syst. Integr. **11**(4), 331–340 (2018)
9. Uwano, F., Kitajima, E., Takadama, K.: Sigmoid-based incorrect opinion prevention algorithm on multi-opinion sharing model. Trans. Jpn. Soc. Artif. Intell. **36**(6), B-KB2 (2021)

Effects of Immediate Feedback in Operating Information Device by Finger Tap Gesture

Kyosuke Watanabe, Makoto Oka$^{(\boxtimes)}$, and Hirohiko Mori$^{(\boxtimes)}$

Tokyo City University, 1-28-1 Tamazutsumi, Setagaya-ku, Tokyo, Japan
`{g2091402,moka,hmori}@tcu.ac.jp`

Abstract. In this paper, we proposed a robust finger tap gesture recognition method and examined the feedback function when operating information devices using finger tap gestures. A finger tap gesture recognition method using hall sensors and gyro sensors achieved a high recognition rate without causing false detection. However, when operating information devices with finger tap gestures, there are the following two problems. The first is that it is recognized as a gesture different from the intended gesture, and the second is that the user's subjective gesture success or failure differs from the actual gesture success or failure. If the above phenomenon occurs, the user cannot operate the information device smoothly. In this paper, we aimed to make it possible for the user to quickly grasp the state of the information device and take appropriate actions by presenting the user with immediate feedback according to the type of gesture immediately after the successful gesture. As for the types of immediate feedback, tactile feedback and sound feedback were prepared and compared those feedback condition. As a result, it was found that by giving immediate feedback, the user can properly grasp the state of the information device and quickly per-form appropriate operations. Furthermore, when comparing tactile feedback and sound feedback, the operational performance tended to be higher for tactile feedback, and the subjective evaluation tended to be higher for sound feedback.

Keywords: Input interface · Eyes-free · Finger gesture

1 Introduction

In recent years, it has become possible to carry small information devices such as smartphones, smartwatches, and music players, and we are now in an era where we can benefit from computers anytime, anywhere. However, from the viewpoint of safety and social acceptability, it is difficult to operate information devices seamlessly in the following three situations:

- Situations where users are performing other tasks besides operating information device (For example, while walking or jogging).
- Situations where users can't move and speak something (For example, users are on a crowded train).

S. Yamamoto and H. Mori (Eds.): HCII 2022, LNCS 13305, pp. 166–182, 2022.
https://doi.org/10.1007/978-3-031-06424-1_13

- Situations where users are performing activities of daily living, including fine movements of fingers.

Gesture operation is one of the methods to operate information equipment without looking at it. In operating information devices seamlessly by gestures in the above three situations, it is necessary to fulfil all of the conditions <1> <2> <3> <4>, and, in addition, it is desirable to satisfy the condition <5>. However, none of the studies conducted satisfy all the following five conditions so far.

<1> There are no similar movements in daily life, and there is no need to switch between gesture recognition mode and gesture non-recognition mode by a specific operation.
<2> To make it possible for users to operate information device anytime regardless of the surrounding environment, the operation associated with the gesture should be compact.
<3> There is no need to watch the body part where the gesture is performed.
<4> Users can perform gestures while walking or jogging.
<5> To reduce the time and the effort required to operate information equipment smoothly, it is not necessary to acquire training data and build a classifier for each user.

In this paper, we propose a robust finger tap gesture recognition method that fulfill all above five conditions and examine the feedback function when operating information devices using finger tap gestures.

2   Related Works

The following are the studies that assume the operation of information devices by gestures while performing physical activities at the same time, and studies that examine false detection of gestures when performing various behaviors in daily life. Norieda et al. [1] proposed a gesture of tapping the arm with the other hand. Murao et al. [2] proposed a method for recognizing seven types of gestures (chop, throw, punch, draw a clockwise circle, draw a counterclockwise circle, jump, kick). Yoon et al. [3] proposed a method for recognizing gestures such as finger touch and swipe using a thin device attached to the index finger. However, we have shown that false detection can happen by jogging or finger flexion. Kawahata et al. [4] and Kerber et al. [5] investigated combinations of arm-based gestures that are less likely to cause false detection in activities of daily living. However, they have not made any proposals on how to recognize gestures. Yamamoto et al. [6] proposed a foot gesture that can be performed while jogging.

The following studies proposed gestures using only finger movements. Kubo et al. [7] proposed a method for recognizing 20 types of gestures, such as the posture that the finger is in contact with each other, by implementing piezo elements on the back of the hand. Chan et al. [8] proposed a method for recognizing gestures, such as the posture that the fingers are contacted with each other, by placing a fisheye lens on the hand. Saponas et al. [9] proposed a method for recognizing the state in which a force is applied

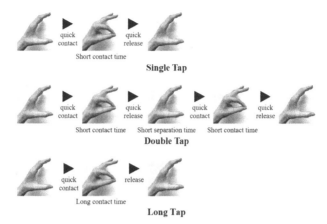

Fig. 1. Description of each gesture

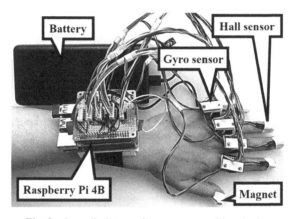

Fig. 2. Overall picture of gesture recognition device

Table 1. The state of satisfaction with conditions in related works

✓: meet the condition   −: unverified   empty field: do not meet the condition

Related works	<1> switching	<2> compact	<3> gaze	<4> walk/jog	<5> classifier
Norida et al. [1]	✓		✓	✓	
Murao et al. [2]	✓		✓	✓	
Yoon et al. [3]		✓	✓		✓
Kawahata et al. [4]	✓		✓	−	
Kerber et al. [5]	✓		✓		
Yamamoto et al. [6]	✓		✓	✓	
Kubo et al. [7]		✓		−	
Chan et al. [8]		✓	−	−	✓
Saponas et al. [9]		✓	−	−	
Zhang et al. [10]		✓	−	−	
Zhang et al. [11]		✓	−	−	
Dementyev et al. [12]		✓	−	−	
Nakamura et al. [13]		✓	✓	−	

to a finger by measuring the electromyogram of the forearm. Zhang et al. [10] proposed a method for recognizing gestures such as the posture in which fingers are in contact with each other and American Sign Language numbers by placing a transducer on the thumb and a microphone on the thumb and wrist. Zhang et al. [11] proposed a method in which a microphone and an inertial sensor are attached to the thumb to recognize the action of rubbing another finger with the thumb. Dementyev et al. [12] proposed a method of recognizing the posture in which the fingers are in contact with each other and the posture in which the palm is kept strongly spread by wrapping a band with a large number of pressure sensors around the wrist. Nakamura et al. [13] proposed a method of recognizing the gesture of tapping each segment of a finger other than the thumb with another finger by attaching an accelerometer to the base of each finger. Table 1 summarizes the condition satisfaction status from <1> to <5> mentioned in Sect. 1 regarding the studies mentioned in this chapter. From Table 1, there is no study that proposes gestures that satisfy all the conditions from <1> to <5> mentioned in Sect. 1 and can be used in all three situations mentioned in Sect. 1.

3 Finger Tap Gesture

3.1 The Types of Finger Tap Gesture

There are three types of finger tap gestures: single tap, double tap, and long tap (Fig. 1). Single tap is a gesture that performs the following three actions consecutively only once as the following processes:

1. Quickly bring the end segment of thumb and the end segment of another finger into contact with each other,
2. The time from contact to release is short,
3. Quickly release the fingers.

Double tap is a gesture of performing single tap twice consecutively.

Long tap is a gesture that performs the following three actions consecutively only once as following processes:

1. Quickly bring the end segment of thumb and the end segment of another finger into contact with each other.
2. Keep a long time from contact to release.
3. Release the fingers.

3.2 Sensors Used for Finger Tap Gesture Recognition

Linear output hall sensors (A1324LUA-T, hereafter hall sensor), a neodymium magnet (magnetic flux density 4200 mT, hereafter magnet), and gyro sensors (MPU9250) are used to recognize gestures. The hall sensor used in this paper has an output voltage of 2.5 V when the magnet is not nearby, and the output voltage increases as the magnet approaches (maximum 5 V). Measurement of sensor data and gesture recognition processing are performed by Raspberry Pi 4B.

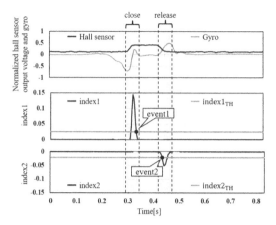

Fig. 3. Relationship between hall sensor output voltage, gyro, index1 and index2

The hall sensor is attached on the fingernail except the thumb, and the magnet is placed on the fingernail of the thumb. The gyro sensors are attached at base of the finger except the thumb (Fig. 2). The hall sensors measure the closeness of the thumb and other fingers, and the gyro sensors measure the speed of the finger. By attaching each sensor and magnet to the back side of the hand as shown in Fig. 2, it is not necessary to cover the palm side of the end segment, which is the most important when handling an object with the fingers.

3.3 Recognition Method of Finger Tap Gesture

We define index1 (Eq. (3)) and index2 (Eq. (4)) to recognize finger tap gestures. The value of index1 changes greatly when the end segment of thumb and the end segment of other fingers are quickly brought into contact with each other. The value of index 2 changes greatly when fingers are quickly separated from each other.

$$Ne(x) = \begin{cases} 1 & \text{if } x < 0 \\ 0 & \text{if } x \geq 0 \end{cases} \tag{1}$$

$$Po(x) = \begin{cases} 1 & \text{if } x > 0 \\ 0 & \text{if } x \leq 0 \end{cases} \tag{2}$$

$$index1_t = \max\left(H_{MA,t} - H_{MA,t-5}, 0\right)\max\left(\Omega_{MA,t} - \Omega_{MA,t-5}, 0\right)Ne\left(\Omega_{MA,t-5}\right) \tag{3}$$

$$index2_t = \max\left(H_{MA,t} - H_{MA,t-5}, 0\right)\max\left(\Omega_{MA,t} - \Omega_{MA,t-5}, 0\right)Po\left(\Omega_{MA,t}\right) \tag{4}$$

Equation (1) is a function that becomes 1 when the argument value is negative and 0 when the argument value is non-negative. Equation (2) is 1 when the argument value is positive and 0 when the argument value is non-positive.

In Eqs. (3) and (4), H_{MA} is the moving average among 5 times of the normalized hall sensor output voltage. We normalize the hall sensor value [2.4 V, 3.0 V] to [0, 1] because the hall sensor output voltage value in being tapped by a man with a thick finger was about 2.6 [V], while the one in being tapped by a woman with a thin finger was about 2.9 [V]. Ω_{MA} is a moving average among 5 times of the normalized gyro sensor values. We normalized the gyro sensor values $[-2000$ [°/s], 2000 [°/s]] to $[-1, 1]$ because the range of the gyro sensor used in this paper was the minimum value -2000 [°/s] and the maximum value 2000 [°/s]. t represents the sampling time.

When the thumb and another finger quickly is bringing closer, the slope of both the hall sensor output voltage value and the gyro become positive (Fig. 3, upper row), and index1 takes a positive value with a large absolute value (Fig. 3, middle row). When the thumb and another finger quickly released, the slope of the hall sensor output voltage value becomes negative and the slope of the gyro becomes positive (Fig. 3, upper row), and index2 takes a negative value with a large absolute value (Fig. 3, middle row).

We explain how to recognize the three gestures of single tap, double tap, and long tap on each finger using index1 and index2. We define two events; first event (event1) occurs when the fingers are brought into contact with each other quickly, second event (event2) occurs when the fingers are quickly separated from each other (Fig. 3).

Event1 is an event that occurs when all following three conditions are fulfilled. Index1$_{TH}$ represents the threshold value for index1 and index2$_{TH}$ represents the threshold value for index2.

- $\text{index1}_{t-1} \geq \text{index1}_{TH}$
- $\text{index1}_t < \text{index1}_{TH}$
- The maximum value of index1 in the past 0.17 s of the event target finger is the largest of other fingers.

Event2 is an event that occurs when all of the following two conditions are satisfied.

- $\text{index2}_{t-1} \geq \text{index2}_{TH}$
- $\text{index2}_t < \text{index2}_{TH}$

Event1 is an event that occurs when index1 falls below index1$_{TH}$, and event2 is an event that occurs when index2 falls below index2$_{TH}$. The third condition of event1 was set to avoid gesture recognition on unintended fingers.

Then, single tap, double tap, and long tap are defined as follows using event1 and event2.

- Single tap recognition occurs when event2 occurs less than 0.3 s after event1 occurs and event1 does not occur within 0.3 s after event2 occurs.
- Double tap recognition occurs when event2 occurs less than 0.3 s after event1, event1 occurs less than 0.3 s after event2 occurs, and event2 occurs less than 0.3 s after event1 occurs.
- Long tap starts when the hall sensor output voltage exceeds 2.51 [V] for 0.5 consecutive seconds after event1 occurs, and long tap ends when the hall sensor output voltage becomes 2.51 [V] or less.

3.4   Effectiveness Verification Experiment of Finger Tap Gesture Recognition Method

Prior to the experiment, index1$_{TH}$ and index2$_{TH}$ were set as follows: index1$_{TH}$ was set to a value slightly higher than the maximum value of index1 when the page turning operation.

- Pinch one sheet of A4 size paper with fingers so as to be easy to pick up
- Separate the picked papers and the unpicked papers as quickly as possible

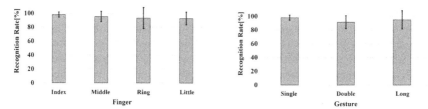

Fig. 4. Recognition rate for each finger   **Fig. 5.** Recognition rate for each gesture

Table 2. Recognition rate of gesture in related works

Related Works	Recognition Rate
Kubo et al.[7]	Entire: 84.4%
Chan et al.[8]	Entire: 84.75%
Saponas et al.[9]	Pinch state: 79% Travel mug gripping state: 85% Weight bag gripping state: 88%
Zhang et al.[10]	State of touching each phalanges: 93.77% American sign language: 95.64%
Zhang et al.[11]	Entire: 89%
Dementyav et al.[12]	Realtime recognition condition: 80.5%
Nakamura et al.[13]	Finger visible condition: 96.2% Finger invisible condition: 95.0%

We considered the page turning operation is the most similar to the finger tap gesture in activities of daily living. Index2$_{TH}$ was set to a value slightly higher than the minimum value of index2 when the finger was tapped quickly. In order to set each threshold, we collected data from two participants (participant 1: 25 years old male, participant 2: 54 years old female). The sampling frequency was set to 300 Hz. As a result of data collection, index1$_{TH}$ was set to 0.025 and index2$_{TH}$ was set to −0.008.

Two verifications were performed using the finger tap gesture recognition method described in Sect. 3.3. First, we verified whether false detections occurred during activities of daily life, and the second, we verified the recognition rate in performing gestures. The number of participants in the experiment was eight (6 male and 2 female).

As a result of the first verification, no false detections occurred even if the page turning motion and the pinch motion, which are activities of daily life similar to the finger tap gesture, were performed. Therefore, it can be said that it is a robust recognition method in daily life.

The explanation and results of the second verification are shown below. Assuming use while walking or jogging, we asked each participant to perform each gesture 30 times in each finger while walking on a spot without looking at the fingers. In addition, we also asked each participant to report whether gesture they subjectively feel failed or not. The average recognition rate for all fingers and gestures was 94.83% (SD: 10.01%). The average recognition rate for each finger is 98.06% (SD: 3.72%) for the index finger, 95.41% (SD: 7.44%) for the middle finger, 93.21% (SD: 15.08%) for the ring finger, and 92.63% (SD: 9.29%) for the little finger (Fig. 4). The average recognition rate for each gesture was 98.13% (SD: 3.78%) for single tap, 91.36% (SD: 9.54%) for double tap, and 95.00% (SD: 13.47%) for long tap (Fig. 5). Table 2 shows the recognition rate of finger gesture mentioned in Sect. 2.2. From Table 2, it can be said that the recognition rate of the finger tap gesture recognition method proposed by us is the highest level among finger gestures.

Though the recognition rate was high, two problems were shown. One is false recognition when user tried a double tap, a single tap was recognized by system (72 out of 957). The other is that there can be a difference between the subjective feelings of success or failure of a gesture and the actual success or failure of a gesture. For example, the user feels that the gesture is successful, but the system does not recognize it as the successful gesture. Of the total of 2866 trials of all experimental participants, the number of miss gestures judged by system was 149 times, and the number of miss gestures judged by the participants subjective feelings was 19 times. Of the 19 miss gestures that the participants judged subjectively, the number of miss gestures that the system judged was 7.

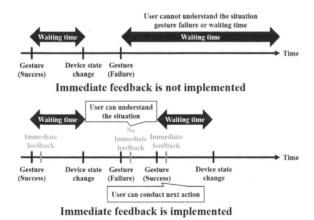

Fig. 6. The effect of immediate feedback

4 Giving Immediate Feedback

4.1 Problems and Their Improvement Plan

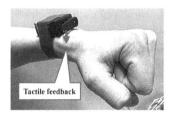

Fig. 7. State when the servomotor is installed

As we showed above, the gesture may be recognized different from the intended gesture, and that there may be a difference between the subjective feelings of success or failure of the gesture and the actual success or failure of the gesture. This problem becomes more serious when there is a time lag from the successful gesture to the change in the state of the information device. This time lag must occur the case such as amount of calculation of the information device are required and the Internet connection is unstable. When there is a time lag, the user cannot judge the success of the gesture and cannot accurately grasp the status of the information device (Fig. 6, top). Therefore, by giving feedback that represents only what type of gesture (hereinafter, immediate feedback) the system recognizes, the user must instantly and accurately grasp the state of the information device and take appropriate actions according to the state of information device (Fig. 6, bottom).

4.2 The Types of Immediate Feedback

We prepared two types of immediate feedback, sound feedback and tactile feedback.

Sound feedback uses earphones to present the user with the sound according to the types of gesture. A click sound is presented once when a single tap is successful, a click sound is presented twice when a double tap is successful, and a buzzer sound is presented when a long tap is successful.

Tactile feedback uses a servomotor (MG996R) to present the upper side of the user's wrist with tactile sensation according to the types of gesture (Fig. 7). A tactile sensation is presented once when a single tap is successful, a tactile sensation is presented twice when a double tap is successful, and the tactile presentation is continued for a certain period of times when a long tap is successful.

5 Experiment to Evaluate the Effect of Immediate Feedback

5.1 Procedure

Figure 8 shows the experimental procedure.

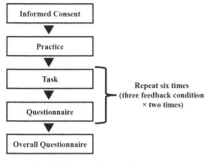

Fig. 8. Experimental procedure

Table 3. Relationship between gestures and functions

Finger	Gesture	Function
Index	Single Tap	Play / Stop
	Double Tap	15 second fast forward
	Long Tap	Next song
Middle	Double Tap	15 second rewind
	Long Tap	Previous song
Ring	Single Tap	Volume up
Little	Single Tap	Volume down

The phase of informed consent, we explained each participant the contents of the experiment based on the ethical guidelines for ergonomics research for humans [14] and obtained their consent.

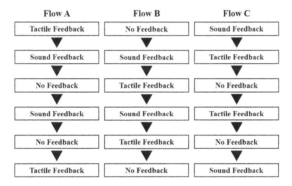

Fig. 9. Task flow

In the phase of training, we attached the experimental device to each participant and asked him/her to operate the virtual music player with gestures to get the knack of the gestures and to learn how to operate the music player (Table 3).

In the phase of task, assuming the operation of a music player, we asked each participant to perform the tasks under three feedback conditions (tactile feedback/sound feedback/no immediate feedback) twice. In order to remove the order effect, we prepared 3 order patterns as shown in Fig. 9 and asked each participant to perform one of the 3 patterns. A total of 26 operations (play and stop were performed 4 times each, and other operations were performed 3 times at random) were conducted for each task. In addition, we instructed each participant not to gaze the finger in performing the gesture and there were no visual feedback of the music player status.

In the phase of questionnaire, after each task, we asked each participant to answer the question of "Do you want to use it in your daily life?" in 5 stages.

In the phase of overall questionnaire, we asked each participant to answer the questions of "The condition that is the easiest to use", "The condition that is the most difficult to use" and "Which is better, the condition with immediate feedback or the condition without immediate feedback?".

16 participants were involved in the experiment (10 males and 6 females).

5.2   Experiment System

Figure 10 shows the overall picture of the experimental system. We used two RaspberryPi 4B, one for virtual music player (device1) and the other for gesture recognition and immediate feedback presentation (device2). The user performs a gesture, and device2 performs the gesture recognition process by the method described in Sect. 3.3. When gesture is recognized as a success, device2 sends a function command corresponding to the gesture to device1 by socket communication and presents immediate feedback to the user. When device1 receives an operation command from device2, it performs the function corresponding to the gesture after time lag (minimum 0.1 s, maximum 2 s, generated in uniform random). The lag time was implemented to mimic the situation where the two problems of the finger tap gesture may become serious mentioned in Sect. 3.4.

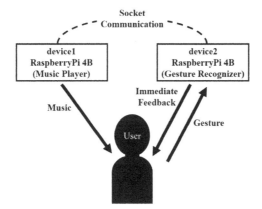

Fig. 10. Experimental system

5.3   Various Settings

The sampling frequency in device2 was set to 100 Hz. While the sampling frequency is different from that in the experiment described in Sect. 3.4, the values of $index1_{TH}$ and $index2_{TH}$ are the same as in Sect. 3.4 ($index1_{TH} = 0.025$, $index2_{TH} = -0.008$). No false detections occurred even when the high-speed page turning operation was performed, and each gesture was performed several times, but almost no false recognition occurred.

6 Results

6.1 Time Required Per Operation

The time for each operation was calculated to objectively evaluate whether each partic-ipant can operate the information device smoothly by finger tap gesture. It can be said that the shorter the time required for each operation is, the smoother the operation of the information device is. We standardized the value of the time in each operation of each participant and each gesture, because the time required for each operation differs depend-ing on each participant and the time required for the next operation differs depending on the type of gesture. Hereinafter, the standardized value is defined as "time required per operation". In calculating the time required for each operation, we removed the waiting time from the time when device1 receives the function command to the time when the function corresponding to the gesture is performed. In addition, by comparing the video recorded in the experiment with the operation log measured during the experiment, we classified into two groups: one is the operation which is performed after the user judged that the operation is incorrect (hereinafter, after error), the other is ne is the operation which is performed after the user judged that the operation is correct (hereinafter, after non-error).

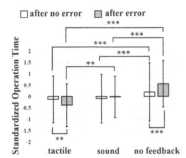

Fig. 11. The time required for each operation

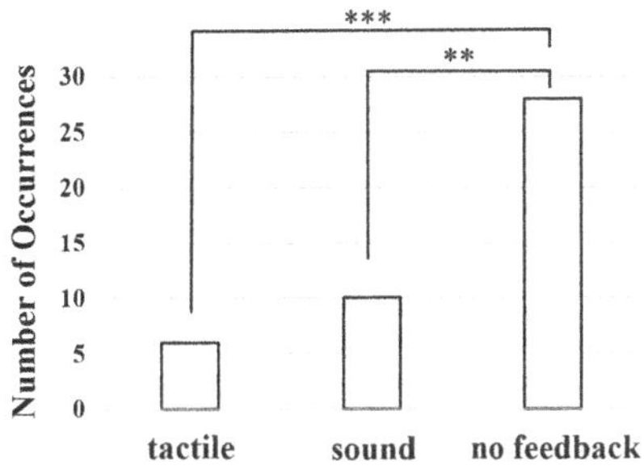

Fig. 12. The number of misunderstandings as success

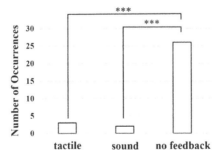

Fig. 13. The number of misunderstandings as failure

A between-subject two-way ANOVA was performed for the time required for each operation. The factors were feedback condition factors (3 levels: tactile feedback condition/sound feedback condition/no immediate feedback condition) and pre-operation factors (2 levels: after non-error/after error). The significance level was set to 5%.

Figure 11 shows the results of the ANOVA. As the result of ANOVA, an interaction between the two factors was observed ($p < 0.001$), a simple main effect test was performed. As the result of a simple main effect test for each level of the feedback condition factor, under tactile feedback condition, the time required for each operation is significantly shorter after error than after non-error ($p < 0.01$) and under no immediate feedback conditions, the time required per operation was significantly longer after error than after non-error ($p < 0.001$). As the result of a simple main effect test for each level of pre-operation factor, a simple main effect was observed both after non-error ($p < 0.001$) and after error ($p < 0.001$), so we conducted multiple comparisons by the Holm method. As a result of multiple comparisons after non-error, the time required for each operation of tactile feedback condition ($p < 0.001$) and sound feedback condition ($p < 0.001$) were significantly shorter than the condition no immediate feedback, respectively. As a result of multiple comparisons after the error, the time required for each operation of tactile feedback condition ($p < 0.001$) and sound feedback condition ($p < 0.001$) were significantly shorter than no immediate feedback condition. Furthermore, the time required for each operation of tactile feedback condition was significantly shorter than sound feedback condition ($p < 0.01$).

From the above results, it can be said that user can operate information device smoothly by giving immediate feedback immediately after a successful gesture in a situation where there is a waiting time. Furthermore, it can be said that by giving tactile feedback, user can deal with the operation error more quickly.

6.2 The Number of Times the User Could not Accurately Grasp the Status of the Information Device

We verified whether immediate feedback can suppress the errors that the user cannot accurately grasp the state of the information device.

We divided into the two types of the errors referring to the recorded video of experiment and the operation log measured during the experiment. One is the number of times that the users judged the operation was completed and moved on to the next operation despite correct operation was not completed (hereinafter, misunderstanding as success). The other is the number of times that the users judged the operation was not completed and performed the same operation again despite the correct operation was completed (hereinafter, misunderstanding as failure).

A chi-square test was performed to investigate whether there was a difference between each feedback condition regarding the number of misunderstandings as success (Fig. 12). As the result of a chi-square test and multiple comparisons by the Holm method, misunderstandings as success of tactile feedback condition ($p < 0.001$) and sound feedback condition ($p < 0.01$) were significantly less than no immediate feedback condition.

A chi-square test was performed to investigate whether there was a difference between each feedback condition regarding the number of misunderstandings as failure (Fig. 13). As the result of a chi-square test and multiple comparisons by the Holm method, misunderstandings as failure of tactile feedback condition ($p < 0.001$) and sound feedback condition ($p < 0.001$) were significantly less than no immediate feedback condition.

From the above results, it can be said that giving immediate feedback has the effect of suppressing the performance that the user cannot accurately grasp the state of the information device.

6.3 Results of Subjective Evaluations

In the experiment, each participant performed each feedback condition twice and the participant were asked the questionnaire "Do you want to use it in your daily life?" for each trial. The average value of the first and second answers for each feedback condition was used for the analysis. We performed a within-subject one-way ANOVA to investigate whether there is a difference for each feedback condition in the results of the questionnaire. The factor was feedback condition factor (3 levels: tactile feedback condition/sound feedback condition/no immediate feedback condition).

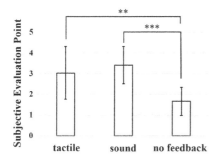 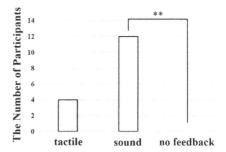

Fig. 14. Result of questionnaire item "Do you want to use it in your daily life?"

Fig. 15. Result of questionnaire item "The condition that is the easiest to use"

Figure 14 shows the results of the ANOVA. Since the main effect was observed ($p < 0.001$), multiple comparisons were performed by the Holm method. The point of tactile feedback condition ($p < 0.01$) and sound feedback condition ($p < 0.001$) were significantly higher than the immediate feedback condition. However, no significant difference was found between tactile feedback condition and the sound feedback condition (Fig. 15).

We conducted a chi-square test to investigate whether there are any differences between the feedback conditions regarding the response results of the "which is the easiest to use?" that were answered at the end of the experimental procedure. As a result of a chi-square test and multiple comparisons by the Holm method, the number of participants that prefer sound feedback conditions were significantly more than the no immediate feedback condition ($p < 0.01$), but no significant difference was observed between the other conditions.

At the end of the experiment procedure, we asked the participants "which is the most difficult to use?". In this question, all the participants answered that "No immediate feedback condition is the most difficult to use". Furthermore, for the question "Which is better, the condition with immediate feedback or the condition without immediate feedback?", The responses of 15 out of 16 participants were that "The condition with immediate feedback is better" and the remaining 1 responded that "Either is fine".

From the above results, it was found that the subjective comfort is improved by giving immediate feedback. In addition, many experimental participants answered that sound feedback was preferable to tactile feedback, but it can be said that there is no big difference.

7   Discussion

7.1   Discussion of Operational Performance

We found that giving the immediate feedback allows the users to reduce the operation time. It is considered that the reason is the user can predict the state of the change before the state change of the information device actually occurs and can prepare for the next operation in advance.

In addition, only the tactile feedback condition was found to shorten the time for the operation after the error. In the experiment, the time lag was set from 0.1 s to 2.0 s, but in the actual situation, the time lag is often longer. In such situations, the tactile feedback condition is the most effective feedback method.

It was found that the immediate feedback suppresses the error that the user cannot accurately grasp the state of the information device. Therefore, even when it is difficult for the user to determine the state change of the information device, it is possible to support the user to accurately grasp the state of the information device by giving immediate feedback. Since the experiment is conducted being supposed the operation of a music player, it was easy for the user to judge the state change of the information device. On the other hand, it should be difficult for the user to judge the change of state in the menu selection operation supposing the situation where the smartwatch or the smartphone is operated without visual information. In such a situation, it can be said that giving immediate feedback makes it easier for the user to grasp the state of the information device and the users can operate comfortably.

7.2   Discussion on Subjective Evaluation

The tactile feedback condition shows the highest in the operation performance, while the sound feedback condition tended to be high in the subjective evaluation. We are considering that the device that gives tactile feedback causes the discrepancy between operational performance and subjective evaluation. The servomotor used in the experiment is relatively large and heavy (Fig. 7). This may have hindered the user's comfort. Therefore, tactile feedback can be excellent in both operation performance and subjective evaluation by reducing the size and weight of the device that presents tactile feedback and devising the mounted position.

8 Conclusion

In this paper, we proposed a robust finger tap gesture recognition method that fulfill all above five conditions and examined the feedback function in operating information devices using finger tap gestures. A finger tap gesture recognition method using hall sensors and gyro sensors achieved a high recognition rate without causing false detection. However, when operating information devices with finger tap gestures, there are the following two problems: one is that it is recognized as a gesture different from the intended gesture, and the other is that the user's subjective gesture success or failure differs from the actual gesture success or failure. To address the above problems, we have added a function to present user with immediate feedback according to the type of gesture immediately after the successful gesture. Tactile feedback and auditory feedback were prepared as the types of immediate feedback. In the experiment, supposing the operation of a music player, we com-pared the three conditions of tactile feedback condition, sound feedback condition and no immediate feedback condition. As the result, it was found that by giving the immediate feedback, the user can properly grasp the state of the information device and quickly perform appropriate operations. Furthermore, when comparing tactile feedback and auditory feedback, the operational performance becomes higher for tactile feedback, and the subjective evaluation becomes higher for sound feedback. By reducing the size and weight of the device that presents tactile feedback and devising the mounting position, it should be able to be an excellent immediate feedback method in terms of both operational performance and subjective evaluation. Since the occurrence of misrecognition is a common problem in operating information device by gesture, the results of this paper will be able to be applied not only to finger tap gesture but also to operating information device by other gestures.

References

1. Norieda, S., Mitsuhashi, H., Sato, M.: ArmKeypad: a new input interface by tapping on user's arm. Trans. Hum. Interface Soc. **13**(4), 315–322 (2011)
2. Murao, K., Terada, T.: A motion recognition method by constancy decision. IPSJ J. **52**(6), 1968–1979 (2011)
3. Yoon, S., Huo, K., Ramani, K.: Wearable textile input device with multimodal sensing for eyes-free mobile interaction during daily activities. Pervasive Mob. Comput. **33**, 17–31 (2016)
4. Kawahata, R., Shimada, A., Yamashita, T., Uchiyama, H., Taniguchi, R.: Design of a low-false-positive gesture for a wearable device. In: International Conference on Pattern Recognition Applications and Methods, pp. 581–588 (2016)
5. Kerber, F., Schardt, P., Löchtefeld, M.: WristRotate - a personalized motion gesture delimiter for wrist-worn devices. In: The 14th International Conference on Mobile and Ubiquitous Multimedia, pp. 218–222 (2015)
6. Yamamoto, T., Terada, T., Tsukamoto, M., Yoshihisa, T.: A FootStep input method for operating information devices while jogging. IPSJ J. **50**(12), 2881–2888 (2009)
7. Kubo, Y., Koguchi, Y., Shizuki, B., Takahashi, S., Hilliges, O.: AudioTouch: minimally invasive sensing of micro-gestures via active bio-acoustic sensing. In: Proceedings of the 21st International Conference on Human-Computer Interaction with Mobile Devices and Services, no. 36, pp. 1–13 (2019)

8. Chan, L., Chen, Y., Hsieh, C., Liang, R., Chen, B.: CyclopsRing: enabling whole-hand and context-aware interactions through a fisheye ring. In: Proceedings of the 28th Annual ACM Symposium on User Interface Software & Technology, pp. 549–556 (2015)
9. Saponas, T., Tan, D., Morris, D., Balakrishnan, R., Turner, J., Landay, J.: Proceedings of the 22nd Annual ACM Symposium on User Interface Software and Technology, pp. 167–176 (2009)
10. Zhang, C., et al.: FingerPing: recognizing fine-grained hand poses using active acoustic on-body sensing. In: Proceedings of the 2018 CHI Conference on Human Factors in Computing Systems, no. 437, pp. 1–10 (2018)
11. Zhang, C., et al.: FingOrbits: interaction with wearables using synchronized thumb movements. In: Proceedings of the 2017 ACM International Symposium on Wearable Computers, pp. 62–65 (2017)
12. Dementyev, A., Paradiso, J.: WristFlex: low-power gesture input with wrist-worn pressure sensors. In: Proceedings of the 27th Annual ACM Symposium on User Interface Software and Technology, pp. 161–166 (2014)
13. Nakamura, Y., Sakai, T., Yazaki, K.: PhKey: an input interface for wearable devices using phalanges as keys. IPSJ J. **62**(2), 701–712 (2020)
14. Japan Human Factors and Ergonomics Society: The ethical guidelines for ergonomics research (2009)

Effectiveness of Diverse Evidence for Developing Convincing Proofs with Crowdsourcing

Nadeesha Wijerathna, Masaki Matsubara$^{(\boxtimes)}$ ⓘ, and Atsuyuki Morishima$^{(\boxtimes)}$ ⓘ

University of Tsukuba, Kasuga 1-2, Tsukuba, Ibaraki, Japan
nadeesha.wijerathna.2017m@mlab.info, masaki@slis.tsukuba.ac.jp,
morishima-office@ml.cc.tsukuba.ac.jp

Abstract. Crowdsourcing techniques have been developed over the past decade to leverage the 'wisdom of crowds' to solve real-world problems and human intelligence tasks. An example of such a task is fact-checking, that asks workers to check whether the shown claim is true or not. Fact-checking tasks are used in many applications such as services to identify fake news. This context motivates us to investigate a crowdsourcing-based framework to find convincing proofs for fact-checking. This study investigates a good crowdsourcing strategy to obtain convincing proofs with evidence. We focus on an iterative workflow in which workers improve the proofs provided by other crowd workers. In this study, we show the results of our experiment, in which we compare the results of two conditions, by which we see the effects of the diversification of shown evidence and proofs. The experimental results with real-world workers show that showing diverse evidence and proofs to crowd workers in the iterative workflow helps them develop more convincing proofs.

Keywords: Crowdsourcing · Diverse evidence · Fact check

1 Introduction

Humans often have the power to improve results considerably compared to computers. Although computer systems have made substantial progress in the past several decades, in many areas, computers have not been able to match the creativity, flexibility, and complexity of human intelligence [8]. Therefore, many attempts to involve humans in crowdsourcing techniques have also been developed to leverage the 'wisdom of crowds' to solve real-world problems and human intelligence tasks, such as verifying natural disasters [11], generating conference programs [9], image tagging for subjective topics [20, 21], understanding topics in microblogs [3], finding approaches to collect data and understanding human health [1, 15], and finding evidence for proof under challenging problems [18].

Fact-checking is one of such tasks that require human intelligence. The explosive growth of information techniques and the internet has made the world a

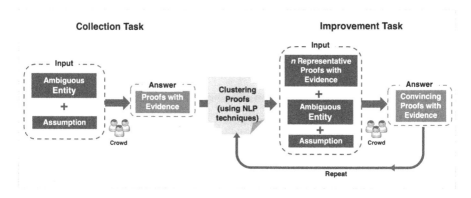

Fig. 1. In this crowd-based workflow, we focus on two phases. First, in the collection task (left), we ask crowd workers to give possible proofs with evidence supporting the shared assumption of an ambiguous entity. Then we cluster the collected answers using different clustering methods (middle) and show n representative proofs evidence for improvement task. In the improvement task, we focus on an iterative workflow in which workers improve the proofs given by other crowd workers and provide convincing proofs with evidence (right).

more connected place than ever before. Digital 2021: Global Digital Overview[1] reports that 59.5% of the world's population already uses the Internet. One consequence is that a large amount of fake information is generated and shared extensively by Internet users. In 2019 the PHYS.ORG[2] conducted a survey with more than 25,000 Internet users in 25 counties and found that 86% of Internet users admitted to being duped by fake information.

The purpose of this study is to find a good crowdsourcing strategy to obtain convincing proofs with evidence for fact-checking. In particular, we focus on an iterative workflow in which workers improve the proofs provided by other crowd workers (see Fig. 1). In each task, some of the proofs by other crowd workers are shown, and we ask another worker to integrate and devise a more convincing proof. Then, a natural question arises. Which proofs should be shown in the task?

Our research question is: What is a good strategy for choosing proofs to be shown in the task? We hypothesize that workers outputs will be more convincing when a set of diverse evidence are selected and shown in the improvement task. We expect that the diverse set will give many different perspectives and provide different paths for the proof based on different evidence. In this paper, we show the results of our experiments in which we compare the results of two conditions, by which we see the effects of the diversification of shown proofs.

The contribution of this paper is as follows. First, we devise an iterative framework to obtain better proofs for fact checking with crowdsourcing. Second,

---

[1] https://datareportal.com/reports/digital-2021-global-overview-report.
[2] https://phys.org/news/2019-06-percent-internet-users-duped-fake.html.

we empirically show that showing a set of diverse evidence help crowd workers to develop more convincing proofs.

2   Related Work

2.1   Crowdsourcing Approaches for Intelligent Tasks

The success of crowdsourcing techniques and the sprawl of crowdsourcing during the past decade has made many attempts to involve humans in crowdsourcing research to exploit human computational capabilities to solve real-world problems and intelligent tasks [1,3,8,9,15,18,20,21]. Hence, it is clear that crowdsourcing is a promising tool, involving multiple people to search for accurate information, providing a solution for real-world problems, and performing difficult tasks such as finding evidence. Crowdsourcing is defined in this study as an approach to solving difficult problems by an individual, a small team, or a computer. Improving the quality of the results is the main focus area in crowdsourcing, and numerous studies have addressed this issue [2,17]. Some major approaches involve assigning the same task to multiple workers and obtaining the results. Another approach consists of deriving the results from self-corrected individuals [9,14]. In this study, we assigned the same task to multiple workers, aggregated possible evidence and proofs, and improved the given set of answers to support the given assumption.

2.2   Approaches for the Fact Check and Verification

There have been efforts to develop websites and web services to detect fake news and information over the last few years. Many of them check the facts related to the political news. There are two ways to summarize the approach of most of these sites and services. First, they make a reference statement or the claim based on some incidents, and then ask web users to measure degrees of truth or false and publish the results. The second approach is that some services investigate the facts by their team collecting some evidence and publishing generally accurate facts. In addition, few services follow both methods together, in either way.

On the other hand, several approaches have addressed the problem of using the power of crowds for the fact checks in academia, such as developing web or mobile applications to collect user comments to verify the information [11, 13]. In contrast to our approach, these applications asked workers to submit a particular type of evidence, such as uploading photos of the event or analyzing user comments. Recently, efforts have also been made to integrate some AI and NLP techniques to check and identify the reference statements to review and understand the content of the reference statements [4–7,10,16,19]. In contrast, we tried to develop a framework for finding proofs with evidence to the facts of ambiguity and the effectiveness of crowdsourcing workflows that we can use human intelligence on that workflow.

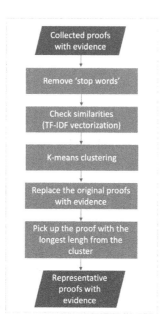

Fig. 2. The process of choosing proofs with diverse evidence for the improvement task.

3   Workflow Design

Workflows have been adopted as a dominant crowdsourcing infrastructure in the field of crowdsourcing today [12]. This section focuses on the workflow design of the study and describes the experiment's configuration of two tasks. As shown in Fig. 1, our workflow consists of two tasks, namely proof collection tasks and improvement tasks. We use the collection tasks to obtain initial set of proofs and then use the improvement tasks to revise them. We do not assume any particular termination condition of the iteration here. We can stop after a fixed number of iterations are done, or we find convincing proofs. We discuss this in our future work.

3.1   Collection Tasks

The collection tasks are used to collect initial set of proofs with evidence for an assumption. The assumption is given in the task as a statement that may be true or false. For example, *"this scenery photo was taken in the morning"*, associated with the photo, is an assumption. The workers enter potential proofs with evidence. To make the workers understand the task instruction clearly, we provide instructions with an example of a task and an answer. All the proofs obtained in the collection task will be supplied to the improvement task.

3.2 Improvement Tasks

The improvement task show some of the obtained proofs and ask workers to integrate them and other evidence in order to develop a more convincing proof. To make workers understand the task instruction clearly, we also provide some examples for the answers along with the instruction of the improvement task.

A problem here is how to choose the shown proofs. Since the space for the task instruction is limited, we need to choose a small number of proofs to be shown to workers. There are many potential ways to do this. For example, we can just randomly choose the fixed number of existing proofs.

Our hypothesis in this paper is that diversity of the shown proofs is effective for devising more convincing proofs. Here we give a procedure to choose a diverse set of proofs from the original set of obtained proofs.

Choosing a diverse set of proofs (Fig. 2**).** First We remove the stop words from the collected proofs and checked their similarities using TF-IDF vectorization. Next, we use the K-means algorithm to cluster them. Then we select the proof descriptions with the longest length from each cluster. This is based on the following assumptions: a) longer proofs are better than the shorter proofs in the same cluster, and b) the different clusters have different advantages than those in the other clusters.

4 Experiment and Results

We examined the effectiveness of showing a set of diverse evidence to develop convincing proofs in the improvement task in our crowdsourcing workflow. In the improvement task, we set the two conditions a) diverse set of evidence, and b) random set of evidence. We compared the workers outcome to verify whether showing diverse evidence affect finding more convincing proofs. Therefore, our experiment focuses on the improvement task and we just used the results of the collection tasks we collected in the past experiment [18].

We published the tasks via a crowdsourcing platform, Amazon Mechanical Turk (AMT)[3]. Since the AMT uses English, English was used to describe the tasks. Afterward, we asked any worker who was interested in published tasks to submit an answer. Finally, we approved the answers and granted them rewards.

4.1 Collection Task

Procedure. For collection task, we selected a scenery image of Mt. Tsukuba along with a poppy flower field at the Kokaigawa Fureai Park in Japan taken by Katsuyoshi Nakahara[4] which has already been published on the web. Based on the photograph, we built the assumption of *"This photograph is taken in the morning"* because it is unclear whether the photograph was taken in the

---

[3] https://www.mturk.com/.

[4] https://www.katsuyoshinakahara.com/spring/.

Fig. 3. The photograph of Mt. Tsukuba along with Kokaigawa Fureai Park, Japan taken by Katsuyoshi Nakahara (See footnote 4). Based on the photograph, we built the assumption of *"This photograph is taken in the morning"*.

morning or the evening (see Fig. 3). The correct answer is that the photograph is taken in the morning.

The task was available for ten days, and crowd workers were asked to complete the task within two hours. We assigned one-hundred crowd workers with a reward of about 0.30 USD when they completed the task.

The task design consists of three parts: a) Inputs: a photograph as an ambiguous entity and the assumption, b) Instruction field, and c) Submission field. In this task, a worker was to find possible evidence and submit the answers to the submission field as text and URL addresses.

Result. As a result of the collection task, we obtained one-hundred possible proofs, among which 41, 12, and 47 answers were obtained as a text description, only a URL link to the web page, and a text description with a URL link to the web page, respectively. The collected answers demonstrated that the crowdsource-based approach could collect diverse possible proofs to prove this fact, and more than half of the collected ones supported this assumption. In addition, it is not easy to identify the most convincing proof by simply collecting several answers. Detailed results were described in our previous study [18].

4.2   Choosing Proofs with Diverse Evidence

Procedure. To generate the five ($n = 5$) proofs with various evidence to show for the improvement task, we re-organized the collected answers into a diverse set using NLP techniques by using TF-IDF vectorization and the K-means algorithm. Then, we selected the proof descriptions with the longest length from each cluster as representative proofs. There were five clusters, and we assumed that since we have one-hundred pieces of evidence, around five similarities can be found.

Results. The following five proofs with evidence were chosen as a result of the NLP techniques. According to the results, only proof number 2 can be recognized as insufficient but correct proof among the five.

1. *From the following URL[5]. Shirley poppies and Mount Tsukuba at dawn. The scenery made me dream! This photo was taken on May 22, 2015. But, by record heavy rain of September 10, 2015 embankment of Kinugawa is outburst, this park was damaged. However, beautiful flower bloom by the effort of the volunteer group this year in the park. Also, that fog/mist that you see is only going to be evident in the morning hours. The picture shows the dawn time. It sky is showing the sunrise is about to begin. And has beautiful flowers giving the essence of new morning.*
2. *The sun looks like it could be rising as it does in the very early morning. You can see light from the sun, which shows that it could be the morning.*
3. Shirley poppies bloom in a field near Japan's Mount Tsukuba, here silhouetted against an early morning sky. From the following URL[6].
4. *From the following URL[7] "If you shoot after sunrise, when the sun becomes visible from behind Mount Tsukuba, it is possible to capture the fleeting glitter of the morning dew on the petals and stems despite the backlit condition, and also portray the colour tones of the flower petals at their most vivid." The evidence picture is shown from the same angle and location.*
5. *The following[8] is an exact match to the photo shown. You may have to go through the images until you see- "DREAMINESS PHOTO AND CAPTION BY KATSUYOSHI NAKAHARA" "This photo was taken on May 22, 2015.". On the following website [9], you can see that if you outlined the mountain from the sky, the outlines would match up curve by curve for the most part on the highest points.*

---

[5] http://travel.nationalgeographic.com/photographer-of-the-year-2016/gallery/week-6-nature/19/.

[6] https://www.nationalgeographic.com/photography/photo-of-the-day/2015/6/mountain-view-poppies/.

[7] https://snapshot.canon-asia.com/article/en/stunning-summer-landscapes-scenic-spots-in-japan-pro-photography-tips-1.

[8] http://travel.nationalgeographic.com/photographer-of-the-year-2016/gallery/week-6-nature/19/.

[9] https://en.japantravel.com/ibaraki/hiking-up-mt-tsukuba/2653.

Table 1. Definition for the categories of the improvement task

Categories	Definition for the Categories		Example
	Claims in the proof are connected correctly	Sub-claims is given a good evidence in the proof	
Convincing	Yes	Yes	The flower blooms in the morning therefore this picture is taken in the morning. And there is an article (link) to show this flower blooms in the morning
Insufficient evidence	Yes	No	The flower blooms in the morning therefore this picture is taken in the morning
Logically incorrect	No	Yes	The flower blooms in the morning therefore this picture is taken in the evening. And there is an article (link) to show this flower blooms in the morning
Not convincing	No	No	I think this picture is taken in the evening

4.3 Improvement Task

Our experiment intended to see if showing a set of proofs with diverse evidence could provide more complete and convincing proofs. We compared two conditions: one shows the diverse set of proofs, and the other shows the set of randomly chosen proofs for the control group. For both cases, we used the exact task instructions and design.

Procedure. We posted five proofs for the improvement task in each condition. We showed the proof descriptions with the longest length from each cluster for the diverse condition and the five randomly selected proofs for the random condition with the image of an ambiguous scenery and its assumption. As an initial study, in this paper, we conducted one iteration, and review the results of improvement tasks.

The task design consists of four parts: a) Inputs, five representative pieces of evidence, a photograph as an ambiguous entity and the assumption, b) Instruction field, c) Example of the answers with the basic structure of the answer that we expect from the crowd worker, and d) Submission field. In this task, a worker were required to carefully read instructions and the diverse evidence, and submit the answers that obtain convincing and complete proof by improving the given proofs with evidence, such as combining and adding new evidence or doing both.

Table 2. Review results of improvement task

Catergories	Diverse set				Random set			
	RW_1	RW_2	RW_3	RW_4	RW_1	RW_2	RW_3	RW_4
Convincing	**5**	**6**	**5**	**5**	**1**	**2**	**1**	**0**
Insufficient evidence	5	4	7	5	6	10	8	4
Logically incorrect	1	0	1	0	0	1	0	0
Not convincing	9	10	7	10	13	7	11	15

We assigned 20 crowd workers with a reward of about 2.00 USD when they completed the task. The task was available for seven days, and crowd workers were asked to complete the task within half an hour.

After completing the 20 proofs in each condition, we asked four colleagues to review the answers according to the four categories shown in Table 1 and considered their agreement ratio to find the most convincing proof as to the final output of the workflow.

Result. The results of evaluation by reviewers are shown in Table 2. We conducted two-way ANOVA at alpha level 0.05, and interaction effect between two conditions and the categories was observed ($p < .01$). We also conducted t-test as a post-hoc test, and the amount of labeled categories in Diverse set condition was significantly larger than Random set condition ($p < .01$). This indicates that the proofs in the diverse set is more effective than the random set to construct convincing proofs.

5   Conclusion

This study investigated a good crowdsourcing strategy to obtain more convincing proofs with evidence. We empirically confirmed that crowdsourcing could help effectively discover the most convincing proofs when we show a diverse set of evidence to the crowd in an iterative framework. In particular, the framework uses numerous crowds with a lower monetary cost and does not require expertise.

Acknowledgments. This work was partially supported by JST CREST Grant Number JPMJCR16E3, JSPS KAKENHI Grant Number 21H03552, Japan.

References

1. Bevelander, K.E.: Crowdsourcing novel childhood predictors of adult obesity. PLoS ONE **9**(2), e87756 (2014)
2. Daniel, F., Kucherbaev, P., Cappiello, C., Benatallah, B., Allahbakhsh, M.: Quality control in crowdsourcing: a survey of quality attributes, assessment techniques, and assurance actions. ACM Comput. Surv. (CSUR) **51**(1), 1–40 (2018)
3. Ghosh, S., Sharma, N., Benevenuto, F., Ganguly, N., Gummadi, K.: Cognos: crowdsourcing search for topic experts in microblogs. In: Proceedings of the 35th International ACM SIGIR Conference on Research and Development in Information Retrieval, pp. 575–590 (2012)
4. Graves, D.: Understanding the promise and limits of automated fact-checking (2018)
5. Guo, Z., Schlichtkrull, M., Vlachos, A.: A survey on automated fact-checking. arXiv preprint arXiv:2108.11896 (2021)
6. Karadzhov, G., Nakov, P., Màrquez, L., Barrón-Cedeño, A., Koychev, I.: Fully automated fact checking using external sources. arXiv preprint arXiv:1710.00341 (2017)
7. Kim, J., Tabibian, B., Oh, A., Schölkopf, B., Gomez-Rodriguez, M.: Leveraging the crowd to detect and reduce the spread of fake news and misinformation. In: Proceedings of the Eleventh ACM International Conference On Web Search and Data Mining, pp. 324–332 (2018)
8. Kittur, A., et al.: The future of crowd work. In: Proceedings of the 2013 Conference On Computer Supported Cooperative Work, pp. 1301–1318 (2013)
9. Kobayashi, N., Matsubara, M., Tajima, K., Morishima, A.: A crowd-in-the-loop approach for generating conference programs with microtasks. In: 2017 IEEE International Conference on Big Data, Big Data, pp. 4394–4396. IEEE (2017)
10. Nguyen, A.T., et al.: Believe it or not: designing a human-ai partnership for mixed-initiative fact-checking. In: Proceedings of the 31st Annual ACM Symposium on User Interface Software and Technology, pp. 189–199 (2018)
11. Popoola, A., et al.: Information verification during natural disasters. In: Proceedings of the 22nd International Conference on World Wide Web, pp. 1029–1032 (2013)
12. Retelny, D., Bernstein, M.S., Valentine, M.A.: No workflow can ever be enough: how crowdsourcing workflows constrain complex work. In: Proceedings of the ACM on Human-Computer Interaction, CSCW, vol. 1, pp. 1–23 (2017)
13. Sethi, R.J.: Crowdsourcing the verification of fake news and alternative facts. In: Proceedings of the 28th ACM Conference on Hypertext and Social Media, pp. 315–316 (2017)
14. Shah, N., Zhou, D.: No oops, you won't do it again: mechanisms for self-correction in crowdsourcing. In: International Conference On Machine Learning, PMLR, pp. 1–10 (2016)
15. Swan, M., et al.: Crowdsourced health research studies: an important emerging complement to clinical trials in the public health research ecosystem. J. Med. Internet Res. **14**(2), e1988 (2012)
16. Thorne, J., Vlachos, A.: Automated fact checking: Task formulations, methods and future directions. arXiv preprint arXiv:1806.07687 (2018)
17. Venetis, P., Garcia-Molina, H.: Quality control for comparison microtasks. In: Proceedings of the First International Workshop on Crowdsourcing and Data Mining, pp. 15–21 (2012)

18. Wijerathna, N., Matsubara, M., Morishima, A.: Finding evidences by crowdsourcing. In: 2018 IEEE International Conference on Big Data, Big Data, pp. 3560–3563. IEEE (2018)
19. Wu, Y., Agarwal, P.K., Li, C., Yang, J., Yu, C.: Toward computational fact-checking. Proc. VLDB Endowment **7**(7), 589–600 (2014)
20. Yan, T., Kumar, V., Ganesan, D.: Crowdsearch: exploiting crowds for accurate real-time image search on mobile phones. In: Proceedings of the 8th International Conference on Mobile Systems, Applications, and Services, pp. 77–90 (2010)
21. Zhai, Z., Kijewski-Correa, T., Hachen, D., Madey, G.: Haiti earthquake photo tagging: lessons on crowdsourcing in-depth image classifications. In: Seventh International Conference on Digital Information Management, ICDIM 2012, pp. 357–364. IEEE (2012)

Visual Design

The Overheard Text Map: A Voice Communication System that Displays Word Clouds of a Conversation in a Virtual Room to Participants Outside the Room

Runa Eguchi, Chika Oshima$^{(\boxtimes)}$, and Koichi Nakayama

Saga University, Saga 8408502, Japan
sj5872@edu.cc.saga-u.ac.jp, knakayama@is.saga-u.ac.jp

Abstract. This paper developed a voice communication system, the Overheard Text Map (OTM), which displays the frequent words of a conversation in a virtual space. Participants who engage in voice communication using the OTM can create conversation rooms. They may move freely among the rooms, if they mutually agree to do so, holding internal departmental meetings, group discussions at seminars, poster sessions, and informal gatherings, for example. The OTM displays frequent words in the current conversation to the participants outside the corresponding room using a word cloud. The word cloud selects multiple words with a high frequency of occurrence in the text data of conversations and displays them in a size corresponding to their frequency. In this way, participants can obtain an overview of the conversation in the room without joining it. Therefore, it is expected that the participants will find it easier to choose and join a room with conversations that match what they want to talk about. In the experiment, participants watched the word clouds and chose an appropriate room where participants were having a conversation that matched what they wanted to talk about. The results showed that word clouds created based on discussions are useful for people who want to join an appropriate conversation room.

Keywords: Conversation room · Frequent words · Overview of the conversation

1 Introduction

In recent years, many people have begun to use voice communication systems (online conference/chat systems). When the number of participants in these rooms increases, they are often divided into smaller online rooms for discussion. Both Zoom [1] and Microsoft Teams [2] are equipped with "breakout rooms." Remo [3] is an interactive virtual event platform that consists of many rooms depicted with a Table and six chairs on a two dimensional map. Remo participants can move themselves to a new Table by clicking on a chair before any table. Similarly, SpatialChat

S. Yamamoto and H. Mori (Eds.): HCII 2022, LNCS 13305, pp. 197–208, 2022.
https://doi.org/10.1007/978-3-031-06424-1_15

[4] is a group video chat tool. Each SpatialChat [4] user has an avatar displayed in a two dimensional virtual space. When the participants move their avatars closer to one another, they can hear each other's voices.

Though these systems are often used for internal departmental meetings, group discussions at seminars, poster sessions at research meetings, and informal gatherings. However, the participants sometimes hesitate to move from one room to another, or to approach another user's avatar.

As an example of a user's hesitation to enter another room, imagine a poster session hosted on Remo [3]. Each presenter at the poster session would be assigned a virtual room in which to explain his or her research. The presenter and the audience in each room cannot hear the voices of those in other rooms. The presenter gives an overview of their research to the audience, and then they all begin discussing the research. Under this system, people who enter the room late may not be able to understand the discussion. It will take time for them to evaluate the current comments and what the presenter and the audience in the room are talking about. The presenter also has to give a polite explanation of what has gone on to the new audience member, so that they can fully understand the discussion.

SpatialChat [4] participants may also hesitate to enter a conversation group by placing their avatar close to those of other participants. For example, about 50 mutually familiar participants in a SpatialChat [4] room will gradually form smaller groups (gatherings of their avatars), depending on who each of them wants to talk to and/or what they want to talk about. However, the formation of these groups is not fixed. They may also want to move among groups in the space, so they can join all of the groups that are talking about something in which they are interested. In the case of a mixer in the real world, participants move little by little and talk with various people; they can also hear what the groups next to them are talking about, albeit vaguely. Therefore, they can move to the other group naturally. SpatialChat [4] also allows participants to hear the voices of others as they approach their avatars. However, the participant is only considered to have joined the conversation group when they have placed their avatar close to those of the other participants. Therefore, some people will hesitate to move their avatars.

If the participants have a way to know what the participants in other rooms or groups of distant avatars are talking about, it may become easier for them to join those rooms and groups. However, if the voices of the conversations are leaked to the outside, the advantage of holding a conversation in a separate room is reduced. At the same time, even faintly leaked words outside the room can allow people to understand the topic of conversation in the room to some degree. Although the voices in the conversation fade over time, if some words, especially nouns and verbs, can be displayed as text, participants outside the room can know what is currently being said in the room.

With the above in mind, this paper develops a voice communication system, the Overheard Text Map (OTM), which displays frequent words (nouns and verbs) in the current conversations of other rooms in the same virtual space. The OTM converts the utterances of each OTM user into text data and creates a constantly updated word cloud [5] based on the text data. The OTM allows users to obtain an overview of the current conversation in each available room before committing to join it.

The next Sect. describes how the OTM was constructed. Section 3 details an experiment to examine the effect of a word cloud for users of a voice communication system. The paper concludes with Sect. 4.

2 System Construction

2.1 Overview

Figure 1 shows a schematic diagram of the OTM. OTM users in the same room can talk with multiple people via SkyWay [6]. The utterances of each user are recognized by the speech recognition features of the Web Speech API [7]. A Japanese morphological analysis engine, kuromoji.js [8], is used for morphological analysis. The obtained word data is shared with all users, and then a constantly updated word cloud [5] is created from the word data, providing an overview of the conversation and displaying this information on the room's screen. The next sections describe the main functions of the OTM.

2.2 User Registration

The system uniquely identifies the users. Users create their own accounts by registering their name, e-mail address, cell phone number, and password, and then they log into the system using their e-mail address and password.

2.3 Calling Function

The call function of the OTM uses SkyWay [6], a multi-platform software development kit that can implement video and voice calls. Users can create a room for calling others and start a conversation by entering the room. In addition, users can add any other user as a member of the room.

When the users log into the system, a list of rooms in which they are registered as a member is displayed. After they enter one of the rooms, they can participate in a conversation with other users registered there.

2.4 Showing an Overview of the Conversation

The OTM informs users of an overview of the room's current conversation before they enter it (Fig. 2). This makes it easier for users to join the conversation. More specifically, the OTM creates a visualization of the current conversation using a word cloud [5]. Figure 3 shows an example of screen image created using a word cloud [5]. Word clouds are a visual representation of selected multiple words with a high frequency of occurrence. They are displayed in different sizes and fonts according to their frequency of occurrence.

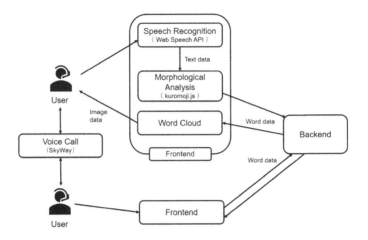

Fig. 1. A schematic diagram of the OTM voice communication system.

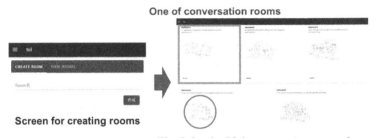

Fig. 2. The OTM interface.

The OTM uses the web speech API SpeechRecognition [7] for speech recognition. This API enables speech synthesis and speech recognition using a Web browser. First, the API converts the voices of the members entering the room into text data.

Second, a morphological analysis is performed on the text data using kuromoji.js [8], a Japanese morphological analysis engine that can be completed with just the front end. It extracts only nouns and verbs from the word data obtained from morphological analysis. The extracted nouns and verbs are shared with all members of the room via WebSocket [9], a communication protocol that enables two-way communication via the Web.

Third, the word cloud is created using the shared word data with vue-d3-cloud [10], a library for creating word clouds in Vue.js [11]. Vue-d3-cloud [10] creates word clouds based on word data and their numbers of occurrences. We counted the number of occurrences of each word from the shared word data and sent them to vue-d3-cloud [10] as objects.

Fig. 3. An example of an image created with a word cloud (in Japanese).

The created word clouds are displayed on the room's screen as image data. The position and color of the words are randomized, and their size corresponds to the frequency of occurrence.

3   Experiment

3.1   Aim

The purpose of this experiment is to show that a word cloud, which represents an overview of a current conversation, is useful for people who are about to join a conversation room.

3.2   Preparation for the Experiment

Figure 4 shows the preparations for the experiment. Five pre-recorded discussions [12,13] were prepared to serve as the conversations in each room (Discussion-A through -E). Five word clouds were created based on each discussion, because one word cloud was created every 10 min (WordCloud-A1 through -E5).

Five fictional scenarios (thoughts) were prepared based on the five discussions (Thought-A through -E). These thoughts expressed what the participants in the experiments wanted to talk about related to a fictitious scenario.

The details of the experiment are indicated in the following Sects.

3.3   Create the Word Clouds Based on the Five Discussions

Summaries of the five pre-recorded discussions are indicated below:

Discussion-A: Fun Even Nine members of the same laboratory discussed what kind of fun event should be held. The final conclusion was "online games."

Discussion-B: Research Project Six members of the same laboratory discussed what kind of research project their laboratory should launch. The final conclusion was an "interactive robot for the elderly."

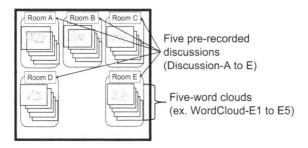

Fig. 4. The five prepared recorded discussions and five word clouds for each room.

Fig. 5. WordCloud-A1: The first word cloud created based on the discussion "A: Fun Event."

Discussion-C: Farewell Party Six members of the same laboratory discussed what kind of farewell party should be held. The final conclusion was "drinking at a pub."

Discussion-D: Event at a Kindergarten (Virtual Reality) Four members of the same laboratory discussed how to entertain kindergarten pupils. The final conclusion was "VR goggles."

Discussion-E: Event at a Kindergarten (Treasure Hunt) Four members of the same laboratory discussed how to entertain kindergarten pupils. The final conclusion was the host a "treasure hunt."

Fig. 6. WordCloud-B1: The first word cloud created based on the discussion "B: Research Project."

Fig. 7. WordCloud-C1: The first word cloud created based on the discussion "C: Farewell Party."

Fig. 8. WordCloud-D1: The first word cloud created based on the discussion "D: Event at a Kindergarten (Virtual Reality) ."

Figure 5, 6 ,7, 8 and 9 shows the first word cloud created based on each of the five discussions. The left image shows the word cloud used in the experiment. The right image shows an English translation of the words created by one of the authors based on the left-side word cloud.

Figure 10 shows one of sheets that the participants looked at during the experiment. Five kinds of word clouds (WordCloud-A1 through -E1) are displayed simultaneously on one sheet (Sheet 1). Similarly, Sheet 2 consists of the word clouds WordCloud-A2 through -E2, and Sheet 5 consists of the word clouds WordCloud-A5 through -E5.

3.4   Method

Thought-A, which corresponds to Discussion-A: Fun Event
"You want to organize a social gathering for new students in your lab."

Thought-B, which corresponds to Discussion-B: Research Project
"You are looking for a research topic."

Thought-C, which corresponds to Discussion-C: Farewell Party
"You want to have a farewell party for graduating seniors."

Thought-D, which corresponds to Discussion-D: Event at a Kindergarten (Virtual Reality)
"You want to entertain kindergarten pupils and help them use the latest technology."

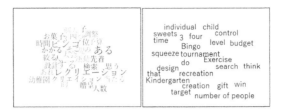

Fig. 9. WordCloud-E1: The first word cloud created based on the discussion "E: Event at a Kindergarten (Treasure Hunt) ."

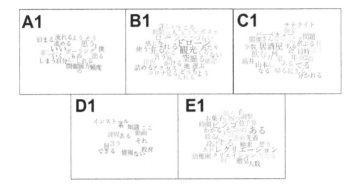

Fig. 10. Sheet 1: WordCloud-A1 to -E1 are displayed simultaneously.

Thought-E, which corresponds to Discussion-E: Event at a Kindergarten (Treasure Hunt)

"You want to entertain kindergarten pupils by playing children's games with them."

One of the thoughts was presented at the same time that one of the sheets was displayed. Table 1 shows the combination of the sheet (Sheet-1 through -5) and the fictional thought (Thought-A through -E). The participants could look at each sheet for up to 40 s. The order in which the five sheets were presented followed the timeline of the discussion.

The participants chose one or two word clouds that matched each fictional thought. If they were unsure of the answer, they could choose up to two answers (their first and second choices). Although there was no limit on the response time, participants were forbidden to go back to previous sheets and revise their answers.

3.5 Results

Table 2 shows the number of participants who chose the correct/incorrect word cloud for each sheet for each thought. "1st" means that the participant could choose the correct one as their first choice from five word clouds on the sheet.

Table 1. Experiment conditions

		Participant												
		P1	P2	P3	P4	P5	P6	P7	P8	P9	P10	P11	P12	P13
Order	Sheet	Fictional thought												
1	1 (A1-E1)	A	B	C	D	E	E	A	B	C	D	A	C	C
2	2 (A2-E2)	B	C	D	E	A	D	E	A	B	C	D	E	A
3	3 (A3-E3)	C	D	E	A	B	C	D	E	A	B	B	B	D
4	4 (A4-E4)	D	E	A	B	C	B	C	D	E	A	E	D	B
5	5 (A5-E5)	E	A	B	C	D	A	B	C	D	E	C	A	E

"2nd" means that the participant could choose the correct word cloud as their second choice. "Incorrect" means that the participant could not choose the correct word cloud. The results indicate that 12 out of 13 participants chose the correct word cloud as their first choice for Sheet-4. Whenever the participants were able to choose the correct word cloud for Thought-B and -C, they chose it as their first choice. For Thought-D, most of the answers were incorrect on all sheets, other than Sheet-4.

Figure 11 shows the correct answer rates for Thought-A through -E. The left vertical bar on each thought means the correct rate among the answers was the first choice. The right vertical bars means that the correct answer rate considered answers that were either the first or second choice to be correct. Thought-B, -C, and -E each had a correct answer rate of 75% for participants' the first choice; by contrast, the correct answer rate for Thought-D was low.

Table 3 shows the answers of the participants who could not answer correctly with their first choice. For example, when Thought-A was presented in Sheet-1, Participant-7 (P7) answered "WordCloud-C" as his first choice and "WordCloud-E" as his second choice. In the same sheet, the participants who answered incorrectly had similar tendencies in their responses.

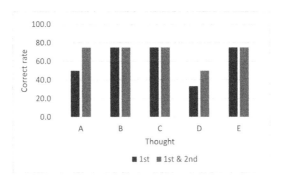

Fig. 11. The correct answer rates for each thought.

Table 2. The number of participants who chose the correct/incorrect word cloud on each sheet.

	Sheet-1 Correct			Sheet-2 Correct			Sheet-3 Correct		
Thought	1st	2nd	Incorrect	1st	2nd	Incorrect	1st	2nd	Incorrect
A	0	2	1	1	1	1	2	0	0
B	1	0	0	0	0	2	3	0	1
C	4	0	0	1	0	0	2	0	0
D	0	0	2	1	1	1	0	1	1
E	2	0	0	3	0	0	2	0	0

	Sheet-4 Correct			Sheet-5 Correct		
Thought	1st	2nd	Incorrect	1st	2nd	Incorrect
A	1	0	1	2	0	0
B	3	0	0	2	0	0
C	2	0	0	0	0	3
D	3	0	0	0	0	2
E	2	0	0	0	0	3

3.6 Discussion

Many systems have been developed in which keywords are used to help people remember details [14], keep one's train of thought [12,13], and generate new ideas [15]. The OTM is a system in which keywords allow people to choose a conversation room that matches what they want to talk about.

The results of the experiment suggested that the word clouds created based on rooms' discussions are useful for people who want to join an appropriate conversation (e.g., the correct answer rate of 75% on Thought-B, -C, and -E).

In contrast, the correct answer rate for Thought-D was only 33.3% as the first choice. The contents of both Discussion-D and -E were discussions on how to entertain kindergarteners. The word clouds created based on Discussion-E included words related to kindergarten and entertainment: Bingo, recreation, kindergarten, sweets, game, playing, quiz, treasure hunt, picture story show, and so on. By contrast, the word clouds created based on Discussion-D did not include the word "kindergarten" even once. Moreover, WordCloud-D's Sheet-1 only had 14 words. Therefore, it was difficult for the participants to choose the appropriate word cloud for this thought.

In the same way, because WordCloud-A's Sheet-1 had only 18 words, and WordCloud-E had many words related to entertainment, P1 and 11 may have mistakenly chosen WordCloud-E.

In Sheet-5, the rates of correct answers were low for Thought-C, -D, and -E. Because Sheet-5 reflected the ends of the discussions, the conversations had often

Table 3. Wrong answers

Correct answer	Sheet	Participant	Answer	
			1st choice	2nd choice
A	1	P7	C	E
	1	P1	E	A (correct)
	1	P11	E	A (correct)
	2	P5	C	D
	2	P8	C	A (correct)
	4	P3	D	–
B	2	P1	D	–
	2	P9	D	–
	3	P12	E	–
C	5	P4	A	–
	5	P8	A	–
	5	P11	A	–
D	1	P4	E	–
	1	P10	E	A
	2	P3	E	–
	3	P7	E	–
	5	P5	C	–
	5	P9	C	–
E	5	P1	D	–
	5	P10	–	–
	5	P13	–	–

shifted to preparations and precautions for carrying out the events. Therefore, it may have been difficult to choose the correct word cloud.

4   Conclusion

This paper developed a voice communication system, the Overheard Text Map (OTM), that displays word clouds to indicate frequent words in conversations held in a virtual space. The OTM's users can estimate what each conversation room is talking about within 10 min. Then, they find it easier to choose and join an appropriate room. In the experiment detailed in this paper, participants chose one of five word clouds according to what they wanted to talk about related to a fictitious scenario. The results of the experiment suggested that the word clouds indicate what each room is talking about, and the users can choose an appropriate room with a high probability of success. However, the word clouds created based on the ends of discussions do not typically express the main themes of each room very well.

In the future, the experiment will be conducted in real conversation rooms in virtual spaces.

References

1. Zoom video communications: Zoom. https://explore.zoom.us/en/about/, accessed 28 Nov 2021
2. Microsoft: Teams. https://support.microsoft.com/en-us/teams, accessed 28 Nov 2021
3. Remo. co: Remo conference. https://remo.co/, accessed 28 Nov 2021
4. Spatialchat Ltd: Spatial Chat. https://spatial.chat/, accessed 28 Nov 2021
5. Cui, W., Wu, Y., Liu, S., Wei, F., Zhou, M. X., Qu, H.: Context preserving dynamic word cloud visualization. In: 2010 IEEE Pacific Visualization Symposium, PacificVis, pp. 121–128. IEEE (2010). https://doi.org/10.1109/MCG.2010.102
6. WebRTC Platform: SkyWay. https://webrtc.ecl.ntt.com/en/, accessed 28 Nov 2021
7. MDN Web Docs: Web Speech API, SpeechRecognition. https://developer.mozilla.org/en-US/docs/Web/API/Web_Speech_API, accessed 28 Nov 2021
8. kuromoji.js. https://github.com/takuyaa/kuromoji.js/
9. MDN Web Docs: WebSockets. https://developer.mozilla.org/en-US/docs/Web/API/WebSockets_API, accessed 28 Nov 2021
10. vue-d3-cloud. https://github.com/makeupsomething/vue-d3-cloud, accessed 28 Nov 2021
11. Vue.js. https://vuejs.org/index.html, accessed 28 Nov 2021
12. Sasaki, C., Oyama, T., Oshima, C., Kajihara, S., Nakayama, K.: Online Discussion Support System with Facilitation Function. Int. J. Adv. Comput. Sci. Appl. **12**(8), 37 (2021). https://doi.org/10.14569/IJACSA.2021.0120837
13. Oyama, T., Sasaki, C., Oshima, C., Nakayama, K.: AI Facilitator Allows Participants to Conduct a Friendly Discussion and Contribute to Feasible Proposals. In: Stephanidis, C., Antona, M., Ntoa, S. (eds.) HCII 2021. CCIS, vol. 1420, pp. 523–530. Springer, Cham (2021). https://doi.org/10.1007/978-3-030-78642-7_70
14. Itou, J., Tanaka, R., Munemori, J.: Chat support system to recall past conversational topics using tags. In: Stephanidis, C. (ed.) HCI 2017. CCIS, vol. 713, pp. 450–457. Springer, Cham (2017). https://doi.org/10.1007/978-3-319-58750-9_62
15. Wang, H.C., Cosley, D., Fussell, S.R.: Idea expander: supporting group brainstorming with conversationally triggered visual thinking stimuli. In Proceedings of the 2010 ACM Conference on Computer Supported Cooperative Work, pp. 103–106 (2010). https://doi.org/10.1145/1718918.1718938

Proposal for Visualization of Affective Image in Three Regions of China

He Jiang[1]([✉]), Keiko Kasamatsu[1], and Takeo Ainoya[2,3]

[1] Tokyo Metropolitan University, Tokyo, Japan
jhe02@sina.com
[2] Tokyo University of Technology, Tokyo, Japan
[3] VDS Co., Ltd., Tokyo, Japan

Abstract. This paper takes the visual design of tea culture in three different regions of China as examples, compares the perceptual impression brought to people by different cultural atmosphere and environmental background in the three regions, and applies it to the visual design related to tea culture. Questionnaire survey was used to analyze the perceptual impression differences between local residents and foreigners in these three regions, and based on the survey results, suggestions were put forward to improve the impression differences between the two sides, and optimization plans were put forward to facilitate intercultural communication. A survey and analysis of perceptual impressions of three regions of China from the perspective of local residents has been published in HCII2020. As an extension of this project, this paper obtains some effective information from the survey of how foreigners feel about different tea cultures and regional image of other countries from the perspective of foreigners. Finally, the above survey and analysis results of perceptual impression from the three regions are integrated into the visual design proposals of tea culture in the three regions. Through the perspective of local residents and foreigners, fully understand the feelings and ideas of both sides, and realize the effective conversion of design language and cultural transmission and communication.

Keywords: Affective image · Impression differences · Visual design proposal

1 Research Background

With the increase of international exchanges, the countries of the world are communicating with all human society through their own culture, at the same time offering an alternative access to get knowledge about different culture types for the whole world. We can see that every country is doing that, and China is one of them. When doing intercultural communication on basis of the cultures of different countries, there are two factors that should always be taken into consideration: the first one is cultural differences between countries and the second one is the differences between receivers.

However, special attention should always be lied on the stressing and emphasis of the communication subject - person. It is person that both launch and receive the communication. The feeling of the communication varies with individuals of distinctive nationalities and ages due to their experience, knowledge, skills and time. Therefore, when the cultures of different countries are supposed to be effectively spread, analysis and designs unfurled on foundation of human communication pattern would definitely be the most effective.

2 Research Purpose

This paper takes the visual design of tea culture in three different regions of China as examples, compares the perceptual impression brought to people by different cultural atmosphere and environmental background in the three regions, and applies it to the visual design related to tea culture. Questionnaire survey was used to analyze the perceptual impression differences between local residents and foreigners in these three regions, and based on the survey results, suggestions were put forward to improve the impression differences between the two sides, and optimization plans were put forward to facilitate intercultural communication.

3 Preliminary Investigation

Here, I want to try and give you a point to understanding China. The point is that China is primarily a civilization instead of a nation state. Without understanding this notion of Chinese civilization, you cannot understand China who is the longest continuously existing polity in the world. The way we think of what China is, is not a function of the last hundred years of being a nation state. It is a function of more than 2000 years of being a civilization state. It is absolutely different from western countries. Western countries are constituted on the basis of national identity, like U.S. China is different; China is firstly and foremost constituted on the basis of civilization. I mean Chinese all regard ourselves to be multiracial multicultural. We have very unique relationship, confusion values, very unusual conception of families.

To make foreigners understand the Chinese cultural diversity and the cultural images of different Chinese regions, the first thing is to divide regions by different culture. In recent years, Chinese scholars have divided Chinese culture regions from different perspectives (e.g. geography, history, politics, nationality, etc.). Qin Liangjie [1] and Wang Huichang [2] divided Chinese culture into 16 regions according to the region's customs. This compartmentalization is more suitable for my research. I made this map [3] as follows (see Fig. 1) to make it easier to understand base on this compartmentalization.

As mentioned above, because China is a civilization state which is different with nation state of western countries, it becomes more necessary to analyze and compare cultures between regions in China. Only then can foreigners be provided a comprehensive and accurate information reference of Chinese culture. The three survey regions (region A, B, C) selected in this study are Poyang region, Qinghai-Tibet region, and Guandong region.

Fig. 1. Chinese culture 16 regions

4   Research Approaches

A survey and analysis of perceptual impressions of three regions of China from the perspective of local residents has been published in HCII2020. As an extension of this project, this paper obtains some effective information from the survey of how foreigners feel about different tea cultures and regional image of other countries from the perspective of foreigners. The respondents of this survey (16 persons) come from 16 different countries, and the questionnaire has 3 questions (1, 2, 3), and the analysis method is the KJ method. Then, the perceptual impression was compared with the results of the two surveys.

5   Research Results

5.1   The Features of the Three Tea Cultures

Topic problem of Question 1: Please explain the features or characteristics of the three tea cultures and your impressions of them. The whole KJ Method Process firstly makes all the answers from respondents into labels one by one, and then classifies these labels according to correlation degree. It is divided into five first-level label groups: Tea, Tea Set, Experience, Environment and Background. Each first-level label group is divided into multiple second-level label groups. After that, a chart was made to sort out the survey results and to make topic explanation according to the chart.

By comparing the survey results of Fig. 2, 3 and 4, it can be seen that four second-level label groups, smell, taste, sight and tea types, can be divided under the first-level label named "Tea". The main differences between the three countries are: There are various types of tea in Chinese style, which is light color and tea leaves can be seen. British tea is bagged tea, dark brown with deep color, taste strong and sweet. Japanese tea is powder tea with a fresh smell, astringent and bitter taste. It tastes like grass with intense creamy visual impression.

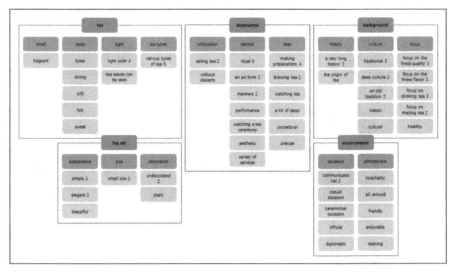

Fig. 2. The features or characteristics of Chinese tea

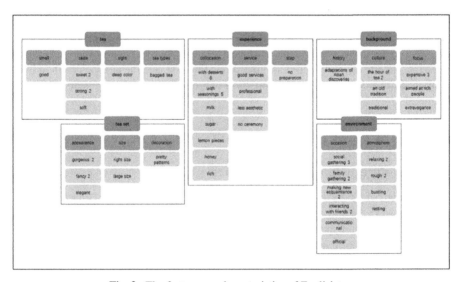

Fig. 3. The features or characteristics of English tea

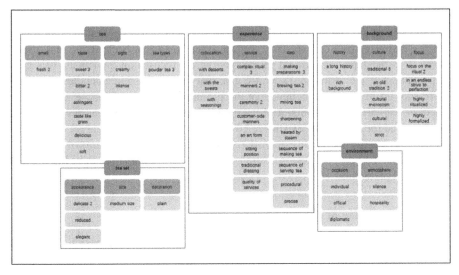

Fig. 4. The features or characteristics of Japanese tea

The first-level label named "Tea Set" is divided into three second-level label groups, appearance, size and decoration. The main differences among the three countries are as follows: The appearance of Chinese tea sets is simple and elegant, the size of tea cups is small, and the decoration of tea sets can be plain or undecorated. The tea set of English tea looks gorgeous and fancy. The size of the teacup is large, which is right size. There are pretty patterns on the tea set. The tea set of Japanese tea is delicate and reduced. The size of the teacup is medium size, and the tea set is decorated with plain.

Under the first-level label named "Experience", there are three second-level label groups, namely "Collocation", "Service" and "Step". The main differences among the three countries are: Chinese tea is served without desserts, but with tea selling. Service is an art form which is a performance with a lot of preparation steps. There is an impression of being precise, ritual, etc. English tea is served with desserts and seasonings. The service is less aesthetic without ceremony or preparation steps. Japanese tea is served with desserts and seasonings to focus on the quality of services and the sequence of making tea and serving tea. There are complex rituals and customer-side manners.

There are two second-level label groups under the first-level label named "Environment", namely occasion and atmosphere. The main differences among the three countries are: Chinese tea drinking environment tend to be more ceremonial with an atmosphere of hospitality and friendliness. The English tea drinking environment is social communicational, including family gathering, making new acquaintance, interacting with friends, social gathering and relaxing atmosphere. Japanese tea drinking environment are both individual and official, bringing silence or hospitable tea drinking atmosphere.

Under the first-level label named "Background", three second-level label groups including history, culture and focus are divided. The main differences among the three countries are: Chinese tea is the origin of tea with a very long history. It is an old traditional culture that pays attention to health, the finest quality, the finest flavor, making tea and drinking tea. English tea is an adaptation of Asian discoveries. It has its own afternoon tea traditions called "the hour of tea" which is aimed at rich people and has an image of being extravagance and expensive. Japanese tea has a rich background and a long history. It is the Japanese cultural microcosm which focuses on the rituals. It is both highly ritualized and formalized and also a pursuit of perfection in an endless strive.

To sum up, respondents believe that the prominent image of Chinese tea is "wide variety of tea leaves" and "pursuit of tea quality"; the outstanding features of English tea are "social function" and "expensive"; The feelings of Japanese tea are "ceremonial" and "emphasizes the tea-making process". According to the survey results of question 1, the perceptual image of Chinese tea different from other tea cultures can be highlighted in the visual proposal.

5.2   The Description of Regional Impression

Question 2 is about the description measurement of regional impression. There are 20 pairs of antisense adjectives and Likert 7-scale measurement method is adopted. Respondents were asked to describe their image of three different regions (regions A, B, C) with adjectives by viewing promotional films and pictures related to natural resources, human resources, lifestyles, celebrities, art forms and ideas. Table 1, 2 and 3 are line charts comparing impressions of region A, B, C between foreigners and local residents.

Table 1. The comparing impressions of region A between foreigners and local residents

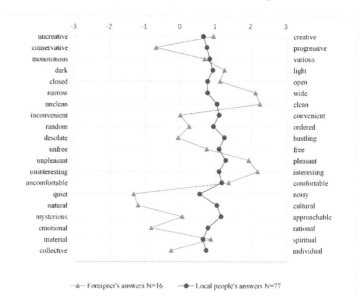

Table 2. The comparing impressions of region B between foreigners and local residents

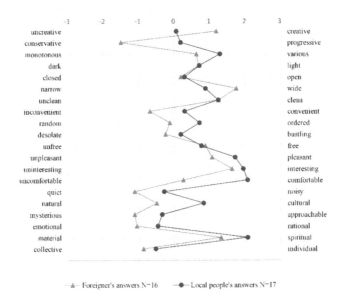

Table 3. The comparing impressions of region C between foreigners and local residents

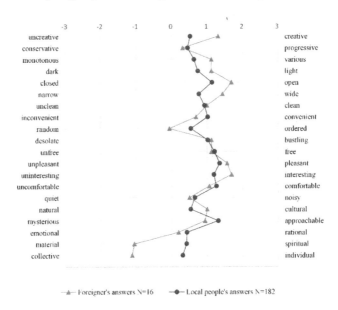

The whole four-Quadrant Analysis Method process was firstly analyzed from the perspective of both sides. The ordinate (from top to bottom) was named "inside-lateral", and the abscissa (from left to right) was named "strong image - weak image. The range of strong impression is set as plus or minus 1 point (excluding 1 point), and the range of weak impression is set as plus or minus 1 point (including 1 point). Rank the adjectives in descending order of score, and compare the perceptual impression of the inside (local residents) with that of the outside (foreigners). Referring to the above results, further comparative analysis was conducted from a lateral perspective. Name the ordinate (top to bottom) as "agreed image - opposite image" and the ordinate (left to right) as "higher rated - lower rated", and arrange the adjectives in descending order of difference. According to the importance level of image improvement, the four quadrants were named as maintaining image (upper left), to be improved (upper right), improving impression (lower left) and in urgent need of improvement (lower right).

According to the survey results, in region A (see Fig. 5 and 6), foreigners and local residents have the same image and higher evaluation of clean, wide, creative, etc. These image need to be maintained. The image that foreigners and local residents have the same but lower evaluation are ordered, approachable, etc., and these impressions need to be improved. The weak image of foreigners opposite to local residents is quiet, emotional, etc., which needs to be improved; The strong image of foreigners opposite to local residents is desolate, natural, which are in urgent need of improvement.

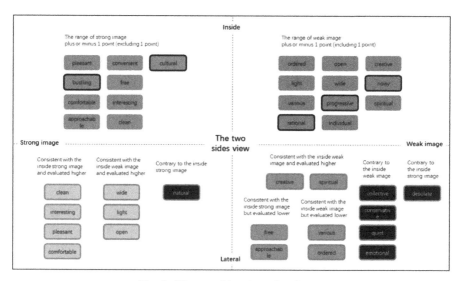

Fig. 5. The two sides view of region A

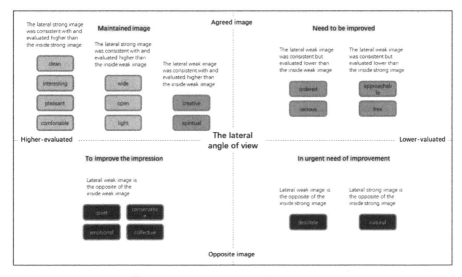

Fig. 6. The lateral angle of view in region A

In region B (see Fig. 7 and 8), foreigners and local residents have the same image and higher evaluation of clean, wide, creative, etc. These image need to be maintained. The image that foreigners and local residents have the same but lower evaluation are spiritual, open, comfortable, etc., and these impressions need to be improved. The weak image of foreigners opposite to local residents is natural, inconvenient, etc., which needs to be improved; The strong image of foreigners opposite to local residents is conservative, which are in urgent need of improvement.

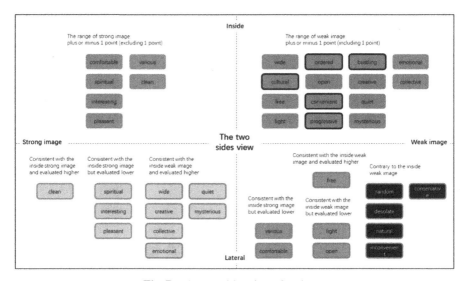

Fig. 7. The two sides view of region B

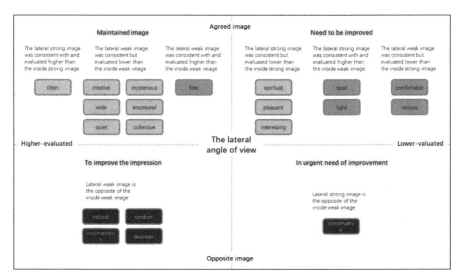

Fig. 8. The lateral angle of view in region B

In region C (see Fig. 9 and 10), foreigners and local residents have the same image and higher evaluation of open, creative, clean, etc. These image need to be maintained. The image that foreigners and local residents have the same but lower evaluation are free, noisy, comfortable, etc., and these impressions need to be improved. The weak image of foreigners opposite to local residents is random, which needs to be improved; The strong image of foreigners opposite to local residents is material, collective, which are in urgent need of improvement.

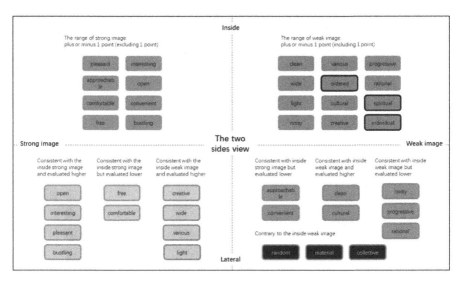

Fig. 9. The two sides view of region C

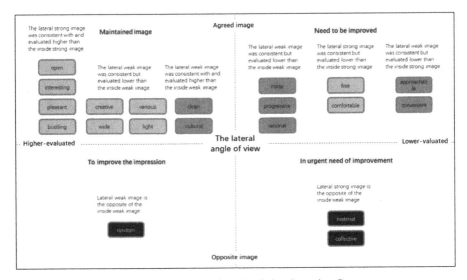

Fig. 10. The lateral angle of view in region C

From what has been discussed above, the perceptual image which varies most significantly between foreigners and local residents is "natural-cultural" and "desolate-bustling" in region A, "conservative-progressive" in region B, "material-spiritual" and "collective-individual" in region C. According to the survey results of Question 2, these differences in the impression of local residents that are deeply felt but not conveyed to foreign respondents are in urgent need of improvement.

5.3 The Selection of Regional Color Impression

Question 3 is about the hue selection of regional color impression and the explanation of the reasons for selection. Respondents were asked to choose a representative color from three to describe the impression that best represented the region, and complete four sets of choices. (The four representative colors are the first four colors from a survey of local residents, published in HCII2020). Table 4, 5 and 6 are bars of comparison between foreigners and local residents for color image of region A, B, C. KJ Method process was used to make all the answers from respondents into labels one by one, and then classify these labels according to the two label groups: things and feelings. After that, a chart was made to sort out the survey results and to make topic explanation according to the chart.

Table 4. The comparison between foreigners and local residents for color image of region A

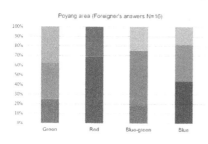
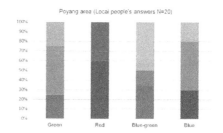

Table 5. The comparison between foreigners and local residents for color image of region B

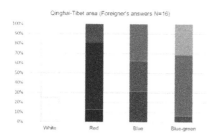
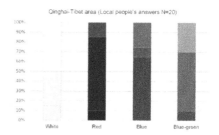

Table 6. The comparison between foreigners and local residents for color image of region C

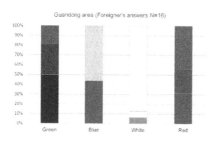
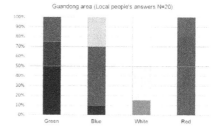

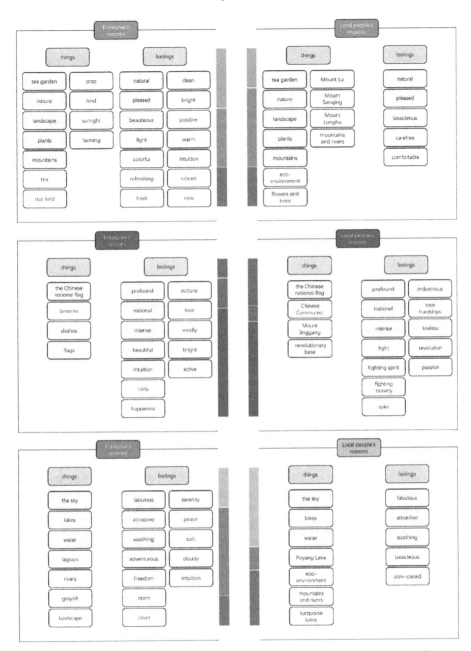

Fig. 11. The comparison of reasons for color selection in region A (Color figure online)

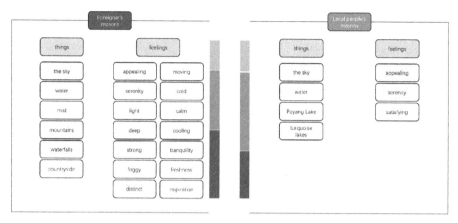

Fig. 11. continued

By comparing the answers of foreigners and local residents (see Fig. 11), it can be found that in region A, the two sides tend to have the same evaluation on the color hue selection of "Green", "Red" and "Blue". In terms of "Green", both sides have the same image including things such as "tea garden" and "nature" and feelings such as "natural" and "pleased". The same image of "Red" has "the Chinese National Flag" "national" "Profound" and so on. The same image of blue is "the sky", "water", "appealing" and "serenity". However, there are obvious differences in the color hue choice of "blue-green". Foreigners have selected reason of "freedom" and "serenity" which are different with local residents. In addition, the same select reasons include things such as "the sky" and "lakes", and feelings such as "fabulous", "attractive" and "soothing".

In region B, as shown in Fig. 12, the two sides tend to have the same evaluation on the color hue selection of "White", "Red" and "Blue-green". The same image of "Green" from both sides include "snow-capped mountains" "clouds" and "pure". The same image of "Red" are "buildings" "spiritual" and "beautiful". In terms of "Blue-green", both sides have the same image including things such as "lakes" "water", and feelings such as "relax". However, the hue selection of "Blue" is slightly different from that of local residents, who choose "vivid" and "freezing". In addition, the same select reasons include things such as "landscape" "lakes", and feelings such as "pure".

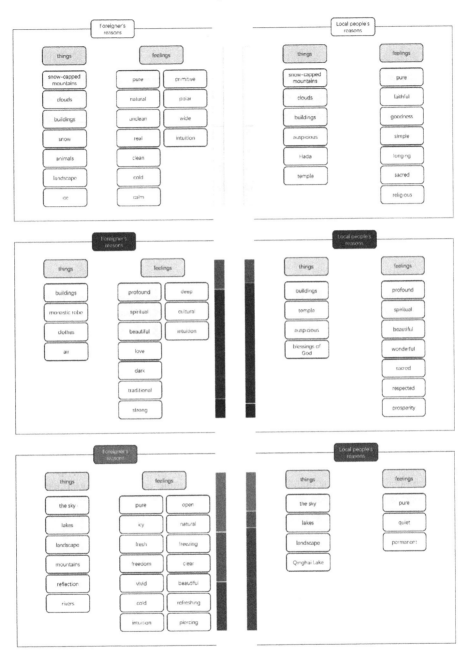

Fig. 12. The comparison of reasons for color selection in region B (Color figure online)

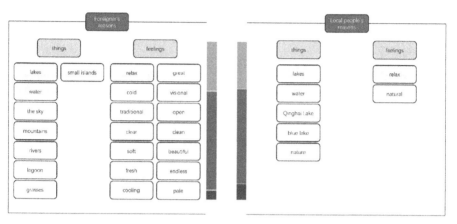

Fig. 12. continued

As shown in Fig. 13, the two sides tend to have the same evaluation on the color hue selection of "Green", "White" in region C. In terms of Green, both sides have the same image including things such as "forest" "forest vegetation", and feelings such as "natural" "lush". In terms of White, both sides have the same image including things such as "snow festival" and "ice sculptures", and feelings such as "cold" and "simply". However, there are obvious differences in the color selection of "Blue" and "Red". Keywords related to "Blue" include "snow", "ice" and "cold". Together with "Clothes and fabrics", "young" and "fresh", which are related to Red, were not mentioned by the local residents as their image. In addition, the same image of "Blue" from both sides include "sea" "the sky" and "balance". And the same image of "Red" from both sides include "festival" "the firecrackers" "bustling" "pleased". In conclusion, the comparison results of question 3 can be applied to the color matching of visual design and corresponding adjustments can be made.

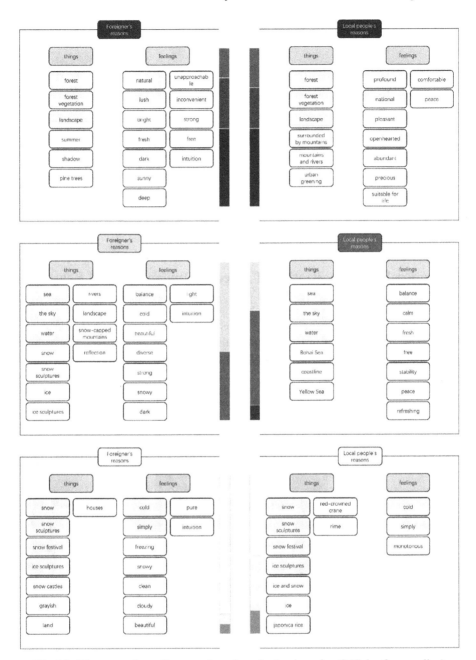

Fig. 13. The comparison of reasons for color selection in region C (Color figure online)

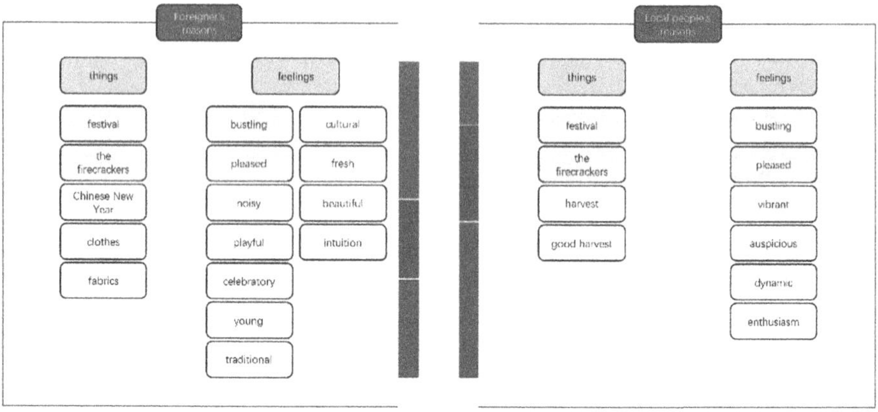

Fig. 13. continued

6   Proposal for Visualization of Affective Image in Three Regions

The picture (see Fig. 14) was designed based on the survey results of local residents on their hometown colors, representative elements and impressions. We investigated the feelings and impressions of foreign respondents on the three illustrations of tea culture in region A, B, C. Using the four-quadrant analysis method, four quadrants were divided into "able to understand the design content", "unable to understand the design content", "personal intention to like and expect" and "personal intention to dislike and reject", and the results were sorted out and summarized.

Fig. 14. The visualization of affective image in three regions

The feelings and image of foreign respondents on the illustrations of tea culture in region A are summarized as follows. Comprehensible design contents include "the scene of collecting green tea", "The pursuit of tea quality" and "the importance of tea to local people". Incomprehensible design contents include "the building in the background" and "the abstract element of the tea tree". Personal likes and expectations include: "traditional style", "natural atmosphere", "fresh and healing feeling", etc. Personal dislikes and rejections include: "Abstract elements," "confusing colors," "lack of story".

The feelings and image of foreign respondents on the illustrations of tea culture in region B are summarized as follows. Comprehensible design contents include "local tradition and natural elements" and "Butter tea is an important local drink". Incomprehensible design contents include "the relationship between packaging and tea". Personal likes and expectations include: "harmony with nature", "spiritual feeling", "strong ethnic identity", etc. Personal dislikes and rejections include: "interspersed relationship between characters and mountains" and "placement of tea elements".

The feelings and image of foreign respondents on the illustrations of tea culture in region C are summarized as follows. Comprehensible design contents include: "scenes to celebrate the festival", "warm and lively atmosphere", "cold climate", "cherish the warm characteristics of black tea" and so on. Incomprehensible design contents include "There are only tea boxes," and "The kinds of food on the table." Personal likes and expectations include: "Reminds me of Christmas", "likes representative elements in illustrations", "happy and interesting feelings", etc. Personal dislike and rejection include "not giving more information".

Finally, the above survey and analysis results of perceptual impression from the three regions are integrated into the visual design proposals of tea culture in the three regions. Through the perspective of local residents and foreigners, fully understand the feelings and ideas of both sides, and realize the effective conversion of design language and cultural transmission and communication.

References

1. Qin, L.: Chinese Culture Region Tourist Literature Collection. Tsinghua University Press, China (2014)
2. Wang, H.: Chinese Cultural Geography. Central China Normal University Press, China (2010)
3. Information source related to the Chinese administration frame: China City Map Homepage. http://www.ditu-map.com/gov. Accessed 20 June 2019. China Administration Divisions Homepage. http://www.xzqh.org/html/show/cn/37714.html. Accessed 20 June 2019

Attention to Medical Warning Labels Using the Flicker Paradigm

James Miles[(⊠)], Kristen Brown, and Michelle Nguyen

California State University, Long Beach, Long Beach, CA 90840, USA
Jim.miles@csulb.edu, {kristen.brown,
michelle.nguyen10}@student.csulb.edu

Abstract. One of the top causes of adverse drug effects is the mislabeling and misreading of instructions or warnings on medical labels. In addition to miscomprehension of these labels, label information may be missed or seen incorrectly due to a lack of sufficient attention and visual processing. Currently, there is little consistency in prescription medical labels across providers, with warning labels containing either icons, text, or a combination of both. The present study examined how the design configuration of iconography and text on medical labels influences attention to specific label elements. A flicker task was used in two experiments in which a set of medical labels were presented on a display. Participants were required to detect and identify changes in a label's icon, text, or both. Overall, the results indicate that viewers tend to focus attention on icons rather than text, and that label information is more likely to be missed on labels containing both icon and text information compared to labels with a single type of information. We discuss how change detection in the current study relates to design considerations for prescription medical warning labels.

Keywords: Attention · Change blindness · Medical warning labels

1 Introduction

Each year, there are approximately 1.5 million cases of preventable adverse drug events related to medication errors in the United States [1]. At least one-third of these medication errors involve patients not administering medicines as intended [2]. A likely source of these errors is the mislabeling or misreading of instructions and warnings on prescription labels. This is not surprising – there is very little consistency between prescription labels across the most common providers; for example, Costco, CVS, Target, and Walgreens (4 of the largest providers of prescription medicines) all use different labeling styles that often involve different text for the same instructions and may or may not include icons (Fig. 1; [3]). Furthermore, a single medical prescription may include 4 or more of these warning labels arranged in a variety of ways. Standardization of these labels may reduce these medication errors. However, further examination is first required in order to better understand how individuals attend to and visually process label information [4].

© The Author(s), under exclusive license to Springer Nature Switzerland AG 2022
S. Yamamoto and H. Mori (Eds.): HCII 2022, LNCS 13305, pp. 228–238, 2022.
https://doi.org/10.1007/978-3-031-06424-1_17

Fig. 1. Examples of medical warning labels from Costco (A), CVS (B), Target (C), and Walgreens (D). Labels greatly vary in type (inclusion of icons and text) and layout.

In addition to miscomprehension, medical label information may simply be missed or seen incorrectly. There is now a large body of evidence demonstrating that people are often unaware of visual information, even when it is being directly viewed [5–7]. Relatedly, people often miss a change in the features of a visual stimulus, known as change blindness [8]. Specific mechanisms underlying change blindness are still debated, but it is generally attributed to one of two causes [9, 10]. First, even if the viewer is fully aware of the pre- and post- change states, they may fail to make a comparison between these states [11–13]. Second, change blindness may be the result of inadequate representation of visual information – changes may be missed because either the pre-change or post change visual information is not fully processed [8, 14, 15]. In accordance with the latter scenario, rates of change blindness may be considered a proxy measure of the degree to which display information is initially attended to and visually processed - higher rates of change blindness indicate lower levels of attention and visual processing.

Change blindness and related issues of attention and visual processing are commonly measured using the flicker task paradigm [15]. In short, participants view a flickering image in which a change occurs, and they must report the change when noticed. The duration needed to notice the change reflects the amount of time before sufficient attention and visual processing is allocated to the changing element. For example, flicker tasks experiments have found that important warnings and instructions can be missed. This indicates that a viewer is not attending to the area of the information to a sufficient degree [16, 17]. Similar studies have examined change blindness in complex driving scenes [18], pilot perception [19], and other complex displays [20].

There are several factors that may affect change detection in the flicker task. In particular, change blindness is more common in complex visual scenes [21–23]. As the visual complexity of a display increases, visual processing of unattended visual objects is diminished, leading to a greater chance of change blindness. Conversely, visually salient information is less likely to suffer from the effects of change blindness because it is more likely to capture attention, leading to improved visual processing [24, 25].

In the current study, two experiments were conducted using the flicker task paradigm in order to evaluate the ability to detect and correctly identify changes to medical warning labels similar to those found on prescription medication bottles. We found that viewers are better at attending to and visually processing icon versus text information on medical labels, and that attention to this information is reduced when the amount of information of a warning label is increased, especially for text (Experiment 1). Further, when medical labels contain both icon and text information, icon changes are more readily noticed, and may prevent viewers from attending to concurrent changes in the text (Experiment 2).

2 Experiment 1

2.1 Method

Participants. One hundred and one participants were recruited from the Introductory Psychology Participant Pool at California State University Long Beach (CSULB). Participants were given experimental credits toward their course research requirement for their participation. Data from 9 participants (8.9%) were excluded due to accuracy scores on the task that were below chance performance on at least 1 of the task conditions ($<12.5\%$ correct trials). The final data set consisted of 92 participants (68 female, 24 male; Mean Age $= 18.83$ yrs, $SD = 1.99$ yrs). Five participants reported being left-handed, 86 right-handed, and 1 ambidextrous.

Materials and Research Design. The experiment was implemented and presented online using the PsyToolkit platform [26, 27]. A full-size computer monitor was required for the experiment, but monitor size varied.

Participants performed a flicker task in which 8 medical labels were presented in 2 columns of 4 labels each (see Fig. 2A). There were 8 distinct medical labels used, and they were arranged such that each label appeared on an equal number of trials at each of the 8 positions. On an individual trial, a label arrangement remained on the screen for 250 ms, followed by a blank white screen for 100 ms. The same label arrangement was then presented again for 250 ms but with a change in one of the labels. Another blank white screen appeared for 100 ms and then the displays repeated. The trial continued until the participant indicated that they noticed the changing label by pressing the space bar or until 10 s had passed. Immediately following the end of the flicker task, participants viewed the original set of labels in the same arrangement and used a mouse to left click on the label that changed.

In total, there were 5 combinations of label types and change types, presented in separate trial blocks: Single-Item/Icon Change, Single-Item/Text Change, Full Label/Icon Change, Full Label/Text Change, and Full Label/Both Change. Figure 2B provides an example of each label combination for one of the medical warning labels. Participants performed 2 blocks of 32 trials of each label combination. Changes were counterbalanced such that there were an equal number of changes in each of the 8 labels at each of the 8 label positions. In total, participants performed 320 trials of the task. Prior to receiving a new Label Type/Change Type combination, participants received detailed instructions, including which change type would occur in the upcoming blocks. The order of combinations was counterbalanced between-participants.

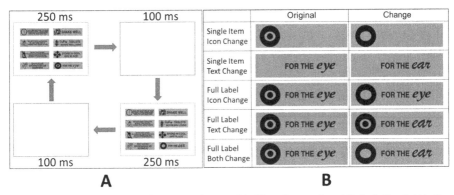

Fig. 2. Stimuli and sample task presentation used in Experiments 1 and 2. Left Panel (A): Presentation of the flicker task. In this example, both the icon and text change in the bottom right label. Right Panel (B): Example of each combination of Label Type (Single Item or Full Label) and Change Type (Icon, Text, or Both) for one of the medical warning labels.

During task performance, data were recorded for how long it took for the participant to press the space bar during the flicker task (detection time), and whether the changing label was subsequently correctly selected (error rate). This data was subject to several analyses, including a 2 (Change Type: Icon vs Text) × 2 (Label Type: Single-Item vs Full) within-subjects ANOVA in order to examine the influence of the amount of label information on change detection. The condition in which both changes occurred concurrently in the full label (Full Label/Both Change) is excluded from this first analysis. Additional paired-sample t-test comparisons between the 3 Full Labels combinations (Full Label/Icon Change, Full Label/Text Change, and Full Label/Both Change) were conducted in order to determine which change type was most detectable when labels contained both icon and text information.

2.2 Results

Detection Time. Figure 3 shows detection time and accuracy for each of the Change Type and Label Type combinations. The 2(Change Type) × 2 (Label Type) ANOVA of detection time indicated that icon changes ($M = 2219$ ms, $SE = 40$ ms) were detected more quickly than text changes ($M = 3338$ ms, $SE = 53$ ms), $F(1, 91) = 525.73, p < .001$. Change detection was faster with Single-Item labels ($M = 2599$ ms, $SE = 42$ ms) compared to Full Labels ($M = 2958$ ms, $SE = 46$ ms), $F(1, 91) = 87.16, p < 001$. Additionally, the increase in change detection time in Full versus Single-Item labels was greater for Text Change ($M_{diff} = 510$ ms) than for the Icon Change ($M_{diff} = 207$ ms), as indicated by a Label Type × Change Type interaction, $F(1, 91) = 11.81, p < .001$.

When comparing change types in Full Labels, paired-sample t-tests showed that detection time was faster for Icon Change ($M = 2322$ ms, $SE = 55$ ms) than Text Change ($M = 3593$ ms, $SE = 61$ ms), $t(91) = 18.39, p < .001$, faster for Icon Change ($M = 2322$ ms, $SE = 55$ ms) than Both Change ($M = 2929$ ms, $SE = 64$ ms), $t(91) = 10.35, p < .001$, and faster for Both Change ($M = 2929$ ms, $SE = 64$ ms) than

Text Change ($M = 3593$ ms, $SE = 61$ ms), $t(91) = 9.23, p < .001$. In other words, for full labels, icon changes were detected the fastest, followed by both changes, and text changes were detected the slowest.

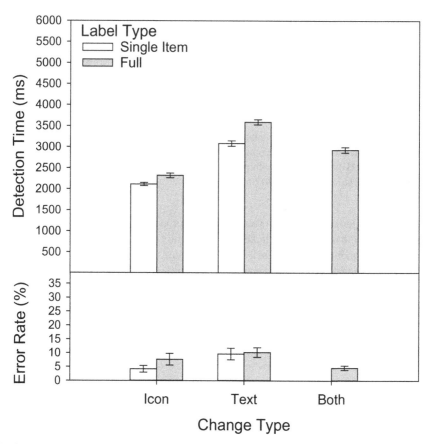

Fig. 3. Mean Detection Time and Error Rate for each combination of Change Type and Label Type in Experiment 1. Error bars represent Standard Errors (*SE*).

Error Rate. As with the analysis of detection time, participants made fewer errors when selecting the changing label for Icon Change ($M = 6.0\%$, $SE = 1.5\%$) compared to Text Change ($M = 10.0\%$, $SE = 1.8\%$), $F(1, 91) = 9.17, p = .003$. No significant difference was found for error rates between Single-Item ($M = 6.9\%$, $SE = 1.5\%$) and Full labels ($M = 9.0\%$, $SE = 1.7\%$), $F(1, 91) = 3.74, p = .056$. Paired-sample t-tests further found that for Full Labels, there was no difference in error rates for Icon Change ($M = 7.7\%$, $SE = 2.1\%$) versus Text Change ($M = 10.2\%$, $SE = 1.8\%$), $t(91) = 1.38, p = .17$. There was also no difference in errors for the Icon Change ($M = 7.7\%$, $SE = 2.1\%$) versus Both Change ($M = 4.6\%$, $SE = .8\%$), $t(91) = 1.49, p = .14$. However, there were significantly more errors for Text Change ($M = 10.2\%$, $SE = 1.8\%$) compared to Both Change ($M = 4.6\%$, $SE = .8\%$), $t(91) = 3.59, p < .001$.

2.3 Discussion

The results of Experiment 1 conclusively show a detection time benefit for icon over text changes, and a general benefit to the detection time of changes in single item versus full labels. These results are consistent with previous findings indicating an attention and visual processing benefit to more salient objects [24, 25] and to less complex displays [23].

Of interest, when comparing different types of changes in the full labels, concurrent changes in both the icon and text were detected more slowly than icon changes alone. This finding is somewhat surprising, considering that participants were simply required to notice a change in one of the labels. In the condition in which both the icon and text concurrently changed, participants could simply look for the icon change to complete the task. If this were the case, one would expect that for the full labels, Both Change detection times should look similar to Icon Change detection times. There are several possibilities that may explain the poorer detection time performance in the Both Change condition. First, as previously indicated, visual salience tends to reduce the occurrence of change blindness. The single change of the icon in the medical label may contrast with the unchanging text, increasing the likelihood of attention to the label. Second, although participants could rely on only the icon change to detect the label in the Both Change condition, this optimal strategy may not have been used. Rather, participants may have looked for both the icon and text changes before responding, which would have increased detection time in comparison to the Icon Only change. This suboptimal strategy could have been driven by the structure of the task – participants received each change type in separate trial blocks and were instructed to the change type prior to each condition.

In order to better understand change detection in the full labels, Experiment 2 focused on change detection in the full labels only. Participants in Experiment 2 also reported the type of change that occurred in each trial. This additional information provides insight into whether participants made systematic errors when reporting the change. For example, in Both change trials, were participants likely to erroneously report only a single change in the label, and if so, were they more likely to report an icon or text change? Conversely, when only a single change occurred in the label, were participants likely to report both items as changing?

3 Experiment 2

3.1 Methods

Participants. One hundred and six participants were recruited from the Introductory Psychology Participant Pool at California State University Long Beach (CSULB), given experimental credits toward their course research requirement for their participation. Data from 14 participants (13.2%) were excluded due to accuracy scores on the task that were below chance performance on at least 1 of the task conditions (<12.5% correct trials). The final data set consisted of 92 participants (65 female, 27 male; Mean Age = 18.9 yrs, SD = .23 yrs). Six participants reported being left-handed, 85 right-handed, and 1 ambidextrous.

Materials and Research Design. The materials and design were identical to Experiment 1 except for the following changes. Only the full label combinations were used in Experiment 2: Full Label/Icon Change, Full Label/Text Change, and Full Label/Both Change. All label changes occurred within the same block of trials, and participants were unaware of the nature of the change in advance. Additionally, after selecting which label changed at the end of a trial, participants received another screen in which they selected the change type (Icon, Text, or Both) from a drop-down menu. Participants performed the task for 8 blocks of 24 trials each for a total of 192 trials.

3.2   Results

Detection Time. Detection time and error rate for each Change Type with the full label are shown in Fig. 4. Paired-sample t-tests indicated that detection time was faster for Icon Change ($M = 4378$ ms, $SE = 81$ ms) than Text Change ($M = 5264$ ms, $SE = 66$ ms), $t(91) = 8.85$, $p < .001$. Unlike in Experiment 1, detection time was faster for

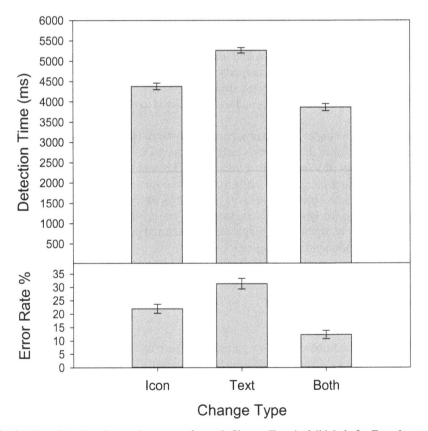

Fig. 4. Mean detection time and error rate for each Change Type in full labels for Experiment 2. Error bars represent Standard Errors (*SE*).

Both Change ($M = 3864$ ms, $SE = 86$ ms) than Icon Change ($M = 4378$ ms, $SE = 81$ ms), $t(91) = 6.78$, $p < .001$, and Text Change ($M = 5264$ ms, $SE = 66$ ms), $t(91) = 15.81$, $p < .001$. Thus, labels with both changes were detected the fastest, followed by icon changes, and text changes were detected the slowest.

Error Rate. Similar to detection times, errors in selecting the changing label were lower for Icon Change ($M = 22.0\%$, $SE = 1.7\%$) than Text Change ($M = 31.3\%$, $SE = 2.0\%$), $t(91) = 6.57$, $p < .001$. Both Change ($M = 12.3\%$, $SE = 1.5\%$) had lower errors than both Icon Change ($M = 22.0\%$, $SE = 1.7\%$), $t(91) = 12.53$, $p < .001$, and Text Change ($M = 31.3\%$, $SE = 2.0\%$), $t(91) = 16.96$, $p < .001$.

Reported Change Type. An additional analysis was conducted on the reported change type for each type of actual change. As shown in Fig. 5, participants were highly accurate at selecting the actual change type for both Icon Change ($M = 93.7\%$ $SE = .6\%$) and Text Change ($M = 94.2\%$ $SE = .7\%$), and there was no difference between their accuracies, $t(91) = .71$, $p = .481$. Participants were much less accurate at selecting the correct change for Both Change ($M = 69.4\%$, $SE = 1.6\%$) compared to Icon Change, $t(91) = 16.03$, $p < .001$ and Text Change, $t(91) = 17.19$, $p < .001$. Of particular interest is the selected change type when the selection was incorrect. For Icon Change, participants were more likely to incorrectly select that a text change occurred ($M = 4.6\%$, $SE = .4\%$) than both changed ($M = 1.6\%$, $SE = .2\%$), $t(91) = 7.20$, $p < .001$. For Text Change trials, icon changes ($M = 3.3\%$, $SE = .4\%$) and both changes ($M = 2.4\%$, $SE = .4\%$) were equally incorrectly selected, $t(91) = 1.82$, $p = .07$. Last, for Both Change trials,

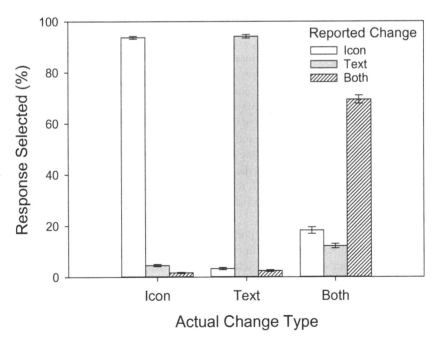

Fig. 5. Reported change for each Change Type. Error bars represent Standard Error (*SE*).

participants were more likely to incorrectly select that an icon change occurred ($M = 18.27\%$, SE 1.3%) than a text change ($M = 12.1\%$, $SE = .9\%$), $t(91) = 4.18, p < .001$.

3.3 Discussion

As in Experiment 1, participants were faster at detecting an icon change compared to text change, indicating that icons received greater initial attention and visual processing. However, unlike in Experiment 1, label changes were detected the fastest when both icon and text changes occurred concurrently. There are a few possible reasons for the Both Change detection benefit in Experiment 2. First, in Experiment 2, participants received each change type within the same trial blocks and did not have foreknowledge of the type of change that would occur in a specific trial. Since the change type could not be predicted, participants may have adjusted their strategy when searching for the change. Specifically, instead of looking for both changes in the Both Change trials, participants may have focused on a single icon or text change. Simply put, participants responded as soon as any change was detected. This view is supported by the analysis of reported change type; the change type in Both Change trials was reported incorrectly over 30% of the time as either an icon change or a text change only. Further, considering that participants incorrectly reported an icon change had occurred rather than a text change more frequently when both items had concurrently changed, it is likely that the icon change was detected first on most occasions.

4 General Discussion and Conclusions

The current study used the flicker task to examine the focus of attention and the degree of visual processing that occurs in different configurations of medical warning labels. The results of Experiments 1 and 2 have several important implications. First, icon changes were detected more quickly than text changes, indicating that salient forms of information such as icons are more detectable in labels. Second, changes were more quickly detected in single-item labels compared to full labels containing multiple elements. This finding is consistent with prior work indicating attention and visual processing deficits in complex environments [23]. Adding both icons and text to labels may offer information redundancy, but also reduces the chance that patients will notice the individual elements. When full labels with both icons and text are used, attention is more often initially allocated to the most salient information at a cost to other information on the label.

Together, Experiments 1 and 2 present a mixed message about the detection of concurrent icon and text changes within full labels. Whereas Experiment 1 found that both changes together were harder to detect than icon changes, the results of Experiment 2 found overall better detection when both changes occur compared to only an icon or text change. It is likely that this difference is related to search strategy. When changes are expected in both icon and text information, viewers may confirm both changes before reporting the change. When the nature of the change is unexpected, as in Experiment 2, viewers may instead respond immediately to the first noticed change, thus missing any additional changes. In relation to medical warning labels, this may indicate that complex labels with many elements could lead viewers to attend to the most salient items at a cost to attending to other label information.

The current study further establishes the usefulness of change blindness paradigms such as the flicker task for the evaluation of label and display design. In particular, the flicker task can provide insight into the design of medical warning labels and similar warnings in order to minimize the chance that information is missed or incorrectly identified. Further research is needed to understand how other factors, such as search strategies, mental workload, and individual differences such as age and expertise influence attention and comprehension of important instructions and warning information on labels.

References

1. Aspden, P., Aspden, P.: Preventing Medication Errors. National Academies Press, Washington (2007)
2. Gurwitz, J.H., et al.: Incidence and preventability of adverse drug events among older persons in the ambulatory setting. JAMA **289**(9), 1107–1116 (2003)
3. Consumer Reports: Can You Read this Drug Label?, June 2011. https://www.consumerrepo rts.org/cro/2011/06/can-you-read-this-drug-label/index.htm
4. Shrank, W.H., et al.: The variability and quality of medication container labels. Arch. Intern. Med. **167**(16), 1760–1765 (2007)
5. Mack, A.: Inattentional blindness: looking without seeing. Curr. Dir. Psychol. Sci. **12**(5), 180–184 (2003)
6. Mack, A., Rock, I.: Inattentional blindness: perception without attention. Vis. Atten. **8**, 55–76 (1998)
7. Simons, D.J.: Current approaches to change blindness. Vis. Cogn. **7**(1–3), 1–15 (2000)
8. Simons, D.J., Levin, D.T.: Change blindness. Trends Cogn. Sci. **1**(7), 261–267 (1997)
9. Levin, D.T., Seiffert, A.E., Cho, S.-J., Carter, K.E.: Are failures to look, to represent, or to learn associated with change blindness during screen-capture video learning? Cogn. Res.: Princ. Implic. **3**(1), 1–12 (2018). https://doi.org/10.1186/s41235-018-0142-3
10. Simons, D.J., Rensink, R.A.: Change blindness: past, present, and future. Trends Cogn. Sci. **9**(1), 16–20 (2005)
11. Hollingworth, A., Henderson, J.M.: Accurate visual memory for previously attended objects in natural scenes. J. Exp. Psychol. Hum. Percept. Perform. **28**(1), 113 (2002)
12. Mitroff, S.R., Simons, D.J., Levin, D.T.: Nothing compares 2 views: change blindness can occur despite preserved access to the changed information. Percept. Psychophys. **66**(8), 1268–1281 (2004)
13. Simons, D.J., Chabris, C.F., Schnur, T., Levin, D.T.: Evidence for preserved representations in change blindness. Conscious. Cogn. **11**(1), 78–97 (2002)
14. Caplovitz, G.P., Fendrich, R., Hughes, H.C.: Failures to see: attentive blank stares revealed by change blindness. Conscious. Cogn. **17**(3), 877–886 (2008)
15. Rensink, R.A., O'regan, J.K., Clark, J.J.: To see or not to see: the need for attention to perceive changes in scenes. Psychol. Sci. **8**(5), 368–373 (1997)
16. Gaschler, R., Mata, J., Störmer, V.S., Kühnel, A., Bilalić, M.: Change detection for new food labels. Food Qual. Prefer. **21**(1), 140–147 (2010)
17. Grissinger, M.: 'Inattentional blindness': what captures your attention? Pharm. Ther. **37**(10), 542 (2012)

18. Galpin, A., Underwood, G., Crundall, D.: Change blindness in driving scenes. Transport. Res. F: Traffic Psychol. Behav. **12**(2), 179–185 (2009)
19. Ahlstrom, U., Suss, J.: Change blindness in pilot perception of METAR symbology. Int. J. Ind. Ergon. **46**, 44–58 (2015)
20. Durlach, P.J.: Change blindness and its implications for complex monitoring and control systems design and operator training. Hum.-Comput. Interact. **19**(4), 423–451 (2004)
21. Austen, E., Enns, J.T.: Change detection. Paying attention to detail. Psyche **6**(11) (2000). http://psyche.cs.monash.edu.au/v6/psyche-6-11-austen.html
22. Cartwright-Finch, U., Lavie, N.: The role of perceptual load in inattentional blindness. Cognition **102**(3), 321–340 (2007)
23. Murphy, G., Greene, C.M.: Load theory behind the wheel; perceptual and cognitive load effects. Can. J. Exp. Psychol./Revue canadienne de psychologie expérimentale **71**(3), 191 (2017)
24. Posner, M.I.: Orienting of attention. Q. J. Exp. Psychol. **32**(1), 3–25 (1980)
25. Pessoa, L., Ungerleider, L.G.: Neural correlates of change detection and change blindness in a working memory task. Cereb. Cortex **14**(5), 511–520 (2004)
26. Stoet, G.: PsyToolkit: a software package for programming psychological experiments using Linux. Behav. Res. Methods **42**(4), 1096–1104 (2010)
27. Stoet, G.: PsyToolkit: a novel web-based method for running online questionnaires and reaction-time experiments. Teach. Psychol. **44**(1), 24–31 (2017)

Analysis of Social Media Usage

Reina Mishima[✉] and Yumi Asahi

Department of Management, Graduate School of Management, Tokyo University of Science,
1-11-2, Fujimi, Chiyoda-ku, Tokyo 102-0071, Japan
8621510@ed.tus.ac.jp, asahi@tsc.u-tokai.ac.jp

Abstract. In recent years, the number of Internet users has been increasing every year. Influenced by the demand for stay-homes in Corona, the current situation is that the Internet is becoming even more popular. In particular, the use of social networking services has increased, indicating that the spread of social networking services among the younger generation is remarkable. From the usage of social networking services, it can be seen that Instagram is the media that shows a large difference among the usage groups. In addition, Instagram is highly effective in appealing to visual information, and is said to be suitable for marketing cosmetics and clothing. (The cosmetics industry has been cited as an industry that has seen a drop in sales in the Corona disaster. Therefore, the cosmetics industry needs to change its marketing methods and aim for recovery in the market. Therefore, this study will focus on the cosmetics industry and discuss effective marketing methods on Instagram. First, we will analyze the characteristics of the cosmetics industry and Instagram users to find common points. Next, we will analyze their behavior on the Internet, focusing on the common point of "fashion-conscious people". Finally, we will examine what kinds of posts on Instagram are most likely to appeal to customers.

Keywords: Social media marketing · Marketing research · Consumer behavior

1 Introduction

The number of Internet users has increased in recent years, and the current situation is one of increasing popularity. In particular, the use of social networking services has been increasing in the previous years.

From Fig. 1, by age group, the usage rate among people in their twenties exceeds 90%, indicating that the use of social networking services is particularly widespread among young people. (Ministry of Internal Affairs and Communications, 2021 White Paper on Information and Communications) Furthermore, based on the usage of social networking services, there is a large difference in the demographics of Instagram users (more young and female users), and it can be predicted that targeted marketing is possible. In order to think about specific measures, we first need to narrow down the industry; Instagram is said to be suitable for marketing cosmetics and clothing because of its strong appeal to visual information. As the coronavirus spreads, sales are slumping in a variety of industries. While sales are recovering in many industries, the cosmetics industry is lagging behind

S. Yamamoto and H. Mori (Eds.): HCII 2022, LNCS 13305, pp. 239–248, 2022.
https://doi.org/10.1007/978-3-031-06424-1_18

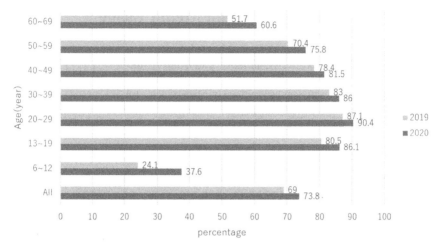

Fig. 1. Usage of social media

in recovering sales from the coronavirus disaster, although it had the highest sales before the coronavirus among cosmetics, clothing, food, and household goods. Based on the characteristics of Instagram and the slump in sales during the Corona disaster, this study will focus on the cosmetics industry. By analyzing the characteristics of Instagram users and customers in the cosmetics industry, we will find common ground. By analyzing the characteristics of Instagram users and customers in the cosmetics industry, we will find common ground, and by analyzing the media that people with common ground use on the Internet at the same time as Instagram, we will find ways to increase mutual effectiveness. In addition, we will further analyze the characteristics of what kind of posts should be made on Instagram to increase the mutual effect.

2   Research Objective

The purpose of this study is to analyze the behavior of customers on social media based on their usage of social media and to propose effective marketing methods on Instagram. The analysis will be done in three stages in conducting the research. First, in order to find out what Instagram users and customers of cosmetic companies have in common, we will analyze the characteristics of each, including their consumption values. Next, to understand the behavior of potential customers on social media, we will focus our analysis on those who have something in common. Finally, by further analyzing the characteristics of customers, the final objective will be to consider how to post in order to increase marketing effectiveness

3   Analysis Method

In this study, we figure out that feature commonalities between Instagram user and customer of cosmetic companies. From that result we analyzed how people use social media. We did three analyses in this study.

3.1 Data

We will use 2,500 questionnaire data provided by Nomura Research Institute. Web usage data and main data will be used from this data.

3.2 Analysis Method

i. **Analyze the characteristics of Instagram users and customers of cosmetic companies.**
    We will analyze the characteristics of Instagram users and cosmetics customers by performing binomial logistic regression analysis. Binary logistic regression analysis is a method of analysis that allows us to find out which factors have a high impact on the cause of a certain event. It consists of a function with each factor $x1, x2, x3, \ldots,$ xn as a variable and a value range of 0 or 1. The model is a linear combination of $x1, x2, x3, \ldots,$ xn, with each b (k $k = 0, 1, 2, \ldots,$ n) as a constant. The model equation is as follows.

$$X = b_0 + \sum_{k=1}^{n} b_k x_k$$

In analyzing the characteristics of Instagram users, Instagram use was set as the objective variable with those who use Instagram more than once a week as users and those who use Instagram less than once a week as non-users. Gender, age, cognitive demands scale, consumption values, REC scale (purchase scale), and control focus scale were set as explanatory variables. Next, customers of cosmetics companies are analyzed. For three products, Canmake (product name: Marshmallow Finish Powder), Maquillage (product name: Dramatic Powdery EX), and Primavista (product name: Beautiful Skin Texture Powder Foundation), the respondents were asked if they "bought the product within the last month," "bought the product within the last Those who answered" "I bought it within the past month" or "I tried it in a store within the past month" were considered customers of the respective companies, and those who answered "I saw it in a store within the past month," "I haven't seen it in a store but I know its name," or "I don't know it" were considered non-customers. For explanatory variables, the same variables as for Instagram users were set.

ii. **Analysis of media used simultaneously with Instagram for "fashion-conscious people"**
    From the analysis of i, we found that the common characteristic of Instagram users and customers of cosmetics companies is that they are "fashion-conscious people". Then, referring to the innovator theory, we classified the "fashion-conscious" into two categories. The innovator theory is a theory proposed by Everett M. Rogers. It is a theory that shows how new products and services will spread in the market by classifying consumers into five layers. Based on the innovator theory, the first step in the penetration of a fad into society is the purchase of a new product by the innovators, followed by the purchase of the product by the early adopters, and then the spread to the early majority, followed by the late majority, and then the laggards. It has been proposed that the transition from early adopter purchases

to early majority purchases is the most difficult task in the penetration of fads. Therefore, we believe that different approaches are needed for early adopters and early majority. In this study, those who answered that they are "more likely to use new products and services or go to new stores before others" were categorized as "those who buy new things before others" and those who answered that they "buy new products and services or go to new stores after waiting a while" were categorized as "those who buy new things before others". Those who answered, "I buy new things before others," and those who answered, "I use new products and services or go to new stores after waiting a little while," were defined as "people who buy what is in fashion". By conducting association analysis, we analyzed which media people in each category use in combination with Instagram. Association analysis is a method of extracting correlations between elements hidden in data in the form of rules (regularities). Rules are expressed as $\{A \Rightarrow B\}$, where A is called the conditional part and B is called the conclusion part. A rule is expressed as $\{A \Rightarrow B\}$, where A is called the condition part and B is called the conclusion part. The most commonly used evaluation indices, support, expected confidence, confidence, and lift, are shown below.

(1) Support: The ratio of the number containing both A and B to the total number (M) $\frac{A \cap B}{M}$.
(2) Expected confidence: The importance is measured by the ratio of the number containing B to the total number (M) ($\frac{B}{M}$).
(3) Confidence: The ratio of the number containing both A and B to the number containing A $\frac{A \cap B}{A}$.
(4) Lift: Confidence divided by expected confidence $\left(\frac{p(B|A)}{P(B)}\right)$. The evaluation will be based mainly on the indicators (1), (3), and (4). The social media Twitter, Facebook, Ameba, LINE, YouTube, Nico Nico Douga, and LINE LIVE were input as variables in the association analysis on media use.

iii. **Analyze the characteristics of each user by focusing on media use.**
From the results derived by ii, the values of customers that differ according to the characteristics of media use are again characterized by performing a binomial logistic regression analysis. (1) Those who use video content (YouTube, Nikoniko video, LINELIVE) at the same time as Instagram, and (2) those who use other SNS (Twitter, Facebook, LINE) at the same time as Instagram are analyzed as objective variables. As variables that characterize each of these variables, we will set "time zone of Instagram use," "product recognition scale for cosmetics," and "consumption values" as explanatory variables.

4   Result of Analysis

4.1   Result of the Characteristics of Instagram Users and Customers of Cosmetic Companies

The results of the binomial logistic regression derived for the characteristics of Instagram users and customers of cosmetic companies are shown in the following figure (Table 1).

Table 1. Feature of Instagram user

	Odds ratio	P-value
Set high goals	0.9202103	3.903870e-02
Focus on color and design even for electrical appliances	1.4464274	6.025989e-03
curious about the reputation of the people who use it	1.5671766	1.301575e-04
Select products based on your lifestyle	1.3730105	2.311323e-03
Buy Japanese products rather than foreign products	0.7069441	1.201329e-03
Buy new products before others when they come out	1.0957723	3.152416e-02
High interest in favorite things	0.8915853	1.387250e-02
Sex (male: 1 ,female: 2	1.9800473	1.342783e-13
Age	0.9656683	1.647942e-15

The following variables were found to have a positive impact on the characteristics of Instagram users: "care about the color and design of electrical products," "care about the reputation of people who use the products," "choose products based on their lifestyle," "buy new products before others when they come out," and "Female" (Table 2).

An analysis of the characteristics of the customers of the three cosmetics companies (Canmake, Maquillage, and Primavista) showed that for Canmake, the variables "buy what is in fashion" and "pay particular attention to the mood and emotion of things" had a positive impact. For Maquillage, "buy custom-made products," "often make expensive purchases with a credit card when I don't have immediate cash or savings," "buy what people around me say is good," and "buy what's in fashion" have positive effects. Finally, for Primavista, "I buy things that are in fashion" and "I pay particular attention to the mood and emotion of things" have a positive influence.

Based on the results of these four binomial logistic regression analyses, it can be said that the common denominator between Instagram users and customers of cosmetics companies is that they are "trendy".

Table 2. Feature of customer of cosmetic companies

	Odds ratio	P-value
Canmake		
buy a trending product	1.8865327	9.913933e-03
Emphasize the mood and emotion of the object	1.4604558	4.549540e-02
Sex (male: 1、 female: 2)	12.8881274	4.574268e-30
Age	0.9730356	3.189491e-04
Maquillage		
Buy custom-made products often	2.3675005	3.625146e-02
Gather various information before they buy products	1.4441479	3.182962e-02
Often make large purchases with credit cards when they don't have immediate cash or savings	1.8152868	2.385828e-03
Chose product by advice from around them	1.8060097	5.486065e-03
Buy a trending product	1.7829448	1.719718e-02
Emphasize the mood and emotion of the object	1.4693307	3.919470e-02
Sex (male: 1、 female: 2)	15.5449846	1.282813e-35
Age	0.9771647	1.587833e-03
Primavista		
Buy a trending product	1.8705328	8.570826e-03
Emphasize the mood and emotion of the object	1.6045716	9.182321e-03
Sex (male: 1、 female: 2)	11.8035882	6.366884e-32

4.2 Result of Analysis of Media Used Simultaneously with Instagram for "Fashion-Conscious People"

Based on the results of Sect. 4.1, it was found that Instagram users and customers in the cosmetics industry have one thing in common: they are sensitive to trends. The results of the association analysis of media use are shown below (Tables 3 and 4).

First, it can be seen that (1) those who buy new things before others use Instagram as well as Ameba, YouTube, Nikoniko movie, and LINE Live. From this, we can see that those who belong to ① use video content at the same time as Instagram more frequently. Next, we see that (2) people who buy trending things use Twitter, Facebook, and LINE at the same time as Instagram. From this result, we can see that people who belong to the category (2) use other SNS at the same time as Instagram. The results derived from association analysis show that people who buy new things before others use Instagram and video content at the same time more frequently. On the other hand, those who buy what is currently in fashion are more likely to use Instagram and other social networking sites at the same time.

Table 3. Media usage of people who buy new things before others

			Support	Confidence	Lift
Instagram, Ameba	$\Rightarrow$	YouTube	0.185484	1.0	1.2156
Instagram, Nikoniko movie	$\Rightarrow$	Twitter	0.177419	1.0	1.4252
Instagram, Nikoniko movie	$\Rightarrow$	YouTube	0.177419	1.0	1.2156
Instagram, Nikoniko movie	$\Rightarrow$	LINE	0.177419	1.0	1.2156
Instagram LINELIVE	$\Rightarrow$	Twitter	0.177419	1.0	1.4252

Table 4. Media usage of people who buy trending things

			Support	Confidence	Lift
Instagram, LINE Timeline	$\Rightarrow$	LINE	0.201708	0.9792	1.2450
Twitter, Facebook, Instagram	$\Rightarrow$	LINE	0.201708	0.9692	1.2322
Facebook, YouTube, Instagram	$\Rightarrow$	LINE	0.21238	0.9613	1.2222
Facebook, Instagram,	$\Rightarrow$	LINE	0.23159	0.9601	1.2207
Twitter, Instagram	$\Rightarrow$	LINE	0.344717	0.9389	1.1937

4.3   Result of the Characteristics of Each User by Focusing on Media Use

Based on the results of ii, we divided the respondents into (1) those who use video content at the same time as Instagram, and (2) those who use other SNS at the same time as Instagram and derived the characteristics of each group of people through binomial logistic analysis. The results are shown below (Tables 5 and 6).

Table 5. Feature of people who use video contents and Instagram simultaneously

	Odds ratio	P-value
Knowledgeable enough to advise others about cosmetics	0.448751	0.024033
There are brands that they always decide to buy	1.672919	0.007461
Often buy disposable products	0.41843	0.022191
Save money to buy things you like, even if they are expensive	0.661811	0.03367
Time of Instagram use: Commuting school or work	1.528213	0.042543

Table 6. Feature of people who use other SNS and Instagram simultaneously

	Odds ratio	P-value
Time of Instagram use: Commuting school or work	2.419556	0.00631
Time of Instagram use: Return home	2.71301	0.00469
Time of Instagram use: Night to before sleep	2.023992	0.002601
Time of Instagram use: Day	1.681858	0.011601
Interested in cosmetics	1.941265	0.023387
Often use rental and leasing	3.342774	0.013659
Often buy disposable products	0.346844	0.053471

For those who belonged to (1), "I have a brand that I always decide to buy" and "I use Instagram on my way to work or school" had a positive impact. On the other hand, "I have the knowledge to give advice to others about cosmetics," "I often buy disposable products," and "I save up to buy what I like, even if it is expensive" have negative effects. These results indicate that people who use Instagram and video content at the same time use Instagram during their commute to and from work, and that they are particular about the brands they buy. On the other hand, they are not confident in their knowledge of cosmetics, and many of them have a tendency to save money. For those belonging to the category (2), we found that "the time of day I use Instagram (commuting to and from work, nighttime to bedtime, during the day, and when I get home)," "cosmetics are of interest to me," and "I often rent or lease products" have a positive influence. On the other hand, "I often buy disposable products" was found to have a negative impact. These results indicate that people who use Instagram and other social networking sites at the same time use Instagram at all times of the day, have a strong interest in cosmetics, and have a tendency to save money and spend only what they need when they need it. From these two results, we can see that the common denominator between those who use Instagram and video content at the same time and those who use Instagram and SNS at the same time is that they have a desire to save money. On the other hand, they use Instagram at different times of the day: those who use Instagram and SNS at the same time use Instagram regardless of the time of day, while those who use Instagram and video content at the same time tend to focus on their commute to work or school.

5 Summary of Result

In this study, we focused on Instagram, which has a large number of young users. In addition, based on the current situation of the cosmetics industry, we thought that the cosmetics industry should focus on marketing on Instagram to recover sales, so we focused our research on a specific industry. First, we analyzed the characteristics of Instagram users and the customers of the three cosmetic companies. We found that they had one thing in common: they were fashion-conscious. Then, referring to the classification of early adopters and early majority in the innovator theory, we divided the "fashion-conscious" into "those who buy new things before others" and "those who buy what is currently in fashion". The results of the analysis were as follows. As a result, it was found that "people who buy new things before others" use video content at the same time as Instagram more frequently, while "people who buy trendy things" use other SNS at the same time as Instagram more frequently. Based on these results, we conducted a binomial logistic regression analysis to determine the characteristics of those who use video content at the same time as Instagram and those who use other SNSs at the same time as Instagram. As a result, the common denominator between those who use video content at the same time as Instagram and those who use other SNSs at the same time as Instagram is that they have a "saving orientation. There is also a difference in the time of day when people use Instagram: those who use video content at the same time as Instagram tend to use Instagram when they are commuting to and from work, while those who use other SNS at the same time as Instagram tend to use Instagram regardless of the time of day. It was also found that people who use other SNS at the same time as Instagram use Instagram regardless of the time of day.

6 Discussion

Based on the results of the analysis, we will discuss effective ways to post on Instagram. First, based on the results of association analysis, since people who buy new products before others use Instagram and video content at the same time, we believe that it is effective to post verification videos about the products of each cosmetics company, short videos explaining how to apply makeup using the performance of the products, promotional videos, and videos on the making of video ads. We think that it would be effective to post videos, or videos of the making of the shooting of video ads. In addition, for those who buy trendy products, it would be effective to conduct projects linked to SNS, increase the number of followers of the company's SNS account, and spread word of mouth on SNS. Next, based on the results of the binomial logistic regression analysis that led to the characteristics of the users of each media, we discuss effective posting. In addition, we found that people who use video content at the same time as Instagram and people who use other social networking services at the same time as Instagram have a common interest in saving money, so we believe that posting information on deals and special campaigns will attract the attention of users.

7 Contributions and Future Challenges

In this study, we focused on "fashion-conscious people" based on the characteristics of Instagram users and customers of cosmetics companies. Based on the innovator theory, we divided "fashion-conscious people" into those who buy new things before others and those who buy what is currently in fashion. The characteristics of each media use were clarified. In addition, we clarified the values of people who have the characteristics of media use. In this study, we first analyzed the customers of cosmetics companies and finally clarified their values regarding cosmetics. Therefore, the research focused on the marketing of cosmetics companies. In the future, we would like to analyze customers in other industries and discuss effective marketing in other industries as well. In addition, although only items related to cosmetics were included as explanatory variables in this study, future analyses should take into account the fact that customers of cosmetics companies can also be customers of other industries.

Thanks.   I would like to express my sincere gratitude to Prof. Yumi Asahi for her a lot of advice in the promotion of this research and the writing of this paper.

References

1. Katsuki, H.: Cosmetic Marketing, Japan Management Association, p. 321 (2005)
2. Niikura, T.: Cosmetics and consumer behavior toward building brand value **37**(3), 192–196 (2013)
3. Watanabe, S.: Young people using social networking as an information tool **69**(5), 38–56 (2019)
4. Sakata, T.: Instagram marketing strategy-advertising communication to gain user engagement **51**(2), 1–33 (2016)
5. Onodera, T.: Public Relations in the Age of Social Media, vol. 68(4) (2018)
6. Nakazawa, H.: Logistic regression **10**(4), 186–191 (2014)
7. Matsuka, T.: Exploratory multi-agent modeling of social structure and innovation emergence, vol. JSAI2013, p. 4F1-4 (2013)
8. Terui, N.: Introduction to Big Data Statistical Analysis, Nihon Hyoron.co (2018)
9. Ministry of Internal Affairs and Communications Japan: White Paper on Information and Communication (2021). https://www.soumu.go.jp/johotsusintokei/whitepaper/ja/r03/html/nd242120.html. Referred 25 Feb 2022
10. Cosmetics Industry Vision Study Group: Cosmetic Industry Vision. https://www.meti.go.jp/policy/mono_info_service/mono/bio/cosme/cosme_vision2021.pdf. Referred 25 Feb 2022
11. Ministry of Internal Affairs and Communications Japan: White Paper on Information and Communication (2019). https://www.soumu.go.jp/main_content/000708015.pdf. Referred 25 Feb 2022

An Analysis of the Writing Japanese Characteristics of Left-Handed Calligraphers ~ Use as Infographics ~

Miho Suto[1][✉], Keiko Kasamatsu[1], and Takeo Ainoya[2,3]

[1] Tokyo Metropolitan University, Asahigaoka, Hino, Tokyo, Japan
112stumh@gmail.com, kasamatu@tmu.ac.jp
[2] Tokyo University of Technology, Nishi-Kamata, Ota, Tokyo, Japan
[3] VDS Co., Ltd., Higashiyama, Meguro, Tokyo, Japan

Abstract. In Japan, there are more right-handed people than left-handed people. For this reason, most of the things in our daily lives are designed with right-handed people in mind. This has led to many inconveniences that left-handed people experience in their daily lives. In spite of the fact that writing is a basic activity that is required from an early age and is performed many times in daily life, the inconvenience felt by left-handed calligraphers is much greater than that of right-handed calligraphers. In this study, we examined the inconvenience felt by left-handed calligraphers when writing Japanese. Therefore, we conducted a meta-analysis of the inconveniences felt by left-handed calligraphers when writing to find out what elements of calligraphy are responsible for the inconveniences they feel. The purpose of this study is to clarify the writing Japanese characteristics of left-handed calligraphers and to summarize them in a form that can be easily understood by people other than left-handers.

Keywords: Left-handed writing · Writing posture · Infographic

1 Introduction

In Japan, there are more right-handed people than left-handed people. For this reason, most of the things in our daily lives are designed to be used by right-handed people.

For example, the automatic ticket gate at the station has the ticket insertion slot and IC card touch panel on the right side of the entrance, and the drop-shaped ladle at the soup bar is difficult to pour because the spout faces the bowl when held with the right hand, but the round side that holds the round soup faces the bowl when held with the left hand. The reason why most of the windows in elementary school classrooms are designed on the left side is to prevent right-handed students from casting shadows on their hands when they write [1].

Indeed, it may be rational to design something so that it is easy for the majority of people to use, because most people will find it convenient.

However, even though they are a minority, there are still approximately 15.08 million left-handed people in Japan in 2022 [2, 3], or about 12% of the population, or one out of every ten people.

In addition, even though writing is a basic activity that is often required from an early age and is performed many times on a daily basis, the inconvenience felt by left-handed calligraphers is much greater than that of right-handed calligraphers.

The purpose of this study is to conduct a meta-analysis of "inconveniences felt by left-handed calligraphers when writing" to find out what elements of writing cause inconveniences, and to conduct experiments to clarify the writing characteristics of left-handed calligraphers and to summarize them in a form that can be easily understood by people other than left-handed people.

2 A Meta-analysis of the Writing Characteristics of Left-Handed Calligraphers

2.1 Focusing on the Elements of Writing Behavior

In order to conduct a meta-analysis of the inconveniences felt by left-handed calligraphers when writing, first of all, we decided to focus on the elements in the writing behavior to predict the elements of the writing behavior that cause the inconvenience, and to find out what they are. Figure 1 shows the decomposition of a writing action into its elements.

Fig. 1. Diagram showing the decomposition of a writing action into its elements.

First, we decomposed the writing behavior into the following ten elements.

- Look at the letters you are writing
- Look for balance as you write
- See where the writing instrument lands
- See where to write and position
- Direction to apply force
- Strength to apply force
- Direction of movement of the writing instrument
- How to hold a writing instrument

- Posture and stance when writing
- Position and angle of the writing target

These could be broadly grouped into three categories: "see", "move hand" and "posture".

2.2   Categorization of Inconveniences Perceived by Left-Handed Calligraphers

Next, we investigated the types of inconveniences felt by left-handed calligraphers, and categorized them according to the three categories mentioned above to determine which elements of the calligraphic motion were causing them.

Inconvenience Felt by Left-Handed Calligraphers. We extracted the inconveniences felt by left-handed calligraphers based on inconveniences that the author, Suto, a left-handed calligrapher, has experienced herself, the interviews with four left-handed calligraphic students in the Department of Industrial Arts, Faculty of System Design, Tokyo Metropolitan University, and a questionnaire survey on the actual status of left-handedness problems conducted by Zebra Corporation (Headquarters: Shinjuku-ku, Tokyo; President: Shinichi Ishikawa) in March 2016 among 104 left-handed people in Japan. [4] The following are some of the inconveniences that emerged.

- When I write horizontally, I can't see the letters that I have just written with my hand.
- The way you hold your writing utensils is strange.
- When I write horizontally, my hand rubs the letters I write and my hand and paper get dirty.
- To begin with, the writing order and the direction of the brush tip, which is considered to be clean, are designed for right-handed people.
- Confused about the stroke order of kanji
- Writing while pressing down on the writing instrument causes the line to be grazed.
- If the model or question text is on the left and the column for writing is on the right, you cannot write while looking at it.
- If you are using a writing instrument that is prone to shaking, such as a brush, you will not be able to draw a straight line due to the effect of pushing.

In particular, "When writing horizontally, the hand rubs the written characters, which stains both the hand and the paper," and "The line is grazed because the writing is done while pushing the writing instrument" were cited in all three of the inconvenience categories.

How to Categorize. This categorization was done by placing and arranging the elements of writing behaviors that are expected to be the cause of each item immediately below the itemized inconveniences of left-handed calligraphers, and tagging each item with the category to which the element of writing behaviors that are expected to be the cause belongs (see Fig. 2).

Fig. 2. Categorizing the inconveniences of left-handed calligraphers.

The inconvenience of left-handed writing is often caused by elements of the "hand movement" category of writing behavior. It was also found that the elements of writing actions in the "hand movement" category alone caused inconvenience, while the elements of writing actions in the "looking" category and the "posture" category caused inconvenience only when they occurred together with the elements of writing actions in other categories.

Therefore, we decided to see how the writing elements of each category are related to each other to cause inconvenience in Experiments A to C.

3   Experiment A: Investigation of the Relationship Between Gaze and Writing Behavior of Left-Handed Calligraphers During Writing

3.1   Hypothesis and Objectives of Experiment C

- Hypothesis
  The way left-handed calligraphers hold their writing utensils is related to the difficulty in seeing the letters they write due to the position of their hands.

  As a supplement to the hypothesis of our experiment, Oshiki et al. (2003) also discussed the relationship between the problem of the hand holding the writing instrument blocking the line of sight during writing and the way the writing instrument is held [5].
- Objective
  To classify left-handed calligraphers by the way they hold their writing instruments.
  To investigate whether the way of holding a writing instrument changes depending on the writing instrument.

To investigate the vision of left-handed calligraphers when writing.
To investigate whether left-handed calligraphers have different writing styles.

3.2 Experimental Methods

The experimental method is as follows.

- Location of the experiment
  Room 307, 3rd floor, Bldg. 4, Hino Campus, Tokyo Metropolitan University
- Experiment period
  July 2021
- Participant
  Four students who are left-handed calligraphers belonging to the Department of Industrial Arts, Faculty of System Design, Tokyo Metropolitan University.

Participants who were left-handed calligraphers were asked to write the specified letters and symbols using the following seven types of writing instruments.

Pencil (Mitsubishi Pencil Hi-uni HB), Mechanical pencil (Mitsubishi Pencil Kultuga Standard Model 0.5 mm HB), Oil-based ballpoint pen (Mitsubishi Pencil Jetstream Standard 0.5 mm), Pressurized oil-based ballpoint pen (Mitsubishi Pencil Power Tank 0.5 mm), fountain pen, Brush pen (Pentel brush, medium size) and Oil-based marker (Zebra Corporation, Macky Extra Fine).

We asked the participants to wear the Tobii Pro, a spectacle-type gaze-measuring device, to record their vision and gaze while writing.

Figure 3 shows the Tobii Pro and an example of the recording screen.

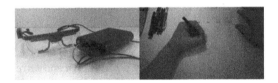

Fig. 3. Example of Tobii Pro and recording screen.

3.3 Experimental Results

Visual Field of Left-Handed Calligraphers During Writing. The main feature of left-handed calligraphers' vision when writing is that the left side of the writing target is hidden by their own hand. There are two factors as to why this leads to inconvenience.

The first factor is that most writing in Japan today is done horizontally, from left to right. [6, 7] In school, textbooks and reference books are written horizontally in all subjects except Japanese, and the writing format is also specified as horizontal. Other official documents, such as marriage certificates, are also written horizontally in a left-to-right format. When left-handed calligraphers write horizontally from left to right in this way, the text written just before the current writing target is hidden by their own hand on top of it. This leads to the inconvenience of having to lift the hand to check underneath each time he wants to check what he has written before.

The second factor is that the writing order is often left-to-right. Therefore, compared to right-handed calligraphers, who have the right side of the writing target hidden by their own hand, they have a disadvantage in vision not only in writing but also in every single letter.

How to Hold a Writing iInstrument for Left-Handed Calligraphers. Among the four participants in our experiment, two different ways of holding the writing utensil were observed, as shown in Fig. 4. The two ways of holding the writing utensil were designated as *holding style a* and *holding style b* respectively.

Fig. 4. How a left-handed calligrapher holds a writing instrument. The left figure shows *holding style a*, and the right figure shows *holding style b*.

Of the four participants, three held their writing utensils in *holding style a* and one in *holding style b*.

In *holding style a*, the left hand is at the back of the writing object, the nib is facing the front, and the wrist is wrapped around the writing object.

Outside of Japan, the "inverted hand position of the left-handers" [8] was used by Jerre Levy and Marylou Reid (1976), the "inverted posture" [9] was used by Jeannine Herron. et al. (1979), "the inverted hand position of left-handers" [10] by Volpe, B. T., et al. (1981), "inverted posture" [11] by Volpe, B. T., et al. (1983) stated that "left-handers who employ an inverted handwriting posture" [8], and Jerre Levy and Marylou Reid (1976) observed that more than 90% of left-handed calligraphers in the U.S. hold their writing implements in a similar manner to this posture. (Jerre Levy, Marylou Reid, 1976, p. 337) [8].

In *holding style b*, the left hand is in front of the object to be written, the nib is pointing toward the back, and the wrist is bent. *Holding style b* is introduced for right-handed calligraphers as a "desirable" and "comfortable" way of holding Japanese calligraphy [5, 12].

After the experiment, we asked each participant why he or she was holding it this way. All three of the participants who were holding the pen in *holding style a* answered, "So that I can see my hand easily." The participant who was holding the pen in *holding style b* answered, "I think it is because I learned calligraphy when I was a child, but it is difficult to see my hand as it is, so I tilt my head to the right so that I can look into it.

3.4 Considerations in Experiment A

From the above results, it can be said that most of the left-handed calligraphers devise a way to hold the writing utensil in order to cope with the field of view when writing.

It can be said that left-handed calligraphers who have the "desirable holding style" of right-handed calligraphers can also cope with the visibility during writing by devising a posture other than holding style.

4 Experiment B: Analysis of Gaze and Writing Behavior of Left-Handed Calligraphers During Writing and Investigation of Inconveniences Felt by the Calligraphers

4.1 Hypothesis and Objectives of Experiment C

- Hypothesis
  There is a similar trend in the gaze and writing behavior of left-handed writers when writing.

  There are different points of inconvenience depending on the writing conditions, such as horizontal and vertical writing, and different writing tools.

  The point of inconvenience differs from those of right-handed calligraphers due to the difference in vision and holding style.
- Objective
  By recording and comparing the gaze and handwriting of left-handed and right-handed writers when they write, we will clarify the differences and find the characteristics of left-handed writing.

  To compare the degree of inconvenience felt by left-handed and right-handed calligraphers in writing situations, we conducted a questionnaire survey on items that may cause inconvenience to left-handed and right-handed calligraphers, and converted the results into a graph using a unique scale called "inconvenience points".

  The results of the survey will be used to compare the degree of inconvenience felt by left-handed and right-handed calligraphers in writing situations, and to compare the causes of the inconvenience felt by each.

4.2 Experimental Methods

The experimental method is as follows.

- Location of the experiment
  Room 307, 3rd floor, Bldg. 4, Hino Campus, Tokyo Metropolitan University
- Experiment period
  November to December 2021
- Participant
  Four students who are left-handed calligraphers (same as the participants in Experiment A) and four students who are right-handed calligraphers belonging to the Department of Industrial Arts, Faculty of System Design, Tokyo Metropolitan University.

The students were asked to write the following specified sentences on ruled paper as instructed. We decided to quote a passage from a famous novel, keeping in mind that the participants' writing of the assigned passage should span multiple lines.

- Specified text

それはだんだんはっきりして、とうとうりんとうごかないようになり、濃い鋼青のそらの野原にたちました。いま新らしく灼いたばかりの青い鋼の板のような、そらの野原に、まっすぐにすきっと立ったのです。

- (Quoted from "Night on the Galactic Railroad" by Kenji Miyazawa)[13]
- Instructions for writing actions

The students were asked to write sentences based on the following 12 instructions.

(1)   Horizontal writing, carefully, with a pencil.
(2)   Horizontal writing, carefully, with a mechanical pencil.
(3)   Horizontal writing, carefully, with a ballpoint pen.
(4)   Horizontal writing, like you're taking a note, with a pencil.
(5)   Horizontal writing, like you're taking a note, with a mechanical pencil.
(6)   Horizontal writing, like you're taking a note, with a ballpoint pen.
(7)   Vertical Writing, carefully, with a pencil.
(8)   Vertical Writing, carefully, with a mechanical pencil.
(9)   Vertical Writing, carefully, with a ballpoint pen.
(10)   Vertical Writing, like you're taking a note, with a pencil.
(11)   Vertical Writing, like you're taking a note, with a mechanical pencil.
(12)   Vertical Writing, like you're taking a note, with a ballpoint pen.

In addition, the participants were asked to answer a questionnaire about the degree of inconvenience they felt in writing each of the 12 instructions. The contents of the questionnaire are described in Subsect. 4.2. "Degree of inconvenience: The contents of the questionnaire about inconvenient points" below.

- Procedure
  After the participants wrote sentences under the instructions from (1) to (6) and answered the questionnaire, additional questions were asked orally based on the results of the questionnaire and their writing behavior, and a 10-min break was provided after their answers. After the break, the participants were asked to write sentences based on the instructions in (7) to (12) and answer a questionnaire, and then additional questions were asked orally based on the results of the questionnaire and their writing behavior. At the end of the session, we asked additional questions orally if there were any points of concern throughout the session.
  The participants wore the Tobii pro to measure their gaze, and their gaze was recorded while they wrote.

Degree of Inconvenience: The Contents of the Questionnaire About Inconvenient Points

The purpose of this experiment was to compare the degree of inconvenience felt by left-handed and right-handed calligraphers in writing situations by conducting a questionnaire survey on items that may cause inconvenience and converting the results into a graph using a unique scale called "inconvenience points". The scale to measure the "inconvenience point" in the questionnaire was set as follows. In the first place, the "scale" often mentioned in this section is based on a psychometric scale [14, 15].

Yokouchi says, "The psychometric scale is a kind of method for measuring psychological phenomena, and is, so to speak, a 'measure of the mind' for understanding invisible psychological phenomena. By scoring the answers to a number of questions, the psychometric scale makes it possible to grasp individual differences in psychological phenomena" (Yokouchi, 2007, p. 1) [16].

In this experiment, a scale was set up to measure the psychological inconvenience felt when writing, a questionnaire was created and responses were collected, and the results were analyzed.

First, in order to extract examples of "inconvenience" suitable for the scale, "inconvenience felt in writing" was identified again.

The difference between the inconveniences identified in this study and those surveyed in Sect. 2.2 "inconveniences felt by left-handed calligraphers" is that the inconveniences include not only those caused by the dominant hand but also those caused by the characteristics of calligraphy itself. Therefore, we conducted an additional interview survey with a right-handed calligrapher friend, and added the inconveniences found in the survey to the list of inconveniences. After dividing the inconveniences into "inconveniences caused by the dominant hand" and "inconveniences of writing itself," the inconveniences that could occur under the writing conditions of Experiment B were extracted. The reason for this categorization process is to predict the degree of inconvenience that may differ between left-handed and right-handed writers.

The elements of inconvenience extracted are as follows.

(i)   Whether the direction of the writing process made it difficult to write.
(ii)   Difficulty in seeing your own hand
(iii) Ease of writing on the writing utensils used
(iv)   Stains on hands and paper
(v)   Feelings of inferiority about my own writing
(vi)   Fatigue when writing
(vii) Evaluation of one's own posture when writing

Of these, (i), (ii), (iv), and (vii) were classified as being caused by the dominant hand, and (iii), (v), and (vi) were classified as being caused by the inconvenience of writing itself. As for (iii), "the degree of writing ease depending on the writing utensil used," the reason why some writing utensils are difficult to use depends on the dominant hand, as confirmed in Experiment A. Therefore, the inconvenience caused by the dominant hand is also included. The above inconvenience factors were set as a scale to measure the inconvenience points as follows, and the participants were asked to rate the points in the range of 1 to 4 points. They were asked to rate the inconvenience in the range of 1 to 4 points. The questions were formulated so that the higher the point, the more inconvenient they felt.

(1) Did the direction of the writing process make it difficult to write?
(2) Was it hard for you to see what you were doing?
(3) Are the writing utensils you used easy to write with?
(4) Did you get your hands or paper dirty?
(5) Do you find it difficult to read back the words you just wrote?
(6) Did you feel tired when you wrote it?
(7) Do you feel that your posture is bad when you write?

4.3 Experimental Results

View of the Field of Views. The following figure shows a chronological sequence on a number line of recordings of the visual field during writing.

Figure 5 shows the observation of the visual field of participant C-l, a left-handed calligrapher with *holding style a.*

Figure 6 shows the observation of the visual field of participant B-l, a left-handed calligrapher with *holding style b.*

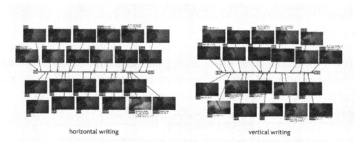

horizontal writing   vertical writing

Fig. 5. The observation of the visual field of participant C-l, a left-handed calligrapher with *holding style a.*

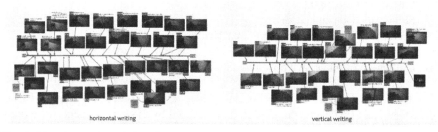

horizontal writing   vertical writing

Fig. 6. The observation of the visual field of participant B-l, a left-handed calligrapher with *holding style b.*

Field of vision of left-handed calligraphers with *holding style a* writing horizontally have the following characteristics: "the content of the previous writing is hidden by their left hand" and "they tilt their head to the right so that they can easily see the writing target". Their field of vision writing vertically have the following characteristics: "the hand is easier to see than in horizontal writing, but the left side of the character is hidden, so the hand is not always in a position where it is easy to see each character" and "when writing on the lower side (front side), the hand is looking into the hand from the upper right. Field of vision of left-handed calligraphers with *holding style b* writing horizontally have the following characteristics: "not only the content of the previous writing, but even the writing target at that moment is hidden by his left hand." and "since the writing target is quite difficult to see, he tilts his head in both directions to make it easier to see the writing target." Their field of vision writing vertically have the following characteristics: "compared to horizontal writing, the hand is easier to see, but I still find it difficult to see, so I tilt my head to the right quite a bit and adjust it to make it easier to see."

Results of Analysis of Responses to Questionnaire About Degree of Inconvenience: Inconvenience Points

The following is an excerpt from a list of items that tended to be more inconvenient for left-handed writers than for right-handed writers.

Figure 7 shows the items for which the inconvenience points tend to be higher for left-handed writers than for right-handed writers.

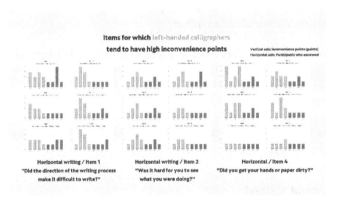

Fig. 7. Graphs of inconvenience point questionnaires for items where inconvenience points tend to be high among left-handed calligraphers. The vertical axis shows the number of inconvenience points and the horizontal axis shows the participants.

The following items tended to be more inconvenient for left-handed writers than for right-handed writers: horizontal writing/(1): "Difficulty in writing depending on the direction of writing", horizontal writing/(2) "Is it difficult to see my hand", and horizontal writing/(4): "Is my hand or paper dirty?

4.4 Considerations in Experiment B

Left-handed calligraphers who use *holding style a* to accommodate their field of vision when writing.

On the other hand, left-handed calligraphers who use *holding style b* have a poor visual field when writing.

Many left-handed calligraphers find it difficult to write horizontally.

The main reasons for this are that it is difficult to see one's own hand when writing horizontally and that left-handed calligraphers often place their hand on the letter just before they are writing when writing horizontally, which causes them to rub the written letter when using a pencil or mechanical pencil, turning their hand and paper black.

5   Experiment C: A Survey on the Ease of Writing Letters and Dots as Perceived by Left-Handed Calligraphers

5.1 Hypothesis and Objectives of Experiment C

- Hypothesis
  There is a tendency for left-handed and right-handed calligraphers to write letters and dots in different ways.

  In addition, there is a tendency for left-handed and right-handed calligraphers to have difficulty writing dots and characters.
  Left-handed calligraphers who do a lot of push writing have relatively higher writing pressure than right-handed calligraphers.
- Objective
  To clarify the elements of dots that are difficult or easy for left-handed calligraphers to write, and to investigate whether there are differences between left-handed and right-handed calligraphers.

  The relative writing pressure will be compared to see if there is a trend between left-handed and right-handed calligraphers.

  By recording their handwriting on video, we can check whether they are trying to make the stroke order of pointillism easier to write.

5.2 Experimental Methods

The experimental method is as follows.

- Location of the experiment
  Room 307, 3rd floor, Bldg. 4, Hino Campus, Tokyo Metropolitan University
- Experiment period
  November to December 2021
- Participant
  Four students who are left-handed calligraphers and four students who are right-handed calligraphers belonging to the Department of Industrial Arts, Faculty of System Design, Tokyo Metropolitan University (same as the participants in Experiment B).

The students were asked to write the following specified sentences on ruled paper as instructed. We decided to quote a passage from a famous novel, keeping in mind that the participants' writing of the assigned passage should span multiple lines.

Using an iPad pro and an Apple Pencil, the participants were asked to write the specified symbols and letters and the evaluation of the ease of writing these prepared in the paint art production application "procreate".

The evaluation method was based on the fact that when we conducted a questionnaire on the symbols and letters that were particularly easy to write and difficult to write in Experiment A, the participants forgot the feeling of writing the symbols and letters at the end of the questionnaire and the evaluation became ambiguous.

For the evaluation options, there were three choices: ○ (evaluation score: 2 points) for "easy to write", △ (evaluation score: 1 point) for "normal" and × (evaluation score: 0 points) for "difficult to write".

When comparing the ratings, an item was considered "difficult to write" if there was a difference of two or more points between the rating scores of left-handed and right-handed calligraphers for the item (one symbol or letter) and if the total rating score for the item was less than one point.

At this time, we asked the participants to wear "Tobii pro" to record their gaze. We also recorded their posture and handwriting while they wrote.

Selection of Symbols and Characters. We selected a set of symbols and Japanese letters: regular kanji, hiragana, and katakana, paying attention to the direction of brush strokes and other pointing elements, based on previous studies [17–20] and the results of a preliminary survey in Experiment A.

In experiment C, we selected a total of 20 symbols: clockwise circles (starting points: top and bottom), counterclockwise circles (starting points: top and bottom), straight lines in eight directions, (straight lines rotated by 45°), horizontal spirals (starting points: left and right, two ways of winding), and vertical spirals (starting points: top and bottom, two ways of winding), as well as 20 types of Japanese letters (see Table 1).

Table 1 summarizes the Japanese letters selected and the reasons for their selection.

Table 1. The Japanese letters we selected and why we selected them.

All participants were instructed to use the same size sheet and brush when filling out the form.

Measurement of Writing Pressure. In order to compare the relative writing pressure between left-handed and right-handed calligrapher, we created and set up a brush with pressure detection that changes the line thickness depending on the writing pressure, and all participants used it under the same conditions.

5.3   Experimental Results

About Dot Elements that are Difficult or Easy for Left-Handed Calligraphers to Write. Tables 2 and 3 summarize the participants' ratings of the ease of writing symbols and Japanese letters.

Participants A-l, B-l, C-l, and D-l are left-handed calligraphers, and participants E-r, F-r, G-r, and H-r are right-handed calligraphers.

Table 2. Participants' evaluation of the ease of writing symbols.

The evaluation of symbols shows that left-handed writers find it more difficult to write "clockwise starting point upper circle," "clockwise starting point lower circle," "eight-way straight line 2," "horizontal spiral c," "vertical spiral f," and "vertical spiral h" than right-handed writers.

Considering the commonalities among these symbols, we can assume that the "eight-way straight line 2" and "vertical spiral h" are difficult to write for left-handed calligraphers because they begin by pressing down. In addition, "horizontal spiral c," "vertical spiral f," and "vertical spiral h" are considered to be difficult to write because they contain a series of clockwise circles, which are also felt to be difficult to write by left-handed calligraphers.

Because they are used to writing letters on a regular basis, they rated writing as easy or normal overall, so we could not determine the tendency of difficulty in writing letters among left-handed calligraphers.

Table 3. Participants' evaluation of the ease of writing Japanese letters.

		北	永	成	才	女	去	及	皮	近	あ	す	せ	つ	ひ	り	ん	シ	ツ	ミ	ヨ
Left-handed calligrapher	A-l	△	○	△	○	○	○	△	△	△	○	○	○	○	○	△	○	○	△	○	○
	B-l	△	△	△	×	×	○	○	△	○	○	○	△	△	○	△	○	△	○	△	○
	C-l	○	○	○	○	△	○	○	○	○	△	○	○	△	○	○	○	○	△	○	○
	D-l	○	○	○	○	○	○	△	△	○	○	○	○	○	△	○	○	○	○	×	○
evaluation score		6	7	6	6	5	8	6	5	7	7	8	7	6	7	6	8	7	6	5	8
right-handed calligrapher	E-r	×	△	○	○	△	○	△	○	△	△	○	△	△	△	△	○	△	△	○	○
	F-r	○	○	○	△	○	△	△	△	△	○	○	△	○	○	○	○	×	△	△	○
	G-r	○	○	○	○	△	○	○	△	○	○	△	○	○	○	△	○	○	△	△	○
	H-r	○	×	△	△	×	△	○	×	○	○	△	△	○	△	×	○	○	△	△	△
evaluation score		6	5	7	6	4	6	6	5	6	7	6	5	7	6	5	8	5	4	5	7

Writing Pressure of Left-Handed Calligraphers. Figure 8 shows a comparison of the relative strength of writing pressure between the handwriting of the participants in Experiment C.

	left-handed calligrapher				right-handed calligrapher			
	A-l	B-l	C-l	D-l	E-r	F-r	G-r	H-r
symbol	7	6	1	2	3	5	4	8
character	7	3	2	5	6	1	4	8
comprehensive	7	5	1	3	5	2	4	8

Ranking the strength of writing pressure

Fig. 8. A relative comparison of the strength of writing pressure between the handwritings of the participants who filled out the form in Experiment C.

As can be seen in Fig. 8, there was no relationship between the strength of writing pressure and handedness.

5.4 Considerations in Experiment C

Both left-handed and right-handed calligraphers felt that it was easy to write lines in the pulling direction and difficult to write lines in the pushing direction.

Left-handed calligraphers find it difficult to draw a clockwise circle.

The letters were generally rated as easy or normal to write, probably because they are used to writing letters on a regular basis. Therefore, we could not identify any tendency of difficulty in writing letters.

The strength of writing pressure was not related to handedness.

6 Proposal for Infographics on Left-Handed Writing Characteristics

An infographics booklet on the writing characteristics of left-handers was produced on the purpose of this study is to clarify the writing characteristics of left-handed calligraphers based on the survey and to summarize them in a form that can be easily understood by people other than those involved.

Figure 9 is a part of the contents of the booklet.

Fig. 9. A part of the contents of the booklet.

I have tried to summarize the characteristics of left-handed calligraphy in a visually clear way, and to describe what left-handed calligraphers can do as well.

In addition to the issue of handedness, the content of the book is designed to encourage people to think about the design of things from the perspective of various people, and to consider designs that make the most of their individuality.

7 Conclusion

The purpose of this study was to conduct a meta-analysis of "inconveniences felt by left-handed calligraphers when writing" to find out what elements of writing cause inconveniences, and to conduct experiments to clarify the writing characteristics of left-handed calligraphers and to summarize them in a form that can be easily understood by people other than left-handed people.

The research method is as follows.

First of all, we decomposed the elements of writing, categorized what elements were responsible for the inconvenience of left-handedness, and predicted the elements of writing that caused the inconvenience of left-handedness.

As a result, we arrived at the following considerations and conjectures.

First, let's look at the way left-handed calligraphers hold their writing instruments.

This can be explained by the observation of the visual field of left-handed calligraphers when writing one letter at a time in Experiment A and the observation of the visual field of left-handed calligraphers when writing a sentence in Experiment B.

Many left-handed calligraphers use *holding style a* to accommodate their field of vision when writing.

On the other hand, left-handed calligraphers who use *holding style b* have a poor field of view when writing because their hand hides the writing target.

The next question is about the factors that left-handed calligraphers find inconvenient when writing.

The results of the questionnaire survey on the inconvenience felt by left-handed calligraphers during writing in Experiment B can be used to explain this.

Many left-handed calligraphers find it difficult to write horizontally.

The main reasons for this are that it is difficult to see their own hand when writing horizontally and that left-handed writers often write with their hand on top of the letter they are writing, so when they use a pencil or mechanical pencil, they rub the letter they have written and their hand and paper turn black.

Finally, there are some symbols and characters that left-handed calligraphers find difficult to write.

This can be considered from the results of the survey on the ease of writing letters and dots felt by left-handed calligraphers conducted in Experiment C.

Left-handed calligraphers find it easier to write lines in the pulling direction and harder to write lines in the pushing direction.

In addition, left-handed calligraphers find it difficult to write clockwise circles.

In addition, since Japanese characters are basically written with the rules of "left to right" and "top to bottom," it can be inferred that left-handed calligraphers, who tend to move their hands in the pushing direction, may find it easier to write at fewer times than right-handed calligraphers, who tend to move their hands in the pulling direction.

We also created an infographics booklet to make the writing characteristics of left-handed calligraphers easier to understand for people other than the left-handed calligraphers.

Therefore, the social significance of this study is to spread knowledge of the problems and inconveniences that left-handed writers, who are in the minority, face in their daily lives to people other than those who are involved in the study, and to promote improvements in society that are considerate of left-handed writers.

References

1. Kawai, T.: School hygiene in Arthur Newsholme: hygienization, government, and morality. Reg. Stud. Bull. Fac. Reg. Stud. Tottori Univ. **12**(2), 61–74 (2015)
2. Statistics Bureau, Ministry of Internal Affairs and Communications in Japan Homepage, Population Projection in Japan (Current as of 1 July 2021 (Constant value)). https://www.stat.go.jp/data/jinsui/new.html. Accessed 18 Jan 2022
3. Kubota, K.: The Hand and the Brain, Revised and Updated Edition, pp. 174–175. Kinokuniya Bookstore, Japan (2010)
4. ZEBRA Homepage. https://www.zebra.co.jp/press/news/2016/0411.html. Accessed 18 Jan 2022
5. Oshiki, H., Kondoh, S., Hashimoto, A.: Desirable ways of holding writing instruments, their rationality and verification methods. Writ. Calligraphy Educ. Res. **17**, 11–20 (2003)
6. WEDGE Infinity, ACADEMIC ANIMAL Homepage: Intellectual Inquirers, How Japanese Went from Vertical to Horizontal Writing (Part 1). https://wedge.ismedia.jp/articles/-/1019. Accessed 21 Jan 2022

7. WEDGE Infinity, ACADEMIC ANIMAL Homepage: Intellectual Inquirers, How Japanese Went from Vertical to Horizontal Writing (Part 1). https://wedge.ismedia.jp/articles/-/1020. Accessed 21 Jan 2022

8. Levy, J., Reid, M.: Variations in writing posture and cerebral organization. Science **194**, 337–339 (1976)

9. Herron, J., Galin, D., Johnstone, J., Ornstein, R.E.: Cerebral specialization, writing posture, and motor control of writing in left-handers. Science **205**, 1285–1289 (1979)

10. Volpe, B.T., Sidtis, J.J., Gazzaniga, M.S.: Can left-handed writing posture predict cerebral language laterality? Arch. Neurol. **38**(10), 637–638 (1981)

11. McKeever, W.F., Hoff, A.L.: Further evidence of the absence of measurable interhemispheric transfer time in left-handers who employ an inverted handwriting posture. Bull. Psychon. Soc. **21**(4), 255–258 (1983). https://doi.org/10.3758/BF03334702

12. Hirakata, S., et al.: The New Calligraphy 2. Tokyo Shoseki, Japan (2020)

13. Miyazawa, K.: Brand-New Edition: The Night of the Milky Way Trai, pp. 171–172. SHINCHO BUNKO, Japan (1989)

14. Hori, H., Matsui, Y.: Psychological Measurement Scales III-Measures of Mental Health <Appropriate and Clinical>. SAIENSU-SHA, Japan (2001)

15. Boateng, G.O., Neilands, T.B., Frongillo, E.A., Melgar-Quiñonez, H.R., Young, S.L.: Best practices for developing and validating scales for health, social, and behavioral research: a primer. Front. Public Health **6**, 149 (2018)

16. Yokouchi, M.: Basic understanding of psychometric scales. J. Jpn. Soc. Intensive Care Med. **14**(4), 555–561 (2007)

17. Ohnishi, A., Oshiki, H.: A basic study on the difference of handedness in writing behavior: focusing on the direction and tilt of stroke and the selection of empty strokes. Joetsu Univ. Educ. Kokugo Stud. **29**, 48–34 (2015)

18. Kobayashi, H.: An analytical study on the relationship between the paper placement and the character form in left-handed calligraphy: a comparison between brush calligraphy and pencil calligraphy. In: Shinshu University Faculty of Education Research Conference, vol. 8, pp. 61–80 (2015)

19. Galina, V., Victor, V.: A method of the analysis of Kanji structure: a new approach based on structural decomposition and coding. Natl. Inst. Linguist. **9**, 215–236 (2015)

20. Galina, V., Victor, V.: Inhibition factors in Kanji study and their elimination for learners of Japanese from a Non-Kanji background: supporting systematic. Kanji Study **12**, 163–179 (2017)

Research and Optimization of Skin Design for Mobile Terminal Input Method Based on Emotional Experience

Rui-Qi Wu[✉] and Xue-Dong Zhang

School of Arts, Anhui Polytechnic University, Wuhu, China
wuruiqi0922@163.com

Abstract. Objective: To provide ideas and schemes for the emotional design of mobile input method skin. Methods: The emotional experience evaluation experiment was designed according to the selected representative skin samples of input method, so as to obtain the emotional response data of each sample under different emotional dimensions. Conclusion: through the analysis of experimental data and the comparison of different sample design elements, the suggestions of skin design optimization of mobile input method based on emotional experience are put forward.

Keywords: Mobile input method skin · Emotional design · Sample · Emotional experience

1 Introduction

With the popularization of smart phones, users have more and more personal needs for mobile phone software, and the mobile input method skin is an indispensable functional software for mobile phones. In the field of mobile input method skin design, the tendency of product homogeneity is becoming more and more serious, and in the design of user experience, almost all of them are limited to the improvement and extension of the vision and function of the input method skin, rarely involving emotional experience. In terms of emotional experience, there is no research on the mobile input method skin, so it is particularly necessary to study the emotional design of the mobile terminal input method skin.

User experience refers to the psychological feelings established by users in the process of using a product. At present, with the development of information technology, on the one hand, users have become more demanding on the user experience of products. On the other hand, designers can quickly explore the potential emotional needs of users through new technologies such as the Internet. Users also have various ways to express their own emotional appeals, even directly involved in product design. The direction of product design has gradually shifted, and the concept of user experience has also expanded the purpose of design from usability and ease of use to the dimensions of emotion and meaning [1]. As an important direction of product design, emotional design has begun to become a new trend in product user experience design.

The goal of emotional design is to connect with users at the personality level [2], so that users can generate positive emotions in the process of interacting with the product, so that users can generate pleasant memories and promote users to continue using the product. As the trend of product homogeneity is becoming more and more obvious today, consumers are more willing to choose products that can touch their emotions, so the research of emotional design is particularly important [3].

2 Sample Selection

2.1 Collection of Input Method Skins

The object of this research is the input method skin of the mobile terminal. Therefore, according to the input method designer and skin type, search and experience 20 different types of mobile terminal input method skins through the web, then in each input method skin, open the nine-grid keyboard and use its interface as a sample of the initial mobile terminal input method skin.

2.2 Determine the Input Method Skin Design Elements and Their Level

According to the collected nine-grid keyboard interface of 20 mobile input method skins, it can be found that the overall structure of most input method skins is exactly the same. After analysis and sorting, the top view of the nine-grid interface of the mobile terminal input method skin is shown in Fig. 1. It should be noted that the function bar of some input method skins will be directly occupied by the text association field, that is, the text association field will not be set separately, and some input methods will not set the input text field, but directly occupy the input of the application column.

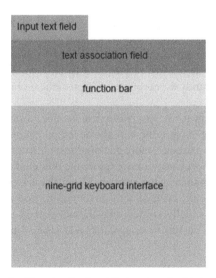

Fig. 1. Thumbnail of mobile input method interface

Next, this experiment invited five teachers and graduate students engaged in related research to determine the design elements of the mobile terminal input method skin using morphological analysis and expert discussion. The process was divided into two steps: In the first step, all participants were required to view and think about the collected 20 initial samples of mobile input method skins, and to list the mobile skin design elements in each region according to the regional division of the mobile interface thumbnails; In the second step, participants are required to form a focus group to analyze and discuss the results obtained by observing the input method skin samples in the first step and explain some of the design elements.

Table 1. Design elements and levels of mobile input method skin that affect user emotional experience

Selected area	Skin design elements	Element level
Input text field	Yes or No (A)	Yes (A1)
		No (A2)
Text association field	Background color (B)	Theme background (B1)
		White (B2)
	Separate column (C)	Yes (C1)
		Occupy the function bar (C2)
Function bar	Logo (D)	Yes (D1)
		No (D2)
	Unified style (E)	Yes (E1)
		No (E2)
	One-click skinning (F)	Yes (F1)
		No (F2)
Keyboard keys	Button form (G)	Three-dimensional (G1)
		Flat (G2)
	Button feedback (H)	Special sound effects (H1)
		No (H2)
Overall	Theme (I)	Yes (I1)
		No (I2)
	Color (J)	Cool colors (J1)
		Warm colors (J2)
	Dynamic effect (K)	Yes (K1)
		No (K2)
	Word Art (L)	Yes (L1)
		No (L2)
	Style (M)	Simplicity (M1)
		Normal (M2)
		Fancy (M3)

According to the listed input method skin design elements, experts discuss again, and combined with 20 initial mobile terminal input method skin samples, determine the skin design elements that affect the user's emotional experience and their levels [4] as shown in Table 1.

2.3 Input Method Skin Code

The initial skin samples (20 skin nine-grid interfaces of mobile input method)are coded according to the level of the input method skin design elements that affect the user's emotional experience, and 27 levels of the 20 groups of design elements for each input method skin are coded. For comparison, when the input method skin belongs to a certain level on a certain design element, mark 1 at the corresponding code position of the level, and mark 0 on the contrary. Use SPSS software to perform cluster analysis on the coding results [5], and obtain a cluster analysis tree diagram as shown in Fig. 2.

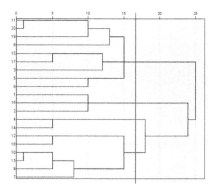

Fig. 2. Cluster analysis dendrogram

According to the dendrogram analysis of cluster analysis in Figs. 1 and 2 above, it can be seen that the results of clustering 20 input method skin samples into 4 categories are relatively stable, which shows that the characteristics of 4 categories are more prominent, so 20 input methods can be divided into 4 categories. In order to select a sample from each class as the representative of the class, using k-means cluster analysis and set the number of clusters to 4. The cluster analysis results are shown in Table 2.

Table 2. Cluster analysis results

Skin number	Category	Distance from center	Skin number	Category	Distance from center
7	1	2.167	6	3	2.041
9	1	1.552	8	3	2.198
10	1	1.457	15	3	1.683
12	1	1.884	17	3	2.041
13	1	1.807	19	3	2.198
16	1	2.356	4	4	1.414
18	1	2.356	5	4	2.280
1	2	1.414	11	4	1.897
2	2	1.414	14	4	2.366
3	3	2.041	20	4	1.897

Select the input method skin sample closest to the center in each category as the representative of each category [6]. Therefore, the input method skin numbers are 10, 1, 15 and 4 respectively, namely the Poker (Baidu), Night factory (Sogou), Interstellar (Xunfei) and Capsule (Sogou) input method skins are used as the representative input methods for the subsequent emotion scale measurement. Experiments (see Figs. 3, 4, 5 and 6).

Fig. 3. Input method skin number A display

Fig. 4. Input method skin number B display

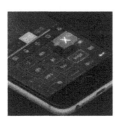

Fig. 5. Input method skin number C display

Fig. 6. Input method skin number D display

3   The Skin Emotion Experience Evaluation Experiment of the Mobile Terminal Input Method

The main purpose of this experiment is to study the emotional response of users in three different dimensions when they experience different input skins by using SAM scale. In this experiment, college students from Anhui Polytechnic University were used as subjects, including 22 males and 18 females. The Experiment was conducted in a well-lit and quiet computer room [7]. Before the experiment, four mobile phones of the same model (Meizu 16x, white, 6+ 64G, 6.0-inch screen), were install installed with four representative input methods selected above, and then replaced the corresponding skins as experimental materials. 40 subjects were asked to input the text materials shown in Fig. 7 on four mobile phones with different input method skins in sequence at the specified time, and pay attention to experience the various functions and appearance design of the input method [8]. Finally, the subjects were asked to fill in the SAM emotional quantification table based on their experience [9].

1、 "都到齐了么？同学们。"老师说，"都到齐了我们就可以出发了。"

2、 {[a-zA-Z]|[0-9]|\W}其实我也很郁闷。

3、 The weather is very good today, but I heard that it may rain in the next few days. You must remember to bring an umbrella when you go out, otherwise it will get wet.今天天气很不错，但是我听说未来几天可能会下雨，你出门要记得带伞，否则会被淋湿。

Fig. 7. Text materials

4   Experimental Data Processing and Analysis

The pleasure degree and activation degree in the emotional quantitative form of SAM were ranked from left to right as 9, 8, 7, 6, 5, 4, 3, 2 and 1, respectively indicating the degree from very happy to very unhappy and from awakening to dormancy. The degree of dominance is marked as 1, 2, 3, 4, 5, 6, 7, 8, and 9 in the order from left to right, indicating the degree from controlling to being controlled. Three pictures representing emotional responses were displayed on each dimension to help participants make choices. Finally, entered the participants' options and used x ± s to describe the final score for each dimension [10].

Use SPSS2.2 statistical software to perform repeated measurement single-factor analysis of variance and multiple comparisons on the experimental data to test whether the pleasure, activation and dominance of the input method skin are significant, and whether the difference between the input method skins is significant. The score is the dependent variable, and the input method skin type is the factor [11].

4.1   The Influence of Input Method Design on Pleasure

On the pleasure dimension, the statistical results of each skin score are analyzed by repeated measurement one-way analysis of variance, and the repeated measurement one-way analysis of variance is shown in Tables 3 and 4.

Table 3. Pleasure score variance homogeneity test form

Levene statistical data	df1	df2	Significance
1.707	3	156	0.168

It can be seen from Table 3 that the significance of the output is 0.168, which is greater than 0.05, so the overall variance of each group can be considered equal.

Table 4. Pleasure score analysis of variance form

	Sum of square	Df	Mean squared	F	Significance
Between groups (merge)	137.825	3	45.942	10.609	0.000
Linear term comparison	54.08	1	54.08	12.488	0.001
Deviation	83.745	2	41.873	9.669	0.000
In the group	675.55	156	4.33	–	–
Total	813.375	159	–	–	–

It can be seen from Table 4 that the variance test F = 10.609, the corresponding significance is 0, which is less than the significance level of 0.05. Therefore, it can be considered that at least one of the four input method skins and the other are present in pleasure significant difference. The results of multiple comparison analysis are shown in Table 5.

Table 5. Pleasure score multiple comparison form

(I) Skin number	(J) Skin number	Average difference (I-J)	Standard error	Significance	95% confidence interval	
					Lower limit	Upper limit
A	B	0.575	0.443	0.196	−0.30	1.45
	C	−0.575	0.443	0.196	−1.45	0.30
	D	−0.100	0.443	0.822	−0.97	0.77
B	A	−0.575	0.443	0.196	−1.45	0.30
	C	−1.150*	0.443	0.010	−2.02	-0.28
	D	−0.675	0.443	0.129	−1.55	0.20
C	A	0.575	0.443	0.196	−0.30	1.45
	B	1.150*	0.443	0.010	0.28	2.02
	D	0.475	0.443	0.285	0.40	1.35
D	A	0.100	0.443	0.822	−0.77	0.97
	B	0.675	0.443	0.129	−0.20	1.55
	C	−0.475	0.443	0.285	−1.35	0.40

From Table 5 score multiple comparison form, where which means the average difference data result with "*" is lower than 0.05 significance level of the pairwise combinations. It can be seen from the Form that only the combination of skin number B and skin number C has a significance of 0.01 lower than the significance level of 0.05, so only this combination has a significant difference in the pleasure dimension. The difference in the average skin score of each input method is shown in Fig. 8 below.

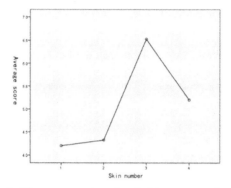

Fig. 8. The average value of each skin score on pleasure

4.2   The Influence of Input Method Design on Activation

On the activation dimension, the statistical results of each skin score are analyzed by repeated measurement of one-way analysis of variance, and the results are shown in Tables 6 and 7.

In the activation dimension, the statistical results of skin scores were analyzed by repeated measures of one-way Anova, and the results were listed in table.

Table 6. Activation score variance homogeneity test form

Levene statistical data	df1	df2	Significance
0.791	3	156	0.501

It can be seen from Table 6 that the significance of the output is 0.501, which is much greater than 0.05, so the overall variance of each group can be considered equal.

Table 7. Activation score analysis of variance form

	Sum of square	Df	Mean squared	F	Significance
Between groups (merge)	26.75	3	8.917	2.276	0.028
Linear term comparison	4.205	1	4.205	1.073	0.032
Deviation	22.545	2	11.272	2.877	0.059
In the group	611.25	156	3.918	–	–
Total	638	159	–	–	–

It can be seen from Table 7 that the variance test $F = 2.276$, and the corresponding significance is 0.028, which is less than the significance level of 0.05. Therefore, it can be considered that at least one of the four input methods and the other are significant in activation differences. The results of multiple comparison analysis are shown in Table 8.

Table 8. Activation score multiple comparison form

(I) Skin number	(J) Skin number	Average difference (I-J)	Standard error	Significance	95% confidence interval	
					Lower limit	Upper limit
A	B	−0.25	0.465	0.789	−1.04	0.79
	C	−2.325*	0.465	0.000	−3.24	−1.41
	D	−1.000	0.465	0.033	−1.92	−0.08
B	A	0.125	0.465	0.789	−0.79	1.04
	C	−2.200*	0.465	0.000	−3.12	−1.28
	D	−0.875	0.465	0.062	−1.79	0.04
C	A	2.325*	0.465	0.000	1.41	3.24
	B	2.200*	0.465	0.000	1.28	3.12
	D	1.325*	0.465	0.005	0.41	2.24
D	A	1.000	0.465	0.033	0.08	1.92
	B	0.875	0.465	0.062	−0.04	1.79
	C	−1.325*	0.465	0.005	−2.24	−0.14

It can be seen from Table 8 that in the activation dimension, the input method skin C is significantly different from other skins, and the significance between the two is lower than the significance level of 0.05. There is no significant difference in other pairwise combinations. The average value of each skin score is shown in Fig. 9 below.

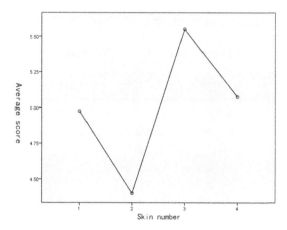

Fig. 9. The average value of each skin score on Activation

4.3   The Influence of Input Method Design on Dominance

On the dominance dimension, the statistical results of each skin score are subjected to repeated measurement one-way analysis of variance, and the results are shown in Tables 9 and 10.

Table 9. Dominance score variance homogeneity test form

Levene statistical data	Df1	Df2	Significance
1.762	3	156	0.157

It can be seen from Table 9 that the significance of the output is 0.157, which is greater than 0.05, so the overall variance of each group can also be considered equal.

Table 10. Dominance score analysis of variance form

	Sum of square	Df	Mean squared	F	Significance
Between groups (merge)	62.669	3	20.890	5.218	0.002
Linear term comparison	24.851	1	24.851	6.208	0.014
Deviation	37.818	2	18.909	4.723	0.010
In the group	624.525	156	4.003	–	–
Total	687.194	159	–	–	–

It can be seen from Table 10 that the variance test $F = 5.218$, and the corresponding significance is 0.002, which is less than the significance level of 0.05. Therefore, it can be considered that at least one of the four input methods and the other are significant in Dominance differences. The results of multiple comparison analysis are shown in Table 11.

Table 11. Dominance score multiple comparison form

(I) Skin number	(J) Skin number	Average difference (I-J)	Standard error	Significance	95% confidence interval	
					Lower limit	Upper limit
A	B	−0.425	0.447	0.344	−1.31	0.46
	C	−01.700*	0.447	0.000	−2.58	−0.82
	D	−0.750	0.447	0.096	−1.63	0.13
B	A	0.425	0.447	0.344	−0.46	1.31
	C	−1.275*	0.447	0.005	−2.16	−0.39
	D	−0.325	0.447	0.469	−1.21	0.56
C	A	1.700*	0.447	0.000	0.82	2.58
	B	1.275*	0.447	0.005	0.39	2.16
	D	0.950*	0.447	0.035	0.07	1.83
D	A	0.750	0.447	0.096	−0.13	1.63
	B	0.325	0.447	0.469	−0.56	1.21
	C	−0.950*	0.447	0.035	−1.83	−0.07

According to Table 11 in the dominance dimension, only the significance of input method skin C and other input method skins is less than the significance level of 0.05, which has a significant difference, and there is no significant difference between the other two combinations. The average value of each skin score is shown in Fig. 9.

From the above single-factor analysis of variance and multiple comparison of scores on the experimental data, it can be concluded that in terms of pleasure, the significant difference between input method skin C and input method skin B is less than the significance level of 0.05, indicating that the difference between this group is significant, but the difference between all other combinations is not significant; In terms of activation, the significant difference between input method skin C and all input method skins is less than 0.05, indicating that the difference between other combinations is not significant; In terms of dominance, the significance of the input method skin C and all input methods is less than 0.05, which means that except for the input method skin C, the differences between the other combinations are not significant (Fig. 10).

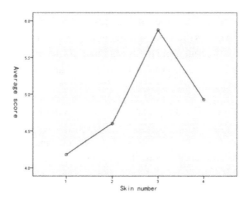

Fig. 10. The average value of each skin score on Dominance

Through the LSD method, the scores of the four input method skins in three dimensions are compared in pairs to verify that the input method skin C is more prominent in three dimensions than the other three input method skins [12].

4.4 SAM Scores in 3 Dimensions

Table 12. SAM scores of subjects after skin stimulation with four different input methods (n = 40)

Project	A	B	C	D
Pleasure	4.2 ± 2.1	4.3 ± 2.2	6.5 ± 1.8	5.2 ± 2.2
Activation	5.0 ± 2.1	4.4 ± 2.0	5.6 ± 2.1	5.1 ± 1.8
Dominance	4.2 ± 1.7	4.6 ± 2.0	5.9 ± 2.0	4.9 ± 2.3

From the experimental data sorted out in Table 12, it can be seen that input method skin C is a high pleasure input method skin, input method skin A is a low pleasure input method skin; input method skin C is a high activation input method skin, input method Skin A is low activation skin; input method skin C is high dominance skin, and input method skin A is low dominance skin.

5   Discuss the Influence of Design Features on Emotional Experience

The following Table 13 summarizes the characteristics of the four input methods skins.

Table 13. Comparison of skin design features of four input methods

	A	B	C	D
Input text field	Yes	No	No	No
Text association field	Yes	Yes	No	No
Logo	Yes	No	No	Yes
Unified style	Yes	No	Yes	No
One-click skinning	No	No	N0	No
Button form	Flat	Flat	Flat	Three-dimensional
Button feedback	No	No	Yes	No
Theme	Yes	Yes	Yes	Yes
Color	Warm colors	Cool colors	Cool colors	Cool colors
Dynamic effect	Yes	No	Yes	Yes
Word Art	No	No	Yes	No
Style	Fancy	Normal	Simplicity	Normal

Compare the features of the skins of the four input methods in Form 3-11, summarize and analyze the impact of the design features of the four input methods on the user's emotional experience.

(1) The reason why the input method skin C can cause more emotional reactions related to the pleasure dimension is:

First, the input method skin C deletes the settings of the input text box and the association text box without affecting the Normal use of the user, which simplifies the interface of the input method to a certain extent. Generally speaking, a cumbersome interface design will give users a sense of psychological pressure and tension, while a simple interface design will make users feel happy and relaxed [13]. Input method is generally defined as auxiliary tool software, too much content sometimes does not bring added value to the input method, but will affect the user experience of the input method.

Second, due to the high frequency of the input method and the high screen-to-body ratio during use, it is necessary to avoid warm-toned color designs in the selection of warm and cold tones. Cool colors generally remind people of empty scenes such as the sky and the sea [14]. They will quickly settle down and give people a quiet and relaxing emotional experience. On the contrary, warm colors can make people excited, and if used improperly, they can even make people feel anxious.

The difference in the interface layout and the choice of warm and cold colors is the reason for the greater difference in pleasure between the input method skin C and the input method skin A.

(2) The reason why the input method skin C can cause more emotional responses about the activation dimension is:

First, compared to the input method skin B, the input method skin C has more dynamic effects and the design of artistic characters. Static visual images are conducive to the transmission of information, but in the input method skin design, dynamic elements are more likely to attract the user's attention and give users a strong visual impact. At the same time, dynamic design can strengthen the emotion of the product to a certain extent [15] and bring users interest. People tend to be new and strange, and the design of artistic characters is more attractive to users than normal fonts.

Second, the input method is a highly interactive product, which is an important software for human-computer interaction. In the process of input method interaction, proper feedback design can improve the user's attention and reduce the user's error rate when typing. In terms of emotional experience, feedback designs such as vibration and sound effects can maintain the user's alertness [16] to a certain extent, and will not make users feel bored and dull.

The differences in dynamic effects, artistic characters and feedback design are the reasons for the greater difference in activation between input method skin C and input method skin B.

(3) The reason why the input method skin C can cause more emotional reactions about the dominant dimension is:

The overall design style of the input method skin C tends to be more concise. In the input method skin design, the more concise the design, the lower the possibility that users will be interfered by complex information, and it is easier to focus on the practical functions of the product, thereby generating more positive emotions about the product. At the same time, compared to the fancy design style, the simple design gives users more control and self-confidence. This sense of control and self-confidence can enhance the user's emotional response in the dominant dimension and bring users more positive emotions.

The simple design and fancy design are the main reasons for the large difference in dominance between input method skin C and input method skin A.

6 Conclusion

According to the analysis of experimental data and the comparison of the skin characteristics of the sample input method, guiding opinions can be put forward for the emotional design of the mobile terminal input method skin from three levels.

1. Pleasure dimension: In the design, delete or optimize unnecessary function settings as much as possible, such as input text field and associative text field, etc. The overall color tone should be biased toward cool colors to avoid excessive warm colors.
2. Activation dimension: Art words and dynamic effects can be added appropriately, and appropriate innovations can be made in the feedback design of the buttons. Generally, design methods such as vibration feedback and sound feedback can be used.
3. Dominant dimension: Design should avoid fancy design style, simplify interface decoration, function and color, avoid redundant decoration, and reduce excessive use of color.

This paper also has the following points that need improvement:

1. The skin sample volume of the input method on the mobile terminal is relatively small.
2. The age structure of the participants in the experiment is too single, and the difference is not obvious.

References

1. Peng, H.: Research on the design of children's scooter oriented to emotion. Mach. Des. **32**(11), 123–125 (2015)
2. (United States) Norman, D.A.: Design Psychology 3: Emotional Design. China CITIC Press, Beijing (2015)
3. Junwu, D., Dongtao, Y., Yadong, C., Lin, W.: Main theories, methods and research trends of emotional design. J. Eng. Des. **17**(01), 12–18+29 (2010)
4. Han, Y.: Research on the elements and trends of interactive design of electronic picture books based on the characteristics of preschool children. Editor's Friends **08**, 85–90 (2020)
5. Li, L., Mou, F.: Research on mobile phone video App design based on usability measurement. Industrial Design Industry Research Center. Industrial Design Research (Fourth Series).Industrial Design Industry Research Center, vol. 5 (2016)
6. Xue, Y., Wu, X., Yu, H., Lin, T., Qiu, D., Yu, Z.: Research on the influence of pearl jewelry design methods on consumers' purchasing tendency. Shandong Text. Econ. **9**, 29–31 (2016)
7. Plass, J.L., et al.: Emotional design for digital games for learning: the effect of expression, color, shape, and dimensionality on the affective quality of game characters. Learn. Instruct **70**, 101194 (2019)
8. Luna-Perejon, F., et al.: Evaluation of user satisfaction and usability of a mobile app for smoking cessation. Comput. Methods Prog. Biomed. **182**, 105042 (2019)
9. Lv, J., Chen, D.: Appraisal of clothing emotion based on consumer psychological cognition. J. Text. Res. **36**(09), 100–107 (2015)
10. Lixiu, Z., Lihong, W.: The application of self-emotion rating scale in senile dementia population. Chin. J. Nurs. **51**(02), 231–234 (2016)
11. Daye, H., Hyeja, C.: Combined effects of physical evidence and functional service at Bulgogi restaurants on customers' store image and purchase behaviors: application of video scenario technique. J. Korean Soc. Food Cult. **35**(2), 181–192 (2020)
12. Iwona, A., et al.: Physical fitness of school-age children after cancer treatment. J. Environ. Res. Public Health **16**(8), 1436 (2019)
13. Meiyu, Z.: Sensibility·Design. Shanghai Science and Technology Press (2011)
14. Pan, Z., Zhang, C., Tang, C.: Research and practice of illustrations in web page emotional design. Design **33**(16), 128–130 (2020)
15. Tian, Y., Zhang, T.: On the role of graphic visual design elements in dynamic media art. Design **43**(18), 133–134 (2015)
16. Song, H.: Creative skin+music keyboard octopus input method 3.0. Comput. Netw. **41**(09), 23 (2015)

Analysis of Situation Map User Cognitive Characteristics Based on Eye Movement Data

Jiayue Zhang[1]([✉]), Wenjun Hou[2], Ximing Zhu[3], and Yufan Wei[3]

[1] School of Digital Media and Design Art, Beijing University of Posts and Telecommunications, Beijing, China
zhang_jiayue82@163.com
[2] Beijing Key Laboratory of Network and Network Culture, Beijing University of Posts and Telecommunications, Beijing, China
[3] The 27th Research Institute of China Electronics Technology Group Corporation, Zhengzhou 450052, China

Abstract. A situation map shows the dynamic changes of the environment within a specific space and time in the form of graphics, which can help users effectively understand the current situation and predict the future situation from multidimensional and massive information. It is an essential tool for users to make decisions in a complex information system. However, the current situation map interface has some problems, such as poor visibility, difficulty in interaction, etc., which has a particular impact on the user's performance of situation awareness and the efficiency in completing tasks.

In order to improve the current problems of the situation map interface, this study hopes to optimize the design of the situation map interface based on the cognitive characteristics of users. A large number of eye movement data of users in the situation map were collected and analyzed to. After analyzing the time series data of eye movement coordinates, the duration of fixation point entering the target area of interest (AOI) for the first time, eye movement speed and other eye movement characteristic indicators, as well as the scanning path chart, it is concluded that the differences of users' eye movement behaviors were mainly manifested in three aspects. They are the differences in visual search strategy, target positioning speed and accuracy, and decision-making speed and accuracy.

Then, according to the differences in cognitive characteristics such as attention distribution mechanism and information processing efficiency reflected by the differences in users' eye movement behaviors, the cognitive types of users are summarized as blind cognition, purpose cognition, learning cognition, and memory cognition. Based on the characteristics of the above four cognitive types, the situation map design elements are extracted and sorted out as the criteria for subsequent interface optimization. The optimization design scheme of the interface elements of the situation map is proposed to help users improve their situation awareness level, information identification efficiency, and task operation efficiency.

Keywords: Situation map · Eye movement · User's cognition

S. Yamamoto and H. Mori (Eds.): HCII 2022, LNCS 13305, pp. 282–294, 2022.
https://doi.org/10.1007/978-3-031-06424-1_21

1   Introduction

Endsley first proposed the definition of situational awareness, which means that the operator understands the current environment and predicts the future state of the environment by perceiving, analyzing, and predicting the dynamic changes of the environment within a certain time and space [1]. Based on this, the operator takes corresponding measures and achieves the purpose of completing the task. The situation map is the interface that supports situational awareness and is the core part of situational awareness visualization. It graphically reflects the evolution state of the overall or local characteristics of the research object in time or space, helping operators review historical situations, analyze current situations, and predict future trends [1].

Situation maps are usually used in large-scale dynamic and complex information systems such as military systems, giant network systems, etc. It visually presents multi-dimensional and massive information, helping users to effectively understand the current situation and make decisions. This means that the situation map interface usually contains a large number of elements and a large amount of information, and the interface structure is usually complex, which makes the user's learning cost and cognitive cost high, and also makes the interaction process more difficult. Therefore, it is very meaningful to improve the user's situation awareness level and improve the task efficiency by optimizing the situation map interface (Fig. 1).

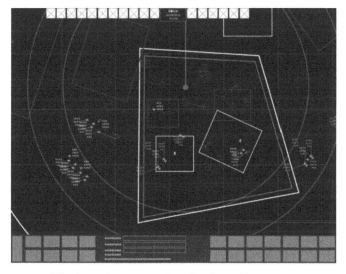

Fig. 1. A situation map interface in a military game

As cognition is an important factor affecting situational awareness and ergonomic, it is of great value to analyze and study users' cognitive characteristics in the optimization process of situational maps. This study is devoted to exploiting the advantages of research on user cognition in the design. Based on the theory of correlation between eye movement behavior and cognitive characteristics, we analyze the users' eye movement data of a military game situation map interface, and summarize the differences in users' eye movement behaviors and the cognitive differences reflected by them. Then the user cognition is divided into four types: blind cognition, purpose cognition, learning cognition, and memory cognition. According to the characteristics of the situation map interface and the cognitive characteristics of users, we extract the design criteria of the situation map.

2 Current Situation Map and Related Research

2.1 Problems in Situation Map and Necessity of Optimization

By analyzing the interface structure and characteristics of the current situation map, we conclude that the current situation map has the following problems:

1. At present, many situation maps, especially in military systems, are most directly developed by technical personnel, and they lack design links. However, the professionalism of the situation map determines that the developer is not the real user, and does not understand the user's cognition and behavioral habits. There is a large gap between the mental models of the two, which leads to certain problems in the process of using the situation map for users.
2. Since the situation map is mostly used in large-scale complex dynamic information systems, the amount of information presented in the diagram is very large and has many dimensions, which requires a good organization layout and visualization scheme for the information. However, at present, the information in the situation map is arranged in a mess, the visual salience of each element is not high, and the visibility of the situation map is low, which leads to the low performance of users in identifying information in the map.
3. The user needs to perform operations based on the understanding and prediction of the current situation in the situation map, but the current interface has a single interaction form, the operation process is cumbersome, and many operations lack timely and effective feedback, which will affect the user's operational performance.
4. The current situation map system has a low degree of automation and poor intelligence, and users still need to complete many mechanical and cumbersome operations, which increases the cognitive load of users. Moreover, the situation map interface cannot be adapted according to the user's characteristics and the current task characteristics, and its flexibility is poor, which will reduce the user's task completion efficiency.

Because complex information systems have the characteristics of massive and multidimensional information, high difficulty in performing tasks, and complex and changeable situational environment, whether the system can effectively achieve situational awareness is a key factor for users to make decisions [2]. As a visualization tool for users to perceive the situation, the situation diagram plays a very important role in the complex information system. However, the above-mentioned problems in the current situation map interface lead to high requirements for users to complete situational awareness and operation and have a great impact on the user's task performance. It is very necessary to optimize the current problems. Reasonable design of the situation map interface is of great value and significance, because it can reduce the requirements of the situation visualization system for users, help users to perform situational awareness efficiently and accurately, effectively improve the user's cognitive efficiency and efficiently complete operational tasks.

2.2 Existing Research on Situation Maps

Since the U.S. Air Force proposed the concept of situation awareness in the 1980s, this concept has had important applications in the military, network security and other fields. There are also many related research on situation maps, the core part of situation awareness visualization. However, the existing research on situation maps mostly focuses on the construction methods, plotting and other technical aspects, and there are little research on the optimization design of situation maps interface.

Yang Song [3] proposed that the battlefield situation awareness interface should have five characteristics, namely on-demand interconnection, flexible display, natural interaction, convenient collaboration and efficient perception, and summed up a situation-based battlefield situational awareness interface model; Zhang Jianmin [1] et al. proposed the generation mechanism of the future forecast dynamic situation map, and preliminarily discussed three key evaluation indicators for the design of the situation map. In addition, Guo Yusong [4] et al. proposed the construction of a user mental model based on situation awareness elements to guide the interface design of the situation map. The mental model was constructed through the results of user interviews, and it was evaluated whether the interface information presentation and interaction design matched the model. The research is user-centered and adopts the idea of "interaction design is user behavior design". The research expectation starts from the user's cognition and behavior, which is very valuable, but because there are only user interviews and no data support in the research, it only stays at the user task process level in the end. The article does not directly analyze the specific cognitive methods of users, but focuses more on the construction method of mental models. However, this idea is worth thinking about and learning from.

3   Cognitive Research and Eye Movement

3.1   The Importance of User Cognition Research in Interaction Design

The user obtains information in the situation map to understand the current situation, and based on this, performs the next operation in the interface, which is the process of interaction between the user and the situation map interface. The process of interaction design is also based on the research on users' cognition and behavior, and integrates the oriented design process of multiple cross-domains [5]. Donald Norman [6] put forward requirements for design from the perspective of users' psychology, cognition and behavior, and transformed the psychological research results about human cognition and behavior into human-centered design principles; Xin Xiangyang [7] also believed that Whether the interaction process design conforms to user cognition is an important factor affecting interaction performance and experience.

To design from the user's point of view, it is necessary to fully tap the user's cognitive characteristics and understand the user's goals and needs in the task process. It's important to understand the user's way of thinking and cognitive habits, as well as the user's mental model in the process of interacting with the product. This helps us effectively meet users' expectations through design, help users achieve a high level of situation awareness, and give users a more efficient and smooth task experience.

3.2 Correlations Between Eye Movements and Cognitive Characteristics

The user's eye movements can well reflect the user's cognitive characteristics. Cognitive psychology believes that there are many correlations and consistency between human eye movement and cognition, and eye movement is an integral part of many cognitive processes, reflecting human thinking processes (Yarbus 1967). Usually, eye movements are not automatic or reflex actions made by people, but represent frequent decision-making processes in the human brain (Einhäuser & König, 2010) [8]. Therefore, analyzing the user's eye movement data is an effective method to understand the user's cognition. Eye movement speed, saccade distance, gaze dwell time, and saccade path are all effective indicators for analyzing the cognitive processing process of the brain [9].

At present, the commonly used eye movement data visualization methods include scan path method, heat map method, AOI (area of interest) method and 3D space method. The scanning path method is mainly used to express the correspondence between the user's visual distribution and the visual stimulus objects, as well as the user's attention distribution and difficulties encountered in the task process [10]. In this study, the scanning path method is mainly used to visualize the user's eye movement data collected in the early stage. By analyzing the eye movement saccade path map of different users, the differences in eye movement behavior of users during the task process are summarized, and the characteristics of cognitive differences reflected by the differences in eye movement behavior are explored.

4 Analysis of User Cognitive Characteristics of Situation Map Based on Eye Movement Data

4.1 Experiment

First, we carried out an experiment to collect the eye movement data of users in the situation map. The specific experiment process is as follows:

1. Based on a military game with a situation map interface, four typical tasks in the game are selected, namely, searching for key targets, disposing of dropped targets, target positioning, and monitoring key areas;
2. We invite 8 users of military game situation map to participate in the experiment, and introduce the task objectives and operation procedures of the above 4 tasks to them;
3. Let 8 users complete the above 4 tasks in the situation map, and rest for 1 min between each task. In the process of the user completing the task, the user's eye movement data is collected through the ASee3 eye tracker;

4. Process the eye movement data of 8 users in 4 tasks. Focus on the user's eye movement coordinate time series data, the time when the gaze point first enters the target area of interest (AOI), and the eye movement speed. For each task, 8 users are clustered according to the above datas. After calculating the average of the user's eye movement datas under various categories, the eye movement saccade path maps are generated according to the datas.

4.2   User's Cognition Differentiation and Eye Movement Performance

By comparing and analyzing the eye movement saccade path maps of different types of users during each task, we have sorted out the differences in user eye movement behavior reflected in these maps, which can be summarized into the following three aspects:

1. Differences in visual search strategies
2. Differences in target positioning speed and accuracy
3. Differences in decision-making speed and accuracy

Differences in Visual Search Strategies. By analyzing the scanning path maps of different users during the task process, it is found that there are differences in their visual search strategies, which can be classified into two categories. Taking the observed signal line in the target positioning task as an example. In this step, the user needs to identify the signal line whose radiation source is located in the key area among several signal lines in the situation diagram, and determine whether it is a type A direction finding line, if so, perform target positioning.

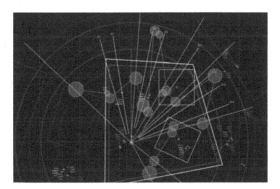

Fig. 2. Scanning path map 1

Observing the two eye movement saccade path maps shown in Figs. 2 and 3, it can be seen that the former user's gaze points are distributed in all the areas where the signal lines are located, and they tend to use the information saccade strategy. The allocation of attention of these users lacks focus, resulting in poor visual search performance for target signal lines. On the other hand, the gaze points of the latter users are mainly distributed in the key areas (white rectangles), and they mainly focus on the signal lines in the key areas. Their attention is more distributed on the signal lines in the key areas, and the visual search performance is better.

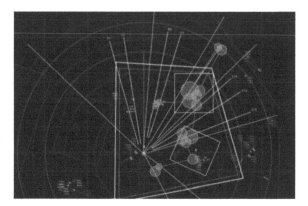

Fig. 3. Scanning path map 2

Different visual search strategies of users reflect the differences in users' cognition. Users who adopt the information saccade strategy are evenly distributed in each part of the interface, and their gaze points are distributed according to the visual clues in the interface, which is bottom-up attention distribution mechanism. The users whose attention is mainly distributed in the key areas are reasonably distributed according to the mission objectives and combat plans, which is a bottom-up attention distribution mechanism.

Differences in Target Positioning Speed and Accuracy. Users need to locate the key targets of this mission in the situation map based on the mission objectives, their own experience and knowledge reserves. We found that there are differences in the speed and accuracy of users in locating the targets. Taking the process of locating the dropped target as an example, the user needs to lock the dropped target in the situation map and perform operations on it. The dropped target will have some characteristics, such as the icon does not move for a long time, the icon changes gray or the icon suddenly disappears, depending on the user's previous settings for the target.

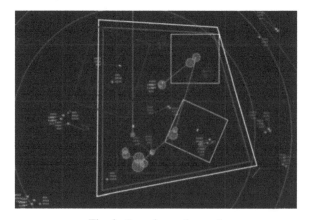

Fig. 4. Scanning path map 3

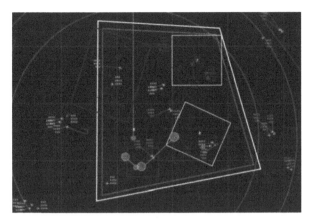

Fig. 5. Scanning path map 4

Observing the saccade path map of the first type of users as shown in Fig. 4, it is found that their gaze points stay in multiple areas in the situation map. After spending a period of time judging whether each target was dropped, their eyes then shifted to the dropped target, and they stayed there for a long time. It can be seen that the target positioning speed of such users is relatively slow, and it takes a long time to judge whether their judgment is accurate after positioning. However, in the saccade path map of the second type of user as shown in Fig. 5, the gaze points are few and are basically located at the drop target, and the fixation durations are short. It can be seen that such users can quickly lock the target and quickly determine whether the target positioning is accurate.

Differences in Decision-Making Speed and Accuracy. After users understanding the acquired information in the situation map, they need to make decisions based on the current situation. After observing the users' eye movement saccade path maps, it can be seen that there are differences in the decision-making speed and accuracy of different users. Taking the target positioning task as an example, in the task, the user decides whether to perform target positioning according to the aggregation of historical signal lines.

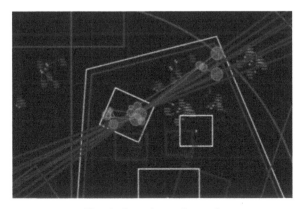

Fig. 6. Scanning path map 5

As shown in Fig. 6, the gaze points of the first type of users stay at the convergence point of the historical signal lines for a long time, and there are multiple sight line backtracking at the last positioning result (yellow triangle) and the convergence point. During this period, the sight line also jumped to other places to observe the distribution of historical signal lines, indicating that such users are slow in judging and making decisions about whether the convergence of historical signal lines meets the positioning conditions, and have low confidence in the accuracy of decision-making. As shown in Fig. 7, the second type of users have few gaze points, the fixation time at the convergence point and the last positioning result is shorter, and there is no redundant saccade path. It can be seen that such users have a faster decision-making speed.

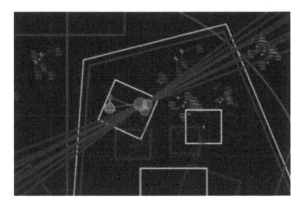

Fig. 7. Scanning path map 6 (Color figure online)

4.3 Classification of User's Cognition Characteristics

According to the above differences in users' eye movement behaviors, the cognition differences reflected by them are excavated. The differences in visual search strategies of different users reflect that users have adopted different mechanisms in the allocation of attention resources, namely the up-bottom purpose-driven allocation mechanism and the bottom-up data (cue)-driven allocation mechanism. The differences in the speed and accuracy of their positioning and decision-making reflect the differences in the efficiency of users in processing the acquired information.

Based on the characteristics of cognitive differences reflected by the differences in users' eye movement behaviors, the cognitive types of users can be divided into four types: blind cognition, purpose cognition, learning cognition and memory cognition:

1. Blind cognition: A bottom-up attention distribution mechanism is adopted, and attention is distributed at various visual cues in the situation map, rather than collecting information explicitly according to the task goal;
2. Purpose cognition: adopt a up-bottom attention distribution mechanism, effectively allocate attention according to task goals and expectations, and quickly obtain information related to the current goal;

3. Learning cognition: The user is still in the learning stage of the system-related knowledge hierarchy, and has not yet formed long-term memory, so the efficiency of processing the acquired information will be slightly lower;
4. Memory cognition: Relevant knowledge has been transformed into long-term memory and stored in the user's brain, which can be quickly recalled and matched with the acquired information, and the information processing efficiency is high.

After that, we select two typical tasks, "target positioning" and "processing dropped targets", to sort out the different eye movement behaviors of users involved in the task process, and correspond the eye movement behavior characteristics to cognition types, such as Table 1 shows:

Table 1. Users' eye movement behaviors and cognition types

Task	Eye movement behaviors	The cognition types reflected
Target positioning	Gaze points stay on the signal lines in the key area for a long time	Purpose cognition
	Gaze points are evenly distributed on all signal lines in the situation map	Blind cognition
	Quickly determine the type of signal lines based on their features	Memory cognition
	The sight line does not consciously check the position of the signal line features, and the type of the signal line cannot be judged quickly and accurately	Learning cognition
	View the parameters of the target and quickly decide whether to locate the target according to the parameters	Memory cognition
	The sight line stays on the signal lines for a long time, and the parameters of the target are not checked in time	Blind cognition
	Gaze points are concentrated at the convergence point of history lines	Purpose cognition
	There are many gaze points, and the sight line jumps sharply on the historical signal lines	Blind cognition

(continued)

Table 1. (*continued*)

Task	Eye movement behaviors	The cognition types reflected
	After observing the convergence point of historical signal lines, quickly decide whether to perform target positioning	Memory cognition
	There are many redundant gaze points, and the sight line stays at the convergence point for a long time	Learning cognition
Processing dropped targets	The sight line moves between multiple key targets in the situation map to observe the movement status of the targets	Purpose cognition
	The gaze points are distributed in each region of the situation map, and there is no focus object	Blind cognition
	Quickly notice that the target has dropped and look at the dropped target	Memory cognition
	Look around the situation map, can not quickly find the dropped target	Learning cognition
	Quickly predict the possible position of the dropped target, and fix on the position	Memory cognition
	The distribution of gaze points is chaotic and it is difficult to accurately predict the possible location of the dropped target	Blind cognition

4.4   Extract Design Criteria from the Characteristics of Cognition Differences

According to the four different cognition types of situation map users, including blind cognition, purpose cognition, learning cognition and memory cognition, and their characteristics, we extract some design criteria for the situation map interface:

1. Enhance the visibility of information in the situation map interface, improve the saliency of visual elements, and provide users with reasonable and effective visual clues. Ensure that the user's allocation mechanism is reasonable when relying on data (clues) to drive attention allocation, and can effectively achieve situation awareness based on visual clues;

2. Optimize the layout and organization of information in the interface, so that the element layout conforms to the user's cognitive habits and task flow, which can

improve the user's visual search efficiency. At the same time, give users reasonable and effective feedback to help users efficiently accomplish task goals;

3. Ensure the interaction consistency in the situation map system and optimize the interface function structure. The process in the system should conform to the user's mental model as much as possible to reduce the user's learning cost and cognitive load;

4. Enhance the adaptability of the system. For different types of users, the situation map system can set corresponding interface schemes according to users' preferences, which conform to the user's behavior and cognitive habits and help improve task performance.

5 Summary and Prospect

Based on the correlation between eye movement and cognition characteristics, this study conducts an experiment to collect the eye movement datas of users in the situation map during the task process, and analyzes and summarizes the differences in users' eye movement behaviors and the characteristics of cognition differences reflected. We divide users' cognition into four types: blind cognition, purpose cognition, learning cognition and memory cognition. Based on the characteristics of different cognition types, the guidelines for the optimization and design of the situation map interface are proposed, hoping to achieve the goal of helping users improve situation awareness, information identification efficiency and task operation efficiency.

As an important tool to help users achieve situation awareness in complex information systems, how to make the situation map play a greater role, better help users to perceive the current situation and complete the task is of great research significance and value. This paper is mainly based on the existing situation map interface for analysis and research, and with the development of science and technology, the situation map will definitely develop in a more flexible, diverse and intelligent direction. Situation map can help users deal with complex situational information and efficiently achieve situation awareness. Users will allocate more attention resources in the decision-making process. How to realize the human-machine intelligence integration between users and the situation map system, and how to reasonably and effectively allocate human-machine resources will become a problem worthy of research and solution in the future.

References

1. Zhang, J., Chen, H., Chen, J., Zhou, M., Zhuang, X., Chen, Y.: Smart grid situation awareness diagram modeling and conceptual design of situation awareness visualization. Autom. Electr. Power Syst. **38**(09), 168–176 (2014)
2. Hu, H., Guo, H.: Architecture and techniques of common operational situation picture. Command Control Simul. **5**, 28–32 (2006)
3. Yang, S., Yang, Q., Yang, Z.-H., Zhou, L.: Battlefield situation-aware interface model on context. Command Control Simul. **39**(02), 81–84 (2017)
4. Guo, Y., Gong, X., Chen, W.: Construction method of mental model based on situation awareness elements. Ind. Eng. Des. **2**(05), 1–9 (2020)

5. Peng, J.: Research on interactive design method based on user's cognition and behavior. Art Des. **2**(08), 80–82 (2017)
6. Donald, N.: The Psychology of Everyday Things. Basic Book (1998)
7. Xin, X.: Interaction design: from logic of things to logic of behaviors. Art Des. **1**, 58–62 (2015)
8. Konig, P., Wilming, N., Kietmann, T.C.: Eye movements as a window to cognitive processes. J. Eye Mov. Res. **9**(5), 1–16 (2016)
9. Ren, Y., Meng, F.: Cognitive values and polygraph testing applications of eye movement indicators. Psychol. Tech. Appl. **7**, 26–29 (2015)
10. Cheng, S., Sun, L.: A survey on visualization for eye tracking data. J. Comput. Aided Des. Comput. Graph. **26**(05), 698–707 (2014)

Visualization and Big Data

Detection and Mitigation Method of Bottlenecks in Data Stream Based on Program Net

Mohd Anuaruddin Bin Ahmadon[✉] and Shingo Yamaguchi

Graduate School of Sciences and Technology for Innovation, Yamaguchi University,
16-1 Tokiwadai 2-chome, Ube, 755-8611 Yamaguchi, Japan
{anuar,shingo}@yamaguchi-u.ac.jp

Abstract. In this paper, we proposed a method to detect and improve bottlenecks in the data flow of IoT systems. Various IoT devices such as sensors and actuators are used in IoT systems, and millions of data flow through the edge nodes to be processed. Data exchange between edge routers is processed in buffers in sorted order of the event-driven flow. However, because buffers in edge routers are limited, link interference and power instability always reduce the latency of the system. Even a small misalignment in data flow may cause minor incidents that will later cause a chain of breakdown. In this study, we model the data flow with program nets to capture the stagnation of data tokens in order to detect bottlenecks. The data flow is modeled with Program net, and we can visualize the flow of data represented by tokens. We also proposed a mitigation method to tackle the bottleneck problem. Then, we demonstrate the effectiveness of our approach by quantitative evaluation. The evaluation result showed that the proposed method could detect bottlenecks in IoT systems and reduce the buffer to below the 80% of the threshold value.

Keywords: IoT system · Data stream · Bottleneck · Program net

1 Introduction

1.1 Background

In recent years, the Internet of Things (IoT) systems has been gaining popularity to realize a society where people and things are connected by information, as in Industry 4.0 and Society 5.0. IoT systems that are supported by heterogeneous sensors and actuators are changing lifestyles. Example of these systems includes the smart home, smart factory, self-driving system, logistics, and agriculture. For example, in the smart home, house temperature and humidity can be controlled autonomously using ambient intelligence. In smart factories, many

This research is partially supported by Interface Corporation, Japan.

of the machines and equipment are managed using sensors and actuators to improve productivity. IoT systems are also gaining popularity in the transportation industry, where sensors and actuators are used to control the quality of goods.

IoT devices takes data from sensors and send them over the Internet through the appropriate application layer protocols such as MQTT, XAMPP, and CoAP. In general, these protocols transfers data through wireless networks which are called as wireless sensor networks (WSN). In WSN system, data that are produced by sensors are sent to the edge computer within the networks so that they can be processed in the cloud. In order to connect and exchange data seamlessly in real time, data transmission and processing must be very agile and precise. One of the main factors that affect the performance of WSN is the latency. Reduced latency in an event-driven system may cause inappropriate system response. An edge nodes in an IoT systems process data received from sensors before sending it to the actuators or cloud. In order to process these data, edge nodes uses buffer in the system.

In this paper, we tackle the problem of detecting and mitigating bottlenecks in the data flow of IoT systems. In this study, we model the data flow with program nets to capture the stagnation of data tokens called as data pile-up. The data flow is modeled with Program net, and we can visualize the flow of data represented by tokens. We also proposed a mitigation method to tackle the bottleneck problem. Then, we demonstrate the effectiveness of our approach by quantitative evaluation. The evaluation result showed that the proposed method could detect bottlenecks in IoT systems and reduce the buffer to below the 80% of the threshold value.

1.2   Related Work

There are several works related to handling congestion in the data stream. In these works, we consider three factors that are important in our work which are stream model and strategy.

Fu et al. [1] proposed a Stream Processing Engine (SPE) that considers congestion using a scheduler. The SPE proposed by Fu et al. also incorporates a fixed-sized worker pool. They showed that their proposed SPE improved the throughput while keeping the latency low. In the work proposed by Fu et al., SPE uses a data flow programming model. The data flow programming model (directed acyclic graph) consists of a source, sink, and operation nodes. It represents the data flow topology, and the scheduler selects the operation in the data queue that flows through the data flow model by prioritizing the longest queue to be processed by the worker pool.

Khan et al. [2] stated that buffers are related to the access link of edge routers, and it is important to consider the latency by managing the buffer provisioning and queuing delays. They proposed a method to manage *under-provisioned* and *over-provisioned buffers* in edge routers where adjusting the buffer size is difficult. They proposed a buffer calculation method based on the congestion window and evaluated the proposed buffer sizing scheme with link utilization and latency. They showed that their buffer sizing scheme improved the flows of the data packet.

Shaikh et al. [3] proposed a query execution scheme in an event-driven stream. They tackled a problem in a basic query system where queries from all event stream tuples are processed even though there is no data tuple that may trigger the event. They mainly focused on the continuous query (CQ) in a data stream and proposed the execution strategy for CQ. They proposed a smart window to buffer stream data when there is no data to trigger any event. The data in the buffer are flushed out after the window expires.

In the context of the streaming model, Fu et al. proposed the scheduler method to queue queries into data flow. The topology is a model using a data flow programming model which consists of three basic nodes; sink, source and operation. Our approach uses a Program net where each node has attributes to represent event-driven and conditional mechanisms such as AND, OR, and SWITCH. Regarding the strategy, Khan et al. proposed the buffer sizing method to increase the transmission latency. However, in the case of lightweight edge routers with very small buffer sizes, it is impossible to resize the buffer as there is a minimal buffer available. For example, they evaluated their method on NS-3 simulator [4] where buffer size is adjustable. Our method enables us to implement the mitigation strategy regardless of buffer size. Shaikh et al. proposed a smart window to buffer query and flush out the query when no event rises within specific time intervals. Our work focus on data that are continuously needed in data accumulation, such as statistics calculation and visualization. However, when a queue of data reaches the limit of its buffer, our approach mitigates the congestion by performing a data accumulation strategy to reduce the number of queues.

2 Preliminary

2.1 Program Net

In this study, we use Program net [5] to represent the data stream. A Program net is a four-tuples represented by $PN=(N, E, \alpha, \beta)$. Its elements are as follows:

(1) N is a finite set of nodes. Each node $n \in N$ is either AND, OR, or SWITCH. There is a source node named start node s and a sink node named termination node t. All nodes are on the connected path from s to t.

(2) E is a finite set of connected edges with the First-In-First-Out (FIFO) function. Each connected edge $e \in E$ is either a data flow edge or a control flow edge.

(3) $\alpha : E \rightarrow \{1, 2, 3, ...\}$ and $\beta : E \rightarrow \{1, 2, 3, \cdots\}$ are the weights of the edge. For an edge e, α_e is the weight for its end point and β_e is the weight for its start point.

A token in the program net represents a single piece of data with value and is placed on a directed edge.

In a program net, data streams are denoted by tokens, an AND node becomes fireable when each input edge $e_{in} \in E$ has at least $\alpha_{e_{in}}$ of tokens. When an AND node fires, $\alpha_{e_{in}}$ tokens are removed from each input edge e_{in}, and $\alpha_{e_{out}}$ tokens

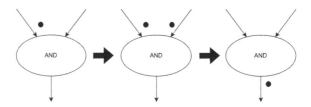

Fig. 1. Illustration of AND node.

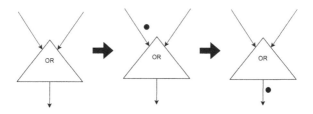

Fig. 2. Illustration of OR node.

are added to each output edge e_{out}. An OR node becomes fireable when any one of its input edges (i.e. e_{in}) has at least $\alpha_{e_{in}}$ tokens. When a fireable OR node fires, $\alpha_{e_{in}}$ tokens are removed from the input edge e_{in} and $\beta_{e_{out}}$ tokens are added to the output edge e_{out}. A SWITCH node becomes fireable when there are at least $\alpha_{e_{in}}$ tokens in the data flow edge e_{in} and at least one token in the control flow edge. When a fireable SWITCH node fires, $\alpha_{e_{in}}$ tokens are removed from the data flow edge e_{in} and one token is removed from the control flow edge. If the value of the token removed from the control flow edge is true, then $\beta_{e_{True}}$ tokens are added to the output edge e_{True} labeled *True*. If the value of the token removed from the control flow edge is false, then $\beta_{e_{False}}$ tokens are added to the output edge e_{False} labeled as *False*.

When represented as a graph, AND nodes are drawn as $\bigcirc$, OR nodes as $\triangle$ and SWITCH nodes as $\triangledown$ while data flow and control flow edges are drawn as $\rightarrow$. Tokens are drawn as dots $\bullet$ on the valid edges. It is represented using nodes and tokens as shown in the figure. Figures 1, 2, and 3 show the operation of an AND node, OR node, and SWITCH node, respectively. The AND node fires when there are tokens on all input edges, and the OR node fires when there are tokens on any input edge. The SWITCH node sets a condition and fires as shown in Fig. 3 if the condition is *True*. For example, if a token carries a value X, if $X \ll 3$, then output the token to the edge labeled *True*.

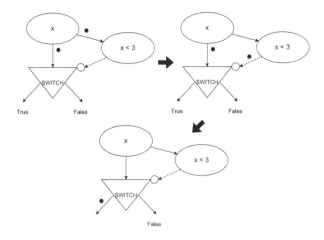

Fig. 3. Illustration of SWITCH node.

3　Detection and Mitigation Method of Bottlenecks

This section describes the definition and approach to identifying bottlenecks. The definition of a bottleneck is given as follows:

Definition 1 (Bottleneck). *In a data flow $D = (PN, Q)$, given the buffer size ω at each node $e \in E$ in PN, a bottleneck is defined if the buffer usage ratio $r = |Q_e|/\omega$ at time t is greater than a threshold h where Q is the set of tokens, and Q_e is the set of tokens at edge e.*　□

Given a system D with buffer Q, we define the problem of detecting bottleneck when buffer threshold h and buffer size ω is known.

Definition 2 (Bottleneck Detection Problem)
Input: Data flow $D = (PN, Q)$, threshold h, buffer size ω
Output: Set of edges with bottlenecks $\mathcal{E}$　□

3.1　Method for Detecting Bottleneck

Based on the definition, we can detect bottlenecks by calculating the usage of buffer in data flow D. If the buffer usage ratio r is over the specified threshold h. Then, a set of edges with bottleneck Σ is output. We give an example of identifying a bottleneck using the proposed procedure as shown in Figs. 4 and 5. The modeled system D_1 is a cold chain system which implements temperature sensor n_1, humidity sensor n_2, and ambient light sensor n_3. Temperature and humidity data is processed at edge node n_1 and cold chain control is performed on edge node n_2 which accumulates data from edge n_1. We give the procedure as follows:

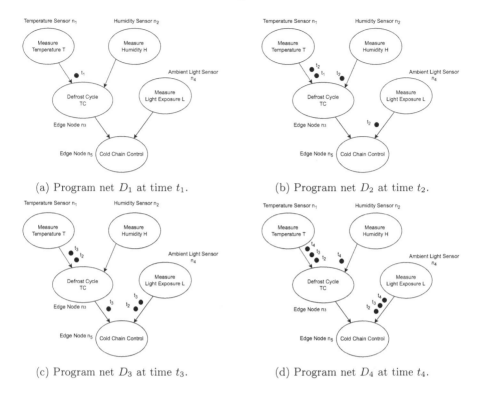

(a) Program net D_1 at time t_1.

(b) Program net D_2 at time t_2.

(c) Program net D_3 at time t_3.

(d) Program net D_4 at time t_4.

Fig. 4. Illustration of a cold chain system represented by Program net D_1.

≪Bottleneck Detection Procedure ≫
Input: Data flow $D = (PN, Q)$, threshold h, buffer size ω
Output: Set of edges with bottlenecks $\mathcal{E}$

1° Create an $m \times m$ matrices $A_1, A_2, \cdots, A_k$ for each edges $e \in E$ of PN of the data flow at time $t_1, t_2, \cdots, t_k$.
2° Create matrices $A'_1, A'_2, \cdots, A'_f (f \leq k)$ by calculating moving average (window size f) of matrices $A_1, A_2, \cdots, A_k$.
3° Calculate the percentage of buffers $r = q_{(m,n)}/\omega$ and if $r \geq h$, assign edge (m, n) into the set $\mathcal{E}$ where $q_{(m,n)}$ is the value of buffer usage ratio in A_k.
4° Output the set $\mathcal{E}$ and stop.

By using moving averages, we can determine if a bottleneck exists by looking at trends of tokens pile up. Also, by using a matrix, we can represent the buffer usage ratio of each edges in the data flow D.

Consider an example where the data sent by the humidity sensor is delayed. In normal operation, only one token is accumulated between each node, but because of the delay in the humidity sensor n_2, there are three tokens between

	n_1	n_2	n_3	n_4	n_5
n_1	0	0	0	0	0
n_2	0	0	0	0	0
n_3	0.2	0	0	0	0
n_4	0	0	0	0	0
n_5	0	0	0	0	0

(a) Matrix at time t_1.

	n_1	n_2	n_3	n_4	n_5
n_1	0	0	0	0	0
n_2	0	0	0	0	0
n_3	0.4	0.2	0	0	0
n_4	0	0	0	0	0
n_5	0	0	0	0.2	0

(b) Matrix at time t_2.

	n_1	n_2	n_3	n_4	n_5
n_1	0	0	0	0	0
n_2	0	0	0	0	0
n_3	0.4	0	0	0	0
n_4	0	0	0	0	0
n_5	0	0	0.2	0.4	0

(c) Matrix at time t_3.

	n_1	n_2	n_3	n_4	n_5
n_1	0	0	0	0	0
n_2	0	0	0	0	0
n_3	[0.6]	0.2	0	0	0
n_4	0	0	0	0	0
n_5	0	0	0	0.4	0

(d) Bottleneck at (n_1, n_3) at time t_4.

Fig. 5. Illustration of each nodes in Program net.

(n_1, n_3), one between (n_2, n_3), and two between (n_4, n_5) in the state t_4 shown in Fig. 4 (d). Since n_3 is not processed in the previous state, there is no token between (n_3, n_5). Looking at n_5, tokens accumulate between (n_4, n_5). At time t_5, no new token is supplied from n_2 because it has been delayed by the humidity sensor. Therefore, the tokens accumulate between (n_1, n_3). In t_4, the token is accumulated in (n_4, n_5). Let the buffer size $w = 5$ and the threshold value $h = 0.6$ are given. From the matrix, shown in Fig. 5, we can see that the bottleneck is detected at (n_1, n_3) at time t_4.

3.2   Method for Mitigating Bottleneck

We propose a method using the reconstruction of Program nets using a new type of arc. The arc is called OV-Arc (Overwrite Arc). OV-Arc holds only one token. If a token t_a exists on the OV-Arc in one state S_t, and when the node that supplies the token to the OV-Arc fires a new token t_b in the next state S_{t+1}, token t_a is replaced with token t_b. At this time, it will discard token t_a, which was fired at the previous state. If the input edge e_{in} of the AND node contains an OV-Arc, the token exists on the arc when there are $\alpha_{e_{in}}$ tokens on edge other than the OV-Arc. It is used for accumulating tokens into one token if buffer usage is over h value. If the buffer is below h, then the output nodes can fire any time if enough tokens are available.

As shown in the example in Figs. 6 and 7, this method determines the accumulation of tokens at the bottleneck location detected in ≪Bottleneck Detection Procedure ≫. The mitigation method is conducted by reconstruction of the

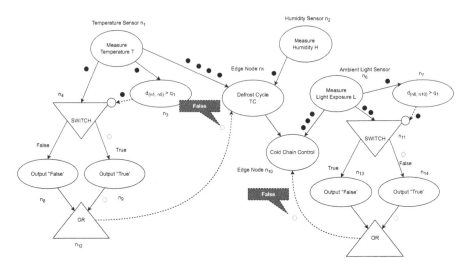

Fig. 6. Mitigation method using OV-Arc at time t_k.

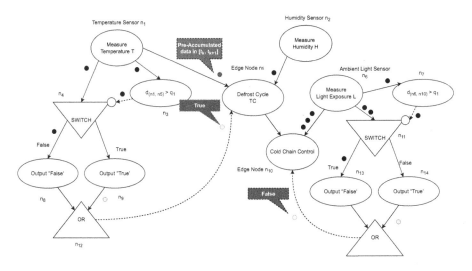

Fig. 7. Mitigation method using OV-Arc at time t_{k+1}.

Program net. The method can be implemented by adding a SWITCH node that outputs is *True* if multiple tokens are accumulated or *False* otherwise. If there is a true token on the OV-Arc, it will take the average value of the tokens piled up in the input arc of the target node. The token will be processed as a single token with accumulated value.

4   Evaluation

4.1   Evaluation of Detection Method

In the previous example, there was only one bottleneck detected, but it is quite possible that two or more bottlenecks will be detected depending on the buffer capacity, threshold, and window size of the moving average. However, it is important to consider the window size. If the window size is too large, it may not be able to respond to sudden changes. On the other hand, if the window size is small, there is the problem of increased computation and over-sensitivity, so it is necessary to set a window size suitable for the buffer capacity and system characteristics.

Figures 8 and 9 show the result of evaluation. In the experiment, we check the bottleneck when the humidity sensor is delayed and the moving average of these values with different window sizes of 2 and 3. When the number of tokens increases monotonically, the smaller the window size, the faster the bottleneck can be detected. When the number of tokens repeats the same amount of increase and decrease as in the graph, the possibility of a bottleneck is low, so a larger window size reduction may reduce the sensitivity of detecting the bottleneck. In the proposed method, by using moving average, a bottleneck can be identified before it exceeds the capacity of the buffer.

4.2   Evaluation of Mitigation Method

For any type of edge node, the buffer utilization is set to h (usually 80% or less). Reducing the buffer utilization does not affect the system, but for a given buffer size, the size of the buffer can be reduced if normally the utilization does not reach 100%. This is suitable for an edge system with a small buffer size. We propose concurrent token processing by accumulating queued tokens into one token when the buffer reaches the threshold h.

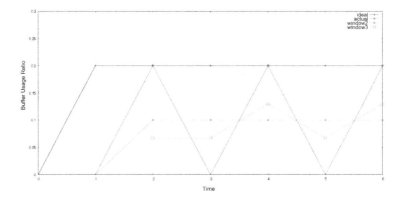

Fig. 8. Detection of buffer usage ratio at edge (n_1, n_3).

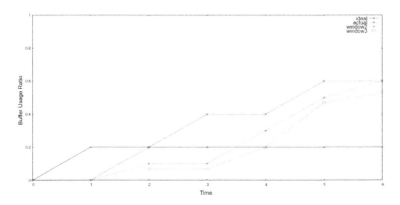

Fig. 9. Detection of buffer usage ratio at edge (n_2, n_3).

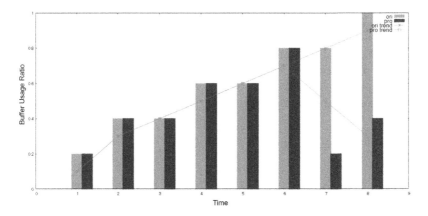

Fig. 10. Evaluation of mitigation method at bottleneck point at (n_1, n_5).

The method of concurrently processing tokens is shown in Fig. 6 where the bottleneck is identified at (n_1, n_5). The figure shows the flow of tokens from time t_k to t_{k+1}, respectively. The token accumulation between (n_1, n_5) is determined by the SWITCH node, which adds a node and an arc with the ability to output a token with *True* value if the buffer usage is 80%. If the buffer q_1 or q_2 are not reached, the AND nodes process the input tokens in a regular way. Figure 10 shows when mitigation method is applied to (n_1, n_5). The blue bar shows after the mitigation method are applied, and the yellow bar shows the buffer usage ratio without applying the mitigation method. We can see that buffer usage is reduced when the buffer reaches the limit h. Figure 11 also shows the mitigation result at (n_6, n_{10}). The trend line shows an overall reduction when the bottleneck occurs at the edge where bottlenecks were detected.

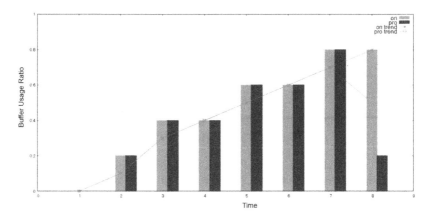

Fig. 11. Evaluation of mitigation method at bottleneck point at (n_6, n_{10}).

5 Conclusion

In this paper, we proposed two methods; (i) detection of bottleneck and (ii) mitigation of bottleneck in the data flow. The detection method uses moving average to calculate the number of tokens piled up at certain edges. By monitoring the changes in the trend of buffer usage using moving average, we can identify the edges where bottlenecks occur. In the mitigation method, we proposed a reconstruction approach using arc that overwrites true or false data in order to trigger token accumulation. The accumulated token is grouped into one token when the buffer usage ratio of the input edge of the target node reaches the specified threshold. In future work, we will consider a mitigation detection and mitigation method that can be controlled when the bottleneck changes rapidly.

References

1. Fu, X., Ghaffar, T., Davis, J., Lee, D.: Edgewise: a better stream processing engine for the edge. In: Proceedings of the 2019 USENIX Conference on Usenix Annual Technical Conference, pp. 929–945 (2019) Technical Conference , pp. 929–945 (2019)
2. Khan, J., Shahzad, M., Butt, A.: Sizing buffers of IoT edge routers. In: Proceedings of the 1st International Workshop on Edge Systems, Analytics and Networking, pp. 55–60 (2018). https://doi.org/10.1145/3213344.3213354
3. Shaikh, S., Watanabe, Y., Wang, Y., Kitagawa, H.: Smart scheme: an efficient query execution scheme for event-driven stream processing. Knowl. Inf. Syst. **58** (2019)
4. NS-3 Discrete-event network simulator. https://www.nsnam.org/. Accessed 11 Feb 2022
5. Dennis, J.B.: First version of a data flow procedure language. In: Robinet, B. (ed.) Programming Symposium. LNCS, vol. 19, pp. 362–376. Springer, Heidelberg (1974). https://doi.org/10.1007/3-540-06859-7_145

The Use of Digital Reports to Support the Visualization and Identification of University Dropout Data

Rodolfo S. S. dos Santos[✉][iD], Moacir A. Ponti[iD],
and Kamila Rios da Hora Rodrigues[iD]

University of São Paulo, São Carlos, SP, Brazil
rodolfosanches@usp.br, {moacir,kamila.rios}@icmc.usp.br
https://icmc.usp.br/en/

Abstract. University dropout is a concern for educational institutions since it directly impacts management and academic results, as well as being directly related to social problems. The literature points out that analyzing this phenomenon is a positive factor for developing programs to combat dropout, in addition to planning interventional actions and academic monitoring, making it possible to identify students at risk of dropout through techniques that use Machine Learning, for example. This paper presents a panoramic study of a public university, in which the school data were analyzed and classified using Machine Learning. The analysis of the data allowed to obtain an overview of the dropout data of the studied university. In addition, the main stakeholders were interviewed to report their main difficulties to know statistics about dropout. Considering these different data sources, we created digital reports to professors, chiefs and academic assistants, with information and statistics to assist university managers in decision-making related. These reports were validated by stakeholders and we hope that the next decisions can minimize any problems related to mental health, thus improving the quality of life of students, as well as their academic trajectory.

Keywords: University dropout · Mental health · Machine learning · Digital reports · Validation · Public university

1 Introduction

Students of higher education are exposed to several positive and negative events during the educational process. The successes often outweigh the efforts from the enrollment until the student effectively earns a degree, however adversities may lead to dropout [32,34]. This phenomenon is common to public and private higher education, directly interfering in their management and in the results of education quality [27,31], which consequently generates a necessary concern, as the students' departure from the study cycle induces several consequences [18,28].

The costs associated with college attrition include hindering of future job prospects with impacts in the countries economy, the personal and professional costs for the former student, waste of institutional and federal resources, a potential damage to university reputation and demoralization of students still in the school [3,14].

Several factors influence dropout, the main ones being related to financial and family reasons, unfulfilled expectations and lack of motivation [3]. Likewise, in a survey carried out by FONAPRACE [12], issues related to academic requirements are also discussed, which were also considered preponderant to dropout. Xenos, Pierrakeas and Pintelas [35] state that the identification of these factors is essential to provide special assistance to students, and categorizes them as follows: Internal factors - related to students' perception; Factors related to the course and professors and; Factors related to student demographic characteristics.

Studies point out that the prevalence of mental health problems in universities among students is high, with the majority being in university students subjected to relational stressors and with low social support [9,21]. In a survey conducted at an American University, Eisenberg et al. [9] observed that the prevalence of depressive or anxiety disorders was 15.6% for undergraduate students and 13.0% for graduate students, and also, there is suicidal thought reported by 2% of students. According to Leonhardt and Sahil [18], in American higher education, in 2018, about one in three students who enroll in college never earn a degree. They looked at 368 colleges arranged by what they would expect their graduation rates to be, based on the average for colleges with similar student bodies concluding that colleges with higher success rates study academic data and use it to remove hurdles for students, in addition, students' connection to other people, financial issues, and university structure also influence to increase success.

In Brazil, a special committee on dropout studies was established in 1995, from the Ministry of Education ordinance, with the purpose of evaluating the performance of Federal Higher Education Institutions (FHEI; IFES, in Portuguese). In 2002, this became a major concern with the significant increase in the number of places offered by IFES in Brazil [34].

Since this, data visualization techniques have been explored to prevent dropout in terms of providing management support in order to identify students at risk of dropping out [4,8,10,26]. Some studies also see Data Mining (DM) and Machine Learning techniques (ML) to predict possible dropout [1,5, 15,16,20,23,29,30].

This paper presents the report of the panoramic study of a Brazilian public institution of higher education through the data visualization of its students and interviews with different stakeholders, seeking to identify students in a possible situation of risk of dropout and who may need support services due to emotional difficulties, financial, among others. We hope that this study can motivate other institutions to use the concepts and techniques proposed, to support students in vulnerable situations more effectively. We also highlight that this study went through the validation of the Brazilian ethical committee, CAAE number: 34343920.5.0000.5504.

The paper is structured as follows: Sect. 2 describes related works; Sect. 3 describes university data and techniques to collect data; Sect. 4 describes the prototype designed; Sect. 5 presents the validation carried out in prototype; Sect. 6 shows the metrics of the reports usage and, finally, Sect. 7 relates the final considerations and future work.

2 Related Works

Previous studies found that college attrition depend on the type of course [6,35], student's year at college [6,18,19,32], social issues such as parental background [2,6], class-cultural discontinuities [17] and economic profile [25]; as well as quantitative academic data [23].

Lozano et al. [19] found the first and second years to be crucial when it comes to retention as it allows for more numerous and more intensive interventions. According to Casanova et al. [6], the first years are particularly difficult for students who enrolled in the course as a second option. The authors suggest improving motivation in students who have to adapt to this situation.

Hippel and Hofflinger [13] conducted a study to identify students at risk of dropping out at 8 Chilean public universities using Logistic Regression (LR). The authors used both personal/family data, e.g. parents' education, high school grades, and entrance exam scores, as well as academic data collected during college. They studied the effect of programs focused on helping students adapt to university life, develop study skills and manage anxiety. The assisting programs dictated a reduction of 30–40% in the chances of dropping out in 2 of 4 universities where such programs existed. They found the dropout risk to be inferior for older students, and also for those receiving scholarships. This makes it evident there is no clear consensus on the causes of dropout and also the variety of factors protecting against it.

Coutinho et al. [8] analyzed dropout data using related metrics and developed visualization interfaces covering: a) dropout index; b) the main factors that lead to this phenomenon and c) data related to teaching methodology, in order to support decision making. In the same methodology, Reino [26] carried out an analysis of the main causes of dropout in a distance undergraduate course and showed the results through statistical visualizations.

Already Barbosa et al. [4] performed the classification of students at risk of dropout using machine learning techniques and also performed an analysis of the results to support management.

Ferreira et al. [10] extracted and processed a dataset from a Brazilian institute using all courses and degrees since 2002. They analyzed applications for data visualization based on interactivity, client and API support, data modeling, multiple visualizations on a single screen and active community tutorials. After choosing the visualization tool, they applied eight different report pages, including monthly tracking and comparison, overall performance, achievement by profile and personal information, concluding that data visualization allows to detect and adopt measures to prevent dropout situations.

After identification of students that are prone to dropout college, interventions may be employed to assist students. Those may represent a positive approach to improve retention, as shown by the experience of a Brazilian public university, which points out a dropout decrease of 12.3% in 2018 when compared to 2017 [33]. This reduction was due to institutional interventions that increased the number of registered students, accounting for new admissions and the re-inclusion of students who had taken time off from college. In addition, the number of these students decreased from 10,686 (2017) to 1,142 (2018).

This paper describes the analysis of dropout in a higher education institution, as well as offering support decision-making by managers in order to decrease dropout rates and minimize the consequences and losses caused by it.

3   Data Collection Step

The data collecting step was carried out by using three different sources: (1) literature study (described above); (2) mining of university's data and; (3) analysis of stakeholders' questionnaire responses. These three sources allowed us to understand the context and also to propose some interventions for different stakeholders to consider.

The university where this study was carried out has several computational systems for managing institutional processes. They are separated by purpose for example: under-graduation; postgraduate studies; university restaurant; library, among others. The main systems used to manage academic and student data are integrated used in this study to collect data are: **Integrated Academic Management System**: responsible for the academic processes related to the student, lecturers and the main activities, such as course enrollments, registration of grades and frequencies, teaching plans, subjects, courses, among other activities; **Integrated University Management Support System**: general management of the university including registration of people, permissions, and applications student cards; **Dean of Extension**: management of outreach and extension courses, as well as postgraduate courses *lato sensu* e *stricto sensu*.

By considering source (2) to data collecting and, aiming to find out the relevant data to be collected to assess dropout risk, we follow the empirical evidence found by Pal [24], Hippel and Hofflinger [13]; and Souza [31], in which: personal data, academic information prior to college enrollment, academic information collected during college, as well as economic information, are sufficient to investigate college attrition and student dropout.

Note that, Brazilian federal universities have affirmative actions, so that the category of admission defines quotas of student places related to social/economic status of the student as well as race.

We obtained data from students who entered the university between 2008 and 2020, from all undergraduate courses offered by the institution during this period. In each year, between 2000 and 3000 students are admitted. In total, information was collected from 32.892 students, separated by course, year and period/semester.

Based on the data collected, the biggest problems related to dropout are found in the departments of exact sciences and, for the most part, occur in the 1st, 2nd and 3rd scholar semesters. There are other metrics that can be analyzed in the fight against dropout, for example: fees from academic centers and evasion by type of admission. These and other information were made available in the university's academic management system, actually validated by stakeholders and described in the following section.

Finally, in the source (3) of data collection, we analyzed the information obtained through an online questionnaire, which aimed to understand how the monitoring and combat dropout actions are carried out by teachers, heads and managers. In addition, we seek to understand the perception of these users regarding the dropout scenario, collecting the views of monitoring, combating and preventing dropout, which are not currently used and applied at the university.

The questionnaire was divided into 5 parts to assist in the planning and development of indicators/reports, those: 1) participant identification; 2) profile survey and activities performed at the university; 3) follow-ups performed with students and/or groups of students; 4) perception of dropout; 5) needs, ideas for data visualization in the systems and final suggestions.

Among the information collected from the 32 participants who answered the questionnaire, it was observed that individual and group monitoring of students is carried out according to the teacher's subjects. The coordinators of undergraduate courses, especially, also monitor the students by profile and characteristics, including: a) indigenous people; b) students with special needs; c) students with learning disabilities and d) scholarship holders.

The perception of school dropout by participants reflects the literature and reaffirms the different factors that influence this phenomenon, among them, difficulties in basic high school subjects, lack of motivation, lack of interest in classes and courses, financial difficulties and family problems. In addition to the literature, the data also included the lack of dialogue between teacher and student, difficulty with the Portuguese language (foreign and indigenous students), use of illicit drugs, immaturity, problems with gender identity and difficulty in self-regulation and planning.

Mental health conditions impact the conduct of basic actions, such as: getting out of bed to attend classes and staying in the classroom, with students having panic and anxiety attacks.

Issues related to gender identity highlight adaptation in courses—transgender people experience violence and discrimination. On the other hand, problems related to planning occur due to a difficulty in delineating academic life in the long and medium term, which directly affects the payment of credits.

As a preventive approach to dropout, interventions were suggested by the participants in the first semesters of the course, in order to introduce the student to higher education and equalize the knowledge of incoming students, through complementary high school teaching activities; psychological support to face the responsibilities and adaptations in the university; pedagogical tutoring; facilitate access to motivational assistance and smaller classes.

In addition, among the solutions cited to assist in these approaches, was mentioned the use of graphs, indicators, simulators of real data, extract from semiannual dropout and progress reports of each student, in a way that they are able to visualize the students who dropped out in semester, and the student data according to the monitoring groups.

In line with the actions suggested above by the main stakeholders, this group of researchers proposed the development of graphical reports to be inserted into the main management system for leaders and teachers, in order to give visibility to information related to students and dropout trends. The next section describes the design of these reports.

4   Reports - Graphical Interface Design Step

We followed four stages to design digital reports to support university managers: a) Identifying the main requirements from a survey with different stakeholders of university (described above); b) Definition of reports to be developed according the requirements and interested stakeholders; c) Prototyping graphic interfaces with relevant information (to be available in the university management system) and, d) Validating of the prototyped interface with a sample of stakeholders who participated from step a).

In step (b), among the stakeholders interested in viewing statistics and monitoring the dropout, stand out five user profiles that were defined for the purpose of this study, namely: 1) the undergraduate rectory managers, 2) academic centers heads, 3) departments heads, 4) coordinators of undergraduate courses and 5) professors. Each of these profiles should follows the visualization of the interesting data according to the organizational hierarchy, in this way, the profile with the highest visualization capacity (1) can also view information from the other profiles: **Undergraduate rectory managers**: It has an overview of the data without hierarchy restrictions, being able to also visualize the data of academic centers, departments, courses and professors; **Academic centers heads**: It is restricted to only viewing data related to the center, being only the departments, courses and professors that are under its management; **Departments heads**: It has the visualization of the data of the courses and professors that are related to the department; **Coordinators of undergraduate courses**: It is restricted to viewing data related to the course and professors who are under his/her coordination; **Professor**: Can view the data of the subjects and students, as well as the number of approvals and disapprovals related to them over the years.

In the (c) stage, we prototyped digital reports for data visualization based on the collection of data from the questionnaire, from the literature review [4, 8, 26] and data mining step. Ten reports, divided into 2 groups of profiles, were prototyped to be made validated. For the first group - profiles of undergraduate rectory managers, centers, department heads, and coordinators of undergraduate courses - these users can view: the history of dropout rates, dropout rates by academic center, general situation of students per semester and by type of admission; historical evasion by student profile; Number of credits enrolled, approved, disapproved per student. For the second group - the professors profile - they can view: failures, approvals and cancellations; subjects' failures; historical overview of semester data; general situation of students by subject.

The interface design followed all the system's interface and language standards. The person in charge of the UX/UI area of the university also analyzed the reports' interface.

Figure 1 illustrates three different graphs that present an overview of dropout rates at the university, making it possible to verify the variations by period and which academic centers have the highest rates. Finally, the students' situations are shown according to the division already used by the university. The Fig. 2 illustrates the teacher's indicators, with the number of students, approvals and disapprovals, in order to provide performance data and subjects that need further monitoring. Finally, Fig. 3, illustrates the visualization of student credits in a table format and allows the identification and monitoring of groups of students (defined by the manager), as well as students who enrolled in a few credits in that semester, also being able to cross information of credits taken and final deadline for completion of the course.

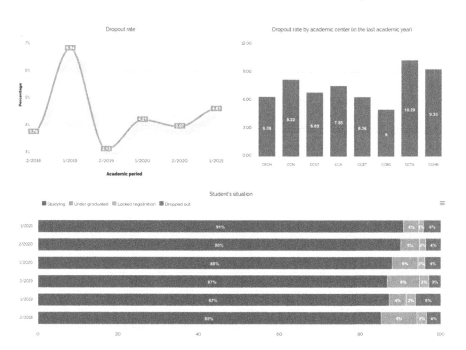

Fig. 1. Visualization of dropout rate, dropout by academic center and student situation graphs.

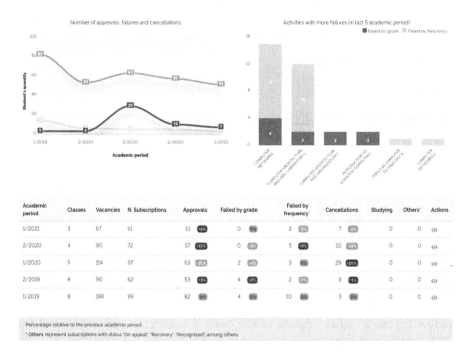

Academic period	Classes	Vacancies	N. Subscriptions	Approvals	Failed by grade	Failed by frequency	Cancellations	Studying	Others*	Actions
1/2021	3	67	61	51 +4%	0 0%	3 -2%	7 -2%	0	0	👁
2/2020	4	90	72	57 +15%	0 -2%	5 +3%	10 -16%	0	0	👁
1/2020	5	114	97	63 -2%	2 -4%	3 0%	29 +26%	0	0	👁
2/2019	4	90	62	53 +3%	4 +2%	2 -7%	3 +1%	0	0	👁
1/2019	8	188	99	82 0%	4 0%	4 0%	10 0%	3 0%	0	0	👁

Percentage relative to the previous academic period.
* Others represent subscriptions with status "On appeal", "Recovery", "Recognized", among others.

Fig. 2. General graphs and summary table of the teacher's profile.

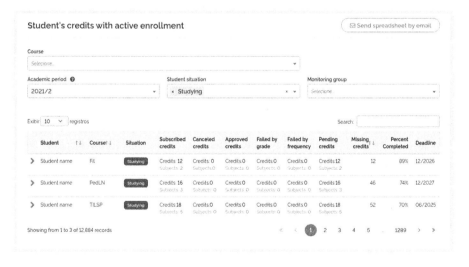

Fig. 3. Student's credits with active enrollment.

Finally, the last stage included the validation of the interface with stakeholders of different levels. This step is described in detail in the next section.

5   Validation Step

The validation of the requirements listed from different sources and made available in the reports interface is relevant to ensure that they have achieved the purpose for which they were created, as well as to ensure that target users are able to use the features, even with little knowledge of the system [7,11].

Usability tests [22] are used to evaluate interfaces of computer systems under development. This was the technique used here.

To conduct the validation, high-fidelity prototypes of the reports were developed in the university's management system. Thus, the profile representatives (who answered the questionnaire to gather requirements) were able to access the prototype and provide feedback on the available data, and on the interface and interaction elements arranged in the reports. It should be noted that the data provided are fictitious data.

The profile that carried out the use test was the profile of the Dean of Undergraduate Studies - in the figures of the head of the sector and two administrative technicians of the academic and pedagogical monitoring coordination. They carried out 10 tasks via web conference, with a recorded screen, in which the researchers in charge were able to observe the user's interaction with the report screens available on the SAGUI system.

System logs were also being collected. It was observed the ease with which the user interacted and understood the actions of the system. In these tasks, the user should answer some associated questions to ensure that the correct information has been found. The following metrics were evaluated. a) Number of clicks; b) Time required to complete the task; c) Number of successfully executed interactions; d) Unexpected behaviors; e) Ease of learning.

The tasks carried out were made available in a questionnaire and it consist of: a) Logging in; b) Consult the avoidance reports; c) View the general dropout data of the university; d) Find the number of canceled credits for student 2; e) Find foreigners who made an external transfer of the physics course in 2020/1; f) Find indigenous students who locked the Environmental Engineering course in 2018/2; g) Finding students of the Administration course dropping out in 2018/1 who entered the University through the PcD PPi, modality with an income ≤1.5; h) Find out which department has the highest dropout rate considering the management and technology center; i) Find the course with the second highest dropout rate in the physics department; j) Find the subject with the most disapproval from any professor. The tasks to be carried out on the prototype should vary according to the stakeholder profile performing the validation.

Tables 1 and 2 illustrate the results obtained by this first stakeholder, comparing them to the data collected in the pilot test evaluation.

In general, participants showed ease in performing what was requested, with only partial difficulty being observed in some tasks, which did not prevent them

Table 1. Results of the **amount of clicks** and unexpected behavior, comparing the values obtained and the expected value.

	Number of clicks				Unexpected behaviors		
	P1	P2	P3	Expected	P1	P2	P3
Task a	3	3	3	3	0	0	1
Task b	4	6	2	2	0	0	0
Task c	7	3	3	3	0	0	0
Task d	5	0	0	0	1	0	0
Task e	7	19	9	4	0	0	0
Task f	6	15	13	6	1	1	0
Task g	8	5	15	4	0	0	0
Task h	9	9	5	5	0	0	0
Task i	6	9	5	5	0	0	0
Task j	13	8	14	8	0	0	0

Table 2. Result of the **time** required to carry out the Tasks, comparing the values obtained and the expected value.

	Time			
	P1	P2	P3	Expected
Task a	15 s	23 s	21 s	30 s
Task b	40 s	34 s	23 s	1 min
Task c	2 min 3 s	1 min 33 s	1 min 06 s	1 min
Task d	1 min 40 s	58 s	48 s	3 min
Task e	1 min 25 s	2 min 06 s	1 min 32 s	3 min
Task f	42 s	2 min 45 s	1 min 18 s	1 min 30 s
Task g	1 min 33 s	1 min 42 s	2 min 54 s	2 min 30 s
Task h	1 min 32 s	1 min 47 s	1 min 02 s	1 min
Task i	1 min 50 s	2 min 01 s	57 s	1 min 30 s
Task j	3 min 11 s	2 min 04 s	3 min 54 s	2 min

from being carried out. Among the difficulties, there were efforts beyond what was expected to relate a requested task to the information presented in the interface, in addition to confusion between the data of the visualizations, which were overcome with a more careful analysis of the system. The participants, however, pointed out several doubts, needs and suggestions for availability in the interfaces of the reports:

1. Specification of the concepts used visually, detailing the meaning of the information;

2. List of students who fit the dropout factors (grade, attendance, credits enrolled, credits canceled);
3. Division of dropout rates into course dropout and institution dropout;
4. Add option to filter data by "Non-scholarship holders" and also select several items, such as: Foreign Scholars;
5. Change the chart of dropout by academic center due to the large amount of information;
6. Differentiate the courses by Graduation Degree (Bachelor's Degree/Bachelor's Degree) and Shift (Night/Afternoon/Day);
7. Correction of some of the used nomenclatures.

During the validation of the reports, it was possible to observe that they were relevant to assist managers in decision making through the different profiles. The collection of requirements through the online questionnaire confirmed the information found in the literature and in the university data mining stage, in addition to highlighting the evasion scenario in the university. The reports developed in prototypes were validated by the main representative of all profiles and had positive results with regard to acceptance, satisfaction and usability requirements.

6   Reports Implementation and Real Usage

After the validation stage, we implemented and made the reports available in the university's management system with minor adjustments, including the issues raised by the participants, which proved to be relevant and significant for the improvement of the system and the effectiveness of the reports.

The technology used in the implementation of the system was the Angular 12[1], a Javascript-based framework maintained by Google, and, for the development of reports, the libraries apexcharts[2] and datatable[3], which cover full chart implementation and table visualization, respectively.

Two formal presentations of the system were made to all stakeholders, including those who participated in data collection and usability tests. Also, during the presentations, new changes and functionalities were suggested, among them: a) List of disciplines and the number of students missing to take it; b) Information on the amount of credits allowed for a student to take in the semester and calculate if it is possible to take the missing credits until the end of the course; c) Expansion of the data view in more academic periods. Suggestion a) is intended to meet a managerial need for the planning of semesters and is indirectly related to dropout, while suggestions b) and c) are features directly linked to improving student monitoring and will be implemented with priority.

In order to collect information related to the use of reports, we implemented the features provided by Google Analytics and Google BigQuery, in order to

---

[1] https://angular.io/.
[2] https://apexcharts.com.
[3] https://datatables.net.

identify, in practice, the profiles most interested in truancy and also the frequency of access to the system. Among the functionalities, we collect information related to the time spent on the page, information about the profile that requested the report and which report was requested.

The data was collected during the period of September 27, 2021 and January 21, 2022. Table 3 shows the number of page views, number of unique users, average queries per user and the average time spent on the page. Figure 4 shows the distribution of the users' profile, and finally, Fig. 5 shows the relationship between the type of information and the number of times in which it was requested.

Table 3. Number of views, unique users, average queries per unique user, and average engagement time.

Views	Unique users	Average queries per unique user	Average engagement time
386	110	3,5	3 min 12 s

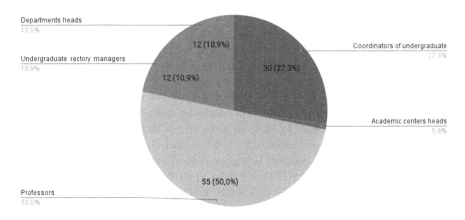

Fig. 4. Unique users profile distribution.

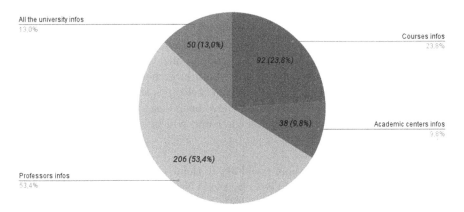

Fig. 5. List of the type of information and the number of queries carried out.

It is observed in Fig. 4 that of the 110 users who consulted the forms, 50% belonged to the professor profile, which was already expected, since this is the category with the largest number of representatives. We had, however, representatives of all categories accessing the reports.

Regarding the type of information researched, Fig. 5 illustrates that information from professors was researched 53.4%, information about courses in 23.8% of the time, information from all the university in 13% of the time and information from academic centers in 9.8% of the time.

7   Final Remarks and Future Works

Obtaining, analyzing and providing data related to university dropout is an important step towards understanding the main causes and consequences of this phenomenon, especially to provide support in decision-making by managers of educational institutions.

In this article, issues related to dropout were explored using the collection of data from the academic systems of a public institution, and also, through an online questionnaire about the perception of this phenomenon *versus* the reality of the university. Then, ten reports with data visualizations were implemented to provide information to managers. Finally, a validation of the design of these reports was carried out with three participants who represent the undergraduate pro-rector profile.

We had positive perceptions regarding the use of reports in the dropout combat. That is, to make decisions and carry out more punctual interventions, managers and teachers need, in fact, to have access to information. Once they are available, monitoring becomes more feasible and viable.

Based on the results obtained, it was possible to confirm the empirical evidence from the literature, and the need to identify information on university dropout in the institution where this study was applied, to carry out interventions in all instances. The evaluation carried out encouraged us to continue with the study, considering that the evaluators highlighted the relevance of the work carried out, as well as the quality and importance of the reports made available.

In future works, we intend to analyze the effects of the use of reports in the fight against university dropout. A second stage, in progress, includes creating intervention models to be matched through a gamified computational solution. This solution should support students in the organization and planning of studies. Currently, at the studied university, these interventions are applied manually by an internal university program that welcomes students with difficulties in their academic life. The interventions have been designed and conducted with the support of the program's psychologists and will be evaluated together with the authors of this project.

Acknowledgments. The authors would like to thank the CAPES, Brazilian agency, for their financial support. The authors also would like to thank the participants in the requirements gathering and validation stages of the graphical reports. We would also like to thank the Federal University of São Carlos - Brazil, specifically the IT sector, for all the support given to the research.

References

1. Abu-Oda, G.S., El-Halees, A.M.: Data mining in higher education: university student dropout case study. Int. J. Data Min. Knowl. Manage. Process **5**(1), 15 (2015)
2. Aina, C.: Parental background and university dropout in Italy. High. Educ. **65**(4), 437–456 (2013)
3. Ataíde, J., Lima, L., De, E., Alves, O.: A repetência e o abandono escolar no curso de licenciatura em física: um estudo de caso. Physicae 6 (January 2006). https://doi.org/10.5196/physicae.6.5
4. Barbosa, A.M., Santos, E., Gomes, J.P.P.: A machine learning approach to identify and prioritize college students at risk of dropping out. In: XXVIII Simpósio Brasileiro de Informática na Educação SBIE (Brazilian Symposium on Computers in Education), November 2017, Recife, pp. 1497–1506 (2017). https://doi.org/10.5753/cbie.sbie.2017.1497
5. Burgos, C., Campanario, M.L., de la Peña, D., Lara, J.A., Lizcano, D., Martínez, M.A.: Data mining for modeling students' performance: a tutoring action plan to prevent academic dropout. Comput. Electr. Eng. **66**, 541–556 (2018)
6. Casanova, J.R., et al.: Factors that determine the persistence and dropout of university students. Psicothema **30**, 408–414 (2018)
7. Costa, L.F., Ramalho, F.A.: A usabilidade nos estudos de uso da informação: em cena usuários e sistemas interativos de informação. Perspectivas em Ciência da Informação **15**, 92–117 (2010). http://www.scielo.br/scielo.php?script=sci_arttext&pid=S1413-99362010000100006&nrm=iso
8. Coutinho, E., Horta Bezerra, J., Bezerra, C.I.M., Moreira, L.: Uma análise da evasão em cursos de graduação apoiado por métricas e visualização de dados (October 2018). https://doi.org/10.5753/cbie.wie.2018.31
9. Eisenberg, D., Gollust, S., Golberstein, E., Hefner, J.: Prevalence and correlates of depression, anxiety, and suicidality among university students. Am. J. Orthopsychiatry **77**, 534–42 (2007). https://doi.org/10.1037/0002-9432.77.4.534
10. Ferreira, F., Santos, B.S., Marques, B., Dias, P.: FICAvis: data visualization to prevent university dropout. In: 2020 24th International Conference Information Visualisation (IV), pp. 57–62 (2020). https://doi.org/10.1109/IV51561.2020.00034
11. Ferreira, S.B.L., Leite, J.C.S.: Avaliação da usabilidade em sistemas de informação: o caso do Sistema Submarino. Revista de Administração Contemporânea **7**, 115–136 (2003). http://www.scielo.br/scielo.php?script=sci_arttext&pid=S1415-65552003000200007&nrm=iso
12. FONAPRACE, F.N.d.P.R.d.A.C.e.E.: V pesquisa nacional de perfil socioeconômico e cultural dos (as) graduandos (as) das ifes. Technical report (2018)
13. Hippel, P.T.V., Hofflinger, A.: The data revolution comes to higher education: identifying students at risk of dropout in Chile. J. High. Educ. Policy Manage. **43**, 1–22 (2020). https://doi.org/10.1080/1360080X.2020.1739800
14. Ivankova, N.V., Stick, S.L.: Students' persistence in a distributed doctoral program in educational leadership in higher education: a mixed methods study. Res. High. Educ. **48**(1), 93–135 (2007)
15. Kelly, J.O., Menezes, A.G., de Carvalho, A.B., Montesco, C.A.: Supervised learning in the context of educational data mining to avoid university students dropout. In: 2019 IEEE 19th International Conference on Advanced Learning Technologies (ICALT), vol. 2161, pp. 207–208. IEEE (2019)

16. Kotsiantis, S.: Educational data mining: a case study for predicting dropout-prone students. Int. J. Knowl. Eng. Soft Data Paradigms **1**(2), 101–111 (2009)

17. Lehmann, W.: "i just didn't feel like i fit in": the role of habitus in university dropout decisions. Can. J. High. Educ. **37**(2), 89–110 (2007)

18. Leonhardt, D., Chinoy, S.: The college dropout crisis. The New York Times (May 2019). https://www.nytimes.com/interactive/2019/05/23/opinion/sunday/college-graduation-rates-ranking.html

19. Lozano, J.M., Rua Vieites, A., Bilbao-Calabuig, P., Casadesús-Fa, M.: University student retention: best time and data to identify undergraduate students at risk of dropout. Innov. Educ. Teach. Int. **57**, 1–12 (2018). https://doi.org/10.1080/14703297.2018.1502090

20. Martins, L.C.B., Carvalho, R.N., Carvalho, R.S., Victorino, M.C., Holanda, M.: Early prediction of college attrition using data mining. In: 2017 16th IEEE International Conference on Machine Learning and Applications (ICMLA), pp. 1075–1078. IEEE (2017)

21. da Matta, K.W.: Evasão Universitária Estudantil: Precursores Psicológicos do Trancamento de Matrícula por Motivo de Saúde Mental. Master's thesis, Universidade de Brasília (2011)

22. Nielsen, J., Molich, R.: Heuristic evaluation of user interfaces. In: Proceedings of the SIGCHI Conference on Human Factors in Computing Systems, pp. 249–256 (1990)

23. Nistor, N., Neubauer, K.: From participation to dropout: quantitative participation patterns in online university courses. Comput. Educ. **55**(2), 663–672 (2010)

24. Pal, S.: Mining educational data using classification to decrease dropout rate of students. Int. J. Multidisciplinary Sci. Eng. **3**, 35–39 (2012)

25. Powdthavee, N., Vignoles, A.: The socio-economic gap in university dropout. B.E. J. Econ. Anal. Policy **9**(1), 1–36 (2009)

26. Reino, L., Hernández-Domínguez, A., Freitas Júnior, O., Carvalho, V., Barros, P., Braga, M.: Análise das causas da evasão na educação a distância em uma instituição federal de ensino superior (October 2015). https://doi.org/10.5753/cbie.sbie.2015.91

27. Ribeiro, M.: O projeto profissional familiar como determinante da evasão universitária: um estudo preliminar. Revista Brasileira de Orientacao Profissional **6**, 55–70 (2005)

28. dos Santos Baggi, C.A., Lopes, D.A.: Evasão e avaliação institucional no ensino superior: uma discussão bibliográfica. Avaliação: Revista da Avaliação da Educação Superior (Campinas) **16**, 355–374 (2011)

29. Sarra, A., Fontanella, L., Di Zio, S.: Identifying students at risk of academic failure within the educational data mining framework. Soc. Indic. Res. **146**(1), 41–60 (2019)

30. Solís, M., Moreira, T., Gonzalez, R., Fernandez, T., Hernandez, M.: Perspectives to predict dropout in university students with machine learning. In: 2018 IEEE International Work Conference on Bioinspired Intelligence (IWOBI), pp. 1–6. IEEE (2018)

31. de Souza, A.M.: Machine learning e a evasão escolar: análise preditiva no suporte à tomada de decisão. Master's thesis, Faculdade de Ciências Empresariais (April 2020). https://repositorio.fumec.br/xmlui/handle/123456789/420

32. Stein, C.: The push for higher education: College attrition rates. PA Times Org. (July 2018). https://patimes.org/the-push-for-higher-education-college-attrition-rates/

33. UFAL: Ufal comemora a redução do índice de evasão de estudantes de graduação. Technical report (2019). https://ufal.br/ufal/noticias/2019/10/ufal-comemora-a-reducao-do-indice-de-evasao-de-estudantes-de-graduacao
34. Veloso, T.C.M.A., de Almeida, E.P.: Evasão nos cursos de graduação da universidade federal de mato grosso, campus universitário de cuiabá - um processo de exclusão. Série-Estudos - Perioódico do Mestrado em Educação da UCDB **13**, 133–148 (2002)
35. Xenos, M., Pierrakeas, C., Pintelas, P.: A survey on student dropout rates and dropout causes concerning the students in the course of informatics of the Hellenic Open University. Comput. Educ. **39**(4), 361–377 (2002)

Default Factors in Motorcycle Sales in Developing Countries

Ryota Fujinuma[✉] and Yumi Asahi

Graduate School of Management, Department of Management, Tokyo University of Science,
1-11-2, Fujimi, Chiyoda-ku 102-0071, Tokyo, Japan
8621510@ed.tus.ac.jp, asahi@tsc.u-tokai.ac.jp

Abstract. A basic concept of loan is reconsidered all over the world by the new BIS regulations. However, many people in Latin America still have a vague way of thinking about loans. It is due to the global recession. As a result, companies have not been able to recover their manufacturing costs. However, a large potential market has been formed in Latin America. Therefore, the challenge for companies is how to formulate product strategies that can meet the needs of the market. Therefore, in this study, we create a classification model of whether customers will default or not. In addition, we explore the characteristics of the default customers. Propose a sales strategy for the product based on these characteristics. This would help companies to improve their financing problems and secure profits. In this study, we compare the accuracy of Logistic Regression, Random Forest and XGBoost. Since the data handled in this study were unbalanced data, data expansion by Synthetic Minority Over-sampling Technique (SMOTE) was effective. Finally, we analyze analyzes what variables contribute to the model by using SHapley Additive exPlanations (SHAP). From this analysis result, we will explore the characteristics of what kind of person is the loan unpaid customers. The variables with the highest contribution were the type of vehicle purchased, the area where the customer lives, and credit information. We propose sales strategy by focusing on the variables that are significant to the model.

Keywords: Marketing research · Loan bankruptcy · Credit risk model · Sales strategy · Developing country

1 Introduction

The U.S. subprime mortgage crisis, which came to light in the spring of 2007, has thrown the world's financial markets into turmoil. The problem started when the delinquency rate of SPLs, mortgages with low credit quality, increased in the U.S., raising the risk of default. However, the problem that emerged from the SPL problem was not only securitization and credit ratings, but also the fact that banks were embarking on extremely risky businesses. In preparation for the introduction of the new capital adequacy regulations (new BIS regulations), which were created based on the lessons learned from this event, the establishment of an appropriate internal rating system and its verification have become major issues worldwide [1].

While the new BIS regulations are causing people around the world to rethink the way they think about loans, many people in Country X, which is located in southeastern Central and South America and has the largest area and population in Central and South America, still have an ambiguous attitude toward loans. This is due in large part to the national character of Country X: "Country X is generally optimistic and does not worry about trivial matters". In addition to this national character, in response to the economic damage caused by the Lehman Shock, the government of Country X lowered interest rates. In 2011, there was a sovereign debt crisis in Europe, and the value of the country's currency fell, so the government of Country X lowered interest rates during this period as well. As a result of these two policy interest rates, even the poorest citizens of Country X were able to obtain loans more easily, which led to vigorous consumption and a rapid increase in personal debt. As a result, it has become common for individuals in Country X to take out loans to purchase goods. The purchase of Japanese products is no exception, and many customers are paying for them with loans. In this study, we focus on motorcycles among the products purchased with loans. In country X, where the infrastructure is not perfect, motorcycles are a practical means of transportation and are indispensable for commuting, farming, and other economic development. Motorcycles are a commodity that can be considered a necessity in the lives of X citizens.

Strategic default is a problem in country X and internationally. Fukumitsu [2] defines default as a default when the borrower cannot afford to pay the mortgage, and a strategic default when the borrower can afford to pay but chooses not to. While this is mainly a problem in housing loans, customers who deliberately default on their loans have also become a problem in two-wheelers. In addition, there are cases where customers take out new loans despite non-payment of loans. The new BIS regulations make late payments a high risk for companies. In addition, it is important to note that customers who are late in making payments have a very high probability of becoming bankrupt. This is why it is important to identify customers with a high risk of bankruptcy in advance. In addition, it is necessary to pay attention to customers who are late in paying their loans.

2   Previous Research

The BRICs and other emerging markets have emerged from the global recession caused by the Lehman Shock and are attracting attention as the next generation of growth markets. In particular, it is the middle class, not the rich or the poor, that is driving economic growth in emerging countries. Although a large potential market has been formed, it is not easy to enter these areas, penetrate the middle class market with products and businesses, and secure profits. Focusing on the motorcycle market, since the late 2000s, local consumers and governments have learned various lessons, and demand has grown for products that offer high value for money in terms of safety, security, driving performance, durability, and design, taking quality and functions into consideration rather than just price. The issue is how to formulate a product strategy that can respond to the needs of this middle-class market [3].

In addition, a problem that has been gaining importance in developing countries in recent years is the sufficiency of financial services. One of the obstacles is that the poor do not have access to financial services. This is because it is difficult to verify the identity of the poor and determine their creditworthiness, so financial institutions need to select those who have the ability to repay, which itself is expensive, and as a result, financial services are difficult to provide. In addition, the inability of small businesses and sole proprietors to obtain loans when they need them has even greater negative effects than for individuals, as they miss opportunities to grow their businesses and are unable to continue operating in times of emergency [4].

Miyoshi [5] analyzed what dependent variables affect the bankruptcy rate by using a fixed effects model with the bankruptcy rate as the independent variable. The results of this study showed that the size of the proportion of the population aged 20–24 is a variable that lowers the personal bankruptcy rate. Similarly, an increase in GDP per capita is also a variable that lowers the bankruptcy rate. This suggests that age and income are related to unpaid loans in Country X. Guiso, Sapienza & Zingales [6] discuss what factors increase strategic default. First, those who consider default immoral do not want to default, while those who are angry about the economic situation, want to reduce confidence in banks, and want to increase regulation are more likely to default strategically. The key reason for strategic default is not high prices, but deteriorating security in the region. In the case of country X, where regional disparities are strong, it can be predicted that regional variables have a strong impact on loan unpaid customers.

Traditionally, statistical methods such as Logistic Regression have been used for credit risk models. However, in recent years, various machine learning methods have been proposed and their accuracy has been significantly improved [7]. Sawaki et al. [7] constructed credit risk models using various machine learning methods on data of domestic small and medium-sized enterprises, and examined which methods can achieve high accuracy. In machine learning, it is generally known that ensemble learning, which combines multiple models, often yields higher accuracy than learning only a single model. Methods such as bagging, boosting, and stacking are known in the field of ensemble learning. In addition, Neural Network, Gradient Boosting Decision Tree, Random Forest [8], and Support Vector Machine are representative machine learning methods that have attracted attention in recent years. Each of them has its own characteristics, and which method is optimal depends on the field of application and the characteristics of the data set. Among them, Random Forest, which is an ensemble learning method, can be used for regression and classification problems in supervised learning. For classification problems, it is a method that gathers several different decision trees based on the bagging of ensemble learning, and discriminates by majority voting of the multiple decision trees. While decision trees on their own have the disadvantage of being prone to overlearning, Random Forest adds diversity to the data set by randomly sampling features and duplicate random samples when creating multiple decision trees. This is one of the methods to deal with the problem of overlearning. In addition, eXtreme Gradient Boosting (XGBoost) [9] is an ensemble learning method that combines gradient boosting and decision trees. Gradient boosting is a method in which weak learners are built one by one in sequence. When constructing a new weak learner, the results of all weak learners constructed so far are used. A gradient boosting tree is one that uses a decision tree as the weak learner. Compared to Bagging, in which all weak learners are trained independently, this method cannot parallelize the computation and takes more time to learn, but is known to produce higher accuracy.

The Synthetic Minority Over-sampling Technique (SMOTE) [10] is a method for dealing with unbalanced data such as those in this study. SMOTE is a method of oversampling using neighboring data rather than simply copying a small number of data. Reducing the number of variables through feature selection has the advantages of increasing accuracy, improving interpretability, and reducing learning time by reducing computational cost. As a method for feature selection, Hall [11] mentions a correlation-based approach among filter methods. In many cases, the correlation-based filter method provides results comparable to the wrapper method and runs many times faster than the wrapper method, making it suitable for large data sets such as the one in this study. Correlation-based filtering means that a good feature set is a model that contains features that are highly correlated with the independent variable, but that are not correlated with each other among the features.

In models that use decision trees such as Random Forest and XGBoost feature importance of features can be defined using the trained model. The default feature importance calculation method of XGBoost is Gain. However, Yoshida, Tajima, and Imai [12] showed in experiments that the feature importance of XGBoost may cause the contribution of the model to be calculated incorrectly. Therefore, the feature importance of a model that uses decision trees as a weak learner is not synonymous with the contribution of the model. In addition to feature importance, another way to define the impact on the model is SHApley Additive exPlanations (SHAP) [13], which is a framework to improve the interpretation of predictions for ensemble learning and deep learning, which are considered difficult to interpret models. SHAP calculates the SHAP calculates the SHAP value and interprets the model.

3   Research Objectives

In this study, we identify the default factors of motorcycle sales in developing countries. Based on the results, we propose a sales strategy for motorcycles. a large potential market has been formed in emerging countries such as country X. Nowadays, we propose a strategy for selling motorcycles in developing countries. The challenge for companies in developed countries is how to enter these regions and form a sales strategy to penetrate their products and businesses. However, it is not easy to secure profits. The reason for this is that developing countries have customers who default on different factors than developed countries due to lack of loan experience and strategic default problems. In this study, we focus on the two-wheeler market and create a credit risk model for country X. The results show which features are most important for loan performance. The results of this study indicate that it is possible to develop a sales plan that is acceptable to both firms and customers, even in developing countries immediately after the start of the loan system.

4   Data Summary

In this study, we used data on motorcycle sales loans provided by motorcycle sales companies. The target country is Country X, and the data for the period from September 1, 2010 to June 30, 2012 is used. Although financing is normally provided by financial institutions, in Country X, financing is provided by manufacturers. The number of data after removing missing values and outliers is 13,059, and 54 variables are used. In the following, the variables used in the analysis are listed by information category.

4.1 Customer Information

The variables in the customer information include gender, marital status, age, income, years of employment, education, real estate value, home ownership, variables indicating the region in which the customer lives, and occupation. Age, income, years of employment, and real estate value are quantitative variables, while gender, marital status, education, home ownership, variables indicating the region of residence, and occupation are qualitative variables. There are four types of education: graduate school, high school, junior high school, and elementary school. The education system in country X differs from that in Japan in that elementary school students are 6–10 years old, junior high school students are 11–14 years old, high school students are 15–17 years old, there is no university, and graduate school students are 18 years old or older. Up to junior high school, education is compulsory as in Japan. The relationship between education and loan unpaid customer is illustrated in Table 1. Income rises as education increases, but there are a certain number of loan unpaid customers in every educational background. The regions in which the customers of country X reside are divided into five regions based on the administrative divisions issued by the government of country X: North,

Table 1. Characteristics by background.

Academic background	Number of customers	Unpaid rate (%)
Completed graduate school	109	5.5
High school graduate	1327	15.8
High school dropout	763	21.8
Junior high school graduate	9279	24.4
Junior High school dropout	639	23.5
Elementary school graduate	504	23.4
Elementary school dropout	137	30.7
No educational background	301	20.3

Table 2. Characteristics by region.

Region	Average commodity price (yen)	Average debt (yen)	Average income (yen)	Unpaid rate (%)
North	145.6	138.1	30.1	28.7
Northeast	134.4	127.3	26.0	25.9
Midwest	149.1	137.6	31.0	24.6
Southeast	180.4	156.1	37.5	18.3
South	183.4	156.7	34.5	16.7

Northeast, Midwest, Southeast, and South. The characteristics of each region are shown in Table 2. The unit of measurement is the closing price of the currency of country X on September 1, 2010, the date when the data used in this study were first collected, in Japanese yen. In the south and southeast, customers with relatively high incomes live. The number of poor people tends to increase in the northern part of the country. The variables representing occupation include self-employed, freelance, salaried, housewife, civil servant, military, agricultural worker, student, businessman, pensioner, and investor. The three occupations of civil servants, self-employed, and salaried workers account for 90 percent of the customers who purchased motorcycles. Since every customer group has a certain number of loan unpaid customers, it is necessary to know which customer characteristics have a strong impact on non-payment of loans.

4.2 Product Information

The variables of the product information are trade-in value, interest rate, debt, product price, down payment, and the product purchased. Interest rates, loans, commodity prices, and down payments are quantitative variables. The trade-in value and the purchased goods are the qualitative variables. There are three levels of trade-in value: high, medium and low. Among the products purchased, Product 11 is purchased the most followed by Product 12. The displacement classes of Products 11 and 12 are placed in the small motorcycle category. Table 3 shows the characteristics of product.

Table 3. Characteristics by Region.

Product	Average product price (yen)	Average down payment (yen)	Average interest rate (%)	Unpaid rate (%)
Product 1	1194.4	624.3	8.4	6.3
Product 2	687.5	343.8	1.5	0.0
Product 3	642.0	274.8	12.4	2.1
Product 4	616.8	256.5	7.6	7.3
Product 5	591.0	227.3	7.2	7.7
Product 6	524.0	321.2	5.6	16.7
Product 7	263.7	72.4	12.1	26.2
Product 8	252.8	58.8	9.7	19.4
Product 9	205.5	106.0	6.3	7.0
Product 10	147.0	20.6	11.5	24.1
Product 11	140.8	17.0	10.8	29.3
Product 12	107.6	5.5	6.2	16.6

4.3 Credit Information

Credit information is a variable that represents a customer's credit information. All credit information is binary data. The details are shown in Table 4.

Table 4. Credit information details.

Credit Information	Details
Credit Information 1	Indicates whether the bank has received an inquiry from a commercial association in country X
Credit Information 2	Indicates whether the bank has received an inquiry from a consumer credit company in country X
Credit Information 3	Indicates whether the bank has received an inquiry from a car loan company in country X
Credit Information 4	Indicates whether there are different names listed for the same customer
Credit Information 5	Indicates whether the customer is restricted by the bank to borrowing less than 10.4 yen
Credit Information 6	Indicates whether the customer has ever had an outstanding loan payment of 10.4 yen or less.
Credit Information 7	Indicates whether the customer has any credit restrictions
Credit Information 8	Indicates whether the customer has been using the bank for more than 5 years
Credit Information 9	Indicates whether the bank has set a credit limit for the customer

4.4 Independent Variable

In this study, we set as the independent variable whether a loan payment delay has occurred or not. We distinguish between loan unpaid customers and loan paying customers according to whether the loan payment was delayed at least once during the loan repayment period, resulting in unpaid loans, or whether the loan was paid off without any delay during the loan repayment period. The data used in this study is unbalanced, with 77% (10042 data) of the loan paying customers and 23% (3017 data) having not repaid their loans.

5 Main Experiment

The credit risk model in this study is not a model that estimates the default probability for firms, but for individuals. The credit risk model essentially estimates the probability of default based on the number of times the same person has defaulted. However, due to the nature of the data used in this study, we define a default as a customer who defaults on a loan at least once during the 18-month period of the data period. In contrast, customers who pay off their loans in full within 18 months without any late repayment are defined as non-defaulters. For example, we consider a customer who defaults on a loan repayment in the sixth month of the 18-month period, and it is unlikely that this customer will recover from the loan delay in the sixth month or later and be defined as a fully repaid customer in the 18th month. As a result, the credit risk model in this study determines whether a customer has delayed loan repayment at least once or has paid off the loan without delay.

In this study, we use a holdout method to evaluate the accuracy of the test data. We randomly divide the learning data and test data in a ratio of 7 (9141 data):3 (3918 data). After that, we tune the hyperparameters to increase the prediction power of the test data. In this study, we created models using Random Forest and XGBoost, which are ensemble learning methods among the methods presented by Sawaki et al. [7] as representative machine learning methods that have attracted attention in recent years. In addition, we created models using Logistic Regression, which is used in conventional credit risk models, and compared the accuracy of the three methods. We then determine which biographical information affects loan unpaid customers and which biographical information affects loan paying customers.

In the evaluation of credit risk models, the ROC-AUC is suitable for predicting default using models that calculate the probability of default [1]. Therefore, in this study, the model is evaluated using ROC-AUC.

6   Result

The depth of the decision tree used in the Random Forest can be continued until the data set assigned to it becomes 1, but this would result in overlearning, so it is necessary to introduce a stop condition. One way to do this is to stop when the information gain from splitting falls below a certain value. Therefore, in this study, the depth of the tree is varied in order from 1, and learning is stopped when the ROC-AUC decreases. In addition, the prediction accuracy of Random Forest tends to improve as the number of trees is increased. However, once a certain number of trees is reached, the accuracy tends not to improve any further. Therefore, it is necessary to examine the optimal number of trees in order from 1. For this reason, the depth of the tree is set to 1 and the number of trees is set to 1 as the initial value of Random Forest.

For the number of rounds in XGBoost, as in the Random Forest, the values that best discriminate loan unpaid customers are examined and adopted in order from 1. For this reason, the number of rounds was set to 1 as the initial value of XGBoost. XGBoost sets the threshold by myself. Even a small change in the threshold value can significantly change the classification accuracy. For these reasons, we adopted a threshold value of 0.5 as the initial value to prevent the classification from being weighted one way or the other.

The accuracies of Logistic Regression, Random Forest, and XGBoost are shown in Table 5. The models are not able to handle unbalanced data and the accuracy is extremely poor.

Table 5. Accuracy comparison of initial values.

	ROC-AUC (95%CI)
Logistic Regression	0.501 (0.500, 0.522)
Random Forest	0.500 (0,500, 0,522)
XGBoost	0.524 (0.503, 0.546)

We use SMOTE to extend the training data. In this way, the model is created as a 5:5 data set with 7032 fully repaid loans and 7032 unpaid loans, and applied to the test data. The results are shown in Table 6. The conditions for all models are the same as before the data expansion, indicating that the data expansion using SMOTE was effective for the model.

Table 6. Accuracy comparison after data expansion.

	ROC-AUC (95%CI)
Logistic Regression	0.578 (0.566, 0.608)
Random Forest	0.520 (0.500, 0.542)
XGBoost	0.588 (0.567, 0.609)

We tune the tree depth and the number of trees, which greatly affect the accuracy among the hyperparameters of Random Forest. As mentioned above, the depth of the trees is changed in order from 1, and learning is stopped when the accuracy of ROC-AUC drops. After that, the optimal number of trees is investigated by changing the number of trees until no improvement in accuracy is observed. As in the case of Random Forest, we tune the hyperparameters of XGBoost. In this research, we tune the number of rounds, which has a large impact on accuracy among the hyperparameters of XGBoost. As mentioned above, the number of rounds is increased in order from 1 to investigate the best number of rounds to discriminate customers. After that, the optimal threshold is examined. As for the size of the threshold to be changed at a time, we used 0.01 as a value that does not change the accuracy drastically to understand the transition of accuracy. The optimal size of the threshold change is a subject for future study. The results are shown in Table 7. When comparing the two models, the accuracy of the XGBoost model was higher.

Since the accuracy of XGBoost is high, feature selection using the correlation-based filter method is performed on XGBoost. For those with correlations between features, the feature selection was performed so that variables with high correlations with the independent variable would remain. However, the accuracy after feature selection was significantly reduced. This was thought to be due to the reduction of important features.

Table 7. Accuracy comparison after tuning.

	ROC-AUC（95%CI）	Hyperparameter
Random Forest	0.562（0.541，0.584）	Depth=9
		Number=1
XGBoost	0.623（0.602，0.644）	round=2
		Threshold=0.50

Therefore, in this study, we reduced the features in order of the variables with the lowest correlation with the independent variable. In this way, the correlations among the features can be alleviated without reducing the important features. For each reduction, the accuracy was evaluated using the same procedure as that for changing the hyperparameters of XGBoost. As a result, the highest accuracy was obtained for the 23 variables with high correlation. Table 8 shows the accuracy results and the hyperparameters at that time.

Table 8. Accuracy after feature selection.

	ROC-AUC（95%CI）	Hyperparameter
XGBoost	0.628(0.607，0.648）	round=10
		Threshold=0.53

In this study, we adopt the XGBoost model. The final accuracy of the model is ROC-AUC = 0.624. Due to the change in macroeconomic environment caused by the Lehman shock, the AR value of the credit risk model will decrease significantly. In the case of companies with annual sales of less than 0.5 billion after the Lehman Shock, the AR value was reported to be 20% [14]. Therefore, in this study, which focuses on small firms in developing countries after the Lehman Shock, we adopt the above model of XGBoost.

Find the SHAP value of the adopted XGBoost. Table 9 shows the results of the SHAP in order of increasing contribution rate. The correlations by SHAP can only be examined for the top 20 variables with the highest contribution rate at a time. Therefore, the three variables with low contribution rates, credit information 3, credit information 2, and completion graduate school, were examined separately, and their contribution rate rank was set to 21. As an example, for Product 12, which has the highest contribution rate, the correlation is negative, indicating that customers who purchased Product 12 are variables that affect loan paying customers. Conversely, if the correlation is positive, the variable affects loan unpaid customers. The variables with high contribution rates in both positive and negative are those related to products.

Table 9. SHAP result.

Variable	Contribution Ratio Rank	Correlation
Product 12	1	Negative
Southeast	2	Negative
Marital status	3	Negative
Credit information 8	4	Negative
South	5	Negative
Credit Information 7	6	Negative
Trade-in Value (Medium)	7	Negative
High School Graduation	8	Negative
Product 11	9	Positive
Salaried	10	Negative
Credit Information 1	11	Positive
Self-employed	12	Positive
Northeast	13	Negative
Civil servant	14	Negative
Credit Information 4	15	Negative
Home ownership	16	Positive
Credit Information 6	17	Negative
Junior high school graduate	18	Negative
Gender	19	Negative
Product 4	20	Negative
Credit Information 3	21	Positive
Credit Information 2	21	Positive
Completed graduate school	21	Negative

7 Discussion

The variable with the largest contribution to the model was the product variable. The number of motorcycles purchased as a precondition was skewed, with Commodity 12 and Commodity 11 accounting for 80% of the total. Therefore, it was determined that, among the two products, the customers who purchase Product 12, which has a low loan unpaid customer ratio, tend to become loan paying customers, while the customers who purchase Product 11, which has a high non-paying customer ratio, tend to become non-paying customers. When comparing these two products, the major difference is the average interest rate. It can be considered that the citizens of Country X who have little experience with loans have a limited understanding of interest rates and purchase products that do not fit into their budget. The contribution of variables related to residence is high among the customer information. In the south and southeast, customers with relatively high incomes tend to live in these areas and thus tend to become loan paying customers. As for customers living in the northeast with relatively low incomes, living in the northeast had an impact on loan paying customers. Today, the economy in the northeast of Country X is growing. This is the current situation that supports the growth of the motorcycle market. Although the northeast is a region where the poor live, from the viewpoint of loans, companies do not need to change their sales strategy according to the region. In this study, there was no effect of strategic default as in previous studies. This is because the southern and southeastern regions were as safe and fewer people were dissatisfied with the economic situation and banking regulations. In terms of credit information, customers with credit information 1, credit information 2, and credit information 3 tend to become loan unpaid customers. Table 9 shows that credit information 1 is the most likely characteristic to become loan unpaid customers. It can be seen that customers who were late or defaulted on their loans in the past are more likely to be late or default again on their loans. Therefore, it can be said that country X, as well as developed countries, needs to be cautious about giving loans to these customers. Credit Information 8, Credit Information 7, and Credit Information 6 all show the tendency of loan paying customers. These variables were found to be credit information unrelated to unpaid loans. Credit information 8 is information on the banking history. The longer the banking history, the more the characteristics of loan paying customers. The longer the banking history, the stronger the perception of loan repayment. Credit information 7 is a variable that indicates whether there are credit restrictions. In the case of country X, whether or not credit restrictions have been imposed is not a variable that can be used to identify loan unpaid customers. Credit information 6 is a variable that indicates whether the customer had unpaid loan payments of 10.4 yen or less in the past. Therefore, it is not possible to identify a loan unpaid customers if the amount of outstanding payments is as small as 10.4 yen.

There are four risk factors of credit risk defined in the new BIS regulations: PD, LGD, EAD, and Maturity. In this study, we focused on PD, which has been the focus of much research. In future research, we need to plan to model LGD, EAD, and Maturity based on the results of this study.In this study, we modeled for customers in country X. Therefore, it is necessary to examine the countries to which the model of this study can be applied and the countries to which it cannot. In terms of products, we dealt with motorcycles, an expensive product. It is necessary to examine whether the model of this study can be applied to other expensive or inexpensive commercial products.

References

1. Yamashita, T., Kawaguchi, N., Tsuruga, T.: A Study and Comparison of Evaluation Methods for Credit Risk Models. Financial Research and Training Center, Financial Services Agency, Discussion Paper (2003)
2. Fukumitsu, H.: On strategic default. Seijo Univ. Keizai Kenkyu **193**, 179–234 (2011)

3. Amano, T., Shintaku, J.: ASEAN strategy of Honda's motorcycle business: introduction of low-cost model and innovation of product strategy. Akamon Manage. Rev. **9**(11), 783–806 (2010)
4. Matsunaga, T.: Interpretability of a Data-Driven Credit Scoring Model for Developing Countries: An Analysis of Customer Data from a Vietnamese Shipping Commercial Bank (2021)
5. Miyoshi, Y.: An empirical study of adverse selection in consumer finance markets. Kagawa Univ. Econ. Rev. **88**(4), 529–553 (2016)
6. Guiso, L., Sapienza, P., Zingales, L.: The determinants of attitudes toward strategic default on mortgages. J. Financ. **68**(4), 1473–1515 (2013)
7. Sawaki, T., Tanaka, T., Kasahara, R.: Building a Credit Scoring Model for Small and Medium Enterprises Using Machine Learning, Artificial Intelligence Research Group Materials (2017)
8. Breiman, L.: Random forests. Mach. Learn. **45**(1), 5–32 (2001)
9. Chen, T., Guestrin, C.: XGBoost: a scalable tree boosting system. In: Proceedings of the 22nd ACM SIGKDD International Conference on Knowledge Discovery and Data Mining, pp. 785–794 (2016)
10. Chawla, N.V., Bowyer, K.W., Hall, L.O., Kegelmeyer, W.P.: SMOTE synthetic minority over-sampling technique. J. Artif. Intell. Res. **16**, 321–357 (2002)
11. Hall, M.A.: Correlation-based feature selection for machine learning (1999)
12. Yoshida, H., Tajima, Y., Imai, Y.: A test of the usefulness of SHAP values in the interpretation of decision tree models. In: Proceedings of the 34th National Convention of the Japanese Society for Artificial Intelligence. Japanese Society for Artificial Intelligence (2020). 3E5GS204-3E5GS204
13. Lundberg, S.M., Lee, S.I.: A unified approach to interpreting model predictions. In Proceedings of the 31st International Conference on Neural Information Processing Systems, pp. 4768–4777 (2017)
14. Ogi, K., Toshiro, M., Hibiki, N.: The relationship between the robustness of the business history function and the amount of personal assets of the manager in the credit scoring model for small firms. Japan. J. Oper. Res. **59**, 134–159 (2016)

Analysis of Declining Fertility Rate in Japan by Focusing on TFR and Women Moving

Shigeyuki Kurashima[✉] and Yumi Asahi

Tokyo University of Science, Kagurazaka, Shinjuku-ku, Tokyo 1628601, Japan
sk81tk34@gmail.com

Abstract. In Japan, birth rates are declining year by year. If this goes on, half of municipalities will disappear. Recently, there have been many studies on fertility using TFR as a benchmark for municipal unit data. However, when considering the municipal level, it is not sufficient to focus only on the TFR in investigating the reason for the declining birthrate. In this paper, we conducted an analysis of fertility decline by focusing on TFR and women moving in and moving out of regions. We used OLS regression that do not take into account regional differences and Geographically Weighted Regression (GWR) which allows to include regional differences. We could infer that low income and women's social advancement, which are generally considered to be factors in declining fertility, do not have much of an impact from the results. We also found that there are regional disparities in TFR that cannot be explained by the variables incorporated in this study, and regional disparities were a trend of west high and east low. In addition, when we looked at the policies of regions that have been successful in maintaining their populations, we also found that there are common steps in policies that are successful in maintaining population.

Keywords: Fertility rate · Female moving in and moving out · Declining birthrate · Geographically weighted regression model

1 Introduction

In 2005, Total fertility rate (TFR) in Japan was 1.26, which was the worst rate ever in Japanese modern history. These days, it has been improved somewhat compared to then, but it is still very low. If this phenomenon goes on, 11 million people will decrease in a decade. It is about 10% of population. However, by region, TFR is both high and low in some areas. Some research background on declining birthrate have been done by using TFR as a benchmark. Sasai (2005) advocated, "Regional fertility rates vary in their levels and patterns of change, and the factors that contribute to them are also diverse. It fluctuates in an extremely complex context. However, it can be explained by two large demographic factors, marriage trends and couple's fertility, to some extent [1]." Another study conducted a geographically weighted regression (GWR) with parameters varying by region, pointing out that most studies use least squares (OLS) regression and that the factors contributing to TFR are the same everywhere, even though they vary by region (Kamata, Iwasawa 2009) [2].

© The Author(s), under exclusive license to Springer Nature Switzerland AG 2022
S. Yamamoto and H. Mori (Eds.): HCII 2022, LNCS 13305, pp. 337–353, 2022.
https://doi.org/10.1007/978-3-031-06424-1_25

However, region with high TFR will not guarantee to sustain their population in the future. Maeda (2005) has given a hint insisting that TFR is the ratio of the number of children to the number of women, and even if the number of children decrease accompanied by the number of women in the denominator decrease, the TFR remains unchanged [3]. Her opinion points out the importance of number of women aged 15–49. The figure below is a scatter plot. The X-axis shows TFR and the Y-axis is FMI, an indicator of women moving in and out of the region, which will be discussed later (Fig. 1).

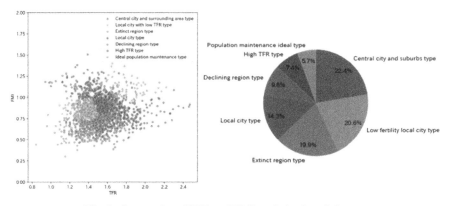

Fig. 1. Scatter plot of TFR and FMI, and pie plot of clusters

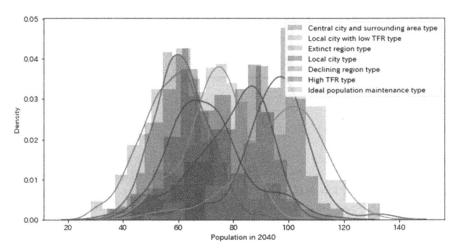

Fig. 2. Histogram of future population by clusters

In addition, based on TFR and FMI, we did a cluster analysis and named the clusters as shown in the legend on the upper right.

The Fig. 2 shows a histogram of the future population for each cluster. The future population is based on the year 2015 as 100. The regions with high TFR and FMI, which is the most ideal type for maintaining population, can keep their population. The region with high TFR and low FMI, which we named High TFR type, cannot keep their population. From these, it is clear that it's not enough to focus only on TFR when considering the issue of declining birthrate and population, but it is also necessary to pay attention to FMI.

In this paper, we discuss the declining birthrate from two aspects, TFR and moving in and moving out of women, considering regional differences.

Briefly, we explain about each region in Japan.

Hokkaido region is located at the northernmost tip of Japan, which is about the same latitude as southern Europe, and is largest prefecture. The area is as same as Ireland. The dairy and fishery industries are flourishing. Sapporo, the capital of the Hokkaido Prefectural Government, is the most prosperous area in Hokkaido, with a population of about 2 million, which accounts for about 40% of the population of Hokkaido.

Tohoku region is the northernmost region of Honshu, which is the main island of Japan. It is an area where agriculture is thriving. In recent years, the population has been flowing out to Tokyo, and it is one of the areas with the largest population decline.

Kanto region is a region located south of Tohoku region. Tokyo exists in this region. In addition to Tokyo, there are other cities such as Yokohama, Chiba, and Saitama, and the urban functions of Japan are concentrated in this region. About 35% of Japan's population lives in this region. Many of the areas in this region have especially low birth rates.

Chubu region is a region located west of Kanto region. The area is sandwiched between Tokyo and Osaka, making it one of the most prosperous areas in Japan. Nagoya City in this region, in particular, is said to be one of the three largest cities along with Tokyo and Osaka. The region is home to Toyota and other automobile and other manufacturing companies.

Kinki region is a region located west of Chubu region. Cities such as Osaka, Kyoto, and Kobe are in this region. Kyoto is Japan's ancient capital and is often visited by foreigners as a tourist destination.

Chugoku region is a region located west of Kinki region. Like the Chubu region, this area also has a thriving manufacturing industry, with oil complexes and steel mills.

Kyushu region is located at the western end of Japan. It is the western gateway to Japan, close to China, Korea and other Asian countries. It has one of the highest birth rates in Japan and is one of the fastest growing regions in the country.

2   Methods

2.1   Data Source and Data Processing

We got statistical data of all cities, towns, and villages in Japan from Japanese Statistics Bureau, except for evacuation zone near the Fukushima nuclear power plant. Geographic data was gained from Ministry of Land, Infrastructure, Transport and Tourism and previous research, and we got university campus location data from university's website. The table below is the list of variables we used (Table 1).

Table 1. All variables we used

Resoponse variable	TFR	FMI
	FMI	TFR
Explanatory variable	Male Ratio	Number of Persons Per Household
	Nuclear Family Household Ratio	Nuclear Family Household Ratio
	Number of Marriages Per Population	Number of Marriages Per Population
	Ratio of Employees in The Construction industry	Ratio of Single-Person Households
	Ratio of Workers in Primary industry	Ratio of Workers in Primary industry
	Ratio of Workers in Secondary industry	Ratio of Workers in Secondary industry
	Ratio of Workers in Tertiary industry	Ratio of Workers in Tertiary industry
	Total Unemployment Rate	Ratio of Employees in Manufacturing industry
	Average Annual Salary	Ratio of Medical And Welfare Employees
	Number of Kindergarten Per Population Aged 0~3	Number of Kindergarten Per Population Aged 0~3
	Percentage of University Graduates	Percentage of University Graduates
	Male Employment Rate	Male Employment Rate
	Female Employment Rate	Female Employment Rate
	Percentage of Female Civil Servants in Managerial Positions	Percentage of Female Civil Servants in Managerial Positions
	Percentage of Female Legislators	Percentage of Female Legislators
	Day/Night Population Ratio	Housing Expense Ratio
	Financial Strength Index	Financial Strength Index
	Child Welfare Expense Ratio	Child Welfare Expense Ratio
	Agriculture, Forestry And Fisheries Expense Ratio	Firefighting Expense Ratio
	Labor Expense Ratio	Distance from Tokyo
	Number of Retail Stores (Per 1,000 Population)	Number of Retail Stores (Per 1,000 Population)
	Number of General Hospitals (Per 100,000 Population)	Number of General Hospitals (Per 100,000 Population)
	Number of University Campuses within 20 km	Number of University Campuses within 20 km
	Latitude	Latitude
	Longitude	Longitude
	Average Elevation	Average Elevation
	Average Slope	Average Slope

Regarding the earth as sphere, we calculated distance between region A and region B from latitude (lat) and longitude (lon) as the below formula.

$$Distance = 6371 * \arccos\left(\begin{array}{c} \cos(latA) + \cos(latB) * \cos(lonB - lonA) \\ + \sin(latA) * \sin(latB) \end{array}\right) \quad (1)$$

To add an explanation to the variables, those with the word "expense" in the item name are related to municipal expenditures. For example, housing expense ratio refers to the ratio of the expense spent on the development of residential areas to the total expenditure of the municipality.

2.2 Create an Indicator of Women Moving in and Moving Out

We created an indicator named Female Migration Indicator (FMI) by dividing the number of women aged 15–49 moving in by the number of women aged 15–49 moving out. The intention was to use this indicator to show how the population is flowing in and out, and we used this indicator as response variable when we performed regression analysis.

2.3 Analysis Procedure

OLS regression was performed with TFR and FMI as the response variable, and two types of OLS regression analysis were conducted for each of the two indicators. One is the model which is involving geographical data in explanatory variables, and the other is the model which is not involving geographical data in explanatory variables. The latter explanatory variable is also incorporated into the GWR. GWR is the model which allows parameters to vary by region. GWR is characterized using a kernel function. Since the kernel function is a distance decay function in which the spatial weighting increases when the distance is small, the spatial weighting on the location changes according to the distance from the regression point to the sample point. The kernel function used for GWR has mainly two types, Gauss and Bi-square. In this paper, Gauss was used because the accuracy was superior. Furthermore, there are two ways to set the bandwidth of a kernel function: fixed and adapted. The fixed type is a method in which the bandwidth from the regression point is constant at all points, while the adaptive type is a method in which the bandwidth is determined for each point so that the number of sample points included in the bandwidth is equal, and we used fixed type.

To gain the best model of OLS regression analyses, the model was created by adding explanatory variables in order of increasing value of partial correlation coefficient and considering R-squared, Adjusted R-squared and AIC, and we excluded explanatory variable whose VIF score is over 4 to avoid multicollinearity. Using GWR and the same explanatory variables of prior model which is not involving geographical data in explanatory variables, we could obtain another two models. Now we get six models: OLS regression with geographic variables for TFR (TOwG), OLS regression without geographic variables for TFR (TOwoG) and GWR regression for TFR (TG) OLS regression with geographic variables for FMI (FOwG), OLS regression without geographic variables for FMI (FOwoG) and GWR for FMI (FG).

3 Result

3.1 TOwG and TOwoG

Table 2 gives a summary of TOwG and TOwoG. Both regression analyses are statistically significant. It is shown from probability of F-statistic. R-squared and Adj. R-squared tell us that geographic variables are important to regress for TFR because the score of those is quite different.

Table 2. Summary of result of TOwG and TowoG

	R-squared	Adj. R-squared	F-statistic	Prob (F-statistic)	AICc
TOwG	0.569	0.565	161.5	1.47E-300	-2051.24
TOwoG	0.337	0.332	72.65	1.38E-143	-1311.12

The figure expresses the value of coefficients. Before we do regression analysis, we performed a z-score normalization on every explanatory variable. A z-score normalization uses following formula, taking x for data, μ for average of data and σ for variance of data. Therefore, we can compare the coefficients regardless of unit or value of variables (Fig. 3).

$$z\_score = \frac{x-\mu}{\sigma} \tag{2}$$

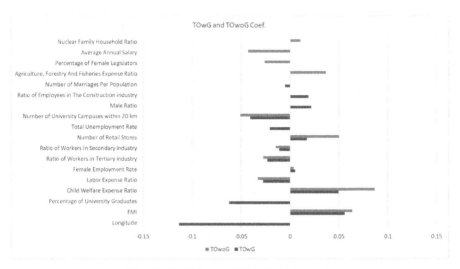

Fig. 3. Coefficients of TOwG and TOwoG

Focusing on the coefficients of TOwG, which are blue bars, we can understand longitude has large negative score. This means TFR tend to be low in eastern area and high in western area. Percentage of university graduates and number of university campus within 20 km also have negative score. On the other hand, FMI, child welfare expense ratio and number of retail store have positive value.

Focusing on the coefficients of TOwoG, which are orange bars, they show almost same score of TOwG. In addition, coefficients of agriculture, forestry and fisheries expense ratio and nuclear family household ratio have positive value. Percentage of female legislators and average annual salary have negative value. According to cabinet office, declining incomes is the one of the factors of declining birthrate [4]. Another questionnaire from cabinet office shows 40% of unmarried people under the age of 49 don't desire to have child because of economic issue [5], but the result of TOwoG was different. The coefficient of annual salary being negative value means if the annual income goes down, the TFR goes up, and if the annual income goes up, the TFR goes down.

3.2 FOwG and FOwoG

The following table is the result of FOwG and FOwoG. At the significance level of 5%, these analyses are statistically significant. As opposed to regression analysis for TFR, there are little difference in R-squared.

	R-squared	Adj. R-squared	F-statistic	Prob (F-statistic)	AICc
FOwG	0.544	0.541	204.7	3.24E-284	-2274.085
FOwoG	0.531	0.528	194.5	5.96E-274	-2226.319

The figure below is the coefficients bar graph. FOwG and FOwoG have almost same coefficients values. Percentage of university graduates has largest positive value. Number of university campuses within 20 km also have positive score, so it seems that university has some kinds of positive effect on FMI. On the other hand, number of persons per household has largest negative value. This means the region with many single-person household tend to have high FMI and the region with many large families tend to indicate low FMI.

As for focusing on blue bar, latitude is positive, so it seems to be high FMI in north and low in south, but the coefficient is relatively small, so the relationship seems to be weak. Focusing on orange bar, female employment rate has positive value (Fig. 4).

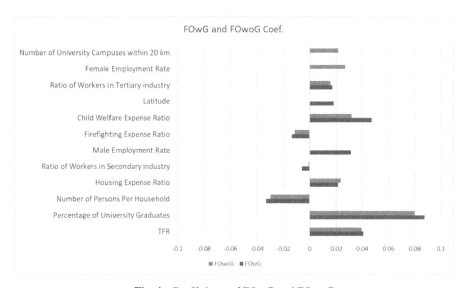

Fig. 4. Coefficients of FOwG and FOwoG

3.3 TG and FG Result

Table 3 is summary of TG and FG. From R-squared and AICc, these GWR models are improved from OLS regressions analyses. The right two columns of Table 3 show results of Leung's F test [6]. Leung's F test has three types. F1 test is the test that confirms whether GWR is better fitted than OLS which is TOwoG or FOwoG in this paper. F2 test verifies whether there is statistically significant difference between GWR and OLS. F3 test decides if the regional differences in coefficients are statistically significant. Table 3 shows that both GWR models, TG and FG, are better fitted model and the difference with

OLS are statistically significant. The result of F3 test is Table 4. Variables marked with * indicate regional differences, and variables marked in yellow do not indicate regional differences.

To add a note about TG and FG, Ogasawara village was excluded because optimize bandwidth was too small to regress TFR and FMI of there. The following section, statistically significant coefficients of TG and FG are visualized, provided that Tokyo's island areas and part of Kagoshima's island areas are excluded from the visualization because isolated islands tend to be outliers.

Table 3. Summary of result of TG and FG

	R-squared	AICc	Leung et al. (2000) F(1) test	Leung et al. (2000) F(2) test
TG	0.7100158	-2385.717	p-value < 2.2e-16	p-value < 2.2e-16
FG	0.6694341	-2561.379	1.102E-07	p-value < 2.2e-16

Table 4. The result of F3 test

Leung et al. (2000) F(3) test				
TG		FG		
Intercept	***	Intercept	*	
Child Welfare Expense Ratio	***	Child Welfare Expense Ratio	***	
FMI	***	Female Employment Rate	***	
Number of University Campuses within 20 km	***	Firefighting Expense Ratio		
Agriculture, Forestry And Fisheries Expense Ratio	***	Housing Expense Ratio	***	
Percentage of Female Legislators	***	Number of Persons Per Household	***	
Average Annual Salary	***	Number of University Campuses within 20 km		
Female Employment Rate	***	Percentage of University Graduates	***	
Ratio of Workers in Tertiary industry	***	Ratio of Workers in Secondary industry	***	
Ratio of Workers in Secondary industry	***	Ratio of Workers in Tertiary industry		
Nuclear Family Household Ratio	***	TFR	***	
Number of Retail Stores				
Labor Expense Ratio				

Signif. codes: 0 '***' 0.001 '**' 0.01 '*' 0.05 '.' 0.1 ' ' 1

3.4 TG Coefficients

Figure 5 express how coefficients of region vary. Most of regions have positive values of child welfare expense ratio and FMI, and negative values of number of university campus within 20 km. Other variables have both positive and negative values in some regions.

Then, we focus on Fig. 6. The coefficient of child welfare expense ratio has highest value in Kyushu region, and lowest in southern Hokkaido region, and only there is a negative value. Northern Tohoku region and Kanto region have small values but have positive. In other words, most of regions have positive correlation between TFR and child welfare expense ratio, so government need to consider providing better financial support for children. In Hokkaido region and Kanto region whose coefficient value is positive but almost 0, raising child welfare expenses needs to be carefully considered. The coefficient of FMI is also positive in most of regions. Especially, the value is large in Kanto region, Chubu region and Kinki region.

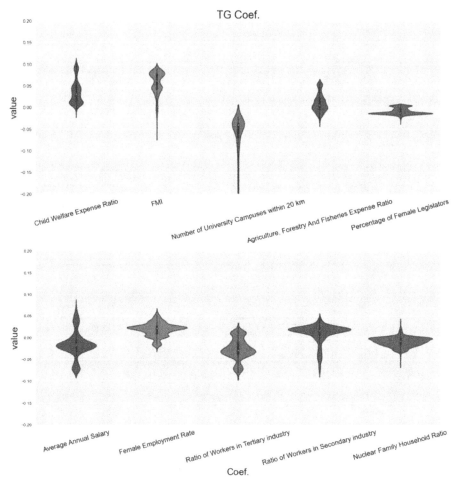

Fig. 5. Coefficients of TG

The coefficient of number of university campus within 20 km have negative values in the most region. This is consistent with Tsutsumi's paper (2020) [7]. He pointed out university students are included in the denominator of the TFR, but they don't give birth, so if they increase, TFR decrease.

Agriculture, Forestry and Fisheries expense ratio and percentage of female legislators are high in Kinki region. As for Agriculture expense, most of regions have positive value. However, there is negative value in Chubu region. Area where this expense is high can

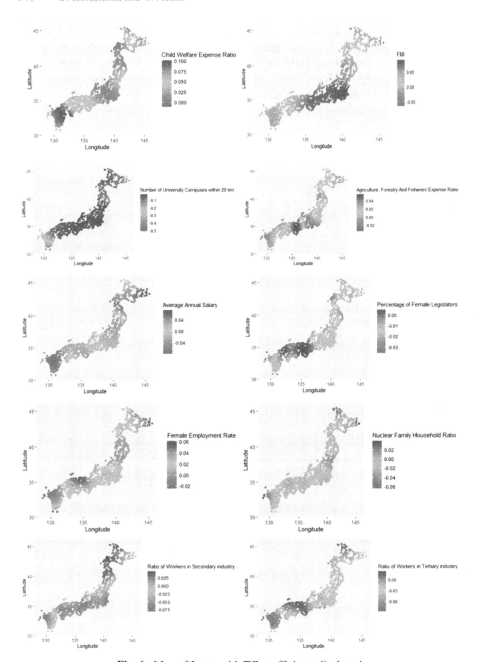

Fig. 6. Map of Japan with TG coefficients displayed

be regarded as rural area, and these areas tend to score high TFR. However, the trend doesn't exist in Chubu and Kyushu region. As for percentage of female legislator, most of areas have negative value. Percentage of female legislator often used as a measure of women's social advancement and is considered to be negative in most areas because it is generally believed that TFR decreases as women's social advancement increases. Even the area with the highest coefficient, the score is almost 0, which means percentage of female legislators doesn't effect TFR.

Female employment rate is largest value in Tottori Pref. and lowest in Kyushu region. Other region takes small value, but positive excluding Kyushu region. Generally, it is said that the advancement of women in society has accelerated the decline in birthrate, but this result is opposite to common belief and result of percentage of female legislator. Nuclear family household ratio has slightly positive value in Kanto region, Chubu region and Kansai region, and also has values closer to 0 in the other region.

When regarding industry factors, the ratio of workers in secondary industry has positive coefficient in 80% regions. In part of Hokkaido region, Miyagi and Kyushu region, there are negative. At the same time, tertiary industry has negative coefficient in 80% areas. Positive values are seen only in Kinki region and Chugoku region.

Lastly, we focus on intercept. The intercept can be regarded as representing the TFR, stripped of the influence of explanatory variables. Therefore, if there are still regional differences in the intercept, it means that there are disparities that are not explained by these variables. The figures below are about intercept. From left figure, the values tend to be higher in the west and lower in the east. We knew the trend from the coefficient of longitude in TOwG, and this result means the trend is inadequate to be represented by the explanatory variables we used here. The right figure is scatter plot of intercept and TFR. A simple regression analysis shows that R-squared is 0.19. This means that 19% of the variance of TFR is explained by the intercept and 50% is explained by explanatory variables in the TG analysis (Fig. 7).

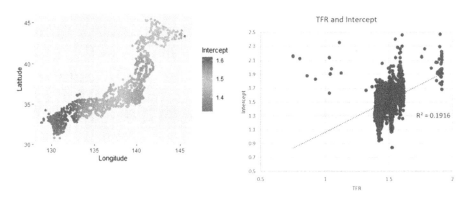

Fig. 7. Map of Japan with TG intercept displayed and scatter plot of TFR and intercept

3.5   FG Coefficients

Figure 8 is violin plot of FG coefficients. As can be seen from the figure, percentage of university graduates has largest value, and TFR is the second largest. Number of persons per household and ratio of workers in secondary industry are negative value in more than 85% region (Fig. 9).

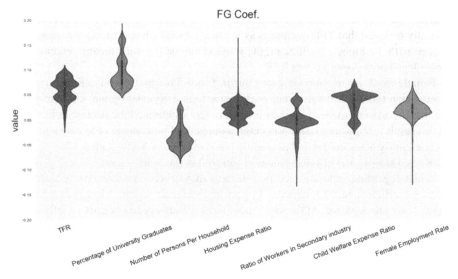

Fig. 8. FG coefficients

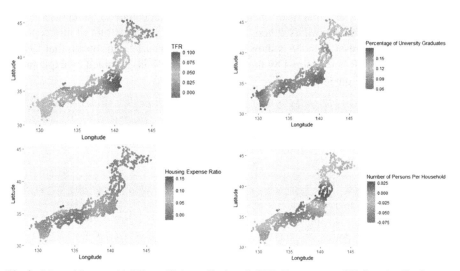

Fig. 9. Map of Japan with FG coefficients displayed, TFR, Percentage of University Graduates, Housing Expense Ratio and Number of Persons per Household

Focusing on TFR, almost all regions have positive coefficients and especially high in Kanto region. Chubu region and Kinki region are also high, although not as high as Kanto region. Comparing the previous analysis, there is likely to exist correlation between TFR and FMI in Kanto region area because the coefficients of FMI in TG were high in Kanto region and the coefficients of TFR in FG were also high. In fact, there is correlation in Tokyo metropolitan area excluding Tokyo 23 wards and remote islands. The correlation coefficient is 0.47. In the Kanagawa, Chiba and Saitama, the correlation coefficient is 0.57. If we expand the scope a little more, there is a correlation, for example, the correlation coefficient is 0.32 in Tokyo metropolitan area excluding Tokyo 23 wards, Aichi, Kyoto, Osaka and Hyogo. In all regions in Japan, correlation coefficient is 0.11. From these results, it can be said that there is some kind of tendency for women to gather in areas with high TFR, or for areas where women gather to have high TFR in cityside.

The coefficient of percentage of university graduates takes the highest value in Kyushu region, especially in Fukuoka, middle in Hokkaido region and Tohoku region, and lowest in Honshu except for Tohoku region. As for Fukuoka, this strong tendency exists because many people from Kyushu region gather here and there are many universities. Housing expense ratio is relatively high in Kanto region and Chubu region. Number of persons per household have highest and only positive value in Tohoku region, and in the other area, have negative value, especially low in Chubu region and Kinki region. In the result of OLS regression analysis, the coefficient of number of persons per household was negative, but from this result, it varies by region and there are positive coefficients (Fig. 10).

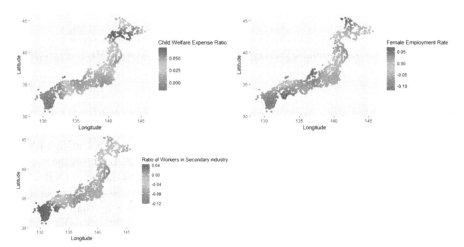

Fig. 10. Map of Japan with FG coefficients displayed, Child Welfare Ratio, Female Employment Rate and Ratio of Workers in Secondary industry

Child welfare expense ratio have the lowest value in Kyushu region. In case of TG, the value was highest in Kyushu region, but not in this analysis. This is because there is no correlation between TFR and FMI in Kyushu region. Regardless of the value of FMI, TFR is around 1.5 to 2 there. Female employment rate takes negative value in few regions, and since the value is close to zero in most areas, it seems to be no relationship between FMI and female employment rate.

Ratio of workers in secondary industry takes high value in Kyushu region and relatively high in Chubu region. Eastern Tohoku region also has high score. There are many semiconductor factories in these areas, which may have something to do with it. In addition, it is difficult to imagine that the rise of the secondary industry will be a factor in increasing the number of women moving into the area, but we think that the underlying mechanism is that the rise of the secondary industry will attract men, and these men will create a new economic zone that will increase the population of both men and women.

Just like TG, we will focus on the intercept at the end here as well. From figures below, the explanatory variables seem to explain the regional disparities to some extent (Fig. 11).

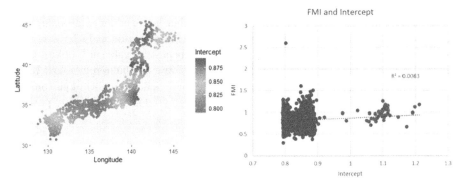

Fig. 11. Map of Japan with FG intercept displayed and scatter plot of FMI and intercept

3.6 Successful Policies for Region Maintaining Population

In this section, we pick up some policies of regions which is high TFR and high FMI.

Firstly, we take a look at Nagaizumi Town, Shizuoka Prefecture. This is the town in eastern Shizuoka, located about 100 km from Tokyo and about 300 km from Osaka. The town has a well-developed transportation network, with two JR (the company of public transportation in Japan) stations in the town, and from nearby Mishima Station, you can take the Shinkansen (bullet train) to Shinagawa Station in 35 min. This town has highest TFR and FMI is also high level. The town did not originally take measures against the declining birthrate, but rather worked to attract companies to build a stable financial base and developed the town by taking advantage of the convenience of transportation. As a result, young people have been attracted to the city, leading to an increase in the number of births and population growth. As a result, the number of births has increased and the population has grown. Since the companies are located locally, the number of people moving out to find work has decreased, and the population can be maintained.

Secondary, we pick up Tsukuba City, Ibaraki Prefecture. The city is located in the southernmost part of Ibaraki Prefecture, about 40 km from Tokyo. The city has a day/night population ratio of 86% and seems to function as a bedroom community. The city has 20 university campuses within a 20 km radius, so it is expected that many students will move here. In addition, the city has focused on attracting companies and has promoted the relocation of factories. Recently, there has been an increase in the relocation of head office functions and research institutes. The city is also focusing on childcare support.

After observing the areas discussed in this report and other areas that have been able to prevent decreasing the birthrate, it was found that there are common steps to take in order to prevent decreasing the birthrate as the figure shows it. Successful municipalities had first implemented policies to reduce the outflow or increase the inflow of population in the municipality. For example, they reduced the number of people moving out of the city for employment reasons by attracting companies. There were some municipalities that had not done the second step, but those that had done the first step, such as attracting companies, generally fulfilled the second step. Finally, by implementing childcare support policies that raise the TFR, the government has succeeded in maintaining the population by increasing the number of children in the numerator while maintaining the population in the denominator of the TFR (Fig. 12).

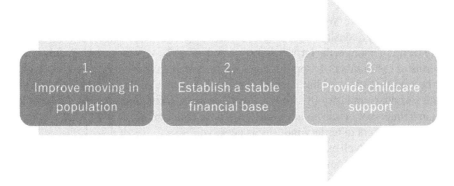

Fig. 12. Common steps of successful policies

On the other hand, according to Maeda (2005), Nagaoka City in Niigata Prefecture and Tohno City in Iwate Prefecture focused on child-rearing support in order to counter the declining birthrate, and although they were able to improve TFR as a result, their future populations declined, indicating that they could prevent the declining birthrate in the long run [3]. The reason for this is thought to be that the government skipped the first step and started with the third step.

4   Discussion

We can say TFR was well explained from the result of TG. The factors that contribute to TFR vary from region to region, and the implementation of policies and other measures must be tailored to the region rather than uniformly implemented. In other words, we need to look at each region for consideration. In addition, the intercept showed a trend of west high/east low, and a trend that could not be fully explained by the explanatory variables.

For instance, we focus Kanto region. Comparing to west Japan, the intercept is small and the TFR does not rise that high to begin with. Although we do not know the causal relationship with FMI, thinking deeply about women's in-migration and implementing policies to promote women's in-migration may lead to an improvement in TFR because the highest coefficient was FMI. As for the economic issue, according to the result of questionnaire from cabinet office, people answered that they don't give birth because of financial problem. However, the coefficients of the economic variables, such as child welfare expense and average annual salary, has very small value and even as for average annual salary has negative value. Therefore, TFR declining is not caused by economic problem, but other factors. For example, there may be the length of commuting and working hours, opportunities to interact with people, and the psychology of people living in Kanto region. The female employment rate was also found to be positively correlated with TFR, contrary to the general perception and reality, but the coefficient of the percentage of female legislators, seen as an indicator of women's advancement in society, is negative.

When focusing on industry, ratio of secondly industry was positive and tertiary industry was negative. Working hours seem to be a factor in this. Recently, working hours in the secondary industry, including manufacturing and construction, are decreasing, while working hours in the tertiary industry, including the service sector, are increasing. In terms of the number of working days and the percentage of workers getting paid, it can be said that the working environment is often worse in the tertiary industry than in the secondary industry [8]. Tertiary workers are working more hours and have less personal time, so they can no longer afford to have children, which is why the coefficient of ratio of workers in tertiary industry is negative.

FMI was also well explained. The difference from TFR is that there is no correlation between the intercept and the actual FMI, so there is a large regional difference in the part represented by the explanatory variables. The coefficient of percentage of university graduates was high in the most region. Increasing employment opportunities for university graduates may be a factor in increasing FMI.

As for FMI in Kanto region, the intercept is extremely high. The coefficient of TFR has biggest value in coefficients. Therefore, it might go even higher if TFR improve, but as with the others, it should be noted that this is a correlation and does not yet prove causation. The second highest coefficient is percentage of university graduates. This seems to be difficult to increase because there are already enough job opportunities for university graduates. Additionally, in terms of increasing FMI, increasing child welfare spending may be a good idea because the coefficient of it was relatively high.

In this way, by focusing on the intercept, we can roughly check the extent to which TFR and FMI can be raised, and by focusing on the coefficient, we can find clues on how to deal with the declining birth rate in each region.

5   Conclusions

In this paper, we analyzed fertility decline by focusing on two factors, TFR and FMI. OLS regression analysis was used to narrow down the variables that are necessary to explain TFR and FMI. GWR analysis was used to vary the intercept and coefficients.

With this method, we were able to create a model with high explanatory power. Since each region has different parameters, as mentioned in the discussion, by focusing on a particular region, it became possible to get clues to consider improvement measures tailored to the region.

By focusing on case studies of municipalities that have been successful in maintaining their populations, we found that there is a common trend to improve FMI and then TFR in order to improve the birthrate.

Future development may include finding variables that can explain the trend of west high/east low in TFR, and conducting analysis that proves causality rather than correlation. An analysis that takes into account the impact of coronaviruses will also be necessary.

References

1. Sasai, T.: Trends in fertility rates by municipality and factors causing changes. J. Popul. Prob. **61–3**, 39–49 (2005)
2. Kamata, K., Iwasawa, M.: Spatial Variations in Fertility: Geographically Weighted Regression Analyses for Town-and-Village-level TFR in Japan. Demographic Research, vol. 45 (2009)
3. Maeda, M.: Child-rearing support measures by local governments and the reality of declining birthrates and population decline. Hirao Sch. Manage. Rev. **5**, 1–16 (2015)
4. Cabinet office. https://www5.cao.go.jp/keizai-shimon/kaigi/special/future/sentaku/s3_1_2.html. Accessed 01 Feb 2022
5. Cabinet office. https://www8.cao.go.jp/shoushi/shoushika/research/h25/taiko/2_1_1.html. Accessed 01 Feb 2022
6. Leung, Y.: Statistical tests for spatial nonstationary based on the geographically weighted regression model. Environ. Plan A **2000**(32), 9–32 (2000)
7. Tsutsumi, K.: Impact of Social Change on Total Fertility Rate. Statistical Data Analysis Competition (2020)
8. Yuka, S.: Actual Conditions and Issues of Long Working Hours by Industry. Daiwa Institute of Research (2018). https://www.dir.co.jp/report/research/policy-analysis/human-society/20180330_020030.pdf. Accessed 09 Feb 2020
9. Masumi, Z., Takashi, O., Yuichi, K., Akiko, T., Shiro, K., Masakazu Y.: Relationships between Distribution of Japanese Residential Areas and Topography (2005). http://www.csis.u-tokyo.ac.jp/dp/dp68/68.pdf. Accessed 11 Feb 2022
10. Nagaizumi Town, Shizuoka Prefecture: A Town Where It's Easy to Give Birth and Raise a Child - Measures to Support Child Rearing in the Town of Niko Niko. https://www.zck.or.jp/site/forum/1319.html. Accessed 08 Feb 2020
11. Tsukuba Mirai City has the highest population growth rate in the prefecture! What is "Japan's No. 1" in Tsukuba Mirai City? https://tochiten.com/work/changejob/news/ibaraki-147.html. Accessed 08 Feb 2020

Characteristic Analysis of Midfielder in Japanese Professional Football League (J1 League) Using Grouping and Tactical Analysis

Shunsuke Mitani$^{(\boxtimes)}$ and Yumi Asahi

Graduate School of Management, Tokyo University of Science, Shinjuku, Japan
8621515@ed.tus.ac.jp, asahi@rs.tus.ac.jp

Abstract. The level of soccer in Japan is getting higher and higher. This is due to the fact that more and more players belong to overseas teams. However, if this trend continues, there is a possibility that the level of soccer in Japan will decline again. One of the reasons why j-league players are not selected for the national team is that there are few objective indicators of player characteristics, and they are easily influenced by the judgment of their team's coaches and managers. Therefore, the purpose of this paper is to analyze and visualize the characteristics of players. In this study, the analysis was conducted on midfielder players in the J1 League. The reason why we chose the position of midfielder among many positions is that it plays an important factor in both offense and defense. The analysis was initially done by principal component analysis to create new variables to understand the characteristics of the players. Then, a hierarchical cluster analysis was conducted on the principal component scores to divide the players into several groups and identify their characteristics. As a result, we were able to classify them into seven distinctive groups.

Keywords: Big data · Sports science · Grouping

1 Introduction

Figure 1 shows the transition of Japan's FIFA ranking [1]. The FIFA rankings are published by the Federation Internationale de Football Association (FIFA) and are based on the results of international matches played by the national teams of the member countries and regions of FIFA. Japan's FIFA ranking had been consistently low since 2013. The reason for this is that the power of the players who were at the forefront of foreign leagues, such as Keisuke Honda and Shinji Kagawa, is waning and they are no longer getting good results. Japan had been eliminated from the preliminary league at the FIFA World Cup in Brazil. But since 2019, Japan's FIFA ranking had been higher again. This can be attributed to the fact that Japan had been able to consistently achieve good results. In fact, Japan made it to the Round of 16 at the 2018 FIFA World Cup in Russia. In this way, the level of Japanese soccer is improving. One of the reasons for the good results is that more and more players are playing in foreign leagues.

S. Yamamoto and H. Mori (Eds.): HCII 2022, LNCS 13305, pp. 354–363, 2022.
https://doi.org/10.1007/978-3-031-06424-1_26

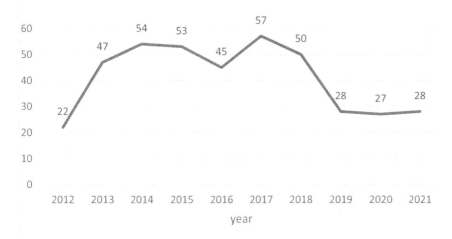

Fig. 1. Transition of FIFA ranking in Japan

Table 1. 2014 World Cup Japan vs Colombia Starting Members

GK	Eiji Kawashima(Ligue 1)
DF	Atsuto Uchida(Bundesliga)
DF	Maya Yoshida(Premier League)
DF	Yasuyuki Konno(J.LEAGUE)
DF	Yuto Nagatomo(Serie A)
MF	Makoto Hasebe(Bundesliga)
MF	Toshihiro Aoyama(J.LEAGUE)
MF	Keisuke Honda(Serie A)
MF	Shinji Kagawa(Premier League)
MF	Shinji Okazaki(Bundesliga)
FW	Yoshito Okubo(J.LEAGUE)

Table 2. 2021 World Cup Qualifier Japan vs Australia Starting Members

GK	Shuichi Gonda(Premier League→J.LEAGUE)
DF	Hiroki Sakai(Ligue 1→J.LEAGUE)
DF	Maya Yoshida(Serie A)
DF	Takehiro Tomiyasu(Premier League)
DF	Yoto Nagatomo(Ligue 1→J.LEAGUE)
MF	Wataru Endo(Bundesliga)
MF	Hidemasa Morita(Primeira Liga)
MF	Ao Tanaka(2. Bundesliga)
MF	Takumi Minamino(Premier League)
MF	Junya Ito(Jupiler Pro League)
FW	Yuya Osako(Bundesliga→J.LEAGUE)

Table 1 shows the starting lineup for the 2018 World Cup in Brazil against Colombia, a time when there were no good results, and Table 2 shows the starting lineup for the 2021 World Cup qualifier against Australia, a time when there were good results. While the starting lineup for the 2014 World Cup in Brazil consisted of 3 out of 11 players from the J. LEAGUE, the starting lineup for the 2021 World Cup qualifiers consisted of all 11 players with experience in foreign leagues. The players represented by the right arrow are those who were on foreign teams until the summer of 2021. The starting lineup for 2021, with its good results, has more players who were part of foreign teams than the starting lineup for 2014, with its bad results. The same can be said for the reserve members. In 2014, 8 out of 12 reserve members were from the J.LEAGUE, while in 2021, 1 out of 12 reserve members were from the J.LEAGUE. And that one player was a GK. One of the factors behind this improvement in the level of Japanese soccer is the increase in the number of players playing for overseas teams.

However, if the current situation continues, the level of Japanese soccer may decline again. There are three main ways for a J.LEAGUE player to transfer to an overseas team.

The first is to take the selection of a foreign team by yourself and join the team. In this case, it is very difficult to join a team in a strong league, and most of the time they belong to a team that is not so strong.

The second way is that when a coach who was in charge of a J.LEAGUE team becomes a coach of an overseas team, he brings in players from the J.LEAGUE. This way is not very common, but it happened recently. Ange Postecoglou, who is currently the manager of the prestigious Scottish Premiership team Celtic, was previously the manager of the J.LEAGUE team Yokohama F Marinos.

So when he took over at Celtic, he acquired three players from the J.LEAGUE: Daizen Maeda, Reo Hatate and Yosuke Ideguchi.

The third way is to get an offer from an overseas team to the J.LEAGUE team. This is the most orthodox way. In this method, it is very important to perform well in international competitions and to attract the attention of scouts from foreign teams.

However, at present, the Japanese national team has very few players who belong to the j-league, and the opportunity for j-league players to appeal to overseas teams is lost. Therefore, if this trend continues, the number of players transferring from J.LEAGUE teams to overseas teams will decrease, and the level of Japanese soccer will decline. Therefore, in order to maintain the level of soccer in Japan, many j-league players need to be selected for the Japanese national team.

What are the reasons why J.LEAGUE players are not selected for the national team? The quality of players in the J.LEAGUE is getting higher and higher every year. The reason for this is that players who have proven themselves in prestigious teams overseas are moving to the J.LEAGUE. For example, Andrés Iniesta, David Villa, Fernando José Torres, etc. The quality of players in the j-league has improved as these players have given back their experience and skills. However, the J.LEAGUE lags far behind the rest of the world in terms of tactics. J.LEAGUE teams have not been able to develop tactics that take advantage of the characteristics of their players [2]. Therefore, no matter how good a player is, the scouts of the national team may have missed him because he is not able to show his characteristics due to tactics. Therefore, the purpose of this paper is to analyze and visualize the characteristics of players. In this study, the analysis was conducted on midfielder players in the J1 League. The reason why we chose the position of midfielder among many positions is that it plays an important factor in both offense and defense.

2   Data Summary

In this paper, we used ball touch data from all 45 matches of the 2020 J1 League season, from the 19th to the 23rd. The data for this study was provided by Data Stadium, Inc. and the Sports Statistics Section of the Japan Statistical Society. The following data were selected for analysis: Shoot, Shoot assist, Dribble, Pass, Through-pass, Cross, Intercept, Block, Tackle, Recovery of a lost ball, Clear, Enter "penalty area", Enter the area 30m from goal. These data were selected by the author if they were considered to have an effect on the characteristics of the players. Table 3 is a description of the variables used.

Table 3. Mainly used variables

Shoot	Shoot
Shoot-assist	Pass if the next teammate shoots (including the previous pass if the shooter traps and then shoots)
Dribble	Dribble
Pass	Play which is passed a ball to a teammate
through-pass	Through-pass
Cross	Cross
Intercept	A play in which the player actively moves to cut off an opponent's pass and either holds it or connects it to a teammate
Block	A play in which the player passively prevents the opposing team's shot or pass from hitting his or her body at a relatively short distance
Tackle	Tackle
Recovery of a lost ball	Play when the previous play was a clear, block, or hand clear (regardless of the team that made the previous play)
Clear	A play made to avoid a dangerous situation without the intention of connecting it to a teammate, such as kicking it outside or recovering a position
Enter "penalty area"	The next time a player is able to play by himself or by a teammate in the enemy penalty area. Refer to fig2
Enter the area 30m from goal	The next play is within 30 meters of the enemy goal line. Refer to fig2

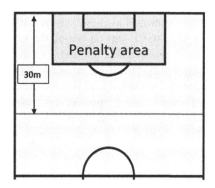

Fig. 2. Area name near the goal

In addition, two midfielders with the most official appearances for each team in the J-League in 2020 were selected for analysis [3]. The selected players, their teams and their playing time are shown in Table 4 (Fig. 2).

Based on these data, we conducted a principal component analysis and created new variables to understand the characteristics of the players. A hierarchical cluster analysis was then performed on the principal component scores to separate the players into groups and identify their characteristics. In the hierarchical cluster analysis, the distance between each individual was measured by Euclidean distance and combined using the Ward method.

Table 4. Playing time of selected players

Player	Team	Time
Ao Tanaka	KAWASAKI FRONTALE	433
Hidemasa Mirita	KAWASAKI FRONTALE	376
Shuto Abe	F.C. TOKYO	297
Yojiro Takahagi	F.C. TOKYO	240
Hotaru Yamaguti	VISSEL KOBE	385
Andrés Iniesta	VISSEL KOBE	385
Yosuke Ideguchi	GAMBA OSAKA	450
Shu Kurata	GAMBA OSAKA	428
Teruki Hara	SAGAN TOSU	405
Daiki Matsuoka	SAGAN TOSU	360
Hayao Kawabe	SANFRECCE HIROSHIMA	450
Shunki Higashi	SANFRECCE HIROSHIMA	420
Leandro Desábato	CEREZO OSAKA	450
Tatsuhiro Sakamoto	CEREZO OSAKA	425
Keiya Shihashi	VAGALTA SENDAI	382
Kunimitsu Sekiguchi	VAGALTA SENDAI	337
Ewerton	URAWA RED DIAMONDS	384
Kazuki Nagasawa	URAWA RED DIAMONDS	274
Takahiro Ougihara	YOKOHAMA F · MARINOS	313
Takuya Kida	YOKOHAMA F · MARINOS	270
Reo Yasunaga	YOKOHAMA F.C.	437
Kohei Tezuka	YOKOHAMA F.C.	334
Kento Misao	KASHIMA ANTLERS	433
Kei Koizumi	KASHIMA ANTLERS	322
Daiki Kaneko	SHONAN BELLMARE	450
Satoshi Tanaka	SHONAN BELLMARE	373
Renato Augusto	SHIMIZU S · PULSE	450
Mitsunari Musaka	SHIMIZU S · PULSE	368
Yushi Hasegawa	OITA TRINITA	401
Toshiro Shimagawa	OITA TRINITA	335
Masatoshi Mihara	KASHIWA REYSOL	394
Richardson	KASHIWA REYSOL	370
Takuma Arano	CONSADOLE SAPPORO	434
Takuro Kaneko	CONSADOLE SAPPORO	390
Sho Inagaki	NAGOYA GRAMPUS EIGHT	450
Takuji Yonemoto	NAGOYA GRAMPUS EIGHT	442

3 Analysis Results and Discussion

Table 5 shows the results of principal component analysis. The results of the principal component analysis showed that the cumulative contribution rate of the fourth principal component exceeded 70%, so the fourth principal component was adopted.

Table 5. Results of principal component analysis

Principal component	Eigen-value	cumulative contribution rate	contribution rate
1	4.146287	31.01%	31.01%
2	2.548447	50.07%	19.06%
3	2.052129	65.41%	15.35%
4	1.10352	73.67%	8.25%

Table 6. Interpretation of principal components

	Principal component			
	1	2	3	4
Shoot	0.307	−0.104	0.387	−0.033
Shoot-assist	0.395	−0.034	−0.200	0.089
Dribble	0.305	0.265	0.339	0.210
Pass	0.129	−0.472	−0.246	0.120
Through-pass	0.399	0.034	−0.216	−0.031
Cross	0.340	0.328	0.165	0.040
Intercept	−0.143	−0.202	0.423	0.199
Block	0.044	−0.213	0.424	0.393
Tackle	0.019	−0.346	0.241	−0.573
Recovery of a lost ball	0.214	−0.346	0.248	−0.282
Clear	−0.068	−0.410	−0.154	0.549
Enter "penalty area"	0.414	0.084	−0.063	0.125
Enter the area 30 m from goal	0.347	−0.292	−0.235	−0.107

Table 6 shows the eigenvectors of each principal component. The first principal component was named "offensive MF" because of its high value related to attack, the second principal component was named "wide MF" because of its high value related to attack from the side, the third principal component was named "balanced MF" because of its high value related to both offense and defense, and the fourth principal component was named "defensive MF" because of its high value related to defense.

Next, hierarchical cluster analysis was conducted from the principal component scores.

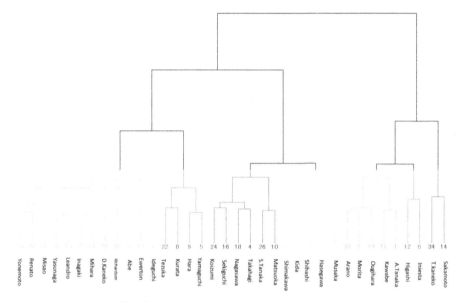

Fig. 3. Results of hierarchical Cluster Analysis

Figure 3 shows the results of the hierarchical cluster analysis. The results of the hierarchical cluster analysis were classified into seven clusters. As for the characteristics of these clusters, cluster 1 was interpreted as "polyvalent MF" because it recorded high values for all variables and could handle any position. Cluster 2 was designated as a "super offensive MF" because high values were recorded for both principal components 1 and 2. Cluster 3 was designated as "offensive MF (Central)" because of the high value of Principal Component 1. Cluster 4 was designated as "hard-working MF" because of the high values of principal components 2 and 4. Cluster 5 was designated as "offensive MF (wide)" because of the high value of principal component 2. Cluster 6 was classified as "defensive midfielder" because of the high value of principal component 4. Cluster 7 was classified as "balanced MF" because the highest value was recorded in Principal Component 3. The principal component scores for each cluster are shown in Table 7.

We can also predict some of the team's tactics from these results. For example, focusing on the VISSEL KOBE players Iniesta and Yamaguchi, Iniesta was classified as a super offensive midfielder while Yamaguchi was classified as a defensive midfielder. This indicates that both players complement each other in the game. Focusing on the next two KAWASAKI FRONTALE players, Ao Tanaka and Hidemasa Morita are classified as Cluster 3. This suggests that Kawasaki FRONTALE's attacks start in the center of the field. Thus, we can predict some of the team's tactics from these results.

Table 7. Principal component scores by cluster

Cluster	Player	Team	PC1	PC2	PC3	PC4
1	Tatsuhiro Sakamoto	CEREZO OSAKA	2.81	2.31	1.86	0.10
1	Takuro Kaneko	CONSADOLE SAPPORO	3.57	3.75	3.64	1.89
2	Andrés Iniesta	VISSEL KOBE	5.58	0.34	-2.02	-0.32
2	Shunki Higashi	SANFRECCE HIROSHIMA	3.61	1.73	-0.89	-0.04
3	Ao Tanaka	KAWASAKI FRONTALE	2.08	-1.76	0.84	-0.71
3	Hayao Kawabe	SANFRECCE HIROSHIMA	3.34	-1.81	0.22	-0.47
3	Takahiro Ougihara	YOKOHAMA F・MARINOS	1.47	-0.35	-2.70	-0.29
3	Hidemasa Mirita	KAWASAKI FRONTALE	1.51	-1.67	-1.57	0.07
3	Takuma Arano	CONSADOLE SAPPORO	2.10	-1.01	-1.71	-0.80
4	Mitsunari Musaka	SHIMIZU S・PULSE	-1.52	0.67	-1.30	-0.86
4	Yushi Hasegawa	OITA TRINITA	-1.75	-0.14	-1.04	-0.46
4	Keiya Shihashi	VAGALTA SENDAI	-2.15	0.04	-0.40	1.20
4	Takuya Kida	YOKOHAMA F・MARINOS	-1.91	0.85	-1.19	1.00
4	Toshiro Shimagawa	OITA TRINITA	-1.66	0.13	-1.39	0.53
5	Daiki Matsuoka	SAGAN TOSU	-3.24	2.16	-0.61	0.00
5	Satoshi Tanaka	SHONAN BELLMARE	-3.23	3.22	0.13	-0.55
5	Yojiro Takahagi	F.C. TOKYO	-1.24	2.48	-0.95	-1.13
5	Kazuki Nagasawa	URAWA RED DIAMONDS	-1.27	1.11	-0.26	-1.15
5	Kunimitsu Sekiguchi	VAGALTA SENDAI	-0.18	2.27	0.77	-0.06
5	Kei Koizumi	KASHIMA ANTLERS	0.26	1.96	-0.71	-0.75
6	Hotaru Yamaguti	VISSEL KOBE	-1.06	-0.77	-0.38	1.82
6	Teruki Hara	SAGAN TOSU	-1.74	-1.19	-0.54	2.62
6	Shu Kurata	GAMBA OSAKA	1.40	0.35	-0.40	1.68
6	Kohei Tezuka	YOKOHAMA F.C.	0.64	-0.71	-1.47	1.94
7	Shuto Abe	F.C. TOKYO	0.33	0.01	1.70	-1.42
7	Yosuke Ideguchi	GAMBA OSAKA	-0.25	-2.57	2.59	0.60
7	Leandro Desábato	CEREZO OSAKA	-1.26	-1.09	1.38	-0.25
7	Ewerton	URAWA RED DIAMONDS	-0.82	-1.55	2.94	-0.84
7	Reo Yasunaga	YOKOHAMA F.C.	-0.53	-1.18	1.26	-0.30
7	Kento Misao	KASHIMA ANTLERS	0.62	-1.42	-0.33	-1.31
7	Daiki Kaneko	SHONAN BELLMARE	-1.66	-0.63	0.81	-0.44
7	Renato Augusto	SHIMIZU S・PULSE	-0.85	-1.59	-0.12	0.40
7	Masatoshi Mihara	KASHIWA REYSOL	-0.64	-0.97	0.86	0.43
7	Richardson	KASHIWA REYSOL	-0.89	-0.35	0.68	-1.96
7	Sho Inagaki	NAGOYA GRAMPUS EIGHT	-0.93	-1.49	1.04	0.23
7	Takuji Yonemoto	NAGOYA GRAMPUS EIGHT	-0.55	-1.12	-0.73	-0.40

4   Future Tasks

In this study, we investigated the characteristics of MFs using ball touch data. Many types of MF were born from the results of this study. However, this study limited the number of players to two per team, so the influence of team tactics may have been more pronounced. Therefore, it is necessary to increase the number of target players of MF players and need to analyze again. We also want to use player tracking data to classify player characteristics in more detail.

References

1. https://fifaranking.net/nations/jpn/ranking_d.php. Accessed 24 Feb 2022
2. Hirashima, Y., Asai, T., Fukayama, K., Nakayama, M.: Verification of a regression equation to predict the probability of a football goalkeeper's failure to stop shots at goal. Jpn. J. Phys. Educ. Health Sport Sci. **63**, 315–325 (2018)
3. https://data.j-league.or.jp/SFPR01/. Accessed 24 Feb 2022

Designing for Interaction: Determining the Most Influential Aesthetic Factors for Effective Visualisation of Uncertainty

Joel Pinney[✉] and Fiona Carroll

Cardiff School of Technologies, Cardiff Metropolitan University, Llandaff Campus, Western Avenue, Cardiff CF5 2YB, UK
{jpinney,fcarroll}@cardiffmet.ac.uk

Abstract. Visualisations offer a variety of novel ways to depict data to a wider range of users. Moreover, they provide the ability to transform raw data into intuitive visual mechanisms for communication. Despite the developments in visualisation techniques, an area of depiction that has struggled to advance is uncertainty. The visualisation of uncertainty offers an additional dimension for the data by presenting confidence and error rates. Whilst nearly all predictive data sets visualised contain uncertainties, there is still little impulse to actively represent uncertainty. A growing area of interest in the visualisation world is the field of aesthetics; the authors ask the question 'could aesthetics be applied to address the issues surrounding visualising uncertainty'. This paper reports on the design and delivery of a study to evaluate the effectiveness of aesthetics for the depiction of uncertainty. In particular, the evaluation of how to practically determine how we assess the influence of aesthetic dimensions for the presentation of uncertainty. The paper reports on the strategies employed in this study to assess user's decision around aesthetic designs, whilst determining what aesthetic combinations elicit the most uncertain visual representation. The findings show that certain aesthetic combinations in a line graph visualisation portrayed a higher level of uncertainty than others and that particular combinations triggered affective responses based on how the visualisation influenced/impacted a participant. In detail, how the textured line characteristics can be displayed aesthetically (combined with either emphasis or scale) to encourage optimal user experiences of uncertainty in a diverse participant group. The paper highlights how a user's decision on which texture was most uncertain can be overturned when presented with varying levels of emphasis and scale. In summary, this paper contributes to a more in-depth understanding of how to design for and evaluate aesthetic uncertainty visualisations that encourage interaction with the data.

Keywords: Uncertainty · Visualisation · Aesthetics

S. Yamamoto and H. Mori (Eds.): HCII 2022, LNCS 13305, pp. 364–383, 2022.
https://doi.org/10.1007/978-3-031-06424-1_27

1   Introduction

Aesthetics are an important factor for visualisation experts to consider when wanting to engage user attention, create an appropriate emotional interaction and most importantly, provide an opportunity for a deeper insight into the data. It is the authors' opinion that this is particularly true for the visualisation of uncertainty in data. Certainly, understanding what visual aesthetics afford what 'uncertainty' affect is crucial for visualisation experts to enhance their knowledge and skills of how they might apply aesthetics to the design of uncertainty in data visualisations. However, few studies have been done to explore the relationship between visual aesthetics and the visualisation of uncertainty, more commonly research explores only a basic visual encoding of uncertainty [43]. This research aims to propose a framework to support data visualisation experts in the design and use of aesthetics for the presentation of data uncertainty. In detail, the framework aims to support visualisation experts to effectively identify the appropriate aesthetics to present the right levels of uncertainty in the data. Specifically, this paper will focus on the journey to determining what visual aesthetics afford what level of uncertainty. The paper not only presents the findings from a 'determining aesthetic factors for uncertainty' study with over one thousand participants but more importantly, documents the design and development of this questionnaire-based study to ensure that appropriate questions are asked. The following sections cover the important literature influencing the study on aesthetics, visualisation methods, uncertainty and decision making techniques.

2   Aesthetic Factors

2.1   Aesthetics as It Exists Today

Aesthetics has had a long and flowery history; it belongs within the field of philosophy, though at the same time, it has strongly defined ties within the fields of art (i.e. visual aesthetics), anthropology (i.e. aesthetic realism), psychology (i.e. aesthetic perception) and now technology, to name a few. More recently, aesthetics is a research area at the intersection of psychology and neuroscience that aims to understand how people experience, evaluate, and create objects aesthetically [28]. Indeed, this empirical approach aims to understand how people experience, evaluate, and create objects aesthetically [13]. As Wassiliwizky et al. [58] suggests researchers are now thinking in terms of temporal dynamics and interactions between: the stimulus and the perceiver; different systems within the perceiver; and different layers of the stimulus. Following this thinking, the authors are also particularly aligned to a vein of aesthetics called Pragmatic Aesthetics (i.e. Dewey (1934), the idea of the aesthetic experience). In detail, the authors present the aesthetic interaction as a process of interaction which through the use of aesthetics, 'engages' the user in the data visualisation to influence the 'what' and 'how' they experience the data. In terms of the nuts and bolts, the authors are interested in the patterning of design elements and principles to 'engage' the senses, intuition, past experience as well as the intellect. In doing so, the authors are keen to understand how we can promote the interaction with data to a new experiential level. How we can ensure that a user can draw a deeper and more intuitive insight from the data?

2.2   Aesthetic Interaction

Aesthetic Interaction is about the use of aesthetics in the design of the interface/visualisation to sensually attract and arouse the user into a deeper cognitive and affective understanding of the experience/data [3]. For clarity, the authors do not see the aesthetic interaction as an added bonus or bi-product of the data visualisation. In fact, it is seen as an interaction in itself and as a process of interaction which promotes a richer and more insightful means of communication, storytelling and problem solving. In their paper, Skov and Nadal [53, p. 1] define 'aesthetics as the study of how and why sensory stimuli acquire hedonic value'. And there is a convincing line of research that shows that the physiological experience can contribute to the comprehension of visualisation of scientific data, especially artistic approaches [4,15,40,48]. Indeed, emotions afforded by the aesthetics 'entail motivational approach and avoidance tendencies, specifically, tendencies toward prolonged, repeated, or interrupted exposure and wanting to possess aesthetically pleasing objects' [38, p. 171]. In reference to information visualisation and decision making, it is the authors' belief that these emotions can have a key influence on judgments and choices made. Undeniably, it has been found that visual information plays a critical role in the human decision-making process [61].

In his paper, Markovic [34] notes, three crucial characteristics of aesthetic experience: fascination with an aesthetic object (high arousal and attention), appraisal of the symbolic reality of an object (high cognitive engagement), and a strong feeling of unity with the object. Furthermore, Kim et al. [21] discuss three factors of aesthetic interaction: freedom of interaction, interaction pattern, and richness of motor actions. Whether active and/or passive, aesthetics not only has the power to capture user attention but also to afford a deeper engagement/understanding of what they are experiencing. In fact, designing an aesthetic interaction is an important issue for Interaction Design (ID) and Human-Computer Interaction (HCI) [30]. For example, Lenz et al. [30] discuss particular interaction attributes (e.g., 'fast') are systematically related to particular experiential qualities (e.g., 'feeling competent') and that interaction 'feels better' if interaction matches the intended experience. In product design, research shows that the effects of product aesthetics have an enduring impact on people's consumption experiences [59]. Likewise, in information visualisation, 'visual artefacts should have a functional dimension, allowing the analysis of information, and an aesthetic dimension, to seize the users' attention to the information being displayed' [36, p. 1]. Nonetheless, in the world of visualisation, a growing body of work in InfoVis explores the user experience (UX), however, emotions still largely remain under explored [23]. As Deng et al. show the current research on human-machine interaction interface layout focuses on ergonomic analysis, while the research on aesthetics and aesthetic degree calculation of interface layout was insufficient [10].

Inspired by the works of Colin Ware (*Visual Thinking for Design*), Edward R. Tufte (*The Visual Display of Quantitative Information*) and Jacques Bertin (*Semiology of Graphics*), this paper is particularly focused on the design of line graph visualisations and how we might design for the more insightful data experiences around uncertainty. The authors align with contemporary research such as the *Online Visual Aesthetics Theory Model* (which proposes that the perception of online data is directly influenced by the eight web design categories: graphics, text, simplicity, animation, layout, unity, emphasis, and balance [33]); recommendations for visualization research on uncertainty communication [16] and the book *Beautiful News* [37], to name a few. The paper aims to document what combinations of design elements and principles can trigger the aesthetic interaction to afford more insight into the uncertainty of the data.

3   Data Visualisation

Data visualisations offer a graphical depiction of large and complex data-sets to provide an interactive dynamic tool to facilitate new discoveries [11]. Moreover, providing users the ability to discover trends and patterns in which may have gone unnoticed in the raw data format [20]. Different visualisation methods can be made use of depending on the analysis required (i.e. comparative, two-dimensional variation etc.) or based on the users requirements [49]. Visualisations hold immense potential in facilitating engagement with users. Such as, providing benefits including portraying a visual representation of vast amounts of data immediately, expediting insights, identification of errors and enhancing understanding of large and small scale data sets [32]. Recent advancements have empowered experts (i.e. researchers, statisticians, data annalists, etc.) to leverage the vast potentials of visualisations [12]. However, there is a growing interest in the power of visual depictions of data for a lay audience. Moreover, researching the benefits visualisations may have for wider groups of people who are non-experts [29]. Despite the interest to engage a wider group of people, it is important to consider that different visualisation approaches must be taken that do not rely on previous experience. Moreover, the design of the visualisation will play an important role in appealing to an inexperienced audience. The intended audience and design of a visualisation must be carefully considered as those without prior knowledge will not be able to acquire the intended insight [45]. It has been said that in order for a user to make sense of visualisations they first require a general understanding of how to operate the tool, and secondly an understanding of how to interpret the content [5].

The design of a visualisation can play an essential role in accomplishing both of these requirements and fundamentally whether or not the visualisation will achieve its goal of providing analytical insight to its users. Research has shown how design elements as simple as manipulating the colour can drastically influence a users comprehension [52]. Whilst the authors propose strongly the use of aesthetics to engage users, it is often said that scientists lack the knowledge surrounding design principles to generate effective visuals [39]. After all, visualisations were not originally intended to be heavily influenced by design, instead their purpose was to provide analytical insights in an effective but efficient manner [48]. Exploring the use of aesthetics and design in visualisations displays a strong separation between those with creative background (designers etc.) calling for the inclusion of aesthetics and design considerations in a visualisation, and those strongly against (scientist etc.). This divide is caused by those with a scientific mindset taking a cautious approach to putting the data on a 'back-seat'. Moreover, fearing that creativity may be influenced by the designers subjectively and result in ignoring clarity [48]. Nevertheless, there is a rise in non-expert users benefiting from creatively designed visualisation of everyday data such as those display by McCandless [37]. Furthermore, it is important to consider aesthetics in visualisation as more than simple 'pretty pictures' but instead as an integral part of science [27].

Whilst visualisations methods have witnessed improvements through the use of aesthetics [4], the authors ask the question 'can aesthetics play a role in improving the depiction of uncertainty in data visualisations?'. In order to begin to address this question, we must first explore the influence and current climate of uncertainty in visualisations and data.

3.1 Uncertainty in Data

The term uncertainty has been categorised by multiple definitions, from the cognitive limitations in the decision making process [51] to limits in data [26] and unpredictable factors [17,56]. Furthermore, the definition of what makes something uncertain can differ between people. A scientific perspective would classify something as uncertain when there is a lack of certainty, whilst those with a social science perspective would assert an association with the term risk [56]. While the term uncertainty does portray the idea of unpredictability and imperfect knowledge, visualising uncertainty does hold its benefits. These include the ability to view the data as a whole [60], improve decision quality [9,19] and promoting scientific transparency [43]. For these reasons understanding uncertainty in data has become a focus for many areas including (but not limited to) health care [54], geography [24], business [46], and the stock market [6]. It is important to note that different forms of uncertainty may be present in data when modelling, including both direct and indirect quantitative uncertainty. Direct quantitative uncertainty refers to uncertainty surrounding the numbers and facts, while indirect delineates the quality of knowledge relating to how effective the numbers and facts represent reality [44]. Whilst uncertainty in data may be a result of sampling errors [35] or a product of estimation [42], it is often a misconception that data sets are free from uncertainty [60]. Furthermore, in reality, nearly all data sets contain a form of uncertainty, and the decision to portray it falls with the visualisation designer [42].

Whilst Tufte [57] claims that a visualisation should be designed for simplicity, it raises the question of does adding uncertainty information as additional dimension to the visualisation become too complex? Research suggests that the inclusion of the supplementary information furthers the visualisations ability to improve how people understand statistics [60].

Although there are multiple reasons in support of presenting uncertainty, there are still many reasons why visualisation designers and authors avoid it. Reasoning includes the viewers perception of the uncertainty, the necessity of including more information and selecting the correct visual methods, detail briefly why uncertainty visualisation is uncommon [16]. Moreover, in order to successfully implement uncertainty in a visualisation there must be better techniques available that are socially-agreed upon for depiction [2], thus not bespoke for experts.

When visualising uncertainty to provide further credibility to the data, the issues remains that the communication and interpretation of uncertainty is a challenge for both experts and a lay audience [18]. Furthermore, it is important to consider that there is no 'one way fits all' technique when it comes to visualisation methods and consideration must be made on a case-by-case basis [31]. Whilst there are commonly used approaches for depiction [42], existing visualisation methods fall into two categories, graphical annotations of distributional properties (such as error bars etc.) and visual encoding (such as location, transparency etc.) [43]. Whilst more commonly uncertainty visualisation methods are utilising distributional properties which require previous expert knowledge to be correctly interpreted [42]. It will be use of visual encodings through aesthetic depictions that the authors are interested in exploring further to represent uncertainty. Visualisation methods that focus on creating stronger intuitive impressions of uncertainty may be a favourable method of depiction for non-expert audiences [42].

While methods are available to visualise uncertainty, the design and expression of uncertain information must be carefully considered as it can influence a user's decision-making [9].

3.2 Decision Making: Cognitive and Intuitive

The decision making process can be defined as 'whereby an individual, group or organization reaches conclusions about what future actions to pursue given a set of objectives and limits on available resources.' [50, p.1]. With the decision-making process a contributing factor to whether or not a venture succeeds [41], it is important to understand the relationship between uncertainty visualisation and decision-making.

Intuition based decision making can be conceived as decisions which are automatic, effortless and unconscious [14], whilst cognitive decisions are based on memory and attention [47]. Moreover, the authors differentiate intuition decision making as the immediate acquisition of knowledge without prior understanding which is experienced through instinct and feelings, whilst cognitive decision making as utilising rational processes and conscious thought processing. It is the intuitive response which is of particular interest to the authors for this research and understanding the influence of the aesthetic to portray/trigger the intuitive instinctual/feeling led decision. Research has shown that decisions based solely on intuition play an important role in completing tasks that may be highly complex or time sensitive [8].

A recent study has found that a common factor influencing the decision-making process is 'uncertainty resulting from lack of information and data, time, availability of resources and funding' [25, p. 2382]. It is the uncertainty originating from the lack of information and data that the authors are particularly interested in. There has been vast research in understanding the influence of uncertainties on the decision making process [22, 55]. It has been said that the communication of data uncertainties are important for the decision making process and more importantly when the decision have potential dramatic consequences [24]. However, there is a need for set practices and processes to represent uncertainty effectively that are widely agreed upon [7].

4   Design and Delivery of Questionnaire Study

4.1   Introduction

The study conducted as part of this research involved developing a questionnaire to evaluate the influence of aesthetics factors on the visualisation of uncertainty. The study was conducted by Cardiff Metropolitan University from 11th August 2021 till 14th August 2021. Full ethics approval was granted by the university for this research. The questionnaire was developed using the online software Qualtrics.

4.2   Participant and Recruitment

During the period the questionnaire was live, one thousand, one hundred and forty two completed questionnaires were gathered. Of which were, six hundred and four Female, five hundred and third two Male and six prefer not to say. Participants were all over the age of eighteen and all residents in the UK. Thirty percent were aged between eighteen and thirty four, thirty nine percent aged between thirty five and fifty four and thirty one percent over the age of fifty five. Ninety five percent have a formal education, with forty three percent holding a bachelor's degree or higher. Participants ranged in experience in working with data with forty two percent confirming they do utilise data, forty five percent stating they do not and thirteen percent unsure. Visuals for the questionnaire study were built using both Adobe editing software and inspired by D3.js. The visuals involved in the study were designed to be minimal. This was to ensure that participant attention was fully on the line and not distracted by external factors. In order to collect sufficient data, the questionnaire was developed and disseminated virtually. To obtain a diverse range of participants throughout the UK, the authors utilised a third party distribution company. The Company, Dynata, collects multiple data-points on participants when they express their interest to sign up for participation in studies. Dynata then matched those data points against the requirement specified by the authors to find relevant participants. The only specification raised by the authors was that participants must be eighteen years and older, this allowed for the adoption of a form of random sampling and ensured the unbiased collection of data which represented the population (UK residents).

4.3   Questionnaire Method and Structure

In order to evaluate the influence of the aesthetic, it was important to make careful considerations during the design of the study. In detail, the questionnaire included a range of quantitative and qualitative questions which had to go through several iterations. Overall, it had a strong visual element which was at the forefront of every question presented to participants. The questionnaire was split into multiple sections each containing a different design element paired with design principles. To elicit the aesthetic the questionnaire combined three design elements (colour, texture, and line) with three design principles (emphasis, movement, and scale), each of the design elements had 4 levels of contrast (i.e. the degree of emphasis added were 1pt, 2pt, 4pt, and 8pt line weight (Fig. 2 (B2))). Because of the vast number of combinations there were over two thousand one hundred questions contained within the questionnaire. However, as a participants decision in a question would continuously influence the reaming questions, the participants journey would only consist of maximum 35 questions (excluding demographic). This paper will report on the findings of the textured line with both emphasis and scale.

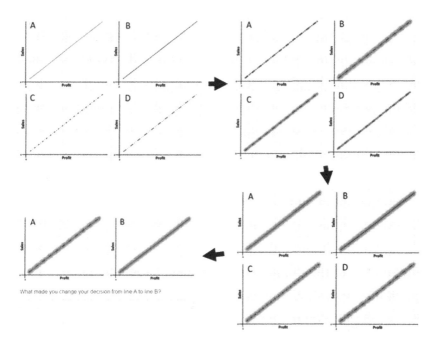

Fig. 1. Example segment of a question from the study

4.4 Procedure for Questionnaire Study

In order to help participants envisage the context they were presented with a simple scenario. This scenario was presented to participants after the demographic questions but before any visuals were shown. Scenario: "You are a company director who needs to make a decision to buy a new product for your business. You view a set of data visualisations to help make your decision. The visualisations show the Sales Vs Profit". This scenario was chosen to help facilitate participants comprehension of the reasons these decisions were being made. Figure 1 presents the four phase approach implemented to determine the aesthetic that most effectively affords uncertainty. In this instance the question is displaying the design element 'texture' with design principle 'emphasis'. Firstly a participant would be presented with all variations of the design element texture (dot line, dashed line, dot dash, and dot-dot dash). The next phase asked participants to rank which graph depicts the most uncertainty (1 being the most uncertain, 4 being the least uncertain). Once the participant selects an option (in this instance D is selected dot-dot-dash as the most uncertain (rank 1)), they were then presented with the selected option combined with the design principle. In this example the participant is presented with their chosen line (dot-dot-dash) but now with four variations (5pt, 8pt, 11pt and 18pt emphasis) of the design principle emphasis applied. Once again, the participant was asked which they felt was the most uncertain (participant selects either A, B, C or D). Once the participant selects the level of variation they felt is the most uncertain, they are now presented with all textures (from question 1) with the same level of emphasis as their selection. In this example, all textures are now presented with the 18pt emphasis (as selected in the second stage). The participant is asked for a final time which of the 4 textured lines they feel is the most uncertain. The next question presented is dependant on the participants selection. If their decision is to remain with the same texture, they were asked "Why do you feel this line was the most uncertain?". If the participant changes their decision they will be asked "What made you change your decision from line A to line B?". This format allows the authors to collect further insight into the influence of the aesthetic. For example, the authors can see if the added principle influences the original decision, but also gather qualitative reasoning as to why this is.

4.5 Creation of the Questionnaire Assets: Textured Line

As discussed, several design elements and principles were explored during this research (i.e. colour, line, texture etc.). This paper solely reports on the textured line which was displayed through using different patterned lines. This method of displaying textures as line patterns is supported by the principles proposed by Bertin [1]. Moreover, that texture is the variation in sensations resulting from a series of pattern of marks, the texture is the number of separable marks contained in an area (i.e. the line). [1]. Figure 2 displays the textures used for this study with no added principle (A: Dot, B: Dash, C: Dot-Dash, D: Dot-Dot-Dash).

Despite the design of the study displaying the final output of the questionnaire, the design process went through multiple designs and considerations. The

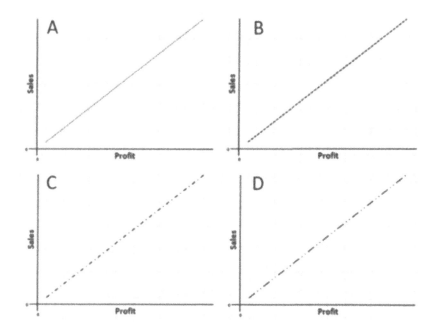

Fig. 2. Textures used in the study

authors feel it is important to share this development process with the HCI community to further inform how we set about designing to understand the influence of aesthetics on uncertainty visualisation.

4.6   Iterative Design Journey of Questionnaire

Many iterations of the questionnaire were undertaken in order to successfully measure and evaluate the use of aesthetics to depict uncertainty. In order to develop a questionnaire which could successful determine the most uncertain aesthetic combination, many drafts were made. For instance, it was important that no combination of design element and principle intentionally stood out over the rest causing a bias response. For example, in the second iteration is was suggested to compare 4 line graphs (3 with regular black line depiction and one applying the aesthetic qualities). On further consideration it was clear that method would induce bias as the participant would be selecting the one which was different not the one which elicited the most uncertain qualities. Furthermore, the inclusion of potential bias could hinder the authors the ability to conclude if the aesthetic was the determining reason for selection (Fig. 3).

Through multiple drafts of the questionnaire the authors were able to determine issues influencing the potential end results. Figure 2 displays three drafts of a question assessing the influence of a solid black line accentuated by different

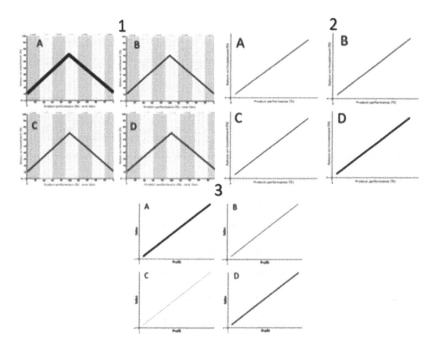

Fig. 3. Development of questionnaire: Phase 1–3 example question

levels scale. In the first draft (no. 1) issues were raised with the addition of unnecessary details such as the complexity of the axis and the direction of the line. In order to be certain that the aesthetic was the determining factor in decisions, it was important to minimise distraction and external influences. Moreover, the detail of the axis may cause a participant to question their decision. Additionally, the direction of the line showing a positive up trend followed by a steep downtrend may solely present a negative and uncertain impression. The second draft (no.2) of the question visual addressed the raised issue but introduced the complication of bias. When inspecting the second question it is clear that one stands out (line D) more than the other three line. With uncertainty often based on the 'unknown' the authors felt this line solely standing out would greatly influence a participants decision. The final draft (no.3) addressed this issue by presenting all four lines with different scales. This solution not only addressed the concern of bias, but also introduced further opportunities to collect data. In the third draft no one line stood out distinctly, there were minimal distractions and participants were able to select from a range of scales (whether they determined larger scales as most uncertain or smaller scales as most uncertain).

5   Outcomes of the Questionnaire Study Texture

This research shows that a participants original decision on what they felt was the most uncertain texture can be highly influenced when applied with a design principle to elicit an aesthetic reaction. When asked to rank which texture (see Fig. 2) was the most uncertain, participants stated that the texture dot (Fig. 2: A) was the most with over 38.6% ranking it first (most uncertain). This was closely followed by dot-dot-dash (Fig. 2: D) with 30.8%. Proceeding dash with 16.8% and dot-dash last with 14% of participants ranking it as the most uncertain texture. Interestingly, with the addition of the design principles emphasis and scale, many participants decisions were swayed to change what they deemed the most uncertain textured line.

5.1   Texture + Emphasis

As shown in Fig. 1 (B2), participants were exposed to 4 levels of emphasis. These levels included 5pt, 8pt, 11pt, and 18pt of emphasis added to the texture. The results in Table 1 display the number of participants to select each variation of texture and design principle (emphasis). Of the 441 participants who selected the Dot line as the most uncertain, 227 believed that the variation with 18pt emphasis displayed the most uncertainty. However, only 127 participants felt it was the most uncertain once exposed to the same level emphasis on other textures. Of those who's decision remained, when asked why the **dot line texture with 18pt emphasis** was the most uncertain, participants said: *"Very blurry and difficult to differentiate" (P1059), "Because the dots of the line are smaller" (P786), "The bolder line exaggerates the width of the shaded line" (P526), "The fuzzy highlighting suggests uncertainty." (P1087), "Largest area" (P19), "Most variation" (P785) , and "Widest variation" (P584)*. Despite the dot texture eliciting the most uncertainty in the first round of questioning and similarly with the added 18pt emphasis. When participants were given the choice of the Dot texture with 18pt emphasis or any of the other textures with the same degree of emphasis, 44% changed their decision (Table 2).

The majority of participants (30%) in the second round of questioning now decided that the dot-dot-dash with 18pt emphasis now presented the most uncertainty. Participants raised reasoning including:: *"The line is broken which suggests unpredictability" (P773), "Erratic pattern and too thick" (P686), "It stood out as a more prominent line" (P1049), "Too thick to see properly" (P66), "too many dots indicating unknown data" (P746), "its got a much wider margin of uncertainty" (P738), "This line has the largest shadow, which could indicate standard error or the interval of uncertainty." (P263) and "The least regular and most fuzzy" (P782)*. The texture dot-dot-dash with combined emphasis has gained the majority of votes for being the most uncertain with 47% (536) of participants, with the majority (360/536) held by the 18pt emphasis. Interestingly, when exploring participants reasoning for other degrees of emphasis with the dot-dot-dash texture, the lowest degree of 5pt emphasis was not the cause for the uncertainty. Participants responses to the dot-dot-dash texture included: *"Too many breaks" (P571), "There is a lot of gaps" (P243), "The breaks in the line" (P213), "Its too busy with not enough definition"*

Table 1. Participants original decision (Emphasis)

Texture	Level of Emphasis	Participants
Dot	5pt	89
Dot	8pt	79
Dot	11pt	46
Dot	18pt	227
	Total	**441**
Dashed	5pt	36
Dashed	8pt	35
Dashed	11pt	43
Dashed	18pt	78
	Total	**192**
Dot-dash	5pt	39
Dot-dash	8pt	24
Dot-dash	11pt	17
Dot-dash	18pt	77
	Total	**157**
Dot-dot-dash	5pt	50
Dot-dot-dash	8pt	36
Dot-dot-dash	11pt	30
Dot-dot-dash	18pt	236
	Total	**352**

Table 2. Once exposed to all textures with same degree of emphasis

Texture	Level of emphasis	Participants	Line change	Total line % change
Dot	5pt	48	−46%	−46%
Dot	8pt	23	−71%	
Dot	11pt	42	−9%	
Dot	18pt	127	−44%	
	Total	**240**		
Dashed	5pt	19	−47%	−23%
Dashed	8pt	56	+60%	
Dashed	11pt	15	−65%	
Dashed	18pt	58	−26%	
	Total	**148**		
Dot-dash	5pt	70	+79%	+48%
Dot-dash	8pt	54	+125%	
Dot-dash	11pt	24	+41%	
Dot-dash	18pt	85	+10%	
	Total	**233**		
Dot-dot-dash	5pt	77	+54%	+48%
Dot-dot-dash	8pt	41	+14%	
Dot-dot-dash	11pt	55	+83%	
Dot-dot-dash	18pt	348	+47%	
	Total	**521**		

(P953), "Inconsistent" (P972), and "The spaces" (P997). The influence of the added emphasis to create the aesthetic was not initiating a response, only the texture was eliciting the response when dealing with lower degrees of emphasis (Tables 3 and 4).

5.2 Texture+scale

Table 3. Participants original decision (Scale)

Texture	Level of emphasis	Participants
Dot	1pt	102
Dot	2pt	82
Dot	4pt	62
Dot	8pt	195
	Total	**441**
Dashed	1pt	40
Dashed	2pt	54
Dashed	4pt	32
Dashed	8pt	66
	Total	**192**
Dot-dash	1pt	40
Dot-dash	2pt	21
Dot-dash	4pt	11
Dot-dash	8pt	85
	Total	**157**
Dot-dot-dash	1pt	42
Dot-dot-dash	2pt	23
Dot-dot-dash	4pt	30
Dot-dot-dash	8pt	257
	Total	**352**

Similar results were seen when experimenting with the same textures (dot, dash, dot-dash, and dot-dot-dash) but with the added design principle of scale. The initial dot line experienced large drops in participant numbers when exposed to other textures with same degrees of scale. In total the dot line seen a 71% drop in participants going from 441 to 209, whilst the dot-dash seen a 69% increase (192 to 266) and dot-dot-dash 52% increase (352 to 536). The findings show that 47% (536) of participants selected the dot-dot-dash as the most uncertain, of which over half (360) selected the degree of scale 8pt as the most uncertain. Participants response to why this aesthetic (dot-dot-dash and 18pt scale) created the most

Table 4. Once exposed to all textures with same degree of scale

Texture	Level of emphasis	Participants	Line % change	Total line % change
Dot	1pt	51	−50%	−71%
Dot	2pt	42	−49%	
Dot	4pt	40	−35%	
Dot	8pt	76	−61%	
	Total	**209**		
Dashed	1pt	30	−25%	−38%
Dashed	2pt	19	−65%	
Dashed	4pt	23	−28%	
Dashed	8pt	59	−11%	
	Total	**131**		
Dot-dash	1pt	83	+108%	+69%
Dot-dash	2pt	42	+100%	
Dot-dash	4pt	33	+200%	
Dot-dash	8pt	108	+27%	
	Total	**266**		
Dot-dot-dash	1pt	60	+43%	+52%
Dot-dot-dash	2pt	77	+235%	
Dot-dot-dash	4pt	39	+30%	
Dot-dot-dash	8pt	360	+40%	
	Total	**536**		

uncertain impression included: *"Line is most intermittent" (P1095)*, *"the gap between the data points is the largest among all graphs" (P314)*, *"The boldness, thickness of the lines, the blank spaces are off-putting" (P973)*. When asking participants who changes from another texture to dot-dot-dash (8pt) why they made the switch, the large majority indicated that the *"larger gaps"* indicated a less certain line. Other observations also indicated reasoning including *"Lack of consistency" (P123)*, *"unusual pattern" (P373), and its "unusuality" (P89)*. Conversely, when reviewing the same texture (dot-dot-dash) but with 1pt scale, participants attention was mainly focused on the visual as a whole rather than the texture/principle presented. Participants comments included *"The line is faint"*, *"It is the least bold of the examples"*, *and its "least visible"*.

6   Discussion

Interestingly when participants were exposed to the texture with emphasis 66% of the participants selected a texture with combined features (consisting of both dot's and dashes). Similarly, when exposed to textures with scale 70% of participants selected the combined featured textures. Ignoring the type of texture and focusing on the inclusion of the design principle displays 54% of participants

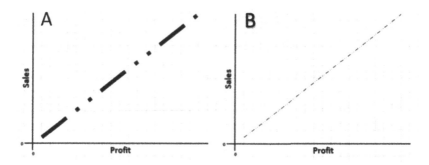

Fig. 4. Scale dot-dot-dash 1pt and 8pt - I feel this needs to be included but risks with the length of the paper.

selected a combination with 18pt emphasis (highest level of emphasis tested) as the most uncertain. When focusing on the influence of scale only, 53% selected the 8pt scale (highest level of scale tested) as the most uncertainty. Interestingly, only 20% selected the 1pt scale as the most uncertain. The findings highlight that when considering the use of emphasis and scale that the degree of intensity can play an important role. In those examples where 5pt emphasis were tested, the response by participants was rarely about the modification but inherently focused on the texture itself. On the other hand, when applying 1pt scale participants did take on board the change through expressing the limited visibility of the data which could signify weakness and uncertainty. When analysing the findings from the study we can see the true influence the aesthetic has had on a participants decision of what makes a textured line uncertain. Whilst the dot line texture can be seen as the most uncertain in the first stages of questions, when adding the design principle scale or emphasis to create the aesthetic we can distinguish the influence it has had on a participants decision. In the context of this research we provided the participant a scenario that may occur in a business setting as a basis to their decision. The focus on the business setting has been designed in order to complement the case study for this research. The case study explores how we may visualise uncertain data for intuitive interaction in the business world when dealing with predictive analytics. Moreover, how we may present to customers/clients who may not have required experience in dealing with data and uncertain data. When applying the findings from this study we can explore how for a lay audience this intuitive impression may bridge the gap of communicating analytical insight in an effective but comprehensible manner.

7   Conclusion and Future Work

This paper presents the detailed design of a questionnaire study to determine how and what aesthetics have the ability to create an intuitive representation of uncertainty in data visualisations. As shown, we can see how the inclusion of certain aesthetic combinations can elicit a greater impression of uncertainty.

This research has shown how different levels of the design principles emphasis and scale can create different impressions on the users decision making. When exploring the use of emphasis it appeared the larger degree (18pt) created a higher degree of uncertainty, whilst lower degrees (5pt) were not as prominent in influencing the decision making process. On the other hand, when exploring the use of scale we found that both the larger degree of scale (8pt) and lowest degree (1pt) both could create strong impressions of uncertainty (See Fig. 4). Whilst aesthetic depictions of uncertainty may not be a favourable approach for those in the scientific community, the research has displayed the benefits for a wider lay audience by creating an intuitive impression of uncertainty.

This study was conducted as part of a wider research project that aims to explore the influence of aesthetics on the visualisation of uncertainty. This research will investigate multiple combinations of design elements and principles to determine their influence to visualise uncertainty. Going forth, the authors will be utilising these findings to help inform the construction of an aesthetic uncertainty visualisation framework. This interactive framework will equip visu-alisation designers with the means to consider the depiction of uncertain infor-mation in their visualisation from an intuitive perspective. The framework will allow visualisation designers to select their desired levels of uncertainty and then the aesthetic means to present these. In doing so, opening up the doors to more engaging, insightful and affective data visualisations.

References

1. Bertin, J.: Semiology of Graphics, 1st edn. Esri Press, New York (2011)
2. Boukhelifa, N., Duke, D.J.: Uncertainty visualization - why might it fail? In: Con-ference on Human Factors in Computing Systems - Proceedings (April), pp. 4051–4056 (2009). https://doi.org/10.1145/1520340.1520616
3. Carroll, F.: Designing (for) experiences in photorealistic VR environments. New Rev. Hypermedia Multimedia **16**(1–2), 181–194 (2010). https://doi.org/10.1080/13614561003710250
4. Cawthon, N., Moere, A.V.: The effect of aesthetic on the usability of data visualiza-tion. In: Proceedings of the International Conference on Information Visualisation, pp. 637–645 (2007). https://doi.org/10.1109/IV.2007.147
5. Chen, C.: Top 10 unsolved information visualization problems. IEEE Comput. Graph. Appl. **25**(4), 12–16 (2005). https://doi.org/10.1109/MCG.2005.91
6. Chuliá, H., Guillén, M., Uribe, J.M.: Measuring uncertainty in the stock market. Int. Rev. Econ. Finan. **48**, 18–33 (2017). https://doi.org/10.1016/j.iref.2016.11.003
7. Comes, T., Adrot, A., Rizza, C.: Decision-making under uncertainty (2017). https://www.researchgate.net/publication/324792356
8. Dane, E., Pratt, M.G.: Exploring intuition and its role in managerial decision making. Acad. Manage. Rev. **32**(1), 33–54 (2007). https://doi.org/10.5465/AMR.2007.23463682
9. Deitrick, S., Edsall, R.: The influence of uncertainty visualization on decision mak-ing: an empirical evaluation. In: Riedle, A., Kainz, W., Elmes, G. (eds.) Progress in Spatial Data Handling, pp. 719–738. Springer, Heidelberg (2006). https://doi.org/10.1007/3-540-35589-8_45

10. Deng, L., Wang, G.: Quantitative evaluation of visual aesthetics of human-machine interaction interface layout. Comput. Intell. Neurosci. **2020**, 9815937 (2020). https://doi.org/10.1155/2020/9815937
11. Gandhi, P., Pruthi, J.: Data Visualization. Springer, Singapore (2020). https://doi.org/10.1007/978-981-15-2282-64
12. Gatto, M.A.C.: Making Research Useful: Current Challenges, vol. 54, May 2015
13. Greb, F., Elvers, P., Fischinger, T.: Trends in empirical aesthetics: a review of the journal empirical studies of the arts from 1983 to 2014. Empirical Stud. Arts **35**(1), 3–26 (2017). https://doi.org/10.1177/0276237415625258
14. Hallo, L., Nguyen, T.: Administrative sciences holistic view of intuition and analysis in leadership. Adm. Sci. **12**(4), 25 (2022)
15. Hohl, M.: From abstract to actual: art and designer-like enquiries into data visualisation. Kybernetes **40**(7/8), 1038–1044 (2011). https://doi.org/10.1108/03684921111160278
16. Hullman, J.: Why authors don't visualize uncertainty. IEEE Trans. Visual. Comput. Graph. **26**, 130–139 (2020). https://doi.org/10.1109/TVCG.2019.2934287
17. Jedynak, P., Bąk, S.: Understanding uncertainty and risk in management. J. Intercultural Manage. **12**(1), 12–35 (2020). https://doi.org/10.2478/joim-2020-0030
18. Joslyn, S., Savelli, S.: Communicating forecast uncertainty: public perception of weather forecast uncertainty. Meteorol. Appl. **17**(2), 180–195 (2010). https://doi.org/10.1002/met.190
19. Joslyn, S., Savelli, S.: Visualizing uncertainty for non-expert end users: the challenge of the deterministic construal error. Front. Comput. Sci. **2**, 1–12 (2021). https://doi.org/10.3389/fcomp.2020.590232
20. Kemal, M.: Data Visualization: Methods, Types, Benefits, and Checklist, March 2019. https://doi.org/10.13140/RG.2.2.19618.48324
21. Kim, C., Self, J.A., Bae, J.: Exploring the first momentary unboxing experience. Des. J. **21**(1), 1–22 (2018). https://doi.org/10.1080/14606925.2018.1444538
22. Kleineberg, J., Levontin, P., Walton, J.L.: Analysis under uncertainty for decision makers network, pp. 1–29 (2019)
23. Koningsbruggen, R.V., Hornecker, E.: "It s just a graph" the effect of post-hoc rationalisation on InfoVis evaluation (2021). https://doi.org/10.1145/3450741.3465257
24. Korporaal, M., Ruginski, I.T., Fabrikant, S.I.: Effects of uncertainty visualization on map-based decision making under time pressure. Front. Comput. Sci. **2**(August), 1–20 (2020). https://doi.org/10.3389/fcomp.2020.00032
25. Kozioł-Nadolna, K., Beyer, K.: Determinants of the decision-making process in organizations. Procedia Comput. Sci. **192**, 2375–2384 (2021). https://doi.org/10.1016/j.procs.2021.09.006
26. Krickx, G.A.: The relationship between uncertainty and vertical integration. Int. J. Organ. Anal. **8**(3), 309–329 (2000). https://doi.org/10.1108/eb028921
27. Lang, A.: Aesthetics in information visualization. In: Proceedings of the Working Conference on Advanced Visual Interfaces - AVI 2008, p. 384 (2008)
28. Leder, H., Pelowski, M.: Empirical aesthetics (2021). https://doi.org/10.1093/oxfordhb/9780198824350.013.43
29. Lee, B., Choe, E.K., Isenberg, P., Marriott, K., Stasko, J.: Reaching broader audiences with data visualization. IEEE Comput. Graph. Appl. **40**(2), 82–90 (2020). https://doi.org/10.1109/MCG.2020.2968244
30. Lenz, E., Hassenzahl, M., Diefenbach, S.: Aesthetic interaction as fit between interaction attributes and experiential qualities. New Ideas Psychol. **47**, 80–90 (2017). https://doi.org/10.1016/j.newideapsych.2017.03.010

31. Levontin, P., Lindsay Walton, J.: Visualising uncertainty a short introduction, vol. 1 (2020)
32. Li, Q.: Overview of data visualization. In: Embodying Data, pp. 17–47. Springer, Singapore (2020). https://doi.org/10.1007/978-981-15-5069-0_2
33. Longstreet, P., Valacich, J., Wells, J.: Towards an understanding of online visual aesthetics: an instantiation of the composition perspective. Technol. Soc. **65**, 101536 (2021). https://doi.org/10.1016/j.techsoc.2021.101536
34. Marković, S.: Components of aesthetic experience: aesthetic fascination, aesthetic appraisal, and aesthetic emotion. i-Perception **3**, 1–17 (2012). https://doi.org/10.1068/i0450aap
35. Mazzi, G.L., Mitchell, J., Carausu, F.: Data Uncertainties: their Sources and Consequences, pp. 1–33 (2019)
36. MaçAs, C., Lourenço, N., MacHado, P.: Evolving visual artefacts based on consumption patterns. Int. J. Arts Technol. **12** (2020). https://doi.org/10.1504/IJART.2020.107693
37. McCandless, D.: Beautiful News: Positive Trends, Uplifting Stats, Creative Solutions. Harper Design, New York (2022)
38. Menninghaus, W., et al.: What are aesthetic emotions? Psychol. Rev. **126**, 171–195 (2019). https://doi.org/10.1037/rev0000135
39. Midway, S.R.: Principles of effective data visualization. Patterns **1**(9), 100141 (2020). https://doi.org/10.1016/j.patter.2020.100141
40. Moere, A.V., Purchase, H., Leuven, K.U.: On the role of design in information visualization. Inf. Visual. **10**, 356–371 (2011). https://doi.org/10.1177/1473871611415996
41. Olalekun, A., Olubunmi, O., Samson, O., Oluwatoyin, F.: Effective management decision making and organisational excellence: a theoretical review. Int. J. Bus. Manage. **9**(1), 144–150 (2021). https://doi.org/10.24940/theijbm/2021/v9/i1/bm2101-049
42. O. Wilke, C.: Fundamentals of Data Visualization. O'Reilly Media, Sebastopol (2019)
43. Padilla, L., Kay, M., Hullman, J.: Uncertainty visualizations. J. Cogn. Eng. Decis. Making **6**(1), 30–56 (2020). https://doi.org/10.1177/1555343411432338
44. Padilla, L.M., Powell, M., Kay, M., Hullman, J.: Uncertain about uncertainty: how qualitative expressions of forecaster confidence impact decision-making with uncertainty visualizations. Front. Psychol. **11**, 1–23 (2021). https://doi.org/10.3389/fpsyg.2020.579267
45. Perkhofer, L., Walchshofer, C., Hofer, P.: Does design matter when visualizing Big Data? An empirical study to investigate the effect of visualization type and interaction use. J. Manage. Control **31**(1-2), 55–95 (2020). https://doi.org/10.1007/s00187-020-00294-0
46. Pinney, J., Carroll, F., Chew, E.: Valuable insights into the visualisation of uncertainty in data as a means to navigating business risks and making better strategic decisions. In: Cardiff, AMI Conference, p. 22 (2021)
47. Prezenski, S., Brechmann, A., Wolff, S., Russwinkel, N., West, R.L.: A cognitive modeling approach to strategy formation in dynamic decision making. Front. Psychol. **8**, 1–18 (2017). https://doi.org/10.3389/fpsyg.2017.01335
48. Quispel, A., Maes, A., Schilperoord, J.: Aesthetics and clarity in information visualization: the designer's perspective. Arts **7**(4), 72 (2018). https://doi.org/10.3390/arts7040072
49. Sadiku, M., Adebowale, S., Musa, S., Akujuobi, C.: Data visualization. Int. J. Eng. Res. Adv. Technol. (IJERAT) **2**(12), 11–16 (2016)

50. Schoemaker, P.J., Russo, J.E.: Decision-making (2018). https://doi.org/10.1057/9781137294678.0160
51. Schumpeter, J.A.: Theory of Economic Development: An Inquiry into Profits, Capital, Credit, Interest and the Business Cycles. Harvard University Press, Cambridge (1934)
52. Sinar, E.: Data visualization. In: Tonidandel, S., King, E.B., Cortina, J.M. (eds.) Big Data at Work, 1st edn., Chap. 5, p. 43. Routledge, New York (2015). https://doi.org/10.1080/15228959.2015.1060147
53. Skov, M., Nadal, M.: A farewell to art: aesthetics as a topic in psychology and neuroscience. Perspect. Psychol. Sci. **15**, 630–642 (2020). https://doi.org/10.1177/1745691619897963
54. Smith, A.F., Messenger, M., Hall, P., Hulme, C.: The role of measurement uncertainty in health technology assessments (HTAs) of In Vitro tests. PharmacoEconomics **36**(7), 823–835 (2018). https://doi.org/10.1007/s40273-018-0638-1
55. Sniazhko, S.: Uncertainty in decision-making: a review of the international business literature. Cogent Bus. Manage. **6** (2019). https://doi.org/10.1080/23311975.2019.1650692
56. Spiegelhalter, D.: Risk and uncertainty communication. Annu. Rev. Stat. Appl. **4**, 31–60 (2017). https://doi.org/10.1146/annurev-statistics-010814-020148
57. Tufte, E.R.: The Visual Display of Quantitative Information, 2nd edn. Graphics Press, Cheshire (1983)
58. Wassiliwizky, E., Menninghaus, W.: Why and how should cognitive science care about aesthetics? (2021). https://doi.org/10.1016/j.tics.2021.03.008
59. Wiecek, A., Wentzel, D., Landwehr, J.R.: The aesthetic fidelity effect. Int. J. Res. Mark. **36**, 542–557 (2019). https://doi.org/10.1016/j.ijresmar.2019.03.002
60. Yan Yu, Z.: Visualizing uncertainty. Ph.D. thesis, Northeastern University (2018). https://doi.org/10.1075/idjdd.12.3.07erv
61. Yu, W., et al.: Visually aware recommendation with aesthetic features. VLDB J. **30**(4), 495–513 (2021). https://doi.org/10.1007/s00778-021-00651-y

Neural Network Visualization in Virtual Reality: A Use Case Analysis and Implementation

Dirk Queck[1], Annika Wohlan[2], and Andreas Schreiber[2]

[1] Department of Electrical and Computer Engineering, Serious Games Engineering, TU Kaiserslautern, Paul-Ehrlich-Straße, 67663 Kaiserslautern, Germany
`queck@eit.uni-kl.de`
[2] Institute for Software Technology, German Aerospace Center, Linder Hoehe, 51147 Cologne, Germany
`{annika.wohlan,andreas.schreiber}@dlr.de`

Abstract. Software systems and components increasingly rely on machine learning methods such as Artificial Neural Networks (ANNs) to provide intelligent functionality. Therefore, software developers and machine learning users should have a basic understanding of such methods. However, since ANNs are complex and thus challenging to grasp, novel visualization approaches can contribute to a better comprehension. We conducted an online survey to identify use cases and requirements for visualizing ANNs. Based on our results we designed and implemented an ANN visualization in virtual reality (VR) specifically targeted at machine learning users. Our approach is particularly suitable for teaching purposes and machine learning novices or non-experts who want to get an impression of the general functionality of neural networks.

Keywords: Virtual reality · Visualization · Neural networks

1 Introduction

In the ongoing process of digitalization, *artificial neural networks* (ANNs) are increasingly used in industrial and scientific fields. The group of people who need to understand the functioning of these algorithms, such as common programmers, increased. Thus, there may be a growing need for effective learning materials and broader forms of visualizations to achieve a greater understanding. Most visualization approaches for neural networks are tailored to developers of machine learning (ML) libraries—such as TensorBoard [6] for TensorFlow—or require prior knowledge [14]. Hence, a novel representation is required to enable non-experts to obtain a basic understanding of the functionality of ANNs.

A severe challenge in visualizing AI models is the enormous size and complexity of neural networks, consisting of thousands of neurons. While 2D visualizations are easier to navigate and interact with, they do not scale particularly well

S. Yamamoto and H. Mori (Eds.): HCII 2022, LNCS 13305, pp. 384–397, 2022.
https://doi.org/10.1007/978-3-031-06424-1_28

for large data sets. To avoid a cluttered view, 2D visualizations rely on multiple views that may strain and confuse beginners. Consequently, two-dimensional visualization approaches are only somewhat suitable for introducing ANNs. The inclusion of the third dimension is required to increase the information density of the visualization, without exposing users to additional cognitive load. Especially virtual reality (VR) environments may be well suited to analyze n-dimensional models. Objects in VR do not have to be grabbed and turned to be observed, users simply walk around objects. Moreover, the virtual space offers enough room to allow the comparison of several neural networks [9]. Furthermore, VR technology has the potential of supporting studying processes by providing an immersive environment [3]. Previous research has shown that a 3D-visualization of *convolutional neural networks* (CNNs) in VR has positive effects on the learning outcome and learning experience of users [8,13].

Based on a use case analysis, we will collect use cases and requirements for an ANN visualization depending on the target group. Further, we will present a VR prototype that is able to visualize different ANNs, starting with a CNN. Our goal is to create an immersive, virtual learning environment in which users can fully engage with the ANN. Therefore, our contribution is twofold:

- We present a use case analysis in which we identified target groups and corresponding requirements for visualizing ANNs (Sect. 2).
- Based on our findings, we present a user-friendly ANN visualization for machine learning novices in VR (Sect. 3).
- Finally, we summarize related work, especially on visualization neural networks for non-experts and on visualization in VR (Sect. 5).

2   Use Case Analysis

To identify use cases and main requirements of an ANN visualization to derive design implications, we conducted a use case analysis through a survey questionnaire.

2.1   Methodology

We conducted an online survey addressed to machine learning experts. The survey aimed 1) to determine in which cases experts require ANN visualization tools, 2) to identify specific essential features and functionalities, and 3) to evaluate beneficial effects of VR technology. To do so, the survey consisted of two sections. In the first section, questions referred to ANN visualization tools in general. The second section focused on ANN visualizations in VR. We deliberately chose to include free text answers instead of pre-selected options to get qualitative data to provide a deeper insight of the participants' needs. The survey took an average of 30 min to complete.

2.2   Results

We received 17 responses. All participants stated to have an advanced or expert knowledge in ML. To evaluate the data, we conducted a qualitative content analysis [7]. To evaluate the data, we conducted a qualitative content analysis. First, we classified the responses to categories based on our collected data. For each question, we first analyzed the free written data by formulating statements from the participants' answers. Then, we identified related answers between participants and grouped them according to their frequency. Finally, we coded all statements into a category. For example, we coded statements regarding the structure of an ANN to the category network architecture.

ANN Visualization. First, we asked participants about their experiences with pre-built tools and frameworks as well as visualization tools (e.g., TensorBoard, Pytorch and SciPy). Eleven participants stated that they did not see the necessity to use visualization tools because they are not conductive to their daily work. However, six participants reported that they use ANN visualization tools. Reasons for using a tool are, to get an overview of the underlying structures (three participants), and wish to track the training process, especially when something is not working as expected (five participants). We further asked them to state what they like about the(se) visualization tool(s) and how they could be improved. Three participants stated that they like the intuitive and interactive interaction. Two participants stated that they appreciate graph visualizations and one participant emphasises getting insights in the training process through activation and weight histograms. Nevertheless, all six participants stated that complex deep ANNs are challenging to visualize properly. Moreover, two participants indicated that they do not necessarily gain additional knowledge from these visualizations.

We then asked all 17 participants in what situations they wish to use a suitable visualization tool and what use cases they can imagine for others. Within the qualitative content analysis, we categorized the participants' free written answers into use case categories. For example we categorized answers such as *"understanding what the black box is doing"* and *"I am interested in understanding the mighty black box"* into the use case *"Getting inside the black box"* and answers such as *"Visualizations should serve to better implement and debug an ANN"* and *"Error detection in the sense of a visual debugging assistant"* into the use case *"Debugging and improving models"*. In addition, we have further clustered these use cases into main categories *explainability, evaluation,* and *presentation* (Fig. 1).

The results show that most answers concern explainability and evaluation purposes. More precisely, debugging and improving models as well as gaining knowledge has been named most often.

Furthermore, we asked the participants to name important features and information that has to be represented in an ANN visualization. Table 1 shows a list of the responses clustered by network architecture and network status.

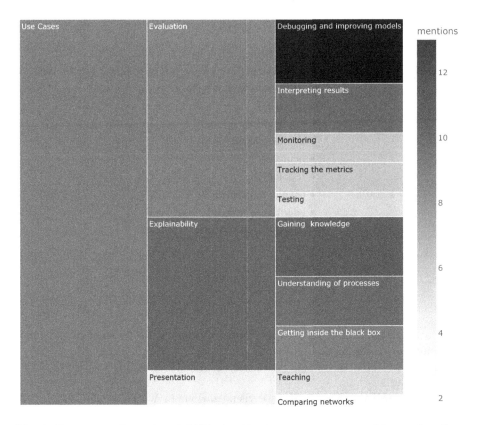

Fig. 1. Frequency of mentioned ANN visualization use cases grouped by explanation, evaluation, and presentation. The Icicle chart shows the clustered results with three columns: the first column ("root") represents the totality of use cases, the second column represents our three clusters, and the third column shows the individual use cases mentioned. The size of the individual areas is proportional to the frequency with which they are mentioned.

ANN Visualization in Virtual Reality. The second part of the survey aimed to determine the conditions under which the use of VR technology would be a feasible way to visualize ANNs. We first asked participants about their experience with ANN visualizations in VR. Then we asked them about *possible use cases* and about *possible benefits* of VR technology. None of the participants had previous experience with ANN visualizations in VR.

Six Participants could not image any reason for visualizing ANNs in VR since you can simply use desktop-based tools. Eight Participants stated that ANN visualizations in VR could be useful, especially for teaching purposes since the architecture of the networks can be displayed in a more detailed and accurate way. Six participants stated that VR technology may be useful for marketing purposes and exhibitions since you could show ANNs quite well on a lower level. Only three participants could imagine using VR technology in their daily work. In summary, we could identify three use cases:

Table 1. Required information to be displayed in interactive ANN visualization.

Category	Requirements
75emNetwork architecture	• model structure (layers, filters, weights, output, inputs)
	• mathematical functions
	• patterns
	• gradients
	• learned abstractions
	• neurons
	• topology
65emNetwork status	• change of parameters
	• adaption of weights
	• classification process
	• activations
	• data flow
	• backpropagation paths

1. Teaching: ML teachers could use visualizations in VR to explain the functioning of ANNs to their students.
2. Presenting: ML researchers could use visualizations in VR to present AI to non-experts.
3. Learning: ML students could use visualizations in VR to explore ANNs and gain knowledge.

When asking about VR benefits, nine participants emphasized the use of the virtual space because it could be possible to walk or fly through a large net. Moreover, four participants stated that the virtual space is more effective for showing higher dimensional data. One participant could imagine comparing different ANNs in the virtual space and two participants emphasized the immersive effect of virtual environments. However, six participants did not see any benefit in using VR technology. In summary, we could identify four benefits for using VR technology:

1. Usage of the virtual space to explore large networks
2. Comparison of different networks
3. Having an immersive environment
4. Having new ways to interacting with the network

2.3   Implications

In summary, we asked 17 machine learning experts about possible use cases and requirements of ANN visualizations tools. Most of them had no prior experience with ANN visualization tools and did not see the benefit in using them since they seem not conductive to their daily work. Nevertheless, most participants

Table 2. Summary of results: users, use cases, requirements and VR benefits for visualizing ANNs.

Users	Use cases	Requirements	VR
Developers	Error detection, evaluation of own models, interpretation of results, monitoring, quick overview	Upload own model, tracking the metrics, show backpropagation, use live input	Visualizing high dimensional networks
Students	Understanding of training, understanding of architecture, understanding of processes	Have different views, show network status, show network properties, upload own model, algorithm animation, use live input	Visualizing any ANN, comparing different ANNs
Non-experts	Getting an overview of ANNs	Have different views, show input and output, show network properties	Reduced 3D model

could imagine that adequate ANN visualizations would be useful for evaluation and explainability purposes. Since our main goal is to determine under which conditions VR technology may be beneficial for visualizing ANNs, we then asked the participants about possible benefits VR can offer. Most of the participants could imagine that the usage of the virtual space may be beneficial for exploring higher dimensional and large neural networks. However, using VR would mostly be necessary for teaching, presenting or learning purposes. Based on our findings, Table 2 summarize our results by combining different use cases with the respective requirements and the benefits of VR technology.

We found three main user groups for ANN visualizations: developers such as ML experts or ML researchers, students such as ML beginners or users with a need to gain basic understanding of ANNs, and non-experts such as managers or saleswomen. These different user groups have different use cases and therefore different requirements to an ANN visualization. While developers primarily need to focus on evaluation processes, students need to gain a basic understanding of the underlying structures and functionalities first. Non-experts do not necessarily have the need to explore ANNs to a detailed level. For them a reduced view of ANNs may be favorable. We conclude that the virtual environment may be beneficial in cases of visualizing different ANNs to gain a basic understanding of the underlying structures and the functioning. This is consistent with our premise that VR can provide a conducive learning environment. Moreover, our analysis supports the findings of Meissler et al. [8].

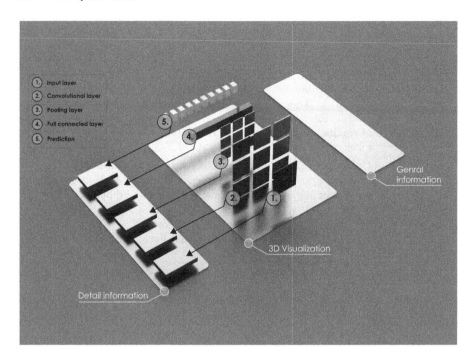

Fig. 2. Schematic overview of the virtual environment: main area with the 3D visualization (middle), detail information area with details of the corresponding model layers (left), and general information area with information about different neural networks (right).

3 Neural Network Visualization

In this section, we will present our approach to create an engaging virtual environment for exploring ANNs. Based on our analysis, we decided to address ML beginners. The visualization was developed in Unity 2019.3.0 for HTC Vive.

3.1 Design Goals

The results of the use case analysis were used to derive design implications for the ANN visualization. We define the following design goals for an interactive ANN visualization in VR to help ML beginners to gain a basic understanding of the architecture and the functioning of different ANNs:

- Construct an immersive and engaging learning experience: We want to ensure a user-friendly interaction and high user experience through an engaging environment.
- Require no prior technical knowledge: We want to provide users all necessary information they need to understand the functionality and architecture of the different ANNs.

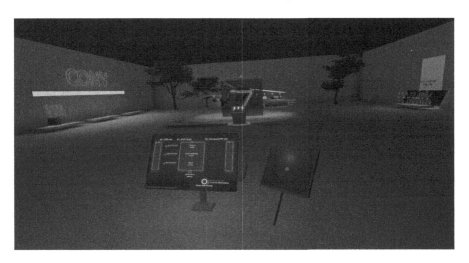

Fig. 3. Start position: overview of the detail area (left), the CNN model (middle), and the general information area (right). In front are an information panel and a portable map.

3.2   Implementation

We started with visualizing a convolutional neural network (CNN). We used digit recognition based on the MNIST dataset as a representative starter example. In addition, a step-by-step development of the individual components was necessary. In the first step, the CNN had to be modeled, trained, and tested. Exploratory testing resulted in splitting the trained hyperparameters for exporting the CNN data into different file formats. This was done due to performance constraints and the associated minimization of user experience. In addition, treating a single CNN component as a single development increment showed advantages in development and testing. We imported the exported and separated components of the CNN into the game engine. Then, we visualized and tested each layer of the CNN individually.

3.3   Environment

Due to the complexity of the construction of neural networks and the resulting potential information overload, we have decided to provide users with three sources of information in the virtual environment instead of putting all information into one model (Fig. 2).

The main focus of the application is the 3D model located in the main area in the center of the room. Additional information is displayed to the left and right of the main area. The detail information area provides additional information about the ANN model according to the model layer. The general information area provides general deep learning information as well as information about other neural networks. Users can move through the virtual space freely. Figure 3 gives an overview of the implementation from the start position. We added an information panel and a portable map for orientation.

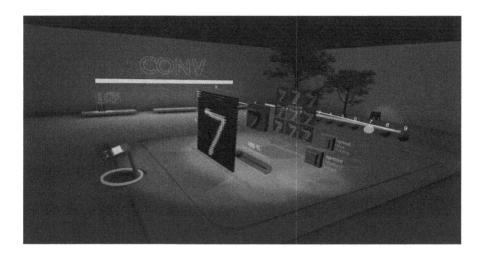

Fig. 4. Overview of the 3D CNN model in the virtual environment.

3D Visualization. The Main area corresponds to the main information source. The 3D-model includes all major components of CNN. Figures 5 shows the conceptual structure of the 3D model.

The visualized components are input layer, convolutional layer, pooling layer, fully-connected layer and output layer. Each element is clearly separated from the others and can be viewed in the entire virtual space, for example the user can walk around the model as well as step between the individual layers (Fig. 4). Individual pixel values are represented as three-dimensional pixel elements and can thus be perceived by the user as semantic objects. In addition, the main area contains all direct layer connections, such as weights and biases (Fig. 6a).

Detail Information. The detail information area displays the corresponding mathematical functions and provides additional information about parameters. Within the detailed information area there are sub-areas associated with the respective location of each level of the main area. Thus, all additional information of the corresponding level has a local and content-related reference.

General Information. The general information area contains additional information relevant for the understanding of deep learning and ANNs. Here, the functionality of a perceptron, the historical development of deep learning and various other ANN networks are presented.

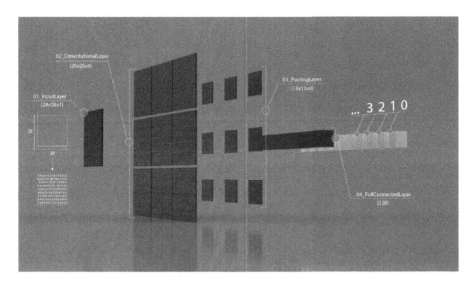

Fig. 5. Schematic structure of the 3D model for a CNN: input layer, convolutional layer, pooling layer, fully-connected layer and output layer are mapped in sequence.

3.4 User Interaction

To have an engaging VR experience, we focused on creating an intuitive interaction and navigation.

Navigation. To help the users' locomotion in the virtual environment, we have placed teleportation points at all information areas (Fig. 6b). However, users are not bound to the teleportation points, they can freely explore the virtual environment.

Moreover, teleportation enables users to quickly move between the areas. However, to fully explore the 3D model, users need the freedom of movement and precision. Therefore, users can simply step between the different layers of the model and explore the visualized information from different angles.

General Interaction Concepts. To interact with the 3D model, users can use the input panel in front of the model (Fig. 6c) and the interaction panels next of the respective model component. The input panel enables users to choose between different input data. These are 30 randomized examples of the training data set. Moreover, the user can show and hide the individual model components. Thus, they have the possibility to explore the individual CNN components separately.

Moreover, we created a self-explanatory interaction at each component of the CNN. Each interaction element offers the opportunity to encode the complexity of the represented object. For example, at the input layer the user has the possibility to change the transparency of the individual neurons with a 3D-slider

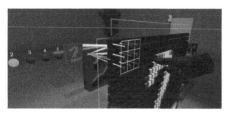

(a) Visualization of filter calculation to generate feature maps.

(b) Highlighted teleportation point in front of the input panel.

(c) Input panel in front of the 3D model. Users can select the input and show or hide different model components.

(d) 3D slider to change the transparency of the neurons.

Fig. 6. Interaction and navigation in the virtual environment.

to explore their numerical input values (Fig. 6d). At the convolutional layer and the pooling layer the user has the possibility to dissolve the layered arrangement and to view the individual maps separately via a 3D-button.

4   Proof of Concept

For the proof of concept we had five participants at our disposal. The participants were between 23 and 27 years old. The user group consisted of four male and one female user. All users had prior academic-technical knowledge, but had no prior knowledge of ML or KNN. Thus, the user group corresponded to the identified target group (Sect. 2.3). We used the prototype with all components and interaction modalities as mentioned before. The goal was to determine if the application contributes to the understanding of CNN and we checked whether the primary requirements were met. In addition, we investigated whether all features and interactions within the VR work.

4.1   Set Up and Procedure

We used the *Thinking Aloud* method [11]. The participants explored each area of the environment regarding its comprehensibility. During this process we documented the participants findings, hints and impressions.

We used the Unity 3D engine to develop the VR environment. An HTC Vive VR system was used in the proof-of-concept. The space available to the users for free movement corresponded to a square movement space 3.50 m long and 2.00 m wide. During the performance, each subject was provided with an exploration guideline time of approximately 10 min.

User testing was conducted primarily through self-exploration and was carried out with the help of small hints. The goal was to allow users to move freely in the virtual space and understand the individual CNN components in the process. In the course of the tests, the users were encouraged to verbalize their thoughts, impressions, and problems. This was done throughout the test phase. After the test, qualitative interviews were conducted to discuss the presentation of each CNN component.

4.2   Feedback

Navigation and Interaction. All users found the navigation to be pleasant. The navigation model was considered intuitive by the users. The interaction concepts were found to be helpful. All desired user movements and inputs functioned without restrictions.

CNN Model. For the participants the representation of the input layer as pixel cubes was understandable and contributed to a gain of knowledge. The layered structure of the feature maps led to an understanding of the multidimensionality of the convolutional layer and showed the data reduction as well as the feature expression of the layer. Nevertheless, some users found it difficult to understand the relationship between the input layer and feature map. In addition, the two-dimensional representation of the feature maps made it difficult to understand neuron activation. The same applied to the visualization of the pooling layers, which did not stand out from the feature maps in their form of presentation. Two users also wished for info texts on the feature maps to better understand connections. Only one user understood the context of the layers. The static visualization of the filters led to misunderstandings and ambiguities in some cases. The transition from the pooling layer to the flattening layer was understandable and conveyed the functionality of its identity. The output layer was well understood by the user group. During the overall visualization of the CNN, it was noted that the individual layers were too close together. This resulted in some users feeling a sense of crowding. In addition, the layers being too close together resulted in some interactions not being performed correctly.

5   Related Work

Much research focuses on teaching non-experts about neural networks. For example, Carney et al. [2] developed the web-based application *Teachable Machine*, which allows machine learning novices to learn about their own ML classification models. In 2015, Harley et al. [4] presented an interactive visualization for large-scale CNNs. Machine learning novices could draw digits in the web application, which then were classified by the algorithm. Users were able to observe activation patterns reacting in real-time. Based on the work of Harley et al., Bellgardt et al. [1] developed an immersive node-link visualization of ANNs in VR where nodes represent individual activations and edges represent the weights between them. Their visualization explicitly targets ML experts and a small user study gave positive results.

In 2019, Schreiber et al. [10] developed an interactive 3D visualization for deep learning models, which are implemented with TensorFlow. They designed their prototype to be suitable for both experts and beginners. Wang et al. [13] identified key requirements for an interactive CNN visualization. Their *CNN EXPLAINER* addresses non-experts to explore CNNs.

In terms of prospective benefits of using VR technology, Meissler et al. [8] showed that machine learning beginners gained a good understanding of the functioning and training of CNNs when exploring the *LeNet-5* architecture [5] visualized in VR. Likewise, Van Horn et al. [12] underlined that a virtual environment has benefits on the users learning motivation. Users reported that they did not feel a mental barrier when learning about complex AI models. In addition, the authors claimed that they consider the large space in VR to be necessary when comparing different models. Furthermore, users tend to be more comfortable observing complex models from different angles when they had the option to walk around the model instead of turning it [9].

6 Conclusion and Future Work

We present use cases for ANN visualizations in virtual reality. From our use case analysis, we derived the requirements for a visualization. Based on our analysis of the interview, we developed a virtual environment for machine learning beginners, focusing on our design goals.

The next step is to evaluate our findings in a user study. Moreover, we want to conduct a requirement analysis by interviewing data science students. Based on the evaluation, the prototype will be enhanced in the future.

The different areas are still missing some relevant information. For example, users can currently only explore the CNN 3D model. In the future, we plan to visualize further models. Moreover, we plan to improve the explanation of individual layers and their interrelationships by didactic and visual communication methods.

Based on this visualization approach, we are working on a concept to develop an ANN building block system for VR that shows the individual layers as interactive building blocks within the architecture. In our vision, ML beginners can build their own ANNs in VR by using drag and drop interaction. However, the model and the associated hyperparameters would be in an untrained state and the training process must be initiated after assembly. In addition, the user would need to have access to training data within the VR. To enable access to training data, we plan to develop an interactive input layer. This layer has the ability to process pixel data written in VR and feed it directly into the neural network.

Acknowledgements. This work was partially supported by the DFG within the SPP 2199.

References

1. Bellgardt, M., Scheiderer, C., Kuhlen, T.W.: An immersive node-link visualization of artificial neural networks for machine learning experts. In: 2020 IEEE International Conference on Artificial Intelligence and Virtual Reality (AIVR), pp. 33–36 (2020). https://doi.org/10.1109/AIVR50618.2020.00015
2. Carney, M., et al.: Teachable machine: approachable web-based tool for exploring machine learning classification. In: Extended Abstracts of the 2020 CHI Conference on Human Factors in Computing Systems, pp. 1–8 (2020)
3. Chavez, B., Bayona, S.: Virtual reality in the learning process. In: Rocha, Á., Adeli, H., Reis, L.P., Costanzo, S. (eds.) WorldCIST'18 2018. AISC, vol. 746, pp. 1345–1356. Springer, Cham (2018). https://doi.org/10.1007/978-3-319-77712-2_129
4. Harley, A.W.: An interactive node-link visualization of convolutional neural networks. In: Bebis, G., et al. (eds.) ISVC 2015. LNCS, vol. 9474, pp. 867–877. Springer, Cham (2015). https://doi.org/10.1007/978-3-319-27857-5_77
5. LeCun, Y., Bottou, L., Bengio, Y., Haffner, P.: Gradient-based learning applied to document recognition. Proc. IEEE **86**(11), 2278–2324 (1998). https://doi.org/10.1109/5.726791
6. Mané, D., et al.: Tensorboard: tensorflow's visualization toolkit (2015)
7. Mayring, P.: Qualitative Content Analysis - A Companion to Qualitative Research, vol. 1. Sage Publications, London Thousand Oaks (2004)
8. Meissler, N., Wohlan, A., Hochgeschwender, N., Schreiber, A.: Using visualization of convolutional neural networks in virtual reality for machine learning newcomers. In: 2019 IEEE International Conference on Artificial Intelligence and Virtual Reality (AIVR), pp. 152–156. IEEE (2019)
9. Naraha, T., Akomoto, K., Yair, I.E.: Survey of the VR environment for deep learning model development. In: The 35th Annual Conference of the Japanese Society for Artificial Intelligence, vol. 35 (2021). https://doi.org/10.11517/pjsai.JSAI2021.0_2N3IS2b04
10. Schreiber, A., Bock, M.: Visualization and exploration of deep learning networks in 3D and virtual reality. In: Stephanidis, C. (ed.) HCII 2019. CCIS, vol. 1033, pp. 206–211. Springer, Cham (2019). https://doi.org/10.1007/978-3-030-23528-4_29
11. Someren, M.V., Barnard, Y., Sandberg, J.: The Think Aloud Method: A Practical Approach to Modelling Cognitive, vol. 11. Academic Press, London (1994)
12. VanHorn, K., Çobanoğlu, M.C.: Democratizing AI in biomedical image classification using virtual reality. Virtual Real., 1–13 (2021)
13. Wang, Z.J., et al.: CNN explainer: learning convolutional neural networks with interactive visualization. IEEE Trans. Vis. Comput. Graph. **27**(2), 1396–1406 (2020)
14. Yosinski, J., Clune, J., Nguyen, A., Fuchs, T., Lipson, H.: Understanding neural networks through deep visualization. In: In ICML Workshop on Deep Learning (2015)

Quantitative Progress Evaluation
for Open Source Project with Application
to Bullseye Chart

Hironobu Sone[1], Yoshinobu Tamura[2](✉), and Shigeru Yamada[3]

[1] IBM Japan, Ltd., 19-21, Nihonbashi Hakozaki-cho Chuo-ku, Tokyo 103-8510, Japan
[2] Graduate School of Sciences and Technology for Innovation, Yamaguchi University,
2-16-1, Tokiwadai, Ube-shi, Yamaguchi 755-8611, Japan
`tamuray@yamaguchi-u.ac.jp`
[3] Graduate School of Engineering, Tottori University, Minami 4-101, Koyama,
Tottori-shi 680-8552, Japan
`yamada@tottori-u.ac.jp`

Abstract. Open source software (OSS) are used under the various situations, because OSS are useful for many users to make cost reduction, standardization, and quick delivery. While OSS have many advantages, it is difficult for us to quantitatively grasp the progress of development such as general software development because OSS are developed by many different people around the world. In general software development, Earned Value Management (EVM) is often used to quantitatively evaluate the progress of a project. However, it is difficult to apply EVM directly in terms of the characteristic of the open source project. Therefore, EVM in open source projects has not been sufficiently researched.

In this paper, we apply the progress data of open source projects to EVM. We also try to derive the bullseye chart by using the Cost Performance Index (CPI) and Schedule Performance Index (SPI) known as the indexes of EVM. Also, we apply the derivation method discussed in this paper to actual open source project data in order to quantitatively evaluate the project.

Keywords: Data visualization and big data · Decision support systems · Open source project · Project management · Bullseye chart · Earned value management

1 Introduction

The source code of open source software (OSS) is freely available for use, reuse, fixing, and re-distribution by the users. OSS are used under the various situations, because OSS are useful for many users to make cost reduction, standardization, and quick delivery. Many OSS programs are known as high performance and reliability, even though many OSS are free of charge. In particular, OSS are developed using the bazaar method [1] under the situation of the free and

© The Author(s), under exclusive license to Springer Nature Switzerland AG 2022
S. Yamamoto and H. Mori (Eds.): HCII 2022, LNCS 13305, pp. 398–409, 2022.
https://doi.org/10.1007/978-3-031-06424-1_29

the opened source code. Then, OSS are promoted by an unspecified number of users and developers. The bug tracking system is also one of the systems used to develop OSS. The bug tracking system registers a lot of defect information, such as the status of fixes, the details of fixes, and the priority of fixes. These information are used to manage the OSS project.

While the quality of OSS is high because it is developed and maintained by the OSS community, many faults reported to the OSS community are not always resolved quickly. The previous research has shown that there are large differences in the time to resolve individual faults in OSS [2]. In addition, the result of investigating in terms of the resolving time for OSS faults reported within one year after the release of three OSS is shown in a previous research [3], this research has shown that the time to resolve faults has varied greatly according to several OSS's.

Although there are several previous researches [4–6]. In the project evaluation for the predicting development effort in open source project, it is difficult to apply EVM directly because of the characteristics of open source project.

In this paper, we consider an appropriateness of EVM for open source projects. Then, we focus on the OSS-oriented EVM and a bullseye chart from the results of numerical examples. We also discuss the applicability of the proposed method by applying it to actual open source project data.

2   EVM Overview

In this paper, we use an earned value management (EVM) for the OSS development. The EVM is one of the project management techniques in order to measure the project performance and progress. The EVM has been developed for the success of the US national projects.

The EVM can observe the current schedule condition and cost in the project. The EVM basically measures the project performance and progress by using three indexes: Planned Value (PV), Earned Value (EV), and Actual Cost (AC) as shown Fig. 1. Also, we can quantitatively grasp the current status of the project by comparing three indexes such as Table 1. In the previous research [6], we could not derive the PV value and the related value by applying the existing EVM to the open source project.

3   OSS-oriented EVM

In order to apply EVM in open source projects, we consider to derive AC, EV, PV and BAC. The open source projects involve an indefinite number of people from all over the world. Then, the progress of the project becomes the irregular status. Therefore, we consider irregularities for the effort in open source projects. In this paper, we discuss the irregularities of the effort in open source projects by using the stochastic model of Wiener process.

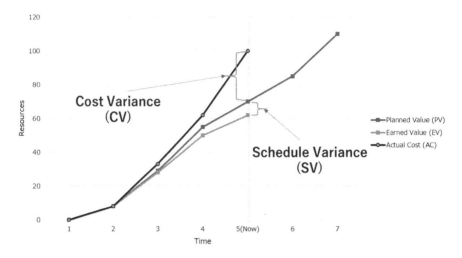

Fig. 1. The example of EVM.

Table 1. Several examples of the indexes used in EVM.

EVM Elements	Explanation
Planned Value (PV)	a supposed work value at any given point in the project schedule
Earned Value (EV)	a value of work progress at a given point in time
Actual Cost (AC)	AC is an amount of resources that have been expended to date
Budget at Completion (BAC)	represents the total PV for the project
Cost Variance (CV)	shows whether a project is under or over budget. CV=EV-AC
Cost Performance Index (CPI)	evaluates how efficiently the project is using its resources. CPI=EV/AC
Schedure Variance (SV)	determines whether a project is ahead of or behind schedule. SV=EV-PV
Schedule Performance Index (SPI)	evaluates how efficiently the project team is using its time. SPI=EV/PV
Estimate at Completion (EAC)	shows the final cost of the project in case of continuing current performance trend. EAC=BAC/CPI
Estimate to Complete (ETC)	shows what the remaining work will cost. ETC=(BAC-EV)/CPI

3.1   Effort Prediction Model for Open Source Projects

Considering the characteristic of the operation phase of OSS projects, the time-dependent expenditure phenomenon of maintenance effort keeps an irregular state in the operation phase, because there is variability among the levels of developers' skill. Then, the time-dependent effort expenditure phenomenon of maintenance phase becomes unstable.

The operation phases of many OSS projects are influenced from the external factors by triggers such as the difference of skill, and the time lag of development and maintenance activities. Considering the above points, we apply the stochastic differential equation modeling to the managing of the OSS project. Then, let $\Omega(t)$ be the cumulative maintenance effort, such as finding software faults and improving functionality up to operational time t ($t \geq 0$) in the OSS project. Suppose that $\Omega(t)$ takes on continuous real values. Since the estimated maintenance effort are observed during the operational phase of the OSS project, $\Omega(t)$ gradually increases as the operational procedures go on. Based on software reliability growth modeling approach [7,8], the following linear differential equation in terms of the maintenance effort can be formulated as:

$$\frac{d\Omega(t)}{dt} = \beta(t)\{\alpha - \Omega(t)\},\tag{1}$$

where $\beta(t)$ is the increase rate of maintenance effort at operational time t and a non-negative function, and α means the estimated maintenance effort expenditures required until the end of operation.

Therefore, we extend Eq. (1) to the following stochastic differential equation with Brownian motion [9]:

$$\frac{d\Omega(t)}{dt} = \{\beta(t) + \sigma\nu(t)\}\{\alpha - \Omega(t)\},\tag{2}$$

where σ is a positive constant representing a magnitude of the irregular fluctuation, and $\nu(t)$ a standardized Gaussian white noise. By using Itô's formula [10], we can obtain the solution of Eq. (2) under the initial condition $\Omega(0) = 0$ as follows:

$$\Omega(t) = \alpha\left[1 - \exp\left\{-\int_0^t \beta(s)ds - \sigma\omega(t)\right\}\right],\tag{3}$$

where $\omega(t)$ is the Wiener process which is formally defined as an integration of the white noise $\nu(t)$ with respect to time t. Moreover, we define the increase rate of maintenance effort in case of $\beta(t)$ defined as [11]:

$$\int_0^t \beta(s)ds \doteq \frac{\frac{dF_*(t)}{dt}}{\alpha - F_*(t)}.\tag{4}$$

In this paper, we assume the following equations based on software reliability models $F_*(t)$ as the cumulative maintenance effort expenditures function of the proposed model:

$$F_i(t) \equiv \frac{\alpha\{1 - \exp(-\beta t)\}}{1 + c \cdot \exp(-\beta t)},\tag{5}$$

where $\Omega_i(t)$ means the cumulative maintenance effort expenditures for the inflection S-shaped software reliability growth model with $F_i(t)$. The inflection S-shaped type model is one of the famous software reliability growth models.

Therefore, the cumulative maintenance effort, Ω_i up to time t are obtained as follow:

$$\Omega_i(t) = \alpha \left[1 - \frac{1+c}{1+c \cdot \exp(-\beta t)} \exp\{-\beta t - \sigma \omega(t)\} \right]. \tag{6}$$

In this model, we assume that the parameter σ depends on several noises by external factors from several triggers in open source projects. Then, the expected cumulative maintenance effort expenditures spent up to time t are respectively obtained as follows:

$$E[\Omega_i(t)] = \alpha \left[1 - \frac{1+c}{1+c \cdot \exp(-\beta t)} \exp\left\{-\beta t + \frac{\sigma^2}{2}t\right\} \right]. \tag{7}$$

3.2   Derivation of OSS-oriented EVM

In OSS-oriented EVM, the period of data used for Planned Value (PV) and Actual Cost (AC) have the different values. Both PV and AC use the data obtained from the bug tracking system and required by the fault reporters and the fault correctors. In the open source projects, we assume that the project period is from OSS release to EOL. Then, we can use the maintenance effort data until OSS release and equations (6)–(7) in order to derive PV. In particular, the parameter α in Eqs. (6)–(7) mean as the estimated maintenance effort at the time OSS is released. Therefore, the parameter α can be rephrased as Budget at Completion (BAC) in OSS-oriented EVM. AC uses the maintenance effort data obtained from the bug tracking system, including after the OSS release required by the fault reporter and the fault corrector. Therefore, the start time of the data used to derive PV and AC is the same.

Earned Value (EV) is the cumulative maintenance effort viewed on the same scale as the project budget (BAC). Therefore, if the OSS development effort increases but the fault is not resolved, the value of EV becomes small and it is regarded as an inefficient OSS project. In the derivation of EV value, the number of potential faults predicted from the fault data reported up to the time of OSS release is used. We use Eqs. (6)–(7) to predict the number of potential faults. We derive the "fault resolving cost", i.e., the value obtained by dividing the number of potential faults from the BAC, as follows:

$$\gamma = \frac{BAC}{p}. \tag{8}$$

Then, γ means the fault resolving cost, and p means the potential faults at OSS release. We can derive the EV in cases of $F_i(t)$ by using the fault resolving cost γ and the cumulative number of resolved faults up to the operating time t.

$$EV_i(t) = \gamma \cdot \alpha_f \left[1 - \frac{1+c_f}{1+c_f \cdot \exp(-\beta_f t)} \exp\{-\beta_f t - \sigma_f \omega(t)\} \right]. \tag{9}$$

Then, α_f, β_f, c_f, and σ_f are parameters used to predict the cumulative number of resolved faults at time t. Therefore, the expected EV required for OSS maintenance until the end of operation time t are respectively obtained as follows:

$$\mathrm{E}\left[EV_i\left(t\right)\right] = \gamma \cdot \alpha_f \left[1 - \frac{1 + c_f}{1 + c_f \cdot \exp\left(-\beta_f t\right)} \exp\left\{-\beta_f t + \frac{\sigma_f^2}{2}t\right\}\right]. \quad (10)$$

Then, the resolved cumulative number of faults is counted when the fault status is "Closed" in the bug tracking system.

In this paper, OSS-oriented EVM uses the dataset obtained from bug tracking system to derive PV, AC, and EV. We assume the following terms in the Table 2 as the OSS-oriented EVM in the open source project considering the derivation of these EVM indexes.

Table 2. Explanation for OSS-oriented EVM.

OSS-oriented EVM elements	Explanatory
Planned Value (PV)	Cumulative maintenance effort as planned value up to operational time t considering the fault reporter and fault corrector
Earned Value (EV)	Cumulative maintenance effort up to operational time t viewed on the same scale as BAC
Actual Cost (AC)	Cumulative maintenance effort up to operational time t considering the fault reporter and fault corrector
Budget at Completion (BAC)	Total budget in the end point as the specified goal of OSS project
Cost Variance (CV)	$\mathrm{E}[CV_e(t)]$ and $\mathrm{E}[CV_s(t)]$ obtained from EV-AC
Cost Performance Index (CPI)	$\mathrm{E}[CPI_e(t)]$ and $\mathrm{E}[CPI_s(t)]$ obtained from EV/AC
Schedure Variance (SV)	SV obtained from EV-PV (Explanation of formula omitted in this chapter)
Schedule Performance Index (SPI)	SPI obtained from EV/PV (Explanation of formula omitted in this chapter)
Estimate at Completion (EAC)	$\mathrm{E}[EAC_e(t)]$ and $\mathrm{E}[EAC_s(t)]$ obtained from BAC/CPI
Estimate to Complete (ETC)	$\mathrm{E}[ETC_e(t)]$ and $\mathrm{E}[ETC_s(t)]$ obtained from (BAC-EV)/CPI

4   Bullseye Chart

The bullseye chart is a variance diagram of the Schedule Performance Index (SPI) and Cost Performance Index (CPI) calculated based on the basic indexes of EVM collected periodically. In this paper, we use the results of SPI and CPI derived by OSS-oriented EVM in the bullseye chart. The approach on the bullseye chart is as follows:

– Quadrant 1: Both progress and cost progressing within the planned progress and cost
– Quadrant 2: Progress is slow, but cost overruns are not occurring
– Quadrant 3: Slow progress, excessive costs
– Quadrant 4: Progress is on schedule. but cost overruns are occurring

5   Numerical Examples

5.1   Used Data Set

In this paper, we use the data set of open source project to derive the bullseye chart by using OSS-oriented EVM. For applying the proposed model to actual project data set, we use the data of LibreOffice [12] obtained from Bugzilla. The LibreOffice is OSS as an office software. In particular, the effort and fault data were obtained from Bugzilla are version 7. For estimating PV and AC, in this paper, the cumulative number of reported faults are 267 and 3073, respectively. In particular, we use the project data for about 37 weeks, before LibreOffice was released to predict PV. For prediction AC, we also use project data for about 112 weeks after LibreOffice released. Also, each data is weekly unit data.

5.2   Numerical Examples for OSS-oriented EVM

Table 3 shows the results of parameter estimation of maintenance effort, and AIC (Akaike's Information Criterion) for reference. Also, the parameter α in the PV data can be rephrased as BAC.

Table 3. Parameter estimates of maintenance effort in case of LibreOffice.

		Planned value	Actual cost
parameter	α	1.499×10^7	1.575×10^7
	β	8.318×10^{-2}	5.426×10^{-2}
	c	3.727×10^2	9.877×10^1
	σ	1.695×10^{-4}	5.488×10^{-3}
AIC		723.164	2892.647

In addition, we used Eqs. (6)–(7) to derive parameters for the cumulative number of faults. Table 4 shows the results of parameter estimation of number of fault, and AIC for reference. Also, the parameter α in the PV data can be rephrased as potential faults at OSS release. In other words, from Eq. (8), we can calculate the fault resolving cost $\gamma \fallingdotseq 14335$ (man · days).

Table 4. Parameter estimates of number of fault in case of LibreOffice.

		Estimated number of potential faults at OSS release	Estimated number of potential faults after OSS release
parameter	α	1.046×10^3	2.305×10^4
	β	8.020×10^{-2}	3.822×10^{-2}
	c	5.304×10^1	4.544×10^2
	σ	3.122×10^{-3}	7.929×10^{-4}
AIC		204.0702	987.783

Figures 2 and 3 show the estimated cumulative maintenance effort as PV and AC at operation time t in case of $\Omega_e(t)$ and $\Omega_s(t)$. In Figs. 2, the training data and prediction results for 37 weeks are close, and the sample path is very small. Therefore, we can assume that the irregularity peculiar to the open source project was small and the OSS development was stable before the project started. On the other hand, in Figs. 3, we can see that there is some noise in the prediction results.

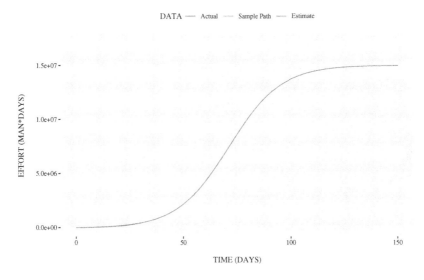

Fig. 2. Cumulative maintenance effort as PV of LibreOffice project by using Eqs. (6) and (7).

For deriving EV value, we need to estimate the "fault resolving cost" and the number of faults shown in Eqs. (8)–(10). Figures 4 shows the estimated cumulative number of potential fault as of starting project. Also, Fig. 5 shows the estimated cumulative number of resolved fault. There is a large difference between the estimated cumulative number of faults estimated at the time of

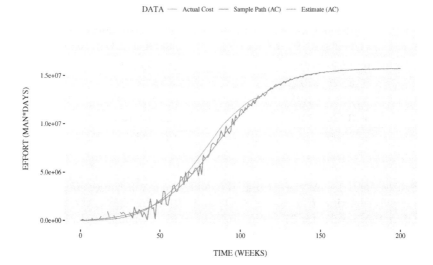

Fig. 3. Cumulative maintenance effort as AC of LibreOffice project by using Eqs. (6) and (7).

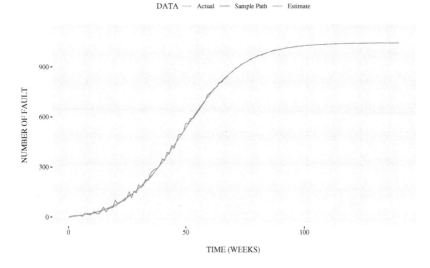

Fig. 4. The estimated cumulative number of potential fault of LibreOffice project by using Eqs. (6) and (7).

LibreOffice release and the estimated number of resolved faults at 112 weeks after the release.

Figure 6 shows the result of deriving EV value by using Eqs. (9) and (10). From Eq. (10), in case of more resolved fault than the number of potential faults

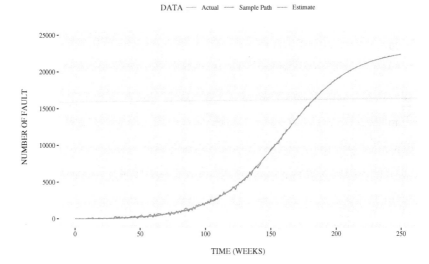

Fig. 5. The estimated cumulative number of fault of LibreOffice project by using Eqs. (6) and (7).

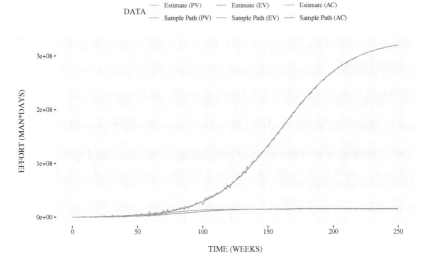

Fig. 6. The estimated AC, PV, EV in LibreOffice project.

at OSS release, the EV value will be larger than BAC. Therefore, the same result was obtained in the LibreOffice project used this time.

We used the EVM indexes derived in Fig. 6 to draw the Fig. 7 bullseye chart. The bullseye chart showed that the chart remained in the first quadrant for all periods, initially approaching the origin. However, the moving away from the

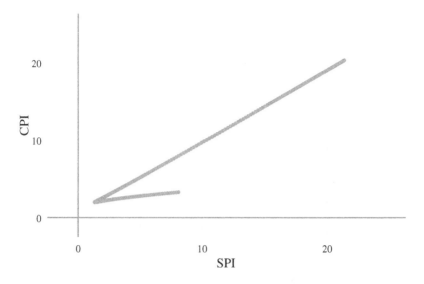

Fig. 7. The bullseye chart in LibreOffice project.

origin as the values of both SPI and CPI increased. This means that the value of EV became very large. Therefore, the bullseye chart shows that the LibreOffice project is stable in terms of schedule and cost.

6   Conclusion

In this paper, we have derived a bullseye chart to quantitatively evaluate the progress of the open source project. In this paper, we have been able to draw a bullseye chart by deriving the information necessary to calculate the EVM indexes.

In the future, we will use multiple model equations and project data to examine the appropriate model equations, and conduct a detailed evaluation of open source projects.

Acknowledgments. This work was supported in part by the JSPS KAKENHI Grant No. 20K11799 in Japan.

References

1. Raymond, S.E.: The Cathedral and the Bazzar: Musings on Linux and Open Source by an Accidental Revolutionary. O'Reilly and Associates, Sebastopol (1999)
2. Sone, H., Tamura, Y., Yamada, S.: Prediction of fault fix time transition in large-scale open source project data. Data **4**(3), 1–12 (2019)
3. H, Sone., Y, Tamura., S, Yamada.: Comparison of stabilities for open source project. In: Proceedings of the 2021 IEEE International Conference on Industrial Engineering and Engineering Management, Singapore, CD-ROM (Reliability and Maintenance Engineering 2, Virtual mode) (2021)

4. Robles, G., Gonzälez-Barahona, M.J., Cervigön, C., Capiluppi., A., Izquierdo-Cortäzar, D.: Estimating development effort in Free/OSS projects by mining software repositories: a case study of OpenStack. In: Proceedings of the 11th Working Conference on Mining Software Repositories, pp. 222–231. India (2014)
5. Mishra, R., Sureka, A.: Mining peer code review system for computing effort and contribution metrics for patch reviewers. In: Proceedings of the 2014 IEEE 4th Workshop on Mining Unstructured Data, pp. 11–15. Canada (2014)
6. Sone, H., Tamura, Y., Yamada, S.: Statistical maintenance time estimation based on stochastic differential equation models in OSS development project, Comput. Rev. J. **5**, 126–140 (2019)
7. Yamada, S.: Software Reliability Modeling: Fundamentals and Applications. Springer, Tokyo (2014). https://doi.org/10.1007/978-4-431-54565-1
8. Lyu, M.R.: Handbook of Software Reliability Engineering. IEEE Computer Society Press. Los Alamitos (1996)
9. Wong, E.: Stochastic Processes in Information and Systems. McGraw-Hill, New York (1971)
10. Arnold, L.: Stochastic Differential Equations-Theory and Applications. Wiley, New York (1971)
11. Yamada, S., Kimura, M., Tanaka, H., Osaki, S.: Software reliability measurement and assessment with stochastic differential equations. IEICE Trans. Fundamentals **E77-A**(1), 109–116 (1994)
12. LibreOffice. https://ja.libreoffice.org/. Accessed 9 Jan 2022

Visualization and Reliability Analysis for Edge Computing Open Source Software

Yoshinobu Tamura[1]([⊠]), Adarsh Anand[2], and Shigeru Yamada[3]

[1] Yamaguchi University, Yamaguchi, Japan
tamuray@yamaguchi-u.ac.jp
[2] University of Delhi, Delhi, India
[3] Tottori University, Tottori, Japan
yamada@tottori-u.ac.jp
http://www.tam.eee.yamaguchi-u.ac.jp/

Abstract. At present, there are various software services by using the cloud computing. In particular, the edge computing expanded from the cloud computing is embedded in various situation because of the avoidance of whole system down. Also, the technologies of cloud services based on edge computing and 5G are very important to keep our convenient lifestyles. The appropriate control of the software faults detected in OSS project will directly relate to the quality, reliability, and cost. In particular, the fault correction time is very important factor in order to keep the edge computing service. We focus on the visualization of the estimation results of fault correction time for the assessment of operation performance of edge computing open source software. Then, we discuss the estimation method of fault correction time based on the characteristics of several components by using the deep leaning. We use the deep learning in order to estimate the fault correction time. In particular, we discuss the characteristics of fault trend by using the three dimensional graphs as the visualization of fault big data. Thereby, we can show the recognizability of the proposed method for fault big scale data based on deep learning from the standpoint of edge open source software. In particular, this paper analyzes the fault correction time from the standpoint of the characteristics in the fault content for the actual data sets. Then, we make a visualization based on three dimensional graph by using the estimation method based on deep learning. Moreover, we discuss the estimation results obtained from the three dimensional graphs. Furthermore, we show several numerical examples based on the proposed estimation method by using the actual fault big data. We analyze the fault big data in terms of the fault correction time in OSS component of edge computing in cloud computing in OpenStack. We can obtain the fault correction times from several characteristics of the factor in the bug tracking system. In this paper, we discuss two kinds of characteristics from the bug tracking system.

Keywords: Fault big data · Fault correction time · Deep learning · Software reliability · Open source software

© The Author(s), under exclusive license to Springer Nature Switzerland AG 2022
S. Yamamoto and H. Mori (Eds.): HCII 2022, LNCS 13305, pp. 410–420, 2022.
https://doi.org/10.1007/978-3-031-06424-1_30

1   Introduction

In the past, several researchers have discussed open source software (OSS) reliability assessment methods [1]. In the method of traditional reliability assessment, software reliability growth models have been applied to various software projects as a reality [2–5]. Moreover, our research group has discussed the method of OSS reliability assessment [1]. However, plausible researches focused on the reliability assessment based on deep learning for OSS fault big data have not been proposed. Recently, there are many software services by using the cloud computing. Especially, the edge computing developed from the cloud one is used in various situation because of the avoidance of whole system down. Also, the technologies of cloud services based on edge computing and 5G are very important to keep our convenient lifestyles. The proper control of the software faults detected in OSS project will directly relate to the quality, reliability, and cost. In particular, a fault correction time is very important factor in order to maintain the edge computing service. Many users of edge computing will fully satisfy, if we can estimate the fault correction time in the future. The edge service time becomes large when the fault correction time becomes small. Therefore, it is very important to manage the operation time of edge service by estimating the fault correction time.

This paper discusses the software fault correction time in OSS component under the edge computing service. In particular, this paper analyzes the fault correction time based on fault severity level for the actual data sets. Then, we make a visualization based on three dimensional graphing by using the estimation method based on deep learning. Then, we discuss the estimation results obtained from the three dimensional graph based on two kinds of fault severity level. Furthermore, we show several numerical examples based on the proposed estimation method by using the actual fault big data.

2   Estimation of Correction Time of OSS Faults Based on Deep Learning

There are several approaches for software reliability assessment by using the machine learning [6,7]. Traditionally, the comparison researches based on the software reliability growth models and the method of machine learning have been proposed in the past. Especially, the past research papers based on the machine learning have been used only the fault data. On the other hand, we use several different data types depended on software reliability in the proposed method. The unique characteristic of our research is to use 12 kinds various data for the input data.

Several researchers have proposed deep learning algorithms. As the examples, the application method based on deep learning for the min-cut theorem are shown [8]. Also, the deep learning is used for the automatic recognition in terms of the speech recognition [9,10]. Moreover, many deep learning algorithms have been proposed in terms of the image recognition [11–13]. In particular, the optimized algorithms based on deep learning for each research area have been developed by many researchers. As above mentioned several research papers based on deep learning, many methods based on deep learning have been used for many research areas. Then, we focus on the deep learning approach for the OSS reliability area. We will be able to apply the deep learning as the discrete time model considering the correction time of software faults.

In this paper, we use the deep neural network to learn the fault big data on bug tracking systems of open source projects. We apply the following amount of information to estimate the parameters of pre-training units. Then, the objective variable is given as the correction time of software faults.

We define the for each item recorded on the bug tracking system as follows:

Opened: D^o
Changed: D^c
Product: N^p
Component: N^c
Version: N^v
Reporter: N^r
Assignee: N^a
Severity: N^l
Status: N^s
Resolution: N^r
Hardware: N^h
OS: N^o
Summary: S

We convert above all items from the characteristic data to the numerical values by using the frequency encoding. In particular, we use the correction time of software faults. The correction time of software faults will be useful to measure the property of software stability. Then, we define the instantaneous correction time of software faults as follows:

$$I_k = D_k^c - D_k^o. \tag{1}$$

where I_k is the k-th instantaneous correction time of software faults. Also, D_k^c is the k-th changed date of OSS fault. Similarly, D_k^o is the k-th opened date of OSS fault. We define I_k as the explanatory variable of deep learning, i.e., the output value for the learning data.

In particular, we focus on the fault occurrence phenomenon in terms of the vulnerability and reliability. Then, the "unspecified" means the unspecified fault, i.e., the unknown origin. the fault named as "unspecified" of the fault factor is difficult to remove from the source code. Therefore, "unspecified" fault depends on the reliability and vulnerability. Considering the "unspecified" fault, we define as follows:

$$I_k^{and} \Leftarrow N_k^{uh} \cap N_k^{ul} \cap N_k^{uo}, \tag{2}$$

$$\text{subject to} \begin{cases} N_k^{uh} \subseteq N_k^{h}, \\ N_k^{ul} \subseteq N_k^{l}, \\ N_k^{uo} \subseteq N_k^{o} \end{cases}$$

N_k^{uh} means k-th "unspecified" fault in terms of Hardware. Also, N_k^{ul} means k-th "unspecified" fault in terms of Severity. Similarly, N_k^{uo} means k-th "unspecified" fault in terms of OS. Therefore, I_k^{and} is the k-th instantaneous correction time of software faults under the conditions of Eq. (2).

Similarly, we consider that the reverse condition in Eq. (2). Then, we define as follows:

$$I_k^{or} \Leftarrow N_k^{uh} \cup N_k^{ul} \cup N_k^{uo}, \tag{3}$$

$$\text{subject to} \begin{cases} N_k^{uh} \subseteq N_k^{h}, \\ N_k^{ul} \subseteq N_k^{l}, \\ N_k^{uo} \subseteq N_k^{o} \end{cases}$$

Similarly, N_k^{uh} means k-th "unspecified" fault in terms of Hardware. Also, N_k^{ul} means k-th "unspecified" fault in terms of Severity. Similarly, N_k^{uo} means k-th "unspecified" fault in terms of OS. Therefore, I_k^{or} is the k-th instantaneous correction time of software faults under the conditions of Eq.(3).

The procedure of our deep learning is shown in Fig. 1.

1. The correction time of software faults as the objective variable I_k^{and} are learned in case of $N_k^{uh} \cap N_k^{ul} \cap N_k^{uo}$.
2. The correction time of software faults as the objective variable I_k^{or} are learned in case of $N_k^{uh} \cup N_k^{ul} \cup N_k^{uo}$.
3. Several reliability assessment measures are illustrated after completion of the learning phase.

3   Numerical Examples

We analyze the large-scale fault data in terms of the fault correction time for the edge computing software included in cloud software such as OpenStack [14].

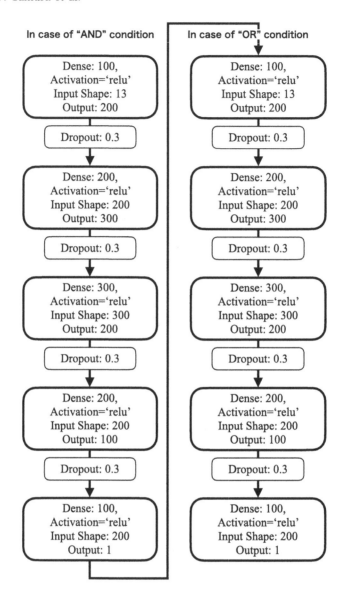

Fig. 1. The learning procedures in deep learning.

We can obtain the correction time of software faults for the objective variable I_k^{and} in case of $N_k^{uh} \cap N_k^{ul} \cap N_k^{uo}$ in the bug tracking system, and the correction time of software faults for the objective variable I_k^{or} in case of $N_k^{uh} \cup N_k^{ul} \cup N_k^{uo}$.

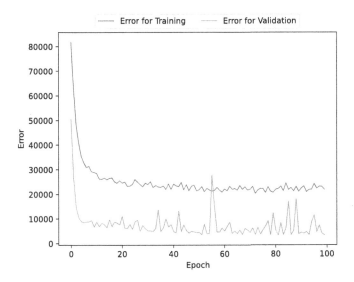

Fig. 2. The estimated error between validation and training in case of 10% testing data and I_k^{and}.

In this paper, we discuss two kinds of fault contents such as I_k^{and} and I_k^{or} in terms of "unspecified".

Figure 2 shows the estimated error between validation and training in case of 10% testing data of I_k^{and}. Also, Fig. 3 is the estimated instantaneous correction time of software faults in case of 10% testing data of I_k^{and}. Moreover, Fig. 4 shows the estimated comparison results between estimate and testing for the cumulative correction time of software failure in case of 10% testing data of I_k^{and}. Furthermore, Fig. 5 is the cumulative correction time of software faults in case of 10% testing data of I_k^{and}.

Similarly, we show from the estimated error between validation and training in case of 10% testing data of I_k^{or} to the cumulative correction time of software faults in case of 10% testing data of I_k^{or} in Figs. 6–9, respectively.

Above mentioned results, we have found that the I_k^{and} fits better than I_k^{and} in case of 10% testing data. We can be considered a cause that the variation in instantaneous correction time of software faults become large from Figs. 3 and 7.

Anyway, I_k^{and} is larger than I_k^{or} in terms of the level of unspecified. Therefore, we consider that the proposed model is useful to assess the reliability of edge OSS, because our method can estimate I_k^{and} accurately.

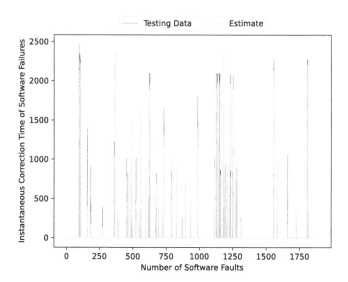

Fig. 3. The estimated instantaneous correction time of software faults in case of 10% testing data and I_k^{and}.

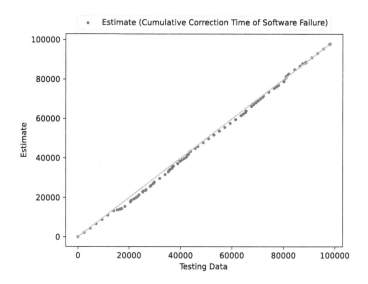

Fig. 4. The estimated comparison results between estimate and testing for the cumulative correction time of software failure in case of 10% testing data and I_k^{and}.

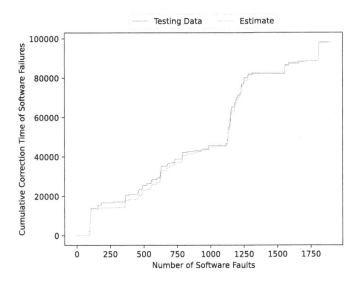

Fig. 5. The cumulative correction time of software faults in case of 10% testing data and I_k^{and}.

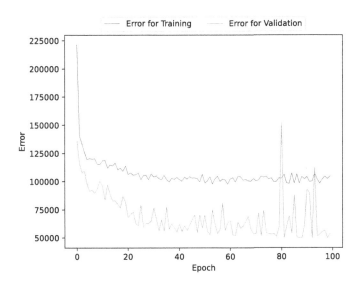

Fig. 6. The estimated error between validation and training in case of 10% testing data and I_k^{or}.

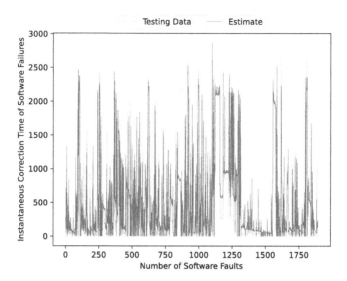

Fig. 7. The estimated instantaneous correction time of software faults in case of 10% testing data and I_k^{or}.

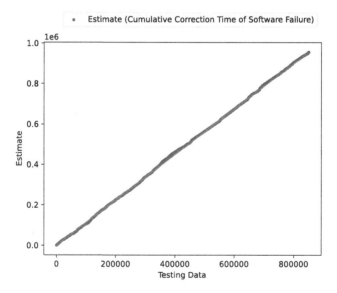

Fig. 8. The estimated comparison results between estimate and testing for the cumulative correction time of software failure in case of 10% testing data and I_k^{or}.

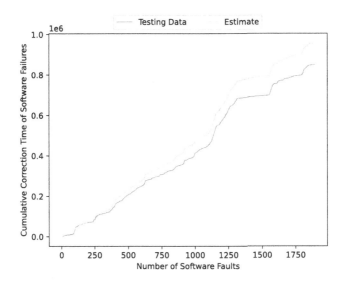

Fig. 9. The cumulative correction time of software faults in case of 10% testing data and I_k^{or}.

4 Concluding Remarks

In the operation of edge service on the cloud computing, several edge OSS components are embedded in the cloud OSS. In the bug tracking system of OSS used under the edge computing, there are large-scale software fault data. The edge operation managers can assess the reliability of edge OSS, if we can comprehend the trend of OSS fault correction time. Then, we have discussed the estimation method of fault correction time in two cases of the identified fault and the non-identified one.

In this paper, we have proposed the estimation method of fault correction time in the cases of I_k^{and} and I_k^{or}. It will be useful to analysis the OSS reliability under the environment of edge computing service, if the edge operation managers can estimate the fault correction time. Also, the reliability assessment method based on the deep learning considering the cases of I_k^{and} and I_k^{or} has been discussed in this paper. In particular, the proposed method can understand the reliability trend based on the fault correction time from the standpoint of the identified fault.

Acknowledgments. This work was supported in part by the JSPS KAKENHI Grant No. 20K11799 in Japan.

References

1. Yamada, S., Tamura, Y.: OSS Reliability Measurement and Assessment. SSRE, Springer, Cham (2016). https://doi.org/10.1007/978-3-319-31818-9
2. Lyu, M.R. (ed.): Handbook of Software Reliability Engineering. IEEE Computer Society Press, Los Alamitos (1996)
3. Yamada, S.: Software Reliability Modeling: Fundamentals and Applications. Springer, Tokyo/Heidelberg (2014)
4. Kapur, P.K., Pham, H., Gupta, A., Jha, P.C.: Software Reliability Assessment with OR Applications. Springer, London (2011)
5. Kingma, D.P., Rezende, D.J., Mohamed, S., Welling, M.: Semi-supervised learning with deep generative models. In: Proceedings of the 27th International Conference on Neural Information Processing Systems, pp. 1–9 (2014)
6. Karunanithi, N., Whitley, D., Malaiya, Y.K.: Using neural networks in reliability prediction. IEEE Softw. Mag. 9(4), 53–59 (1992)
7. Dohi, T., Nishio, Y., Osaki, S.: Optimal software release scheduling based on artificial neural networks. Ann. Softw. Eng. 8(1), 167–185 (1999)
8. Blum, A., Lafferty, J., Rwebangira, M.R., Reddy, R.: Semi-supervised learning using randomized mincuts. In: Proceedings of the International Conference on Machine Learning, pp. 1–8 (2004)
9. George, E.D., Dong, Y., Li, D., Alex, A.: Context-dependent pre-trained deep neural networks for large-vocabulary speech recognition. IEEE Trans. Audio Speech Lang. Process. 20(1), 30–42 (2012)
10. Vincent, P., Larochelle, H., Lajoie, I., Bengio, Y., Manzagol, P.A.: Stacked denoising autoencoders: learning useful representations in a deep network with a local denoising criterion. J. Mach. Learn. Res. 11(2), 3371–3408 (2010)
11. Martinez, H.P., Bengio, Y., Yannakakis, G.N.: Learning deep physiological models of affect. IEEE Comput. Intell. Mag. 8(2), 20–33 (2013)
12. Hutchinson, B., Deng, L., Yu, D.: Tensor deep stacking networks. IEEE Trans. Pattern Anal. Mach. Intell. 35(8), 1944–1957 (2013)
13. Kingma, D.P., Ba, J.L.: Adam: a method for stochastic optimizations. In: Proceedings of the International Conference on Learning Representations, pp. 1–15 (2015)
14. The OpenStack project, build the future of open Infrastructure. https://www.openstack.org/

Visualization of Judicial Precedents on Power Harassment Issues Using Relationship Chart

Soichiro Tanaka[1]([⊠]), Toru Kano[2], and Takako Akakura[2]

[1] Department of Information and Computer Technology, Graduate School of Engineering, Tokyo University of Science, 6-3-1 Niijuku, Katsushika-ku, Tokyo 125-8585, Japan
4618048@ed.tus.ac.jp
[2] Department of Information and Computer Technology, Faculty of Engineering, Tokyo University of Science, 6-3-1 Niijuku, Katsushika-ku, Tokyo 125-8585, Japan
{kano,akakura}@rs.tus.ac.jp

Abstract. Power harassment has become a problem in Japan recently. However, it has been found that reading judicial precedents is one of the ways to prevent it. In this paper, in order to promote the reading of judicial precedents, we visualized the relationships between people in judicial precedents, which are not easy for non-experts to read. We first extracted the words from the text of judicial precedents that represent people using morphological analysis. Next, we then extracted information about the relationship between the persons using dependency analysis. We then determined the direction of the extracted relationship. Finally, based on the automatically extracted relations between the persons, we visualized the structure of the case as relationship charts and fishbone diagrams. To confirm the usefulness of the proposed diagrams in reading judicial precedents, we conducted an evaluation experiment using both judicial precedents and diagrams on six Tokyo University of Science students. The results suggest that diagrams make it easier to read judicial precedents.

Keywords: Learning support system · Judicial precedents · Natural language processing · Power harassment

1 Introduction

1.1 Research Background

Increase in Power Harassment. In Japan, power harassment has become a problem in recent years. According to a national survey, the number of consultations with the Labor Bureau about bullying and harassment has been on the rise, and exceeded 80,000 in 2019 (Fig. 1).

S. Yamamoto and H. Mori (Eds.): HCII 2022, LNCS 13305, pp. 421–434, 2022.
https://doi.org/10.1007/978-3-031-06424-1_31

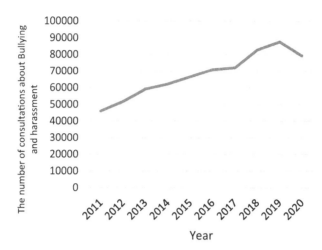

Fig. 1. Transition of the number of bullying and harassment consultations.

Efforts to Address Power Harassment. Various efforts have been made to prevent power harassment in recent years. In May 2019, mandatory measures against power harassment were enacted by the government and in December of the same year, guidelines for action on power harassment in the workplace were issued [1]. However, it is difficult for individuals to distinguish the line between what constitutes power harassment and what does not. There are also challenges in preventing and identifying power harassment. Watanabe et al. [2] stated that knowledge of judicial precedents is effective in preventing power harassment. However, judicial precedents are somewhat hard to read due to the presence of certain factors, such as difficult words and complicated relationships. Therefore, for those who are not accustomed to reading judicial precedents on a regular basis, it is difficult to gain knowledge from reading.

1.2 Related Research

Goto et al. [3] thought that when viewers search for a broadcast program, they can check its introduction. However, they may not be able to read the text because it is difficult to do so in such a short time. Therefore, Goto et al. generated relationship charts using the program introduction in order to let people instantly grasp its contents. By using machine learning, persons and relations were extracted from a total of 79 sentences, which automatically generated relationship charts (Fig. 2).

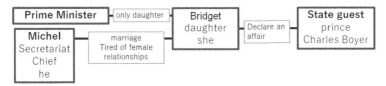

Fig. 2. Relationship charts result [3].

However, the generated relationship charts were undirected graphs. It was also difficult to understand and distinguish the relationships. Therefore, we think that there is room for improvement in understanding the sentences, such as making the relationship chart a directed graph.

1.3 Purpose of the Research

This study aims to assist students who are about to enter the workforce and wish to deepen their knowledge of power harassment by reading and understanding case law. We focused on "complicated relationships" and proposed a method to visualize such relationships between people using a person correlation diagram and a fishbone diagram to support reading comprehension.

2 Visualization Procedure

First, we collected PDF files of the judicial precedents whose texts are to be extracted. After extracting the text data, they were converted to json files. Next, we performed morphological analysis and extracted the persons from the analysis results. Then, we performed a dependency analysis and extracted the part of the sentence that corresponds to the relation based on the analysis and extraction results of the person. We then determined the direction of the relationship between the extracted people and turned it into a csv file, which we used to generate relationship charts and fishbone diagrams.

2.1 Extraction of People Expression

Table 1. Rules of people expression on judicial precedents.

Rule	Example
defendant	被告
plaintiff	原告
(plaintiff or defendant) + noun	被告ら，被告弁護人
noun + alphanumeric	上司P4，株式会社N
alphanumeric + noun	I教諭
alphanumeric	M, O

In ordinary writing, such as in newspapers and novels, personal names like "Taro" and "Hanako" or pronouns such as "he" and "she" are often used. However, personal names are rarely used in judicial precedents. Instead, in addition to "defendant" and "plaintiff," they use forms of "noun + alphanumeric" and "alphanumeric + noun," as shown in Table 1. Hence, we devised a method that can extract a person's expressions based on rules by utilizing the characteristics of judicial precedents. We then performed a morphological analysis on the sentences of the judicial precedents. Based on the word segmentation and parts of speech obtained from the analysis results, we determined whether the sentence is a person or not using the rules set in Table 1.

Morphological Analysis. A morpheme is the smallest unit of meaningful expression, such as a word or a symbol. Morphological analysis is the process of dividing a sentence into morphemes and determining the part of speech of each morpheme. In this study, we used MeCab [4], which is a fast morphological analysis engine.

2.2   Extraction of People Relation

In this section, we described a method for extracting relational sentences between the detected person expressions. We defined a relation sentence as one that describes a relationship between two persons and fits into the format of Table 2.

Table 2. Example of relation sentences in judicial precedents.

From whom	To whom	Direction
「person は」 or 「person が」	「person に」	right
「person は」 or 「person が」	「person を」	right
「person は」 or 「person が」	「person と」	none
「person は」 or 「person が」	「person から」	left

Dependency Analysis. Dependency in natural language processing is the relation between clauses, such as subject-predicate, modifier-verb, and so on. Dependency analysis is the process of splitting the text into clauses to determine the structure of texts, and which clauses depend on other clauses. In this study, we used CaboCha [5], which is a fast-working dependency analyzer.

Parse Tree. In this study, we analyzed the sentences and converted them into a syntax tree to extract the relevant sentences. As shown in Fig. 3, CaboCha splits the sentence into clauses and classifies each clause. For example, in Fig. 3, the clauses, "解雇する(fire)" and "旨の(content of)" belong to "メールを(the mail)."

```
平成 -D
  26年 -D
     7月 -D
      30日,  - - - - - - - - - - -D
        被告は - - - - - - - - -D
原告P2に対し,  - - - - - - -D
           解雇する -D  |
               旨の -D  |
              メールを -D
              送信した.
```
EOS

Fig. 3. Example of analyze result of CaboCha.

This study follows the following method and procedures.

1. Mark phrases in the syntax tree that signify a person.
2. Detect the words "person は" or "person が" as the subject of a sentence in the parse tree and search the parse tree starting from that word.
3. When we reach a clause marked as an expression signifying a person, we consider the set of clauses on the path to be the relational sentences between the persons.
4. If, during the search, we arrive at a clause that contains a noun other than person, we do not search the clause related to that clause.
5. Extract person-related sentences from the subjects of the sentences such as "person は" or "person が," or end the extraction when all the clauses have been searched.

This procedure is repeated for all sentences in the precedent to extract character relationships from the precedent.

Defining the Direction of Relation. To make the relationship chart by directed graph, we define the direction of the extracted relation. To define the direction, we focused on the types of the person clause's auxiliary verbs. Table 2 shows how we defined the direction. Here, the order in which "from whom" and "to whom" appear in a sentence is sometimes interchanged. The direction of relationship is reversed, as shown in Table 2. Moreover, sentences that describe a person and a person who do not fit this format is not considered a relational sentence.

2.3 Creation of Graph

To make it easy to read the text and follow the flow of judicial precedents, we created the relationship chart and fishbone graph.

Relationship Chart. A relationship chart is a visualization of how people involve others using a graph like Fig. 4.

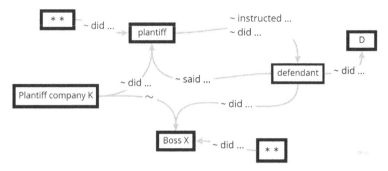

Fig. 4. Example of relationship chart.

In this study, we created relationship charts with persons as nodes and relations as edges, based on the persons that fit the rules defined in Table 1.

Fishbone Diagram. A fishbone diagram is a graph like the one in Fig. 5.

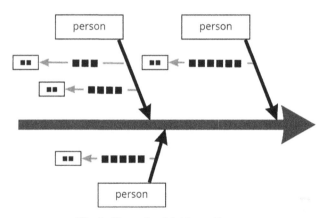

Fig. 5. Example of fishbone diagram.

It is difficult to read events chronologically in a relationship chart to determine which relationship and relation occurred first. Thus, we also created a fishbone diagram to show the time series of the relationships between the people.

3   Analysis Result and Discussion on Relation Extraction

3.1   Evaluation Method

We evaluated the accuracy of extracted people and relations. Referring to Goto et al.'s study [3], we analyzed the accuracy of the extraction by calculating the similarity between the manually created relationship chart C_H and the automatically generated relationship chart C_S. We compared the recall and precision of the nodes (people) and edges (relationships) of the correlation diagram between manual and automatic methods. We showed the node's equations in Eq. 1 and Eq. 2.

$$\text{node's recall} = \frac{\text{the number of } C_H \text{ and } C_S' \text{s mutual people expression of both node}}{\text{the number of } C_H' \text{s people expression}}$$

(1)

$$\text{node's precision} = \frac{\text{the number of } C_H \text{ and } C_S' \text{s mutual people expression of both node}}{\text{the number of } C_S' \text{s people expression}}$$

(2)

3.2 Result

We extracted seven judicial precedents about power harassment from 2015 to 2020. From each judicial precedent result, we calculated the recalls and precisions. We summarized the results in Table 3.

Table 3. Results of each judicial precedents

ID	Person (node)		Relation (edge)	
	Recall	Precision	Recall	Precision
A	0.800 (8/10)	0.889 (8/9)	0.722 (13/18)	0.722 (13/18)
B	0.412 (7/17)	1.000 (7/7)	0.625 (5/8)	0.625 (5/8)
C	0.778 (7/9)	0.700 (7/10)	0.643 (9/14)	0.600 (9/15)
D	0.600 (15/25)	0.833 (15/18)	0.652 (30/46)	0.612 (30/49)
E	0.529 (18/34)	0.529 (18/34)	0.489 (46/94)	0.511 (46/90)
F	0.875 (7/8)	0.875 (7/8)	0.778 (28/36)	0.718 (28/39)
G	0.636 (14/22)	0.824 (14/17)	0.730 (8/11)	0.400 (8/20)
Avg.	0.661	0.807	0.662	0.598

3.3 Discussion

According to the accuracy of Table 3, the lowest values for both recall and accuracy are recorded in E. One possible explanation for this is that in this precedent, many of the alphabets representing the internal evaluation and contribution of the company have been detected as persons.

3.4 Result of Relationship Charts and Fishbone Diagrams

From the results of the manual and automatic extractions, relationship charts and fishbone diagrams were created by dividing the extracted relations using the sections of the judicial precedents. Examples of the results are shown in Fig. 6 and 7.

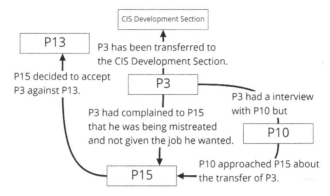

Fig. 6. Example of created relationship chart.

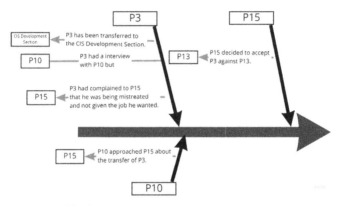

Fig. 7. Example of created fishbone diagram.

3.5 Discussion of Created Relationship Charts and Fishbone Diagrams

For judicial precedents D in Table 3, we showed an example of created relationship charts in Fig. 8, 9, and 10. These relationship charts show the arguments of the plaintiff and defendant, and the judgment of the court in a specific case.

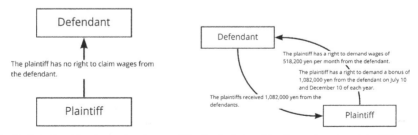

Fig. 8. Relationship charts showing defendant's argument.

Fig. 9. Relationship charts showing plaintiff's argument.

Fig. 10. Relationship charts showing judgment of the court.

These figures reflect the part of the argument that show whether the plaintiff has the right to claim wages from the defendant, which was automatically extracted from the judicial precedents. From the extracted relations, we show the claims of the plaintiff and the defendant. The final judgments of the court are represented by the relationship charts. Hence, we were able to show which side the court has favored after both sides have argued. In order to show the relationship between people as an edge, we showed the extracted sentences on the edge.

We also discussed about the creation of the fishbone diagram. The diagram of Fig. 7, we can follow the relation in order from top to bottom and left to right and understand the flow of the judicial case like below.

1. P3 had complained to P15 that he was being mistreated and not given the job he wanted.
2. After that, P10 approached P15 about the transfer of P3.
3. Thus, P15 decided to accept P3 against P13.
4. This feature is not found in the relationship charts. Therefore, the combination of relationship charts and fishbone diagrams is expected to effectively facilitate the understanding of the precedents.

4 Evaluation Experiment

4.1 Overview

In order to verify whether or not the relationship charts and the fishbone diagrams help in reading judicial precedents, we conducted an evaluation experiment. The target subjects will be university students who will be job hunting and are expected to be interested in power harassment in the workplace. Participants read a judicial precedent that consists of 22 pages. The flow of the evaluation experiment is as follows.

1. Explanation of the experiment: We explained the content of the evaluation experiment and how the judicial precedents are structured (5 min.)
2. Pre-questionnaire: We determined how much the participants are aware of power harassment, the law and judicial precedents (5 min.)

3. Experiment A: We gave a hand out of judicial precedents only to participants and participants read the first 11 pages (20 min.)
4. Experiment B: Participants read the remaining 11 pages of judicial precedents using both judicial precedents and diagrams (20 min.)
5. Post-test: We conducted a survey to see how well students understood the content of the judicial precedents (5 min.)
6. Post-questionnaire: We asked their opinions and impressions on reading comprehension using graphs (5 min.)

4.2 Result and Discuss of Evaluation Experiment

This section describes and discusses the results of the questionnaire and test conducted in the evaluation experiment. The evaluation experiment was conducted on six university students.

Pre-questionnaire Results. We showed the result of pre-questionnaire in Table 4.

Table 4. Pre-questionnaire results. 5-point scale, where 5 = positive

No.	Question	Avg.	SD
Q1	Have you ever been aware of power harassment, sexual harassment, or other forms of harassment?	3.50	1.64
Q2	Have you ever worried or felt uneasy about power harassment when you thought about finding a job?	3.50	1.22
Q3	Do you want to acquire knowledge and have the means to defend yourself in order to prevent power harassment?	4.50	0.84
Q4	Are you interested in law and court cases?	3.50	1.38
Q5	Have you read legal texts and case law texts?	2.67	1.51

Post-test Results. We tested participants to confirm how they grasped judicial precedents. The test is a six-point scale whose results are shown in Table 5.

Table 5. Post-test results. 5-point scale, where 5 = positive

Participant	A	B	C	D	E	F	Avg.	Percentage
Points	5	5	6	5	4	4	4.833	0.806

From the post-test, the percentage of correct answers was over 80%, indicating that the subjects can grasp the contents without any problem.

Table 6. Post-questionnaire results on the relationship charts. 5-point scale, where 5 = positive

No.	Question	Avg.	SD
Q1	Did the relationship charts helped you understand where people stand in the case?	4.17	0.75
Q2	Do you think that the use of relationship charts can effectively track the flow of events along the timeline?	2.67	1.51
Q3	Were relationship charts helpful as a reading comprehension aid?	4.00	0.63
Q4	Did looking at the relationship charts interfere with your reading of the cases?	4.17	0.98
Q5	When studying about power harassment, would you like to use relationship charts?	4.33	0.82
Q6	When you have a class on law, do you want them to use relationship charts?	4.00	0.89

Table 7. Post-questionnaire results on fishbone diagrams. 5-point scale, where 5 = positive

No.	Question	Avg.	SD
Q9	Did the fishbone diagrams help you understand where people stand in the case?	3.50	1.22
Q10	Do you think that the use of fishbone diagrams can effectively track the flow of events along the timeline?	4.50	0.84
Q11	Were fishbone diagrams helpful as a reading comprehension aid?	4.50	0.84
Q12	Did looking at the fishbone diagrams interfere with your reading of the cases?	4.33	1.21
Q13	When studying about power harassment, would you like to use fishbone diagrams?	4.67	0.52
Q14	When you have a law class, do you want them to use fishbone diagrams?	4.33	0.52

Post-questionnaire Results. The average of the evaluation for each question is shown in Table 6.

As a result of the questionnaire survey on fishbone diagrams, the average of the evaluation for each question is shown in Table 7.

Pre-questionnaire Discussion. As a result of the questionnaire survey from Table 4, the average answer to the question, "Do you want to acquire knowledge and have the means to defend yourself in order to prevent power harassment?" was 4.50. Hence, it can be seen that most of the subjects gave a positive opinion. Therefore, it is possible that university students are interested on the issue of power harassment.

Post-questionnaire Discussion. We compared the evaluation of the relationship charts in Table 6 and the fishbone diagrams in Table 7.

Table 8. Comparison of post-questionnaire results. 5-point scale, where 5 = positive

Question	Average points	
	Relationship charts	Fishbone diagrams
Did the graphs help you understand where people stand in the case?	4.17	3.50
Do you think that the use of graphs can effectively track the flow of events along the timeline?	2.67	4.50
Were graphs helpful as a reading comprehension aid?	4.00	4.50
Did not looking at the graphs interfere with your reading of the cases?	4.17	4.33

Based on Table 8, it can be seen that the relationship charts can be used to easier understand the position of the person in the case than by using fishbone diagrams. In addition, the fishbone diagrams show that it is easier to follow the flow of the case along the timeline than the relationship charts. The results suggest that the fishbone diagrams can be used to understand the general flow of the case, and the relationship charts can be used to understand the details and the structure of the case. In the post-questionnaire, we also asked the participants to write freely and we received comments about the content of the judicial precedents such as those provided below.

- People and companies were written with the symbol "P~", which made it difficult to understand.
- The first half of the text of the judicial precedents was difficult to read. There were many new words that were difficult to understand.

Therefore, reading judicial precedents without assistance may be difficult for university students to understand, suggesting that reading assistance may be necessary.

In the post-questionnaire result about relationship charts, there were some positive comments like the following.

- It was easy to understand who did what to whom clearly.
- It was convenient and easy to understand who did what to whom.

From the above, it can be said that the person correlation chart can support the understanding of the structure of the case of power harassment. Moreover, from this comment:

- I felt that it would help me understand if I could see at a glance who did what. Also, the arrows made it more useful.

it was suggested that the graph could be made easier to understand by using a directed graph to represent the relationship charts. However, it can be said that the shortcomings of the relationship charts are that they do not clearly show the time series as can be seen from the comments below.

- Personally, I tend to look at them in the direction of the arrows, so I sometimes mistake them for chronological order.
- The timeline is difficult to understand. The sentences marked with arrows are extracted from the text, and the meaning of some sentences is difficult to understand from the diagram alone.

From the questionnaire result on the fishbone diagrams, we saw comments that said the timeline of the incident was easy to understand. Therefore, the fishbone diagrams can be effective in supporting the reading of the time series of judicial precedents. However, there were comments saying it was difficult to compare the text of the judicial precedents with the text of the cases, and that some parts were difficult to understand. This was also the case with the relationship charts, as some students commented that some of the relationship sentences were not correct. Some examples are provided below.

- Some of the correspondence between the sentences is difficult to understand. When there is only one type of action, it is difficult to follow it in chronological order.
- It was a little difficult to compare with the text.

5   Conclusion

5.1 Summary

In recent years, the number of consultations about "bullying and harassment" has been on the rise and the issue of power harassment has been attracting attention as measures to prevent power harassment have been enacted. In addition, it is said that knowledge of judicial precedents is necessary for countermeasures against power harassment. However, it has been difficult for job hunters who are worried about power harassment in the new environment to read unfamiliar sentences and acquire knowledge of how to draw a line between power harassment acts. In this study, in order to visualize the relationships between people in judicial precedents for the purpose of supporting reading comprehension, we used morphological analysis to automatically extract people and their relationships based on rules and visualized them with diagrams to make it easier to grasp the contents of judicial precedents. For visualization, we used a relationship chart and a fishbone diagram. An evaluation experiment was conducted with university students using the diagrams, which were shown to be effective in supporting reading judicial precedents.

5.2 Future Work

In the future, we would like to expand the definition of the relevant sentence to include other sentences so that we can better visualize the situation of the judicial precedents. In addition, in the expressions of persons appearing in the judicial precedents, "the same~" was found as a way to omit the immediately preceding person expression, such as "the same company" or "the same teacher." In the future, we would like to consider the context and extract these expressions correctly.

Acknowledgments. This research was partially supported by a Grant-in-Aid for Scientific Research (B) (#20H01730; Principal Investigator: Takako Akakura) from Japan Society for the Promotion of Science (JSPS).

References

1. Nagami, M.: Power Harassment Boushi Taisaku ga Gimuka Sarete. J. Kansai Univ. Welf. Sci. **14**, 7–11 (2020). (in Japanese)
2. Watanabe, Y.: A study on the regulation of harassment in the workplace. J. Inf. Commun. Stud. **20**, 81–93 (2021). (in Japanese)
3. Goto, J., Yagi, N., Aizawa, A., Sekine, S.: Generation of correlation charts from TV programs based on Anaphora resolution. In: The 22nd Annual Conference of the Japanese Society for Artificial Intelligence, vol. 187 (2008). (in Japanese)
4. Mecab: Yet another part-of-speech and morphological analyzer. https://taku910.github.io/mecab/. Accessed 17 Nov 2021
5. Kudo, T., Matsumoto, Y.: Japanese dependency analysis using cascaded chunking. J. Inf. Process. **43**(6), 1834–1842 (2002). (in Japanese)

Information, Cognition and Learning

Automatic Generation Rules for Auxiliary Problems Based on Causal Relationships for Force in a Mechanics Learning Support System

Nonoka Aikawa[1(✉)], Kento Koike[1], Takahito Tomoto[2], Tomoya Horiguchi[3], and Tsukasa Hirashima[4]

[1] Graduate School of Engineering, Tokyo Polytechnic University, Atsugi, Kanagawa, Japan
`n.aikawa@st.t-kougei.ac.jp`
[2] Faculty of Engineering, Tokyo Polytechnic University, Atsugi, Kanagawa, Japan
[3] Graduate School of Maritime Sciences, Kobe University, Kobe, Hyogo, Japan
[4] Graduate School of Advanced Science and Engineering, Hiroshima University, Higashi-Hiroshima, Hiroshima, Japan
`https://www.takahito.com/members/aikawa/`

Abstract. In mechanics, it is important to understand the relationships between forces acting on objects. To help learners understand these relationships, a number of mechanics-based learning support systems have been developed. Many of these systems deal with drawing problems. Drawing problems require learners to draw the forces acting on objects in a given physical system using arrows. However, when the relationships between forces are complicated, learners may get stuck. It has been shown that providing auxiliary problems to learners who get stuck can be effective. An auxiliary problem is one that helps the learner understand the original problem. When a learner is presented with an auxiliary problem, they can solve that problem and use errors noticed in it to assist in solving the original problem as well. However, learning by solving auxiliary problems may confuse learners if they are not given ones that are appropriate to the original problem. In order to create appropriate auxiliary problems, it is necessary to create them using consistent rules. We have been working on the automatic generation of auxiliary problems for mechanics. Specifically, based on Mizoguchi et al.'s causal reasoning theory of force and motion, we investigated how to generate problems with consistent deletion. In this paper, we elaborate the rules for generating auxiliary problems, aiming for the automatic generation of them by the system.

Keywords: Auxiliary problem · Error-based simulation · Another keyword

S. Yamamoto and H. Mori (Eds.): HCII 2022, LNCS 13305, pp. 437–450, 2022.
https://doi.org/10.1007/978-3-031-06424-1_32

1   Introduction

In mechanics, it is important to understand the relationships between forces acting on objects. To help learners understand these relationships, a number of mechanics-based learning support systems have been developed [4,5]. Many of these systems deal with drawing problems, which require learners to draw the forces acting on objects in a given physical system using arrows. However, when the relationships between forces are complicated, learners may get stuck, and they may give up trying to solve it. Therefore, this research aims to provide support for resolving these sorts of impasses.

It has been shown that providing auxiliary problems to learners who get stuck can be effective [1,2]. An auxiliary problem is one that helps the learner understand the original problem. When a learner is presented with such a problem, they can solve it and use errors noticed in it to assist in solving the original problem as well. Since there are various patterns of learner errors, it is necessary to present auxiliary problems appropriate to those errors.

However, learning by solving auxiliary problems may confuse learners if they are not given ones that are appropriate to the original problem. In order to create appropriate auxiliary problems, it is necessary to create them using consistent rules.

We have been working on the automatic generation of auxiliary problems for mechanics [3]. Specifically, we first characterized the problem based on Mizoguchi et al.'s causal reasoning theory of force and motion [6]. Next, we examined how to generate problems that are valid with consistent feature deletion. The auxiliary problems were then classified with the intent of generating them into three types.

However, the authors have not yet implemented and generated auxiliary problems in an actual system. In this paper, we elaborate the rules for generating auxiliary problems for system implementation.

2   Three Types of Auxiliary Problems

2.1   Characterization Using Causal Reasoning

To generate an auxiliary problem, the characteristics of the original problem need to be discussed, and the relationship between the original problem and the auxiliary problem needs to be discussed based on those characteristics. In this study, we refer to the causal reasoning theory of force and motion developed by Mizoguchi et al. [6] and create auxiliary problems based on causality. Therefore, the characterization of the problems is treated based on the causal relationships between forces in those problems. Mizoguchi et al. organized the causal relationships among forces acting on physical systems in elementary physics. Based on this, causal relationships in this study are added to the arrows representing the forces acting on objects in EBS problems [3].

In this case, causality refers to the relationships between the order of the forces. In this research, we look at a physical system in which forces are acting on an object in that system. For these forces, we have arranged the relationships between the order of occurrence and propagation.

Figure 1 shows the forces acting on an object in an example problem in which the object is pushed sideways. Figure 2 shows the features of Fig. 1, which are characterized based on causal relationships. The following five points are the main steps in the characterization.

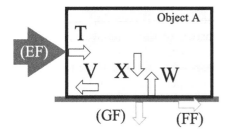

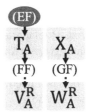

Fig. 1. Example of a problem.   **Fig. 2.** Characterization of Fig. 1.

1. Order the forces acting on an object.
2. Describe the forces according to their sources.
3. Describe forces acting on other objects as existing in the causal series.
4. Describe which object the force is acting on.
5. Separately describe the forces that act on, and those that return to, objects.

In this study, we will generate auxiliary problems by manipulating the features of similar problems. The manipulation of problem features involves deleting a single force arrow and then deleting or adding causally related forces to it, ensuring that the problem situation does not become physically unnatural.

2.2   Three Types of Force

Based on the characterization described in Sect. 2.1, we propose that auxiliary problems should be generated by manipulating forces based on causal relationships. Specifically, when we focus on a particular force in a problem, we generate an auxiliary problem from the original by referring to the causal relationship for that force and then adding or deleting operations to the adjacent forces in the relationship. Three operations are defined for generating the auxiliary problem based on the specific force of interest and the force to which the operation is applied.

As a premise, this study defines three types of forces when focusing on a particular force (Fig. 3). The first is denoted (1) in Fig. 3. This is the force that occurs when an object is subjected to an external force or a force from another system. In the figure, this force is generated when object A receives a force from object B's system.

The second is the returning force, denoted as (2). This is the force that is balanced by force (1). It acts on the same object as the force of interest but in the opposite direction and with the same magnitude.

The third is the causal force, denoted as (0). This force is causally adjacent to (1) and acts on object B, while (1) itself acts on object A. It is the same force as (1) in both magnitude and direction.

The three operations in auxiliary problem generation are operations that delete these forces; balanced delete, simple delete, and replace. Balanced delete is the deletion of force (1), where it and the returned force (if any) are deleted as a set. Simple delete is the deletion of the returned force (2), and only the returned force is deleted from the set comprised of the focused force and the returned force. Replace is the deletion of the causal force (0), where it is then replaced by an external force. With these three operations, we believe that we can automatically generate auxiliary problems to compensate for causal relationships that cannot be visualized, such as those in complex phenomena that are difficult to support with EBS.

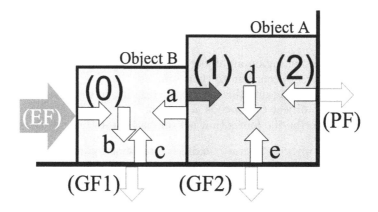

Fig. 3. The basic problem.

2.3   Use of the Three Types of Auxiliary Problems

In this study, we generate three types of auxiliary problems for a single original problem based on the learner's incorrect force (Fig. 4).

First, when the learner does not understand a particular force, it is important to check whether the auxiliary problem that does not include that force can be solved. Since the incorrect force corresponds to the acting force in Sect. 2, we call the auxiliary problem with the incorrect force the auxiliary problem by balanced delete.

Next, there are cases in which the auxiliary problem by balanced delete is solved, but the particular force is not understood. In such a case, we consider that if we give the learner an auxiliary problem that clarifies the source of the force, then they will be able to notice the force. Therefore, we generate an auxiliary problem in which the force that causes the incorrect force is replaced by an external force. Since the force that causes the incorrect force corresponds to the force that causes (0) in Sect. 2, the auxiliary problem with this force removed is called the auxiliary problem by replace.

If the learner can solve the auxiliary problem by balanced delete and the auxiliary problem by replace, then they will be able to resolve the incorrect force. However, if the learner still does not understand, then they do not understand what the effect of that particular force is. Therefore, we generate an auxiliary problem in which the force associated with the effect is deleted. This force corresponds to the returning force (2) in Sect. 2, so the auxiliary problem with this force removed is called the auxiliary problem by simple delete.

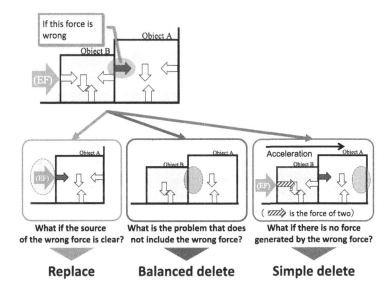

Fig. 4. Three auxiliary problems.

3 Auxiliary Problem Generation Rules

3.1 How to Create a Rule

To generate auxiliary problems, two lists of rules were developed in this research. First, we need a rule for generating auxiliary problems by manipulating the features of the problem. We call these rules "generation rules" (Table 1). For example, Rule 1 is to be applied when the system tells us to generate an auxiliary problem by balanced delete. When this rule is applied, the system executes a balancing and deletion operation. The operations are explained in Sects. 3.2–3.3. The auxiliary problem is generated by applying one or more of these generation rules.

Table 1. List of generation rules.

	If	Then
Rule 1	If a command is issued to the balanced delete	Execute balanced delete operation
Rule 2	If a command is issued to the replace	Execute replace operation
Rule 3	If a command is issued to the simple delete	Execute simple delete operation
Rule 4	If there is a force or object that has no causal connection to the force of interest	Delete the force or the object

Table 2. List of constraint violation rules.

	If	Then
Rule v1	If there is a force that lacks action or reaction And if the force is not caused by gravity or external force	Cancel the operation as it is not a valid problem
Rule v2	If there are multiple objects And if there is gravity on only one of the objects	Cancel the operation as it is not a valid problem
Rule v3	If there are multiple objects And if only one of the objects has acceleration	Cancel the operation as it is not a valid problem
Rule v4	If there is no gravity	Cancel the operation as it is not a valid problem

When an auxiliary problem is generated, it is necessary to verify whether it is a valid problem. In this research, we studied and summarized the conditions under which the problem is not valid. We call these rule "constraint violation rules" (Table 2). For example, from Newton's third law of motion, we know that in a physical system, if there is an action then there is an equal and opposite reaction; If the problem does not satisfy this law, the physical system is wrong and the problem is not valid. This is described in rule v1. This kind of confirmation enables us to provide auxiliary problems that are valid.

In the next section, we will give a detailed explanation of each operation used to generate auxiliary problems, using Fig. 3 as an example.

3.2 Balanced Delete

In this section, we explain how an auxiliary problem is generated when performing a balanced delete operation. The flow graph for the operation is shown in Fig. 5. Balanced delete occurs by applying Rule 1 (Table 1). The content of Rule 1 is "If a command is issued to the balanced delete execute balanced delete operation." Table 3 summarizes the conditions and contents for the balanced delete operation.

Table 3. Operation list by balanced delete.

	Applicable conditions	Execution contents
OP:b1	None	Delete (1), Execute OP:b2, and Execute OP:b3
OP:b2	If there is a causal force for a given force	Delete its force and Execute OP:b2
OP:b3	If there is a force that is being generated by a force	Delete its force and Execute OP:b3

The operations are executed from OP:b1. First, refer to the application condition for OP:b1, and execute the contents if it is applicable. OP:b1 has no applicable conditions, and its execution contents are "Delete (1)," "Execute OP:b2," and "Execute OP:b3." Therefore, delete force (1). Then execute OP:b2 and OP:b3, which are the execution contents of OP:b1, in order.

Next, execute OP:b2. In OP:b2, the application condition is "If there is a causal force for a given force," and the execution contents are "Delete its force" and "Execute OP:b2." Therefore, since force (1) has a causal force (0), delete force (0). In addition, there is "Execute OP:b2" in the execution contents, and since (0) has a causal force (EF), we apply OP:b2 again and delete (EF). However, since (EF) does not have a causal force, OP:b2 cannot be applied to it. Therefore, the OP:b2 process ends here.

Next, execute OP:b3. In OP:b3, the application condition is "If there is a force that is being generated by a force," and the execution contents are "Delete its force" and "Execute OP:b3." Therefore, since force (1) has a force (PF) that is being generated, delete (PF). In addition, there is "Execute OP:b3" in the execution contents, and force (2) is being generated for (PF); apply OP:b3 again and delete (2). Similarly, delete force a. Since force a has no force being generated, OP:b3 cannot be applied to it. Therefore, the process of OP:b3 ends here. This completes the operation for Rule 1.

However, the generated auxiliary problem still has wall objects with no causal connection, so Rule 4 can be applied. The resulting problem is shown in Fig. 6. This is a problem in which two objects are stationary side by side.

This problem is not applicable to any of the constraint violation rules (Table 2). Therefore, this problem is assumed to be valid.

Figure 11 includes three auxiliary problems, namely, P2, P3, and P4, that were generated by the balanced delete operation. These were generated by focusing on the forces T1, T2, T3, and Q from the original problem P1.

3.3 Replace

In this section, we explain how an auxiliary problem is generated when performing a replace operation. The flow graph for the operation is shown in Fig. 7. Replace occurs by applying Rule 2 (Table 1). The content of Rule 2 is "If a

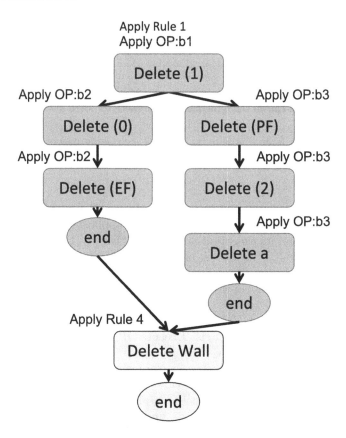

Fig. 5. Procedure for generating auxiliary problems by balanced delete.

command is issued to the replace, then execute replace operation." Table 4 summarizes the conditions and contents for the replace operation.

The operations are executed from OP:r1. First, refer to the application condition for OP:r1 and execute the contents if it is applicable. OP:r1 has the applicable condition "If (0) is present," and its execution contents are "Delete (0)" and "Execute OP:r2." Therefore, delete force (0). Then, execute OP:r2, which is the execution contents of OP:r1.

Next, execute OP:r2. In OP:r2, the application condition is "If (0) is not external force," and the execution contents are "Delete the object on which (0) acts" and "Add (EF) as the force that causes (1)." Therefore, since the force (0) is not (EF), delete the object B on which (0) acts. Since there is nothing more to be done in OP:r2, the process for OP:r2 ends here. This completes the operation for Rule 2.

However, the generated auxiliary problem still has (EF) with no causal connection, so Rule 4 can be applied. The resulting problem is shown in Fig. 8. This is a problem in which only object A is pushed toward the wall.

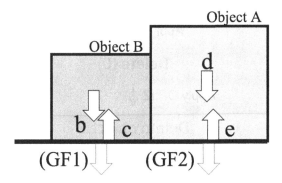

Fig. 6. Generated auxiliary problem by balanced delete.

Table 4. Operation list by replace.

	Applicable conditions	Execution contents
OP:r1	If (0) is present	Delete (0) and Execute OP:r2
OP:r2	If (0) is not an external force	Delete the object on which (0) acts and Add (EF) as the force that causes (1)

This problem is not applicable to any of the constraint violation rules (Table 2). Therefore, this problem is assumed to be valid.

Figure 11 includes two auxiliary problems, namely, P8 and P9, that were generated by the replace operation. These were generated by focusing on the forces Z, T3, and Q from the original problem P1.

3.4   Simple Delete

In this section, we explain how an auxiliary problem is generated when performing a simple delete operation. The flow graph for the operation is shown in Fig. 9. Simple delete occurs by applying Rule 3 (Table 1). The content of Rule 3 is "If a command is issued to the simple delete, then execute the simple delete operation." Table 5 summarizes the conditions and contents for the simple delete operation.

The operations are executed from OP:s1. First, refer to the application condition for OP:s1 and execute the contents if it is applicable. OP:s1 has the applicable condition "If (2) is present," and its execution contents are "Delete (2)," "Execute OP:s2," and "Execute OP:s4." Therefore, delete force (2). Then, execute OP:s2 and OP:s4, which are the execution contents of OP:s1, in order.

Next, execute OP:s2. In OP:s2, the application condition is "If there is a force with an action-reaction relationship in (2)," and the execution contents are "Delete the force with an action-reaction relationship in (2)" and "Execute OP:s3." Therefore, since force (2) has an action–reaction relation force (PF),

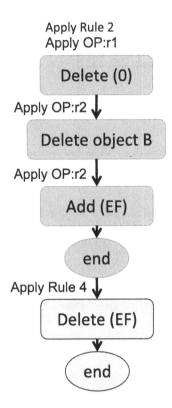

Fig. 7. Procedure for generating auxiliary problems by replace.

delete (PF). In addition, there is "Execute OP:s3" in the execution contents, and the application condition of OP:s3 is "If the force with action-reaction relation (2) acts on the object." Since (PF) is acting on the wall, OP:s3 is executed to delete the wall. Since there is nothing more to be executed in OP:s3, the processing of OP:s3 ends here.

Next, execute OP:s4. In OP:s4, the application condition is "If there is a causal force (0) such that a force (1) balances force (2)," and the execution contents are "Increase (0) so that it is equal to the acceleration of the object on which (1) acts" and "Execute OP:s5." Therefore, since force (1) has a causal force (0), increase force (0) so that it has the same acceleration as object A. Furthermore, there is "Execute OP:s5" in the execution contents, and the application condition of OP:s5 is "If there is a force that has an action-reaction relationship with the force increased by OP:s4 or OP:s6." However, OP:s5 cannot be applied to the force increased by OP:s4 (0) because there is no force related to the action–reaction relationship. Therefore, the process of OP:s5 ends here.

This completes the operation of Rule 3. Figure 6 shows the problem that was created by applying Rule 3. This is a problem in which two objects are pushed from the side and are accelerating.

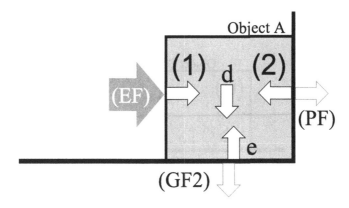

Fig. 8. Generated auxiliary problem by replace.

This problem is not applicable to any of the constraint violation rules (Table 2). Therefore, this problem is assumed to be valid.

Figure 11 includes three auxiliary problems, namely, P5, P6, and P7, that were generated by the simple delete operation. These are auxiliary problems generated by focusing on the forces W1, W2, V, and H from the original problem P1.

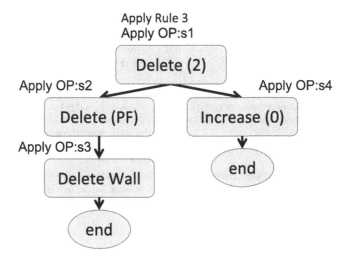

Fig. 9. Procedure for generating auxiliary problems by simple delete.

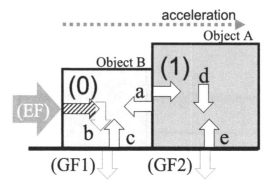

Fig. 10. Generated auxiliary problem by simple delete.

Table 5. List of operation rules by simple delete.

	Applicable conditions	Execution contents
OP:s1	If (2) is present	Delete (2), Execute OP:s2, and Execute OP:s4
OP:s2	If there is a force with an action-reaction relationship in (2)	Delete the force with an action-reaction relationship in (2) and Execute OP:s3
OP:s3	If the force with action-reaction relation in (2) acts on the object	Delete the object on which the force with action–reaction relation in (2) acts
OP:s4	If there is a causal force (0) such that force (1) balances force (2)	Increase (0) so that it is equal to the acceleration of the object on which (1) acts and Execute OP:s5
OP:s5	If there is a force that has an action-reaction relationship with the force increased by OP:s4 or OP:s6	Increase both the force that is increased by OP:s4 or OP:s6 and the force related to the action/reaction to the same magnitude as the force increased by OP:s4 or OP:s6 and Execute OP:s6
OP:s6	If there is a force that results in another force that is balanced by the force increased by OP:s5	Increase the causal force so that it is the same as the acceleration of the object exerted by (1) and Execute OP:s5

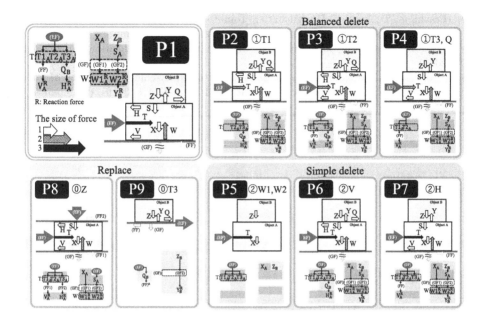

Fig. 11. Example of an auxiliary problem generated using the rules.

4   Conclusion

In this paper, we developed a method for automatically generating auxiliary problems in a mechanics learning support system, and we examined the rules for automatic generation of three types of auxiliary problems based on the learner's incorrect force. In the future, we will implement these rules in the system and examine whether auxiliary problems can actually be generated.

References

1. Aikawa, N., Koike, K., Tomoto, T.: Analysis of learning activities with automated auxiliary problem presentation for breaking learner impasses in physics error-based simulations. In: Workshop Proceedings of the International Conference on Computers in Education ICCE 2020, pp. 72–83 (2020)
2. Aikawa, N., Koike, K., Tomoto, T.: Proposal and preliminary evaluation of a system that presents auxiliary problems to break learners' impasse based on tendency of the error in error-based simulation. IEICE Trans. Inf. Syst. (Japanese edition) **103**(9), 644–647 (2020). (in Japanese)
3. Aikawa, N., Koike, K., Tomoto, T., Horiguchi, T., Hirashima, T.: Characterization of auxiliary problems for automated generation in error-based simulation. In: Yamamoto, S., Mori, H. (eds.) HCII 2021. LNCS, vol. 12766, pp. 3–13. Springer, Cham (2021). https://doi.org/10.1007/978-3-030-78361-7_1
4. Hirashima, T., Horiguchi, T., Kashihara, A., Toyoda, J.: Error-based simulation for error-visualization and its management. Int. J. Artif. Intell. Educ. **9**(1–2), 17–31 (1998)

5. Hirashima, T., Imai, I., Horiguchi, T., Tomoto, T.: Error-based simulation to promote awareness of error in elementary mechanics and its evaluation. In: Proceedings of International Conference on Artificial Intelligence in Education, pp. 409–416 (2009)
6. Mizoguchi, R., Hirashima, T., Horiguchi, T.: Causality-compliant theory of force and motion. Trans. Japan. Soc. Artif. Intell. **31**(4), A-F44_1 (2016). (in Japanese)

Category Creation Between Digital and Analog Sensemaking Tools in a Cognitive Immersive Environment

Shannon Briggs[(✉)], Matthew Peveler, Jaimie Drozdal, and Jonas Braasch

Rensselaer Polytechnic Institute, Troy, NY 12180, USA
briggs4@rpi.edu

Abstract. This paper compares the category creation process during a user study experiment in a cognitive immersive sensemaking environment between an analog and a digital sensemaking tool. The digital sensemaking tool is situated in an immersive environment, comprised of a global view, a personal view, and verbal and gestural technology that allows users to be fully engaged in their tasks. The user study ($n = 26$) examined the words used in both analog and digital tools, and compared the frequency of words generated by users, as well as the representativeness of categories to the materials given to participants. The sensemaking tool in this experiment is a novel brainstorming tool that utilizes interactive technologies which allow participants to seamlessly create knowledge artifacts like sticky notes and categories, while also leveraging the affordances of digital technology to help streamline sophisticated cognitive processes, like sorting and deciding the most salient information and collaborating with group members.

We found that while frequency of words differed little between tools, users were more conservative in their word choices with the digital sensemaking tool, making their choices more representative of the source material.

Keywords: Sensemaking · Human-computer interaction · User evaluations

1 Sensemaking Cognitive Immersive Environment

This paper compares the category creation process during a user study experiment in a cognitive immersive sensemaking environment between an analog and a digital sensemaking tool. The cognitive immersive room is discussed in previous literature, and prior use cases have involved a language learning environment, and a business analytics environment (Divekar et al. 2019). The digital sensemaking tool is situated in an immersive environment, comprised of a global view, a personal view, and verbal and gestural technology that allows users to be fully engaged in their tasks (Peveler et al. 2019). The user study ($n = 26$) examined the words used in both analog and digital tools, and compared the frequency of words generated by users, as well as the representativeness of categories to the materials given to participants. The sensemaking tool in this experiment is a novel brainstorming tool that utilizes interactive technologies which allow participants to seamlessly create knowledge artifacts like sticky notes and categories, while

S. Yamamoto and H. Mori (Eds.): HCII 2022, LNCS 13305, pp. 451–460, 2022.
https://doi.org/10.1007/978-3-031-06424-1_33

also leveraging the affordances of digital technology to help streamline sophisticated cognitive processes, like sorting and deciding the most salient information and collaborating with group members. Previous papers have discussed user generation of user's word choice in their sticky notes as well as concept chunks (Briggs et al. 2020).

We found that while frequency of words differed little between tools, users were more conservative in their word choices with the digital sensemaking tool, making their choices more representative of the source material. In this paper we evaluate the capacity of a digital brainstorming tool to permit participants (n = 26) in a collaborative experiment to create representative categories based off of a pre-determined text sample. Each session was an hour long, with participants conducting first a thirty minute analog sensemaking session, then participating in a second thirty minute session using the digital sensemaking tools in the cognitive immersive room. Participants were given two texts to read and produce sticky notes from, with the analog and digital sessions having separate texts to prevent over familiarity of the material falsely inflating participants' results in the digital session. Users were directed in the process of both divergent and convergent brainstorming during the introduction to the experiment, and therefore were aware that a group decision needed to be reached for category creation. This especially was important for the group to reflect the variety of views and perspectives while still agreeing on an agreed word or two to encapsulate groups of notes. We also noted that ideas that remained uncategorized indicated a weaker or fragmented sensemaking process, which was more apparent in the analog sensemaking session. We found that participants created more concise and representative category names compared to the analog sticky note brainstorming method, and that participants categorized more digital notes than physical notes. We anticipate that more explicit category names are due to pre-existing attitudes to disambiguating digital technology, which is a tendency that will benefit the schema-generation portion of the sensemaking cycle described by Pirolli and Card (2005).

Sensemaking Environment

Global View. The sensemaking environment uses the Watson AI to allow users to give verbal commands to the system. Kinect technology registers gestural commands to allow users to interact with the system via the global screen. The global view is the 360-deg screen that users can conduct collaborative work. On this screen, users can move notes using the drag and drop gesture around the screen, as well as issue voice commands to create notes and categories. This view is important for users to collaborate ideas about notes and potential category names (Briggs et al. 2019) (Fig. 1).

Personal View. The personal view is accessed on any personal device, such as a laptop, smartphone, or tablet. This view allows users to create digital sticky notes that other participants can't see. However, the personal view also allows users to create notes and categories on the global screen, as well as move notes into categories.

Prior Research. Our research framework to create the digital sensemaking tool drew from cognitive science and research that has been conducted in the intelligence analysis domain. Our goal was to create a cognitive immersive environment that would capitalize on procedures and movements users were already familiar with, and therefore lessen the amount of cognitive load needed to use the system. We designed the sticky notes tool

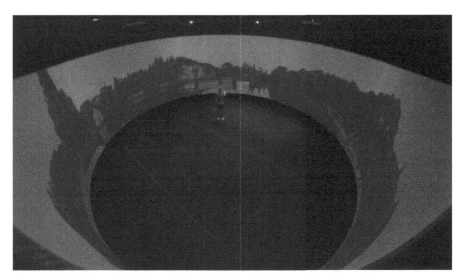

Fig. 1. Overhead view of the global screen in the cognitive immersive room.

to be similar to the analog method already found in intelligence analysis course books (Beebe and Pherson 2014).

Sensemaking. Our sensemaking framework for the sensemaking room is informed by Pirolli and Card's (2005) article. This describes how analysts typically move through two major cognitive loops during the analysis process, the information foraging loop and the sensemaking loop. These loops are comprised of sixteen discrete steps. The digital sticky notes tool was designed to help analysts move through the information foraging process, in order to allow users to find information and extract topics of interest. Other sensemaking theories that informed our approach were Klein's data/frame theory (Klein et al. 2006), which allowed us to understand how a user might use our sticky notes tool to assimilate new information to existing cognitive schemas.

Intelligence Analysis. The sticky notes analysis method is a technique that is described in Beebe and Pherson's book (2014). This method allows a group of analysts working from shared text sources to analyze and produce major themes of interest that they can use through the analysis process. Their method is carried out over eight steps and is timed in order to control the process. This brainstorming method is different from other brainstorming methods in that it uses both convergent and divergent brainstorming methods, usually called group and nominal brainstorming. Divergent brainstorming categorizes the first parts of this method, where participants read, create topics on sticky notes, and then create personal categories by themselves, without input from others. Finally, convergent brainstorming is used to create large note clusters of shared ideas, forming topics that are similar across the group. In our user study, we focused on similarity of topics within user categories in order to determine the digital brainstorming tool's ability to aid users in the sensemaking process.

2 User Study

2.1 Methodology

The user study was conducted over nine sessions, with a study population of 26. Our goal for the user study was to determine if the cognitive immersive technology reliably changed the way in which the users engaged in the sensemaking process. Users participated in small group sessions, each group 2–3 people. Each session was an hour long, with participants conducting first a thirty minute analog sensemaking session, then participating in a second thirty minute session using the digital sensemaking tools in the cognitive immersive room. Participants were given two texts to read and produce sticky notes from, with the analog and digital sessions having separate texts to prevent over familiarity of the material falsely inflating participants' results in the digital session. However, the procedure between the analog and digital sensemaking sessions remained the same to determine it was the technology, and not the analysis method, that was producing any divergent results. Before each session, users were assured at any point they were allowed to leave testing with no consequences, as according to IRB policy. Users who completed the full hour received compensation for their participation.

For the analog session, participants were instructed in the method of the analysis method they were to use for the thirty minute analog session. They were then distributed a sheet of paper with the sample text, and given five minutes to read the text. After this, users were given five minutes to write sticky notes about topics they felt were salient to the text. Following this, participants were instructed to create personal sticky note clusters on a shared wall. Through this period, no discussion is allowed, as per the analysis method. Finally, participants are allowed to discuss the notes and create shared topics and note clusters by creating broad categories for notes. After this, users are encouraged to report their findings.

The digital session was conducted largely the same with a few differences. The participants are distributed a sheet of paper with the session text, but the session text was also available as a fixed field on the global screen for the digital session. Users could also access the session text on their personal devices. Participants were given five minutes to read the text, then five minutes to create sticky notes on their personal devices. After this, participants sent their notes to the global screen, and arranged their notes into personal clusters using the gestural system and the global screen. Finally, participants were given five minutes to discuss and create shared categories. The digital tool had a create category function that allows users to create names containers on the screen, and to then drop sticky notes into these containers. Finally, users were encouraged to report on their findings, any difficulties they had with the technology, as well as any differences they felt were present between analog and digital methods.

2.2 Analysis

Analysis was carried out over video and audio recordings captured of the sensemaking sessions, which allowed us to determine when a category creation was finalized. We also recorded the category names from participants verbally during the analog sessions, and wrote these names on sheets of paper that were used to collect and store the analog sticky notes. Logs of digital sticky note categories were obtained from the system and analyzed. We used content analysis and thematic analysis to qualitatively compare the words participants used to the words used within the sample text given to participants. We also used frequency analysis to determine the rate participants used particular words across all nine sessions. The categorization period of the structured analytic brainstorming technique described by Beebe and Pherson (2014) requires that participants engage in divergent and convergent brainstorming. This elicits the individual participants' personal cognitive schema, as well as a collaborative representation of the groups' shared cognitive schema, which is displayed through groups of sticky notes as well as verbal discussion. For our brainstorming sessions, we followed analysis procedures for interaction analysis so that we could understand how participants engaged in category creation to highlight the broad themes of the brainstorming session. According to Marsh and White, group decision making in interaction analysis is concerned with, "…four fundamental tasks, called functional requisites: a. Thorough and accurate understanding of the choice-making situation; b. Identification of a range of realistic alternative courses of action; c. Thorough and accurate assessment of the positive qualities or consequences associated with alternative choices; and d. Thorough and accurate assessment of the negative qualities or consequences associated with alternative choices" (White and Marsh 2006, p22).

Following these four points, we wanted to understand how participants fulfilled these four steps during the category creation process. We used content analysis and thematic analysis to qualitatively compare the words participants used to the words used within the sample text given to participants. We also used frequency analysis to determine the rate participants used particular words across all nine sessions. We concluded that the digital brainstorming tool was able to enable a more concise category creation section of the sensemaking session that was more representative of the sample text given to the participants.

Results

Analog. The category names for the analog brainstorming session contained 43 unique words, with a total word frequency of 66. Twenty-nine words were used only once in these sessions, comprising 67% of all words in the categories, with a further 23% of words appearing only twice across nine user sessions. One word was used 8 times ("money"), indicating it was of strong interest to participants across all nine sessions. As will be discussed below in recoding participant categories, there are many synonyms in the overall wordlist that show that despite the variety of words, participants focused on many of the same ideas.

In the text segment, there are three major ideas that can be considered as relating to Jonathan Luna's death: 1. Luna's work, 2. Luna's sex life, and 3. Luna's financial debt. For clarity and brevity during coding and annotation, I have condensed these concepts into the following three categories: 1. Work, 2. Sex, 3. Debt. Over the nine user study sessions, participants created roughly 3 categories per session, with a maximum of 5 and a minimum of 2, as can be seen in Table 1.

When coded and recategorized under the three primary concept categories of "Work," "Sex," and "Debt," Table 2 shows that over nine user study sessions, participants created 10 categories that were about Luna's work, 8 that were about Luna's sex life, 10 that

Table 1. Analog category creation across 9 sessions.

Session	Category 1	Category 2	Category 3	Category 4	Category 5
1	Luna's money/Job	Missing money from case	Mystery trips he made to Philly	Habit/Website	Personal life
2	Missing money/court stuff	All things Philly			
3	Debt	Drugs/Travel	Communications		
4	Money	Official investigation	Marriage		
5	Personal debt	Trips to Philly	Internet Communication		
6	Work	Debt	Sex	Life	
7	Sex	Money	Travel	Authorities	
8	Unusual trips to Philadelphia	Where his body was found			
9	Business	Adult websites	Money		

were about Luna's debt, and 3 categories that were either about Luna's death or the investigation into his death. Understanding the ways in which participants described category names alone isn't sufficient to understand how effective the categorization section was for sensemaking. One method of understanding if the category creation portion of the brainstorming process aided in sensemaking is to compare the percentage of users' category names in the three major concept groups to the text segment concept chunks. This comparison allows us to understand if users were able to faithfully represent the content in the text segment given to them in their sticky- notes. The participant concept percentages are Work: 35%, Debt: 29%, and Sex: 26%, with another category, marked as "other," including categories that did not fit any of these three concepts, such as "authorities."

Table 2. Frequencies in analog sessions.

Work	Debt	Sex	Misc
Total frequency 10	Total frequency 8	Total frequency 10	Total frequency 3

When comparing the percentages of the concept chunks within category names to in-text content, I compared the category names with the concept chunks in the text segment. As it shows in Table 3, the text segment has proportionately more content related directly to Luna's work; however, participants have reassigned the significance of "work" in-text concepts to other categories, resulting in a smaller number of categories related to Luna's work. In fact, the percentage of category names and in-text concept chunks. for both the sex and debt concept categories are nearly identical between users and the in-text segment.

Table 3. Analog word concept comparisons between analog notes and analog text segment.

Work concepts	Debt concepts	Sex concepts	Other
In text: 48%	In-text: 28%	In-text: 24%	10%
Users: 35%	Users: 29%	Users: 26%	0%
Difference: 13%	Difference: 1%	Difference: 2%	Difference: 10%

The words with the highest frequency range are displayed in the chart below (Fig. 2). As can be seen in the Fig. 3, tend to be subgroups within those three major groups. Synonymous phrases are also apparent in the breakdown, with concepts like "travel" and "trips" falling into the same concept category, but called different things across sessions. This points to a certain level of variability in category names between participants across the analog sessions.

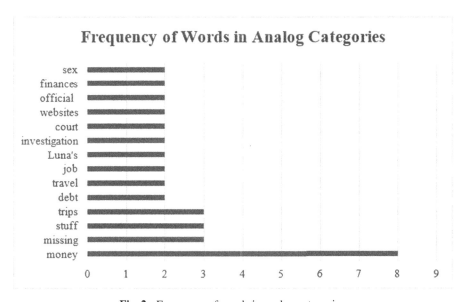

Fig. 2. Frequency of words in analog categories.

Digital. The digital notes category names showed overall less variability and diversity than the analog tool, with a total count of unique words of 21 and a total frequency of all words in category names of 32 (Table 4).

Table 4. Digital categories

Digital	Category 1	Category 2	Category 3	Category 4	Uncategorized
S1	Body	Knife			
S2	Murder	Suicide	Questionable		
S3	Cause of death	Work	Contradictory evidence		Uncat
S4	Body	Knife	Job		
S5	Body wounds	Employment	Penknife	Medical and psychological evidence	
S6	Scene	Job	Luna		
S7	Autopsy	Employment	Knife	Suicide	Uncat
S8	Job	Death			
S9	Stab	Knife	Work	Suicide	

Following a-priori coding, participants' notes should ideally represent the major themes in the text segment given to them, I coded each of the category names to the four major concepts that can be found in the text segment that was used for the digital brainstorming session, "work," "body," "knife," and "death" (Table 5).

Table 5. Frequencies of concepts in digital sessions

Work	Body	Knife	Death
Total frequency: 7	Total frequency: 5	Total frequency: 9	Total frequency: 8

Overall, we found that the participants' responses weren't appreciably different from the text segments, with the exception of the "body" category, with a difference of 18%. This is attributable to users grouping notes with mixed concept categories under different category names, with some users linking wounds to the body to the knife later found at the scene, or opinions of consistency of wounds to the body linking to manner of death (Table 6).

In examining the word frequency of participants' digital brainstorming categories, Table shows the most frequently used words assigned within the four major categories. This is important to consider, as the table shows that the most frequent words represent 58% of the content of category names. This means the digital notes category names are more consistent across the nine user sessions, with fewer unusual or rarely mentioned words becoming category names. This again indicates more consistent participant category names across the digital session, indicating that participants within and across sessions were able to come to a stronger consensus about the category names.

Table 6. Percentage comparisons between digital categories and text categories.

Work concepts	Body concepts	Knife concepts	Death concepts
In text: 17%	In-text: 32%	In-text: 28	29%
Users: 25%	Users: 18%	Users: 26%	25%
Difference: −8%	Difference: 14%	Difference: 2%	Difference: 4%

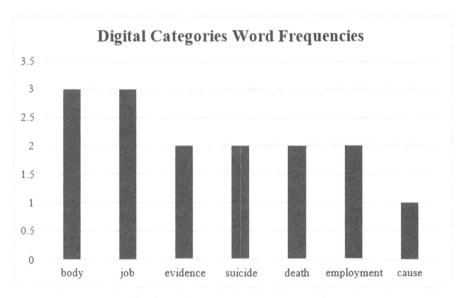

Fig. 3. Digital categories word frequencies

3   Conclusion and Future Work

We found that the category creation in the digital sticky notes tool was more representative and concise in their word use than the analog sticky notes tool. We reached this finding after comparing the number and similarity of words in categories produced across all nine sessions to the words used in the text segment given to participants. Due to this finding, we concluded that the digital sensemaking tool allows users to have a more efficient, concise sensemaking session than the traditional analog technique. Future work for the sensemaking room includes integration of NLP technology, as well as increased visualization techniques, and more user-in-the-loop opportunities for users to influence information flow and schema generation.

References

Beebe, S.M., Pherson, R.H.: Cases in Intelligence Analysis: Structured Analytic Techniques in Action. CQ Press, Washington, D.C. (2014)

Briggs, S., Drozdal, J., Peveler, M., Balagyozyan, L., Sun, C., Su, H.: Enabling sensemaking for intelligence analysis in a multi-user, multimodal cognitive and immersive environment. In: ACHI 2019 the Twelfth International Conference on Advances in Computer-Human Interactions (2019)

Briggs, S., Peveler, M., Drozdal, J., Balagyozyan, L., Braasch, J., Su, H.: Brainstorming for sensemaking in a multimodal, multiuser cognitive environment. In: Stephanidis, C., Marcus, A., Rosenzweig, E., Rau, P.-L., Moallem, A., Rauterberg, M. (eds.) HCII 2020. LNCS, vol. 12423, pp. 66–83. Springer, Cham (2020). https://doi.org/10.1007/978-3-030-60114-0_4

Divekar, R.R., et al.: CIRA: an architecture for building configurable immersive smart-rooms. In: Arai, K., Kapoor, S., Bhatia, R. (eds.) IntelliSys 2018. AISC, vol. 869, pp. 76–95. Springer, Cham (2019). https://doi.org/10.1007/978-3-030-01057-7_7

Klein, G., Moon, B., Hoffman, R.R.: Making sense of sensemaking 2: a macrocognitive model. IEEE Intell. Syst. **21**, 88–92 (2006). https://doi.org/10.1109/MIS.2006.100

Peveler, M., et al.: Translating the pen and paper brainstorming process into a cognitive and immersive system. In: Kurosu, M. (ed.) HCII 2019. LNCS, vol. 11567, pp. 366–376. Springer, Cham (2019). https://doi.org/10.1007/978-3-030-22643-5_28

Pirolli, P., Card, S.: Sensemaking processes of intelligence analysts and possible leverage points as identified through cognitive task analysis. In: Proceedings of the 2005 International Conference on Intelligence Analysis, McLean, Virginia (2005)

White, M.D., Marsh, E.E.: Content analysis: a flexible methodology. Libr. Trends **55**, 22–45 (2006)

TAME: A Method of Teachable Agent Modeling for Error-Visualization

Kento Koike[1]([✉]), Izumi Himura[2], and Takahito Tomoto[2]

[1] Graduate School of Engineering, Tokyo Polytechnic University, Atsugi,
Kanagawa, Japan
k.koike@t-kougei.ac.jp
[2] Faculty of Engineering, Tokyo Polytechnic University, Atsugi, Kanagawa, Japan
https://www.koike.app/en/

Abstract. In the context of learning, the effectiveness of learning-by-teaching (LbT) is widely recognized. LbT is a method through which learners deepen their understanding by teaching others what they have learned. In order to realize LbT, it is necessary to have the behavior of the teachable person, such as the knowledge of other and an attitude towards receiving instruction, as well as the existence of the teachable presence. One technology for approaching this challenge is called a teachable agent. A teachable agent is an agent that behaves as if it is learning what is taught by the learner. Another effective learning method is error-visualization. Error-visualization is a feedback-based approach to simulating the answers by the learner as (abnormal) behavior. However, no modeling methods have been proposed that combine teachable agents with error-visualization. In this paper, we propose teachable agent modeling for error-visualization (TAME) as a teachable agent modeling method that aims to combine teachable agent with error-visualization. As a case study, we realize a teachable agent using the TAME modeling method based on a conventional learning support system called Monsakun.

Keywords: TAME · Teachable agent · Error-visualization · Learning-by-teaching · Problem-posing

1 Introduction

One typical way for learners to deepen their understanding of a topic is to explain it to others. Learning-by-teaching (LbT) is a learning method that utilizes this approach [3]. It is known that a person can deepen their own understanding of a topic by teaching it to others through LbT [4,5].

In order to realize LbT, it is necessary to have the behavior of the teachable person, such as the knowledge of other and an attitude towards receiving instruction, as well as the existence of the teachable presence. For example, if one's own knowledge is comparable to that of the other, or if there is a wide gap between one's own knowledge and that of the other, then teaching activity

© The Author(s), under exclusive license to Springer Nature Switzerland AG 2022
S. Yamamoto and H. Mori (Eds.): HCII 2022, LNCS 13305, pp. 461–474, 2022.
https://doi.org/10.1007/978-3-031-06424-1_34

between them is expected to be difficult. LbT is also difficult to realize if the other is not willing to accept the teaching. Furthermore, when LbT is implemented in a classroom or lecture, LbT can be realized by only the teacher side, and since the minimum possible configuration is a pair of learners, only half of them are able to benefit from LbT.

The teachable agent is a technology that can solve both problems of controlling the behavior of the teachable person and ensuring the existence of the teachable presence [1,13,14]. A teachable agent is a technology that behaves as if it is learning what is taught to the learner. The teachable agent ensures that there is a teachable presence on a computing device, such as a PC or tablet, so that all learners can benefit from LbT. In addition, by integrating the teachable agent with an intelligent tutoring system or a learning support system, it is possible to determine the knowledge level of the learner, and then to equip the teachable agent with the knowledge that can be taught by the learner at their current knowledge level, or to deepen the knowledge of the learner one step at a time from that knowledge level.

Even though the teachable agent is a mere metaphor attached to a learning support system, it is known to bring about a social schema that makes the learner recognize themselves as a co-learner [1,2]. The effects of introducing such a social schema have been recognized in various ways [2,6,15,19]. Among them, recursive feedback provided by teachable agents has been shown to be effective for learner learning [15]. Recursive feedback is a recursive process in which learners teach what they have learned to others and receive feedback based on how the others behave.

The effect of such recursive feedback is thought to be due to the fact that the teachable agent serves not only as a social schema but also as a simulator for hypothesis testing by learners. Since learning support has focused on the latter, there have been a series of studies on error-visualization [9,11,12]. Error-visualization is a learning approach that makes a learner aware when they have gotten the wrong idea by demonstrating through simulations that the wrong answers lead to inappropriate results. In error-visualization, the conditions to be understood are first defined as constraints in advance, and the answers by the learner are diagnosed based on the constraints. The simulation is then visualized based on the constraints that are satisfied or violated in the answer by the learner with the aim of making the learner aware of their error.

In this paper, we propose teachable agent modeling for error-visualization (TAME) as a modeling method for designing teachable agents that visualize errors based on constraints by applying error-visualization techniques to recursive feedback of teachable agents. As a case study, we implement and evaluate a teachable agent using the proposed TAME modeling method based on Monsakun [7,8,10,16–18], a conventional learning support system.

2   Related Work

2.1   Teachable Agent

Teachable agents are usually implemented as an adjunct to learning support systems that have some kind of learning task. For example, SimStudent by Matsuda et al. is a teachable agent that can act as if it is learning in the same environment as the learner in an intelligent tutoring system called APLUS [14]. In this framework, SimStudent behaves as if it does not understand the knowledge in the environment, and encourages teaching by learners who have learned the knowledge from the environment. SimStudent then learns the knowledge taught by the learner using machine learning methods. This approach ensures that SimStudent learns in the same way as a normal learner, that is, through cognitive fidelity. As another example, Betty's Brain by Biswas et al. was designed to make the thinking and reasoning processes of the agent predictable in order to make it usable by students with less educational experience or domain knowledge [1,13]. Specifically, Betty's Brain does not learn from examples or by induction, but only from what they are taught by learners using concept maps, and Betty's Brain uses their concept maps as the reason for their errors.

The impact of the social schema of these teachable agents is significant. For example, Chase et al. showed that such social schemas lead to the protégé effect [2]. The protégé effect is an effect in which the learner recognizes the teachable agent in the system as a person to be guided (protégé), and thus tries to fulfill they responsibilities as a tutor. This effect is known to make learners work harder than when they learn for themselves, because they feel a sense of responsibility to teach the tutee (teachable agent). Okita et al. showed that recursive feedback, in which learners externalize what they have learned by teaching it to a teachable agent and then observe how the teachable agent behaves as a result, is effective in helping learners learn [15]. Specifically, we conducted an experiment in which we divided the teachable agent into two groups: one in which we observed how the teachable agent behaved using the content taught after the subject taught it to the teachable agent, and one in which we did not. The results showed that the former group had a significantly higher learning effect, indicating that teachable agents provide recursive feedback to learners. The introduction of social schemas has also been found to affect cognitive states such as learner gaze control [6] and self-efficacy [19]. In other words, when teachable agents are recognized as social beings for learners, they bring about these various benefits.

2.2   Error-Visualization

Error-visualization is a learning approach proposed by Hirashima et al. that induces learning by making the learner aware of errors by generating simulations with (abnormal) behavior based on the (incorrect) answers by the learner [9,11, 12].

In error-visualization, the presence of constraints (rules to be learned in the learning task) is important. In other words, different simulations are generated depending on which constraints are satisfied or violated by the learner's answer. To illustrate, we take an example of error-visualization in physics (elementary mechanics). When solving the problem of drawing arrows and determining the forces acting on stationary object on the floor, there are two constraints that must be satisfied: gravity is acting and a normal reaction is acting. If the learner only draws and answers gravity, the former constraint is satisfied and the latter is violated. As a result, the system simulates that the object sinks to the floor. In this way, in the error-visualization framework, the learner inputs a hypothesis based on their own ideas, and repeats the trial-and-error process to verify the correctness of the hypothesis by simulation.

2.3   Contribution and Novelty

Teachable Agent. If we focus on recursive feedback from the teachable agent, it is difficult to control the teachable agent in such a way that the learner can infer their own errors from the responses obtained from the teachable agent by using the teachable agent behavior control methods in previous research. For example, since SimStudent uses a machine learning approach, the teachable agent behaves in a probabilistic manner. Betty's Brain uses a knowledge modeling approach that defines a minimum set of primitives, and is designed so that all behaviors are interpretable. However, since it is possible to combine an unlimited number of minimal primitives, the learner may not necessarily be able to infer their own errors from the responses obtained from the teachable agent. In other words, these methods cannot define the search space that the learner should explore.

In this paper, we propose a modeling method that focuses on the error-visualization by a teachable agent with the aim of shifting from interpretable to explorable. Specifically, in order for the teachable agent to behave appropriately, we propose a design method in which the teachable agent is equipped with knowledge for the target learning task in advance, and can simulate and behave appropriately depending on the answers (hypothesis) from the learner.

Error-Visualization. In error-visualization, when a contradiction occurs between the constraints representing the hypothesis input by the learner and the correct constraint set of the simulator, some of the latter are relaxed so that the whole becomes consistent to make all the hypotheses input by the learner valid. In this case, previous studies have used domain-specific heuristics to resolve the inconsistencies in the computation, and it has been pointed out that this approach lacks versatility [11]. Horiguchi et al. proposed a framework for resolving inconsistencies among constraints by explicitly identifying the sources of inconsistencies in the constraint set for computable constraints.

In the proposed TAME method, when the constraint set answered by the learner contains a contradiction, the constraint set that is most similar to the constraint set but contains no contradictions is selected. By processing the constraints in this way, we can resolve the inconsistency of the constraints in a domain-independent manner, although this sacrifices some certain degree of validity as a simulation. In addition, the method is innovative in that it can be applied to learning topics other than those for which computable constraints can be defined.

This paper also presents a novel approach to simulation in error-visualization. Whereas conventional error-visualization simply interprets the answers of the learner and then presents the resulting simulation, this paper realizes an environment in which constraints are taught step by step by using a teachable agent. This allows the learner to obtain a simulation in which the constraints change with each step. These simulations provide a new environment for observing how the satisfaction or violation of each constraint affects the behavior of the simulation.

3   Proposed Method

3.1   Summary

Many teachable agents assume a context in which the teachable agent learns the same topic as the user (learner) at the same time as the user (SimStudent [14] and Betty's Brain [1,13] are typical examples). Thus, after learning from the system, the learner performs LbT on a teachable agent that has learned the same things as the learner, but does not fully understand them (or behaves as if it does not). When a teachable agent is viewed in this way, it is necessary to consider in its design the knowledge of the components of the teaching material, the knowledge of the constraints to be satisfied by the relationships among the components, and the mechanism for generating behavior based on the answers by the learner. In this paper, we propose TAME as a teachable agent modeling method that realizes recursive feedback based on error-visualization by applying the error-visualization method [9,11,12].

This method firstly abstracts the correct answers as patterns of constraints to be satisfied. The patterns of constraints that are satisfied by the answers by the learners are then determined based on the abstracted constraints. Finally, behaviors are generated based on the patterns of constraints. In this way, TAME uses learner answers as constraints and has a mechanism for generating behavior based on these constraints. Therefore, in order to introduce a teachable agent into any learning support system, the creator of the teaching materials needs only to prepare a description of the elements that make up the materials and the rules for the constraints that the relationships between the elements must satisfy. Furthermore, the interaction with the learner is designed as an interaction to which the constraint satisfaction problem is applicable. Based on the premise of this interaction, the input (hypothesis) from the learner is represented as a constraint satisfaction problem, and the computer (teachable agent) can automatically generate behavior by solving the constraint satisfaction problem.

3.2   Constraints

Because of the nature of TAME, which is ultimately solved as a constraint satisfaction problem, it is necessary to define the constraints that must be satisfied in the answer by the learner. These constraints can be described as rules that the elements of the solution must satisfy. At the same time, it also means that the solution itself must be expressible as a combination of elements. The answer must be defined so that it is correct when all the constraints are satisfied, and at the same time, it must be defined so that it is wrong when any of the constraints are not satisfied. In other words, the constraints are the concepts that we want the students to learn in the targeted learning activity. For example, let's take a simple example of constraints on answers in a hypothetical syllogism. In the hypothetical syllogism, if (a), then (b); if (c), then (d); therefore, if (e), then (f), then the constraints to be satisfied can be listed as agreement between (a) and (e), agreement between (b) and (c), and agreement between (d) and (f). If the constraints are specified in this way, the answer is correct if all the constraints are satisfied, and is wrong if any of the constraints are not satisfied. Although it is desirable for constraints to be independent of each other, overlapping and dependencies are not a problem in TAME framework.

This kind of constraint definition has been used in conventional learning support systems. For example, in the arithmetic word problem task (e.g., create a story that can be solved by the equation $30 \times 4 = 120$), the teacher workload is high because there can be multiple correct answers. Therefore, Monsakun [7, 8, 10, 16–18], which was selected as a case study for this paper, uses constraints to diagnose the solution by structuring the solution scheme as a combination of cards. For instance, there are three cards required for the correct answer combination, such as "Apples are 30 grams apiece," "There are four apples," and "Apples are 120 grams," and two dummy cards, such as "There are four oranges" and "Apples are 60 grams apiece." In this case, if the answer by the learner is a combination of "Apples are 30 grams apiece", "There are four oranges," and "Apples are 120 grams," the constraint that the relationships among the objects in the sentences (apples, oranges, etc.) are correct is violated. TAME applies these constraints to generate answers such as "Apples are 30 grams apiece," "There are four oranges," and "Apples are 120 grams," as the behavior of a teachable agent that lacks only the understanding of the constraint that the relationships among objects in the sentences (apples, oranges, etc.) are correct.

3.3   Behavior Generation and Interaction

This section discusses how to generate specific behaviors. In the following explanation, we assume that there are four constraints (A to D) that must be satisfied by the answer in the target learning activity. If all the constraints are satisfied, the answer is correct; if any of the constraints are not satisfied, the answer is wrong.

In TAME, each answer of a learner is collected as a history in the learning support system that performs the learning activity. For each answer in the history, we record the constraint satisfaction pattern of each answer between 0000 and 1111, where 1 is satisfied and 0 is not. For example, for each ABCD constraint, 0111 is used when all constraints except A are satisfied, and 0101 is used when only B and D are satisfied.

The learning support system assumes that the learner solves the problem and comes to the correct answer after repeatedly answering incorrectly. When the learner is able to answer correctly, the system switches to interaction with the teachable agent. First, the most frequent constraint satisfaction pattern in the answer history is identified (e.g., when answers that satisfy only B and D are most frequent, 0101 is the most frequent constraint satisfaction pattern). Note that this is not the most frequent constraint violation alone. Since the answers by a learner may consist of one or more constraint violations, we need a combination of constraint violations to visualize the error by the learner, not a single constraint violation.

Based on the constraint satisfaction pattern identified, the agent solves the constraint satisfaction problem using a combination of elements that can be realized in the target learning activity. At this point, the same constraint satisfaction pattern is generated, namely, wrong answers are generated based on the learner constraint errors. Therefore, they do not necessarily generate exactly the same wrong answers. In other words, we can say that we are visualizing errors that reflect the knowledge state of the learner. If there are multiple answers that satisfy the constraints, one of them is selected. If there is no pattern that contains a constraint violation in the learner's answer history (e.g., only 1111), we present the answer that violates all constraints (e.g., 0000) as the wrong answer. At this point, we can say that the visualization of errors reflects the knowledge state of the learner.

Next, the learner performs LbT based on the wrong answers presented by the teachable agent. At this point, the learner teaches by pointing out the constraints that the teachable agent violates. Specifically, when the constraint violation of the answer given by the teachable agent is 0110 ($[\neg A, B, C, \neg D]$), if the learner teaches the teachable agent that the constraint A is violated, the teachable agent searches again for an answer that satisfies the constraint satisfaction pattern of 1110. During the search, if 1110 does not exist in the possible combinations of elements, the agent chooses the solution that can correct the constraint and is closest to the original constraint satisfaction pattern. For example, if we have the combinations 1010, 0111, or the correct answer 1111, then 1010 or 0111 can be realized with only one modification from the original constraint satisfaction pattern 0110. In this case, in order to modify the pointed out constraint, the teachable agent selects and presents an answer that satisfies the constraint satisfaction pattern of 1010. In the LbT (teachable agent) phase, the teachable agent corrects its understanding (constraint satisfaction pattern) based on the constraints pointed out by the learner, and each time it presents an answer based on the understanding, it visualizes the error and realizes interactive learning that encourages the learner to correct the constraint satisfaction pattern.

4   Case Study

4.1   Summary

We apply TAME to the learning activities of Monsakun [7,8,10,16–18] as a case study for evaluating the feasibility of TAME by implementing additional teachable agents. Monsakun is a learning support system for learning arithmetic word problems by problem-posing as a sentence-integration. In Monsakun, students are presented with a set of cards as sentences, and they answer the questions using combinations of the cards.

The following is a description of the system we developed based on the Monsakun framework. This system consists of two phases: the problem-posing phase (Fig. 1) and the LbT phase (Fig. 2).

The problem-posing phase is an exercise equivalent to traditional Monsakun. In the system interface shown in Fig. 1, the students construct their answers by dragging and dropping the cards from the list on the right to the answer column on the left. When the learner finishes combining cards, they can answer the questions by clicking the button at the upper right. Whenever the learner answers one question correctly in the problem-posing phase, the system switches to the LbT phase for the same question that the learner just solved.

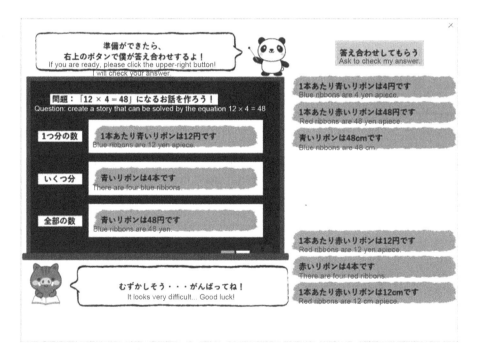

Fig. 1. User interface of the developed system in the problem-posing phase.

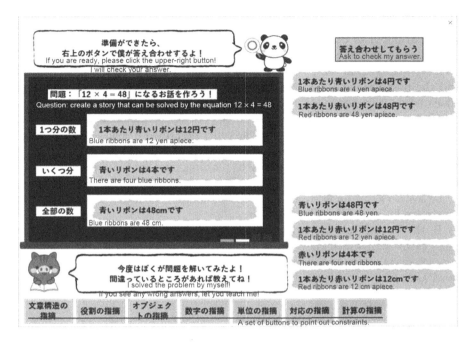

Fig. 2. User interface of the developed system in the LbT phase.

The LbT phase is the exercise of teaching the teachable agent based on TAME. In the system interface of Fig. 2, the seven buttons at the bottom are the constraint violation buttons corresponding to each constraint. The teachable agent reconstructs the answer to correct the pointed-out constraint violation. If the learner thinks that the answer by the teachable agent is correct, they can ask for a diagnosis of that answer by using an answer button in the upper right, the same as in the problem-posing phase. If the teachable agent answers correctly in the LbT phase, the system switches again to the next question in the problem-posing phase.

4.2   Evaluation

Procedure. To evaluate the effectiveness of the proposed system, we conducted an evaluation experiment on 15 undergraduate students in the faculty of engineering who were divided into an experimental group of 8 students and a control group of 7 students. Both groups were given a pre-test for a total of 20 min, and then each group was divided into two groups to perform system-based learning for 20 min. After that, both groups were given a post-test for a total of 20 min and a questionnaire for 5 min. In the system-based learning, the experimental group learned using the proposed system while the control group learned using only the problem-posing phase of the our system (i.e., the same as conventional Monsakun). In order to prevent differences in learning effects between the experimental and control groups, explanatory materials for the seven constraints were distributed to both groups.

The pre-test and post-test consisted of five different tests of eight questions each (40 questions in total). The type of test was the same between the pre-test and the post-test, and only the questions in the test were changed. The time allocated to each test as described below was determined through a preliminary experiment on undergraduate students of engineering. The tests were also conducted during the experiment in the order described below.

In the first test, the "error-identification test," learners have four minutes to find one of the three cards in each question, and find the element of the sentence on that card that is incorrect. The purpose of this test is to determine if the learners can understand the sentence and the elements that violate the constraint by identifying the mistakes.

In the second test, the "role-identification test," learners are presented with three cards with which they have two minutes to assemble the correct answer for each question, and they must assemble them in the correct order in the role slots, as shown on the left side of the system interface. The purpose of this test is to test whether the students understand the role of sentences, which is the most basic of all constraints.

In the third test, the "card replacement test," learners have four minutes to select the wrong card and replace it with the correct card from the choices presented. The purpose of this test is to test the ability of the learners to select the appropriate card from the choices and correct the error.

In the fourth test, the "problem-posing test," learners are required to construct a card from the card choices presented in each question to fit the problem statement, similar to the learning activities in the system, in five minutes. The purpose of this test is to test the overall problem-posing ability of the students.

In the fifth test, the "constraint-identification test," students are given five minutes to point out all the wrong constraints in each question. The purpose of this test is to test whether the students understand each constraint.

It should be noted that previous research has confirmed that even university students have the same tendency to make errors in constraints as elementary school students in Monsakun for addition and subtraction, and has also shown that Monsakun has a learning effect on university students as well [8]. In other words, it shows the difficulty of learning constraints. Therefore, we believe that the experiment on the university students has some validity because the same is expected to hold for multiplication and division, which are generally more difficult than addition and subtraction.

Result. The four tests, except for the constraint-identification test, were scored by assigning one point for each completed question. For the constraint-identification test, one point was given for each identified constraint, because the number of constraints to be identified differs between the questions. In the constraint-identification test, full points are always obtained if all the constraints are identified. Therefore, we decided to evaluate not only the number of correct

Table 1. Results of each test.

	Error-identification		Role-identification		Card replacement	
Group	Pre	Post	Pre	Post	Pre	Post
Exp.	2.13 (1.27)	6.50 (1.66)	4.38 (1.22)	6.13 (1.69)	2.63 (0.99)	2.88 (1.76)
Ctrl.	2.86 (1.46)	4.00 (1.60)	4.43 (1.68)	6.29 (1.28)	1.71 (1.03)	2.57 (1.92)

	Problem-posing		Constraint (correct)		Constraint (incorrect)	
Group	Pre	Post	Pre	Post	Pre	Post
Exp.	4.25 (2.05)	5.25 (2.38)	10.75 (3.15)	12.25 (4.58)	-7.00 (3.97)	-3.13 (2.20)
Ctrl.	2.86 (1.36)	4.71 (1.58)	11.43 (3.45)	14.00 (4.72)	-7.14 (3.83)	-6.86 (3.80)

Note: Numbers outside parenthesis indicate averages, numbers inside indicate S.D.

identifications but also the number of incorrect identifications that are not violated constraints. For each incorrectly identified constraint, a separate score of -1 was given. The results of each test are shown in Table 1.

A 2×2 ANOVA was conducted on the scores of each test, with the group (experimental and control) as the between-subjects factor and the timing of the test (pre- and post-test) as the within-subjects factor.

A significant difference ($p < 0.05$) was found between the groups in the error-identification test. Since an interaction was confirmed, a simple main effect test was conducted. As a result, significant differences ($p < 0.05$) were found between the pre- and post-tests in the experimental group, between the pre- and post-tests in the control group, and between the experimental and control groups in the post tests.

In the role-identification test, there was a significant difference only within the groups ($p < 0.05$).

There was no significant difference in the card replacement test.

In the problem-posing test, there was a significant difference only within the group ($p < 0.05$).

In the constraint-identification test, there was no significant difference in the number of correct identifications, while a simple main effect test was conducted on the number of incorrect identifications because an interaction was confirmed. As a result, there was a significant difference between the pre- and post-tests in the experimental group and between the experimental and control groups in the post-test ($p < 0.05$).

4.3   Discussion

We now discuss the experimental results of each test. For the sake of discussion, we discuss the results in a different order from that in which they were conducted in the experiment.

First, the results of the error-identification test suggest that the activities in the LbT phase are effective for understanding the sentence and its elements that violate the constraints. In addition, the number of errors in the constraint-identification test decreased in the experimental group, suggesting that the activities in the LbT phase improved the accuracy of constraint-identification. This suggests that the activities in the LbT phase promoted the understanding of constraints.

The results of the role-identification test and the problem-posing test suggest that the conventional activities conducted by the control group alone can have some effect on problem-posing learning. At the same time, the experimental group spent less time in the problem-posing phase and more time in the LbT phase than the control group, but the results were the same as those in the problem-posing phase alone.

For the results of the card replacement test, although we expected to see some improvement in the scores of both the experimental group and the control group, there was no such improvement.

The overall results suggest that the LbT activities realized by TAME are useful for understanding problem-posing as a conventional problem-posing support, and that the understanding of constraints and errors is better than conventional problem-posing support.

Therefore, it was confirmed through this case study that the learning activities realized by TAME have some usefulness.

5   Conclusion

This paper proposed TAME as a teachable agent modeling method that realizes recursive feedback based on error-visualization. As a case study, we developed a learning support system with a teachable agent based on TAME for the existing learning support system, "Monsakun" [7,8,10,16–18]. The results of evaluation experiments using the system suggested that the TAME-based teachable agent has some effectiveness in learning.

Although we tried to summarize the value of this paper by focusing on the design and modeling methods of the teachable agent, we believe that it also has some value in the field of problem-posing learning support, which we examined in the case study. For example, in Monsakun, it is important for learners to understand the constraints that must be satisfied in a learning task. Therefore, in order to investigate how learners understand constraints in Monsakun, analysis of the learning process has been actively conducted (and these studies have revealed patterns of constraints that are difficult for learners to understand and frequent violations of constraints) [7,8,16–18]. The TAME-based teachable agent developed in this paper can be positioned as a novel means of approaching the understanding of constraints, which is thought to be important for supporting learning by problem-posing.

In order to expand the scope of application of TAME, it is necessary to investigate whether it can be applied to learning objects and activities in other fields. In addition, we would like to consider more specific design procedures using TAME and compare the cost of implementation.

Acknowledgement. This work was supported by JSPS KAKENHI Grant Numbers JP19H04227, JP20H01730, and JP21H03565.

References

1. Biswas, G., Leelawong, K., Schwartz, D., Vye, N., The Teachable Agents Group at Vanderbilt: Learning by teaching: a new agent paradigm for educational software. Appl. Artif. Intell. **19**(3–4), 363–392 (2005)
2. Chase, C.C., Chin, D.B., Oppezzo, M.A., Schwartz, D.L.: Teachable agents and the protégé effect: increasing the effort towards learning. J. Sci. Educ. Technol. **18**(4), 334–352 (2009)
3. Duran, D.: Learning-by-teaching. Evidence and implications as a pedagogical mechanism. Innov. Educ. Teach. Int. **54**(5), 476–484 (2017)
4. Fiorella, L., Mayer, R.E.: The relative benefits of learning by teaching and teaching expectancy. Contemp. Educ. Psychol. **38**(4), 281–288 (2013)
5. Fiorella, L., Mayer, R.E.: Role of expectations and explanations in learning by teaching. Contemp. Educ. Psychol. **39**(2), 75–85 (2014)
6. Gulz, A., Londos, L., Haake, M.: Preschoolers' understanding of a teachable agent-based game in early mathematics as reflected in their gaze behaviors-an experimental study. Int. J. Artif. Intell. Educ. **30**(1), 38–73 (2020)
7. Hasanah, N., Hayashi, Y., Hirashima, T.: An analysis of learner outputs in problem posing as sentence-integration in arithmetic word problems. Res. Pract. Technol. Enhanc. Learn. **12**(1), 1–16 (2017). https://doi.org/10.1186/s41039-017-0049-5
8. Hasanah, N., Hayashi, Y., Hirashima, T.: Posing arithmetic word problems in a sentence integration learning environment in English and Indonesian: a utilization analysis. J. Inf. Syst. Educ. **18**(1), 51–62 (2019)
9. Hirashima, T., Horiguchi, T., Kashihara, A., Toyoda, J.: Error-based simulation for error-visualization and its management. Int. J. Artif. Intell. Educ. **9**(1–2), 17–31 (1998)
10. Hirashima, T., Yamamoto, S., Hayashi, Y.: Triplet structure model of arithmetical word problems for learning by problem-posing. In: Yamamoto, S. (ed.) HIMI 2014. LNCS, vol. 8522, pp. 42–50. Springer, Cham (2014). https://doi.org/10.1007/978-3-319-07863-2_5
11. Horiguchi, T., Hirashima, T.: Robust simulator: a method of simulating learners' erroneous equations for making error-based simulation. In: Ikeda, M., Ashley, K.D., Chan, T.-W. (eds.) ITS 2006. LNCS, vol. 4053, pp. 655–665. Springer, Heidelberg (2006). https://doi.org/10.1007/11774303_65
12. Horiguchi, T., Imai, I., Toumoto, T., Hirashima, T.: Error-based simulation for error-awareness in learning mechanics: an evaluation. Educ. Technol. Soc. **17**(3), 1–13 (2014)
13. Leelawong, K., Biswas, G.: Designing learning by teaching agents: the Betty's Brain system. Int. J. Artif. Intell. Educ. **18**(3), 181–208 (2008)
14. Matsuda, N., et al.: Cognitive anatomy of tutor learning: lessons learned with SimStudent. J. Educ. Psychol. **105**(4), 1152 (2013)
15. Okita, S.Y., Schwartz, D.L.: Learning by teaching human pupils and teachable agents: the importance of recursive feedback. J. Learn. Sci. **22**(3), 375–412 (2013)
16. Supianto, A.A., Hayashi, Y., Hirashima, T.: Visualizations of problem-posing activity sequences toward modeling the thinking process. Res. Pract. Technol. Enhanc. Learn. **11**(1), 1–23 (2016). https://doi.org/10.1186/s41039-016-0042-4
17. Supianto, A.A., Hayashi, Y., Hirashima, T.: An investigation of learner's actions in posing arithmetic word problem on an interactive learning environment. IEICE Trans. Inf. Syst. **100**(11), 2725–2728 (2017)

18. Supianto, A.A., Hayashi, Y., Hirashima, T.: Model-based analysis of thinking in problem posing as sentence integration focused on violation of the constraints. Res. Pract. Technol. Enhanc. Learn. **12**(1), 1–21 (2017). https://doi.org/10.1186/s41039-017-0057-5
19. Tärning, B., Gulz, A., Haake, M.: Instructing a teachable agent with low or high self-efficacy-does similarity attract? Int. J. Artif. Intell. Educ. **29**(1), 89–121 (2019)

Research on the Design of In-Cockpit Display Interface for Fighter Aircraft Based on Visual Attention Mechanism

Linjian Li[1] , Jing Lin[2] , Zhen Luo[1] , and Zhejun Liu[1](✉)

[1] Tongji University, Shanghai, People's Republic of China
{2033670,wingeddreamer,milkaholic0}@tongji.edu.cn
[2] No. 808 Institute of Shanghai Academy of Spaceflight Technology, Shanghai, China

Abstract. The advances of aviation technology continue to boost the performance of fighter aircrafts and to complicate future sky battlefields, which continually add more and more information that must be presented to the pilot via the cockpit interface, significantly increasing his/her cognitive workload. This study analyzes the evolution of contemporary in-cockpit display interface of warplanes, identifies the general rules of the interface design and looks ahead to future development trends. By doing so, this study brings forward principles of cockpit display interface design from the perspective of visual attention mechanism and tests their effectiveness and feasibility via comparative experiments using simplified prototypes.

Keywords: In-cockpit display · Visual attention mechanism · Interface design

1 Introduction

In the era of great power competition, fighter aircrafts have become backbone nodes in the air-space integrated combat system, with networked intelligent fighting capabilities, excellent situation awareness and quick decision-making abilities. The fighter cockpit display interface serves the "brain" of the fighter, namely the pilot. It is a central information output terminal for all types of onboard data and equipment, as well as a vital communication portal between the fighter and the pilot [1].

The fighter cockpit is the core component of the man-machine interaction, which plays a controlling and commanding role for the aircraft during the operation. Its design is directly related to the pilot's operational effectiveness and life safety. Designing and implementing a cockpit interactive interface is a cost-efficient option for reducing the pilot's workload and improving the pilot's operational performance. An efficient cockpit interactive interface can enhance man-machine information exchange, convey fighter information to the pilot quickly, and speed up and improve the pilot's decision-making process. It's a promising solution to deal with the paradox of a flood of information and a limited amount of information display space.

The vast amount of visual data makes it necessary for pilots to allocate their attention efficiently and precisely [2]. When pilots perform flight and combat tasks, they must constantly acquire data, analyze information, make decisions, issue orders, and perform other processing jobs. This demands the pilot's brain to process a wide range of complex information and generate quick decisions [3]. The pilot's visual attention, on the other hand, is restricted, which means he or she cannot cognize all visual information at the same time. As a result, the cockpit interface should be designed based on the human visual attention mechanism to meet the pilot's operational needs without overburdening his/her cognitive capacity. By enhancing the efficiency of information delivery, the performance of the fighter crafts in real combats may improve consequently.

2 Related Work

2.1 In-Cockpit Display Interface for Fighter Aircraft

The down-view display is a comprehensive electrical/optical display that uses a cathode ray tube or other electronic display characters and images and is installed on the instrument panel and operational console. The head down display interface is not only a vital interactive channel for pilots to comprehend the fighter, but it is also the primary medium for functional operation in the fighter's interactive system. The fighter's flight information and combat mission should be more properly provided through the interface design, so that the pilot can quickly get useful information, accurately recognize the situation awareness (SA), and correctly control the combat operation.

Fig. 1. The development of cockpit display technology from the first-generation to the fourth-generation aircraft

Feng (2020) summarized the evolution of the fighter cockpit display interface [4]. This paper gives an overview of how fighter aircraft displays have evolved over time (see Fig. 1). The first-generation fighters use mechanical instruments scattered inside the cabin space to display equipment status. In addition to supporting new equipment such as missiles, radar and other weapons, the second-generation interface also made use of cathode ray tube displays (for radar) and optical sights (for aiming). The third-generation interface replaced mechanical instruments with flat screens and electronic displays, allowing the presentation of various information on a single screen. Among the fourth-generation interfaces, the F22 series replaced all traditional instruments with digital screens completely. The interface of the more advanced F35 series combined several screens into a large flat one and relocated some information from the screen to the integrated helmet display [5].

The fighter's cockpit interface is a window through which a pilot and a fighter could exchange information. The pilot collects information from the display system through this window, evaluates and interprets the data, and makes judgments [6]. From the perspective of functional and emotional design of information visualization, Wang (2009) suggested the consistency and experience design objectives of the integrated display interface of the fighter cockpit [7]. Ling (2019) employed reaction accuracy and response time as performance indicators to assess a pilot's ability to perceive distinct color information in various flying circumstances and to serve as a foundation for HUD information coding design [8]. Shao (2016) investigated several applications of head-mounted display interfaces from the viewpoint of visual cognition in a systematic manner [9]. Xiong (2016) investigated the impact of Chinese and English icons, as well as their various layout forms, on the pilot's cognition of the fighter jet's multi-function display menu [10].

External information is mostly received by pilots through visual channels, with visual information accounting for over 70% of all information received [11]. Pilots can search, identify, and make choices on interface information more rapidly with a reasonable visual attention distribution, which improves cognitive efficiency [12]. Therefore, studying the influence of pilots' visual attention on information and cognition is critical. The usefulness and convenience of the head down display interface of the fighter's cockpit is improved by the interface's appropriate interaction and aesthetic design.

2.2 Visual Attention Mechanism

We can filter redundant information from a vast amount of visual information, identify valuable information, and speed up the processing capability of information by selectivity of visual attention [13]. The human visual system is constantly receiving information. The information that is important to the subject can enter the processing channel to complete the in-depth study of information, whilst the meaningless information is selectively discarded by individuals from these huge volumes of data [14]. Visual attention refers to the selective processing of visual information described above: the human visual system can focus on the most important information in a limited amount of time and with limited attention resources due to this mechanism [15].

Li (2014) investigated the visual scanning pattern of pilots' attention distribution while seeking dynamic targets [16]. Eye-tracking techniques were then coupled with flight simulators to enhance pilots' training efficiency, based on the studies on the influence of visual scanning mode on pilots' situational awareness [17]. According to Li's (2014) research, pilots used both bottom-up and top-down visual processes depending on the value of the information or previous experience [18]. Li (2015) used an eye tracker to collect diverse human eye movement data in real time and investigated the link between the cockpit human-machine interface layout design and the pilot's attention allocation when performing various activities [19]. Eye trackers and the F-16 flight simulator for air-to-ground missions can help system designers understand pilot attention allocation (Li et al. 2016) [20].

The cognitive processes of human-machine interaction between pilots and interface design can be explained by using visual attention mechanisms [21]. For interface design during flight operations, visual cues provide an opportunity to establish the connections between the pilot's situational awareness and visual stimuli [22]. Prominent visual cues might effectively attract the pilot's attention [23]. Pilots frequently confront time-sensitive circumstances, and an interface based on the visual attention mechanism helps them to optimally distribute their attention [24]. Failure to carry out a high-priority operation in a timely manner might have disastrous effects.

3   Our Framework

3.1   In-Cockpit Display Interface for Fighter Aircraft

An analysis of the cockpit display technologies ranging from the first to fourth generation fighters reveals the future path of development: from complicated electromechanical instruments to more concise electronic displays, which will eventually be superseded by multi-modal multi-functional output devices. The arrangement of information evolved from a casually scattered layout to an ergonomic "T" shape, then to a mixture of forward and downward displays. It is generally believed that since F35's large widescreen display, the trend toward integrated cockpit interface has become obvious.

The major portal for information exchange between pilots and fighters is the head down display interface. This channel transmits situational information for all fighters' tasks including take-off, approach, navigation, cruise, operation, attack, formation, and so on, as well as pilots' decision-making orders to aircraft. As a result, analyzing the categories of presented information and typical flying missions is the cornerstone of appropriate and effective interface information presentation.

Generally, a fighter's display interface is mainly divided into three parts: navigation, main interface layer and sub interface layer [25]. The main interface is divided into fifteen modules [26]: Horizontal Position Interface (his), Heads Up Interface (HUD), Radar Interface (RDR), Aircraft External Mount Management Interface (SMS), Forward Looking Infrared Image Interface (FLIR), Marine Forward Looking Infrared Image Interface (NFLR), Checklist Interface (CHK), Engine Parameters Interface (ENG), Situational Awareness Interface (SA), Automatic Landing Interface (ACL), Attitude Control Display Interface (ADI), Fuel Tank Interface (FPAS). These are the fighter system's 15 major functioning modules Used by pilots to get fighter information, operate the fighter, communicate with the ground, and accomplish airborne missions.

Although the information provided on each module's interface is essentially independent and thus may be examined independently, once a fighter is in a dynamic scenario, the pilot normally need data from many module interfaces in order to accurately gauge the external environment and the fighter's internal status. In this situation, the most typical solution used by a fighter cockpit is to alter the interface via hardware buttons on the same display, to display many viewports at once, or to use a comprehensive interface to include all of the essential information.

Information provided by each module is closely related to each other, however, due to technological limitations, they can only be presented on separate screens. The switch between interface display modes is relies on a hardware button. The performance of a pilot using this information display mode highly depends on his/her memory. In terms of response time and accuracy, a pilot's retention is important, but the correspondance between a display mode and a button is also significant. As a result, it's crucial to optimize the human-computer interaction interface based on visual attention mechanisms and use them to guide the design of fighter cockpit interfaces so that pilots can get accurate and efficient visual interface information.

3.2 Visual Attention Mechanism Method

Visual attention is an important regulating mechanism of the human visual system. The sensory process of visual information is parallel, whereas perceptual process of visual information is serial. As a consequence, the amount of information obtained via the visual sensory process may greatly exceed the capacity of visual perceptual process. As for interface design, the visual attention mechanism directs the visual perception process and is important to the display interface's efficiency and reliability. When used properly, it may serve as a bridge that "conceals" the gap between these two unmatched processes and ensures that a pilot can always obtain the significant information quickly and precisely, which is the ultimate purpose of this research.

In general, the information filtering process of human visual system is influenced by two types of factors: internal subjective factors and exterior objective factors. A goal is the former, which is primarily regulated by the brain recognition system. Subjective cognition, including individual subjective intention and present task aim, guides selective visual attention. The latter is commonly referred to as exogenous attention, and is primarily influenced by stimuli. The visual attention mechanism tends to overlook the current task at hand and the individual's subjective motivation and focus on a few conspicuous stimuli in the visual field, which cannot be regulated by the subjective cognitive system.

The two attention modes above coexist in the real working scenarios of the visual system. They influence the selection, perception, and cognition processes of visual inputs in an interactive manner. Because the brain's ability to comprehend visual information is restricted, attention allocation and information selection become more critical. When confronted with the interactive interface, a pilot's visual system is presented with complicated data that will have difficulty to digest it in a short period of time, necessitating proper information sorting and presentation.

It may be explained as follows using the three-dimensional patterns of visual attention [27]: Firstly, fundamental visual aspects such as the form, color, order, and motion status of the viewed object in the field of vision are received by the pilot's visual receptors. The visual nerve system then filters the data using the attention mechanism, reconstructs and restores the image in the field of view, and generates a clear cognition of the interface content. Finally, the brain uses the memory to recall more target-related experience in order to comprehend and characterize the task.

3.3 Interface Information Division

The increased stress on military pilots is due to conflict between the intrinsic limits of human visual cognition and the delivery of a huge amount of flight data. The increased workload may have a detrimental influence on the pilot's SA performance, resulting in raised risks. Hopefully, human-centered design has the potential to alleviate the burden on pilots caused by the explosion of visual information.

During the flight mission of fighter jets, visual attention is affected by the interplay of two attention modes: endogenous (flight tasks, search targets, etc.) and exogenous (emerging obstacles, warnings and other information). Pilots used both depending on the prominence of the information or existing knowledge, based on previous experience. Endsley identified three levels of SA, which are closely related to the key elements of the cognitive process [28]. Perceiving visual signals, such as alert reminders in the cockpit interface, is the first level. Processing visual clues based on knowledge and experience is the second level. Predicting probable future situations, as well as associated measures and solutions, is the third level.

These visual cues on the fighter interface are crucial for comprehending information, and more than 75% of pilot errors are caused by perception failures [29]. To minimize misunderstanding and distraction, it's vital to provide the pilot with optimized visual information. Fighter cockpit interface design must maintain the pilot's attention and SA with sufficient visual stimuli. A fundamental design principle is that the interface must keep a pilot consistently informed of the interface's goal and current operation mode.

4   The Experiment

The interface design of a head down display system must comply with the habits of pilots have developed as a result of the development of the head down display interfaces. National military standards (GJB) have regulated the design of the most important elements, such as SA, flight altitude, flight direction, airspeed, engine information, navigation information, fuel information, and so on. However, for special elements such as warning information and timely notice of vital tasks, there are no design standards. It's still in the early stage of development and needs to be understood better via further research. The warning information in the interface must be prominent and easily accessible, and feedback information must be sent in a timely way.

The experiment aims to study the effectiveness of the communication of warning information in the head down display interface, and to improve the efficiency of pilots' timely response and decision-making. The alarm information presentation mode of the head down display system is designed based on visual attention mechanism. Looking into subjects' response time and accuracy, the efficiency of alarm information acquisition from different presentation formats is compared and examined.

4.1   Experimental Materials

The major goal of emulating a fighter cockpit's digital interface is to find abnormal information about fighter launch parameters. In the present condition, the fighter interface prioritizes information with a greater priority. The fighter interface gives priority to the information with higher priority in the current state. Because not all of the essential alarm information is currently presented on the interface when a sudden alert occurs, it is important to present the alarm information that is not already displayed on the interface so that the pilot may immediately recognize it. The display interface under the fighter's cockpit, as depicted in Fig. 2, is made up of branch interfaces including situation radar, fuel tank, horizon director, and aircraft plug-in management. It is necessary to display the engine abnormal parameters that are not presented in the existing interface when the engine is abnormal.

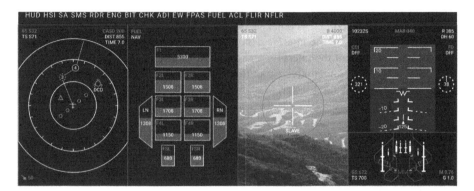

Fig. 2. The interface of eye movement experiment

The experimental materials are presented at a resolution of 2560 * 1024. The background of the experimental interface is pure black in order to decrease distraction. According to the character color standards, when the interface information is green (wavelength 500–650 nm), the visual recognition is greater, thus RGB (0,255,0) is chosen as the primary color code. Furthermore, the national military standards for ergonomic design of military visual display specifies that alert information should be shown in red and yellow. As a result, the alarm's presentation color is red, RGB (255,0,0).

4.2 Experimental Design

This study focuses on the design of special information displays, using alarm data as an example. The goal is to outline the best method for obtaining display information in order to improve the pilot's performance effectively. It is important for pilots to notice vital information quick enough to make correct decisions promptly because in emergent scenarios, a short period of time may make a significant difference.

The classic theory of visualism holds that spatial position has a significant influence on the visual system's selection of information. The spatial position is the first and foremost factor that influences visual attention [30]. In the process of visual perception, attention tends to naturally focus on certain areas in the field of view, searching for a specific stimulus, which is followed by further processing and understanding.

It is a generalized design principle and a model used to represent the visual scanning order, according to the Gutenberg diagram stated in William Lidwell, Kritina Holden, and Jill Butler's book *Universal Principles of Design* [31].

When browsing through the interface, the visual flow starts from the top left corner to the lower right corner, according to the "F" type visual scanning track of human eyes. Significant information should be put in the upper left corner of the interface, the secondary information in the upper right corner and lower left corner, and the least important information in the lower right corner, according to the zoning concept of the Gutenberg diagram for display media. To ensure that users can discover relevant material quickly with their visual habits is also a key tenet of succinct layout design.

The interface design of a fighter generally follows this principle, but the alarm information is not included in the regular design layout. The alarm information is presented in two ways: one is to compress other sections to make room for the alarm information in the upper left corner of the interface; the other is to display the alarm information in the lower right corner of the interface and discard the section with lowest priority (see Fig. 3). We then use comparative experiment to discover which one allows a user to acquire accurate information faster.

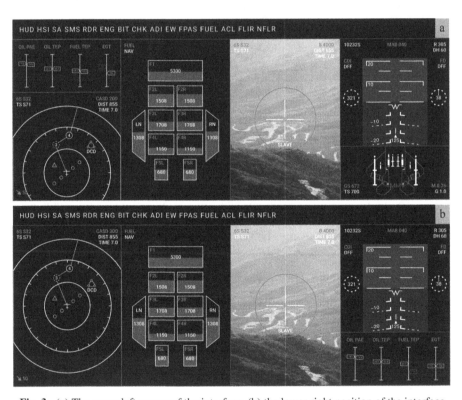

Fig. 3. (a) The upper left corner of the interface, (b) the lower right position of the interface

The participants were 60 college students, 39 males and 21 females, aging from 19 to 29, with normal or corrected-to-normal vision and no color blindness or color weakness. The subjects were instructed to acquaint themselves with the procedures and operations before the experiment. All of the participants had sufficient experience using computer software, but they had never seen a fighter cockpit's interface before.

The experimental material is presented as a series of web pages that can be accessed online. Subjects finished reading the instructions and began the experiment by pressing any key on the keyboard in each trial (see Fig. 4). The initial fighter information is displayed in the middle of the screen for 500 ms, and then the warning information is displayed at either the upper left or lower right of the interface randomly. After detecting the warning message, the participants were asked to confirm by pressing the space key, and their response time was recorded. Then the subject waited for 500 ms before entering the matching judgment interface, where he/she picked the answer by pressing the left or right key on the keyboard.

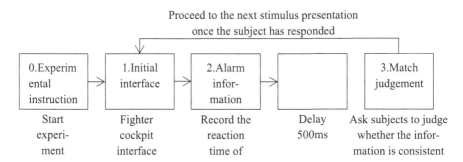

Fig. 4. The interface of eye movement experiment

We obtained quantitative data - reaction time and accurate rate of warning information recognition in the fighter interface - through experiments. Firstly, when task performance is measured in terms of reaction time or correctness, it is found that human performance effectively improves as visual attention is directed to the task. The participants' reaction time to recognize the alert information was recorded, and the accurate rate was calculated. Secondly, when task performance is measured in terms of reaction speed or correctness, visual attention to the task efficiently boosts human performance. The participants' reaction time to recognize the alert information was recorded, and the accurate rate was calculated as well. By comparing and analyzing data, we can draw the conclusion that which interface design method is more effective in transmitting alert information.

5   Result

According to data collected, the alarm information shown at the lower right corner of the interface yielded a faster response time (M = 3380.2556 ms) than the that at the upper left corner (M = 4672.1125 ms) (see Table 1). The difference is 1291.8569 ms, which is significant. As for correctness, the information displayed at the lower right corner resulted in a greater correctness (M = 0.8744) than that at the upper left corner (M = 0.8374), as shown in Table 2.

The data of response time and accurate rate of warning information in different locations were statistically analyzed, and extreme data were omitted from the analysis. SPSS was used to perform an independent T test on the response time and accurate rate (F represents the significant difference level, P represents the test level). The warning

Table 1. Descriptive statistics of reaction time

	Region	N	Mean	Std. deviation	Std. error mean
Reaction time	Right	60	3380.2556	2290.00264	295.63807
	Left	60	4672.1125	4431.63053	569.79725

Table 2. Descriptive statistics of accuracy

	Region	N	Mean	Std. deviation	Std. error mean
Accuracy	Right	60	.8744	.25247	.03259
	Left	60	.8374	.25669	.03314

information displayed the reaction time of different location areas (F = 11.558, P = 0.001 < 0.05), which was statistically significant at the 0.05 significance level (see Table 3). The influence of different areas of the warning information on the accurate rate (F = 0.112 P = 0.738 > 0.05) was not significant, according to the accurate rate analysis (see Table 4). As a result, the diverse display regions of the warning information have a substantial influence on the subjects' cognitive speed under the fighter flying task;

Table 3. T-test analysis of reaction time

		Levene's Test for Equality of variances		t-test for Equality of Means		
		F	Sig	t	df	Sig(2-tailed)
Reaction time	Equal variances assumed	11.558	.001	-2.012	118	.046
	Equal variances not assumed			-2.012	88.619	.047

		t-test for Equality of Means			
				95% Confidence Interval of the Difference	
		Mean Difference	Std. Error Difference	Lower	Upper
Reaction time	Equal variances assumed	-1291.85694	641.92739	-2563.04794	-20.66595
	Equal variances not assumed	-1291.85694	641.92739	-2567.42847	-16.28541

nevertheless, they have no significant impact on the subjects' visual cognitive ability and accuracy.

Table 4. T-test analysis of accuracy

		Levene's Test for Equality of variances		t-test for Equality of Means		
		F	Sig	t	df	Sig(2-tailed)
Accuracy	Equal variances assumed	.112	.738	.855	118	.395
	Equal variances not assumed			.855	117.968	.395

		t-test for Equality of Means			
				95% Confidence Interval of the Difference	
		Mean Difference	Std. Error Difference	Lower	Upper
Accuracy	Equal variances assumed	.03972	.04648	-.05232	.13177
	Equal variances not assumed	.03972	.04648	-.05232	.13177

From a statistical standpoint, there was a substantial difference in reaction times between the two groups. The analysis shows that, when compared with displaying alarm information at the upper left corner by compressing the rest of the interface, it is more effective to replace existing least important content with alarm information and display it at the lower right corner of the interface.

6 Discussion

This study suggests two approaches to provide fighter warning information based on the components and design methodologies of the visual attention mechanism, in order to increase the cognitive efficiency of fighter interface design. The findings of this study's experiments show that creating interfaces based on the visual attention mechanism can enhance cognitive efficiency significantly. The designer can assist the pilot's visual transfer using design methodologies while developing the visual presentation of the information level, enabling the pilot to operate according to the designer's wishes.

According to the F mode area priority division, the upper left of the interface is the region that the user notices first, and the lower right is least observed. However, the experimental results show that the warning information displayed in the lower right of the interface is more effective than the recognition displayed in the upper left. This contradicts the F-suggested mode's browsing movement, and we believe the following factors are to blame:

1. The main variable utilized to measure the subject's reaction time and accurate rate was the position of the interface. The reduced interface or the replacement content are designed to be displayed at the same time. Minimize the influence of the remaining variables as much as possible. The results of the experiment reveal that, in addition to location, design strategies have an impact on visual attention attraction.
2. Content replacement is a swift and immediate change, but interface compression is a slow and subtle change. Visual signals can help guide visual attention to the target area in dynamic situations.
3. Content substitution, as opposed to interface compression with smaller visual stimuli, might draw people's visual attention. As a result, dynamic visual stimuli will affect the human eye even if it moves along the F-pattern. It displays visual selection when receiving alert information. People are more inclined to pay attention to dynamic, shifting visual stimuli than static, unchanging stimuli.
4. Because people are accustomed to receiving information in the upper left corner first, a sudden change in the bottom right corner draws visual attention instead. Specific stimuli, as opposed to habituation stimuli, are more likely to draw people's visual attention.

Based on the foregoing analysis, we should design the fighter cockpit interface using the following design principles: To begin, prompt the pilot to pay attention to the target condition in a clear way. The pilot's visual attention is then directed to the target area of the interface via visual cues. Motion effects can be used to enhance visual stimulation throughout this process. Finally, the pilot can quickly identify the required target information by using objects in the visual field with distinct stimuli that are different from habituation.

7   Conclusions

This paper proposes information display design principles for fighter cockpit interface based on the idea of visual attention mechanism to direct the pilot's attention to the most crucial mission goals. Two different design schemes were proposed and inspected via a comparative experiment. The result reveals that it is better to replace the least important information section with the alarm information and place it at the lower right corner of the interface than compressing the interface and making room for it at the upper left corner.

In conclusion, the proposed design principle for in-cockpit display interfaces of fighter aircraft based on visual attention mechanism can hopefully lower pilots' cognitive load, reduce the chances of information misread, and thus improve safety and performance of pilots' flight or combat missions. We hope this paper may provide some meaningful insight to the design of future fighter aircraft's in-cockpit interfaces.

References

1. 吴文海, 张源原, 刘锦涛, 周思羽, 梅丹: 新一代智能座舱总体结构设计. 航空学报 **37**(1), 290–299 (2016)
2. Bonnardel, N., Piolat, A., Le Bigot, L.: The impact of colour on website appeal and users' cognitive processes. Displays **32**(2), 69–80 (2011)
3. Heinke, D., Humphreys, G.W., Tweed, C.L.: Top-down guidance of visual search: a computational account. Vis. Cogn. **14**(4–8), 985–1005 (2006)
4. 冯悦, 王言伟, 耿欢: 战斗机智能座舱人机交互方式发展及应用. 飞机设计 (2020)
5. 张洋: F-35 战斗机驾驶舱的功能设计. 国际航空 (4), 32–34 (2008)
6. 康卫勇, 王黎静, 袁修干, 柳忠起: 战斗机座舱人机界面基本模型分析. 中國安全科學學報 **16**(1), 49–54 (2006)
7. Wang, H., Xue, C., Wang, H., Qiu, C.: Research on the visualization design of fighter cockpit integrated display interface. In: 2009 IEEE 10th International Conference on Computer-Aided Industrial Design and Conceptual Design, November 2009, pp. 1502–1505. IEEE (2009)
8. Ling, B., Bo, L., Bingzheng, S., Lingcun, Q., Chengqi, X., Yafeng, N.: A cognitive study of multicolour coding for the head-up display (HUD) of fighter aircraft in multiple flight environments. J. Phys. Conf. Ser. **1215**(1), 012032 (2019)
9. 邵将: 基于视觉认知理论的头盔显示界面信息编码方法研究. 东南大学出版社 (2019)
10. 熊端琴, 王嫣嫣, 刘庆峰, 郭小朝, 姚钦, 杜健, 白玉: 战斗机多功能显示器显示菜单标识和编排格式对飞行员认知的影响. 人类工效学, **22**(4), 1–4 (2016)
11. 刘伟, 袁修干, 林海燕: 飞机驾驶员视觉信息流系统工效综合评定研究. 北京航空航天大学学报, **27**(2), 175–177 (2001)
12. Le Callet, P., Niebur, E.: Visual attention and applications in multimedia technologies. Proc. IEEE **101**(9), 2058–2067 (2013)
13. Deutsch, J.A., Deutsch, D.: Attention: some theoretical considerations. Psychol. Rev. **70**(1), 80 (1963)
14. Dill, E.T., Young, S.D.: Analysis of eye-tracking data with regards to the complexity of flight deck information automation and management-inattentional blindness, system state awareness, and EFB usage. In: 15th AIAA Aviation Technology, Integration, and Operations Conference, p. 2901 (2015)
15. Shieh, K.K., Lai, Y.K.: Effects of ambient illumination, luminance contrast, and stimulus type on subjective preference of VDT target and background color combinations. Percept. Mot. Skills **107**(2), 336–352 (2008)
16. Li, W.C., Yu, C.S., Li, L.W., Greaves, M.: Pilots' eye movement patterns during performing air-to-air mission (2014)
17. Yu, C.S., Wang, E.M.Y., Li, W.C., Braithwaite, G.: Pilots' visual scan patterns and situation awareness in flight operations. Aviat. Space Environ. Med. **85**(7), 708–714 (2014)
18. Li, W.-C., Braithwaite, G., Yu, C.-S.: The investigation of pilots' eye scan patterns on the flight deck during an air-to-surface task. In: Harris, D. (ed.) EPCE 2014. LNCS (LNAI), vol. 8532, pp. 325–334. Springer, Cham (2014). https://doi.org/10.1007/978-3-319-07515-0_33
19. Yu, C.S., Wang, E.M.Y., Li, W.C., Braithwaite, G., Greaves, M.: Pilots' visual scan patterns and attention distribution during the pursuit of a dynamic target. Aerosp. Med. Hum. Perform. **87**(1), 40–47 (2016)
20. Li, W.C., Braithwaite, G., Greaves, M., Hsu, C.K., Lin, S.C.: The evaluation of military pilot's attention distributions on the flight deck. In: Proceedings of the International Conference on Human-Computer Interaction in Aerospace, September 2016, pp. 1–6 (2016)

21. Kearney, P., Li, W.C., Lin, J.J.: The impact of alerting design on air traffic controllers' response to conflict detection and resolution. Int. J. Ind. Ergon. **56**, 51–58 (2016)

22. Ahlstrom, U., Friedman-Berg, F.J.: Using eye movement activity as a correlate of cognitive workload. Int. J. Ind. Ergon. **36**(7), 623–636 (2006)

23. Li, W.-C., White, J., Braithwaite, G., Greaves, M., Lin, J.-H.: The evaluation of pilot's situational awareness during mode changes on flight mode annunciators. In: Harris, D. (ed.) EPCE 2016. LNCS (LNAI), vol. 9736, pp. 409–418. Springer, Cham (2016). https://doi.org/10.1007/978-3-319-40030-3_40

24. Bybee, S.M., Bracken-Grissom, H.D., Hermansen, R.A., Clement, M.J., Crandall, K.A., Felder, D.L.: Directed next generation sequencing for phylogenetics: an example using Decapoda (Crustacea). Zoologisc. Anzeig. J. Comparat. Zool. **250**(4), 497–506 (2011)

25. Pazul, K.: Controller Area Network (Can) Basics, vol. 1. Microchip Technology Inc. (1999)

26. 王海燕, 卞婷, 薛澄岐: 新一代战斗机显控界面布局设计研究. 电子机械工程, **27**(4), 57–61 (2011)

27. Ware, C.: Visual thinking for design. Elsevier. (2010)

28. Endsley, M.R.: Toward a theory of situation awareness in dynamic systems. Hum. Fact. **37**(1), 32–64 (1995)

29. Jones, D.G., Endsley, M.R.: Sources of situation awareness errors in aviation. Aviat. Sp. Environ. Med. (1996)

30. Tkachuk, M., Martinkus, I.: Model and tools for multi-dimensional approach to requirements behavior analysis. In: Mayr, H.C., Kop, C., Liddle, S., Ginige, A. (eds.) UNISCON 2012. LNBIP, vol. 137, pp. 191–198. Springer, Heidelberg (2013). https://doi.org/10.1007/978-3-642-38370-0_19

31. Lidwell, W., Holden, K., Butler, J.: Universal principles of design, revised and updated: 125 ways to enhance usability, influence perception, increase appeal, make better design decisions, and teach through design. Rockport Pub (2010)

A Knowledge Sharing Platform for Learning from Others' Code

Shintaro Maeda[1]([✉]), Kento Koike[1], and Takahito Tomoto[2]

[1] Graduate School of Engineering, Tokyo Polytechnic University,
Atsugi, Kanagawa, Japan
`front4.shintaro@gmail.com`
[2] Faculty of Engineering, Tokyo Polytechnic University, Atsugi, Kanagawa, Japan
`https://www.takahito.com/members/maeda/`

Abstract. Learning from code written by other programmers is one of the most important ways of learning how to program. However, reading the code of a skilled programmer can be difficult for a beginner. Put differently, learning how to program can be challenging when the learners have different levels of programming proficiency. To lessen these difficulties, it is necessary to present model code that corresponds to the proficiency level of the learner. However, since proficiency levels in programming may vary by learner, preparing model code matching the proficiency level of every possible learner in advance may not always be practical. Therefore, we propose a platform for sharing knowledge among various learners participating in a given lecture. Functionality for sharing code alone may be insufficient for presenting code appropriate to the level of a given learner. Therefore, we also propose code quality indicators for understanding the degree of proximity in proficiency between a learner and a given programmer whose code is being used as a model. To this end, in this paper, we propose a platform with functionality for sharing, evaluating, and ranking written code. In addition, in order to understand the relationship between code written by other programmers and the behavior of the code at runtime, we propose a platform that involves programming a robot in order to allow the learner to visualize the behavior of the code as movement of the robot.

Keywords: Knowledge sharing · Behavior visualization · Learning programming · Ranking · Code reading

1 Introduction

An important aspect of learning how to program is learning from samples of code written by other programmers in order to improve one's own code [1,7,8]. From the perspective of education in programming, other researchers have pointed out that activities involving learning from others' code, especially activities that involve reading code written by a more experienced programmer, can facilitate the learning process[2–4]. However, when a novice programmer reads code

S. Yamamoto and H. Mori (Eds.): HCII 2022, LNCS 13305, pp. 489–504, 2022.
https://doi.org/10.1007/978-3-031-06424-1_36

written by a more experienced programmer, the experience may not necessarily facilitate learning because of the difference in proficiency level between the two. Oeda et al. [5] also described the challenge involved when a novice programmer attempts to understand code written by a more experienced programmer. Therefore, this research investigates activities involving learning from code written by other programmers, which is a process that is considered to be vital in programming education.

In order to encourage learners to learn from others' code in a programming lecture, various potential problems must be addressed: First, (1) in a programming lecture, only knowledge of programming itself is taught, and few opportunities are presented that allow learning from code written by other programmers. Second, (2) even if a teacher provides an opportunity for sharing code written by other programmers in the lecture, the opportunity may not facilitate learning because of a difference in proficiency level among different learners in the lecture. To solve the problem in (2), the teacher could share various samples of code corresponding to the level of each learner, but this solution may not be practical when the burden that would be placed on the teacher is taken into consideration. Finally, (3) learners may be unable to learn from code written by another programmer because of a lack of understanding of behavior of the code that they are attempting to use as a model.

In order to solve these problems, we propose the following: To solve problem (1), we propose a code-sharing function that can share code written by learners connected in a network. To solve problem (2), we propose a mechanism for ranking learners in a lecture and sharing only code written by other learners who are similar in rank. We also propose quality indicators for calculating the current rank of learners in facilitating this ranking process. To solve problem (3), we propose a system that allows learners to observe the behavior of their code by visualizing it through programming of a virtual robot.

Therefore, in this research, we developed a platform that provides learners with a knowledge-sharing environment in which they can study others' code, and in which the learners can learn programming one step at a time with support from the system. In this paper, we investigate evaluation of the developed code-sharing and ranking functions. We also verify differences between the developed quality indicators and evaluations by experienced programmers.

2   Proposed System

2.1   Functional Requirements of Proposed System

In order to learn from others' code and to improve one's own code, the following requirements are specified:

1. Objectives of the learners' code and code of others must be consistent.
2. The proficiency level of the others' code must match that of the learner.

First, based on (1) and (2), we adopted a method for preparing a common learning task to be shared among multiple learners. By doing so, we expect multiple learners to create various code samples that satisfy (1). However, the code samples written by each learner may not always be actively (mutually) shared. Therefore, the following requirement is also necessary:

3. An environment for sharing of code must be prepared.

In addition, in order to facilitate this activity, the following requirements are desirable:

4. Behavior at runtime of shared code written by others should be known.
5. Advantages of shared code written by others should be understood.

Therefore, in this research, we developed a code-sharing platform with functionality based on the above requirements (1) to (5).

First, based on requirements (1) and (4) above, we propose a farm game involving programming of a virtual robot in a virtual environment as our task. By choosing this task, we expect that the assigned task will be common among learners, and that runtime behavior of the shared code will be reflected in the robot's movements, thereby promoting understanding. Furthermore, in response to requirement (2), we provided an evaluation mechanism for code samples in which a code sample that has received an evaluation similar to that of the learner's own code is shared with the learner. In addition, based on requirement (3), we included gamification as an element in stimulating a spirit of competition among learners by posting the code samples that have been run to all learners in an evaluation-based ranking system. Finally, based on requirement (5), we proposed multidimensional metrics for evaluation of the code so that learners can easily understand how the shared samples of code are superior to their own (e.g., in terms of productivity or processing time).

2.2   System Overview

In order to understand a sample of code written by another programmer, it is important to understand how the code behaves. In this research project, we use programming of a robot to allow a learner to visualize the behavior of the robot on the basis of code written by the learner. This enables the learner to recognize differences between his or her own code and the code of others as differences in behavior of the robot, and thus to understand the code of others.

In this manner, results of execution can be visualized in facilitating understanding of programming by a learner [6].

An example of the system screen developed in our research is shown in Fig. 1. This system is based on a crop-harvesting game in which a learner programs a robot to "move around the field," "plant seeds," and "harvest crops." In this task, learners are presented with panels that have been arranged in two dimensions. There are two types of panels: a field panel and a puddle panel. The field panel can be used for planting seeds and harvesting crops, while the puddle panel will cause failure if a learner's robot enters it.

Figure 2 shows a list of instructions for the robot prepared in this system. First, we prepared movement functions numbered 1–4, which are necessary for

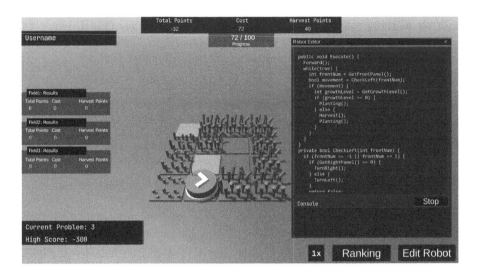

Fig. 1. Example of developed system interface

moving the robot. Using these functions, the learner writes code to move the robot around the field panel. "Planting" is a function for planting seeds in the field panel if there is a field panel at the current location of the robot, and "Harvest" is a function for performing harvesting if there is a grown crop at the current location of the robot. Seeds and crops grow each time that the robot performs an action. In other words, the seed planting phase and the harvesting phase must be separated in order for the robot to correctly patrol the field. The design of this task is expected to facilitate learning by allowing easier understanding of the relationship between each line of code and the corresponding behavior of the robot.

2.3   Scoring Function with Quality Indicators of Code

In order to learn from others' code, it is desirable to learn from code that is appropriate to one's own level. However, in a programming lecture, learners of various proficiency levels, from beginner to experienced programmers, may participate. Therefore, in this study, we propose an evaluation index for measuring similarity in the level of the written code. As described above, we designed a task using a crop-harvesting game. We propose a quality indicator based on this task. First, it is necessary to evaluate how well the code written by the learner is able to perform. In this research, we treat the activity of harvesting crops as an achievement and define the corresponding index as the "harvest count." The number of harvested crops increases with the growth rate of the crop, so it is necessary to perform other tasks for a certain period of time after planting seeds. Next, it is necessary to evaluate cost incurred in addition to evaluating the corresponding result. In this study, we propose a "cost" that indicates cost

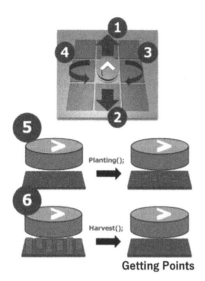

No	Function Name	Cost
1	Forward	1
2	Back	1
3	TurnRight	1
4	TurnLeft	1
5	Planting	1
6	Harvest	1

Fig. 2. Function list of our robot

incurred for an outcome. This cost is designed to be incurred every time the robot's instruction function, described in the previous section, is called. In other words, every activity must be designed in such a way as to minimize this cost. Finally, we propose a "total point" index, which is the sum of the "number of harvests" and the "cost." In this manner, we define "valuable code" as that which allows the robot to harvest a large number of crops at a low cost.

We thought it was necessary to write generic code that could cope with changes in given values in the design of the algorithm. However, if the presented task is fixed, a potential problem arises in which a learner may write code that corresponds only to the specific task and that earns a high score. Therefore, in order to evaluate general-purpose code, we proposed an evaluation method that uses test cases. In our system, a test case is a method in which multiple similar fields are prepared as cases for each problem, and in which all cases are executed during the evaluation. For example, in a problem involving rectangles with field panels, the number of field panels per side differs depending on the case. In this problem, we need to write generic code that traverses the fields even if the lengths of the edges differ. The final score is the sum of the scores calculated for all cases.

2.4   Ranking and Code-Sharing Functions

The ranking function allows scores earned by a learner (Harvest Points, Cost, and Total Points) to be ranked by category. The system also has a code-sharing function that allows the learner to view the code of other learners by selecting a rank that has been presented by the ranking function. However, the code-sharing function is restricted so that only the code of a learner whose rank is lower than his or her own and the code of one of the top learners can be viewed. For example, if the rank of a given learner is 8th, all code of rank 7th and below become visible to that learner, but not that of rank 6th or higher. This solves the problem in which viewing code of a proficiency level very different from that of a given learner does not facilitate learning, while supporting step-by-step learning.

2.5   Flow of Learning

The following procedure describes how learners can perform learning activities using this system. First, the system displays field panels on the screen in accordance with an arrangement that has been predetermined by the learner. The learner then considers how the robot should move based on the presented field panels. Next, the learner starts the code editor by clicking the "EditRobot" button and writes code based on a corresponding strategy. After writing the code, the learner clicks the "Play" button to run the code. When the "Play" button is clicked, the system compiles the code written by the learner. If the compilation is successful, the system executes the code internally and outputs the results sequentially on the learner's screen. Common programming control statements such as "if" and "for" are executed as usual, and the robot behaves according to its own instruction functions, such as "Forward" and "Harvest." The learner then observes the behavior of the robot on the screen, and, by trial and error, repeatedly edits the code and observes the corresponding behavior of the robot on the screen until a satisfactory result is achieved . Even if the behavior of the robot is inadequate at an early stage, the behavior of the robot and the real-time feedback from the robot in the form of harvested points and incurred costs will inform the learner of the degree toward completion of the algorithm. This process will assist the learner in writing better code by leading the learner to the discovery of the next advantageous modification to be made.

The ranking function and the code-sharing function can be used when the learner has created an ideal algorithm, or when the learner's knowledge learner does not allow attainment of the highest score. This function can be used at any time by clicking the "Ranking" button on the system screen. Rankings of learners in a class can be viewed by category; for example, if the current code has a problem in obtaining a certain number of harvests, a ranking of learners with the number of harvests attained can be viewed in ascending order. For instance, if the current code has a problem in obtaining a certain number of harvests, the learner may browse a ranking of learners, with the number of harvests displayed in descending order. Upon selection of a score of another learner in the ranking, the code corresponding to the selected score will be presented to the learner. In addition, since the code-sharing function presents only code that has earned a score similar to that of the current learner, the potential problem of difficulty in learning due to a substantial difference in proficiency level is avoided, thus leading to activities in which the learner learns from the code of others. After learning from the code of others, the learner is allowed to incorporate the code into his/her own code, and to verify results using the behavior of the robot.

2.6   System Infrastructure

The system infrastructure developed in this research is shown in Fig. 3. Since this system is intended to be used by multiple learners, we adopted a client-server model. We adopted Unity as the client because Unity can easily support multiple platforms and can be used on various personal computers owned by learners in a classroom. In addition, Unity has an API that includes many libraries useful for drawing, thus allowing achievement of a very low coding cost and enabling implementation of a system in a short period of time. The client and server communicate with each other using the gRPC framework, and the server is implemented using the C# Console Application. Therefore, code written by the learner needs to follow the specification of the C# programming language. The server receives code written by the learner from the client, and compiles and runs the code using Roslyn, a code analysis API. Results of execution are saved in a database (MongoDB).

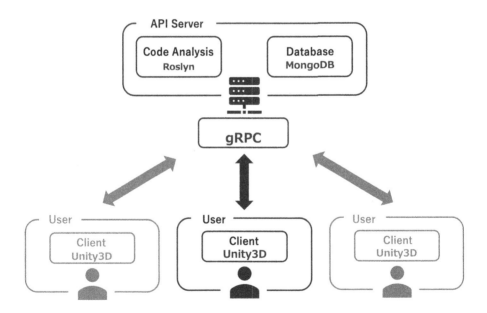

Fig. 3. System infrastructure

3   Evaluation and Discussion

3.1   Method

In this research, we verify whether the developed code-sharing function and ranking function facilitate learning. Participants were 12 university students who had completed a programming course. Experiments were conducted in the following order: tutorial, pre-test, learning with the platform, and post-test. In the pre-test and post-test experiments, the code-sharing function and ranking function were disabled because all functions were subsequently enabled for the experiment involving learning with the platform.

Evaluation was performed over a period of two days. On the first day, a tutorial was given to explain the task design of the system. Subsequently, the participants were asked to use the system with limited functionality for a period of 30 min. On the second day, the participants used the system with all functions enabled for a period of 60 min, and then used the system with limited functionality for another period of 30 min. Finally, a questionnaire was administered.

3.2   Results

Table 1 shows the difference in Harvest Points between the pre-test and post-test experiments. The experimental results suggest that the code-sharing function and ranking function had a certain positive effect on learning, since scores improved across all problems. Table 2 shows the results of the questionnaire using the six-point method. First, the mean value of responses to the question "Do you think that the code sharing function of this system leads to the improvement of understanding of the program?" was 4.8. Second, the mean value of responses to the question "Do you think that the code sharing function of this system leads to motivated learning?" was 4.6. These results suggest that the code-sharing function has certain positive effects on learning and motivated learning.

Table 1. Results of Pre-test and Post-test Harvest Points (Mean SD)

	Pre-test	Pre-test Max	Post-test	Post-test Max	Difference	p-value (t-test)
P1	245.0 (389.2)	1200	842.5 (803.2)	2320	597.5 (760.3)	< 0.05
P2	125.8 (237.8)	760	440.0 (451.0)	1320	314.2 (430.7)	< 0.05
P3	142.5 (274.7)	720	865.0 (608.0)	2100	722.5 (607.0)	< 0.05

Table 2. Results of questionnaire

	Question	Average
1	Do you think that the code-sharing function of this system leads to an improvement in understanding of the program?	4.8
2	Do you think that the code-sharing function of this system leads to motivated learning?	4.6

4 Experiment to Compare Evaluation by the System with Evaluation by an Experienced Programmer

4.1 Overview

For the quality indicators proposed so far, only such execution results as "how much harvesting was done" or "how few steps were needed" have been evaluated. In other words, the quality indicators that we have proposed were based only on behavior generated by running the code. However, when considering code-refinement activities that occur in the process of learning from others' code, it is necessary to evaluate not only code that produces satisfactory results of execution, but also its readability, structure, and reusability. Our hypothesis is that there will be a difference between evaluation by the system and evaluations by experienced programmers. In this research, we conducted an experiment to investigate the difference between evaluation of code by the developed system and evaluations of code considered to be useful for learning by experienced programmers.

4.2 Method

Three experienced programmers participated in this experiment. The first has 28 years of experience in systems development, and has been developing systems for a company. The second has five years of programming experience and two years of systems development experience, and the third has nine years of systems development experience and experience in developing systems for companies.

In this experiment, the experienced programmers were presented with code created by learners in previous experiments. Specifically, we sorted 201 created code samples in descending order of total points, and presented 10 code samples extracted from the list at intervals of 20. For the presented code samples, we instructed the students to sort them in an order that they thought would be beneficial for learning when sharing the code samples in the classroom. The students were also asked to describe their reasons for reordering.

4.3 Results and Discussion

The code samples presented to the subjects in this evaluation are shown in Figs. 4, 5 and 6, the reasons for the reorderings are shown in Table 3, and the scores for each code sample and the rankings by the subjects are shown in Table 4.

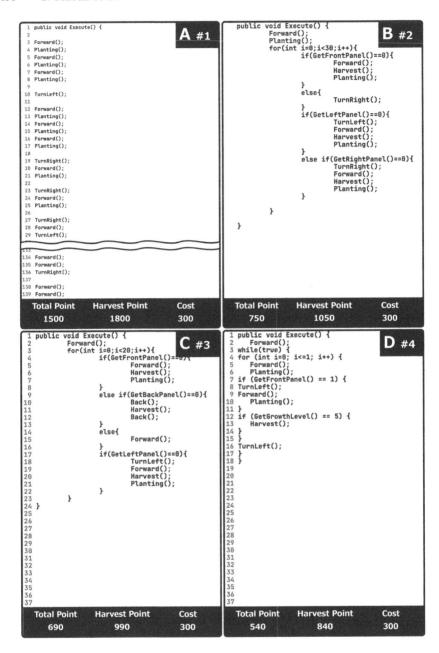

Fig. 4. (1) Code samples presented to participants

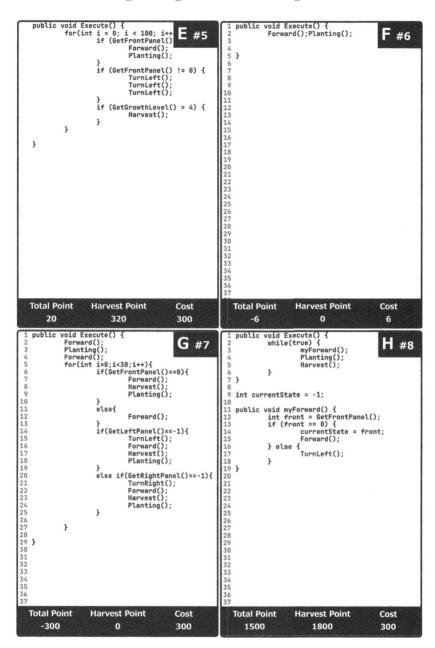

```
public void Execute() {                        E #5
    for(int i = 0; i < 100; i++
        if (GetFrontPanel()
            Forward();
            Planting();
        }
        if (GetFrontPanel() != 0) {
            TurnLeft();
            TurnLeft();
            TurnLeft();
        }
        if (GetGrowthLevel() > 4) {
            Harvest();
        }
    }
}
```

Total Point	Harvest Point	Cost
20	320	300

```
1  public void Execute() {                      F #6
2      Forward();Planting();
3
4
5  }
```

Total Point	Harvest Point	Cost
-6	0	6

```
1  public void Execute() {                      G #7
2      Forward();
3      Planting();
4      Forward();
5      for(int i=0;i<30;i++){
6          if(GetFrontPanel()==0){
7              Forward();
8              Harvest();
9              Planting();
10         }
11         else{
12             Forward();
13         }
14         if(GetLeftPanel()==-1){
15             TurnLeft();
16             Forward();
17             Harvest();
18             Planting();
19         }
20         else if(GetRightPanel()==-1){
21             TurnRight();
22             Forward();
23             Harvest();
24             Planting();
25         }
26
27     }
28
29 }
```

Total Point	Harvest Point	Cost
-300	0	300

```
1  public void Execute() {                      H #8
2      while(true) {
3          myForward();
4          Planting();
5          Harvest();
6      }
7  }
8
9  int currentState = -1;
10
11 public void myForward() {
12     int front = GetFrontPanel();
13     if (front == 0) {
14         currentState = front;
15         Forward();
16     } else {
17         TurnLeft();
18     }
19 }
```

Total Point	Harvest Point	Cost
1500	1800	300

Fig. 5. (2) Code samples presented to participants

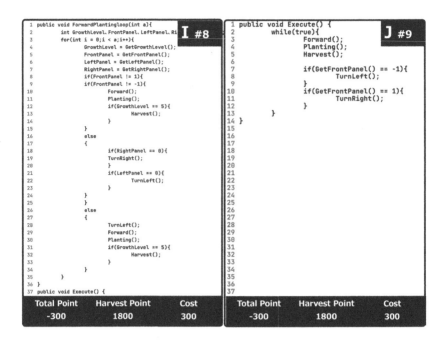

Fig. 6. (3) Code samples presented to participants

Table 4 shows the "combined ranking" of the subjects' rankings, where the first and tenth place were evaluated to be 9 and 0 points, respectively. First, these results show that certain code samples, such as B, C, D, and G, were evaluated similarly to one another. However, for other code samples, such as I and H, the total score evaluated by the system was lowest at -300 points, even though learners with a high proficiency assigned very high ratings. Code A, which had the highest score among the code samples presented, was also rated relatively low by the proficient learners. These results suggest that there is a difference between evaluation by the system and evaluation by an experienced programmer.

In this section, we initially discuss code samples I and H, which were highly evaluated by the experienced programmers. Stated reasons why the code of sample I was chosen included "It uses functions and variables to store state" and "The score is not high, but the program uses functions and is well-structured as code. In particular, it takes the output result of the function as a variable to improve reusability, which I think is most helpful." The same reasons were given for code sample H. From the reasons for the high rankings, use of variables for functions and storage of state and use of control statements were found to be important elements of code samples that were highly evaluated by the skilled users.

Next, we discuss the code sample A, which was not evaluated well by the experienced programmers. The reasons given for the reordering were as follows:

"It is hardcoded" and "It is a program that works only on a specific map, and is not controlled by any loops. However, it is a good first code for learning basic movement." This suggests that the skilled programmers emphasized use of functions and control statements as reasons in assigning high evaluations, and that lack of such use in code sample A was a factor in the low evaluations by the experienced programmers.

From the above results and discussions, we discovered that some code samples were evaluated similarly by the developed evaluation system and the reordering by the experienced programmers, but some code samples were evaluated differently. This result confirms the hypothesis of the authors that a difference exists between evaluation by scoring and evaluation by experienced programmers. One of the reasons for this difference is that we proposed an index that changes evaluation depending only on movements of the robot. In other words, we believe

Table 3. Reasons for Reordering by Participants

	Reason by participant (1)	Reason by participant (2)	Reason by participant (3)
A	It is a program that only works on a specific map, and is not controlled by any loops. However, it is a good first code for learning basic movement.	No structure.	It is hardcoded
B	It is almost the same as C. The score is slightly higher because program B has a slightly better score.	There were no good points, but there were no bad points, either.	It uses `for`
C	B and C are almost the same program, using `for` and `if` statements to determine the panel and to work adaptively.	I don't understand lines 14 and 15; you don't seem to understand the condition of `If`.	This code uses `for`, but its earned score is lower than that of B
D	It is an improved version of E. It has been developed from E and has actually been able to obtain a score.	Indentation is messy and hard to read.	We're using `while` because there's an unnecessary `for`
E	Although there is a waste of time in using "TurnLeft" three times, the algorithm has been well thought out in separating the positions of "Planting" and "Harvest," and in making the condition of "Harvest." The algorithm is well thought out. The score is low, but it could be better.	You are not using "else" correctly in line 7. You are writing an "if" statement that does not need to be written if you use "else."	This code uses `for`, but not `else if` or `if`
F	This code has absolutely nothing to learn as code.	There is too little to fill out.	There is no code written
G	The program uses the `For` statement for iterative processing and the `If` statement for flexible responses to conditions. However, it is structurally immature, with `Forward`, `Harvest`, etc., appearing many times.	I don't understand line 12.	This code uses `for`, but the condition of `if` is wrong
H	The score is not high, but the code is structured, using functions, and someone skilled in B, etc., can give suggestions on how to structure it next time.	It uses functions and variables to store state.	We are using `while`, and we are saving the state
I	The score is not high, but the program uses functions and is well-structured as code. In particular, it takes the output results of functions as variables to improve reusability, which I think is most helpful.	Functions are used, but the range is too large to be of much use. Indentation is messy.	We are using functions, saving and reusing state, and we are using `while`
J	It is written with more structure than G, using `While` statements, so there is less waste. It is more structured and less wasteful than G. Therefore, it can be used as a reference for creating code. However, the score is low, so it is placed here.	This code doesn't use `else`; if line 7 is `true`, we don't need to look at line 10.	It uses `while` in the code

that the fact that we did not evaluate the actual code written by the learner at all, but only the behavior of the robot, was a factor that led to the occurrence of the difference in evaluations.

For future versions of the developed system, it is necessary to consider adding an index that evaluates the actual code written by the learner, in addition to including current evaluation indices, such as number of Harvest Points and incurred Cost.

Table 4. Scores and rankings for each code sample

1	2	3	Rank (Points)	Ranking by system	Total points	Harvest points	Cost
I	H	I	I (26)	A	1500	1800	300
H	I	H	H (25)	B	750	1050	300
B	B	J	B (19)	C	690	990	300
C	C	D	C (16)	D	540	840	300
D	G	B	J (14)	E	20	320	300
E	J	C	D (12)	F	-6	0	6
J	E	G	G (10)	G	-300	0	300
G	A	E	E (9)	H	-300	0	300
A	D	A	A (4)	I	-300	0	300
F	F	F	F (0)	J	-300	0	300

4.4 Consideration of Quality Indicators to Be Added

From the results of the evaluation, we discovered a need for a quality indicator that evaluates the written code itself, in addition to the current evaluation indices. First, two types of evaluation methods exist in programming learning support systems: dynamic evaluation methods and static evaluation methods.

In this system, evaluation changes depending on the behavior of the robot that has been programmed by the learner. Therefore, we believe that we should use dynamic evaluation methods in this system. In other words, we do not perform any static evaluation. When relying on the dynamic evaluation method, we do not analyze the actual code written by the learners themselves, so even if the code does not use a control statement, it will be evaluated based on the robot's movement alone, without any points being deducted. In other words, code that consists of a series of commands for the robot without using any control statement will be evaluated very highly.

Therefore, it is desirable to add a static quality indicator that analyzes content of code written by a learner. In particular, we believe that it is important to add evaluations of the code by experienced programmers, such as evaluations of the use of control statements and functions, and evaluations of the structuring of the code, which were frequently cited as reasons in evaluation by the skilled learners. At present, there are two methods to achieve these evaluations. One is to extract control statements and functions from the code, calculate their types and their frequency of occurrence, and to evaluate them. The other is to use a program slicing method, which enables extracting a set of statements that have an effect on a single variable as a dependency. Therefore, we believe that program slicing can be used to quantify dependencies among statements, and thus to provide an evaluation index for code structuring in terms of coherence of processing.

For future research, we would like to include further study of static quality indicators and discussion of their concrete implementation methods.

5   Conclusion

We focused on learning from code written by other programmers, which is one of the most essential ways to learn programming, and proposed functions for promoting this method as a platform. The results of the evaluation experiments suggested that the developed code-sharing function and ranking function have certain positive effects on learning.

We believe that programming evaluations should address not only satisfactory results of execution, but also reusability of written code and use of functions. Therefore, as an additional step in evaluation, we attempted to differentiate between evaluation by the proposed evaluation index and evaluation by experienced programmers. From the results of the evaluation, we discovered that some of the code samples were valid, but some code samples caused differences in evaluation between the system and the experienced programmers. In the current evaluation method, only dynamic code evaluation is performed, so static code evaluation should be added.

Future work would include proposal and implementation of static code evaluation.

References

1. Busjahn, T., Schulte, C.: The use of code reading in teaching programming. In: Proceedings of the 13th Koli Calling international conference on computing education research, pp. 3–11 (2013)
2. Campbell, W., Bolker, E.: Teaching programming by immersion, reading and writing. In: 32nd Annual Frontiers in Education, vol. 1, pp. T4G–T4G. IEEE (2002)
3. Kölling, M., Rosenberg, J.: Guidelines for teaching object orientation with Java. ACM SIGCSE Bull. **33**(3), 33–36 (2001)
4. Miliszewska, I., Tan, G.: Befriending computer programming: a proposed approach to teaching introductory programming. Inform. Sci. Int. J. Emerg. Transdiscipline **4**(1), 277–289 (2007)
5. Oeda, S., Kosaku, H.: Development of a check sheet for code-review towards improvement of skill level of novice programmers. Procedia Comput. Sci. **126**, 841–849 (2018)
6. Sorva, J., Karavirta, V., Malmi, L.: A review of generic program visualization systems for introductory programming education. ACM Trans. Comput. Educ. (TOCE) **13**(4), 1–64 (2013)

7. Spinellis, D.: Reading, writing, and code: the key to writing readable code is developing good coding style. Queue **1**(7), 84–89 (2003)
8. Tomoto, T., Akakura, T.: Report on practice of a learning support system for reading program code exercise. In: Yamamoto, S. (ed.) HIMI 2017. LNCS, vol. 10274, pp. 85–98. Springer, Cham (2017). https://doi.org/10.1007/978-3-319-58524-6_8

Influence of Communication Environment on Feeling and Degree of Transmission

Masashi Okubo[(✉)], Asuka Iwai, and Akihiro Tatsumi

Doshisha University, Kyotanabe, Kyoto 610-0321, Japan
mokubo@mail.doshisha.ac.jp

Abstract. It is well known that nonverbal information plays the important role for smooth communication. On the other hand, it is also suggested that limiting transmitted nonverbal information leads to accurate comprehension. Further, it is shown that the face-to-face environment and the video chat environment have different influences on the talkers. However, it has not been verified that influences of visual nonverbal information in interactive communication on the feeling/degree of transmission in a video chat environment. Therefore, in this research, we try to verify the influence of varied communication environments on the feeling/degree of transmission and speech/body motion of the talkers in interactive communication by natural dialogue. In communication experiment, we prepared three experimental conditions which are controlled visual nonverbal information by using the dimming glass. As the result of experiment, it was shown that the suppression of the visual nonverbal information causes the decrease in the feeling of transmission and the head motion and, the increase in the degree of transmission and the arm motion. Furthermore, in the environment that can only be seen participants partner's body motion, there is a possibility that the feeling of transmission is worse, and the degree of transmission is most excellent in three experimental conditions. Secondly, the video chat environment was compared with the face-to-face environment. As the results of experiment, this condition is similar to the environment that participants can only be seen partner's physical motion. Furthermore, it was suggested that this environment may affect the increase the degree of transmission, the increase in the arm motion, and the decrease in the utterance rate.

Keywords: Embodied communication · Nonverbal information · Visibility · Feeling of transmission · Degree of transmission · Attention resource

1 Introduction

It is well known that the non-verbal information plays important roles for smooth communication in face-to-face situation [1–3]. On the other hand, Sugitani suggested that human communication should be evaluated by not only the smoothness but also coincidence between sending information and receiving information [4]. And we performed the experiment that compare the three situations which are text chat communication, voice chat, and face-to-face communication from the points of view of smoothness: Feeling of Transmission (FoT) and coincidence: Degree of Transmission (DoT). As a

© The Author(s), under exclusive license to Springer Nature Switzerland AG 2022
S. Yamamoto and H. Mori (Eds.): HCII 2022, LNCS 13305, pp. 505–515, 2022.
https://doi.org/10.1007/978-3-031-06424-1_37

result of study, face-to-face communication shows best performance form the point of view of FoT among the three type of communication. However, it doesn't show the best from the points of view of DoT. And, we investigate the influence of the visual non-verbal information on the communication from the point of view of FoT and DoT in face-to-face communication. In this study, the talker told the story to the listener, and DoT could be measured by the test about the story for the listener. As a result of experiment, we couldn't confirm the influence of visual non-verbal information [5].

In this paper, in free discussion situation, it is investigated the influence of visual non-verbal information on FoT and DoT by changing the visibility.

2 How to Evaluate the Communication

In this research, Feeling of Transmission and Degree of Transmission is used to evaluate the quality of communication. And, talker's speech and body motion, which plays an important role in smooth communication, are recorded for evaluation.

2.1 Feeling of Transmission

Some questionnaires are used to measure the FoT. Table 1 shows the contents of the questionnaires.

Table 1. Questionnaire of FoT

Question #	Content
Q1	I felt that I was able to understand stories of the partner well
Q2	I felt that stories came well from a partner
Q3	I felt that stories reached the partner well
Q4	I felt that it was easy to hear the story of the partner
Q5	I felt that a conversation was fun
Q6	I felt a sense of unity with the partner by a conversation
Q7	I felt that I was able to concentrate on a conversation

2.2 Degree of Transmission

In case of storytelling, DoT can be measured by the score of the test about the story for the listener. However, in case of free talking, this method can't be use. Therefore, we have proposed the method by using Doc2vec. Doc2vec is an extension of word2vec and the technique to make a document of any length the vector. So, DoT can be measured by Cosine Similarity between some keywords which are obtained from talkers after free talking [6].

2.3 Speech Activity

To obtain the speech activity, the directional microphones are used. Speech activity and simultaneous speech are used to evaluate the communication.

2.4 Body Motion

It is said that the entrainment of body motions is seen in case of smooth communication. Therefore, body motions are recorded by using perception Neuron2.0. Figure 1 shows the nodes used in evaluation.

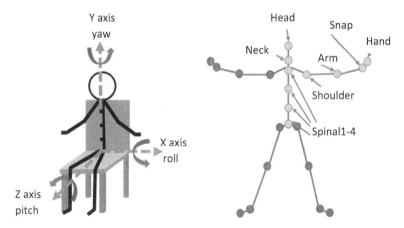

Fig. 1. Coordinate axis and Rotating axis (left) and nodes used in analysis (right).

3 Experiment

To investigate the influence of visuality on the face-to-face communication and video communication from the point of view of FoT and DoT, and speech activity and body motion. The participants are 4 pairs in their twenties.

3.1   Experimental Method

To control the visibility, dimming glass is used. The visibility of dimming glass changes when the voltage of the electric current flowing in the glass is changed. In the experiment, three kinds of visibility are used. In case of low visibility, the participant can't see even the silhouetted partner. In case of middle visibility, the participant can't see the facial expression, however he/she can see the body motion. In case of high visibility, the participant can see the partner clearly. Figures 2 and 3 shows the visual conditions and experimental setup.

Condition	Low visibility	Middle visibility	High visibility
Transmittance	4%	14%	63%
Visibility			
Expression	-	-	✓
Body motion	-	✓	✓

Fig. 2. Visual condition using by the dimming glass

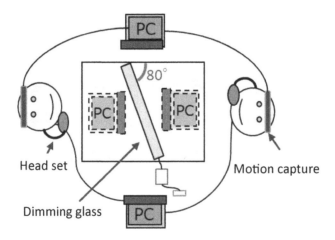

Fig. 3. Experimental setup.

3.2   Experimental Procedure

First, the participants were explained about the experimental objectives and procedure, and all of them understood them. After the system calibration, the participants 6 min. talked freely in three visual conditions. They answered the questionnaire and gave the five keywords about the contents of free talking in each visual condition.

4   Experimental Results

4.1   FoT: Feeling of Transmission

Figure 4 shows the results of questionnaires. The high visibility case is most preferred in all questions, especially there is significant difference between high visibility condition and middle and low visibility condition in Q6: sense of unity and in Q7: concentration. And the second-best condition cannot be decided in comparison between middle and low visibility conditions.

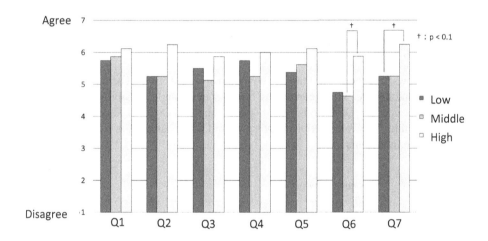

Fig. 4. Average of questionnaire of Table 1

4.2   DoT: Degree of Transmission

Figure 5 shows the average of Cosine similarity between participant's giving keywords.

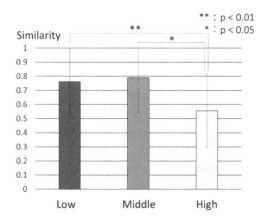

Fig. 5. Average and standard deviation of cosine similarity between talker's keywords.

DoT in case of high visibility condition shows worst performance among three conditions. And there is significant difference between in high visibility condition and low visibility condition and middle visibility condition.

4.3 Speech Activity

Figure 6 shows the average and standard deviation of voice activity. There isn't significant difference among three visual conditions, however in the middle visibility condition, the performance is worst. On the other hand. Table 2 shows the speech activity in each pair. From this table. The voice activity in case of middle visual condition show the worst performance in all pairs.

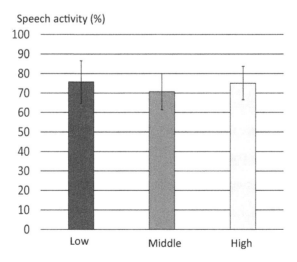

Fig. 6. Average and standard deviation of speech activity (%).

Table 2. Speech activity (%) in each group.

	Group1	Group2	Group3	Group4
Low	*84*	*86*	*76*	58
Middle	**79**	**74**	**74**	**55**
High	80	83	75	*61*

4.4 Body Motions

Figure 7 shows the average and standard deviation of magnitude of center of body's motion in three visual condition. The participants moved their body most frequently in case of high visibility condition and they didn't moved in case of middle visibility condition, however there is not significant difference.

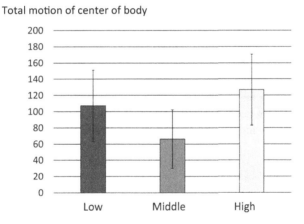

Fig. 7. Average and standard deviation of magnitude of center of body's motion.

And, Fig. 8 shows the average of synchronism number of nodding. The number of synchronisms increased so that visibility rose. On the other hand, the participants moved their arms most frequently in case of low visibility condition.

As a result of experiments, the high visibility condition was most preferred from the point of view of FoT, and the middle visibility condition was worst. On the other hand, the middle visibility condition tended to give the best result from the point of view of DoT.

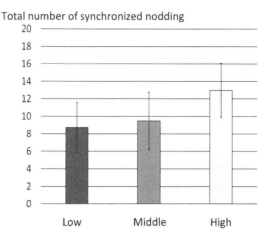

Fig. 8. Average and standard deviation of synchronized nodding between talker's

4.5 Comparison Between High Visibility Condition and Video Chat

We performed another experiment in which we investigated the quality of video chat compared with face-to-face communication.

FoT. Figure 9 shows the average of questionnaire which is described in Table 1. There isn't significant difference between the high visibility condition and video chat, however, for most question the high visibility condition tended to be preferred.

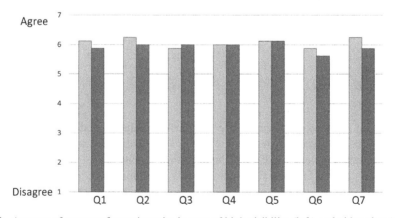

Fig. 9. Average of answer of questionnaire in case of high visibility (left) and video chat (right).

DoT. Figure 10 shows the average and standard deviation of Cosine similarity between participant's giving keywords. The similarity in case of video chat is better than it in case of high visibility condition.

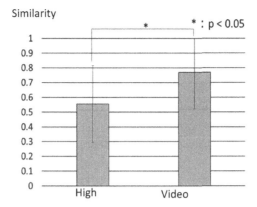

Fig. 10. Average and standard deviation of Cosine similarity in case of high visibility (left) and video chat (right)

Head Motion and Body Motion. Figure 11 shows the average and standard deviation of magnitude of head motion in case of high visibility condition is bigger than it in case of video chat, and there is significant difference between them. Also, Fig. 12 shows the average and standard deviation of magnitude of center of body motion. These results show that the participants didn't move their body in case of video chat situation.

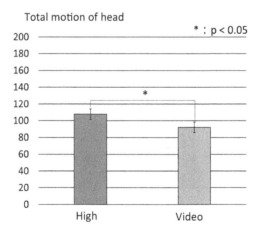

Fig. 11. Average and standard deviation of magnitude of head motion in case of high visibility (left) and video chat (right)

Total motion of center of body

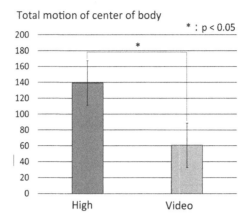

Fig. 12. Average and standard deviation of magnitude of center of body's motion in case of high visibility (left) and video chat (right)

On the other hand, Fig. 13 shows that the average of magnitude of arm motion in case of video chat condition is bigger than it in case of high visibility condition, and there is significant difference between them. It means that the participants moved their body which is not able to be seen by partner in case of video chat situation.

Total motion of arm

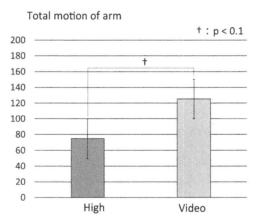

Fig. 13. Average and standard deviation of magnitude of arm motion in case of high visibility (left) and video chat (right)

5   Conclusions

In this research, influence of controlled visibility in face-to-face communication and video chat situation on quality of communication, from the point of view of FoT, DoT, speech activity and body motion. As a result of experiment, the controlled visibility lead to decrease the FoT and body motion, on the other hand, to increase the DoT and arm motion. Middle visibility condition, in which the talker can see only the partner's body motion, lead to worst FoT, speech activity however, best DoT.

Some research indicates the relations of the inverse correlation are seen between FoT and DoT. Especially, FoT in face-to-face communication is highest than in any other communication condition, and Dot isn't highest. Because attention resources are used to non-verbal information, understanding to verbal information may fall. In our research, the similar results were obtained. This indicate that the attention resources should be considered to evaluate the quality of communication.

Acknowledgements. This work is partially supported by JSPS KAKENHI Grant Numbers 21K11988.

References

1. Birdwhistell, R.L.: Kinesics and Context. University of Pennsylvania Press (1970)
2. Mehrabian, A.: Communication without words. Psychol. Today **2**(4), 52–55 (1968)
3. Watanabe, T., Okubo, M., Nakashige, M., Danbara, R.: erActor: speech-driven embodied interactive actor. Int. Natl. J. Hum. Comput. Interact. **17**(1), 43–60 (2004)
4. Sugitani, Y.: Opinion book about the difference of the information transmission in Internet communication and the face-to-face communication (in Japanese). https://www.kantei.go.jp/jp/singi/it2/kaikaku/dai3/siryou3_2_2.pdf
5. Okubo, M., Terada, A.: Effectiveness of visual non-verbal information on feeling and degree of transmission in face-to-face communication. In: Yamamoto, S., Mori, H. (eds.) HIMI 2018. LNCS, vol. 10904, pp. 279–290. Springer, Cham (2018). https://doi.org/10.1007/978-3-319-92043-6_24
6. Le, Q., Mikolov, V.: Distributed representations of sentences and documents. In: Proceedings of the 31st International Conference on Machine Learning (2014)

Interactive Reading Note Generation Utilizing Gaze Information

Satoko Yoshida[1][(⊠)], Madoka Takahara[2], Erina Makihara[1], Ivan Tanev[1], and Katsunori Shimohara[1]

[1] Doshisha University, 1-3 Tatara Miyakodani, Kyotonabe-shi, Kyoto-fu, Japan
yoshida2016@sil.doshisha.ac.jp, kshimoha@mail.doshisha.ac.jp
[2] Muroran Institute of Technology, 27-1 Mizumoto-cho, Muroran-shi, Hokkaido, Japan

Abstract. Reading gives readers intellectual stimuli, elicits their imagination and creativity, and expands their inner world. We introduce the concept to postulate that reading is communication between a reader and a book. An idea is to change a book into a reactive entity and to achieve interactions between a reader and a book. We have introduced a mechanism to feedback a reading note as a response from a book to a reader's gaze information that the reader generates during reading. Reader's gaze information generated during reading shows his/her mind about the book. The goal of this study is to build an automatic reading notes creation system that automatically generates reading notes based on gaze information that a reader naturally generates during reading. We conducted experiments to measure a subject's gaze coordinate data, and to verify whether we could identify eye movements for specific four reading patterns through the analysis of the acquired data. As the result, we have confirmed it possible to identify a reader's reading patterns from the change of gaze information.

Keywords: Reading · Reading notes · Communication · Media · Gaze information

1 Introduction

People have considered that "reading" has many advantages for a long time. Recent research found that childhood reading experiences have a good influence on adult consciousness, motivations, and activities [1]. On the other hand, recently, the increase of young people who don't read books has become a serious problem in Japan. According to the latest survey about college students which is conducted by the National Federation of University Co-operative Associations (NFUCA) every year, the percentage of students who spend no time reading books in a day is 48.0% [2].

Reading gives readers intellectual stimuli that excite imagination and creativity, and expands their inner world. If the reading has such importance, the survey result shows that many people don't understand the importance of reading.

The research concept we introduced is to postulate that reading is communication between a person and a book [3–6]. Communication between people is the activity or process of expressing ideas and feelings or of giving information to each other so that they can share ideas, feelings, and/or information, and can get mutual understanding. Visual and auditory information is in general used as media of communication between people [7, 8]. Reading is the activity or process in which a person as a reader tries to share and/or understand the contents of a given book. Accordingly, we can postulate that reading is communication between a reader and a book, even though a book is not a reactive but non-reactive entity.

An idea is to change a book as a non-reactive entity into a reactive one and to achieve interactions between a reader and a book. Here, we introduce a mechanism to feedback a reading note as a response from a book to a reader's gaze information that the reader generates during reading as a stimulus to the book. A reading note is a record that a reader makes about a book, based on the reader's interest, intention, and/or sense of value. The contents of a reading note include much information; for example, the title of the book, the author, favorite sentences and expressions, ideas and impressions the reader comes up with, and so on. A reader records his/her feelings and thoughts about the book in a reading note. Thus, we can regard that a reading note is rich and useful as a response from a book to a person.

To enable people to re-recognize and rediscover the importance of reading, we propose reading notes as media that intermediates interactions between a person and a book. However, to make reading notes, people have to take considerable time and effort. In this research, we use gaze information generated through his/her reading behaviors. Readers change reading patterns depending on the difference of interest in and difficulty of the contents of books. Therefore, gaze information shows the reader's mind about the book. We think it is useful to create reading notes. Researches on gaze information and reading have been conducted so far. However, these studies don't aim to create reading notes that reflect the reader's mind.

The research objective is to build a system that creates automatic reading notes by gaze information during reading. This paper reports an outcome of the basic research toward the goal. Concretely, we set four reading patterns that readers often apt to have during their reading as the experiment conditions and acquired coordinate data of a reader's gaze with an eye-tracking system. After conducting smoothing on the acquired data, we confirmed that they indicate characteristics inherent to the four reading patterns.

2   Reading Notes as Media for Communication

2.1   Communication Between a Reader and a Book

There is an idea that the importance of communication between people is defined as the expansion of one's inner world by eliciting imagination and creativity from each other [9]. We cannot completely understand and predict someone to communicate with. However, we feel various emotions and get unexpected information by communicating with unpredictable people.

Even in reading where there is no explicit interaction, readers can get intellectual stimuli, elicit their imagination and creativity, and then expand their inner world. If we could make reading into explicitly interactive process between a reader and a book, we could envision a possibility to extract new advantages of reading different from the one-directional normal reading.

2.2   Media Functionality in Reading Note

A book itself is a non-reactive entity by nature, and interactive communication between a book and a reader is not presumed. To achieve interactions between them, we need to change a non-reactive book into an entity reactive to a reader.

To solve this problem, we use reading notes as a kind of feedback from a book to a reader's gaze information during reading as a kind of stimuli from the reader, as shown in Fig. 1. The reason why we employ reading notes as feedback from a reader was already described in Sect. 1, and the reason why we utilize a reader's gaze information to create a reading note is explained in Sects. 2.4 and 2.5.

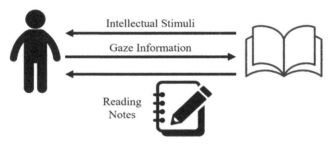

Fig. 1. Communication between a reader and a book.

2.3   Reading Notes as Media

Reading notes record words and sentences which extend the reader's inner world: unknown knowledge, favorite expression, idea, and so on. Reading the notes again after time passes, people remember various emotions, thought, and memory, and get discoveries about themselves and feel their changes. Reading the notes possibly make people re-read the book. And then, a new reading note should be created and new interactions are naturally generated. Through comparing the new reading note with the old one, a reader could realize some change and/or his/her growth in way of thinking. Through comparing his/her reading one with the other's one, a reader could find a difference in way of thinking and feeling to the same book, and it means that reading notes can function as media between people as well as between people and books.

3   Automatic Reading Notes Creating System

3.1   Gaze Information During Reading

We use gaze information generated through his/her reading behaviors to create the reading notes. People change reading patterns depending on the difference of interest in and difficulty of the contents of books. For example, they repeatedly read a part difficult to easily understand, and re-read a part with backtracking. We have a Japanese proverb saying "Read a hundred times over, and the meaning will become clear of itself." It means that people could see the meaning naturally by repeatedly reading many times. In the same way, we could see the same functionality of repeatedly reading not only a book itself but also a part of a book; if the same part of a book gazed, it would be difficult for a reader to understand the meaning of the part. If some parts of a book are skipped over, the parts would not be important and interesting to a reader.

In the case that we study a thing unknown so far, we sometimes read and study several books that contain the same unknown thing. Those books frequently have a common description of basic ideas, a reader who knows the basic ideas should skip the corresponding parts in those books. If some parts and/or pages of a book are intentionally skipped in reading, those parts and/or pages should not be attractive to the reader.

Hence, the gaze is rich in useful information to show the reader's will, interest, intention, and mind about a given book. We employ, thus, reader's gaze information as the useful stimuli from a reader to a book to create reading notes as the feedback from a book to a reader.

3.2 Gaze Information as Reader's Honest Signal

We employed the gaze information to identify a part of a book to interest a reader, although other modalities such as line maker and voice utterance are available.

The gaze information doesn't pose any action and operation to extract sentences from a book to a reader. If you use line marker and/or voice utterance to note, for example, you have to trace it with your finger and/or make your voice. Those actions and operations should give inconvenience to the reader under some situations in which he/she feels difficult to do so.

In addition, the gaze information often implies a reader's unconscious mind and will on the content of the book. If you create reading notes with line maker and/or voice utterance, you should intentionally select words and sentences to take it. You can do the same thing too with eye movement defined for such action, for example, blinking 3 times, at the starting and finishing point to record.

However, we emphasize again that gaze information implies the reader's unconscious mind and will. The reader might read repeatedly not only an interesting part but also a difficult part to understand. In this research right now, we investigate a possibility of gaze coordinate only, but there should be a possibility for a system to be able to judge that the coordinate would be selected whether consciously or unconsciously by introducing other parameters such as the speed of eye movement and the change of pupil diameter into a system.

We postulate that a reading note involving parts that a reader doesn't select should make some difference as media from one involving only part that the reader intentionally selects for the record.

3.3 Process of Creating Reading Notes

We are trying to achieve the following 3 goals, aiming to enable people to re-recognize and rediscover the importance of reading:

1. Presenting reading notes automatically generated by using a reader's gaze information during reading.
2. Investigating the influence of reading notes on the reader's cognitive aspects such as memory and recall.
3. Suggesting new interactions between the reader and the book by utilizing media functionality of reading notes.

For that purpose, we have proposed an automatic reading Notes creating system that consists of a PC equipped with an eye tracker. Figure 2 shows the process to create reading notes in the proposed system. Automatic creation of reading notes is not executed in real-time during reading but after a reader finishes reading. Gaze information including coordination data of eye movement, the diameter of the pupil, and time stamp during reading is stored in Gaze Data Base (GDB).

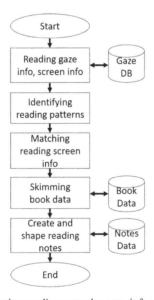

Fig. 2. Process of creating reading notes by gaze information during reading.

We used Tobii Pro Fusion which is the eye tracker provided by Tobii Technology Company [10]. It gets coordinates of the left eye and right eye per 1/120 s: the sampling rate is 120 Hz. The axis of coordinate puts (0, 0) on the upper-left of the screen and (1, 1) on the lower-right. In the document area for this experiment, the range of X coordinate is 0.20–0.78, the range of Y coordinate is 0.17–0.93.

3.4 Reading Patterns from Gaze Information

To guess a reader's mind about the contents of a book, specific reading patterns should be identified by analyzing gaze information stored in GDB. Reading patterns that should be identified are not specified yet because gaze information is now examined. Through matching analysis to identify some text parts in the reading screen that correspond to specific reading patterns, the text information of the book is skimmed accordingly. The text information is extracted based on one sentence or multiple ones to keep readability for a reader.

Reading notes are automatically generated and shaped based on the skimmed text data. As the first step, right now, only the skimmed text data in a book is contained, and any memorandum of a reader is not done. In that sense, the current version of reading notes is a sort of document to summarize pieces of sentences in a book.

4 Related Research

Studies on gaze information and reading have been conducted so far. For example, there is a study to use eye features to detect reading behaviors [11]. The final goal of this research is to create a reading lifelog automatically. The reading lifelog is the long-term digital recording that when what, and how people read in daily life [12]. They conducted experiments to detect reading behavior in daily activities with a mobile eye tracker. Concretely they compared the accuracy of 4 methods: one by Bulling et al. [13], one by Yoshimura et al. [14], one by Kunze et al. [15], and one combined by all these methods. The purpose of this study is to detect reading behaviors, not creating reading notes.

Another study is on a reading support system by using machine learning for gaze movement feature [16]. This study proposed the system to provide a user with appropriate reading support by identifying the user's situation from gaze movement. This research aims to complement the existing gaze input interface that requires longer input time and has the restricted visual information collection function. The proposed system supports the user's intention reading based on the user's features obtained from gaze information for viewing behaviors. The usage of the system is limited, and the authors evaluate that it is not superior to a mouse and keyboard.

In the support of reading by eye-tracking, there is a study to track eye movement during reading an e-book and show the point at where people leave off reading [17]. The point of leaving off reading is shown by changing the color of a part that people finish reading so that the reader can easily return to the right point to re-start reading.

These studies don't aim to create reading notes that reflect the reader's mind.

5 Experiment

This research aims to build the automatic reading notes creating system introduced in Sect. 3.3. As the first step for that purpose, we conducted experiments to acquire a subject's gaze coordinate data with an eye-tracking system, and verify whether we could identify eye movements for specific reading patterns through the analysis of the acquired data. The number of subjects was eight: four women and four men. The range of their ages was 21–24. Three of them wore contact lenses and others wore naked eyes during the experiment. Figure 3 shows the reading screen and the coordinates acquired by the eye tracker.

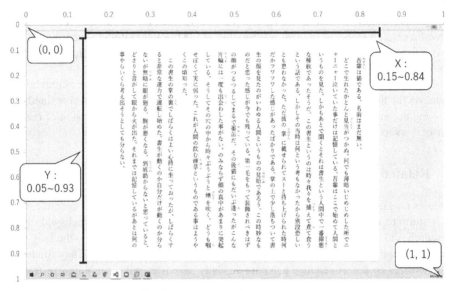

Fig. 3. Coordinates of reading screen.

5.1 Reading Patterns

We measured gaze information of the following 4 reading patterns on sentences directed:

1. Normal reading: a subject reads the document from the beginning to the end along with sentences.
2. Repeated reading: a subject reads the directed sentence within a line twice repeatedly.
3. Returned reading: after reading until the directed sentences of the end side, a subject rereads them from the beginning side.
4. Skipped reading: after reading until the directed sentences of the beginning side, a subject skips to that of the end side.

The experimental conditions are set based on the reasons described in Sect. 3.4 and the author's reading experience.

The directed sentences for conditions 2–4 are changed to red.

5.2 Document for Experiment

To create a document for this experiment, we referenced Soseki Natsume's "I am a cat" published on the Internet [18]. Table 1 shows the layout detail of the document. In Table 1, "furigana" is kana over or beside kanji to indicate pronunciation. A participant reads only one page displayed on the screen in each condition. Table 2 shows the coordinates of the direction sentences for conditions 2–4.

Table 1. Layout details.

Paper orientation	Lateral
Character orientation	Vertical writing
The number of lines	20 lines
Size of the font ("furigana")	16 pt (8 pt)
Margin sizes	Upper, Under, Left, Right: 12.7 mm

Table 2. Coordinate of sentences changed red.

	X	Y
Condition 2	0.49–0.51	0.22–0.80
Condition 3	Beginning side: 0.52–0.53 Tail side: 0.31–0.33	Beginning side: 0.11–0.63 Tail side: 0.39–0.87
Condition 4	Beginning side: 0.67–0.71 Tail side: 0.31–0.36	Beginning side: 0.11–0.88 Tail side: 0.11–0.88

6 Results and Discussion

When people stare at a point voluntarily, eyes vibrate involuntarily. It is called involuntary eye movement during fixation. It causes the experiment result to include many vibrations. Therefore, we performed the smoothing processing by sliding window. A sliding window needs a window width and a sliding width. We decided that the window width is 6 and the sliding width is 2. It means that these values are calculated by averaging data for 600 ms with every 200 ms difference.

Figures 4, 5, 6, 7, and 8 show results of data averaged and processed by smoothing with a sliding window. The sampling rate of the eye tracker is 120 Hz, but the raw data is too many for analyzing it. We took the average of every 12 data: per 1/10 s. In the figures, the ranges of red and green indicate the coordinates of the direction sentences shown in Table 2. In the conditions that have 2 direction sentences, the blue is the beginning side, the red is the end side. The range of yellow indicates the section in which the characteristic eye movement of each condition occurs.

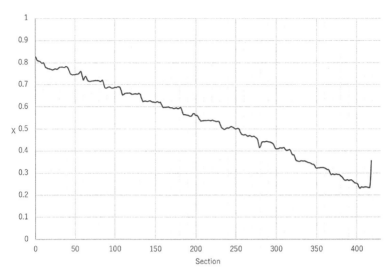

Fig. 4. Result of condition 1 (X coordinate).

Figures 4 and 5 show the results of condition 1. An experiment participant moves eyes from upper to lower and from right to left in Fig. 3. The expected eye movement of the X coordinate is from (1, y) to (0, y). One of the Y coordinates is the oscillation between (x, 0) and (x, 1). Figures 4 and 5 records the explained motion.

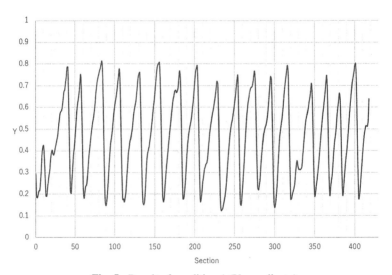

Fig. 5. Result of condition 1 (Y coordinate).

The result of the Y coordinate of condition 2 is shown in Fig. 6. In the second experiment, a participant read the direction sentence twice repeatedly. In Fig. 6, the motion that the eyes move from the end of the direction sentence to its beginning is observed.

The result of the X coordinate of the third experiment is shown in Fig. 7. The X-axis motion is expected that eyes move from (0, y) to (1, y). In Fig. 7, the expected movement is observed. The result of the X coordinate of condition 4 is shown in Fig. 8. The motion is expected that eyes move from (1, y) to (0, y). In Fig. 8, the expected movement is observed.

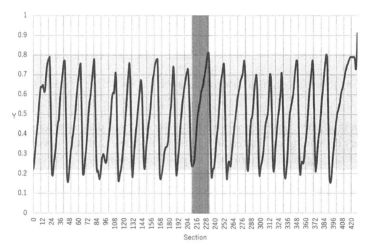

Fig. 6. Result of condition 2 (Y coordinate/R: y = 0.22–0.80).

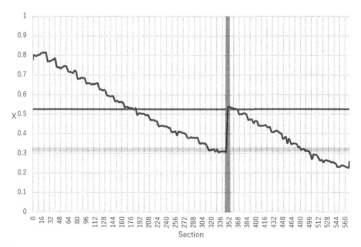

Fig. 7. Result of condition 3 (X coordinate/B: x = 0.52–0.53, R: x = 0.31–0.33).

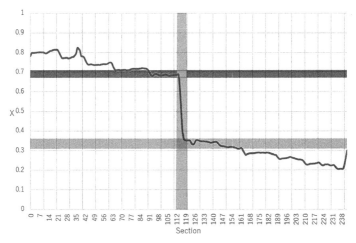

Fig. 8. Result of condition 4 (X coordinate/B: x = 0.67–0.71, R: x = 0.31–0.36).

To sum it up, through the experiments, we verified that the characteristic eye movement differs depending on the reading patterns. It shows that it is possible to identify the reader's reading patterns from the change of gaze coordinate. Especially, in vertical sentences, the analysis of the eye movement of the X coordinate is useful for identifying the 4 patterns measured in this experiment. In addition, the analysis of Y direction is useful for identifying where the eye movement started and ended within a line.

7   Conclusion

This study aims to enable people to re-recognize and rediscover the importance of reading. For that purpose, we introduced the concept to postulate that reading is communication between a reader and a book. An idea is to change a book as a non-reactive entity into a reactive one and to achieve interactions between a reader and a book. Here, we proposed a mechanism to feedback a reading note as a response from a book to a reader's gaze information that the reader generates during reading as a stimulus to the book. The technological goal of this study is to build an automatic reading notes creation system that automatically generates reading notes based on gaze information that a reader naturally generates during reading.

As the first step for that goal, we conducted experiments to measure a subject's gaze coordinate data with an eye-tracking system, and to verify whether we could identify eye movements for specific four reading patterns through the analysis of the acquired data. The results show that the characteristics of eye movements can be classified depending on the 4 reading patterns. Thus, we have confirmed it possible to identify a reader's reading patterns from the change of gaze information.

As future works, since we controlled to focus on one specific reading pattern in every experiment, we need to conduct experiments for actual cases of reading and investigate whether we could classify reading patterns based on actual reading behaviors. That is, we need experiments to allow subjects to read freely, and analyze and classify reading patterns based on a subject's interest and intention about a book, reading his/her reading experience and custom, and so on. It means that we have to tackle the situation where not a single but multiple reading patterns are simultaneously generated.

References

1. Hamada, H., Akita, K., Fujimori, Y., Yagi, Y.: The effects of childhood reading experiences on adult consciousness, motivations and activities. Sci. Read. **58**(1), 29–39 (2016)
2. 54th Summary of Field Survey for Campus Life, National Federation of University Cooperative Associations. https://www.univcoop.or.jp/press/life/report.html
3. Yoshida, S., Takahara, M., Tanev, I., Shimohara, K.: Automatic reading notes creation: identifying reading patterns by Gaze information during reading. Proc. SICE Annu. Conf. **2020**, 1965–1970 (2020)
4. Yoshida, S., Takahara, M., Tanev, I., Shimohara, K.: Reading notes as media to enrich communications between reader and book. In: 2020 IEEE Asia-Pacific Conference on Computer Science and Data Engineering (CSDE), pp. 1–5 (2020)
5. Yoshida, S., Takahara, M., Tanev, I., Shimohara, K.: Effect of media functionality by reading note on reading experience over time. Proc. SICE Annu. Conf. **2021**, 506–508 (2021)
6. Yoshida, S., Takahara, M., Tanev, I., Shimohara, K.: Possibility of reading notes as media to enrich communications between reader and book. Human interface and the management of information. Inf. Present. Visual. **12765**, 113–124 (2021)
7. Matsumura, A.: Daijirin, 3rd edn. Sanseido, Tokyo (2006)
8. Kitahara, Y.: Meikyo Kokugo Dictionary, 2nd edn. Taishukan Publishing, Tokyo (2010)
9. Shimohara, K.: Artificial Life and Evolving Computer. Kogyo Chosakai Publishing, Tokyo (1998)
10. Tobii Technology. Tobii Pro Fusion. https://www.tobiipro.com/ja/product-listing/tobii-pro-fusion/
11. Nakajima, K., Utsumi, Y., Iwamura, M., Hirose, K.: Selection of Gaze-based Characteristics Useful for Detecting Reading Actions. IPSJ SIG Technical Report 2016-CVIM-202(28), pp. 1–6 (2016)
12. Kunze, K., et al.: Quantifying reading habits: counting how many words you read. In: Proceedings of the 2015 ACM International Joint Conference on Pervasive and Ubiquitous Computing (UbiComp 2015), pp. 87–96. Association for Computing Machinery, Inc., New York (2015)
13. Bulling, A., Ward, J.A., Gellersen, H., Tröster, G.: Eye movement analysis for activity recognition using electorooculoraphy. IEEE Trans. Pattern Anal. Mach. Intell. **33**(4), 741–753 (2011)
14. Yoshimura, K., Kawaichi, H., Kunze, K., Kise, K.: Relationship between document understanding and gaze information acquired by eye-tracker. Tech. Rep. IEICE **112**(495), 261–266 (2013)
15. Kunze, K., Ustumi, Y., Shiga, Y., Kise, K., Bulling, A.: I know what you are reading: recognition of document type using mobile eye tracking. In: Proceedings of the 2013 International Symposium on Wearable Computers, pp. 113–116. Association for Computing Machinery, New York (2013)
16. Nakazono, A., Hamakawa, R.: Reading support system using Gaze movement feature. IPSJ Interact. **2018**, 1060–1065 (2018)
17. Imamura, M., Cho, I.: Research on Reading Support with Eye-tracking – Attempt for Ambient Interface. Undergraduate Research of the Department of Intermedia Art and Science, Waseda University (2016)
18. Soseki Natsume: I Am a Cat. https://www.aozora.gr.jp/cards/000148/card789.html

Gaze Analysis and Modeling of Cognitive Process During Debugging for Novice Programmers' Learning

Kohei Yoshimori[1(✉)], Toru Kano[2], and Takako Akakura[2]

[1] Graduate School of Engineering, Department of Information and Computer Technology, Tokyo University of Science, 6-3-1 Niijuku, Katsushika-ku, Tokyo 125-8585, Japan
4621523@ed.tus.ac.jp
[2] Faculty of Engineering, Department of Information and Computer Technology, Tokyo University of Science, 6-3-1 Niijuku, Katsushika-ku, Tokyo 125-8585, Japan
{kano,akakura}@rs.tus.ac.jp

Abstract. Recently, the demand for IT human resources has increased. Therefore, the expansion of programming education should be considered to strengthen the supply of it. This study aimed to propose debugging learning support for novice programmers using experts' gaze behavior. First, we gave feedback to proficient users on their gazing behavior during program debugging and interviewed them about their cognitive processes. Based on the results, we developed a cognitive process model of expert debugging. However, most of the visualized information was based on gaze transitions, and it was difficult to see the characteristics of the cognitive process. This study helped to improve the previously proposed model and developed one that focuses more on the cognitive process during program debugging. Data from students with little programming experience were collected and compared with the cognitive process model of programming experts. This enabled the identification of the characteristics of the program debugging process of non-experts.

Keywords: Programming education · Program debugging · Gaze behavior · Learning support · Cognitive process model

1 Introduction

1.1 The Demand for IT Resources

Currently, Society 5.0 is considered as the form of society that Japan should aim for. It calls for the widespread use of the Internet of Things (IoT) and the development of AI technology [1]. Thus, the demand for IT human resources is increasing [2]. However, the supply of IT personnel is unable to fulfill the demand. According to a report by the Information-technology Promotion Agency of Japan (IPSJ), the shortage of IT human resources in user companies is high in quantity and quality, regardless of the company size [3].

© The Author(s), under exclusive license to Springer Nature Switzerland AG 2022
S. Yamamoto and H. Mori (Eds.): HCII 2022, LNCS 13305, pp. 528–537, 2022.
https://doi.org/10.1007/978-3-031-06424-1_39

Therefore, the expansion of programming education should be considered to strengthen the supply of IT human resources. Programming is included in primary and secondary education curricula. However, a problem associated with programming education is the difficulty encountered by novice learners during program debugging [4]. This has led to a polarization of programming learners in the university education field [5].

1.2 Gaze Behavior During Program Debugging

To address this, we focus on learners' gaze information during program debugging. In a related study, Lin et al. [4] tracked learners' eye movements when searching for bugs in the source code and analyzed their thought process by ability. Moreover, Kano et al. [6] tracked eye movements during program debugging and modeled the program error resolution process. These studies determined the gaze patterns during debugging based on programming ability; however, they were limited to analysis and did not provide learners with recommendations on how to debug successfully. Matsumoto et al., in contrast, used heat maps to support programming education [7]. A heat map is a visualization graph in which the individual values of two-dimensional data are represented by colors and shades. The aforementioned researchers presented a heat map illustrating the gazing behavior of expert to non-expert programmers; the results suggested that the heat map made the gazing behavior of non-expert programmers closer to that of the experts. However, the presented data did not contain time-series information and could not convey the thought process of the expert programmers.

Therefore, in this study, we develop a system to present the gaze information of expert programmers when program debugging to learners, including sequential information, and let novices experience this system. Through evaluation experiments of learning to use the system, we will confirm the effect of the transfer of the cognitive process of experts. To evaluate the learning support system using the gaze information of proficient learners, we track experts' gaze behavior during program debugging and ask them to verbalize the results and their thought states at that time and analyze the connection between the cognitive process and the accompanying gaze transition in this report. The results will be used to create a model that visualizes the relationship between cognitive processes and gaze behavior. The model's construction enables verification of the usefulness of the proposed learning support by comparing the changes in the learners' cognitive process model before and after learning with that of the expert programmers in the evaluation experiment to be conducted.

2 Previous Study

First, to construct a model of the cognitive process during program debugging, in a previous study [8], we gave feedback on the gaze behavior to experts and interviewed them about their cognitive process. Based on the results of the interviews and the analysis of the gaze behavior, we constructed a model of the cognitive process of experts during debugging as a directed graph. Figure 1 shows an example of the construction of the model created in the previous study. Each node represents a thought state (and the gazing point), and each edge represents its transition.

However, most of the visualized information was based only on eye movements, and it was difficult to see the characteristics of the cognitive process. Considering the prospects for system development and evaluation experiments, it is necessary to develop a model-building method that focuses more on the characteristics during programming and debugging.

In this study, we improve the previously proposed model and develop a model that focuses more on the cognitive process during program debugging. Moreover, we conduct additional experiments in the same way as in the previous study. By increasing the number of subjects to include non-experts as well as experts, we compare the cognitive processes of both, and examine the characteristics of their cognitive processes based on their programming abilities.

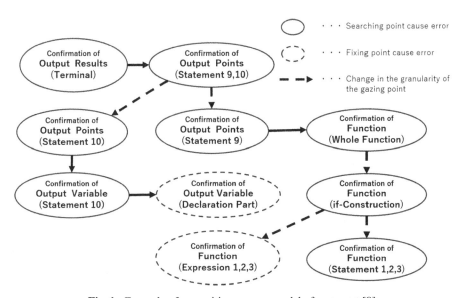

Fig. 1. Example of a cognitive process model of an expert [8]

3   Methodology

The previously proposed model [8] showed gaze transitions and their thought states in an effective graph. In other words, it only labeled the nodes of the thought states with the gazing points and did not show the debugging process regarding the subject's strategy and so on. To focus more on the characteristics of the cognitive and debugging processes, we visualize the changes in the thought state and the accompanying gaze transitions.

The format of the model is a directed graph, as in the previous study [8]. The components are summarized in Table 1.

Table 1. Components of a cognitive process model

Component	Information
Node	Thought state, gazing point
Edge	The thought state and the accompanying gaze transitions

The thought state provides information on the debugging process that the subject is attempting to perform, such as checking the output result, understanding the entire program structure, checking the output process, and predicting the part that causes the error. The range of gazing points is labeled from the entire function to a single sentence based on the subject's feedback. The following is a summary of the improvements made to the model-building method of the previous study.

- The nodes of the thought state and the gazing point were classified.
- We added more granular nodes for the debugging process, such as "prediction of the part that causes the error," along with thought states such as "confirmation of ~."

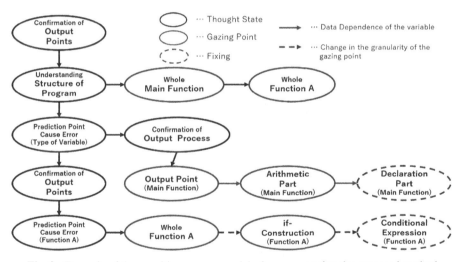

Fig. 2. Example of the cognitive process model of an expert using the proposed method

Figure 2 shows an example of the proposed method for modeling the cognitive process of an expert. First, the flow of the cognitive process was made more visible by dividing the cognitive process and gaze transition by the node type. In the model shown in Fig. 1, only the node "Confirmation of ~ " was used, and the changes in the gazing points could only be seen there. However, by placing the gazing points node under the those of thought states such as "Confirmation of output process" and "Understanding the structure of the program," we can see the changes in the thought states of experts as a whole. Moreover, the proposed method expresses the characteristics of the cognitive process by adding more granular thought states that were not visualized in the previous study [8], such as "predicting the part that causes errors" and "checking the output process."

4 Data Collection Experiment

4.1 Experiment Outline

We conduct a data collection experiment on non-experts. Compared to the subjects in the previous study [8], the subjects in this experiment had fewer years of experience in system development through programming. The outline of the experiment is shown in Table 2.

Table 2. Experiment outline

Subjects	University students majoring in information engineering
Number of subjects	Four
Experimental details	Acquisition of gaze information during program debugging and feedback of cognitive process from subjects
Number of questions	Three
Answer time	Maximum 15 min per question
Whole experiment time	About 1 h
A gaze tracking device	Tobii Eye Tracker 4C
Environment	Space blocked from view from the outside

To collect gaze information during program debugging, we ask the subjects to solve a problem in which they have to modify a program containing an error and reproduce the specified output result (hereinafter referred to as "program debugging problem"). The language used for the problem is C, which the subject has already learned. We used Tobii Eye Tracker 4C, a gaze tracking device, to acquire their gaze data while answering the questions. It was acquired at 20 fps, and a CSV file was created containing each gaze coordinate and its time stamp on the display. The OS used in this study is Windows 10, and the display used is 27 inches with a resolution of 1920×1080.

4.2 Program Debugging

The program contents are related to four arithmetic operations, iterative processing, pointers, and so on. The error patterns are limited to result errors in the output. The subject uses Visual Studio Code to solve the problems. Figure 3 shows the problem-solving screen, which consists of a problem column, text area, and terminal. The subject modifies the source code in the text area and compiles and executes it in the terminal. For the program debugging screen, we record the screen while answering.

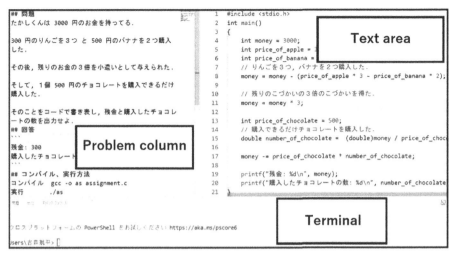

Fig. 3. Program debugging problem

4.3 Explanation by the Subjects

We developed a system that superimposes the gazing behavior on the recorded video of the program debugging process. By inputting the CSV file containing the gazing coordinates and the recording of the program debugging screen into the system, the video to be presented to the subject is outputted. Figure 4 shows the screen on which the gazing behavior is superimposed. The gazing behavior is presented by mapping the gazing points for 0.5 s using the gazing data obtained when solving the program debug problem; the data were displayed in time series. The controller can change the playback speed and control it using a seek bar.

We asked the subjects to check their debugging process and give us an explanation of the changes in their thought states caused by the changes in the gazing points.

5   Results

As for the results of the program debugging problems, the subjects were able to answer all the questions.

The following are some examples of their explanation observed in this experiment.

- To understand the programs' structure, I traced the source code one sentence at a time from the top.
- Looking at the output results, there was a problem with the variable arithmetic, so I checked it in the main function.
- The number of iterations seems to be insufficient, so I checked the definition of the *for* statement.

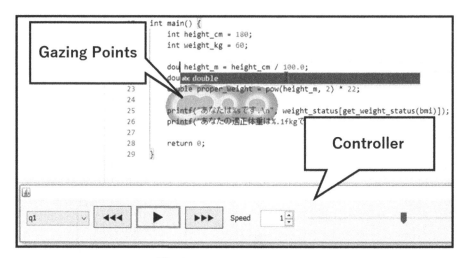

Fig. 4. Display of gaze behavior

Based on these explanations, we constructed a cognitive process model. For one student, many common features of experts' thought process, which were confirmed in previous studies, were true.

The common features of the cognitive processes of these experts were as follows.

- After checking the output results, look at the entire source code to understand the program structure and find the output points.
- Check the variables that are being outputted from the output location and trace their data dependencies. (The blue edge (thin solid line) in Fig. 2)
- After making a rough prediction of the part that causes the error, the granularity of the gazing point is increased (black edge (dashed line) in Fig. 2) to search for the part that needs to be corrected (red node (dashed line) in Fig. 2).

In contrast, for the other three subjects, no noticeable trends in gaze behavior or cognitive processes were observed, but the following similarities in the debugging process were identified.

- They try to understand the programs' structure by reading the program from top to bottom.
- It is not possible to make predictions about the cause of the error; therefore, the search for a fix is done ad hoc.

Figure 5 shows an example of a model of the cognitive process of one of the three students.

Comparing this result with the cognitive process of the experts, it was confirmed that the three students differed from the expert as they read the source code to understand the programs' structure, and could not make predictions about the part that caused the error.

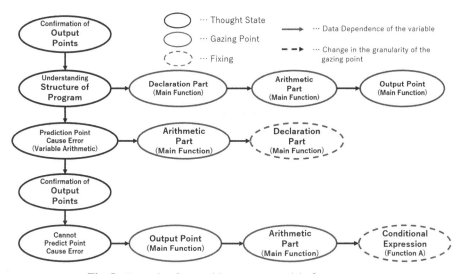

Fig. 5. Example of a cognitive process model of a non-expert

6   Discussion

6.1   Characteristics of the Debugging for Non-experts

Based on the interview results, we can assume that there are no noticeable trends in the cognitive process and the accompanying gaze behavior of the non-expert programmers.

Regarding the similarities among the three subjects mentioned in Chapter 5, the first point, that they read the entire program, could be because the program to be debugged was new to them or because of their low program reading ability. The second point, the ad hoc search for correction points, may be due to the lack of programming experience required to find the point that causes the error.

Since the programs used in this experiment were simple, the subjects were able to correct them. However, when debugging a complex program, debugging will be difficult if these two points are lacking.

6.2   Gaze Feedback for Debugging Learning Support

The same is true for novices regarding low programming reading ability and lack of experience. We believe that we can compensate for these two points by transferring the debugging process of experts to novices. For this, we can use gaze feedback to transfer the cognitive process and accompanying gaze behavior unique to experts as described in Chapter 5. Specifically, the mapping of the gazing points shown in Fig. 4 is modified. As shown in Figs. 6 and 7, by changing the radius and color of the mapping, we can express the changes in the granularity of the gazing points and the gaze behavior when predicting the error points.

```
int main() {                       int main() {
    int height_cm = 180;               int height_cm = 180;
    int weight_kg = 81;                int weight_kg = 81;

    int height_m = height_cm           int height_m = height_cm / 1
    double bmi = weight_kg /           double bmi = weight_kg / pow
    double proper_weight = po          double proper_weight = pow(h

    printf("あなたは%sです.\n"           printf("あなたは%sです.\n", w
    printf("あなたの適正体重は%          printf("あなたの適正体重は%.1

    return 0;                          return 0;
}                                  }
```

Fig. 6. Changing the radius of the mapping

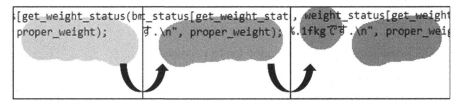

Fig. 7. Changing the radius of the mapping

7 Conclusion

This report reveals improvements to the method of constructing a model of the cognitive process of expert programmers proposed in a previous study [8]. By using different nodes to represent thought states and gazing points and adding a node for detailed thought states, we made a model that focuses more on the cognitive process. Data collection experiments were conducted with students who had little programming experience, and by comparing the models with those of experts, the characteristics of the program debugging process of students considered to be non-experts were identified.

In the future, we plan to implement the gaze feedback that is useful for new learners as described in the discussion, and conduct evaluation experiments using it. In the evaluation experiment, we will be able to verify the effectiveness of the learning support by gaze feedback based on the changes in the cognitive process model of the novice programmers before and after learning.

Acknowledgments. We would like to thank Editage (www.editage.com) for English language editing.

References

1. Cabinet Office. Society 5.0 –Science and Technology Policy–. https://www8.cao.go.jp/cstp/society5_0/. Accessed 23 Jan 2022
2. Ministry of Economy. Trade and Industry: Priority of Economic and Industrial Policy for FY 2020. https://www.meti.go.jp/main/yosangaisan/fy2020/pdf/02.pdf. Accessed 23 Jan 2022
3. IPA Independent Administrative Law Officer Intelligence Processing Agency. White Paper on IT Personnel. https://www.ipa.go.jp/files/000085255.pdf. Accessed 23 Jan 2022
4. Lin, Y., Wu, C., Hou, T., Lin, Y., Yang, F., Chang, C.: Tracking students' cognitive processes during program debugging–an eye-movement approach. IEEE Trans. Educ. **59**(3), 175–186 (2016)
5. Hanahusa, R., Matsumoto, S., Hayashi, Y., Hirashima, T.: Analysis based on data dependencies of program reading patterns using eye movements–for programs consisting of assignment and arithmetic operations. Trans. Jpn. Soc. Inf. Syst. Educ. **35**(2), 192–203 (2018). (in Japanese)
6. Kano, T., Sakagami, R., Akakura, T.: Modeling of cognitive processes based on gaze transition during programming debugging. In: The 2021 IEEE 3rd Global Conference on Life Sciences and Technologies (LifeTech 2021), pp. 416–417 (2021)
7. Matsumoto, K., Wakahara, T.: A proposal for programming education support based on analysis of eye movement information. In: The 80th National Convention of Information Processing Society of Japan (2018). (in Japanese)
8. Yoshimori, K., Kano, T., Akakura, T.: Proposal of a cognitive process model for programming experts based on gaze behavior. In: Japan Society for Educational Technology 2021 Autumn National Conference, pp. 203–204 (2021). (in Japanese)

Author Index

Author Index

Printed in the United States
by Baker & Taylor Publisher Services